PENGUIN BOOKS

# The Musicians' Bible

'Something to replace Gideon's Bible in the right-hand draw of your hotel room. This book will definitely compete with *Music Week* and *The White Book* in terms of up-to-date and accurate information'
*Mike Champion, Manager, the Prodigy*

'Buy a cheap Strat copy – that's great advice [from the chapter on 'Equipment']; and don't forget the money's in the publishing. Very good, practical guide'
*Antony Wilson, Factory Records and In the City*

'The music business is a tricky, cliquey beast. But in this short and readable book John Collis manages to explain how it all works and how it all fits together – or not as the case may be'
*Paul Conroy, President, Virgin Records UK*

'John Collis has seen them all and talked to most of them as the wise words within testify'
*Richard Ogden, Manager of Vanessa-Mae and the Bomfunk MCs; formerly manager of Paul and Linda McCartney; ex-Senior Vice-President, Sony Music Europe; and former Managing Director, Polydor Records*

'Rock-solid advice and a full resource pack, o happy day!'
*Mark Featherstone-Witty, Principal/Chief Executive, Liverpool Institute for Performing Arts*

'I thought Paul Fenn's chapter on 'Booking Agents' was extremely insightful. All too often people who work in the industry simply tell people what they want to hear; which of course is of no use to the up-and-coming musicians. Fenn has told it like it is, which is extremely valuable . . . it will test those who really want to be in the music business!'
*Chris Jenkins, Founder of the National Student Music Awards*

'It would be rare to find that music is excluded from any form of entertainment throughout the world. Whether it be an auditorium concert by a contemporary band; a televised opera or incidental music for a film or play. 'Bible' is indeed the definitive word – it is a must for all musicians and everyone involved in music in any way'
*Bob James, President, Agents' Association*

'I found it to be very comprehensive with up-to-date references, a must-read for anyone wanting to get into the industry'
*Nick Young, Studio Manager, Miloco, who has worked with the Chemical Brothers, Oasis, Coldplay, Badly Drawn Boy, Black Box Recorder, the Prodigy and Robbie Williams*

'A great, simple overview of the music industry . . . A must for everyone, not only those starting out, who will benefit from the advice, but also a useful contact directory for anyone in the business'
*Rupert Withers, Assassination Music*

'The book . . . is an excellent and accessible tool for anyone wanting to work in music . . . There are big winners in the music business but there are also big losers. Knowing how the business works is one sure way to keep out of the second category'
*Caroline Robertson, Director, Westbury Music*

'A must for anyone wanting to make it in the music business, the directories alone make this book invaluable'
*Justin Coll, Managing Director, www.liveclub.co.uk*

'Excellent. I'm sure this will be a must-have for many within the current world of music since it contains good elementary guides and source info'
*Daniel Koety, MCPS/PPL Sound Recordings Copyright Researcher*

## About the Author

John Collis is a freelance writer and music journalist.
A former music editor of *Time Out*, he is the author
of several books, including *The Story of Chess
Records* (Bloomsbury, 1998) and *Van Morrison:
Inarticulate Speech of the Heart* (Little, Brown, 1996).
He is also a cricket writer for the *Guardian*.

JOHN COLLIS

# the
# musicians'
# bible 2002

## the complete guide
## to the music business

PENGUIN BOOKS

PENGUIN BOOKS

Published by the Penguin Group
Penguin Books Ltd, 80 Strand, London WC2R 0RL, England
Penguin Putnam Inc., 375 Hudson Street, New York, New York 10014, USA
Penguin Books Australia Ltd, Ringwood, Victoria, Australia
Penguin Books Canada Ltd, 10 Alcorn Avenue, Toronto, Ontario, Canada M4V 3B2
Penguin Books India (P) Ltd, 11 Community Centre, Panchsheel Park, New Delhi – 110 017, India
Penguin Books (NZ) Ltd, Cnr Rosedale and Airborne Roads, Albany, Auckland, New Zealand
Penguin Books (South Africa) (Pty) Ltd, 5 Watkins Street, Denver Ext 4, Johannesburg 2094, South Africa

Penguin Books Ltd, Registered Offices: 80 Strand, London WC2R 0RL, England

First published 2001
1

Copyright © John Collis, 2001
All rights reserved

The moral right of the author has been asserted

Set in TheSans and Minion
Typeset by Rowland Phototypesetting Ltd, Bury St Edmunds, Suffolk
Printed in England by Omnia Books Limited, Glasgow

# Introduction

1

This book is dedicated to real musicians and songwriters – those who have something to say and who want to retain some control over how they say it. In the story of post-war pop music there has always been another type of performer, more puppet than prodigy, and yet the real thing keeps shining through. This is true even today, when sometimes it seems that the puppets have taken over the theatre.

During the late 1950s there came 'the Frankies and the Bobbys', pretty boys whose good looks and willingness to do what they were told, without taking too much interest in the small print, were their most important characteristics. To a large extent rock 'n' roll took power away from the old-fashioned Tin Pan Alley operators. It was an exhilarating development of folk music performed by working-class blacks and whites, and for them the music came before the industry. They were accidental rebels, ignorant and uninterested in the way things had been done previously. Tin Pan Alley struck back with artists like Fabian: handsome, amiable and musically rootless.

If the 1960s belonged to the Beatles, the Rolling Stones and Bob Dylan, it was also the decade of session-men bands. Some of these short-lived outfits were great, like Capitol's raucous Piltdown Men. Some were literally cartoons, like the Archies. But in neither case did they have any history, nor any future. And there were always people willing to dress in chicken costumes or clowns' trousers, jump up and down on television to someone else's studio confections, and sink once more into the background with a few quid in their pocket.

In the 1970s Boney M were a disco phenomenon, selling records by the tens of millions. Even today there are still a group of artists trading under the name – some of the touring England cricket team went to see them in Pakistan, in autumn 2000. But the group came second, after the sound – German producer Frank Farian made a session record called 'Baby Do You Wanna Bump?' and, when it began to sell throughout Europe, had to create a band to promote the sound. Farian and unseen session performers were the real Boney M, assuming that the word 'real' can be usefully applied to them.

With the success of rap and hip-hop some genuine artists, with an individual voice, did indeed emerge. So did innumerable bunches of kids, strutting their stuff all too briefly to someone else's noise. And at the turn of the century, one of the pop music successes in the UK was a stream of dancing kids under any number of names, good-looking, well-scrubbed, energetic dancers – not musicians, in spite of those curious little dummy microphones that so many wore strapped to their heads. Good luck to them all, but they won't need this book.

These are the 'manufactured' groups. In America, a middle-aged former airline executive, Lou Pearlman, has refined the manufacturing process to great effect. Backstreet Boys, NSync, LFO, O-Town, Marshall Dyllon and C-Note are among those who have rolled off the Pearlman conveyor belt, recruited through advertisements, selected to provide a precise mix of images (shy, moody, ethnic, boy-next-door and good-looker), taught the rudiments of stagecraft and set in front of screaming children.

In the UK, the production company of Stock, Aitken and Waterman laid down the ground rules in the 1980s while Louis Walsh (Boyzone, Westlife) updated them for the 90s. Early in 2001 television viewers watched the skin-crawling embarrassments of *Popstars*, in which wannabees strutted their often woefully inadequate stuff in bleak rehearsal rooms, trying to impress a group of grim Svengalis.

Meanwhile, established artists went on record to bemoan the fact that Radio 1 – funded by the public but apparently answerable to no-one – was hurtling downmarket, catering for an ever younger and more gullible audience. The charts, said Blur, were 'a load of shite', while U2's Bono railed against 'processed and hyped pop bands'. Andy Kershaw, the disc jockey whose eclectic tastes once found their natural home on Radio 1, moved to Radio 3, a solemn channel once exclusively devoted to classical music and impenetrable drama written by Czechoslovakians. Pop, usually the broadest of cultural churches, entered 2001 in danger of being overrun by its dancing children and former soap stars.

On the other hand, genuine talent has always emerged from the most unlikely of sources, from this confectionery-stall end of the pop spectrum. The success of the Monkees in the 1960s may have been as much to do with the expertise of the session men actually playing on the group's early records, and the songwriters behind them, as it owed to the cheeky charm of the four hired hands performing as the band. Mike Nesmith, however, went on to become a respected country-rock performer with hits like 'Joanne', and the other three could perform with conviction when the band was revived in their middle age.

When the duo Wham! were scoring hit after hit it was clear that one of them didn't actually seem to contribute very much beyond adolescent sex appeal, but the other became one of the biggest solo stars in the world. And from the boy-band stable such thoroughbreds as Robbie Williams and Ronan Keating have emerged. No doubt by the time this book is published one or two more puppets will have found a real musical voice.

But the soul of popular music will always rest with those who get involved because first and foremost they burn to communicate a musical message, not because they fancy being photographed leaving the Ivy restaurant. With very, very few exceptions, a desire to succeed is absolutely essential, because success rarely comes easily. And unless that desire is backed by a commitment to the music rather than to the fame and the money, even the elusive prize of success will remain a short-lived one.

Pop music's reference points get ever wider. As equipment has become increasingly cheap and versatile, allied to ingenious computer software, the individual at home can create sounds that once would have required a professional studio, and engineer, a producer and a whole bunch of musicians. From techno wizz-kids creating robotic noises to the dance group Steps, fashions come and go.

One that never seems to go away for long, though, is the time-honoured group format. In its classic form it arose in the mid-50s from hillbilly and small-scale blues outfits, in bands like Buddy Holly and the Crickets, and Gene Vincent's Blue Caps. Elvis had a similar line-up, though when his career took off into the stratosphere Scotty Moore, Bill Black and D J Fontana were clearly seen as backing musicians rather than partners in a group.

At the time of writing this introduction the Beatles, who formed their band in obedience to the prototypes of Holly and Vincent, were at the top of the album charts once again, with a 'greatest hits' package. And Oasis, another guitar-bass-drums band, were still the biggest current name in the business, even though one daily expected a formal announcement of their dissolution.

If the thrust of the book tends to keep this Holly/Beatles/Oasis model clearly in mind, the information should be equally relevant to the lone operator as well as to the big band. It brings together a variety of information relating to the music business, collected into one convenient package. It is aimed at everyone involved in the effort of making music, as well as those who are simply thinking about the possibility of a musical career. For the beginner, it includes detailed discussion of every aspect of the business, in the hope that pitfalls can be avoided and correct decisions made. For those already involved, it offers a full range of essential listings and directories.

Wherever possible, and appropriate, the listings are annotated to make them of more use than a bald list of contact details. If you are a traditional folk singer, for example, it might be useful to know that the record company handily placed a few streets away actually specializes in reggae. In deciding what to include and, inevitably, leave out I have taken advice as widely as possible.

For the beginner, I have tried to envisage what you need to know, and in what order. I then consulted as many experts as possible, and with their help (they are all gratefully acknowledged below) assembled a series of pieces leading you through each aspect of the business as it arises. In some cases, as will be apparent, their involvement consisted of more than simply answering my questions. There has been a general enthusiasm for this project that I have found most encouraging and helpful.

Musical instruments and equipment, the business of forming or joining a band, making a demo, submitting it and protecting your work, finding agency and management representation, publishing and copyright, gigging, recording studios, music and the law, self promotion and approaches to the music press – these are just some of the potential minefields that the tyro musician must tiptoe through, and hopefully this book will help them to avoid a certain amount of learning by bitter experience.

This is intended to be an annual, with all the information checked, corrected, updated and added to each year. Any constructive and helpful comments would be much appreciated, and will be duly acknowledged. Please contact the author c/o The Musicians' Bible, Penguin Books Ltd, 80 Strand, London WC2R ORL. Equally importantly, if you ought to be listed in one of the directories but have been omitted, send in your full details. When the time comes to update the information, we will check with you that it is accurate.

One issue that will continue to reverberate is the relationship between the music business (dedicated to extracting its financial percentage) and the strange new democracy of the Internet. While Peter Whitehead looks to the future in the chapter Music in Space, the day-to-day ramifications continue to develop.

In January the row between music publishers and Napster, the Internet site that allows free downloading and swapping of music files, took a significant turn. The chief executive of the vast Bertelsmann group, Thomas Middelhoff, announced at the World Economic Forum that his company was close to establishing a subscription system (or what Napster preferred to term a 'membership fee') that would enable revenue to be collected for Internet access to music.

This was the next logical step in the controversial co-operation between Bertelsmann and Napster, who were regarded by most of the industry as pirates. 'Napster will continue to be easy to use', the company's interim chief executive Hank Barry told the *Independent*, 'and it will pay artists individually. Copyright is about maintaining the balance between the owner of the rights and the user.' He also argued that services like Napster actually stimulated, rather than suppressed, retail demand.

Not everyone was convinced that Napster was interested in balance, however. Also in Davos, Switzerland, for the Forum was the composer and performer Peter Gabriel. 'As artists we have always been screwed by the music majors', he said. 'Napster and the file sharers are screwing us all over again.' He foresaw a possible return to the bad old days when the artist was bought off with a flat fee that bore no relationship to the revenue earned by a hit.

And the majority of the music industry, those accused by Gabriel of screwing artists, actually agreed with him over Napster. In March, following further moves in court, Napster began the process of preventing copyrighted songs from being swapped on its site. It even began to employ a complex filtering system to identify deliberate misspellings of band names, used by fans to evade the ban.

Still its opponents were not satisfied. A lawyer for Metallica, the band who had always been most prominent in objecting to Napster's infringement of their copyright, was quoted in the *Guardian*, 22 March, as saying: 'They're not trying hard enough.' Napster also found itself landed with a law suit by the 'legal' site Emusic.com, which pays a licence fee to artists.

As always in America, the lawyers are the winners in all this confusion. And in the end an accommodation will have to be found – if Napster shuts down, pirate versions will then arise, always staying a step ahead of the law. Licensing by some agreed formula is the only way forward.

Many experts agree with Peter Whitehead in predicting a system where an artist offers, say, one track of an album free over the Internet as an inducement to buy the whole set. One thing is certain, that current reasons for resisting consumption of music from the Internet will disappear – files will occupy less disk space, hard disks will have vastly more capacity, downloading will be almost instantaneous, and we will not be expected to sit tapping our toes at the ever-present screen. In the face of such speedy change, agreement between the various parties seems inevitable, for the only possible reason – that it is in everyone's interests.

I am most grateful to brothernature, Adrian and Melvin Duffy, and their manager, Michelle Hopkins, for their help with this book. Artist manager Ed Bicknell, who is always ready to 'put something back' into the industry that has brought him such success, was generous with his time, as was that evangelist for music on the Internet, Peter Whitehead. Charlie Gillett gave me many useful leads, while Nigel McCune and Horace Trubridge of the Musicians' Union were enthusiastic about the project from the start. Cliff White, Alasdair Blaazer and Rob Hughes of the Mechanical Copyright Protection Society, record promotor Michael Peyton, Steve Simmonds of the Truelove Label Collective, impresario Denis Vaughan, Alison Wilson of the 'brokers' Tribal Manufacturing, equipment salesman Keith Davis, studio owner Charlie Hart, Paul Fenn of the Asgard agency, Ross Fortune, music editor of *Time Out*, for his survey of the press, and everyone's favourite disc jockey, John Peel, were very helpful in leading me through their particular areas of the business. Thank you to James Fisher of the Music Managers' Forum for many useful comments on the text, which I have taken on board, and to all those who kindly looked through the proofs and were willing to provide endorsements.

At Penguin, I would like to thank Molly Mackey and Rochelle Levy for their great efforts in organizing the huge mail-out and to thank my editor, Martin Toseland, whose hands-on approach to this book was a great help throughout the year of preparation. Finally, thanks to my son, Tom, whose flying fingers helped input much of the information.

In spite of a general suspicion of the influence wielded by multinationals on the creative endeavour of making music, and of quiet despair at the 'manufactured' nature of so much contemporary pop, what came over most strongly was the level of enthusiasm and even optimism that informs their work. I hope, therefore, that this book is both enthusiastic and optimistic.

John Collis, March 2001

# Equipment

2

Keith Davis, a senior salesman at Len Stiles' music shop in Lewisham, is optimistic about the future of live music. And he is well placed to know, since like many of those who sell musical equipment by day he uses it at night, and so he can assess the business from both sides. He plays lead guitar in a 60s cover band, Flashback, and takes three guitars to gigs – an Epiphone Sheraton, a Fender Stratocaster and an electro-acoustic Yamaha, put through a 120-watt Crate combo. Next morning, he's back in the shop. As he says:

In music retail there's always been a tradition of having two jobs. It so happens that I've never wanted to play full-time, because I wouldn't want it to be just a job. You'd lose the fun of playing. But I remember years ago when I was working at Boosey & Hawkes in the West End, there was Chris Squire, the bass player with Yes, in the packing department, Peter Knight, who went on to play violin in Steeleye Span, was in retail and sales, the trombonist Paul Rutherford and the drummer John Stevens, who were in the Spontaneous Music Ensemble, they were in the music hire library. Of course, they all moved on, but I've always been happy to mix the two careers.

There's a big revival in live music. We're now selling more drum kits than drum machines, whereas ten years ago it was the other way round. In fact we were selling more electronics in general. And I see this trend back to music in the pubs and clubs as well. People prefer to see a band rather than a solo act with a keyboard. There's less karaoke, less discos than there were – I think their popularity has peaked. Naturally, there'll always be a demand for discos, and obviously they go out for less money than a band, but people are willing to pay for real music once again.

You also see this in the fact that youngsters are coming in again to buy electric guitars. There's more interest in the instrument than for a long time. Of course, heavy metal bands never go out of fashion, so there's always been a certain demand for guitars, but in the last five years bands like Oasis have sparked a real increase in guitar sales.

This is comforting news to all real musicians. At times during the past year, usually when switching on the television, it has seemed that pop groups consists only of dancing children, jigging about to a backing track. No musicians at all, it seems, just a middle-aged Svengali in a studio somewhere. This is not to denigrate the energy, determination and athletic ability of these non-bands – there's room for them, as long as their audience moves on to the hard stuff.

In the years that Keith Davis has worked in music shops the trade has become more professional.

When I started, the training consisted of standing on the floor and working it out for yourself. Opening drawers to see what was in them. Now there are proper training courses. But they can never totally replace the experience of actually doing the job. And there's so many developments in equipment you've got to keep yourself up to date.

So what advice does he have for someone starting out as a musician? Music shops can be a little daunting, after all.

Yes, it's easy to be conned into buying the wrong equipment. Or not being conned, necessarily, but being unable to find out exactly what you need. The most reliable way is to go on recommendation, on reputation. This will mean getting to know someone locally who's already made a start. Maybe get to know a band who play a residency in the area.

When you're in the shop you should ask questions. You should be able to tell whether the salesman knows what he's talking about. Those rules apply whether you're going up to the West End or shopping locally. But bear in mind that you need service, and that might mean after-sales service as well as good advice to start with. That might decide where you go to buy equipment. It's easier to do that with a local shop, but on the other hand there's a wider range in the West End, both of shops and of stock in the individual stores.

Clearly the more you can afford to pay, the better the equipment ought to be. With guitars you see it in the smoothness of the action, and the response of the pick-ups. Remember that a solid-wood body is better than one made up of laminate. It will actually improve with age.

Tom McGuinness – who has been a professional musician all his working life, playing guitar or bass with Manfred Mann, McGuinness Flint and The Blues Band – has bought countless guitars over the years and so has built up a fund of expertise. This leads him to say: 'I would always tend to buy second-hand. The prices in the West End are a rip-off.'

However, he has decades of experience, and a deep knowledge of the vintage guitar market. Keith Davis feels that the beginner might be better off buying new, although he admits that the trade has changed since he started.

Back then it was almost all second-hand. Now I'd say it's 80 per cent new, and there's not a lot of part-exchange. In the old days the music shops used to go to America to buy second-hand, but there's been such a boom in the vintage market that prices for really collectable old guitars have shot up. Don't forget, though, that nowadays you can get on the Internet – you can literally shop around all over the world. And that's true whether you opt for new or second-hand.

For the beginner learning to play one of the instruments that make up a typical rock band, a minimum outlay of £500-plus is necessary.

If you want to be a guitarist, you can buy a new Fender Squire for £120. It's Fender's budget brand, one of our biggest sellers. I wouldn't recommend going below that. Little practice amps, 10 watts, start at £59 for Marshalls, £69 for Crate. Marshalls are made in Korea these days, Crates are American. I prefer American myself. I think they give more tonal variation. But it's at a price – across the range you could be paying double the price of a Korean amp. For playing in a band you want to start with, say, a 50 watt amp. I'd say you need an outlay of £500 minimum.

Synthesizers start at £500. The most popular brands are Yamaha, Korg or Roland. You won't see many bands using a portable keyboard these days. They're more for the old-fashioned pub duos. A keyboard is very limited in what variations you can get out of it, so I'd say always go for a synthesizer instead. And drum kits start from £269, including the sticks and a stool but not the cases. A good starting price for playing in a band, though, would be around £625-plus.

This is the way bands have always got started. However, in 2001 just as many singles start life in a back-bedroom studio as in a rehearsal room. Miniaturization has made almost anything possible technically, and hardware prices have tended to move in the opposite direction to inflation. One successful backroom operator is Charlie Hart, who, as a multi-instrumentalist and producer, played with such bands as Ian Dury's Kilburn and the High Roads, Ronnie Lane's Slim Chance and Juice on the Loose. Now he spends most of his time off the road, creating musical soundtracks for film and television, in particular for animation projects. His home-produced music has even brought him an Oscar nomination.

Hart's first piece of advice is to take what you are doing seriously, rather than regard it as simply playing with electronic toys:

Even if you're sitting in a bedroom with a cheap computer, you are a *producer*. The industry tends to call home studios 'project studios'. It sounds better, but it also reminds you that it exists for a specific purpose.

He has been doing the job long enough to have moved through several advances in the standard equipment used.

When I started producing you needed to be able to run a tape machine and a mixing desk. I progressed from a Revox to a cassette portastudio, and later an eight-track quarter-inch machine. Then I moved on to an ADAT machine – digital eight-track tape. From there I moved to computer-based hard-disc recording, sequencing, sampling and editing. In each case this piece of equipment is in effect the heart of the studio – it's what transcribes the sound.

The cheapest way is to do everything – all these functions and others, like mixing and applying effects – within the computer, using appropriate software. You should first decide what programmes you can afford. Common ones are Logic Audio, Cubase, and ProTools. They all exist in different forms, and you can buy add-ons and plug-ins depending on what you want to do. Nearly all of the functions of a conventional studio can now be contained within the computer and its software. You'll also need a microphone, a keyboard, a system for monitoring the sound – which could just be headphones. And a chair, of course!

For professional results, though, you usually need quite a lot of 'outboard', which is equipment outside the computer. For example, there are old-fashioned valve compressors, which inject the warmth and depth that are often missing in digital recordings. They give the recording something nearer an analogue sound. Then there are sound modules, which are really like several synthesizers rolled into one, but without the keyboard. They generate different sounds, although they can also be installed inside the computer. And then there's effects like reverb and echo, chorus and delay. If you add this sort of equipment you will give breadth and variety to a computer-based set-up.

Most people, presumably, don't start from scratch with a well-loaded credit card.

No, they don't. With a few thousand to spend you could go out and buy one of the latest complete digital workstations, which are amazing pieces of equipment. But, in practice, most people cobble stuff together bit by bit, gradually building up what they want, trading pieces they have outgrown. And, of course, you could still be using an old-fashioned analogue studio based on a tape machine and a mixing desk. Or a bit of both: part computer-based, part analogue. The minimum outlay to get going, assuming you've already got a PC, is only a few hundred pounds. The digital revolution has put very sophisticated potential into people's hands. But it is also worth investing in as good a DAT machine or CD burner as you can afford. From these pieces of equipment you will be able to produce not just a good demo, but even a production master.

However versatile and ingenious modern technology is, it will never do away with the need for a proper work discipline. Hart says:

You must learn the basic engineering rules. Whatever the system, you should spend as much time as you can learning how to get the best out of it. Even with simple equipment you can produce recordings of professional quality as long as you know exactly what you are doing.

Unless you have grown up with the developments in technology it would be a good idea to consider enrolling in a college course. When I was trying to diversify from just playing in bands I went to Goldsmiths' to study composing, and producing what they call 'music to picture'. In my case this is usually writing and recording soundtracks to fit to animation films.

The most vital quality that will never be replaced by technological magic is the creative spark. Hart agrees:

It is very important not to get so involved in the technology that you overlook the creative side. All the equipment in the world won't make a bad idea sound good. The premium will always be on creativity. And the ideas are not usually conceived while you are sitting at the computer. Beware of spending your whole life in front of the screen. Sort out your creative ideas first – go for a walk, whatever. You must be in charge of the technology, not vice versa, because in the end the equipment is only a vehicle to allow you to transmit your idea. It isn't the idea itself. So, if for example you are basically a songwriter, complete the song before you sit down at the computer. On the other hand, of course, if you are working in a field like techno or house you might only need one good lyric line!

Which leads one to ask, who let the dogs out? I bet you can still hear that one good lyric line, months after it faded from the charts. Even then, that line is only the hook of an overall musical conception, one that wasn't thought of by twiddling a few knobs. It was conceived, created and then constructed.

Finally, says Hart:

Don't forget to continue developing your traditional skills, with your instrument or your voice, because they can always be useful. And with a home system you need to be aware that you'll be trying to do four jobs at once – writer, performer, engineer and producer. When you are a performer you can concentrate on just the one. So building a home studio doesn't necessarily rule out also using a conventional one. In theory it is possible to do everything in your back room, but bear in mind that music usually develops communally. It is an interchange of ideas.

# Demonstration Discs and Recording Studios

3

The demonstration record, on CD, tape or email attachment (henceforward the 'demo'), is a vital stage in a new band's development. Along with a photograph (equally important – it's not much good sounding like Ronan Keating if you actually look like me, and the recipient will need to know if this is the case), it is your basic calling card, the one you present to a record company, publisher, agency or promoter.

A demo should consist of your best three or four original songs – no more, because the recipient won't get that far, or will be even more tempted to give each number just a few bars before moving on. If there is only one writer in the band it may be the other musicians who can best offer an objective perspective on which ones to choose. If you are working alone seek out sympathetic opinion, and then take it or leave it. The strongest song should come first, and the rest should fill out an indication of your versatility, without being so varied that you seem to have no 'voice' of your own.

If you haven't already done so, this is the moment to ask yourself if the tempo and arrangement you have habitually applied to a particular number are the ones that best bring out its qualities. Slow down a fast song and it may reveal an unexpectedly soulful mood. Or it may sound like a dirge (in which case, even at the faster tempo, it may not *be* your best). Turning a medium-pacer into a fast rocker may give it new character – or simply make it sound like every other up-tempo number. You won't know unless you try.

Keep the arrangement tight. The lead guitarist may stretch out to wild acclaim when you play live to a local, sympathetic crowd, but whoever you send the demo to will be familiar with the best in the business. The guitarist's expertise should come over perfectly well in a tauter setting. Above all, remember that the way you start the song will determine whether your target persists to the end. Get to the point – hook him with the riff, move the middle eight to the front, shift a killer line into the first verse, whatever. Start with the grabber.

You should now thoroughly rehearse your chosen mini-set. Even if you haven't made any radical changes, you should still work with a newly critical attitude. Sloppy playing, or even bits of a song that haven't been properly resolved structurally, can be masked by the buzz of a live performance, but they won't be in the studio, or in the A&R office. Tape the selection to the best standard you can manage, and analyse it. Listen with fresh ears, as if coming to the songs for the first time. Because that is what is going to happen when you send them out into the world.

Four-track equipment is fine for rehearsing songs, and at a pinch a singer with a guitar and a drum machine can create a decent demo on it. But does the world need a singer with a guitar and a drum machine? If you are building up a demo on your own or with a production partner, using riffs, samples and vocal fragments cut to a repetitive dance beat, each track-to-track transfer will increase the build-up of extraneous noise. The better the equipment your demo is played on, the more intrusive this will be. And A&R people have good equipment, because they don't have to pay for it. By and large, then, eight-track is the minimum requirement.

If you have access to such equipment without paying for a studio, fine. But consider a few things first. The loan of the equipment should include someone expert in its use, or all the nervous energy of the session will soon dissipate while one of you grapples with the inscrutable software. And this amateur expert should be a sympathetic friend of the band, not one of its members. Playing an instrument is one job, recording it should be another.

Also, what sort of ambient sound are you aiming at? What warmth, depth, space? Do you want to capture a live sound? Whatever the answer, can you achieve the desired noise when crowded into a back bedroom? In the rock 'n' roll era, hits were created in any number of conditions. The Decca sound of Bill Haley was produced in a ballroom, the revolutionary noise of young Elvis from a tiny room, Buddy Holly from an all-purpose studio in the middle of nowhere, Joe Meek's spacey British successes from a Holloway Road walk-up flat, the Beatles from a studio built to accommodate a symphony orchestra. These days the back bedroom may well do for the lone maestro (see what producer Charlie Hart has to say in Chapter 2 – Equipment), but it may not give the atmosphere you want for your band.

If you decide that you need a professional set-up, and this is most likely to be the conclusion, you should have some idea of your total budget and of how far it is practical to travel. A bargain rate 100 miles away is less of a bargain if several of the band need to take unpaid leave from a day job, rather than making an evening booking close at hand.

Shop around within your practical radius, and make sure you visit any studio under consideration. The right one will *feel* right. If you have no choice of studio, accept this and determine to use the facilities to your best advantage. And make sure that you take into account all the charges that will be levied, not just the hourly, daily or bargain-offer rate for the studio and its engineer. What will a master tape cost, and how much more would it be to take away the multi-track tape as well? With the latter, you will not necessarily be limited in future to the mixed-down version of your day's work. However, you should never leave until you are happy with the master tape, because that was the whole purpose of the exercise.

You will be paying for studio time from the outset, so this is not the moment to find out that your equipment will not fit into the space, that the drummer has forgotten his hi-hat, that the dodgy lead you've got by with for the last month has finally given up, or that the bass player needs to go in search of replacement strings. Prepare thoroughly, so that you can achieve maximum value from the session.

Remember that if you break off for a wet lunch in the pub (1) you are still paying for the time, (2) you will stay longer in the pub than you intended, and (3) any momentum already underway will have to be stoked up again. On the other hand, if things are going smoothly, there is a natural break in the proceedings, and you have paid for an open-ended day, then a brief release from the windowless claustrophobia of the studio can be beneficial. Use it to plot out the rest of the session, and don't drink too much. If just one player comes back from a break with fat fingers or an idiosyncratic interpretation of time signatures, then the rest of the session could be wasted.

This recording is intended to present the band in the best possible light. It should have a 'live' buzz while utilizing every useful trick the engineer has to offer. But it will not be a Phil Spector production, even if your budget is indulgently generous. In any case, you may well be trying to sell yourselves to someone who fancies *himself* as the next Phil Spector. The more you over-egg the pudding, the more alternative production options you are closing down. Concentrate instead on clarity, immediacy and energy, selling the quality of the material and the musicianship. The string quartet, the massed kettledrums, the bizarrely 'phased' guitar solo – all these are for the future.

And when that future arrives, you will be assigned to a producer and an engineer. The latter, who may come with the studio or travel as a double act with a freelance producer, is the vital link between your music and its representation on CD. Some producers, particularly in small independent set-ups, engineer their own sessions, but many of the breed know exactly the sound they want but have no idea how to achieve it technically. The engineer will have to act as interpreter when asked for 'a more *crunchy* sound' or 'a dirtier bass'.

Your relationship with the recording studio will depend on the deal. You may have your own label and a close working relationship with the producer and engineer. They may even be partners in the label. On the other hand, you could have a contract with a major label and find that everything and everyone are assigned to you without you being consulted. And if you are a 'manufactured' band, it is likely to be the producer who made the mould. Whichever you are, it is very likely that you will end up paying the bills – even if you only find this out five years later, in a frosty legal communication from a now estranged record company. So, lone entrepreneur or puppet of a multinational label, try and ensure that you get the best possible creative use out of your expensive studio time.

# Booking Agents

4

Agents exist in all areas of the arts, and the role they have in common is to generate work for their clients and to negotiate the terms, in return for a commission on monies earned. Their degree of involvement in the process, however, varies.

In Hollywood the film agent is an all-powerful figure at the very heart of movie-making. He builds a star's career just as a boxing manager takes a protégé from promising tyro to world championship contender, by a shrewd process of wheeling, dealing and match-making. In the film business, nothing happens without the agent's say-so.

With writing, the agent's role is less central but equally important – he is the one who knows what publishers are looking for, he may well generate the book idea, he will certainly negotiate the deal, and he may take an interest in the process of writing.

In the music business the agent, or booking agent, has a clearly defined role, as is suggested by the more specific title. He is an intermediary between artist and promoter, organizing the bookings and the schedule, agreeing the deal for live concert performances. However, he has no active interest in the music itself, in songwriting, rehearsal, promotion or recording – unless, of course, he happens to become a close friend of the performer and is asked for advice. So, how do the artist and the agent come together?

Well, we'll begin with the bad news. Paul Fenn, founder of the London booking agency Asgard, has a message for ambitious new bands – please don't call him. He explains why:

There are about ten major agencies in London, and we are all working non-stop to turn over revenue so that we can avoid being taken over by some conglomerate. To put it harshly, a new artist doesn't bring us anything we need. Unfortunately, it doesn't even make any difference if we really like the music. If they knew just how many unsolicited calls and tapes we get, maybe they'd understand. You see, you can't just ring up a venue in Sheffield and get a booking for an unknown, just because they happen to be good. It's being *known* that counts.

And so the local slog has to come first, and even then Fenn admits that there's a problem. 'There's not really a circuit any more, pubs and small clubs, certainly not on the scale that there used to be.'

The refusal of central agencies to take on untested talent, of whatever quality, comes down to simple economics. 'London offices have huge overheads,' says Fenn. 'We simply can't book out £100 bands. We'd go broke, because it wouldn't even cover the phone bill.'

So, what does a fresh provincial talent have to do?

The local band, the new act, needs someone on the phone all the time, hustling. We can't help with that. Once they've got a reputation, though, that's when we'll hear about it.

We're looking for the buzz, the management structure, the record deal, whatever – something we can work with. With hindsight you can always say that those who succeeded, the ones that rose out of the pack, were going to succeed anyway, regardless. Somehow, the word gets out of their own city, and eventually the London-based business wakes up to them. All parts of it – us, the press, the record companies, the promoters. There comes a stage when we *do* want to know. How they do it, though, that I simply don't know. If I did I'd tell them. All I know is that somehow it happens.

It is quite likely that this raw band, trying to make Paul Fenn sit up and listen, has not attracted a successful, well-financed, hugely experienced manager at this stage, but Fenn says that this is not what matters.

As far as managers are concerned, a guy with no experience but endless energy can succeed, simply by hammering away with enthusiasm. It's going back a bit, I know, but a good example is Chris Fenwick with Dr Feelgood.

These Canvey Island heroes of the 1970s were, in essence, simply an R&B revival band with attitude. Of course, if Fenwick had imitated their cocky, onstage strutting, which was an act put on by an intelligent, friendly bunch of dedicated musicians, then doors would have been slammed in his face. He didn't – he made headway with the two qualities identified by Fenn, energy and enthusiasm. 'A heavyweight manager would not have had the time or inclination to make Dr Feelgood a success,' Fenn adds.

Indeed, such a person would probably not have bothered to see beyond the cover versions and retro appearance of the band, and not realized that R&B was inevitably about to enjoy one of its periodic back-to-the-roots revivals. As it was, the Feelgoods moved inexorably from tiny pubs to the country's biggest concert halls, into the Top Ten and to the very top of the album charts. And when they got there, they were exactly the same band that started out, playing the music they loved. Twenty-five years later, having survived the tragic death of their original lead singer and the long-ago departure of their first guitarist, as well as endless shifts in fashion, the Feelgoods are still out there rocking.

The same lesson that applied to them still holds true today – given the energy, given the dedication, given a musical message that speaks to enough people, the top London agents will eventually receive that message loud and clear. In the meantime, the band must get its early gigs through local knowledge, and then maybe graduate to working with someone booking out bands within a somewhat larger radius. It will then be this agent's job to tap into an expanding network of promoters in widening the band's catchment area.

It is an agent's responsibility to consider certain practical matters in return for a commission, which is a percentage of fees received for the gigs. This will normally be 10 per cent, though in the case of a megastar who takes little or no selling – just efficient hands-on organization – the agent may accept being knocked down as far as 5 per cent, while on the other hand, the standard commission could rise to 15 per cent if he is striving to break totally new ground.

Those practical considerations include the nature of the band's music. A heavy-metal group booked into a Darby and Joan social club should look elsewhere for representation. And even if an agent has an excellent relationship with one promoter in Arbroath and another in Truro, if he books the band into these venues on successive nights then they should save their petrol money and get on the phone instead.

On a local level the agent may well attend the gigs, forming a team with the manager, and deal with the money. More usually, he will invoice the band on a regular basis. At the other end of the spectrum, Asgard also find themselves acting as cashiers when bringing in a top American act, as Fenn describes:

In most cases the money comes through us, so we can monitor it. These days the artist barely needs cash when they're on the road. Everything's on a credit card, and the backing musicians will have a wage from the management. So we often act as a bank for the tour. We'll see all the documentation, all the paper work, to make sure it adds up. In fact the payment chain is very well documented these days, all the way down the line.

It may not, however, be quite so transparent back in the local pubs. It is vital, therefore, that a band is aware of all the details of any contract they have with their agent. In fact, they should think carefully before signing such a document. As Fenn, who handles roughly 100 acts, explains: 'Most agencies would like to think they have contracts with their artists, but it doesn't usually happen that way.' In other words, the relationship is usually based on mutual trust, and mutual interest – it has worked in the past, and both parties assume that this will remain the case until the opposite is proved.

The agent's role is usually limited to booking live gigs. Other appearances – in-store promotions, television and radio, films and videos – are the concern of management. Therefore, the agent should only expect to be paid commission on the precise area of their involvement. This would be the case even when a performer is also an actor (and, to complicate matters further, when they appear either as themselves or in character, in a role that involves speaking, singing or both) – either the agency is also involved by agreement with such work, or it isn't. If it is, the agency may also have a claim on a proportion of earnings from soundtrack albums or videos.

When the relationship is confirmed by a signed contract (and these matters should in any case be discussed in any purely verbal agreement) the range of the agent's involvement must be clear, as must also the length of the deal.

And if the artist becomes famous enough to turn themselves into a company, effectively employing themselves for tax reasons and drawing a salary out of gross receipts, then clearly an agent should not expect a percentage of both. For example, the artist's company is paid

£10,000 for a performance but only 'pays' the artist £1,000 from the fee – the agent can expect commission for securing a £10,000 gig, but not a further percentage of the salary element.

By this time, the artist will inevitably have graduated to one of the big agencies with international contacts (not all of which in the UK, it should be stressed, are based in London). Fenn says:

With big names, we are to a certain extent employed to say no, because promoters come looking for the act but the act may not want to work. Some of our acts haven't worked for ten years and I wouldn't be able to persuade them.

These happy souls, with no burning need to be constantly in the public eye, watch the postman come up the garden path with cheques for back royalties, publishing or PRS, and then go off fishing. 'You can't tell an artist when to tour,' says Fenn. On the other hand, he may hear through the grapevine of an artist apparently living in contented retirement who has suddenly got the itch to go back on the road. How would he angle to represent him?

Well, here's an example. It was an artist who last toured Europe 12 years ago, but not through us. Big tour, huge production, trucks driving all over the continent. It lost a quarter of a million dollars. I pointed out to him that nobody comes to see the lights and the sound rigs. Certainly not to admire the trucks. Hire the best people locally, the experts for each venue. Get rid of the trucks. Keep costs low. A simple pitch, but it meant that on a six-week tour we *made* a quarter of a million, not lost it.

Once an agency like Asgard has won such a valuable client, how do they usually operate?

Normally we're given a specific time period to work in – it's typically the time they are promoting a new album. In the ideal world the manager is already thinking globally, planning the States for a particular time, and then telling us what we can have for Europe. It will usually be too little – I have to point out how many countries there are in Europe, how many cities and venues to cover. So we argue the toss and eventually we agree.

In each country the artist may have a loyalty to a particular promoter they've been happy with in the past. We'd always go down that route first, but if we didn't feel that the deal was right then we'd go elsewhere. When you're trying to sell some artists, the promoters' stock response is to say that they'll check out album sales, and then to come back and say that they're not big enough. I have to convince them that there are so many long-established artists around who will sell out concerts, but the audience doesn't necessarily rush out and buy the albums.

Especially, perhaps, if they haven't toured for 12 years. And, anyway, a capacity crowd of 5,000 can provide a very healthy profit for everyone involved in a one-night stand, but in terms of annual album sales across the country it may produce just a tiny blip on the record company's radar.

Such an artist has reached a contented middle-aged plateau, perhaps – from a local agent to international representation, from hits to solid album sales, from no income to a pension in the form of PRS. That can still be the goal of young musicians following in the tradition.

But back at square one, many artists are taking a different route these days. According to Fenn:

They don't work from scratch any more, building up a following, getting a record contract. Now they buy a drum machine, put out a single and then maybe they think about touring.

In which case, they'll need an agent.

# Management

5

Unless you are an unaccompanied folk singer with a head for business, the chances are that you will need a manager sooner rather than later. With a band that has agreed to split everything equally, the manager could well be an extra equal partner when it comes to the share-out. Otherwise, an agreed percentage is likely to be 20 per cent of gross, although if the land is already an established success it could be negotiated. For live work, however, the percentage should be net – a band's receipts on the road tend to get eaten up in paying for transport, hotels, food, additional personnel, agency fees, etc, and for the manager to take his split off the top would clearly be impractical and unfair in most instances.

Already it should be apparent that, from the very outset, even if the manager is just a friend with a van and some spare time (perhaps *particularly* if he is, to avoid matters getting nasty later on), there should be some sort of agreement in writing between the artist(s) and the one who is charged with doing everything except write, rehearse and perform. In the earliest stages it does not have to be a formal contract, but whatever form of words is chosen the agreement should recognize that things could get serious at some stage in the near future. The relationship between the band and their friend with a van should already have been defined at this stage, in case events suddenly outgrow his business expertise and, indeed, his van. James Fisher of the Music Managers' Forum recommends that band and manager enter a Short Term Agreement for a year, which can then be torn up without resort to lawyers if things turn sour.

It may be, for instance, that if a more professional and expert management set-up is necessary, the role of the original manager can be absorbed by negotiation along previously agreed lines – as road manager, for instance, or as salaried assistant. If this possibility is not envisaged in advance, lifetime friendships could dissolve in bitterness and even litigation – after all, there *is* such a thing as a verbal contract.

In the early days of a band's life there will inevitably be an element of mucking in, but whoever's idea is being acted on it will be the manager's responsibility to make sure that everything gets done. He won't actually be performing, but he will have an input into the nature of the performance, and he will also be responsible for making sure that the musicians get to the gig in order to perform. And if any of the band gets the idea that being a creative musician involves lying in bed and expecting everything to be done for them, then of course it will be the manager's job to disabuse them of the notion.

With increasing success, more and more people will come into the orbit of the band, all of them wanting a piece of that success. Suddenly, the manager is no longer dealing with the landlord of the local pub. He needs a high level of skill at negotiating and co-ordinating. He cannot afford to sign away the band to a contract that they will resent ever after – as Ed Bicknell warns later in this chapter, the first deal has implications for ever. Nor can the manager allow conflicting advice from, say, a lawyer and an accountant to remain unresolved.

By now the manager will be dealing with various representatives of a record company – A&R, press office, legal and financial departments. He will be in meetings with the band's lawyer and accountant, with promoters, equipment and transport suppliers, hotels, caterers, fly-posters and merchandisers. And he will never be immune from the personal problems of the individual members of the band, because financial or marital difficulties, use of narcotics, personality disputes and other such aggravations will all affect the performance of the band and, ultimately, it is the manager's job to see that the performance level is maintained. As the band members spend more time with each other, less with their families, the manager's role will increasingly be that of a counsellor, trying to keep careers and personal lives on course. He will need the absolute trust of the band's members, who can be confident of his honest dealings with them. There is a whole lot more to being a successful manager, therefore, than a shrewd business brain.

Ed Bicknell must surely rate as one of the most successful of all. As an agent in the 1970s he represented some of the top acts of the day, including Elton John, The Ramones, Yes and Talking Heads. Turning to management he was associated with such artists as Gerry Rafferty, Bryan Ferry and Scott Walker. It is for his long association with Dire Straits, however, and subsequently in particular with Mark Knopfler, that Bicknell is best known, since he guided the band from being a London pub act to become *the* rock-music phenomenon of the 1980s, one of the most successful groups of all time. The relationship lasted until 2000.

Bicknell has always had a reputation for putting his expertise back into the business for the benefit of others. He gives lectures, question and answer sessions and tutorials on the business side of rock. He also kindly talked to me at length for this book, and what he has to say is illuminating both for those with an ambition to manage music acts, but also for musicians themselves. Armed with Bicknell's wisdom at second hand, they will be better placed to know what to look for in a manager, and what to expect from them.

The main quality needed to be a manager is to believe in the act. To believe in them as people, and in what they want to achieve. Talent is 50 per cent, but it's willpower that brings success. The talented people who have failed did so because they gave up.

Freddy DeMann once told me that when Madonna walked into his office he knew she would succeed, before he'd even heard her music, because she was 'driven'. And within Dire Straits there were two people, Mark and John, Mark in particular, who were similarly driven.

You might think that the main motivation is money, but in the beginning that's the least concern. *Ego* is the driving force: get up on stage, jump up and down, perhaps make a tit of yourself, that's ego. As the Straits developed it became apparent that certain people were going to last the course, and others not. That's exactly what happened.

I don't think any of us thought we were going to sell 105 million albums. I didn't even think of it in terms of commercial success. I'd been an agent for eight years and I was getting stale. So my first motive was escape. The other thing was that Mark had a red Stratocaster. I was a huge Shadows fan, and when I walked into Dingwalls to see them for the first time I said: 'My God, he's got a red Strat like Hank Marvin.' The guitar was part of the dream, part of the lifestyle.

It was less regimented then than now. We didn't have a plan. These days you tour to capitalize on records. In those days you toured to *sell* records, to connect with a live audience. Once it started there was a rapid momentum – by February 1979 we were in America with a No. 2 album and single. The album was Top 5 all over the world.

One thing I learned was to try and create an event. One way is to underplay demand. It's better to have a queue outside. A bit unfair on those who can't get in, but good for the image. We were offered Madison Square Garden, but we looked better on a club stage. They would have been lost in that space, and there would have been empty seats. As it was the club dates we played were absolutely packed, creating great media attention and a real buzz.

Mutual trust and respect are essential in the relationship between an act and their management. You have to be pulling in the same direction. If you're pulling in different directions, it's disaster. I've discussed this with The Blue Nile [another act that Bicknell works with]. They are the nicest people imaginable. And I've said to them that I will always take the most commercial line. If that means breakfast TV and re-edited singles, fine. If you want to be popular you have to prostitute yourself. If you don't, fuck off to the Isle of Arran and become a folk singer.

Pop music is part of show business. That's one of the reasons why these boy and girl bands are so successful. They're working in the world as it is, and they'll do anything to get what they want. Ronan Keating wouldn't think twice about doing the Lottery show, for instance. When you're abroad, you don't always know what to expect. In Spain once we had dry ice over our heads! The band disappeared. The TV crew went on strike in mid-show, it was so bad. But for most television companies pop music is cheap programming. And the record companies have, to an extent, encouraged that view, with promotional videos, free records, and so on.

A manager must be honest. One tip – don't handle your artists' money. Litigation is almost always about money. Women and money! It's an enormous advantage if you can be friends, but now it's commonplace for managers to get fucked by their acts. The act gets successful. A worm-like accountant points out that your 20 per cent, which used to be 20 per cent of nothing, is now a lot of money. In a situation like that acts can forget about the months that the manager paid the phone bills. They forget about overheads. This office costs a quarter of a million a year to run, for example.

You should definitely have a contract with your acts – the tightest you can get. It's like a marriage without the sex. Or, in the case of Elton John and John Reid . . . but even they split up.

Money changes people. Ideally a band needs a manager as early as possible, before the deals begin. At the start the lawyer will send in his bill and disappear. But when it gets to dealing with the record company there's a huge amount of practical stuff to be considered. Tour support? Who pays for the video? All those things. The 'theory' of contracts is useless in practice. One of the things you're doing as a manager is to create a team. The talent makes the act, the manager assembles the rest around the act and then hopefully hangs on.

The first deal you enter into can be the deal you're landed with for good. The record company owns masters, copyrights. They get bigger and bigger, these corporations. You can lose track of who owns you. These companies don't put unrecouped money on their books as a deficit, but as a credit. Because they own the masters they count the advance debt as a credit. A manager has to keep his eye on all these tricks, and he should be there from the beginning. When an act starts out there's a huge inequality of bargaining power. You must have the vision to see beyond that. Nowadays the big companies are so big that most of the independents are actually controlled by them, because they own the pressing and the distribution and so on.

Experience will never be more important than enthusiasm. But experience does help most when dealing with the corporations. One of the biggest global record companies is the best in the world at shifting units, at selling your records for you, but they are the worst of all to deal with. Another major company is like the Civil Service. The most artist-friendly of all is probably Universal. But the one that sells the most efficiently will still get up to all sorts of tricks to reduce the artist's share. All the majors have their own style. You can assess it from the way the business affairs department works. You need to go with a style that suits you – if you have the choice, that is.

In theory, never get involved in your artists' private lives. In reality, you inherit an extended family. Girlfriends, wives even, houses and cars, come and go, but you're still there close to the band. And you're involved if they stop smoking, if they start again, if they buy a car, crash a car, move house, everything. The worst problems are when their private lives go awry. Some divorces are not just a personal tragedy, they also have a catastrophic effect on the professional life. On the other hand, artists can sometimes write best when they are miserable. Mark wrote 'Romeo and Juliet' after a very traumatic break-up. One of his best songs. And Bob Dylan seems to be permanently miserable.

In the end managers earn half their money for doing the job, and the other half for putting up with the grief. Roger Forrester went through terrible problems with Eric Clapton's addictions – drugs, booze, shopping, women, whatever. In the end you can be making professional decisions for personal reasons. There can be a good side to it. Nowadays I can work round things like half-term holidays. But that's a luxury. It's sad to see those for whom the road goes on forever, because it means they've got nothing else.

There is no such thing as a standard deal. There are so many permutations. If I was to take on a new act now I'd want 20 per cent of the gross across the board. But I'm unusual in that I do book out the act, because I used to be an agent. Some managers and bands work on profit-sharing deals, say a six-way split of profits for a five-man band plus the manager, after all costs have been accounted for including office overheads. The important thing is to strike a deal that neither side resents. There's always going to be a problem at the start, without any capital but a lot of phone bills. But talent will be found out, so you find a way.

Peter Grant [Led Zeppelin's manager] used to say: 'Believe in your act. Believe in your act. Believe in your act. Believe in your act.' There will be tough times. And if you don't believe in what you're selling you won't get through them. Once you've had huge success, a Led Zeppelin or a Dire Straits, there's no point in repeating it. You've done it. Peter Grant had a reputation as a heavy but he was fiercely loyal to his artists. The last thing he did before he died was to get The Pretty Things their masters back. He used to say to me that when he started 'it was an adventure'. There were no rules. Of course people –

usually musicians – got screwed, but now we *all* get screwed by the corporations! Management is now a pretty sophisticated operation – you need a basic knowledge of law and accounting as well as the traditional requirements.

In America now there are management companies with 40 acts going to 40 venues with 40 trucks and 40 lighting rigs, staying in 40 hotels. So dull. An artist might have a personal manager, a business manager, a lawyer, a tour manager, a gopher – personal assistant or whatever – and so on. It costs a fortune and it's very boring. In this country small rosters have always been the most successful. And the most rewarding – very hands-on.

Remember that pop music is not worth being precious about. Too many people working in it treat it as if it's a religion. Bullshit. It provides entertainment and employment. At the same time I would suggest that the works of most of the boy bands do not compare favourably with those of Miles Davis. However, we work in an industry that encourages self-importance, in the most superficial of artists. And we have a media that worships celebrity.

So, Ed Bicknell's rules of management can be summed up as follows:

1. Look for determination as well as talent in an artist.
2. Believe in the artist and their music.
3. Be friends with them and work hard at staying friends.
4. Ensure that management and act are pulling in the same direction.
5. Always think in terms of presenting the band in the best light (e.g. selling out a medium-sized venue is better than failing to fill a stadium).
6. Be honest. Don't handle the artist's money. Agree and sign a contract, so that both sides know what they are responsible for.
7. Get involved with an act as soon as possible, to avoid inheriting problems you didn't create.
8. Form relationships with companies whose style seems sympathetic to you.
9. Don't confuse pop music with high art.
10. Don't take on too many acts.

Finally, from bitter experience, Bicknell is of the opinion that

working with bands that have relatives in them is asking for trouble – Dire Straits, Kinks, Oasis. When you go professional there's no room for passengers – if people aren't pulling their weight, don't have the willpower, can't keep up – they've got to go. And when brothers are involved, it's messy.

By the time Bicknell learned that rule, of course, it was too late. Eventually Mark Knopfler parted company with his rhythm-guitarist brother David. And, some 20 years later, the partnership between Bicknell and Knopfler was also dissolved.

Michelle Hopkins, although she has years of experience in various areas of the music business, is a comparative newcomer to management. And she has already broken one of Bicknell's rules, just as he did himself – the band she manages, brothernature, is a duo made up of two brothers! But she seems quite cheerful about it. 'I wouldn't say there's any difference managing brothers,' she says. 'Adrian and Melvin Duffy are very close.'

In a separate chapter of this book Adrian and Melvin take us through the mechanics of setting up a band and progressing in the business, stage by stage, as well as offering tips on how to stay friends, even with your brother.

Michelle says that her first role as a manager was:

to get brothernature a record deal. However, after a while chasing A&R people, I realized that the amount of energy involved in organizing showcase gigs in terms of phone calls, mail shots and advertising wasn't equating with the end result – industry people not turning up, in other words. It seemed a pointless exercise to continue this course of action so we decided to set up our own record company.

The result was Symphony Ray Records. As for the management role in launching a band, Michelle says:

A good lesson I have learned is not to run before you can walk. The small steps may seem huge at the time but once achieved they build a ladder of success. You must always stay focused. I'm going to manage brothernature until I achieve what I set out to do, and not until then will I manage another band. Don't dilute your efforts.

You should also be realistic about your goals. We expected a Top 40 hit almost instantly with the debut single 'Engines Are Pulling Me'. There's inevitably a lot of knock-backs. Competition for national airplay is fierce, when you are competing for playlist positions with the likes of The Corrs and Robbie Williams.

So you have to be very committed. Don't let rejection stand in your way. There's always endless unreturned phone calls. Set aside as much of your available funds as you can for mail-outs and phone calls. Just keep battling on.

Another lesson is to be very open to the experiences of others. There are no golden rules, but people with the do-it-yourself philosophy are keen to come together and help. As a manager it is important to meet these people face to face.

It is also important to be aware of what tours are taking place, and to contact the relevant agent to see what support has been organized. Most tour support slots are only offered as buy-ons, though, and depending on the headline artist it may cost anything from £5,000 to £100,000, say. It's a great way for a band to raise their profile and increase their fan base, but you might have to visit the bank manager first!

Since paying even £5,000 for the privilege of playing on tour while half of the top-of-the-bill's fans are still in the bar is beyond the reach of most new bands, without serious record-company support – a chicken-and-egg situation, since tour exposure could be a good way of attracting record-company interest – this level of exposure will almost inevitably come slowly. Dire Straits were lucky in that their new manager, Ed Bicknell, was an agent – wearing his agent hat he simply booked them on to the Talking Heads tour he was putting together. Such a smooth path to nationwide exposure is available to few new bands.

So, what rules for managers can Michelle Hopkins add to our list?

1. Be realistic about your goals, taking matters step by step even though you know for sure that your unknown band are the next Oasis.

2. Stay absolutely focused on those goals, and don't be disheartened by the inevitable cold shoulder of an indifferent music business – eventually you will find the right ear.
3. Share experiences with like-minded people in the same position, to pool hard-earned knowledge.
4. Consider setting up your own record label both as a calling card and as a way of bypassing industry indifference.

And Michelle's final golden rule is – there are no golden rules.

# Publishing, Copyright and the Law

A writer owns the copyright of a song from the moment it is composed and exists in a tangible form, written or recorded, and the rights are protected by an Act of Parliament, the Copyright, Designs and Patents Act 1988. This means that he owns 'the right to copy' the work, and to authorize others to copy it, in return for a payment. This is fine in theory, but the writer's interests need to be further bolstered by proof of ownership and, hopefully, by an eventual means of collecting income from the song.

A simple and cheap means of initial protection is to post a tape of the song, however basic in its production, to yourself. Write the date of recording on the tape itself, sign your name across the sealed flap of the envelope, and when it arrives back check that the date on the postmark is readable. To make sure, use recorded delivery or registered post. Put the unopened envelope in a drawer for safe-keeping. On any copies that you send to other people, write something along the lines of: 'Songs composed by so-and-so. Copyright [date].' None of this actually prevents anyone from ripping you off, but it gives you ammunition should you ever have to sue.

An alternative is to lodge a copy with a bank or solicitor in return for a dated, itemized and signed receipt. This may only really be worthwhile, however, if the solicitor is a family friend willing to lend a tiny bit of drawer space for the foreseeable future.

However, this rudimentary and time-hallowed method of protection by posting yourself a package does nothing to 'exploit' the work to your financial advantage. In fact, it is simply gathering dust. And, in truth, it offers only very basic protection. If you ever had to go to court against some mega-corporation you would be putting up your yellowing envelope against their limitless financial muscle.

Your best bet is to have a hit with the song as soon as possible, and of course that is exactly what you are trying to do. Once you have done that, you occupy the higher ground. Without this, you would have to prove that the writer/artist you are convinced has ripped you off not only 'established' the work after you but could have come into contact with your version and – this is the trickiest bit – went ahead and deliberately stole it.

The ether is full of snatches of melody and imagery from old songs. To prove in court that you created a totally original melody (is that possible?) and welded it to your own virgin words, that someone else heard your work (how? when?) and then claimed authorship of a successful retread – it's an uphill climb.

There are numerous chilling examples to suggest that, on the whole, courts regard stars as honourable people and unknowns as chancers who are trying to steal a piece of the action. This rule has often applied in the face of substantial evidence to the contrary. It has even been known for a past hit – not exactly 'Imagine' or 'Yesterday', but a hit nonetheless – to be recycled, and for the more recent composition to be adjudged as being in the clear, and resemblances to be coincidental. So, take what protection you can, keep your fingers crossed, and get a hit record. It's as simple as that.

If, and when, the writer signs with a record company as an artist, the likelihood is that the company will make the recorded version of the song. In this case the writer owns the song, and the record company owns its recorded version. If, on the other hand, the writer/artist creates the entire product themselves, perhaps in a home studio or in a commercial studio paid for on an hourly basis, then the record company would either lease the product from its owner, for an agreed time and at an agreed royalty rate, or buy it outright.

Clearly an artist, however financially embarrassed at the time, should think twice before taking the drastic step of surrendering a share in all future profits from a song. History is littered with sad examples, for example, in the 1950s heyday of commercial urban blues, when impoverished artists (in this case invariably black) would sell a song for a hundred dollars to a record company boss or a publisher (often the same person, and usually, though not always, white). If the song went on to be a hit, appeared for decades afterwards on compilation albums, and maybe eventually turned up in a television commercial, the artist surrendered a small fortune to a wily entrepreneur.

However, for the tyro writer such considerations are luxuries for the future. When your song goes out into the world you have two basic rights that will earn revenue for you as the composer. These are the 'mechanical' and the 'performing' rights.

The mechanical right is granted in order to provide revenue when another artist or group records your song. They require the permission of the copyright holder, and the record company must pay an agreed royalty. In the case of record sales this is comparatively straightforward, given honest accounting, but there are other fields where negotiated fees are due, for example, if the song, or a snatch of the song, is used in a film, a television programme, a commercial, an in-store promotion or a video. This could pay dividends years or decades later – at the time of writing, a TV commercial is making use of Maurice Williams and the Zodiacs' 1961 hit 'Stay', 40 years after it appeared in the charts.

In the US a licence for mechanical rights must be issued by the copyright holder to any party wishing to make use of the work – this is known as a compulsory mechanical licence. In the UK there is no such compulsion.

The performing right gives similar entitlement to revenue whenever the song is performed or when a recording of it is broadcast. The two organizations that protect these rights in the UK are, respectively, the Mechanical Copyright Protection Society Ltd (MCPS) and the Performing Rights Society Ltd (PRS), whose functions are explained in more detail below.

However, if you are just starting out, composing material on guitar or keyboard, perhaps joining or building a band, accumulating a repertoire with the aim of looking for a gig locally, then these concerns are still a little way in the future. You should always bear them in mind, but in the meantime, who is going to be performing your material? You are, in private for a while, and even when you go public you won't be invoicing yourself for permission to sing your own songs. As soon as you begin to create some interest, however, it is time to consider surrounding yourself with the protection of such agencies as MCPS and PRS.

MCPS represents composers and publishers, both in the UK and – through reciprocal arrangements with like-minded organizations – throughout the world. It issues licences to record work owned by its members, collects the resulting revenues and distributes them.

Individual membership of MCPS can be taken up by composers, but if their work is represented by a publisher then it is more appropriate for the latter to deal with MCPS on their behalf. It is one of the reasons you assign your work to a publisher, after all – to deal with such matters and allow you to concentrate on composition and performing.

There is no membership fee to join MCPS. Instead, they keep a commission on revenue collected on a member's behalf. This varies between 4.75 per cent and 12.5 per cent, depending on the source of the income.

On the other hand, PRS do charge a joining fee of £50 (£250 for publishers) and deduct a commission on revenue collected to cover administration costs. Of each £1 received PRS claim to distribute 68p to writer and publisher members and 17.5p to members of affiliated societies overseas, spending 14p on licensing and administration costs and 0.5p on other costs. They represent almost everyone in the country who is professionally involved in writing or publishing music.

You may have seen stickers in pubs and similar places where music is played, confirming that a contribution is made to PRS in return for the right to play CDs, radio, television pop channels or to present live music. Naturally, there is no specific evidence of a radio station being switched on in a particular pub and happening to play your song. The airplay on the radio station itself will be logged, and the rights to additional revenue is calculated on a sampling basis.

The minimum qualification for joining PRS and being registered as a composer entitled to a share of the pot is to be able to prove a catalogue of at least one song, each of which has either been recorded commercially, broadcast within the past two years or performed in public at least a dozen times during the same period, as well as having been published commercially. An alternative qualification is to be able to prove that royalties have already accrued from public performance or broadcasting of the work. This could apply, for example, to original material composed for a stage musical.

In the case of publishers, qualification for membership depends on a demonstrable catalogue of at least 15 songs, 10 of which must have been published or recorded. In addition, the composers of the songs must be members of PRS or one of its affiliated organizations abroad, and the publisher must have secured rights for at least 10 of the songs in an EC territory.

As we have wandered from the territory of the artist to that of the publisher, it seems appropriate here to consider the relationship between the two. What does a publisher have to offer a new artist?

A publisher exists to establish copyright in new material, to exploit it on behalf of the writer in return for a percentage, by licensing it and promoting it using contacts and business knowledge (probably beyond the writer's sphere of expertise), to collect royalties and pass on the writer's share, and to offer protection against infringement. But basically, of course, a publisher exists to make profits from the above process. The rights granted by the writer to the publisher to carry out the above functions are known as administrative rights.

It is in the promotion of the work that a publisher offers protection above that given by a dated tape in a drawer and the security of MCPS membership. At whatever stage of their career an artist/writer may be, it is likely that they lack the expertise, time or inclination, and perhaps all three, to explore the full potential of their work. And so the worth of a publisher stands or falls on the energy they put behind the promotion of that work.

All creative people have, at times, to put themselves in the hands of others more skilled at the business side of their craft. As a writer, for example, I suppose I could seek, find and negotiate terms for all the work I do. Occasionally this happens, but since I couldn't negotiate my way out of a paper bag I have an agent. I could also assemble my own tax returns. But my mathematical ability barely extends beyond chalking at darts in the local pub, and so I have an accountant. In return for signing away chunks of any resulting income, I can get on with the scribbling while trusting that they are working in my best interests.

Trust. It so happens that if a writer or his agent are dissatisfied with the relationship, then the chances are that neither party would see any point in holding to the letter of any contract between them. And most people have no contract at all with their accountant. A writer/artist in the music field, on the other hand, needs to take a step into the dark when signing with a publisher, so the next stage is to examine what a music publisher actually does, beyond the basics mentioned above.

The job of a music publisher is also to discover new writing talent, to create new copyrights, to actively promote them and to keep a weather eye open for possible infringements of these copyrights, taking legal action if necessary.

The income will include that earned when part of a record is 'sampled'. Things begin to get murky when a producer samples your music, reproduces it exactly and then uses their counterfeit in their own record. Do you really want to get involved in all of this? On the other hand, if you are the one doing the sampling, remember that each different sample will have to be paid for, and that it will be you, not the publisher, doing the paying.

For various reasons, publishers are less in control of the business than they used to be, but because of the way they have developed and broadened their influence in the past, the big publishing companies remain significant players. The reasons that their overall stranglehold may have diminished are

(a) because it is now the norm for artists to write, and so the central role of the publisher in bringing together writer and artist has shrunk;

(b) because many artists set up their own publishing companies, and simply employ people to administrate the business on their behalf;

(c) because the best writers develop their own contacts with artists keen to use their material, thus cutting out the middle man; and

(d) because, more and more, forms of popular music have come to the fore that depart from the old-fashioned norm of a saleable song, for example, dance, electronic, rap, etc.

A dance track created by one musician in the back bedroom with a basic recording set-up is hardly likely to generate cover versions, and so does not need an external publisher tending its interests. The creator of the track, which can hardly be described as a 'song', might as well simply publish it himself to protect his rights, and then get on with making the next single.

Of course, a songwriter is not obliged to sign away a proportion of future income to a publisher. They can instead rely on the basic protection and collection facility offered by MCPS. But, as suggested above, they should ask themselves if they are best fitted to fulfil a publisher's role by themselves. A 'conventional' pop song with a catchy melody can be used and exploited in so many additional ways beyond the straightforward cover version that it pays to have an expert keeping tabs on it.

Remember that the expert, your publisher, will charge a further percentage on top of their agreed cut for 'administration' – 10 per cent upwards (negotiate). In other words, the writers pay for the publishers' electricity bills. 'Twas ever so. Perhaps the best advice – great in theory, so try and get as close to it as you can – is to go for the biggest advance you can get. You may never see another penny from the deal, but at least you've got the money in the bank. In the end, the publisher holds the aces, and can go on exploiting the work as they wish, meanwhile paying their electricity bills on time. So it is only honourable for the writer – the labourer in this particular vineyard – to get paid as well as he can up front. It may be the only pay day.

The relationship between a songwriter and publisher will be defined in a contract between them. This is likely to require a specified number of works in a particular period of time, and it could, for example, amount to an album's-worth of material in the first year. This may or may not include songs written before the date of the contract, although inevitably a publisher's interest in a writer can only have been awakened by existing material, and unless this is owned by another publisher it will feature in the deal.

The publisher will retain an option to extend the period of the contract. Very often in the case of a writer/artist the publisher is part of the record company to which they are signed as an artist, and it is likely that the recording contract and the publishing contract will mirror each other – for example, options for an extension could be taken up on both, to require a further album's-worth of acceptable material and the resulting album within the following year.

Another time period will be involved, one that extends beyond the length of the actual contract, and this will be the number of years that the publisher retains the right to exploit the material and earn revenue from it, even if the contract itself has come to an end. With a new artist this would normally vary from a decade starting at the end of the contract to 'for ever'. Clearly it is in the artist's interests to negotiate as short a period as possible – the publishing contract will presumably only end as a result of indifference on the part of the publisher or because the writer is offered a better deal elsewhere, which may include buying off the original publishing company. Either way, the writer does not want material remaining with an uninterested or resentful publisher in perpetuity.

Unless a previous deal precludes such an arrangement, the publisher will expect global rights to the songs. This may well suit the writer, but there can always be exceptions. For example, a London-based artist/writer dealing with a British publisher could in fact be writing a particular form of ethnic music in exile, and feel that they could get a better deal in their home country for themselves. Such considerations then have to become a matter for negotiation.

Also to be agreed is the percentage of the income accruing to the publisher from a particular work that is passed on to the writer. Three-quarters, or a little less, is the norm. It is vital, however, in the case of overseas earnings, that the writer is aware of the distinction between the publisher's net receipts from a particular territory and the song's actual earnings there. The publisher may have sub-contracted the rights locally in that territory, and so another company skims off its share before passing on the rest. It is clearly in the writer's interests that their percentage should be based on the at-source revenue raised, not on the smaller amount filtering back to home base.

This, of course, is another item for negotiation. If the publisher succeeds in establishing that his net receipts are the basis for negotiation, the writer should at least hold out for a percentage ceiling on what the sub-contracted publisher can retain.

A writer, of songs just as is the case with books, has a right to expect accounts twice a year, for the periods ending 30 June and 31 December, and to receive a cheque three months later (officially, 90 days). Offset against these receipts will be any advances already paid. In the course of a publishing contract the payment of advances can be an ongoing process, particularly when tied to the release of albums containing the songs.

A beginner may be unable to secure any advance at all. Other deals may pay what amounts to a monthly wage during the period of the contract, recuperable against future earnings. An established star may demand millions. It all depends.

So, to summarize, what does a publisher agree to do in return for the copyrights of the songs? To make their best endeavours to promote them and so raise revenue, and – this should be established – to register the works with such agencies as MCPS worldwide in order to effect the most efficient protection and collection of as much revenue as possible. If the writer becomes dissatisfied with the publisher's effort, as mentioned above, their protection is to serve notice of this dissatisfaction, and to give a time period during which positive signs of action are required.

Where contracts are involved, so are lawyers. From the outset of an artist's career, nothing should be signed without independent advice. As some very high-profile cases over the years have shown, involving artists as varied as Gilbert O'Sullivan, Bruce Springsteen and George Michael, not only are disputes potentially very expensive but they can effectively paralyse a career, preventing an artist from working – either because of legal handcuffs or because of an unwillingness to work within a relationship that has deteriorated to the point of reaching the law courts. So, any piece of paper requiring a signature should be expertly vetted, to ensure that it does not tie the performer unreasonably. The cheapest way, as described in Chapter 7 – Organizations for Musicians, is simply to join the Musicians' Union (MU), since being able to have contracts given the legal once-over is one of the benefits of membership.

However, if a career develops successfully an artist may wish to have a personal relationship with a solicitor who has made a speciality of the music business and its many snares. Consultations are not cheap – a three-figure sum ticking away on the clock every hour – and while an initial meeting may be free of charge (the onus is on the client to check) an advance against the eventual fee – a sum 'on account' – will almost certainly be then required.

One possible advantage of this closer relationship, once you can afford it, is that the solicitor may well be able to offer expert advice uniquely tailored to your case, beyond the letter of the law – they may, for example, know of a record company, someone in A&R or a manager whom they regard as being particularly straight to deal with, and likely to be in sympathy both with your music and with your career aims. Obviously it is not the job of the MU, nor its tame lawyers, to focus their advice quite so precisely.

It should be pointed out at this stage that many people in the industry feel that the union is no longer a force, and is an irrelevance to most featured musicians. This school of thought would claim that an artist's best protection comes from a strong and expert manager.

If you already have a manager at this stage, you should take Ed Bicknell's advice given elsewhere in this book and make sure that you are not legally represented by the same solicitor. To have a potential conflict of interest is no use for either party, because they will never know if advice is impartial or slanted towards the other side. And remember, you are only engaging a solicitor to give you advice – his role is not to issue mandatory instructions. However, once you have engaged a lawyer to negotiate on your behalf, for example with a record company, then you should not be tempted to contact the other party off your own bat – particularly if they get in touch with you, which is likely to be because they hope to get a better deal from you than from your hired expert. Obviously you should remain polite and co-operative while a deal is in the offing, but simply point out that since you have hired a legal watchdog, you cannot be expected to bark yourself.

It may well be, then, that at the early stages the MU will be able to assist sufficiently to get your career underway without the expense of hiring a lawyer. An accountant, however, is a different matter. Unless accountancy is your favourite way of relaxing after a hard day in the studio (in which case you are unlikely to be a musician in the first place) it is essential that an expert shuffles your financial affairs into order from the outset. The MU publishes a list of accountancy firms that either specialize in the music business, or who have partners within the firm that do. Go and see one, ask exactly what records you need to keep, and then relax. If you are self-employed, don't forget your monthly National Insurance contribution either – a direct debit from your bank account is the most painless way.

If you are part of a band, one legal wrinkle it is as well to sort out from the start is exactly who owns the name of the band. In the past, after much bickering, it has been known for a once-successful pop group to spawn three versions, perhaps one with the original name, one with the same name but the word 'original' tacked on to the front, and a third with the name of one of the original artists followed by the band name. The main thing that this sort of mess indicates is that the punter is not going to witness the band he remembers. A legal agreement from the outset could clarify matters, but it will take the expertise of a solicitor to make it watertight.

Another matter to be resolved early on is whether you wish to be a 'sole trader' (or 'partnership' in the case of a group) or to form a limited company. A solicitor will advise you on the pros and cons of both as they affect your particular situation. For example, sole trader status is simpler and therefore cheaper in accountancy and business terms, but is liable for more if things go wrong.

The accountant will also advise you on whether it is better to register for VAT even if you are likely to remain below the turnover threshold that makes registration compulsory – once registered, you can reclaim the VAT you pay out for goods and services, but your accountancy bill will be much higher. As soon as you get serious, you may well conclude that an annual accountancy bill is a price worth paying to let someone else worry about the figures. Particularly if, like me, you tend to stuff any communication about money behind a metaphorical clock on the mantelpiece, simply because you find the language bewildering and frightening, and, therefore, to be avoided.

Once you become successful, you do not wish to have your career suddenly blighted just as it seemed to be going well, simply because legal and financial matters were ignored during the scuffling days. So the best advice must be to get it sorted while it remains straightforward.

# Organizations for Musicians

7

This chapter looks at some of the main organizations set up to help musicians and those working in other sections of the industry. Many of their websites provide useful links one to the other, and will assist you in building up a picture of the network of associations, companies and pressure groups active in the music business. The Musicians' Union (MU) is the main trade organization for working musicians. I asked the MU's Music Business Adviser, Nigel McCune, and its London official, Horace Trubridge, to make the case for joining the union. McCune feels that:

perhaps the biggest reason for joining is the contract advice service. If you are offered a contract you should get it vetted by an expert. If you go to a specialist music-business lawyer he will charge at least £500. The same advice is free to members. For many of our members we are a trade union in the classic sense, particularly the salaried ones. The biggest employer of musicians in the country is still the armed forces, followed by the BBC.

These salaried musicians see us as their negotiators on rates and conditions. But a lot of the freelances get actively involved themselves. They get elected on to committees and affect what happens. The union is fully democratic – it is the members who make the decisions as to what we should do. For the 85 per cent of the membership who are freelance we are like the AA – the fourth emergency service.

Trubridge adds:

We've probably got the largest centralized resource of information on the music industry. Say a member phones up looking for a list of overseas licensees for house music, or a list of European jazz festivals, or whatever, we've got it. Another financial reason is that as soon as you join you have £5 million's worth of public liability insurance, covering you if you or your equipment causes any damage to property or people. If you were doing a driving job you wouldn't hesitate to cover yourself properly as far as liability is concerned. The same should be true of a working musician. If a stack was to topple over and injure someone, you would obviously be in very serious trouble without adequate cover.

As for the free advice, the fact is that if you are a musician you will at some stage get ripped off. So our expert advice is really another form of insurance.

Both agree that the union is of particularly vital interest to musicians on the way up. 'Mind you, people like Mick Jagger and Phil Collins are still members – it's just that they don't need us very much!'

The union, which employs around 45 full-time officials together with some 70 branch secretaries, is also a campaigning organization, both on obvious topics such as entertainments licensing and copyright, and in more surprising areas. Trubridge gives one example – the proposals for a 'congestion charge' levied on private vehicles entering central London, which one might expect a trade union to be in favour of. He argues, however, that musicians are a special case when it comes to commuting into London, for example to play in a West End theatre orchestra, returning home late at night.

It's not just the double bass players who need transport. A violinist could be going home with £30,000-worth of instrument under their arm. Muggers are becoming aware that musical instruments are valuable. To be honest, a lot of our members feel much safer in their car than they do on the last tube home, and however one might be in favour of public transport one has to sympathize with that point of view.

This reminds McCune of another selling point for the union:

You get £500-worth of insurance when you join – in other words, we pay the first £500 of damage or loss you may have to claim for. Usually, an insurance policy will require you to be responsible for the first £50. If you can go to an insurance company and say you will cover not £50 but £500, then your premium is going to drop hugely.

What the union does not and cannot do is act as an informal agent or lawyer for an up-and-coming act. But they do exist to dispense good advice, and they do see their job as going into battle on behalf of musicians in every field. On a purely mercenary level, what they offer in terms of insurance and database information does seem to make membership well worthwhile.

The union publishes a list of music teachers, maintains an updated website (*www.musiciansunion.org.uk*), issues a directory of members biannually, supplies standard contract forms and publishes a quarterly magazine. It also compiles leaflets on various aspects of the business, containing valuable advice for beginners.

Subscription costs are on a sliding scale depending on your earnings from music in the year prior to application for membership, or prior to subscription renewal. At the time of writing, for income below £5,000, the rate is £66 (£60 on a Direct Debit mandate), for income between £5,000 and £10,000 the rate is £102 (£90), for an amount between £10,000 and £20,000 it is £152 (£138) and those who have earned over £20,000 pay £198 (£180).

There is a reduced rate for musicians under the age of 21 years which stands at £33 (£30), for which proof of age in the form of a copy of birth certificate, driving licence or passport details is required. Although even £60 may seem a little daunting if you have just landed your first pub gig, and do not yet know where the next booking is coming from, you should at least contact the MU for their 'bumph' and make up your own mind.

There are various other organizations involved in the promotion and protection of music. For a full list see the Music Organizations directory. Some of the main ones are discussed here.

The MU recommends that musicians whose work already exists on disc should contact the Performing Artists' Media Rights Association. This is a collecting society for performers, and free membership is open, in its own words, to 'all performers, instrumentalists, singers and music directors, in any genre – jazz, rock, pop, rap, dance, classical, folk and soul – who are on a recording which is played in public or broadcast.' There is a 'non-union' alternative called the Association of United Recording Artists, who can be checked out on their website, www.aurauk.com. This is a sister organization of the Music Managers' Forum and also collects and administers royalties. It specializes in representing featured performers, so you should see which suits the best.

In 1996 a directive by the European Union established the right for performers to receive a royalty for such use of their work. The Association is for qualifying UK citizens or those living permanently in the UK, and also for those who have made a recording in a country that recognizes this right (this does not include the USA).

Those qualifications, however, are strict, and potential members should check with the Association to see if they can join. Categories include featured performers, non-featured performers (musicians and singers, for example, employed on a session basis as backing artists) and contracted performers – those who are bound exclusively to a particular record company. The arrangement includes recordings that have been sampled.

The Association is non-profitmaking. Administration is funded by a small fee deducted from money collected in the UK, but anything accruing from overseas sources is paid out in full. It covers all commercial recordings made since the end of the Second World War, but only on broadcasts and other public use since the Association was founded. The starting date is 1 December 1996.

The division of money collected is quite complicated, and varies depending on whether the recording was made in a 'qualifying' territory or one outside its remit. Payment is made within 60 days of the end of a royalty quarter, and the minimum payment level is £25. This figure is linked to the Retail Price Index, however, and any monies below this cut-off point will be retained, together with interest earned, and paid out when they exceed it. The percentage deducted for administration will never exceed 15 per cent, and at the time of writing was 9.5 per cent. A full breakdown of the payment system is available on the Association's website at *p@mra.org.uk*.

Once you have been accepted for membership you can submit a discography of all recordings you have worked on, which the Association checks against its play-list. You may have to provide proof of participation on recordings where you have not received a credit. You can search the UK play-list on the website, though you should print out the instructions on how to carry out the search first and study them in advance. It is then possible to generate a claims form to list relevant recordings.

The Band Register was set up by Peter Whitehead, whose views on the future of music on the Internet are aired at length in Chapter 12 – Music in Space. The Register provides a means by which groups, orchestras and artists can register their names, and allows them to search the database to see if their proposed name is already in use. Once they are registered, a band can post all their contact information on the site. This service is free, and its use is recommended by such bodies as the MU.

The Register has also developed an A&R function over the past ten years, issuing a series of CDs called *Best of, Unsigned*, which are circulated to subscribers. The CDs have in the past been supported by showcase gigs to promote unknowns to the industry. Whitehead claims five subsequent No. 1 hits among the Register's successes. The website contains details of how to submit work, either through the ether as an mp3 e-mail attachment or by post. Among other services, the Register also posts regular articles on the legal aspects of the music business.

The two main royalty-collecting organizations in the UK, the Mechanical Copyright Protection Society and the Performing Rights Society, are discussed in detail in Chapter 6 – Publishing, Copyright and the Law. Their function is to license the recording and subsequent use of music, and to collect royalties for such use on behalf of members. Among other services the MCPS publishes a magazine, *For the Record*, which provides an ongoing update on copyright issues.

Phonographic Performance Limited (PPL) is a non-profitmaking organization working on behalf of record companies, set up to safeguard the public performance and broadcasting interests of those companies. A levy is made on revenue collected to cover administrative costs, and the revenue arises from licence fees obtained from broadcasts and public performance.

A more recent addition to the field of copyright protection is the Copyright Advice and Anti-Piracy Hotline. This has been set up to co-ordinate the mutual interests of the film, music and software industries, in an era when the expansion of the Internet has raised many issues concerning the protection of intellectual copyright.

The Music Publishers Association (MPA) is a non-profitmaking organization representing UK publishers, established in 1881 and dedicated to guarding standards and improving legislation to the benefit of the industry. It is the parent company of MCPS.

The British Academy of Composers and Songwriters (BACS) is an amalgamation of three UK composer societies – the Association of Professional Composers (APC), the British Academy of Songwriters, Composers and Authors (BASCA) and the Composers' Guild of Great Britain (CGGB) – and represents the interests of composers and songwriters working in all genres.

The British Phonographic Industry (BPI) represents the producers, manufacturers and retailers of recordings in all formats, and is active in such thorny issues as anti-piracy. Any UK-based record company is entitled to apply for membership, proposed by two existing members, and the BPI, a non-profit organization, levies an administrative charge based on company turnover. The BPI claims the membership of 220-plus record companies, between them accounting for 90 per cent of the recorded music in the UK. Each member has a single vote regardless of the company's size or turnover.

As well as its lobbying activities and the provision of quarterly industry statistics, the BPI promotes the annual BRIT Awards show, and in conjunction with the British Association of Record Dealers it also promotes the Technics Mercury Music Prize. It runs various courses and supports musical activity through its charity arm, the BRIT Trust. Subscription is calculated as a percentage of a company's turnover, usually 0.3 per cent, with a minimum fee of £75. This is also the charge levied on newly-established companies prior to accounts being available for their first year.

A sister organization, Video Performance Limited (VPL) deals with revenue accruing from the video use of recordings. The Scottish Music Industry Association (SMIA) represents the music industry's interests north of the border, while the Association of Independent Music is an organization for independent record companies who choose to operate outside the BPI. Finally, the Music Managers' Forum (MMF) represents the interests of managers of bands and solo artistes, and hence those of the artists themselves, over such matters as new-technology copyright, performance fees and contracts. Membership rates vary.

# Promotion and Publicity

8

Before investing in even the modest cost of a photo session, with a suitably talented friend as the photographer, it is as well to be sure – as sure as you can be in this turbulent business – that the drummer of your newly formed band isn't about to defect. When you are reasonably confident of a stable line-up for the foreseeable future, what you are looking for is a decent quality of (preferably digital) image that can be manipulated on a computer to serve a number of uses.

The pictorial print quality of the local newspaper may not be particularly high, but it would be even lower if they were to start with a sub-standard photograph. In fact, they'd reject it. The other obvious uses for a striking picture of the band are in press releases, flyers (advertising hand-outs, usually A5 in size), posters (you may need to take a disk to the local print shop, unless you have access to an A3 printer), and even on business cards.

As the duo brothernature point out in Chapter 11 – Diary of a Band, postcards are also a useful medium in raising awareness of a band's 'brand image'. Take a batch wherever you go, dropping them off (politely, and with permission) on the counters of local record shops.

It is also worth considering a logo. I am assuming that, however painfully, you have already agreed on a name for the band, and that it is a crisp, memorable and intriguing one that won't embarrass you in three months' time – not a graphic squiggle, not hard to pronounce correctly, and not so long that it will have to be reproduced in a drastically reduced point size to fit on a poster.

Also, as Nigel McCune of the Musicians' Union suggests, make it original (check with the MU or with the Band Register – see Music Organizations). In other words do *not* call yourself 'Phoenix' – half the bands in the world have risen from the ashes of another, and sometimes it seems as if half of *them* became Phoenix.

The name may suggest a logo – indeed, the simplest and therefore often the most effective logo is a stylish, readable graphic treatment of the name itself, which also avoids the possibility of sending out confused messages. Bear in mind that the relationship between a band name and an unrelated image, or an obscurely connected one, will not be apparent to anyone, since they haven't heard of you yet.

So, you now have the personnel, the repertoire – majoring on original and therefore publishable material, unless you are specifically a 'covers' band – the name and the image. Now you must go out and get a gig before bothering about the next stage. If you *are* a 'covers' band, by the way, there may not *be* a next stage – gigging is all there is. The days of Showaddywaddy are over – except for Showaddywaddy, of course.

And the next stage is some sort of press release. It will be aimed in the first instance at the local papers – weekly 'paid for' title, free sheet, monthly gig guide, you must cover them all – and so you will stress the local angle. You live in the town, and you are playing at the Railway Tavern every Thursday in October. This is not quite enough, but we'll come to that.

Bear in mind deadlines, and that these will be earlier for the 'leisure' pages of a weekly paper than they are for the front-page splash ('Local Man Third Best in Breed at Crufts'). When I edited the music section of *Time Out* years ago, there would be gig-listing phone calls every week – on the day before publication! Only the death of John Lennon could be fitted into that paper-pulping schedule, not a gig at the Hope and Anchor.

So far you have given the paper nothing to editorialize, beyond perhaps the annotation 'local band'. Unless you can write gags that not only make all of you laugh next morning but also on the morning after that, be careful with humour. Comedy is utterly subjective, and is the only topic on which every single person in the world is an expert. Usually dry humour, gentle irony, has a longer shelf life than over-enthusiastic zaniness.

Unless, that is, you want to go the whole hog, dress up in ridiculous costumes and storm the newspaper office. If you do, don't forget to warn them (their photographer is unlikely to be hanging around in the lobby waiting for something to snap), and in any case take your own photographer as insurance. Do *not* shoot a water pistol at the entertainments editor or his computer. That's not zany, that's playground suicide – paint bombs, even worse. A golden rule – *your job is to make his job easier.* No stink bombs, no unpunctuality, no misplaced 'big time' pretensions, no mumbling. You may not be able to afford fine wines, gourmet food and a Park Lane escort service, but at least be enthusiastic, coherent, helpful and polite. The offer of a pint at the nearest pub might appeal to a deskbound hack, and can't do any harm.

If you want to take the silly costume route, there still has to be some internal logic behind the stunt. If you have called yourselves the Gorillas, fine. Otherwise, you will be sweating inside those stinking, expensive suits for nothing.

The sober press release option is to give precise and accurate details of who you are. Spell your names correctly (leave it to the paper to get two of them slightly wrong), give your real ages (it might come back to haunt you if you don't) and the instruments you play. Briefly define your influences and style of music, but stress your originality within that style. Just as all daytime shows on local radio used to be listed as 'a lively mixture of music, chat and fun' (Phil Collins, dreary phone-ins and some author like me trying to flog a book) so 'uncanny echoes of Oasis' is unlikely to fire an entertainment editor's curiosity – unless you are an Oasis tribute band, in which case I guess it is quite a useful characteristic. But joining in the depressingly negative vogue for tribute bands won't lead you on to the staple activities of the music industry, recording and publishing.

Find out exactly whom you should be contacting. It may be clearly indicated on a by-lined page, but if not, call the switchboard and ask for the name – ask not to be put through, though. Make your first approach by letter, enclosing your press release, a usable photograph and an invitation to a gig, and follow it up with a phone call three days' later (one for the letter to arrive, and an extra one to show that you are keen but not desperate).

If you can persuade your target to a gig (and be prepared for them to say yes but act no, in which case politely chase them again) then your music has to be your best sales pitch, backed up if possible with a chat at the bar afterwards. And don't forget to put them on the guest list. Nothing brings on the 'don't you know who I am?' syndrome in even the most humble, starvation-waged trainee journalist more than being insulted at the door by an incomplete guest list and a large, flat-nosed man in a dinner jacket. It will not dispose him sympathetically. Also, be prepared for the possibility that the journalist might need an 'angle' to persuade him to show interest. 'Local' is not enough.

What have you got to add? Impressive musical pedigree on the part of at least one member? An unusual day job? An *ordinary* day job shared by all the band? (If you are milkmen, for instance, the journalist will begin to see the puns forming in the ether, and you are halfway there – 'There's nothing pint-sized about this group', 'a gold-top act', 'past your eyes and into your ears', 'they won't go sour', etc., etc.). Any distinction in other areas of music or show-business (jingles, TV extra, stage work)? Involvement, even as innocent bystanders, in a big local news story of recent memory?

Think yourself into the position of the local reporter. They need something to get hold of, to help them produce a shit-hot piece that will go straight into their cuttings file for when they try and get a gig on the *Sun* show-biz page. To repeat, because it is indeed the golden rule – your job is to make his job easier.

And one way is to make sure that the gig information is comprehensive. If you are the support act, the local paper will not be amused to find out that they've listed you but didn't know about the headliner, so be honest. Vice versa, list any band supporting you. Don't just give the name of the venue, but the address and telephone number as well.

The time and price are equally important, and though gigs rarely run to the minute it would be bad public relations to give an 8.00pm starting time when you know that nothing is going to happen until 10.00pm. And of course don't forget (it has happened, in my experience) to mention what day the gig is on.

If you have a whole clutch of appearances lined up, relevant to the local press, list them all. It is a good idea, though, to remind them again of the dates for the following week (remember deadlines) because the original press release may have been binned after use. Out-of-town dates, particularly if prestigious, are best mentioned in the text of the release – they imply that things are beginning to happen for you, and the local paper should want to be in on the ground floor when a local band branches out.

Now consider local radio stations, particularly if you have 'product' to send them as well. But even before your debut CD, local radio will broadcast gig guides and is always in the market to fill free air-time with homegrown talent (send them a tape, or preferably a CD, along with the gig information). But do your research first – flatter them by knowing which slots plug gigs and which segments run interviews or live music, and make specific, personalized approaches. There may even be suitable outlets on your local TV stations – again, find out precisely what they are, and remember the rule about giving them a local angle alongside the music wherever possible. An unfocused mail shot will at first probably sit around doing nothing useful, and then it will be thrown away a few days later, like left-overs in the fridge.

By now, with gigs building up, you are assembling a mailing list rather than just stuffing one or two envelopes. Buy sheets of gummed labels suitable to run through a printer, and set up a template of addresses on the computer, making sure that they correspond with the positioning of the labels on the A4 sheet. Assemble your own database. A word-processed list is fine at this stage, though later on there are programmes like Microsoft Access dedicated to building databases.

At this stage, the national music press (and *Time Out* in London) will remain underwhelmed by your progress as far as their feature pages are concerned. But they do run gig diaries (and a list of gigs might even count as a tour), so make sure that they know about you. Include a picture – these are sometimes selected for publication because of their impact, not just because of the name. They might even fillet your press release for a caption or annotation. The more informative they can make their listings, the better service they are providing.

The chances are, though, that they will ignore you. You must weigh up your budget, and decide. So far, your expenditure is limited to the cost of producing and disseminating information, but the ways that the information reaches the public are still costing you nothing. For the time being, exploit free exposure to the full and don't bother with display ads and other paid-for promotional aids. Once you are working regularly, however, and so have something to back it up, a small display ad in a suitable journal is a good way of getting the band name into the subconscious of a lot of people at a low per-capita cost.

When it comes to posters, you will want them to remain relevant for as long as possible, assuming that you are getting a better deal by having a large number printed. The usual way is to leave a defined space within the design for the specific details of a gig to be written in (or, more professionally, to be processed separately and seamlessly stuck on).

As mentioned earlier, you could take the basic design to a print shop on a disk, for a bulk order. Alternatively, assuming you can create an A4 image and print it out domestically, there will be a photocopier with an enlargement and A3 facility somewhere around – the local library, for instance. For a long run, the print shop will prove cheaper.

As the world becomes more garish and multi-coloured, the force of the monochrome image becomes stronger, so you do not necessarily need to stretch your budget to include colour. It is the strength of the image, and the impact of the message, that count. If you are using the print shop, though, you could always discuss printing a mono image on coloured or tinted paper, if you feel that this reinforces the message.

Posters advertising an upcoming gig will be for supplying to the venue, to any sympathetic local organizations (record shop, musical instrument shop, community theatre) and anywhere else that you can get permission to display them. Do *not* go out at night with a bucket of wallpaper paste. Fly-posting is a territorial and specialist business, and the territory is protected with vigour. The least that will happen is that your posters will be covered over before dawn. The worst that could happen is that you will never play the violin again.

If you want to move up to fly-posting, which will inevitably hike up your budget, make a note of who is advertising locally. You may be able to ask one of the clients discreetly who should be approached. But ask around as well – the local paste baron could be a regular in your local. Check *Yellow Pages* under 'Advertising – Outdoor', though this is *not* an official list of fly-posters.

Once you have begun to establish a local following, you will want your supporters to know what you are up to as your career develops. Always talk to anyone at a gig who wants to talk to you – they could be buying your CD in a few months' time. I cannot see any excuse, however big a star you are, for being stand-offish with fans. If you do make the big time you will want your privacy once you shut your front door, but while in public you are a walking advertisement for your own career. Every pleasant word could translate into a sale.

A step beyond simply talking to supporters is to have postcards printed, as mentioned earlier, giving details of how to keep in touch with the band. Consider making it a two-way process by establishing a mailing list, although these days it might be more cost effective to set up a website, using posters, postcards and business cards to advertise it. Ideally you should use both, and make sure that anyone interested is not only informed of what you are up to, but is made to feel part of the family by being offered advance tickets at a discount, bargains for bringing a group of friends to a gig, and generally by being kept up to date on what you are doing. But do make it a communication among friends, not a sales pitch. For a gig some way away, particularly if you are coming up from the provinces for a showcase in London, talk to a local coach company about the possibility of hiring transport, and then see if you can fill it profitably.

When it comes to spreading the word beyond posters and other forms of printed ephemera, you will need to consider promotional artefacts that could develop into a commercial sideline once the band takes off. Given a simple and striking piece of artwork that conveys the message – at the very least the name of the band – your image can be stamped on to badges, book matches or other simple but appropriate giveaways comparatively cheaply. Get the costings, and work out exactly what you hope to achieve with the investment.

The obvious product that both promotes the band and can be marketed at a profit is a T-shirt (and maybe other clothing items such as nylon bomber jackets and baseball caps). These must start with good quality merchandise (if the T-shirt shrinks and twists at the seams on its first wash, it will not be doing a good promotional job for you). This involves investment, so only take this step when you decide you can afford it, and then shop around for a decent 'blank' product and a local supplier who can transform it into a useful promotional and saleable item.

Your thoughts will then turn to video. Be warned that simply sticking a camera in front of a gig is worse than useless, and if you have been persuaded into this course by an outside company (they scour listings magazines and approach bands 'cold') then you will have wasted your money. Super 8 film stock is technically a better starting point, but you will neither be able to capture useable live sound nor lip-synch satisfactorily. If you know someone with Super 8 equipment who could bring something creative to the exercise, however, it is worth considering. Remember, though, that films of bands walking mistily through autumn woodlands, or sitting moodily on walls in gritty urban wastelands, were old hat by the end of the 1960s. Do you really have something to say that adds usefully to the presentation of the band that you are steadily building up? If not, wait until you can get hold of a tape of your first TV spot. However, imaginative graphics, quick-cut stills and fragments of live action can make a professional-looking package on a budget.

Before too long, the work involved in promoting the band by these various means will not only be beyond the band members themselves, but beyond an overworked manager. This is where a publicist moves in – a hired hand but still the next vital member of the team. How do you find such a person, what can you expect them to do for you, and what sort of financial arrangement will you be entering into?

Well, he's not likely to be Max Clifford at this stage. At the start the easiest way may be simply to add one more enthusiastic body to the team – naturally one with a flair for the job – with a firm understanding about future earnings. They may be willing to work for free with this expectation, but not to be out of pocket.

If the first offer comes from a stranger – perhaps as a result of an approach at a gig – you must agree on what expenses are allowable. As with record companies and managers, publicists have been known to bung in unexpected invoices if things go sour. If you move on to the next stage, and can offer an agreed monthly retainer, ensure that you are fully aware of what you can expect for your money, and what is not included.

Impresario Denis Vaughan, who has worked with everyone from Chuck Berry and Jerry Lee Lewis on the one hand to Public Enemy and Run D.M.C on the other, sees the function of the publicist as being merged into other services.

To work with a new band he would require to act as their agent, with the agreement of a negotiated cut in the future. This is why he styles himself an 'impresario' – a trouble-shooter who arranges the whole deal. However, this is not the only way of working. 'To act as a publicist alone,' he agrees, 'you would be negotiating a monthly fee, a retainer, at every stage, with a clear agreement as to what is involved.'

Although Vaughan prefers to see the broader picture these days, and works with established stars, he can recall the process from the ground floor:

The earlier you get involved, the better. The PR required at that stage is at street level. You'd be working on, say, a London concert. Posters on the street, and a rent-a-crowd – this has happened from the Beatles onwards. You ask the cleaner if she and five friends would like half-a-dozen tickets, you ask your own friends, and so on. The rule of thumb for papering a house is that a third of those you ask will turn up.

Assuming that you also attract some genuine punters with your publicity, what does the band get out of it?

The feelgood factor, experience of a full audience, the feel of a more prestigious venue than they are used to. Most important, we hope, some new fans. Word of mouth begins to work, and you follow up a month later with another show, less 'papered'.

At this stage the manager is often a friend of the group who doesn't have an experienced overview. You see the band at a local gig. They are pretty raw. You make musical suggestions about pacing and so on, assuming they are co-operative. You go to rehearsals, work on appearance, stage presentation, getting it all right.

Hopefully by now they have a record company. So there is input from the A&R department – you are working as a team. A plugger is part of this, to get radio play. He will also help by using his contacts to get people to gigs. You begin work in the printed media. Organize interviews, building an image for the group. At this stage you improve their profile, with better posters, better sites and so on. Hopefully you are soon being rewarded with some chart action.

You now begin to think of some gigs in Europe – a festival, for instance. Back in the 1980s getting into Eastern Europe was a good idea, to cause a bit of a stir. And this year the Manic Street Preachers have played in Cuba – the same principle applies.

So now you've had the push, the first record, a bit of buzz. The hipper end of the media are beginning to take interest. Now the band must think of the next album, and so they come off the road to write and record. At this stage you are planning to start live work again in six months, except perhaps for well-paid one-off gigs – a festival or a private appearance, perhaps. But in six months, you won't be going back into little clubs. You are planning for more prestigious venues. Dates around the country, into Europe, and even into America, assuming you've got a deal there. New York and Los Angeles.

Now start organizing the bigger interviews. The glossy Sunday magazines, Jools Holland or equivalent television, network radio specials. A month of prestige dates. Maybe they can headline at smaller festivals by now. If we assume that the band has taken off, then you have a time problem – gigs, recording, interviews, fitting everything in. You have to plan even harder, and the band must decide on their priorities. Some of the bigger bands tour for a year simply to promote and album. And after the promo tour comes the gigging tour, around the world. After that, the sky's the limit.

It's as simple as that, in the doctrine according to Vaughan. In the meantime, as he has indicated, once you are signed, sealed and delivered to a record company the next arm of publicity is the promotions man, or 'plugger', whose job it is to get your record on to radio station playlists, above all Radio 1, Capital, Virgin and the stations in the major provincial cities, as well as on pop-music television. In the latter case, the big prizes are the terrestrial Saturday-morning shows.

One such publicist is Michael Peyton, who has gained nearly three decades of experience since first joining Bell Records in 1972 and helping Gary Glitter's 'Rock 'n' Roll Parts 1 and 2' to the top of the charts. An independent operator since 1981, Peyton soon scored with Eddy Grant's 'I Don't Wanna Dance', and other successes have included the Walker Brothers, Donna Summer and T'Pau.

Reflecting on the changes in the industry since he first trod the corridors of Broadcasting House, Peyton says:

It's all led by marketing departments and accountants. And now it's become a visual business. The video is the most important asset to a new artist. It's not enough any more just to take the record round to the radio stations. They want something else to pick up on. That's probably the main difference between now and 1972 – nowadays radio plays the hits rather than creating them.

This sounds a depressing situation, but Peyton remains ebullient.

It's just different. Radio stations might say to me, 'Yeh, love the record. When it's Top 20 come back to me.' So now TV is the medium.

Another change, surely, is that groups are more clinically assembled these days?

Yes, most of them are manufactured. A four-girl group recently paid £25,000 as a 'buy-on' to support an established group – also manufactured – on tour. They paid £10,000 to TV companies to screen their video and run an interview. The video cost £50,000. Obviously they had considerable financial backing, from people investing in them as they would stocks and shares.

Then you go to the retailers. In the case of that group, Woolworth's would say that if the video can get shown on *Big Breakfast* and *CDUK*, they'll come in with an order that will guarantee a chart placing. Then, as soon as the second single is serviced, as we call it, the big regional radio stations will pick up on it. Then you're underway. In fact the retailers can do as much for you as the radio stations. If you hear something being played in-store you might enquire about it, and maybe buy it. If you can get the first record away like that, the promotional department of the record company think it's all a piece of cake, and off they go.

Peyton returns to the central role of marketing:

Everything has to be perfect for a record to stand a chance. A record company will always pull deals to get records into the shops. 'Take six of these and we'll give you three of these free.' The free one would be a guaranteed seller, all profit, in return for giving a helping hand to the new act. So they sell cheap to get it moving.

In the 1970s records climbed the charts, week by week. Now everything's geared to getting them straight in somewhere near the top. So it's all about timing. If the record is due out but they haven't got all the TV exposure in place then they'll move the release back. At the concerts there'll be questionnaires on all the seats, and they're used to build a database for mail promotions. It's very scientific.

There are exceptions, fortunately. David Gray is a good example. He was around for years, getting nowhere but gaining experience. Then someone at Radio 1 picked up on him and it all turned around. So the main advice is never to give up. If you think you're good enough, if you're determined to prove it, then you must persevere. Send out your tapes to record companies, managers, publicists, everyone. Try and expand out of your own area, gigs, sessions for local radio, anything. In the end, talent will out.

# Running Your Own Label

Dance music is pop in its purest twenty-first century form. Once a DJ picks up on a particular cut it can be in the shops, sell a barrowload and be forgotten within a few weeks. Meanwhile the artist and his record company are already working on the next variation on the theme.

Because of this intensity it seemed appropriate to seek out a dance expert when pondering the pros and cons of running your own label. There is nothing leisurely about the process once a vibe is created, and so all the stages are concentrated, and the energy level remains high. And since, after the best part of a decade in dance music, Steve Simmonds is beginning to wonder if there isn't more to life than expending all that energy, he is the ideal man to warn would-be record-company magnates of the drawbacks as well as the highs of running your own operation – though naturally we will end up on a positive note.

Steve set up a label called Magnetic North in 1992 in partnership with Dave Clarke and John Truelove. The latter had already had a huge hit in the previous year with 'You Got the Love', a dance groove by The Source featuring Candi Staton. From these beginnings developed the Truelove Label Collective, an umbrella organization that eventually came to shelter some 15–20 labels. Steve says:

There is a huge attraction in running your own business, to be in charge of your own time. You have control and flexibility towards your own career. And the integrity to do things the way you want. How do you start? Get some money, get some artists! In fact people who start labels are usually already artists – they want an outlet without having to go through someone else's A&R process. It so happens that I came in through the management side, but since I'm not a corporate person I found the idea of being in control attractive.

The first problem to be confronted is finance – not just start-up, but as ongoing cashflow. Steve continues:

To press up a thousand records costs, say, £1,000, but then there's plus, plus and plus. The cost of promotion, your own basic living expenses, office expenses and so on. Raising money for music ventures is very difficult. It's a very risky business and investors don't understand it. Banks aren't interested. Ideally you find a benefactor, someone with money who's always wanted to be involved in music, but won't interfere too much.

Without that, then, the hardest hurdle is the first one.

Once you are set up you can go to distributors, but they want something solid. Finished product is a help. They like to see some track record and history to instil confidence – there are too many wannabees. This assumes, of course, that you've already got your artist. It is difficult to start from scratch with a distributor. So you have the artist, you prepare a budget and with luck you get a distribution deal. You should set up a company – it doesn't have to be limited, but given the vagaries and litigious nature of the music business it's a good idea to limit your liability.

Since you are already dealing with an artist in order to show something solid to a potential distributor, presumably the relationship between that artist and the company should be defined.

Yes, you need a contract. One track, or several tracks and an album. Agree the nature of the deal so you know where you stand. Get a package together at this stage. The label artwork, the company logo. It shows you mean business.

What sort of time scale is involved to get to this stage?

The process of manufacture goes from the music to mastering to cutting, and this is when you should also be organizing your artwork. You will have test pressings from the cut, and these can be your initial promotion as well. Then you need pressed-up promo copies for DJs and press. Once you have built a vibe in the clubs, and hopefully you're picking up some radio, then you distribute to the shops, followed by full radio promotion. From manufacture to release would normally need a 10- to 12-week turnaround.

It sounds as if a distributor is the essential middle man in the process? Steve agrees.

Distribution is the key. You can go round the shops doing it yourself, but it's an uphill struggle. And shops can be bad payers. You are most likely to start with a one-stop, who will take a number of records on sale or return. Generally, they will only take product within their field – even within dance music itself there are the different categories and styles, so you need to know what the distributor specializes in. It's a good idea to approach them initially with a demo, to create interest. It's a simple form of market research.

So, with a specialist distributor in place, with an agreed number of the single in stock, what comes next?

Promotion. If you haven't got everything in place you could create a demand before you can supply it. And the demand can be quite brief – it could have evaporated by the time you are up and running.

There are basically seven levels of promotion and marketing in dance music. Start with the clubs, ideally through contacts. If you can get a top DJ behind it you will create the vibe. The radio – know who the specialists are. Thirdly, the press – again, the papers who are into your type of music. Then live appearances – gigs for bands, personal appearances for DJs and dance outfits. Now back it up with advertising – fly-posting, flyers, beer mats, whatever. The sixth step, hopefully, is television. It can be cheap to make a video, and there's a whole new breed of channels looking for material. If you've got a killer track and a decent video it will get shown. Finally there are the licensees. If you can license your track for compilations in all the various foreign territories it may be a small fee individually, but it builds up and can be your real source of profit.

This all sounds too much work for one person to manage in the short time-scale.

Yes, you should be starting to build a team who believe in the idea, and the product. And a lawyer is useful from the initial contract stage. They can be hugely expensive, so try to cultivate one who will relate their fees to your progress. And always remember that planning is vital. You are dealing with something that is both an art form and a fast-moving consumer product. In dance music, very fast-moving indeed. An instant vibe, an instant demand. So it must be planned. Make sure you are registered with the mechanical and performance collection societies – MCPS, PRS, PPL. You are required by law to have a licence with the MCPS to press records.

Steve conveys the potential exhilaration of being intimately involved in this process, and yet he has already indicated that he is thinking of stepping back from it somewhat. So, what are the drawbacks?

First of all, money. It takes a long time to get established, and cash-flow is so slow. There are endless time delays but a constant need for more cash. It is difficult to make money – it took us two years before we could draw any for ourselves. You have to be prepared for that. Even with a very successful release it will take six or nine months before you see any money.

Since we started by pointing out the financial problem, we will assume that anyone thinking of setting up a label now knows that they must solve that problem before any other, and that their budget should allow for up to two years of outgoings with little coming back in. What's the rest of the bad news?

Well, it takes over your life. You've got office hours followed by club hours. If you are also the artist there is simply no time left, what with working in the studio as well. You are constantly juggling these disciplines. And in the end you are running a business. This takes a particular mentality. And when you are involved in a business it can be very wearing dealing with artists, who don't share that mentality – they want their release prioritized, and they want their royalties yesterday. It becomes a distraction.

Dwell on these warnings too much, and no one would ever set up a record label. So we should come back full circle to finish on the up-side. Steve stresses:

You are doing what you want to do with no one to tell you otherwise. And it can be great fun – seeing the whole process through is very satisfying, and you are fully immersed in the scene. And if you are an artist you have complete freedom. When you are dealing with a big label you may have records knocked back because they're not seen as the next big thing, and the company is only interested in dealing with huge volume. But on your own you can serve a niche market, selling one or two thousand of a release and on to the next one. You can react very flexibly to the market, and stay ahead of the game.

Between two of the stages that Steve refers to, producing a finished master and shipping finished copies to a distributor, comes the process of manufacturing, packaging and boxing the records. An independent record company may not want to be involved with this. It could be that the artist roster is not big enough to warrant employing production staff, or that the label lacks the relevant expertise or interest, preferring to concentrate on the music rather than the nuts and bolts of turning it into discs. This is where the brokers come in.

One such is Tribal Manufacturing in Balham, south London, run by Alison Wilson.

We act as a production department for independents. From cutting and mastering to delivering the finished product to the distributor, whether it's CD, vinyl, DVD, minidisc, cassette. We also organize the printing from origination to the finished job. Or we can contribute any part of the chain from the finished master to the distributor – whatever the record company doesn't want to be involved in, because it doesn't have the time or the facilities.

As in the financial world of the stockbroker, the broker in the music business acts as an intermediary.

I don't like the name, but it does describe what we do. There's myself and six other members of staff at Tribal, and we have maybe two or three competitors. Then there are other companies that do bits of the process. In the past a lot of printers and factories have had a go at doing what we do, but they've usually failed. It's a specialized part of the music business, and so they go back to doing what they do best.

Who would Tribal and other brokers normally have a contract with?

The record company itself. We wouldn't ever deal directly with an artist unless he is also his own record company.

In which case, as Steve Simmonds has already suggested, he is likely to be very tired indeed.

The total turnaround time is 15–20 days for vinyl, 10–15 for CDs. Vinyl involves extra processes: the master is cut on to lacquer, then to metal and then to the stampers. We take test pressings at that stage to check for problems. That accounts for the extra five days, because a CD is a digital transfer, so all that physical stuff in the middle is cut out. The factory makes a glass master for a CD, and then the discs are pressed from that.

What about the look of the package? Does that remain the responsibility of the record company?

We don't organize the artwork, although we can recommend various designers. We are supplied with finished artwork and take it from there. At the end of the process the stock is delivered wherever the client wants. The distributor has it 10 days before the release date, and then they batch it up into the orders.

Occasionally we are called in to do work for one of the majors, and we're happy to do it. Obviously they've all got their own operations, but we are more flexible. So maybe they come to us, for instance, to do a promotional CD for one of their artists. We can turn it around in a couple of weeks whereas maybe it would take them eight, with 15 people having to give their approval and everyone having their say. And because we don't have those 15 people it also means that we can give a label a better deal, whether they are an independent or a major.

Given the demands of the job of running your own label, as outlined by Steve Simmonds, it seems most likely that any newcomer – once they have the artist and the distributor in place – will want to consider very seriously the possibility of handing over the mechanics of production to a broker, while they plan the rest of the campaign.

# The Music Press

10

Forty years ago, *Melody Maker* was essential weekly reading. From modest beginnings as *Jazz Journal* it went on to sell more than a million copies at its peak. By the time it imploded in 2000, absorbed by its IPC stablemate and biggest rival *New Musical Express* (*NME*), sales were down to an insupportable 30,000. The merge between the two titles was only symbolic – the once-giant *MM* had become a dead dinosaur, now named simply *Maker*, and had been decently buried. Just as significant, that rising star of the late 1960s, the ground-breaking *NME*, was by then only selling a little over 70,000 in its own right. A million each at one time, now 100,000 between them. Soon after the end of *Melody Maker*, the monthly *Select* also closed. Something had changed in music publishing – and the problem was lack of readers for 'general interest' titles in the age of cable TV.

Meanwhile specialist areas of the music press, once largely the province of amateur fanzines, were thriving. In the heavy-metal field EMAP's *Kerrang!* is a major player, for example. It has flourished for 20 years with its dedication to 'loud, aggressive music' and sells over 45,000 weekly. Alongside it, Future Publishing's *Metal Hammer*, founded in 1994 with a 'mainstream hard rock' policy, ticks over by shifting more than 30,000 copies monthly. These figures would be unacceptable for a magazine trying to cover everything musical, but satisfactory when catering for a focused market, with its more defined advertising profile. From Craig Douglas, the singing milkman of 1960, to Craig David, the wind of change in music journals had swung through 180 degrees.

Ross Fortune, the music editor of *Time Out* magazine, confirms this shift, but puts the blame for the problems of the traditional music press partly on themselves:

I used to find *NME* essential reading, absolutely inspirational. It had broader, bolder ambitions. Now it's narrowed down and seems to be just part of the mainstream PR world. So the old role of the established press doesn't apply any more, and in the meantime specialist areas look after themselves.

Interestingly, Fortune sees the shift of emphasis as reflecting that in the music business in general.

The biggest labels have become global and have less and less time for small bands. In that world REM can consider to have failed if they *only* sell seven million of their latest album. Some artists have learned to adapt. The classic example is Tom Waits. A well-established artist with a huge reputation, but low sales in the eyes of a major label. So his latest album *Mule Variations* is on an independent label, Epitaph, and it's his biggest seller ever. It seems possible that a small label can maximize sales for an artist like that, whereas a major can't be bothered. The relevance to the press is that the established titles follow a safe PR route, leaving any imagination to smaller magazines.

This is reflected in the way in which we experience the media as a whole, compared to the days when *Melody Maker* and *NME* ruled the earth. As Fortune says:

Everything used to impact on the mainstream. Take 'God Save the Queen' by the Sex Pistols. Number 1 in the Queen's Jubilee year. Now everything's dissipated, because there is so much TV and radio. People don't experience things en masse any more. But all the little worlds can thrive on their own.

So what is the future for the print media? Fortune is understandably optimistic:

I think there'll always be a place for browseability, for magazines like *Time Out*. The Internet has got a long way to go. You should be able to search for gigs, decide which one to go to, book tickets to be collected at the door and order a cab to take you there, all in one operation. But that's a long way away.

Personally, I believe that there will always be a place for print, over the breakfast boiled egg, on the bus or the tube, while drinking a lunchtime pint, or in the evening armchair. The thought of squinting at a tiny screen at these times, whether to catch up on the news, read a feature article or finally get down to *War and Peace*, as well as glaring at a bigger screen throughout working hours, is too depressing to contemplate. Fortune continues with a warning.

But things are contracting. As just one example, even *Q* seems to be shifting towards the mainstream, becoming more of a style and fashion title as well as music, and that has caused *Mojo* to move in behind it.

If the music press is indeed changing, what does Fortune feel about its role as an arm of A&R, unearthing new talent? The answer is disturbing.

As I recall it, you used to go out and discover bands.

This was indeed true in the 1970s – in fact, *Time Out*'s core function was to nurture pub rock, fringe theatre and independent cinema in a process of symbiosis.

It's more tied up these days, so you are less likely to stumble upon something. It is unlikely that a journalist would respond to a band approaching them out of the blue. It is more funnelled through the PR process – depressing but true. More fabricated.

Just like the mainstream, it seems.

We do take a responsibility to listen to tapes, though, and if we're interested we go and see them. But the approach is still most likely to be from a company. I'm always surprised at how unclued-up bands can be. Badly recorded tapes. Not having found out the name of the person they should approach. Asking *Time Out* to review a gig, when a glance at the magazine would show that it's not its function. New bands expecting a feature – it's even as if they expect a front cover. It's not going to happen, and that sort of arrogant ignorance doesn't endear them to you.

In response to ignorance, is cynicism creeping into journalism?

Well, I think that most of us do still have a healthy enthusiasm for music. That's what we're here for. But I do sense a jaded feeling across the industry, simply because music has become such a packaged product. Hopefully it's a passing phase. To maintain enthusiasm I can only turn to the music. PR is a necessary evil – and to be fair it's not all bad, in any case. You can build up a good relationship with a publicist and trust what they're saying. But there's such a turnover of staff in press offices and PR companies that some of them aren't even aware of their own bands, let alone what your particular interests are.

And yet new artists do get noticed, and genuine talent does rise to the surface. What hints does Fortune have for them?

Avoid the trap of trying to sound like whatever's big at the moment. After a Travis or a Coldplay comes along, for another six months you'll get young bands trying to sound like them. But by the time they get through the system they will already be outdated, and Travis or Coldplay will have moved on anyway. A band must find its own identity, and stick to it.

You can always sense when there's something there, and it's not just in the music. Bands don't get noticed by a stranger standing at the back of the room any more, like Brian Epstein and the Beatles. That 'something' is an awareness, an intelligence, a sense of being sussed – an indication that you've thought things through. In the end the artist has to make all these connections for himself, not wait for someone to do it for him.

# Diary of a Band

11

When I started to prepare this book I looked around for a band who were still to make the big breakthrough, but who had been around long enough to have a wealth of experiences to share. What I was looking for was a personal account of the challenges and pitfalls that a band encounters in the early stages, and some insight into why people would willingly forsake security in favour of a search for a precarious career in music.

There is a non-musical reason for this, of course – a burning desire to be successful, to become rich and famous in a glamorous field which seems (misleadingly) to offer instant dollops of both riches and fame, and it can sometimes work. Every generation has known examples of artists with no great talent, certainly nothing to enrich music as an art form, who have reached the top by sheer determination – though they probably always needed a pretty face and a share of luck to back up a single-minded yearning to succeed. They also need, and there can be no exceptions to this, a core of ruthlessness.

These are not simply subjective judgements – only legal restraints prevent me from naming performers who privately admit to being comparatively talent-free when it comes to a musical 'voice', but who are richly talented as far as nurturing a career is concerned. There is nothing wrong with this, and it is indeed part of a modern trend. Some of the most famous people on television, to take the most visible example, are famous simply because they *are* on television. Their talent is fairly rudimentary – an ability to smile, to read an autocue, to walk across a studio floor as if it is a natural thing to do, and to be very enthusiastic about everything. One can only admire the steely determination necessary to fashion a 'television personality' out of such thin material. But neither they nor their musical counterparts are relevant here.

What concerns us is the opposite approach, a desire to succeed by making good, honest music in the confidence that, by dint of hard work, it will inevitably find an audience, however long it takes. It struck me that the two-piece band brothernature were ideal to guide me through the hinterland of the music business, and I am most grateful to them for agreeing to help. The fact that they are a duo would be an advantage, it seemed to me – fewer contradictions and arguments. So it proved. They both respect the right of the other to complete a thought before adding their own two-penn'orth.

Brothernature are indeed brothers, Adrian and Melvin Duffy, based in south-west London. They have their own label, Symphony Ray Records, and in partnership with their manager Michelle Hopkins they are a musical cottage industry. They have elected to retain a high degree of control over their destiny, producing carefully-crafted music that (if it has to be put in a bag – sorry, chaps) works along a folk-country-pop axis, with the personal 'voice' always coming through.

In organizing what they had to say I have tried to keep a light editorial touch, in the hope of conveying long and convivial pub conversations as naturally as possible. Adrian and Melvin are committed and experienced musicians – Melvin's 'day job', for example, is as one of the country's top pedal-steel session players, and the Irish side of their family ensured that they were surrounded by music from the cradle onwards.

To start with there are lessons to be drawn from the fact that they are, for the foreseeable future, a double act, even though most musicians are more likely to be drawn to the security blanket of a larger group. Melvin explains:

It was a conscious decision for us to not form a band to start with. The realities of trying to keep a band together and get enough work, with the obvious financial burdens, led us to avoid it. We are self-financing – I do session work, Adrian does work outside music when it's necessary, and we invest the profit in ourselves.

Adrian adds that many larger groups are, in essence, centred around a duo:

We were always doing the writing ourselves, which is another reason it made sense to remain as a duo. Any band needs a core that's absolutely rock solid. It could be the writing team, in fact it often is, but whatever it happens to be, the band will come apart without it. Look at most successful bands and you will see that two of them are the constant element around which the band operates.

Lennon and McCartney, Jagger and Richards, the feuding Davies brothers in the Kinks, the equally volatile Gallaghers, Mark Knopfler and the only other constant Dire Strait, John Illsley, the Jamaican rhythm section of Sly and Robbie, Glenn Tilbrook and Chris Difford in Squeeze – the examples are endless, and the principle does seem to hold good.

Although a naturally cemented partnership with another musician, an instant sounding board for ideas, therefore seems like a good idea, most ambitious musicians will nevertheless graduate first towards a band set-up if they are motivated mainly by a desire to play – the hardcore duo can come later, arising out of the larger grouping. Melvin spells out some of the dangers to watch out for:

My previous experience playing in bands, although it has usually been as part of a backing group to an individual artist, has taught me that it can be a frightening experience. All the arguments and politics are very draining. I wanted us to succeed, and the way to do it was in whatever way is least taxing. If you keep it small you can make more headway. There's less disputed decisions, for instance.

Whatever route you take, musical discipline is vital. Melvin continues:

It is crucial to realize that an awful lot of dedication towards your own instrument is necessary. If people took more responsibility in that way they'd realize how much energy it takes, and maybe they'd be a little more humble when it comes to fitting in with others. Dedication and expertise should be respected, but inexperienced people can be quite arrogant – they mistake it for youthful energy. But dedication to the instrument must come first. I've also found many more problems when individuals aren't clear on their precise role in the band. When the machine is well oiled it runs smoothly, but the only reason that can happen successfully is because the machine was built carefully in the first place.

This means that a clarity of vision is necessary from the outset. You must be in agreement as to what you want the band to achieve, at least in the near future. If one member is looking for a weekly semi-pro residency, and another is already dreaming of the first American tour, then at least they must agree on the ground rules. As Adrian says:

You've always got to tell yourself that this is a job for the rest of your life, and you've got to believe it . . .

To which Melvin adds:

. . . which means that you have to forego some of the expectations that other people have. It takes years to learn your craft, like any other skilled tradesman. That may well mean less comforts, less time down the pub, whatever. We live in a remote-control society – if you don't like something you switch to something else. But a musician *has* to stick to it, otherwise they will not succeed. Youngsters who fancy being musicians – or fancy being pop stars, maybe – can switch on the telly and see a group like Westlife and think it happened instantly, as if it always existed like this. They don't think of the years that might have been spent learning to sing, to play instruments, learning dance movements, learning the craft.

In Adrian's opinion:

People can forget that above all you have to graft. If there's only ten people in the audience you've still got to go out there and work as hard as if it's a full house, otherwise you'll lose the ten who *did* come to see you. We knew we were going to do this 10 or 12 years ago, and yet in another way it seems like we're just starting. That's how long it can take to build the foundations. The gap between the instant aspirations of the young and the success that they see on the television screen is huge.

Melvin adds:

And if it's not happening for you financially, then it's the *rest* of your life that has got to adapt, not your dedication to the music. You have to go without in other ways, but you cannot cut corners with the music.

In the brothers' opinion, musical integrity has to be at the heart of what you do, because you can only hope to succeed in what you believe in. If you hold fast to your principles, the world will catch up with you. According to Melvin:

Sometimes it seems almost as if real music will become an art form, financed by the Arts Council to keep it alive. But if you keep working at it the tide will turn again. It always does. A lot of pop music today consists of young kids dancing, and miming to tracks they had nothing or very little to do with. But the demand for music will always be there in the background, waiting to make a comeback.

Our family is steeped in music, and so I think we learned a lot about the pitfalls of the music business by seeing the experience of our father and uncles. Our uncles were working as a bluegrass duo. The main lesson was how hard it is. And what you learn from that is – if you are doing it for the love of music, then it's everlasting. If you are doing it for instant financial gain, you will undoubtedly be disappointed.

What can a new band do to build momentum, to alert the industry to their talent? Adrian answers:

A couple of years ago we were thinking of targeting record companies, but we soon realized that all that effort could be channelled into doing our own thing. What with the Internet, and the drop in price of the technology to produce CDs, it doesn't cost more these days to do it yourself, to retain your independence.

It makes best sense to write your own material. In terms of longevity, your potential income in the future will come from the songs. So I started doing that when I was about 16 years old, and the next step was to start putting together a very basic studio. The dedication requires that you make time for music, to find time outside your day job to get the work done. And it must be a *lot* of time, because that's what it takes. The studio came together in stages. Each time we earned a little bit more money, we bought a little more equipment. So I've always had to find jobs that earned enough money, and gave me time and energy left for the music.

Then you have to market yourselves. Assume you've got the dedication, assume you've made the time, where do you go next? I'd say, get a manager. You simply don't have time to do that as well – you're earning a living, you're developing your music. That's enough to have to do. So, someone else has to mind the shop. Obviously you're going to have to pay them what you can, in the expectation that things will build, but since it's not going to be much to begin with, their first quality must be enthusiasm for what you're doing.

Melvin agrees:

Being a musician is quite enough work, without trying to be a manager as well. Musicians and managers are different animals. You need a different head to do the one job or the other. And none of us has two heads. On my own instrument I've got the confidence to rip it up with anyone, to play in any company. Selling myself on the phone is a different thing.

Adrian continues:

When you're at a gig, having a manager gives you a buffer between yourself and all the rest. Because, before you go out to play, you do have to protect yourself a bit. After you've played, go out into the bar and be the most sociable person in the world. But before you play, lock yourself away and concentrate on the job in hand. You've got to sell the music before you sell yourself.

Build a database of everyone you know. Use e-mail, and regular mail shots. Do whatever you decide you can afford. Kids these days have the tools and the know-how to run off adverts, posters and so on.

Melvin reckons:

That might be one reason why there's a lack of dedication on the part of some youngsters. Because the technical bits are so much easier these days, maybe they expect the musical skill to be easy as well. But it isn't. It's as hard as it ever was.

So how can the band get heard at the outset? Adrian explains:

There are music magazines that will listen to and review demos. The studio-type mags. *Sound on Sound, Muzik, The Mix.* And the Musicians' Union review demos in their magazine. Once you get reviews, you've got something to take to a record company, or to use however you want to. With the cheapness of gear these days, compared to not so long ago, building your own studio – step by step, as you can afford it – is also a good way of keeping control over your music, over the direction you're going in. The future could lie in delivering a complete package to a record company. Anyway, send the stuff out. The worst that can happen is that they send it back. Meanwhile, everyone should maybe lob a few quid a week into the kitty. That's your promotional budget, for paper, envelopes, stamps, whatever. Create your own website, and put your audiofiles on it. Post it on to other sites.

Melvin does have a word of warning, however:

To start your own record company, which is what we did, is to start with all outlay and no income. You have to be prepared for that. But don't forget that an established record company would only shield you from those expenses for a while. You would be steadily going into their debt, and you may not realize it. We know bands only just starting out who are already a quarter of a million in debt.

Adrian continues:

Contact the distributors, and send them material just as you would send it to a record company. Put a business case together, a practical, hard-headed one. Present yourselves as a going concern, so that it's easier for them to make the decision to take you on. After all, they haven't been required to put any money in at this stage. Prepare sales notes, have postcards printed. Always carry a stack with you, and drop them in to record stores. This is all part of spreading the word.

Do your own press, arrange your own interviews. It always starts with 'Who are you?' But it doesn't take long for them to find out, and then they appreciate the fact that you're not just another plugger from a record company – you are actually the artist, making the effort to keep in contact. The enthusiasm of the do-it-yourself approach is often appealing to them. As you build up local airplay, the PRS begins to come in. Not much at first, of course, but it's a sign that you are professional, and it can only build if you keep putting the time in. You will make the time, if you want to do it.

Keep driving it onwards with mail, postcards, flyers, phone calls. Motor on through rejections – you will get them all the time, so you must move on towards the next acceptance. After a while the PRS begins to flow, and then you begin to get tiny cheques from the distributor. That will seed another CD pressing. And so it goes. As a rough guide we can press up 1,000 singles for around £700 or £800, including the artwork and everything.

Another way of sowing seeds is to take out a small display ad in the music press. In terms of the cost of reaching each reader it's incredibly cheap. Of course they're not all going to rush out and buy your record, but you are building recognition bit by bit. Don't forget to secure your name – check with the Musicians' Union. Which reminds me – join the Union. I was flying back from New York once and even though my guitar was properly secure in a flight case, it got cracked. One call, and the MU paid out £500.

Melvin adds:

If the worst comes to the worst, by being in the MU you are part of an organization that already has lawyers on the case.

So the main lessons offered by brothernature are:

1. Without total dedication to improving on your chosen instrument you will get nowhere.
2. You should always be clear of your role and goals within a band.
3. You should accept that music is a career for life.
4. Be prepared for hard graft, invest in music and adapt the other aspects of your life if money is tight.
5. Only go into the job through a love of music rather than a fantasy of fame.
6. Get a manager as soon as you can.
7. Build a database containing anyone who could be useful.
8. Set aside a promotional budget, however small.
9. Construct a business plan for the band.
10. Make sure all aspects of promotion are covered.
11. Join the Musicians' Union.

All this seems to make very good sense, but other musicians who have travelled a little way down the road may have different ideas, or have other lessons to share. Please let us know for future editions (see Introduction for details).

# Music in Space

12

The Internet is now an established fact of life, and it is already beginning to revolutionize the music business. This is surely the area of the industry that will develop and adapt fastest in the near future, and it is likely to move at a pace hitherto unknown in more traditional areas of the business.

Peter Whitehead is an Internet guru, an evangelist for the potential of music on the web. His website bandreg.com (the Band Register) has proved hugely successful as an A&R service providing a showcase for new bands, and he has now expanded into fresh fields. Last year he launched netthebestmusic.com, a global A&R network, netthebestsongs.com, a proactive, song-driven publishing roster, and an 'artist stock market' designed to raise funds for new musical projects.

The original function of the Band Register was, and is, to enable new bands to check if anyone has already registered the name they were going to use, and to enable them to do so if not (see Chapter 7 – Organizations for Musicians). In addition, Whitehead has issued a series of CDs, 'Best of, Unsigned', which have resulted in record contracts for over 70 of the bands featured, notably Stereophonics and Supergrass. Before he launched the Band Register, it was Whitehead who spotted the potential of Radiohead (then called On a Friday) and recommended them to Parlophone. He is perhaps better qualified than anyone to look into the cyberspace crystal ball for *The Musicians' Bible*:

I believe that the Internet will totally change the way that the music industry operates. But to take advantage of the potential of the new technology it is important to think laterally and constructively. Infrastructures will be developed that will have to be bought at a premium price, by companies that could have developed them for themselves in-house, if they had had the necessary imagination and forethought.

This is a clear warning directed at the more hidebound corners of the record business, and it is one that young musicians, having grown up computer-literate, could well exploit.

In all areas of activity, the ones who will succeed with Internet start-ups are those who have a unique idea, one that offers 'added value' to whatever is already available, and who are totally dedicated to it. Anyone who goes into it first and foremost expecting to make a killing will fail. When I started the Band Register I slept on the office floor for four years. I could manage to pay for an office or a house, but not both. Money was not the motive – I had an idea that I believed in. And if the idea is good enough, eventually the revenue will flow.

In a sense Whitehead sees the Internet as a limitless shop window, or more accurately a virtual listening booth:

One key to the development of the Net is for the music industry to reach out to potential consumers and say, 'If you like this, then try this as well.' The conventional record store is a hopelessly archaic and inefficient way of introducing the public to new music. It provides a stockholding function, but offers no 'added value'. And even as a repository of available stock, it only holds a tiny proportion of what is available. The Internet can provide 100 per cent stock holding, and allow for the product to be sampled before buying.

The Internet can also reach across age barriers (my family recently gave my mother just what she wanted for her 80th birthday – an Internet-ready computer), and attract those who might be reluctant to cross the brash, noisy threshold of a typical chain record store. Whitehead points out:

Most disposable income is held by the older generation of potential music-buyers, and by and large they avoid record stores, because they seem alien and off-putting. Meanwhile the younger audience, the only one that record stores seem to be interested in, can soon get tired of being offered such a limited range of product – whatever the record companies wish to push at them that week.

Whitehead sees an inevitable rise of customer power as a result of increased use of the Internet:

In the future the music industry will be consumer-driven, and the attitude of the conventional record store will be rejected as patronizing, uninformative, limited and outdated. In most high-street stores you can try out the product before buying it, if it is something you are unfamiliar with. With music, all you can do is look at the packaging. This of course is why so much attention is paid to the appearance of the product, because this is actually what the store is selling.

In this view of the future, radio will also be revolutionized. In the past 40 years the main development has simply been the granting of more and more radio franchises – in 1960 pop music was only officially available as part (a small and somewhat 'square' part) of the schedule on the BBC Light Programme, and so we were far more dependent on the variable signal from Radio Luxembourg, 208 on the Medium Wave. The new leap forward, according to Whitehead, will embrace the potential of the digital age:

If the record companies had any sense they would be buying into digital radio, which will also be central to the industry in the future. In a sense radio will come full circle – in the 1950s we could listen to hour-long programmes on Radio Luxembourg sponsored by the various record companies, each putting its wares in the shop window. At present radio hates new music – it knows that people like what they know already, what they feel comfortable with, and so it has no wish to broaden their experience.

In the UK one or two key radio stations wield an unhealthy amount of power. *We* pay for Radio 1 and Radio 2 – they should be the 'people's' stations. In fact they are unregulated, the fiefdoms of the controllers. There is no 'OfBeeb' to ensure that the music that is played demographically represents what the licence-payers want to hear.

So I believe that in future radio will be digital and interactive. The consumer will be able to feed back selective information and will, to some extent, be able to choose exactly what they want to hear. This will mean narrow-casting, as opposed to broadcasting. In fact, this will be the exact opposite of the system whereby a national radio station feeds to a million listeners only what its controllers want them to hear – an involuntary radio stream. In future smaller audiences will be listening to what they choose. The present system denies that important principle of saying to listeners, 'If you like this, try this as well.' But that will be how the market will grow in future – leading the listener through related sounds, giving them access to music that they like, but didn't know existed.

Warming to this theme, Whitehead predicts that:

once this form of radio is on offer, there will be no going back. The present model will be seen as out-dated, patronizing and limited, just like the record store. Advertisers will buy into a range of radio 'streams' that enable them to focus more efficiently on to their audience. Listeners will get a better deal – and buy more music.

With the Internet and narrow-cast digital radio acting as an aural shop window for musicians, it is inevitable that the next change will have to come in the way that we pay for music. According to Whitehead:

In the future, music will be sold in the form of artefacts – CDs, DVDs, and so on – subscriptions, one-off transactions to download and, eventually, micro-billed 'play on demand'. Existing companies selling CDs over the Internet will have to improve their facilities for allowing potential customers to hear before buying, to browse among the virtual racks and then actually sample the music before making up their mind.

When interactive TV and radio stations take off they will allow the customer to respond with a keypad, to buy off the air, and to take advantage of special promotions and discount offers. There will be technical advances in DVD audio and video, allowing the consumers to develop their own programmes and mixes. Mail order will be developed through places licensed to play recorded music – pubs, clubs, hotels, trains, etc. – via information displays and an instant ordering facility using credit or debit cards, both on site and via mobile phone. This will increase impulse buying.

However, to a large extent this is basically a continuation of what is already happening, which is a broadening of the means by which we pay for products – by telephoning an order with a credit-card number, for example, or by tapping it into a website. Whitehead admits that some wrinkles have to be ironed out in the new world of consumerism:

Subscription services will develop whereby consumers can download their choice of music from the Internet in return for a regular subscription debit. The main problem to be solved is how to distribute the revenue fairly. I suspect that it will, at first at least, favour the majors and their established artists. But new artists have the potential to use the Internet to develop a fan base, even giving away music free in order to develop loyalty. For all this to work the selection mechanisms for music on the Internet will have to improve, but they are doing that all the time.

There is an existing model, he says:

A subscription system for music could develop in a comparable way to that already in existence for films. At present you can choose to contribute to a film's revenue stream at a number of chronological points. You can pay to see the film in the cinema on release, pay to see it soon afterwards on Sky Box Office or a similar outlet, subscribe to all the cable and satellite film channels and see it a few weeks later, subscribe to the main Sky channels and wait longer, rent the video, buy the video, buy the DVD, eventually see it 'free' on terrestrial television – or copy it from a friend. Music will develop along similar lines, though obviously with generic differences.

There is, of course, resistance in terms of attitudes and habits. Whitehead observes:

Paying a one-off fee to download has not proved popular so far. Record companies have resisted the idea, seeing it as a threat to their profitability. Their attitude is, why change if we don't have to? The answer is that they *will* have to – when the habit of buying music online reaches a 'critical mass', it will force change.
 The record business attacks on such dotcom ventures as Napster and MP3.com have shown that the vested interests among the companies and their shareholders are more than capable of fighting back. In the long term, however, I believe that they would be wise to embrace these developments. The punter holds most of the aces. The pressures exerted from mechanisms on the web that enable free and low-cost music to be accessed without benefit to the artist or record company will force down the price of 'legal' music. What the web is doing is cutting out the middle man and making possible a far larger market place. The companies will wise up. Remember the saying, 'An open hand holds more than a clenched fist.' On the other hand, it is possible that downloading may never become very popular, particularly if a subscription system can be perfected.

Whitehead continues his journey into tomorrow's musical world by musing on such mysterious concepts as micro-billing and brain implants:

The home and office of the future will include playing and viewing facilities which will allow for both subscription and micro-billing. The attraction of micro-billing is that digital music has embedded in it an 'audit trail', making possible a simple mechanism whereby artist, writer, publisher and company can be rewarded according to an agreed formula. This could foreshadow the end of competing collection societies acting for writers and artists – eventually, it will all be included in the sound itself.

This does envisage a huge leap forward, but it is one in which the problems of revenue-collecting are surely solved once and for all. The consumer's bill for the service they are hooked into will be automatically routed to the relevant parties.

Whitehead continues:

Selection will become voice-activated – eventually, far in the future, it will be thought-activated, delivered through a microchip implant in the brain! It will be paid for monthly, or quarterly, through your telecom or connectivity bill. Pricing will be competitive, because the suppliers will want to discourage ownership of artefacts like CDs in favour of reliance on their service.

Micro-billing should soon become available as part of Microsoft Explorer browser technology. Combined with other technology this will allow artists to notify you when they have new music to offer, with a view to you buying it. Micro-billing could thus lead to Internet 'record labels', levying a small page charge for listening to their music, a bigger charge for downloading, 'owning it', in a higher resolution.

Whitehead sees the Internet as making possible the search for exactly what the consumer wants, even if they didn't know what that was when they logged on:

Luddites have criticized the Internet for promulgating a mass of free music, most of which is rubbish. I have news for them. Most of *all* music is rubbish! It is all a matter of selection. Finding the best new music is my job. Potentially, the Internet is a superb way of finding it. Many music websites offer a search engine mechanism that asks you to state your preferences, leading to an interactive response bringing you like-minded music. Hopefully you will enjoy this and maybe buy it. This is the key to selling music on the Internet and through interactive media. You give away a certain amount, and charge for the rest.

The music industry, Whitehead believes, has misunderstood this principle. He points out:

In 1998, Steve Levine and Marc Marot, who was then Chief Executive Officer of Polygram Island, complained on the BBC's *Money Programme* that free music on the Internet was depriving them of income. They were wrong – the people who were downloading Honeyz music would not have bought the CDs instead. They were in effect acting as unpaid agents for the band, all over the world. Similarly, it has been shown that Napster has actually increased record sales. Although it did undermine copyright, Napster in fact pointed the way towards the ultimate mechanism for distributing music and collecting royalties.

It is hard to see how the industry can police the net effectively – sites can migrate and metamorphose, but still maintain links that allow the punter to use them and stay ahead of the 'authorities'. Now, file-sharing services do not even need a co-ordinating host site. So the lesson is that the industry must learn to work *with* Internet services, not chase after them. However, Napster can admittedly also be seen as the thin end of the wedge – if you are going to use free music to promote sales, you must be in control of the sales. But in the end this is simply another reason why the industry should work co-operatively.

So neither the businessmen nor the musicians should be afraid of the concept of 'free music', he says. It is technically possible to allow comparatively low-quality sampling as an encouragement to invest in higher-definition sound.

The best way to use free tracks to generate revenue is to allow low-quality streaming, or a proportion of the total at higher resolution, coupled with a facility for ordering the CD. Then there are the official and unofficial websites associated with a particular band. If you've got 12 tracks on an album, you can afford to 'give away' a couple of tracks on your official website, and let the unofficial site have another.

Sony shot themselves in the foot, in my opinion, when they imposed stringent requirements on artists that the company should own the official website, and that unofficial ones should be eliminated where possible. There has never been a better way of building a band than by encouraging the growth of a fan base through websites – official or unauthorized. They can be used to develop all kinds of revenue stream including subscription membership of the fan club, bringing with it news of releases, access to bonus tracks, videos and merchandizing – as well as links to similar music throughout the world. Such co-operation would operate to mutual benefit. So Sony's knee-jerk stupidity was stupefying. Particularly as they are, of course, well aware that singles are routinely 'given away' to record shops in order to improve chart position and hence stimulate album sales.

One key to all this, it seems to me, is that we will all want to use the Internet as an information and merchandizing tool, but we will not wish to sit straight-backed at the computer when we wish to relax with our chosen music. We will sample on the Internet, pay on the Internet, maybe download high-resolution sound from the Internet. After that, we may want to listen while cooking the dinner, lying in the bath, moving around the house cleaning up, sitting in a deck-chair, or going to sleep. For new bands, the potential is challenging. Says Whitehead:

They can even move from giving away music to selling it without a conventional record deal.

We come full circle when we consider Peter Whitehead's main interest in the power of the Internet – as an A&R tool:

There are websites like MP3.com, Peoplesound and MusicUnsigned that offer opportunities for new artists, including showcases and marketing outlets. And the company that I started, the Band Register – bandreg.com – is virtually on its own in having scored a whole string of chart successes with bands it has featured. The next step is to improve efficiency by encouraging feedback from the punters, a form of Internet market research, and combining it with A&R expertise. This is the area that I am now moving into. Watch this space . . .

**A selection of current sites**
Another promising web site is Live Club (www.liveclub.co.uk), run by Justin Coll and his wife Eva. Says Justin:

It started in 1997 to promote a bi-weekly live music night, but it quickly outgrew what it had been set up to do. Since it was one of the only web sites at the time to show any interest in unsigned musicians and bands, it established itself very quickly.

The site is interactive, enabling musicians to communicate with each other, swap ideas and promote their music. You can advertise yourself on the site, and there's a classified-ad section for buying and selling instruments. There's no charge for any of Live Club's services, however.

We also have a news and reviews section called Live Scene. It has up-to-date business news and a survey of the unsigned scene. We also review new artists, going to gigs and assessing CDs sent to us. And we guide people towards other web sites.

The site includes a gradually developing national list of music venues, and Live Club has its own Internet radio station featuring new talent. Among complementary sites recommended by Justin are the Band Register (see p. 60 above), which he calls 'the best searchable database of band names on the net'; Digibid (www.digibid.com), 'a great resource for musicians and project studios, featuring an online auction of gear and equipment'; the ever-useful Musicians' Union (see Chapter 7 – Organizations for Musicians); and Studiobase (www.demon.co.uk/studiobase/), which is 'a great site with the biggest list I have seen of record companies, studios, hire, design, distributors, management and rehearsal studios.'

With the Internet developing and changing daily, the best advice that a book like this can give is to log on to sites like Live Club to keep in touch with developments.

# Peel's Postscript

13

In September 1967 the disc jockeys of the newly-launched Radio 1 were photographed outside Broadcasting House. Most were refugees from the offshore pirate stations, outlawed the previous month, or from Radio Luxembourg, the UK's only source of regular pop music before the pirates set sail in the mid-60s.

In 2001 some of those pioneers are dead, some in jail. Many have moved to what Harry Enfield dubbed 'Radio Quiet' – nowadays a somewhat unfair description of Radio 2, which offers popular music right across the range, while Radio 1 gets ever narrower. Others have been put out to pasture in provincial radio. Only John Peel survives, and as Radio 1 and pop-music radio in general becomes more and more formulaic, many regard him as Radio 1's 'conscience', a quiet, wryly humorous and principled renegade who is allowed to ignore the tyranny of the playlists. This is a tyranny that most disc jockeys are happy with, since it saves them the trouble of listening to the music and making choices. Peel, meanwhile, broadcasts whatever he wants.

Born in 1939 and a music broadcaster since the early 60s in America, where his Liverpool accent made him a natural 'Beatles expert', Peel somehow retains an enthusiasm for music that many of his colleagues don't even bother to feign:

There's always the hope of something good in the pile.

And it is a pile that gets bigger and bigger. On the day I spoke to him 10 packages arrived in the post, and a sack of mail brought home from Broadcasting House remained to be opened.

The biggest change I've noticed over the years is that there is simply more and more product. At one time I'd be thinking, 'Well, there's a new Led Zeppelin album due in November, and in the meantime here's some Brinsley Schwarz.' Now, for every track I play there are three or four more that I'd *like* to play.

Although Peel probably hears more new music than anyone else in the country, he can presumably never hear it all.

No, even the selection that I'm sent would take more than 24 hours seven days a week. So I hear as much as I can, and try to use my instinct. There really is just too much stuff. I went into Tower Records the other day, and looked through the section they call 'Indie', or whatever name they use. Most of it was by bands I'd literally never heard of. And this is meant to be my field. When it comes to dance music, I can read through the list of the top ten 'big records on the street' and realize that I've not heard of any of them. Nowadays there are even weird sub-categories like Death Metal. Satanic stuff, deliberately confrontational and blasphemous. There's people out there operating at the extremes of taste, where it bleeds into fascism. And I've no doubt that to keep up with Death Metal – that would be a full-time job as well!

So, we are spared Death Metal on Peel's Radio 1 shows, but is there any link between the records that he does play?

I'd be very hard put to find one. In fact, I wouldn't want to try. You would deprive yourself of the element of surprise, of unexpected pleasure.

The music business has changed considerably in the 40 years that Peel has hovered on its fringes – he proudly claims

. . . to keep it at more than arm's length. Nowadays the industry does seem more and more in control. They seem to have eliminated chance as best they can. Chance, surprise, that's what keeps it exciting. But the cultures that throw up the sort of music I like – whatever that might be – exist independently of the industry. The falling price of technology makes it possible for almost anyone to express themselves cheaply. That's a good thing. Technology also makes the programmes that I do much more of a two-way thing. With e-mail I get reactions instantly. That makes it more exciting. So, in spite of the odds, there's still so much that's good about the present situation. The volume of material makes it harder work, but more rewarding.

And is the future of music going to be more and more Internet-based? Peel answers cheerfully:

I haven't a clue. I have the technology here, but neither the time nor the aptitude to explore it. I'm simply too busy listening to records.

And while he listens, and pitches up at Broadcasting House to present the results of his researches, the industry cannot control everything, cannot manufacture every group. The individual voice, given determination as well as talent, will continue to find an outlet.

# directories

**3MI Recording Studios**
Canalot Building
222 Kensal Rd
London
W10 5BN
T 020 8960 5818   F 020 8960 3739

**Abandon Studios**
31 Churchfield Rd
London
W3 6BD
T 020 8993 3399/07956 280 257
E asis.wishful.abandon@virgin.net
*Booking Manager* Sally Ballet
*Contact* Michael Duvoisin

**Abbey Road Studios**
3 Abbey Rd
London
NW8 9AY
T 020 7266 7000   F 020 7266 7250
E info@abbeyroad.co.uk   w abbeyroad.co.uk
*Director of Operations* Chris Buchanan
*Contact* Colette Barber

**Ace Eyed Studios**
2 Menelik Rd
London
NW2 3RP
T 020 7435 6116   F as phone
*Studio Manager* Mark Albert

**Adelphoi Ltd**
71 Endell St
London
WC2H 9AJ
T 020 7240 7250   F 020 7240 7260
E info@adelphoi.co.uk   w adelphoi.co.uk
*Contact* Charles Hodgkinson

**Air Studios (Lyndhurst)**
Lyndhurst Hall
Lyndhurst Rd
London
NW3 5NG
T 020 7794 0660   F 020 7794 8518
E alison@airstudios.com   w airstudios.com
*Bookings Manager* Alison Burton
*General Manager* Jacqui Howell
*Studio established by* Sir George Martin

## Air Tank Studios
138a Chiswick High Rd
London
W4 1PU
**T** 020 8994 9007    **F** 020 8995 1051
**E** info@airtank.co.uk    **W** airtank.co.uk
*Contact* Brutus McManus

*Ideal for hip-hop and R&B projects*
*Also Rugged Expression Productions (contact Harry*
*Bozadjian, harry@ruggedexpression.com): hip-hop*
*and R&B producers/writers*
*See also Duke Avenue Records*

## Air-Edel Recording Studios Ltd
18 Rodmarton St
London
W1U 8BJ
**T** 020 7486 6466    **F** 020 7224 0344
**E** trevorbest@air-edel.co.uk
*Studio Manager* Trevor Best

*Specialists in the recording of music (synch to*
*picture) and spoken word projects*
*Three studios consisting of large and small facilities*
*plus edit suite and post-production*

## Alaska
127–129 Alaska St
London
SE1 8XE
**T** 020 7928 7440    **F** 020 7928 8070
**E** alaskastudios@yahoo.co.uk
*Studio Manager* Bev Lodge

*24-track analogue desk*
*3 rehearsal rooms*

## Alchemy Mastering Ltd
29–30 Windmill St
London
W1T 2JL
**T** 020 7692 0214    **F** 020 7436 3735
**E** martin@alchemymastering.com
**W** alchemymastering.com
*Contact* Martin Giles

*Vinyl cutting and CD mastering*

## Angel Recording Studios
311 Upper St
London
N1 2TU
**T** 020 7354 2525    **F** 020 7226 9624
**E** angel@angelstudios.co.uk    **W** angelstudios.co.uk
*Studio Manager* Gloria Luck

## Antenna Recordings Corps Ltd
PO Box 17394
London
NW1 9ZA
**T** 020 7267 6785    **F** 020 7681 8034
**E** antenna@cableinet.co.uk
**W** wkweb5.cableinet.co.uk/antenna

## APE Recording
19 Market St
Castle Donington
Derby
DE74 2JB
**T** 01332 810933    **F** 01332 850123
**E** info@ape.co.uk    **W** ape.co.uk
*Studio Manager* Nira Amba

## Apollo Recording
7 Garth St
Glasgow
G1 1UT
**T** 0141 402 3805    **E** jason.famous@btinternet.co.uk
*Studio Manager* Calum Maclean

## Arc Studio
Rectory Farm
The Folly
Cold Ashton
nr. Bath
SN14 8JR
**T** 01225 892222    **F** 01225 892233
**E** george.allen@arcuk.net    **W** arcuk.net
*Contact* George D. Allen

*Neve resedential studio with ProTools*

## Ariwa Sounds
34 Whitehouse Lane
London
SE25 6RE
**T** 020 8653 7744 / 020 8771 1470    **F** 020 8771 1911
**E** ariwa.sounds@btinternet.com    **W** ariwa.com

## Audio Workshop, The

22 Goodwin Rd
London
W12 9JW
**T** 020 8742 9242   **F** 020 8743 4231
*Managing Director* Martin Cook

## AudioEdit

15 Popes Grove
Strawberry Hill
Twickenham
Middx
TW2 5TA
**T** 020 8755 2349
*Studio Manager* Tim Handley

## Axis Recording Studios

3 Brown St
Sheffield
S1 2BS
**T** 0114 275 0283   **F** 0114 275 4915
*Contact* Paul R. Bower

## Backyard Recording

West Pen-y-Llan
Churchstoke
Powys
SY15 6HT
**T** 01588 620 129   **F** as telephone
*Contact* Dave Owen

## Band On The Wall Studio

25 Swan St
Northern Quarter
Manchester
M4 5JQ
**T** 0161 834 1786   **F** 0161 834 2559
**E** guy@bandonthewall.com
**w** bandonthewall.com

## Bandwagon Studios

Westfield Lane
Mansfield
Notts
NG18 1TL
**T** 01623 422962   **F** 01623 633449
**E** info@bandwagonstudios.co.uk
**w** bandwagonstudios.co.uk
*Bookings Manager* Andrea Hall
*Studio Manager* Andy Dawson

*36-track digital, also rehearsal studio*
*Special rates for unwaged, workshops and educational uses*
*Courses run in partnership with New College, Nottingham*

## Bark Studio

1A Blenheim Rd
London
E17 6HS
**T** 020 8523 0110   **F** as telephone
**E** brian@barkstudio.co.uk   **w** barkstudio.co.uk
*Studio Manager* Brian O'Shaughnessy

*24-track analogue recording (Studer), 12-track hard disc (Soundscape), MC1 automated console, some nice old equipment*
*Bark specializes in quality acoustic, lo-fi, alternative pop music*

## Battery Studios

1 Maybury Gardens
London
NW10 2NB
**T** 020 8967 0013   **F** 020 8459 8732
**E** amanda.todd@batterystudios.co.uk
**w** battery-studios.co.uk
*Bookings Manager* Amanda Todd

*Restaurant/bar and off-street parking*
*Four rooms to suit any project or budget, with full facilities*
*CD mastering and restoration*
*Recent clients include Robbie Williams, Craig David and Joe Strummer*

## BBC Resources (London)

Maida Vale Music Studios
Dellaware Rd
London
W9 2LH
**T** 020 7765 4066   **F** 020 7765 3201
**E** nathan.clapton@bbc.co.uk
*Bookings Manager* Nathan Clapton
*Studio Manager* Mark Diamond

*Also contact Nathan Clapton for BBC Resources (UK) at Television Centre*

**Beachpark Studios**
Newtown
Rathcoole
Co. Dublin
Ireland
**T** 00 353 1 458 8500   **F** 00 353 1 458 8577
**E** info@beachpark.com   **W** beachpark.com
*Studio Manager* Daire Winston

**Beethoven Street Studios**
The Yellow Building
56 Beethoven St
London
W10 4LG
**T** 020 8960 1088   **F** 020 8969 5231
**E** studio@beethoven-st.demon.co.uk
*Studio Manager* D. Tai

**Berlin Recording Studio**
Caxton House
Caxton Avenue
Blackpool
Lancs
FY2 9AP
**T** 01253 508670 / 01253 591169   **F** 01253 406899
**E** berlin.studios@virgin.net   **W** berlinstudios.co.uk
*Managing Director* Ron Sharples

**Berry Street Recording**
1 Berry St
London
EC1V 0AA
**T** 020 7608 3977
*Contact* Kevin Poree

**Berwick Street Studios**
8 Berwick St
London
W1V 3RG
**T** 020 7292 0000   **F** 020 7292 0010
**E** studios@bstreet.force9.net
*Contact* Ko Barclay
*Director* Brian Young

**Big Ocean Studios**
Big Moon
PO Box 347
Weybridge
Surrey
KT13 9WZ
**T** 01932 847225   **F** 01932 889802
**E** jamie@tzuke.com   **W** tzuke.com
*Studio Manager* Jamie Muggleton

*Private studio owned by Judie Tzuke*

**Big Picture Music**
295 Regent St
London
W1R 8JH
**T** 020 7494 0011   **F** 020 7494 0111
**E** big.picture@boosey.com   **W** boosey.com/media/bigpicture
*Contact* Andrew Sunnucks

**Black Barn**
3 Dunsborough Cottages
The Green
Surrey
GU23 6AL
Ripley
**T** 01482 222600   **F** 020 8783 0164
**E** blackbarn@aol.com

**Black Mountain Residential**
1 Squire Court
The Marina
Swansea
SA19 3XB
**T** 01792 301500   **F** as telephone
*Studio Manager* Ivor Barnett
*Managing Director* Michael Evans

**Blackwing Recording Studios**
All Hallows Church
1 Pepper St
London
SE1 0EW
**T** 020 7261 0118   **W** blackwing.co.uk
*Contact* Eric Radcliffe

**Blah Street Studios**
The Hop Kiln
Hillside
Odiham
Hants
RG29 1HX
**T** 01256 701112   **F** 01256 701106
**E** nick@blahstreet.co.uk   **w** blahstreet.co.uk
*Contact* Nick Hannan

*Analogue and digital, wide range of instruments and*
*gadgets*
*Clients include Robbie Williams, Kylie Minogue,*
*Snowboy*


**Blakamix International**
Garvey House
42 Margetts Rd
Bedford
MK42 8DS
**T** 01234 302115   **F** 01234 854334
**E** blakamix@aol.com
*Contact* Dennis Bedeau


**Blam!**
Unit 2, 10a Acton St
London
WC1X 9NG
**T** 020 7713 1303   **F** as telephone


**Blast Furnace Studios**
Foyle Arts Centre
Lawrence Hill
Co. Derry
BT48 7NJ
**T** 01504 377870 / 0780 300 1898
**E** Rory@blast-furnace.com   **w** blast-furnace.com
*Bookings Manager* Rory Donaghy


**BlueStone**
11 Uxbridge St
London
W8 7TQ
**T** 020 7243 4101   **F** 020 7243 4131
**E** bluestudio@compuserve.com
*Contact* Chris Wyles


**BMN Music**
28 The Bardfield Centre
Great Bardfield
Braintree
Essex
CM7 4SL
**T** 01371 811291   **F** 01371 811404
**E** rob.fuller@bmn-music.com   **w** bmn-music.com
*Contact* Rob Fuller

*Operates the High Barn Recording Studio: 48-track*
*digital, 2 recording rooms plus control room, etc*
*All musical styles, with resident producers and*
*engineers*


**Bob Lamb's Recording Studio**
122a Highbury Rd
Kings Heath
Birmingham
B14 7QP
**T** 0121 443 2186
**E** boblamb@recklessltd.freeserve.co.uk


**Brain Dead Studios**
PO Box 3775
London
SE18 3QR
**T** 020 8316 4690   **F** as telephone
**E** marc@wufog.freeserve.co.uk
**w** wufog.freeserve.co.uk
*Bookings Manager* Neelu Berry
*Studio Manager* Marc Bell


**Brandon Studios**
187 West Parade
Lincoln
LN1 1QT
**T** 01522 540495
*Studio Manager* Paul Middleton


**Bridge, The**
55 Great Marlborough St
London
W1V 1DD
**T** 020 7434 9861   **F** 020 7494 4658
**E** bookings@thebridge.co.uk   **w** thebridge.co.uk
*Bookings Manager* Angela Parkinson
*Technical Director* Rick Dzendzera

## Brill Building, The

Kings Court
7 Osborne St
Glasgow
G1 5QN
**T** 0141 552 6677   **F** 0141 552 1354
**E** info@brillbuilding.pair.com
**w** brillbuilding.pair.com
*Bookings Manager* Angela Ross

*4 rehearsal rooms; 2 studios; 24 track analogue/digital
In-house production deals*

## Britannia Row Studios

3 Bridge Studio
318–326 Wandsworth Bridge Rd
London
SW6 2TZ
**T** 020 7371 5872   **F** 020 7371 8641
**E** britanniarowstudios@cableinet.co.uk
**w** ukweb5.cableinet.co.uk/britanniarowstudios
*Contact* Kate Koumi

## Broadley Studios

Broadley House
48 Broadley Terrace
London
NW1 6LG
**T** 020 7258 0324   **F** 020 7724 2361
**E** manny@broadleystudios.com
**w** broadleystudios.com
*Managing Director* Manny Elias
*Chairman* Ellis Elias

## Brothers Grimm Studios

The Sound Factory
PO Box 681
Birmingham
B17 9AU
**T** 0121 681 881   **F** as telephone
*Studio Manager* Mark Thorley

## Bryn Derwen Studio

Coed-y-Parc
Bethesda
Gwynedd
LL567 4YW
**T** 01248 600 234   **F** 01248 601933
**E** laurie@brynderwen.co.uk   **w** brynderwen.co.uk
*Contact* Laurie Gane

## Bullseye Studios

AIR House
Spennymoor
Co. Durham
DL16 7SE
**T** 01388 814632   **F** 01388 812445
**E** air@agents-uk.com   **w** airagency.com
*Manager* Lloyd Smith
*Managing Directors* Colin Pearson, John Wray

## Ca Va Sound Workshops

30 Bentinck St
Kelvingrove
Glasgow
G3 7TU
**T** 0141 334 5099 / 0141 334 6987   **F** 0141 339 0271
**E** hclark4422@aol.com
*Contact* Helen Clark

## Cabin Studios

82 London Rd
Coventry
West Midlands
CV1 2JT
**T** 024 7622 0749   **E** cabin82@demon.co.uk/sonar
**w** members.aol.com/cabinltd/home.htp
*Studio Manager* Jon Lord

*2" analogue machine etc, pre-production and
mastering suite, guitar bands (eg Primitives,
Catatonia) a speciality*

## Cadillac Ranch Recording Studios

Cadillac Ranch
Pencraig Uchaf
Cum Bach
Whitland
Carmarthen
SA34 ODT
**T** 01994 484466   **F** 01994 484294
*Studio Manager* Dollar Gonzales
*Bookings Manager* Moose Magoon

## Caleche Studios

175 Roundhay Rd
Leeds
LS8 5AN
**T** 0113 219 4929   **F** 0113 249 4941
*Managing Director* Leslie Coleman

## CAP Recording Studios

Crask Of Aigas
By Beulay
Inverness
IV4 7AD
T 01463 782364    F 01463 782525
*Studio and Bookings Manager* Donna Cunningham

## Castlesound Studios

The Old School
Park View
Pencaitland
East Lothian
EH34 5DW
T 01875 340143 / 0131 666 1024
F as telephone numbers
*Bookings Manager* Helen Clark

## Castlesound Studios (Bonskeid Music)

44 Beauchamp Rd
Edinburgh
EH16 6LU
T 0131 666 1024    F as telephone
E info@castlesound.co.uk    w castlesound.co.uk

*Fully-equipped professional recording studio with
Neve 72-channel console, 48-track Radar II Hard
Disk, 24-track Studer analogue etc*

## Chamber Recording Studio

120a West Granton Rd
Edinburgh
EH5 1PF
T 0131 551 6632    F as telephone number
E jamie@humancondition.co.uk
w humancondition.co.uk
*Studio Manager* Jamie Watson

*All types of live music
Established for 15 years
Also rehearsal rooms and label, Human Condition
Records, the starting point for such bands as Idlewild
and Foil*

## Chapel Studios

Bryants Corner
South Thorseby
Lincs
LN13 0AS
T 01507 480305 / 01507 480761    F 01507 480752

w chapelstudios.com
*Studio Manager* Andy Dransfield

## Chipping Norton Recording Studios

26–32 New St
Chipping Norton
Oxon
OX7 5LJ
T 01608 643636    F 01608 644771    E cnrs@clara.net
*Studio Manager* Barry Hammond
*Bookings Manager* John Bennett

## Chiswick Reach Recordings

Lamb House
Church St
London
W4 2PD
T 020 8995 2647 / 020 8995 6504    F 020 8995 0441
*Contact* Nigel Woodward

## Church Studios/Eligible Music Ltd, The

145 Crouch Hill
London
N8 9QH
T 020 8340 9779    F 020 8348 3346
E julie@eligiblemusic.com
*Managing Director* Dave Stewart
*Studio Manager* Julie Coldwell

## Circle Sound Services

Circle House
14 Waveney Close
Bicester
Oxon
OX6 8GP
T 01869 240051    F as telephone
E john@circle.force9.co.uk
*Owner* John Willett

## Clinic, The

42 Station Rd
West Croydon
Surrey
CR0 2RB
T 020 8686 0176    F 020 8681 2879
*Studio Manager* Richie Sullivan

**Coad Mountain Studios**
Coad
Caherdaniel
Co. Kerry
Ireland
T 00 353 66 947 5171   F 00 353 66 947 5264
E coadmountain@tinet.ie
*Bookings Manager* Simon Taylor

**Compression Studios**
56 Frazer Rd
Perivale
Middx
UB6 7AL
T 020 8723 6158   F 020 7738 1764
E compression@music-room.com
W music-room.com
*Director* S Hirani

**Cordella Music Ltd**
35 Britannia Gardens
Hedge End
Hants
SO30 2RN
T 08450 616616 / 07831 456348   F 01489 780909
E barry@barryupton.co.uk   W cordellamusic.co.uk
*Managing Director* Barry Upton

*Also a production house*
*Barry Upton is the creator of Steps*

**Cottage Recording**
2 Gawsworth Rd
Macclesfield
Cheshire
SK11 8UE
T 01625 420163 / 07767 813533
F as first telephone number
E rogerboden@cottagegroup.co.uk
W cottagegroup.co.uk
*Managing Director* Roger Boden
*Studio Manager* Glenn Lockley
*Bookings Manager* Wesley Boden

**Courtyard Studio**
21 The Nursery
Sutton Courtenay
Abingdon
Oxfordshire
OX14 4UA
T 01235 845800 / 01235 845808   F 01235 847692

E kate@cyard.demon.co.uk
W courtyardstudio.oxfordpages.co.uk
*Contact* Kate Cotter or John Bennett

**Crocodile Studios**
7 Goodge Place
London
W1P 1FL
T 020 7636 4840/020 7580 0080   F 020 7580 0560
E name@crocodilemusicstudios.co.uk
W crocodilemusicstudios.co.uk
*Studio Manager* Suzy Watt

*Audio post-production, original music composition,*
*music recording and radio*

**CTS-Watford/CTS-Lansdowne**
Suite 1a
Lansdowne House
Lansdowne Rd
London
W11 3LP
T 020 7727 0041   F 020 7792 8904
E info (or bookings)@cts-lansdowne.co.uk
W cts-lansdowne.co.uk
*Group Manager / Studio Manager* Chris Dibble
*Bookings Manager* Vicky Pyrkos

**Cuan Audiovisual**
An Spideal
Conamara
Co. Galway
Ireland
T 00 353 91 553838   F 00 353 91 553837
E info@cuan.com   W cuan.com
*Studio Manager* Ellie Lennon
*Bookings Manager* Fionnuala Mannion

**Cutting Rooms, The**
Abraham Moss Centre
Crescent Rd
Manchester
M8 6UF
T 0161 740 9438   F 0161 740 0538
E cuttingrooms@hotmail.com
*Contact* Andrew Harris

## Cybersound

Units C101 and C104
Faircharm Trading Estate
8–12 Creekside
London
SE8 3DX
T 020 8694 9484    F 020 8694 9466
E info@cyber-sound.co.uk    w cyber-sound.co.uk
*Studio Owner* Alan Little

*Facilities (Products and Services): 24-track digital studio using 3xAdat, digital mastering and editing, CD writing and copying, four rehearsal studios, production and promotion, website design and Internet promotion, songwriting/production service*

## Dairy, The

43–45 Tunstall Rd
London
SW9 8BZ
T 020 7738 7777    F 020 7738 7007
E thedairy@dircon.co.uk
*Contact* Mark Evans

## DB Entertainments Ltd

PO Box 147
Peterborough
Cambs
PE1 4XU
T 01733 311755    F 01733 709449
E russ@db-entertainments.freeserve.co.uk
w dbentertainments.com
*Contact* Russ Dawson-Butterworth

## De Brett Studios

Unit 64
Millmead Industrial Centre
Millmead Rd
London
N17 9QU
T 020 8365 0105    F 020 8885 6030
E jwest@debrett41.freeserve.co.uk
*Studio Manager* Jon West

*Recorder: Soundscape R.Ed, 32-track, PC-based D to D system*
*Consoles: Mackie and Yamaha Promix 1*
*Large live room*
*All types of music from bands to TV jingles*

## De-Mix Productions

7 Croxley Rd
London
W9 3HH
T 020 8960 1115    F 020 8962 0359
E martin.lascelles@virgin.net
*Bookings Manager* Ava McDowall
*Contact* Martin Lascelles

## Deep Recording Studio/Deep Production Company

187 Freston Rd
London
W10 6TH
T 020 8964 8256    F 020 8962 0397
E deep.studios@virgin.net
w deeprecordingstudios.co.uk/com/net/org
*Manager* Mark Rose

*Live room for solo up to four-piece*
*Lots of Outboard and valve kit (Atari and G4 computers)*

## DEP International Studios

1 Andover St
Birmingham
B5 5RG
T 0121 633 4742    F 0121 643 4904
*Business Manager* Lanval Storrod
*Bookings Manager* Dan Sprigg

## Discfinder Recording Studio

5 Claremont Grove
Killiney
Co. Dublin
Ireland
T 00 353 1 285 6392    F 00 353 1 845 4082
*Contact* Joe Conway

*Complete audio facilities for narration, commercials, editing etc*
*Vast library of music, nostalgia, comedy material*

## Dog House Residential Studio, The

Little Purbeck
Bolney Rd
Lower Shiplake
Henley-on-Thames
Oxon
RG9 3NS

**T** 01189 403516   **F** as telephone
**E** barrie.barlow@virgin.net

### Dream of Oswald Recording Studio
Park House
Warren Row
Berks
RG10 8QS
**T** 07071 223951   **F** as telephone
**E** monkey@dreamsofoswald.co.uk
*Studio Manager* Keith James

### Dreamcore Studios
4, 3 James Court
493 Lawnmarket
Edinburgh
EH1 2PB
**T** 0131 225 5570 / 0797 144 6986
**E** roddy007@hotmail   **W** edenbrew.com/
*Contact* Rob Habeshaw

### Dreamhouse Studio
Home Park House
Hampton Court Rd
Kingston Upon Thames
Surrey
KT1 4AE
**T** 020 8977 0666   **F** as telephone
*Contact* Philippe Zavriew

### Earth Productions
163 Gerrard St
Birmingham
B19 2AP
**T** 0121 554 7424   **F** 0121 551 9250
**E** earth.p@virgin.net
*Studio Manager* Natasha Godfrey

### Earth Terminal
The Kilns
Snails Lynch
Farnham
Surrey
GU9 8AP
**T** 01252 710244
**E** earthterminal@breathemail.net
**W** earthterminal.co.uk
*Studio Manager* Amanda Baldry

*All musical styles*

*Equipment includes Saturn 824 24-track 2'', ADAT
24-track digital, DDA DMR 12 56-channel mixer*

### Eastcote Studios
249 Kensal Rd
London
W10 5DB
**T** 020 8969 3739   **F** 020 8960 1836
**E** philip (or peggy)@eastcotestudios.co.uk
**W** eastcotestudios.co.uk
*Studio Manager* Philip Bagenal

### Eden Studios Ltd
20–24 Beaumont Rd
London
W4 5AP
**T** 020 8995 5432   **F** 020 8747 1931
**E** eden@edenstudios.com   **W** edenstudios.com
*Studio Manager* Beth Shuttleworth

*Residential studios with full in-house maintenance,
house engineers, catering and on-site parking,
accommodation for up to ten people
Two studios and two programming rooms*

### Eel Pie Recording Ltd
4 Friars Lane
Richmond Green
Twickenham
Middx
TW9 1NL
**T** 020 8940 8171   **F** 020 8940 8172   **W** eelpie.com

### English West Coast Music
The Old Bakehouse
150 High St
Honiton
Devon
EX14 1JX
**T** 01404 42234 / 017767 865360
**F** 01404 45346 / 07767 869029
**E** studio@ewcm.co.uk   **W** ewcm.co.uk
*Studio Manager* Sean Brown
*Contact* Ian Dent

### Epic Head Studios
PO Box 183
Sheffield
S1 2XF
**T** 0114 273 1398

**EQ Studios**
Fortune House
Knowle Lane
Cranleigh
Surrey
GU6 8JF
T 07768 052677    E eqstudios@aol.com
*Studio Manager* Danny Sykes
*Bookings Manager* Helen Bruce

**ESSP**
The Sound House
PO Box 37b
Molesey
Surrey
KT8 2YR
T 020 8979 9997    F as telephone
*Contact* Dave Tuffnell

**Factory Sound, The**
Toftrees
Church Rd
Woldingham
Surrey
CR3 7JH
T 01883 652386    F 01883 652457
E mackay@dircon.co.uk
*Managing Director* David Mackay
*Studio Manager* Ron Challis

*All styles of music and music for television catered for*

**Fairview Music/Duplication**
Cavewood Grange Farm
Common Lane
North Cave
Brough
East Yorkshire
HU15 2PE
T 01430 425546    F 01430 425547
E keith@fairviewstudios.co.uk
W fairviewstudios.co.uk
*Studio Manager* Keith Herd
*Bookings Manager* Jackie Herd

**Faith Studios**
174 Ladbroke Grove
London
W10 5LZ
T 020 8960 0494    F 0870 162 9702
E faithstudios@hotmail.com

*Established production team and fully digital
32-track studio*

**Falconer Studios**
17 Ferdinand St
London
NW1 8EU
T 020 7267 7777    F 020 7284 2022
E falconer.studios@btinternet.com

**Fernbank Studio**
Bonnings Lane
Barrington
Ilminster
Somerset
TA19 0JN
T 01460 55747    F 01460 53396
*Studio Manager* Bob Johnson
*Contact* Ronnie Gleeson

**Fisher Lane Farm**
Fisher Lane
Chiddingford
Surrey
GU8 4TB
T 01428 684475    F 01428 684947
*Contact* Dale Newman

**FJR Studios**
1 Herbert Gardens
London
NW10 3BX
T 020 8968 8870    F 020 8960 0719
*Managing Director* Laurie Jago
*Studio Manager* Lee Edwards
*Bookings Manager* Julie Jago

**Foel Studio**
Llanfair
Caereinion
Powys
SY21 0DS
T 01938 810758    F as telephone
E foel.studio@dial.pipex.com    W foelstudio.co.uk
*Managing Director* Dave Anderson

## Folktrax & Soundpost Studios

Heritage House
16 Brunswick Square
Gloucs
GL1 1UG
T 01452 415110   F 01452 503643
E peter@folktrax.freeserve.co.uk   w folktrax.org
*Studio Manager* Peter Kennedy
*Bookings Manager* Beryl Kennedy

*Acoustic blues, celtic and world music*

## Fortress Studio 2

34–38 Provost St
London
N1 7NG
T 020 7251 6200 / 020 7251 1033   F 020 7251 5892
E fortressstudios@compuserve.co.uk
*Contact* Shaun Harvey

## Fresh Studios

Unit 4
Grand Union Centre
Kensal Rd
London
W10 5AS
T 020 8960 3940   F 020 7221 0088
*Contact* Spencer Brinton

## Frog Studios

Unit 2b
Banquay Trading Estate
Slutchers Lane
Warrington
Cheshire
WA1 1PJ
T 01925 445742   F as telephone
*Studio Manager* Steve Millington
*Bookings Manager* Steve Oates

## Gallery Music Ltd

3d Park Mews
213 Kilburn Rd
London
W10 4BQ
T 020 8960 5801   F 020 8960 5802
E info@manzanera.com   w manzanera.com
*Studio Manager* Vicki Lanes

## Gateway Studio

Kingston Hill Centre
Kingston Hill
Kingston Upon Thames
Surrey
KT2 7LB
T 020 8549 0014   F 020 8547 7337
E studio@gsr.org.uk   w gsr.org.uk
*Studio Administrator* Katy Burton
*Business Manager* Hannah Tuakli

## Giovanni's Room

Lupus House
11–13 Macklin St
London
WC2B 4NH
T 020 7404 5675 / 07958 970970
F as first telephone number
E sultrix.marcus@virgin.net
*Contact* Sultrix Marcus

## Gorse Road Recording Studio

PO Box 95
Ashford
Middx
TW15 3TH
T 01784 255629   F 01784 420672
E cliffrandall@compuserve.com
*Contact* Cliff Randall

*Cubase (on a Mac), 2xDass digital recorders, Mackie
32 desk, 2x Akai CO3000, Novation Supernova etc
Digital editing, mastering, CD duplication*

## Granary Studio, The

Bewlbridge Farm
Lamberhurst
Kent
TN3 8JJ
T 01892 891128   F as telephone
*Studio Manager* Guy Denning

## Grand Central Studios

25–32 Marshall St
London
W1V 1LL
T 020 7306 5600   F 020 7306 5616
E info@grand-central-studios.com
w grand-central-studios.com

Managing Director Carole Humphrey
Studio Manager Oscar Kugblenu
Bookings Manager Louise Allen

## Great Linford Manor Recording Studios
Great Linford Manor
Great Linford
Milton Keynes
MK14 5AX
T 01908 667432    F 01908 668164
E info@greatlinfordmanor.com
W greatlinfordmanor.com
Bookings Manager Sue Dawson
Contact Pete Winkelman

Ballroom studio in Grade II listed manor house
Accommodation

## Greystoke Studios
39 Greystoke Park Terrace
London
W5 1JL
T 020 8998 5529    F 020 8566 7885
E andy@greystokeproductions.co.uk
W greystokeproductions.co.uk
Studio Manager Andy Whitmore
Bookings Manager Tom Garrad-Cole

## H2O Enterprises
The Dairy
43–45 Tunstall Rd
London
SW9 8BZ
T 020 7737 9700    F 020 7737 9707
E robinh@h2o.co.uk    W h2o.co.uk
Studio Manager Robin Crookshank Hilton
Bookings Manager Simon Bohannon

## Hart Street Studios
4 Forth St
Edinburgh
EH1 3LD
T 0131 557 0181    F 0131 557 9521
E hartstreet@cheerful.com
W hartstreet.freeserve.co.uk
Managing Director Roy Ashby
Bookings Manager Toni Ashby

Four studios available

## Hatch Farm Studios
Unit 16 Hatch Farm
Chertsey Rd
Addleston
Surrey
KT15 2EH
T 01932 828715    F 01932 828717 / 01932 829938
E brian.adams@dial.pipex.com
Contact Brian Adams

## Headroom Studios Ltd
9 Thorpe Close
Portobello Rd
London
W10 5XL
T 020 8960 1195    F as telephone
E info@headroomstudios.co.uk
W headroomstudios.co.uk
Studio and Bookings Manager Ralph Ruppert

## Hear No Evil
6 Lillie Yard
London
SW6 1UB
T 020 7385 8244    F 020 7385 0700
E info@hearnoevil.net    W hearnoevil.net
Managing Director Sharon Rose-Parr

## Heartbeat Recording Studio
Guildie House Farm
North Middleton
Gorbridge
Edinburgh
EH23 4QP
T 01875 821102    F as telephone
Contact David L. Valentine

## Heat Recordings Ltd
Unit 8, Shaftesbury Centre
85 Barlby Rd
London
W10 6BN
T 020 8969 2912    F 020 8969 2551
E info@heatrecordings.com
Contact Alex Payne

Incorporates Critical Mass, Nu-Tone and Urban
Heat

## Helicon Mountain
The Station
Station Terrace Mews
London
SE3 7LP
**T** 020 8858 0984   **F** 020 8293 4555
*Studio Manager* Richard Holland

## Hi Level Recording
18 Victoria Terrace
Whitley Bay
Tyne & Wear
NE26 2QW
**T** 0191 297 1807   **F** 0191 251 3331
**E** rayandave@hilevel.demon.co.uk
**w** hilevel.demon.co.uk
*Studio Manager* Ray Laidlaw
*Booking Manager* Steve Cunningham

## Hiltongrove
Hiltongorve Business Centre
Hatherley Mews
London
E17 4QP
**T** 020 8521 2424   **F** 020 8521 4343
**E** info@hiltongrove.com   **w** hiltongrove.com
*Studio Manager* Dave Blackman
*Contact* Guy Davis

## House In The Woods Studio, The
The Yews
White Hill
Bletchingley
Surrey
RH1 4QU
**T** 01883 343027   **F** 01883 341108
**E** houseinthewoods@mail.freeonline.net
*Studio Manager* Giz Vandekleut

## Hydepark Recording Studios
120a Coach Rd
Templepatrick
Ballyclare
Co. Antrim
BT39 0HB
**T** 028 9443 2619   **F** 028 9443 2162
**E** george@emeraldmusic.co.uk
info@emeraldmusic.co.uk

*Manager* George Doherty
*Bookings Manager* Jean Doherty

*Also label Emerald Music (Ireland) Ltd*

## ICC Studios
4 Regency Mews
Silverdale Rd
Eastbourne
East Sussex
BN20 7AB
**T** 01323 643341   **F** 01323 649240
**E** studio@icc.org.uk   **w** icc.org.uk
*Studio Manager* Trevor Michael
*Bookings Manager* Gayle Price

## Impulse Sound Studio
71 High St Est
Wallsend
Tyne & Wear
NE28 7RJ
**T** 0191 262 4999   **F** 0191 263 7082 / 0191 240 2580
**E** mdwood33@aol.com   **w** neatrecords.com
*Studio Manager* Peter Carr

## Innovation Studios
13 Swanyard
London
N1 1SD
**T** 07070 649301
*Managing Director* Roderick Macdonald
*Bookings Manager* Susan Husband

## Intimate Studios
The Smokehouse
120 Pennington St
London
E1 9BB
**T** 020 7702 0789 / 07860 109612   **F** 020 7702 0919
**w** gerrybron.com
*Managing Director* Paul Madden
*Bookings Manager* Cai Murphy

## Jacob's Studios
Ridgway House
Dippenham
Farnham
Surrey
GU10 5EE
**T** 01252 715546  **F** 01252 712846
*Studio Manager* Andy Fernbach

*Two studios available, residential*

## Jazz Specialist Ltd, The
11 Glasgow Rd
London
N18 2EG
**T** 020 8482 6114 / 07956 994089  **F** 020 8482 6114
**E** james@jazz-specialist.com  **W** jazz-specialist.com
*Contact* James C. Henriot

## JD Creative
4 Granville Rd
London
EN5 4DU
**T** 020 8441 3564  **F** 020 8440 4012
*Contact* John Dropik

## Jingle Jangles
156 Hollywood Rd
Belfast
BT4 1NY
**T** 028 9065 6769  **F** 028 9067 3771
*Studio Manager* Mr S. Martin
*Bookings Manager* Hugh Matier

## JRP Music Services
Empire House
Hereford Rd
Southsea
Hants
PO5 2DH
**T** 023 92 738 100/0777 600 6107
**E** jrp@soc.soton.ac.uk  **W** jrpmusic.fsnet.co.uk
*Studio Manager* James Perrett

*Specialist in mastering, small-run CD and cassette
duplication, restoration and live recording
Equipment includes 2″ and 0.5″ 16-track*

## Jumbo Music Complex
387–389 Chapter Rd
London
NW2 5NG
**T** 020 8459 7256  **F** 020 8459 7256
**E** jumbojoe808@netscapeonline.co.uk
*Contact* Facilities Manager

*Also rehearsal studios*

## KD's Studio
78 Church Path
Fletcher Rd
London
W4 5BJ
**T** 020 8994 3142  **F** 020 8995 5006
*Studio Manager* Kenny Denton
*Bookings Manager* Hollie Borwn

## KG Engineering Ltd
Unit 6
Ipplepen Business Park
Edgelands Lane
Ipplepen
Devon
TQ12 5UG
**T** 01803 813833  **F** 01803 813141
**E** keithg@kg-digital.co.uk
*Managing Director* Keith Gould

## Kingsize
28 Lyons Rd
Hersham
Surrey
KT12 3PU
**T** 01932 700400  **F** 01932 702144
**E** labels@kingsize.co.uk  **W** kingsize.co.uk
*Contact* Richard Crowmains

## Konk Studios
84–86 Tottenham Lane
London
N8 7EE
**T** 020 8340 4757 / 020 8340 7873  **F** 020 8348 3952
**E** linda@konkstudio.com
*Studio Manager* Sarah Lockwood

*Two studios available: Neve and SSL*

## Kudos
66 Woodland Park
Lisburn
Co. Antrim
BT28 1LD
**T** 028 92 675951
*Contact* K Duncan

*Production of singles, albums, jingles, commercials
Pop, house, jazz, C&W, rock, indie etc*

## La Rocka
Postmark House
Cross Lane
London
N8 7SA
**T** 020 8348 2822   **F** 020 8347 5390
*Studio Manager* Simon Danials
*Bookings Manager* Pete Chapman

## Ladbroke Grove
27 Advance House
109 Ladbroke Grove
London
W11 1PG
**T** 020 7792 3502   **F** 020 7229 5195
**E** popcorp@aol.com
*Contact* Steve Lovell

## Lansdowne Recording Studios
Lansdowne House
Lansdowne Rd
London
W11 3LP
**T** 020 7727 0041   **F** 020 7792 8904
**E** cts-lansdowne@cts-lansdowne.co.uk
**w** cts-lansdowne.co.uk
*Studio Manager* Chris Dibble
*Bookings Manager* Lucy Jones

## Like No Other
PO Box 21335
London
WC2H 8QH
**T** 020 7379 0999   **F** 020 7379 3399
**E** mark@like-no-other.com   **w** like-no-other.com
*Contact* Mark Lambert Stewart

## Lime Street Sound
3 Lime Court
Lime St
Dublin 2
Ireland
**T** 00 353 1 671 7271   **F** 00 353 1 670 7639
**E** info@limetreesound.ie

## Lime Tree Studios
Welgate
Mattishall
Dereham
Norfolk
NR20 3PJ
**T** 01362 858015   **F** 01362 855016
**E** info@limetreestudios.com
**w** limetreestudios.com
*Contact* Stephen Pitkethly

*24-track 2" analogue, extra hard disk tracks
available, CD mastering and duplication, disabled
facilities*

## Linden Studio (MPG)
The Lindens
Rosgill
Shap
Penrith
CA10 2QX
**T** 01931 716362   **F** 01931 716362
**E** linden@dircon.co.uk
**w** users.dircon.co.uk/-linden
*Studio Manager* Maire Morgan
*Contact* Guy Forrester

## Liverpool Music House
51–55 Highfield St
Liverpool
L3 6AA
**T** 0151 236 5551
*Studio Manager* Colin Hall

## Livingston Recording Studios
The Church Hall
Brook Rd
off Mayes Rd
London
N22 6TR
**T** 020 8889 6558   **F** 020 8888 2698
*Director* Jerry Boys
*Bookings Manager* Alina Syed

*Two studios available (SSL 4056E + G-Series, AMEK Rembrandt)*
*Off-street parking and kitchen facilities*

## Lodge, The
23 Abington Square
Northampton
NN1 4AQ
**T** 01604 475399   **F** 01604 576999
**E** lodge@lodgstud.demon.co.uk
**W** demon.co.uk/lodgstud
*Studio Manager* Max Read

*24-track analogue (on 2" tape) or*
*24-track digital (hard disk based)*
*Large live room, custom built drum room, quality*
*microphones and Outboard*
*Specializing in live rock/indie*

## Logorhythm Music
6–10 Lexington St
London
W1R 3HS
**T** 020 7734 7443   **F** 020 7439 7057
*Managing Director* Lloyd Billing
*Contact* Jeremy Pascoe

## Lost Boys Studio
Hill Green Hill Farm
Bourne End
Cranfield
Beds
MK43 0AX
**T** 01234 750730   **F** 01234 750359
**E** info@lostboysstudio.com   **W** lostboysstudio.com
*Studio Manager* Rupert Cook

## M Corporation, The
The Market Place
Ringwood
Hants
BH24 1AP
**T** 01425 470007   **F** 01425 480569
**E** record@m-audio.co.uk   **W** m-audio.co.uk
*Studio Manager* Rufus Biggs

## Mad Hat Studios
In Town
off Lichfield St
Walsall
West Mids
WS1 1SQ
**T** 01922 616244 / 07973 400021   **F** 01922 616244
**E** studio@madhat.co.uk   **W** madhat.co.uk
*Contact* Mark Stuart

*24/48-track analogue and multi-track hard disk*
*recording*
*Digital editing, compiling and mastering*
*Midi sequencing and programming*
*Inhouse producers and engineers*
*Concessionary rates for unsigned acts*

## Magmasters Sound Studios Ltd
20 St Anne's Court
London
W1V 3AW
**T** 020 7437 8273   **F** 020 7494 1281
**E** info@magmasters.co.uk   **W** magmasters.co.uk
*Bookings Manager* Ellie Walker
*Contact* Scott Jackson

## Malibu Studios
Top Floor
21 Greek St
London
W1V 5PE
**T** 020 7287 7444   **F** 020 78377791
**E** malibustudios@aol.com
*Studio Manager* Stephen Smith

*Specializing in all types of modern dance, pop and*
*some acoustic guitar music*
*Recent clients include Nick Heyward, Drugstore,*
*My Life Story*

## Manic One Studio
1st & 2nd Floors
17 St Anne's Court
London
W1V 3AW
**T** 020 7734 6770   **F** 020 7734 6771
**E** manicones@movingshadow.com
**W** movingshadow.com
*Managing Director* Rob Playford
*Studio Manager* Gavin Johnson
*Bookings Manager* Angela Baptiste

## Marcus Recording Studios
17–21 Wyfold Rd
London
SW6 6SE
**T** 020 7385 3366    **F** 020 7386 5858
**E** marcus@marcus-music.co.uk
*Managing Director* Marcus Osterdahl
*Studio and Bookings Manager* Beverly Sharpe

*Four studios available*
*Accommodation*

## Mark Angelo Recording Studios Ltd
27 Britton St
London
EC1M 5UD
**T** 020 7251 2376 / 020 8443 1523
**F** 020 7490 0474 / 020 8350 4042
**E** sarah@theaudionet.ltd.uk
*Managing Director* Mark Lusardi
*Studio Manager* Sarah Ozelle

## Master Rock Studios
248 Kilburn High Rd
London
NW6 2BS
**T** 020 7372 1101    **F** 020 7328 6368
**E** master.rock@dial.pipex.com
**W** masterrock.co.uk
*Managing Director* Miriam Gottlieb

*Two studios available*

## Matrix Maison Rouge
2 Wandsdown Place
London
SW6 1DN
**T** 020 7381 2001 / 020 7731 3053    **F** 020 7381 8784
**E** maisonrouge@ukgateway.net
*Studio and Bookings Manager* Jason Wallbank

## Mayfair Recording Studios
11a Sharpleshall St
London
NW1 8YN
**T** 020 7586 7746    **F** 020 7586 9721
**E** bookings@mayfair-studios.co.uk
**W** mayfair-studios.co.uk
*Studio Manager* John Hudson
*Bookings Manager* Daniel Mills

*Five studios available*

## Metropolis
The Power House
70 Chiswick High Rd
London
W4 1SY
**T** 020 8742 1111    **F** 020 8742 2626
**E** studio@metropolis.demon.co.uk
*Studio Manager* Lorraine Reid

*Five studios available*

## Mex One Recordings
The Basement
3 Eaton Place
Brighton
BN2 1EH
**T** 01273 572090    **F** as telephone
**E** mexone@tinyonline.co.uk
**W** mexone.50megs.com
*Managing Director* Paul Mex

*Budget project studio specializing in quality digital*
*recording for songwriters and vocalists*
*Post-production facilities for mastering and*
*short-run CDs*

## Miloco
36 Leroy St
London
SE1 4SP
**T** 020 7232 0008    **F** 020 7237 6109
**E** markc@milomusic.co.uk    **W** milomusic.co.uk
*Studio Manager* Nick Young

*Four studios with ProTools*
*Recent clients include Oasis, The Chemical Brothers,*
*Coldplay, Badly Drawn Boy and The Prodigy*

## Modus Music
The Old Rectory
Church Lane
Exning
Newmarket
Suffolk
CB8 7HT
**T** 01638 577324    **F** 01638 577106
**E** trygg@modus.force9

## Moles

14 George St
Bath
BA1 2EN
T 01225 404445/6    F 01225 404447
E moles@moles.co.uk    w moles.co.uk
*Studio Manager* Jan Brown

## Motor Museum Studios

1 Hesketh St
Liverpool
L17 8XJ
T 0151 727 7557 / 0151 726 9808    F 0151 283 3649
E motormu@cableinet.co.uk
*Managing Director* Hambi
*Bookings Manager* Ann Heston
*Contact* Andy McCluskey

## MPF Studio

Bon Marche Building
Ferndale Rd
London
SW9 8EJ
T 020 7737 7152    F 020 7738 5428
E mpf@media-production.demon.co.uk
w media-production.demon.co.uk
*Managing Director* Paul Halpin
*Studio Manager* Tom Leader

## MTS Recording Studios

Dublin Rd
Monasterevin
Co. Kildare
Ireland
T 00 353 45 525009    F 00 353 50 262086
E hazel@iol.ie
*Contact* John Kelly

## Music Barn, The

PO Box 92
Gloucester
GL4 8HW
T 01452 814321    F 01452 812106
*Studio Manager* Vic Coppersmith-Heaven

## Music City Ltd

122 New Cross Rd
London
SE14 5BA
T 020 7277 9057    F 0870 757 2004

E info@musiccity.co.uk    w musiccity.co.uk
*Contact* James Woodward

*Also rehearsal, hire, pro-sales, CD burning and
digital editing*

## Music Factory, The

Hawthorne House
Fitzwilliam St
Parkgate
Rotherham
South Yorkshire
S62 6EP
T 01709 710022    F 01709 523141
E andypickles@mfeg.co.uk    w musicfactory.co.uk
*Managing Director* John Pickles
*Production Director* Andy Pickles

## Network Studios (Nophonex)

Network House
22a Forest Rd West
Nottingham
NG7 4EQ
T 0115 978 4714    F 0115 942 4183
*Studio Manager* Mick Vaughan
*Bookings Manager* Linda Davey

## No Sheep

Wimbourne House
151–155 New North Rd
London
N1 6TA
T 020 7684 9490 / 020 7684 5992    F 020 7684 5991
E sales@nosheep.co.uk    w nosheep.co.uk
*Contact* Carul Yun

## Odessa Wharf Studios

38 Upper Clapton Rd
London
E5 8BQ
T 020 8806 5508/0800 970 7268    F 020 8806 4508
E odessa@mathias.idps.co.uk    w surf.to/odessa
*Studio Manager* Gwyn Mathias

*Studio 1: 500-sq ft live room, 2" 24-track analogue
and hard disk recording, AMEK Angela mixing
console with mastermix automation etc
Studio 2: Yamaha O2R digital mixing console, digital
recording and mastering
All types of music from hip hop to big bands
25 years' experience*

## Old Smithy Recording Studio

1 Post Office Lane
Kempsey
Worcs
WR5 3NS
**T** 01905 820659 **F** 01905 820015
**E** old.smithy@virgin.net
*Bookings Manager* Janet Allsopp

## Olympic Sound Studios

117 Church Rd
London
SW13 9HL
**T** 020 8286 8600 **F** 020 8286 8625
*Studio Manager* Siobhan Paine

## One Hundred Acres Studios

30 Phipp St
London
EC2A 4NR
**T** 020 7613 1126 **F** 020 7613 0021
*Managing Directors* Rodney Levine-Boateng,
Natasha Eggough

## Online Studios

Unit 18
Croydon House
1 Peall Rd
Croydon
Surrey
CRO 3EX
**T** 020 8287 8585 **F** 020 8287 0220
**E** info@onlinestudios.co.uk
**w** onlinestudios.co.uk
*Contact* Rob Pearson

*Specialist midi dance studio, catering for DJs,
producers, vocalists etc
Engineers, programmers available*

## Opaz Studios

293–295 Mare St
London
E8 1EJ
**T** 020 8986 8066 **F** 020 8533 7978
*Studio Manager* Shanin Noronha
*Bookings Manager* Brian Spence

## Outlet Recording Co. Ltd, The

15–21 Gordon St
Belfast
Co. Antrim
BT1 2LG
**T** 028 9032 2826 **F** 028 9033 2671
**E** mail@outlet-music.com **w** outlet-music.com
*Contact* Jim McGirr (Engineer, studio operations)

*Specializes in country, folk, gospel and traditional
OB facilities
In-house publishing, manufacturing and distribution
Neumann microphones, Soundcraft 2400 console,
Studer A80 Analogue, Tascam DA88 Digital
32-track, Sadie-Marantz CDR mastering*

## Panther Studios

5 Doods Rd
Reigate
Surrey
RH2 0NT
**T** 01737 210848 **F** as telephone
**E** panther@dial.pipex.com
**w** dialspace.dial.pipex.com/sema/panther.htm
*Proprietor* Richard Coppen
*Bookings Manager* Kelly Walsh

*Also full video production and editing facilities plus
multimedia*

## Parachute Music Studio

Kings Bromley Wharf
Bromley Hayes
nr Lichfield
Staffs
WS13 8HS
**T** 01543 253576/07885 341745
**F** as first telephone number
**E** parachute.music@virgin.net
*Studio Manager* Jason Fillingham

## Park Lane

974 Pollokshaws Rd
Glasgow
G41 2HA
**T** 0141 636 1218 **F** 0141 649 0042
**E** graccounts@btconnect.com **w** pls.uk.com
*Studio Manager* Alan Connell

## Parkland Studios

Parklands
1 The Spinney
Forest Rd
Denmead
Hants
PO7 6AR
**T** 01705 232335   **F** 01705 264368
**E** den@parklandstudios.demon.co.uk
**W** parklandstudios.demon.co.uk

## Parr Street Studios

33–45 Parr St
Liverpool
L1 4JN
**T** 0151 707 1050   **F** 0151 707 1813
**E** parr.street@ dial.pipex.com
*Studio Manager* Anne Lewis
*Contact* Paul Lewis

## Pelican Studio

185 Drury Lane
London
WC2B 5QD
**T** 020 7405 6629   **F** 020 7405 0611
*Studio Manager* Ray Stiles

## Pierce Rooms, The

Pierce Entertainment Ltd
Pierce House
London Apollo Complex
Queen Caroline St
London
W6 9QU
**T** 020 8563 1234   **F** 020 8563 1337
**E** meredith@pierce-entertainment.com
**W** pierce-entertainment.com
*Studio Manager* Meredith Leung

*Live recording and broadcasting link to the Apollo
Theatre
72/60 Flying Fader Neve VR
5:1 Surround Sound System*

## Pisces Studios

20 Middle Row
Ladbroke Grove
London
W10 5AT
**T** 020 8964 4555   **F** 020 8964 4666

**E** studio@pisces.uk.com   **W** studios.uk.com
*Bookings Manager* Samantha Oliver

## Planet Audio

Metropolis Studios
70 Chiswick High Rd
London
W4 1SY
**T** 020 8742 7114/07711 669392   **F** 020 8950 1294
**E** rod@g2-music.co.uk   **W** g2-music.co.uk
*Contact* Rod Gammons

## Pluto Studios

Hulgrave Hall
Tiverton
Tarporley
Cheshire
CW6 9UQ
**T** 01829 732427/07973 861777   **F** 01829 733802
**E** keith@pluto.prestel.co.uk
*Studio Manager* Keith Hopwood

## Point Blank

28–30 Wood Wharf
Horseferry Place
London
SE10 9BT
**T** 020 8293 4909/07966 268078   **F** 020 8293 4333
**E** studio@point-blank.co.uk   **W** point-blank.co.uk
*Contact* John Robson

*Also offers DJ, music technology and MP3 courses*

## Pollen Studios

97 Main St
Bishop Wilton
York
YO42 1SP
**T** 01759 368223   **F** 01759 368366
**E** music@pollenstudio.co.uk
**W** pollenstudio.co.uk
*Studio Manager* Dick Sefton

*16-track analogue, 24-channel desk, Drawmer OB,
CD Architect, Sound Forge, audio post-production,
CD production including design and printing and
digital recording*

**Pose Recording Studio**
3 Bammf Rd
Alyth
Blairgowrie
Perthshire
PH11 8DZ
**T** 01828 633337 **F** 01828 633330
*Contact* Steve or Rory


**POW**
Unit 11
Impress House
Mansell Rd
London
W3 7QH
**T** 020 8932 3033 **F** 020 8932 3032
*Contact* Jody Sharp


**Power Studios**
Unit 11, Impress House
Mansell Rd
London
W3 7QH
**T** 020 8932 3030 **F** 020 8932 3031
**E** jamie@power.co.uk **W** power.co.uk
*Contact* Jamie Chalmers

*Established in 1997*
*Offer cutting edge technology, specialist engineers*
*available*
*Lounge/bedroom, kitchen, shower, free parking, Sky*
*TV and Playstation*


**Powerhaus**
Unit 5
Willtell Works
Upper St John St
Lichfield
Staffs
WS14 9ET
**T** 01543 303200 **F** 01543 303201
**E** powerhaus@fsnet.co.uk


**Prelude**
Unit 8
Ransome's Dock
35–37 Parkgate Rd
London
SW11 4NP
**T** 020 7978 5501/07973 408870 **F** 020 8871 9733

**E** preludeuk@aol.com
*Studio Manager* Norman Arnold


**Premises, The**
201–205 Hackney Rd
London
E2 8JL
**T** 020 7729 7593 **F** 020 7739 5600
**E** info@premises.demon.co.uk
**W** premises.demon.co.uk
*Studio Manager* Che


**Presshouse**
PO Box 6
Colyton
Devon
EX24 6YS
**T** 01297 553508 **F** 01297 553709
**E** presshouse@znet.co.uk
*Studio Manager* Mark Tucker


**Propagation House Studios, The**
East Lodge
Ogbeare
North Tamerton
Holsworthy
Devon
EX22 6SE
**T** 01409 271111 **F** 01409 271350
**E** bookings@propagationhouse.com
**W** propagationhouse.com
*Contact* Lucy Williams


**Protocol Studios**
23a Benwell Rd
London
N7 7BW
**T** 020 7686 0044 **F** 020 7686 0050
*Studio Manager* David Richardson
*Bookings Manager* Tracey James


**Pulse Recording Studios**
67 Pleasants Place
Dublin 8
Ireland
**T** 00 353 1 4784045/4758730
**F** as second telephone **E** pulse@clubi.ie
**W** pulserecording.com
*Studio Manager* Tony Perrey
*Bookings Manager* Naomi Moore

*Two studios, the Engine Room and Area 51, centrally
located in Dublin
24-track AMEK Rembrandt with Supertrue
Automation and Motionworker Synchronization and
sync to picture facilities
2" Analogue and ProTools 5.1 (TDM)*

## Purple Studios
The Old Parish Hall
The Street
Trowse
Norwich
NR14 8SX
**T** 01603 622550   **F** as telephone
**E** purples@paston.co.uk
*Contact* Richard Hammerton

## PWL In The North
380 Deansgate
Castlefield
Manchester
M3 4LY
**T** 0161 833 3630   **F** 0161 832 3203

## PWL London
4–7 The Vineyard
off Sanctuary St
London
SE1 1QL
**T** 020 7403 0007   **F** 020 7403 8202

## QTEN Studio
Unit Q–10
Queensway Industrial Estate
Glenrothes
Fife
KY7 5PZ
**T** 01592 611327   **F** 01592 610315
*Studio Manager* James Bisset

## Quo Vadis Recording and Rehearsal Studios
Unit 1 Morrison Yard
551a High Rd
London
N17 6SB
**T** 020 8365 1999   **E** quovadis_2002@yahoo.co.uk
*Managing Director* Don MacKenzie

## Raezor Studio
25 Frogmore
London
SW18 1JA
**T** 020 8870 4036   **F** 020 8874 4133
*Studio Manager* Ian Wilkinson
*Bookings Manager* Anni Wilkinson

*48-track SSL, Studer A820 x2, car park*

## RAK Recording Studios
42–48 Charlbert St
London
NW8 7BU
**T** 020 7586 2012   **F** 020 7722 5823
**w** rakstudios.co.uk
*Contact* Hugh Tennant
*Bookings Manager* Trisha Wegg

## React Studios Ltd
3 Fleece Yard
Market Hill
Buckingham
MK18 1JX
**T** 01280 823546   **F** 01280 821840
**E** reactstudios@msn.com   **w** reactstudios.co.uk
*Contact* Alan Shearsmith

## Real Stereo Recording Company, The
14 Moorend Crescent
Cheltenham
Gloucs
GL53 0EL
**T** 01242 523304   **F** as telephone
**E** mitchell@kadmon.demon.co.uk
**w** kadmon.demon.co.uk/mitchell
*Production Manager* Martin Mitchell

## Real World Studios
Box Mill
Mill Lane
Box
Wilts
SN13 8PL
**T** 01225 743188   **F** 01225 743787
**E** owenl@realworld.co.uk
**w** realworld.on.net/studios
*Studio Manager* Owen Leech

*Two studios. SSL desks. Studer A820. Protools
Residential facility (12 bedrooms). Full catering*

**Reborn Studios**
Bramley Meade Hall
Whalley
Clitheroe
Lancs
BB7 9AD
**T** 01254 825144   **F** 01254 823938
**E** ribblerecords.co.uk
*Studio Manager* Leon Hardman

**Red Bus Recording Studios**
Studio House
34 Salisbury St
London
NW8 8QE
**T** 020 7402 9111   **F** 020 7723 3064
**E** eliot@amimedia.co.uk   **W** redbusstudios.com
*Managing Director* Eliot Cohen

**Red Fort Studios**
The Site and Sound Centre
Priory Way
Southall
Middx
UB2 5EB
**T** 020 8843 1546   **F** 020 8574 4243
**E** kuljit@compuserve.com   **W** keda.co.uk
*Managing Director* Kuljit Bhamra
*Bookings Manager* Anita Masih

*48 channel desk, 24-track recording specializing in
live bands, folk, rock, pop and British Asian music*

**Redwood Studios**
20 Great Chapel St
London
W1F 8FW
**T** 020 7287 3799   **F** 020 7287 3751
**E** andrejacquemin@hotmail.com
*Studio Manager* Andre Jaquemin

*Sound design for film, TV, radio using ProTools 24
mix plus
Lots of sound effects and own library*

**Revolution Studios**
11 Church Rd
Cheadle Hume
Cheadle
Cheshire
SK8 7JD
**T** 0161 485 8942/0161 486 6903
**F** as first telephone number
**E** revolution@whatup.com
*Proprietor and Bookings Manager* Andrew
MacPherson

*Analogue and digital, ProTools, large live area, two
control rooms*

**RG Jones Recording Studios**
Beulah Rd
London
SW19 3SB
**T** 020 8540 9881/020 8540 9883   **F** 020 8542 4368
**E** studio@rgjones.co.uk   **W** rgjones.co.uk
*Studio Manager* Gerry Kitchingham

*Oldest independent studio in London
Large 'live' recording area, 25–30 musicians
40-channel SSL desk with 48-track Radar*

**Ridge Farm Studio**
Rusper Rd
Capel
Surrey
RH5 5HG
**T** 01306 711 202   **F** 01306 711 626
**E** info@ridgefarmstudio.com
**W** ridgefarmstudio.com
*Contact* Ann Needham

**River Recordings**
3 Grange Yard
London
SE1 3AG
**T** 020 7231 4805   **F** 020 7237 1424
**E** sales@riverproaudio.co.uk
**W** riverproaudio.co.uk
*Managing Director* Joel Monger

*52 input Soundtracs CP6800
24-track Soundcarft HHDR digital hard disk
recorder etc
Two large live rooms, spacious control room, large
microphone collection (Neumann, AKG etc)
Rock, Jazz, Choral, Classical ensemble etc*

## Rockfield Studios

Amberley Court
Rockfield Rd
Monmouth
MP25 5ST
**T** 01600 712449/01600 713625 **F** 01600 714421
**E** rockfieldstudios@compuserve.com
**W** rockfieldstudios.com
*Owner/Manager* Kingsley Ward
*Bookings Manager* Lisa Ward

*Two studios: Quadrangle (Neve 76-input VR with
Flying Faders) and Coach House (Neve 60-input)
Four natural echo chambers, two live rooms, 16
luxury apartments and cordon bleu cuisine*

## Rollover Studios

29 Beethoven St
London
W10 4LJ
**T** 020 8969 0299 **F** 020 8968 1047
*Studio Manager* Phillip Jacobs

*Four studios*

## Rooster

117 Sinclair Rd
London
W14 0NP
**T** 020 7602 2881/020 7603 7305 **F** 020 7603 1273
**E** roosterand@aol.com **W** roosterstudios.com
*Studio Manager* Nick Sykes

*48-track studio, featuring Otari status board, Radar
hard disk recorder (24x2)
Roster includes Bjork, The Divine Comedy, Sinead
O'Connor, Louise etc*

## Roundhouse Recording Studios

91 Saffron Hill
London
EC1N 8PT
**T** 020 7404 3333 **F** 020 7404 2947
**E** roundhouse@stardiamond.com
**W** stardiamond.com/roundhouse
*Studio Managers* Lisa Shimidzu, Maddy Clarke

*Studio 1: SSL 4056G+SE
Studio 2: SSL 6048E
Studio 3: SSL 6048E
24-hour maintenance
Seven programming rooms*

## Roundway Studios

Unit 9 Morrison Yard
551a High Rd
London
N17 6SB
**T** 020 8808 8882 **F** 020 8808 9885
**E** dave@roundway.com
*Managing Director* Dave Thompson

## Sain

Canolfan Sain
Llandwrog
Caernarfon
Gwynedd
LL54 5TG
**T** 01286 831111 **F** 01286 831497
**E** studio@sain.wales.com **W** sain.wales.com
*Studio Manager* Eryl Davies

*Two studios*

## Sanctuary Studios

45–53 Sinclair Rd
London
W14 0NS
**T** 020 7602 6351 **F** 020 7300 6515
**E** nikki.affleck@sanctuarygroup.com
**W** www.sanctuarygroup.com
*Studio Manager* Nikki Affleck

## Sarm West

8–10 Basing St
London
W11 1ET
**T** 020 7229 1229 **F** 020 7221 9247
**E** lola@spz.com **W** sarmstudios.com
*Group Studio and Bookings Manager* Lola Marlin
*Managing Director* Jill Sinclair

*Four studios in west London. Also Sarm East (studio
in east London) and Sarm Hook End (residential
recording studio in Oxfordshire)*

## Savage Sounds

44 Parkgate Rd
Carshalton
Surrey
SM6 0AH
**T** 020 8647 1708/07956 419511
**F** as first telephone number

*Studio Manager* Mark Cremona
*Bookings Manager* Mike Savage

## Sawmills Studio Residential Recording

Golant
Fowey
Cornwall
PL23 1LW
T 01726 833338/01726 833752   F 01726 832015
E info@sawmills.co.uk   W sawmills.co.uk
*Studio Manager* Ruth Taylor

*Residential, established 1974, with a stunning
location on its own tidal creek*
*Vast range of equipment that has been used by such
bands as Oasis and Supergrass*

## Scarlet Recording Company Ltd

Unit 64
Milmead Industrial
Mill Mead Rd
London
N17 9QU
T 020 8365 0800   F 020 8885 6030
E liz@scarletrecording.co.uk
W scarletrecording.co.uk
*Studio and Bookings Manager* Liz Lenten

*Console: Soundtracs CP6800 and cybermix midi
muting and fader automation*
*Tape machine: Tascam MRS-245 1" analogue*
*Live bands of any style. Studio includes acoustic
Chappell baby grand*

## Scotty's Sound Studio

17–22 Newtown St
Kilsyth
Glasgow
G65 0JX
T 01236 823291   F 01236 825683
E nscott@scotdisc.co.uk/billsong@tinyworld.co.uk
*Director* Bill Garden

*Mackie d8b mixing console, Saturn 24-track
analogue, ProTools, Digital Performer, Westlake and
Genelec speakers, various synths and Outboard
equipment*

## Seagate Studios

97 Seagate
Dundee
DD1 2ER
T 01382 200725   F as telephone
*Contact* Mike Brown

## Sensible Studios

90–96 Brewery Rd
London
N7 9NT
T 020 7700 9900   F 020 7700 4802
E studios@sensible-music.co.uk
W sensible-music.co.uk
*Studio Manager* Pat Tate

## Shambles Studio/Shambles Music Ltd

The Shambles
Westhorpe Rd
Marlow
Bucks
SL7 1LD
T 01628 485363/01628 891003
F as second telephone
W focuson.co.uk/shambles-studio
*Studio Manager* Chris Rae

## Silk Sound

13 Berwick St
London
W1V 3RG
T 020 7434 3461   F 020 7494 1748
E robbie@silk.co.uk
*Contact* Robbie Weston
*Bookings Manager* Paula Ryman

## Silver Road Studios

2 Silver Rd
Wood Lane
London
W12 7SG
T 020 8746 2000   F 020 8746 0180
E enquiries@silver-road-studios.co.uk
W silver-road-studios.co.uk
*Bookings Manager* Samantha Leese

*Four studios*

## SMI/Everday Productions – Basingstoke

TTM Studio (Basingstoke)
c/o Mandarin Place
Grove
Oxon
OX12 0QH
**T** 01235 767171/77157    **F** 01235 717577
**E** smi2@risdon.fsbusiness.co.uk
*Studio Manager* Jane Risdon

*R&B/pop, dance and rock, from demo to master,*
*record label commissions, soundtracks etc*
*Also Miggins Music (publishers): same contact details*

## Snake Ranch

90 Lots Rd
London
SW10 0QD
**T** 020 7351 7888    **F** 020 7352 5194
**E** gerry@snakeranch.co.uk    **w** snakeranch.co.uk
*Studio and Bookings Manager* Gerry O'Riordan

*Two studios*
*Specializing in film and TV soundtracks, small*
*classical and jazz ensembles*
*Studio 1: Live room accommodates up to 25*
*musicians plus Yamaha 7' grand piano*
*ProTools or 2" analogue recording systems*

## Soho Recording Studios

Basement
22–24 Torrington Place
London
WC2E 7AJ
**T** 020 7419 2444/020 7419 2555    **F** 020 7419 2333
**E** dominic@sohostudios.co.uk
**w** sohostudios.co.uk
*Bookings Manager* Dominic Sanders

*Two studios*

## Soleil

Unit 10
Buspace Studio
Conlan St
London
W10 5AP
**T** 020 7460 2117    **F** 020 7460 3164
**E** soleil@recordwk.dircon.co.uk
*Contact* Jose Gross

*32-track analogue/digital facilities*
*2 live rooms with drum kit*
*Full midi/ProTools set up*
*Also The Recording Workshop: phone: 020 8968 8222,*
*e-mail: info@therecordingworkshop.co.uk,website:*
*therecordingworkshop.co.uk*

## Songworks, The

Unit 3
3 Hanover St East
Dublin 2
Ireland
**T** 00 353 1 679 3800/087 237 2787
**F** 00 353 1 679 3876    **E** songworks@esatclear.ie
*Bookings Manager* Tom Byrne
*Studio Manager* Colin Turner

## Songwriting, Composing & Musical Productions

Wheal Close House
Delves Lane
Consett
Co. Durham
DH8 7ER
**T** 01207 580565/01736 762826    **F** 01736 763328
**E** panamus@aol.com    **w** icn.co.uk/gisc.html
*Managing Director* Colin Eade
*Bookings Manager* Ann Eade

## Soul II Soul Studios

36–38 Rochester Place
London
NW1 9JX
**T** 020 7284 0393    **F** 020 7284 0166
**E** sales@soul2soul.co.uk    **w** soul2soul.co.uk
*Studio Manager* Simon Cowie

*Three studios*

## Sound Discs

5 Barley Shotts Business Park
off St. Ervans Rd
London
W10 5YG
**T** 020 8968 7080    **F** 020 8968 7475
*Contact* Peter Bullick

## Sound Joint, The
10 Parade Mews
London
SE27 9AX
**T** 020 8678 1404   **F** 020 8671 0380
**E** chris@soundjoint.fsnet.co.uk
*Contact* Barnaby Smith

*Also production house, client development, offering whole package of studio, engineer, producer and musicians when required. Also management and publishing*

## Sound Recording Technology
Audio House
Edison Rd
St. Ives
Cambridge
PE27 3LF
**T** 01480 461880/020 8446 3218   **F** 01480 496100
**E** srt@btinternet.com
**W** soundrecordingtechnology.co.uk
*Contact* Sarah Pownall
*Bookings Manager* Emma Dooley
*Studio Manager* Nick Watson

*Five studios plus mastering*

## Sound Stage Studio
Kerchesters
Waterhouse Lane
Kingswood
Surrey
KT20 6HT
**T** 01737 832837   **F** 01737 833812
**E** ian@soundstage.co.uk   **W** amphonic.com
*Managing Director* Ian Dale
*Studio Manager* Aaron Briggs

## Sound Suite, The
92 Camden Mews
London
NW1 9AG
**T** 020 7485 4881   **F** 020 7482 2210
*Studio Manager* Peter Rackham

## Soundbyte
81 Charlotte St
London
W1P 1LB
**T** 020 7436 1666   **F** 020 7436 1646
**E** info@soundbyte.ltd.co.uk

## Soundhouse, The
Forth House
Forth St
Edinburgh
EH1 3LF
**T** 0131 557 1557   **F** 0131 557 3899
**E** bookings@thesoundhouse.com
**W** thesoundhouse.com
*Managing Director* David Balfe

## Soundsound Studio
2 Ivy Crescent
Riverway
Douglas
Cork
Ireland
**T** 00 353 21 896250/00 353 21   **F** 00 353 214896 250
**E** soundsound@compuserve.com
*Contact* Dan Fitzgerald

*Specialize in acoustic music. Albums with Mary Black, Altom, the Voice Squad, Donovan*
*No unsolicited material. E-mail first*

## Soundtrack Ltd
46b Cricklewood Lane
London
NW2 1HD
**T** 020 8208 2082/07973 835940   **F** 020 8208 0898
*Contact* Michael Lewis

## Soundtree Music
330a Portobello Rd
London
W10 5RU
**T** 020 8968 1449   **F** 020 8968 1500
**E** post@soundtree.co.uk
*Contact* Peter Raeburn
*Studio Manager* Maya Jenkins

## Southern Studios

10 Myddleton Rd
London
N22 8NS
**T** 020 8888 8949   **F** 020 8889 6166
**E** studio@southern.com   **W** southern.com/studio
*Contact* Harvey Birrell

*Analogue: Studer A870 24-track 2" and Studer A820
two-track 0.5"*
*Digital ProTools TDM mix plus*
*Console: Vintage Raindirk Series III*
*Outboard: Chiswick Reach valve compressor, etc*

## Speech Plus Recording

Unit 32
19 Pages Walk
London
SE1 4SB
**T** 020 7231 0961   **F** 020 7231 3837
**E** sprec@globalnet.co.uk

*Specializing in speech/language recording*

## Spider's Web Recording Studio

3 Hammersmith Grove
London
W6 0ND
**T** 020 8563 9990   **F** 020 8563 9995
*Contact* Clive McDonal
*Studio Manager* Carl Frankland

## Spirit Recording Studios

10 Tariff St
Manchester
M1 2FF
**T** 0161 228 1830   **F** 0161 236 0078
**E** enquiries@s-r-s.com   **W** s-r-s.com
*Studio Manager and Bookings Manager* Chris Mayo

*Five studios*

## SQC Residential Recording Studios

389–394 Alfred St North
Nottingham
NG3 1AA
**T** 0115 941 4488   **F** 0115 941 8866
**E** info@sqc247.com   **W** sqc247.com
*Director of Operations* John Bagguley

*Studio 1 (residential) and four further studios*
*Equipment includes AMEK Mozart 56-channel*

*console with Supertrue automation ProTools 24 Mix
Plus, Apple G3, Neve etc in main studio*
*Full equipment list on request*

## Stab Productions

28 Horton Rd
London
E8 1DP
**T** 020 7254 9257   **F** 020 7254 4928
*Contact* Bradley James

## Stanley House Studios

Stanley House
39 Stanley Gardens
London
W3 7SY
**T** 020 8735 0280   **F** 020 8743 6365
**E** studio@stanley-house.co.uk
**W** stanley-house.co.uk
*Contact* Brian Gaylor

*Music recording complex with seven programming
rooms*
*Recording studios with SSL J desk etc*
*Bar restaurant*

## State 51

Alaska Building
Grange Rd
London
SE1 3BA
**T** 020 7237 9222   **F** 020 7237 9444
*Studio Manager* Louise Smith

## Stepping Stone Studios

57 Windsor Rd
London
NW2 5DT
**T** 020 8459 8790   **F** as telephone

## Stickysongs Ltd

Sticky Studios
Kennel Lane
Windlesham
Surrey
GU20 6AA
**T** 01276 479 255   **F** as telephone
**E** stickysong@aol.com   **W** stickysongs.co.uk
*Managing Director* Pete Gosling

## Stone Room Studio, The
Unit 2b
Askew Crescent Workshop
Askew Crescent
London
W12 9DP
**T** 020 8749 8885   **F** 020 8746 0883
*Studio Manager* Rob Cox

## Strongroom
120–124 Curtain Rd
London
EC2A 3SQ
**T** 020 7426 5100   **F** 020 7426 5102
**E** mix@strongroom.com   **W** strongroom.com
*Managing Director* Rob Buckler
*Studio Manager* Nina Mistry

*Five studios*

## Studio 125
125 Junction Rd
Burgess Hill
West Sussex
RH15 0JL
**T** 01444 871818
*Studio Manager* Ian Herron

*ProTools Mix Plus – Control 24*

## Studio B
2 Beulah Rd
London
SW19 3SB
**T** 020 8255 7775/020 8255 7800   **F** 020 8255 7776
*Studio Manager* Ben 'Jammin' Robbins
*Bookings Manager* Sir Harry

## Studio Miraval, France
c/o JFD Management
Unit 9
Acklam Workshops
10 Acklam Rd
London
W10 5QZ
**T** 020 8968 7159   **F** 020 8960 0298
**E** jfdmanagement@pavilion.co.uk
*Co-ordinator* Ella Macpherson
*Studio Manager* Patrice Quef

## Submarine, The
1b Wolsley St
Heslington Rd
York
YO1 5BQ
**T** 01904 431122
*Contact* Andrew Wass

## Suite 16 Recording Studio
16 Kenion St
off Drake St
Rochdale
Lancs
OL16 1SN
**T** 01706 353789   **F** 01706 657548
**E** shan@suite16.u-net.com
**W** yell.co.uk/sites/suite16
*Studio Manager* Shan Hira

## Sun Studios
8 Crow St
Dublin 2
Ireland
**T** 00 353 1 677 7255/671 1800   **F** 00 353 1 679 1968
**E** sun_studios@yahoo.com
*Studio Manager* Denis Lovett

*See also Temple Lane Recording Studios*
*Band recording studio*
*Saturn 824, 2", 24-track tape machine, Amek*
*Einstein automated console*

## Surrey Sound Studios
70 Kingston Rd
Leatherhead
Surrey
KT22 7BW
**T** 01372 379444   **F** 01372 363360
**E** surrey.sound@pncl.co.uk   **W** surreysound.co.uk
*Managing Director* David Yorath

*Residential studio*

## Swanyard Recording Studios
12–27 Swan Yard
London
N1 1SD
**T** 020 7354 3737   **F** 020 7226 2581
**E** michelle@swanyard.demon.co.uk
**W** swanyard.demon.co.uk
*Studio Manager* Michelle Ward

*Bookings Manager* Samantha Wiltshire

*Two studios*

## Swing City Studios
59 Riding House St
London
W1 7PP
**T** 07000 9993 100   **F** 07000 9993 200
**E** studio@wyze.com   **W** wyze.com
*Contact* Kate Ross

## Tall Order Recordings
The Basement
346 North End Rd
London
SW6 1NB
**T** 020 7385 1816   **F** as telephone
**E** info@tallorder.org.uk   **W** tallorder.org.uk

*Digital hard-disk recording/editing on Cubase VST v.5*
*24 track analogue recording on 2" tape*
*Relaxed, friendly atmosphere, bright live room*

## Taurean Recordings
Old Barn Studios
West St Business Park
Stamford
Lincs
PE9 2PS
**T** 01780 481353   **F** as telephone
**E** studio@taurean.csnet.co.uk
*Contact* Brian Harris

## Temple Lane Recording Studios (Apollo)
8 Crow St
Temple Bar
Dublin 2
Ireland
**T** 00 353 1 677 7255/670 9202   **F** 00 353 1 679 1968
**E** sun_studios@yahoo.com   **W** tbmusic.indigo.ie
*Studio Manager* Denis Lovett

*Four studios (see also Sun Studios)*
*Direct links to 600-capacity venue for live recordings*
*Soundcraft 3200 automated console, Otari MkII 2" tape machine, 24-track recording*

## Temple Music
48 The Ridgway
Sutton
Surrey
SM2 5JU
**T** 020 8642 3210   **F** 020 8642 8692
**E** jh@temple-music.com   **W** temple-music.com
*Contact* Jon Hiseman or Justin Hill

*Digital (Digidesign ProTools24mix) and analogue,*
*with studio capable of taking big bands*

## Temple Records
Shillinghill
Temple
Midlothian
EH23 4SH
**T** 01875 830328   **F** 01875 830392
**E** robin@templerecords.co.uk
**W** templerecords.co.uk
*Studio Manager* Robin Morton

## Timeless Studios
Mudginwell Farmhouse
High St
Upper Heyford
Bicester
Oxon
OX6 3LE
**T** 01869 232340
*Partner* Sue Blunsdon

## Touchwood Audio Productions
6 Hyde Park Terrace
Leeds
LS6 1BJ
**T** 0113 278 7180   **E** bruce.w@appleonline.net
**W** touchwood/20m.com
*Studio Manager* Bruce Wood

## Town House, The
150 Goldhawk Rd
London
W12 8HH
**T** 020 8932 3200   **F** 020 8932 3207
**E** rebecca.duncan@emimusic.com
**W** townhousestudios.co.uk
*Studio Manager* Rebecca Duncan; *Director* Ian
Davidson; *Director of Townhouse Management*
Penny Robinson; *Post-Production Manager* Gay

Marshall; *Manager of Townhouse Vision* Julian MacDonald

*Three studios with SSL 4072G+, SSL 8072G and SSL 4072E. Cutting, mastering and editing. Restaurant, accommodation and parking*

## Trend Studios

9 Prince's St South
Dublin 2
Ireland
**T** 00 353 1 671 3544/0042   **E** trend@iol.ie
*Studio and Bookings Manager* Mark Kettle

## Tribal Sound + Vision

66c Chalk Farm Rd
London
NW1 8AN
**T** 020 7482 6944   **F** 020 7482 6945
**E** tribal.sound@virgin.net   **W** tribaltreemusic.co.uk

*Also Tribal Tree, giving access to high end courses in music and music technology for young people*

## Twin Peaks Studio

Ty Neuadd
Torpantau
Wales
CF48 2UT
**T** 01685 359932   **F** 01685 376500
**E** twinpeaksstudio@aol.com
**W** twinpeaksstudio.com
*Contact* Adele Nozedar

*Highest residential recording studio in the UK in the heart of the Brecon Beacons*

## Underground Sound Studio

127 Dewsbury Rd
Ossett
West Yorkshire
WF5 9PA
**T** 01924 277508/07741 066961
**F** as first telephone number
**E** studio@usound.freeserve.co.uk

## Welsh Media Music

Gorwelion
Llanfynydd
Camarthen
Dyfed
SA32 7TG
**T** 01558 668525/07774 100430   **F** 01558 668750
**E** dpierce@welshmediamusic.f9.co.uk
*Studio Manager* Dave Pierce

*Project studio specializing in music and sound for television*

## West Orange

Unit 1
16b Pechell St
Ashton
Preston
Lancs
PR2 2RN
**T** 01772 722626   **F** as telephone
**E** alan@worange.demon.co.uk
*Studio Manager* Alan Gregson

## Westland Studios

5–6 Lombard St East
Dublin 2
Ireland
**T** 00 353 1 677 4229/679 3364   **F** 00 353 1 671 0421/ 670 8457   **E** westland@indigo.ie
**W** westlandstudios.ie
*Studio Manager* Deirdre Costello

## Westpoint

39–40 Westpoint
Warple Way
London
W3 0RG
**T** 020 8740 1616   **F** 020 8740 4488
**E** respect@dircon.co.uk
*Contact* Cathy Gilliat or Ryu Nishizawa
*Studio Manager* Cathy Gilliat

*Studio GA: SSL G-Plus Series, Sony 3348, ProTool 24 Mix Plus*
*Studio GB: Euphonix CS3000*
*Plus many vintage items of equipment*

## Westside Studios

Olaf Centre
10 Olaf St
London
W11 4BE
**T** 020 7221 9494 **F** 020 7727 0008
**E** info@westsidestudios.co.uk
*Contact* Coral Worman
*Bookings Manager* Coral Worman

*Two studios*

## Westsound

95 Carshalton Park Rd
Carshalton Beeches
Surrey
SM5 3SJ
**T** 020 8647 3084 **F** 020 8395 3560
**E** tomjennings@cwcom.net
*Studio Manager* Tom Jennings

## WestStar Recording Studio

4–6 Priory Way
Southall
Middx
UB2 5EB
**T** 020 8571 4679 **E** westarstudios@cwcom.net
**W** westarstudios.co.uk
*Studio Manager* Graeme Tollitt

## WhiteHouse Recording Studio, The

AL Digital Ltd
Voysey House
London
W4 4GB
**T** 020 8742 0755 **F** 020 8742 5995
**E** scruff@aldigital.co.uk **W** whitehouse.co.uk
*Studio Manager* Scruff

## Whitfield Street Recording Studios

31–37 Whitfield St
London
W1P 5RE
**T** 020 7636 3434 **F** 020 7580 0543
*Managing Director* Matthew Villa
*Bookings Manager* Denise Love

*Three studios*

## Windings Residential Recording Studio, The

Ffrwd Valley
Wrexham
North Wales
LL12 9TH
**T** 01978 720420/720503 **F** 01978 757372
**E** windings@enterprise.net **W** windings.co.uk
*Studio Manager* Max Rooks

## Windmill Lane Studios

20 Ringsend Rd
Dublin 4
Ireland
**T** 00 353 1 668 5567 **F** 00 353 1 668 5352
**E** catherine@windmill.ie **W** windmill.ie
*Studio Manager* Catherine Rutter

*Two studios*

## Wise Buddah Creative

74 Great Titchfield St
London
W1W 7QP
**T** 020 7307 1600 **F** 020 7307 1601
**E** paul.plant@wisebuddah.com
**W** wisebuddah.com
*Studio Manager* Paul Plant

## Wolf Studios

83 Brixton Water Lane
London
SW2 1PH
**T** 020 7733 8088 **F** 020 7326 4016
**E** bret@wolfen.netkonect.co.uk
**W** netkonect.co.uk/w/wolfen
*Contact* Dominique Brethes

## Woodbine St Recording Studios Ltd

1 St. Mary's Crescent
Leamington Spa
Warwickshire
CV31 1JL
**T** 01926 338971
*Managing Director* John Rivers

*ProTools 24 Mix Plus, live rooms, 'real world' monitoring, extensive equipment*

## Woodlands Recording

Unit 20
Raglan Works
Methley Rd
Castleford
West Yorkshire
WF10 1NX
T 01977 517672    F 01977 603180
*Studio Manager* Simon Humphrey

*Comprehensive equipment including DDA AMR24
automated by Optifile, Radar 24-bit hard disk
recorder
DAT, Mini Disc and red-book standard CD digital
mastering
Three rooms with 600 sq ft playing area*

## Wool Hall Studios, The

Castle Corner
Beckington
Bath
BA3 6TA
T 01373 830731    F 01373 830679
E exile@woolhall.demon.co.uk
W sonicstate.com/woolhall
*Studio Manager* Antoinette Corry

## Workhouse Studios, The

488–490 Old Kent Rd
London
SE1 5AG
T 020 7237 1737    F 020 7231 7658
*Studio Manager* Ian Tompson

*Two studios*

## Yojo Working

Studio 112
Canalot Studios
222 Kensal Rd
London
W10 5BN
T 020 8960 5172    F as telephone
*Studio Manager* Errol Jones

## York House Studio

Back Lane
Aughton
York
YO4 4PG
T 01757 288953    F 01757 288363
*Contact* Andy Tompkins
*Studio Manager* Els Tompkins

## A2D Remote Recordings

Warrens Lee
Bell Lane
Nutley
East Sussex
TN22 3PD
**T** 01825 712724/07785 257914
**F** as first telephone number   **E** a2dremote@aol.com
*Contact* Doug Hopkins

## Abbey Road Mobiles

3 Abbey Rd
London
NW8 9AY
**T** 020 7266 7000   **F** 020 7266 7250
**E** richard.hale@abbey-road.com
*Contact* Colette Barber

## Alpha Records (Oxford) Ltd

1 Abbey St
Eynsham
Oxford
OX8 1HR
**T** 01865 880240   **F** as telephone
*Managing Director* H F Mudd

## As The Crow Flies

The Retreat
Pidney
Hazelbury Bryan
Dorset
DT10 2EB
**T** 01258 817214/07971 686961   **F** 01258 817207
**E** petefreshney@compuserve.com
**w** petefreshney.co.uk
*Contact* Pete Freshney

*See website for full specifications*

## B&H Sound Services Ltd

The Old School
Crowland Rd
Eye
Peterborough
PE6 7TN
**T** 01733 223535   **F** 01733 223545
**E** sound@bhsound.co.uk   **w** bhsound.co.uk
*Contact* Russ Dawson-Butterworth

*Location recording of all musical styles*
*Package deals available*

### BBC Live Music Mobiles
407 Western House
99 Great Portland St
London
W1A 1AA
**T** 020 7765 5747/07889 175307   **F** 020 7765 0787
**E** john.pearson@bbc.co.uk
**W** livemusicmobiles.com
*Mobile Recording Manager* John Pearson

### Black Mountain
1 Squire Court
The Marina
Swansea
SA1 3XB
**T** 01792 301500   **F** as telephone
*Managing Director* Michael Evans

### Blue Angel Recording Studios
Derwent Rd
Fulford
York
YO1 4HQ
**T** 01904 658436   **F** 01904 634598
*Studio Manager* Roger Moore
*Bookings Manager* J Wells

### BMP Recording
The Red House
Aswardby
Spilsby
Lincs
PE23 4JU
**T** 01790 75440   **F** as telephone
**E** bmpuk@compuserve.com
*Contact* Ken Blair

### Circle Sound Services
Circle House
14 Waveney Close
Bicester
Oxon
OX6 8GP
**T** 01869 240051/017973 633634
**F** as first telephone number
**E** sound@circle.force9.net   **W** circle.force9.net
*Owner* John Willett

### Classic Sound Ltd
5 Falcon Park
Neasden Lane
London
NW10 1RZ
**T** 020 8208 8100   **F** 020 8208 8111
**E** classicsoundltd@dial.pipex.com
**W** classicsound.net
*Directors* Neil Hutchinson and Jonathan Stokes

*Specialists in all forms of acoustic music recording
and mixing to 5.1 and picture*

### Doyen Recordings Limited
The Doyen Centre
Vulcan St
Oldham
Lancs
OL1 4EP
**T** 0161 628 3799/7776 (24-hr ans)   **F** 0161 628 0177
**E** sales@doyen-recordings.co.uk
**W** doyen-recordings.co.uk
*Contact* Nicholas J Childs or Alison Childs

### Emglow Records
Norton Cottage
Colchester Rd
Wivenhoe
Essex
CO7 9HT
**T** 01206 826342/07974 677532
**E** marcelg@aspects.net
*Contact* Marcel Glover

*Location service for most types of acoustic music,
principally classical and early music. Low-volume
CD production for sale at concerts. Oral history,
weddings, memorial services etc. Computer-based
editing*

### Fleetwood Mobiles Ltd
Bray Film Studios
Windsor Rd
Windsor
Berks
SL4 5UG
**T** 08700 771071   **F** 08700 771068
**E** sales@fleetwoodmobiles.com
**W** fleetwoodmobiles.com
*Studio Manager* Tim Summerhayes
*Bookings Manager* Ian Dyckhoff

**Floating Earth**
Unit 14
21 Wadsworth
Perivale
Middlesex
UB6 7JD
**T** 020 8997 4000    **F** 020 8998 5767
**E** record@floatingearth.com
**W** floatingearth.demon.co.uk
*Contact* Steve Long

*Classical and Jazz production company offering recording, production, post-production and project management (CD, DVD, TV)*

**Green Room Productions**
The Laurels
New Park Rd
Harefield
Middx
UB9 6EQ
**T** 01895 822771    **F** 01895 822771
**E** tony@greenroom2.demon.co.uk
*Contact* Tony Faulkner

**H2O Enterprises**
The Dairy
43–45 Tunstall Rd
London
SW9 8BZ
**T** 020 7737 9700    **F** 020 7737 9707
**E** robinh@h2o.co.uk    **W** h2o.co.uk
*Contact* Robin Crookshank Hilton

**Hazard Chase Productions**
Norman House
Cambridge Place
Cambridge
CB2 1NS
**T** 01223 312400    **F** 01223 460827
**E** patrick.allen@hazardchase.co.uk
**W** hazardchase.co.uk
*Contact* Patrick Allen

**Hiltongrove**
Hiltongrove Business Centre
Hatherley Mews
London
E17 4QP
**T** 020 8521 2424    **F** 020 8521 4343

**E** info@hiltongrove.com    **W** hiltongrove.com
*Managing Director* Guy Davis

**Innocent Ear Ltd**
14 Andrews Way
Marlow Bottom
Bucks
SL7 3QJ
**T** 01628 473918/07890 468044
**F** as first telephone    **E** innocent.ear@which.net
**W** innocentear.com
*Contact* Chris Burmajster

*Specialists in recording, editing and mastering classical and acoustic jazz*

**K&A Productions**
5 Wyllyotts Place
Potters Bar
Herts
EN6 2HN
**T** 01707 661200    **F** 01707 661400
**E** info@kaproductions.co.uk
**W** kaproductions.co.uk
*Contact* Andrew Walton

*Location recording company*

**Manor Mobiles**
Chapel House
Bletchington Rd
Kirtlington
Oxon
OX5 3HF
**T** 01869 351488/07770 788959    **F** 01689 351477
**E** info@manormobiles.com
**W** manormobiles.com
*Manager* Zoe Fawcett-Eustace

**Ninth Wave Audio**
46 Elizabeth Rd
Moseley
Birmingham
B13 8QW
**T** 0121 442 2276/0370 364464    **F** 0121 689 1902
**E** ninthwave@dial.pipex.com
*Contact* Tony Wass

*OB and digital audio post-production for TV, radio and CD, equipped to BBC transmission specification and specializing in classical music, with a studio for presentation or voice-over, using BBC-trained staff*

### OxRecs DIGITAL

Magdelen Farm Cottage
Standlake
Witney
Oxon
OX29 7RN
**T** 01865 300347   **E** info@oxrecs.com
**W** oxrecs.com
*Manager* Bernard Martin

*Not a mobile as such, but specialists in location sound recording. Mainly choirs, orchestras, ensembles and pipe organs. From promo CDs to complete packages including artwork, layout, design, typesetting, digital editing and mastering*

### Pace Mobile

26 South St
Oxford
OX2 0BE
**T** 01865 202119   **F** 01865 202121
**E** peter@pacemobile.com

### Realsound Location Recording

**T** 0115 941 1185/07973 279652
**E** jjohn@realsound.fsnet.co.uk
**W** realsound-uk.com
*Owner* John Moon

*Recording in any location, all formats up to 24-track digital, sound production and editing for CD, etc*

### Regent Records

PO Box 528
Wolverhampton
West Midlands
WV3 9YW
**T** 01902 424377   **F** 01902 717661
**E** regent.records@btinternet.com
**W** regentrecords.co.uk
*Contact* Gary Cole

*Location classical recording, production and editing. Master tapes for majors, and CD packages for private release*

### Sanctuary Mobiles

Sanctuary House
45–53 Sinclair Rd
LONDON
W14 0NS
**T** 08700 771071   **F** 08700 771068
**E** ian.dyckhoff@sanctuarygroup.com
**W** sanctuarygroup.com
*Contact* Ian Dyckhoff

### Silver Road Studios

2 Silver Rd
Wood Lane
London
W12 7SG
**T** 020 8746 2000   **F** 020 8746 0180
**E** enquiries@silver-road-studios.co.uk
**W** silver-road-studios.co.uk
*Bookings Manager* Samantha Leese
*Studio Manager* Matthew Weyer

### Sony Music Studios London

31–37 Whitfield St
London
W1P 5RE
**T** 020 7636 3434   **F** 020 7580 0543
**E** nick_kadrnka@uk.sonymusic.com
**W** sonymusicstudios.co.uk
*Contact* Nick Kadrnka

*Also recording studios and mastering service*

### Sound Moves

The Oaks
Cross Lane
Smallfield
Surrey
RH6 9SA
**T** 01342 844190   **F** 01342 844290
**E** steve@sound-moves.com   **W** sound-moves.com
*Owner* Steve Williams

### The Audiomobile

30 Bentinck St
Kelvingrove
Glasgow
G3 7TU
**T** 0141 334 5099/6987   **F** 0141 339 0271
**E** hclark4422@aol.com   **W** cavastudios.co.uk
*Contact* Helen Clark

## The Classical Recording Co. Ltd

16–17 Wolsey Mews
London
NW5 2DX
**T** 020 7482 2303    **F** 020 7482 2302
**E** info@classicalrecording.com
**W** classicalrecording.com
*Contact* Simon Weir

*Digital location and post-production work for all types of classical music. Major suppliers to BBC Radio*

## The Eureka Factor

St. Michael's House
2 Elizabeth St
London
SW1W 9RB
**T** 020 7259 9903    **F** as telephone
**E** mtj_eureka@compuserve.com
*Contact* Mike Jeremiah

## The Jazz Specialist Ltd

11 Glasgow Rd
London
N18 2EG
**T** 020 8482 6114/020 8357 9118
**F** as telephone numbers
**E** james@jazz-specialist.com    **W** jazz-specialist.com

## Zipper Mobile Studio

272 Cricklewood Lane
London
NW2 2PU
**T** 020 8450 4130    **F** as telephone
**E** jay@zipmob.co.uk    **W** zipmob.co.uk
*Bookings Manager* Jeffery Jay

# 3

## Music Organizations

### Agents' Association (Great Britain)
54 Keyes House
Dolphin Square
London
SW1V 3NA
T 020 7834 0515   F 020 7821 0261
E association@agents-uk.com   W agents-uk.com
*Administrator* Carol Richards
*President* Bob James

### ASCAP
8 Cork St
London
W1S 3LJ
T 020 7439 0909   F 020 7434 0073
E rgreenaway@ascap.com   W ascap.com
*The American Society of Composers, Authors and Publishers*
*Contact* Karen Hewson
*International Vice President* Roger Greenaway
*Senior Director, Membership – UK and Europe* Sean Devine

### Association of British Bhangra Artistes
6 St Benedicts Close
Sanwell Valley
West Bromwich
West Midlands
B70 6TD
T 0121 525 7696/07973 503 044
F as first telephone number
*Contact* Mr A S Kang

### Association of British Jazz Musicians
1st Floor, 132 Southwark St
London
SE1 0SW
T 020 7928 9089   F 020 7401 6870
E admin@jazzservices.org.uk
W jazzservices.org.uk
*Chairman* Adrien Macintosh

### Association of Independent Music
Lamb House
Church St
London
W4 2PD
T 020 8994 5599   F 020 8994 5222
E info@musicindie.com   W musicindie.org
*Chief Executive* Alison Wenham

*Trade association for independent record labels and distributors*

## Association of Professional Recording Services
PO Box 11
Uckfield
Middlesex
TN22 5WQ
**T** 01803 868600  **F** 01803 868444
**E** info@aprs.co.uk  **W** aprs.co.uk
*Chief Executive* Mark Broad

## Association of United Recording Artists
134 Lots Rd
London
SW10 0RJ
**T** 020 7352 4564  **F** 020 7351 3117

## British Academy of Composers & Songwriters
British Music House
26 Berners St
London
W1T 3LR
**T** 020 7636 2929  **F** 020 7636 2212/020 7629 0993
**E** info@britishacademy.com
**W** britishacademy.com
*Head of Membership* Jason Bandy

*Professional organization representing the interests of music writers in all genres, offering artistic and legal advice*
*Administrators of the Ivor Novello Awards, and publishers of The Works magazine*

## British Association of Record Dealers
1st Floor
Colonnade House
2 Westover Rd
Bournemouth
Dorset
BH1 2BY
**T** 01202 292063  **F** 01202 292067
**E** admin@bardltd.org  **W** bardltd.org
*Director General* Bob Lewis

*Formed in 1988 to act as a forum for the retail and wholesale sectors of the music industry*

## British Country Music Association
PO Box 240
Harrow
Middlesex
HA3 7PH
**T** 01273 559750  **F** as telephone
**E** the BCMA@yahoo.com
*Chair* Jim Marshall

*Information service for those interested in British and US Country music. Publish a bimonthly news magazine and an annual directory – the BCMA Yearbook*

## British Federation of Audio
19 Charing Cross Rd
London
WC2H 0ES
**T** 020 7930 3206  **F** 020 7839 4613
*Contact* C I C Cowan

## British Interactive MultiMedia Association
5–6 Clipstone St
London
W1P 7EB
**T** 020 7436 8250  **F** 020 7436 8251
**E** info@bima.co.uk  **W** bima.co.uk
*Chairman* Mike Crossman

## British Music Rights Ltd
British Music House
26 Berners St
London
W1T 3LR
**T** 020 7306 4446  **F** 020 7306 4449
**E** britishmusic@bmr.org  **W** bmr.org
*Director General* Frances Lowe

*Established to promote the interests and concerns of British composers, songwriters and publishers to UK and EU policymakers, and to the wider public*
*Member organizations are the British Academy of Composers and Songwriters, the Music Publishers Association, the Performing Rights Society and the Mechanical Copyright Protection Society*

## British Phonographic Industry
25 Savile Row
London
W1S 2ES
**T** 020 7851 4000  **F** 020 7851 4010

E general@bpi.co.uk  W bpi.co.uk
*Director General* Andrew Yeates

*Also this address for The BRIT Awards*

## Broadcast Music Incorporated (BMI)
84 Harley House
Marylebone Rd
London
NW1 5HN
T 020 7486 2036  F 020 7224 1046  W bmi.com
*Vice President European Writer-Publisher Relations*
Phillip R Graham
*Director UK Writer-Publisher Relations* Christian
Ulf-Hansen
*Performing Rights Executive* Brandon Bakshi
*Executive Assistant/Administrator* Denise Wise
*Executive Assistant* Tabitha Capaldi

## Chart Information Network
3rd Floor
Century House
100–102 Oxford St
London
W1N 9FB
T 020 7436 3000  F 020 7436 8000
E jgillespie@ecinuk.com/pclifford@ecinuk.com
*Contact* James Gillespie, Paul Clifford

## Commercial Radio Companies' Association
The Radiocentre
77 Shaftesbury Avenue
London
W1D 5DU
T 020 7306 2603/2610  F 020 7470 0062
E info@crca.co.uk  W crca.co.uk
*Chief Executive* Paul Brown

## Community Media Association
15 Paternoster Row
Sheffield
South Yorkshire
S1 2BX
T 0114 279 5219  F 0114 279 8976
E cma@commedia.org.uk  W commedia.org.uk
*Director* Steve Buckley

*Members include local and restricted-service radio
and TV stations, and community-based production
groups*

*It provides information, advice, training and
consultancy, publishes a quarterly magazine Airflash,
and administers the Local Independent Television
Network*

## Concert Promoters' Association
6 St Mark's Rd
Henley-on-Thames
Oxfordshire
RG 1LJ
T 01491 575060  F 01491 414082
E carolesmith.cpa@virgin.net

*Representing the interest of concert promoters in the UK*

## Contemporary Music Centre
19 Fishamble St
Temple Bar
Dublin 8
Ireland
T 00 353 1 673 1922  F 00 353 1 648 9100
E info@cmc.ie  W cmc.ie

*The Contemporary Music Centre documents and
promotes new Irish music*

## Copyright Advice and Anti-Piracy Hotline
Unit B, Clivemont House
54 Clivemont Rd
Maidenhead
Berkshire
SL6 7BZ
T 0845 6034567  F 01628 760353
E contact@copyright-info.org.uk
W copyright-info.org.uk
*Contact* Nicholas Watson

*The Hotline is a cross-industry initiative promoting a
safe and lawful environment, providing a point of
contact to anyone who wants to use music, film and
software copyrights. The membership includes British
Music Rights, BPI, The Federation Against Copyright
Theft, The Federation Against Software Theft,
MCPS, MPA and PRS*

## Country Music Association
3rd Floor
18 Golden Square
London
W1R 3AG

T 020 7734 3221   F 020 7434 3025
E cmalondon@compuserve.com
W cmaworld.com
*Director* David Bower

## Federation Against Copyright Theft
7 Victory Business Centre
Worton Rd
Isleworth
Middlesex
TW7 6DB
T 020 8568 6646   F 020 8560 6364
E investigator@factuk.org.uk
*Director General* David Lowe

## Guild of International Songwriters & Composers
Sovereign House
12 Trewartha Rd
Praa Sands
Penzance
Cornwall
TR20 9ST
T 01736 762826   F 01736 763328
E songmag@aol.com   W songwriters-guild.co.uk
*Membership Secretary* Carole A Jones

*Advice, guidance, protection and information for members*
*The quarterly Songwriting and Composing magazine is issued free to members*
*Detailed pamphlet available for potential members*

## Hospital Broadcasting Association
Straithe House
Russell St
Falkirk
FK2 7HP
T 01324 611996

## Incorporated Society of Musicians
10 Stratford Place
London
W1C 1AA
T 020 7629 4413   F 020 7408 1538
E membership@ism.org   W ism.org
*Chief Executive* Neil Hoyle

*Professional association for all musicians*
*Representative, legal and professional advice and services*
*See also Music Journal (press)*

## Independent Publishers' Association
PO Box 3163
London
NW1 5HJ
T 020 7704 8541   F 020 7704 8540

## International Federation of the Phonographic Industry
IFPI Secretariat
54 Regent St
London
W1R 5PJ
T 020 7878 7900   F 020 7878 7950
E info@ifpi.org   W ifpi.org
*Director of Communications* Adrian Strain

## International Songwriters' Association
PO Box 46
Limerick City
Limerick
Ireland
T 00353 61 228837/020 7486 5353
F 00 353 61 229464/020 7486 2094
E jliddane@songwriter.iol.ie   W songwriter.co.uk
*Managing Director* James D Liddane
*Contacts* Anna M Sinden, Bill Miller

## Irish Music Rights Organization
Copyright House
Pembroke Row
Lower Baggot St
Dublin 2
Ireland
T 00 353 1 661 4844   F 00 353 1 676 3125
E info@imro.ie   W imro.ie
*Chief Executive* Adrian Gaffney

## Jazz Services
1st Floor, 132 Southwark St
London
SE1 0SW
T 020 7928 9089   F 020 7401 6870
E admin@jazzservices.org.uk
W jazzservices.org.uk
*Contact* Chris Hodgkins or Celia Wood

## Manchester City Music Network
Ground Floor, Fourways House
57 Hilton St
Manchester
M1 2EJ
T 0116 228 3993   F 0116 228 3773
E network@manchester-music.org.uk
W manchester-music.org.uk
Contact Stuart Worthington

## Mechanical Copyright Protection Society
Copyright House
29–33 Berners St
London
W1P 4AA
T 020 7580 5544   F 020 7306 4455   W mcps.co.uk

*Also at Elgar House, 41 Streatham High Street,
London SW16 1ER*
*MCPS (Ireland), Pembroke Row, Lower Baggot
Street Dublin 2 Ireland*
*T 00 353 1 676 6940*
*F 00 353 1 661 1316*
*E victor.finn@mcps.co.uk*
*Performing Rights Society*
*Address/telephone/fax as for MCPS, Berners Street*
*W prs.co.uk*
*Chief Executive*
*John Hutchinson*
*Mechanical Rights Society, Elgar House address*
*T 020 8378 7221*
*F 020 8378 7220*
*E david.buskell@ mcps.co.uk*
*Contact David Buskell*

## MPA (Music Publishers Association)
3rd Floor, Strandgate
18–20 York Buildings
London
WC2N 6JU
T 020 7389 0660   F 020 7839 7776
E info@mpaonline.org.uk   W mpaonline.org.uk
Chief Executive Sarah Faulder

*MPA Ireland (MPAI)*
*3 Pembroke Row*
*Baggot Street*
*Dublin 2*
*Ireland*
*T 00 353 1 677 9046*
*F 00 353 1 677 9386*
*Secretary: Johnny Lappin*

## MRIB
530 Fulham Rd
London
SW6 5NR
T 020 7731 3555   F 020 7731 8545
E Contactus@mrib.co.uk   W mrib.co.uk
Managing Director Paul Basford

*Content and entertainment research*

## Music Industry Research Organization
8 Montague Close
London
SE1 9UR
T 020 7940 8560   F 020 7407 7081

## Music Managers' Forum
1 Glenthorne Mews
115a Glenthorne Rd
London
W6 0LJ
T 020 8741 2555   F 020 8741 4856
E info@ukmmf.net   W ukmmf.net
General Secretary James Fisher

*Represents the interests of artists' managers, and has
published a book about management, including a
listing of managers and their artists, called MMF
Guide to Professional Music Management (ISBN:
1-86074-355-2)*

## Music of Black Origin (MOBO)
22 Stephenson Way
London
NW1 2HD
T 020 7419 1800/0700 2255 662
F 020 7419 1600/0700 2329 662
E info@mobo.net   W mobo.net
Chief Executive Kanya King
Managing Director Andy Rushell

## Music Producers' Guild
PO Box 29912
London
SW6 4FR
T 020 7371 8888   F 020 7371 8887
E members@mpg.org.uk   W mpg.org.uk
Company Secretary Natasha Peevor

## Musicians' Benevolent Fund

16 Ogle St
London
W1W 6JA
**T** 020 7636 4481   **F** 020 7637 4307
**E** info@mbf.org.uk   **W** mbf.org.uk
*Chairman* Christopher Yates
*Secretary* Helen Faulkner
*Head of Casework* Sara Dixon
*Administrator of Awards & Trusts* Susan Dolton
*Administrator of Public Affairs* Michael White

## Musicians' Union

60–62 Clapham Rd
London
SW9 0JJ
**T** 020 7582 5566   **F** 020 7582 9805
**E** musiciansunion.org.uk
**W** musiciansunion.org.uk
*General Secretary* Dennis Scard
*Music Business Adviser* Nigel McCune

## MWM (Mooney Williams May Ltd)

6 Berkeley Crescent
Clifton
Bristol
BS8 1HA
**T** 0117 929 2393   **F** 0117 929 2696
**E** office@mwmuk.com
*Contact* Craig Williams

*Specializing in entertainment and media clients*

## National Sound Archive

British Library
96 Euston Rd
London
NW1 2DB
**T** 020 7412 7440   **F** 020 7412 7441   **E** nsa@bl.uk
**W** bl.uk/nsa and cadensa/bl.uk
*Director* Crispin Jewitt

*Opened in 1955 and holds over a million discs, 190,000 tapes and many other sound and video recordings*

## National Union of Students' Entertainments

45 Underwood St
London
N1 7LG
**T** 020 7490 0946   **F** 020 7490 1026

**E** waves@mites.co.uk
*Contact* Steve Hoyland

## Nordoff-Robbins

55 Fulham High St
London
SW6 3JJ
**T** 020 7736 5500   **F** 020 7371 8206
*Chairman* Andrew Miller

## Patent Office

Central Enquiry Unit
Room 1L02
Concept House
Cardiff Rd
Newport
South Wales
NP10 8QQ
**T** 0845 9 500 505   **F** 01633 813600
**E** enquiries@patent.gov.uk   **W** patent.gov.uk

*Can advise on band logos and copyright*

## Performing Arts Media Rights Association

161 Borough High St
London
SE1 1HR
**T** 020 7940 0400   **F** 020 7407 2008
**E** office@pamra.org.uk   **W** pamra.org.uk
*Chief Executive* Anne Rawcliffe-King

*Sole purpose is to administer the recorded performance remuneration right
Full details on website*

## Phonographic Performance Ireland

1 Corrig Avenue
Dun Laoghaire
Co. Dublin
Ireland
**T** 00 353 1 280 5977   **F** 00 353 1 280 6579
**E** info@ppiltd.com   **W** iol.ie/ppiltd/
*Director General* Dick Doyle

*The Irish record industry's central collecting society for public performance and broadcast licence fees
Free membership to any label with at least one release in Ireland*

## Phonographic Performance Limited
1 Upper James St
London
W1R 3HG
**T** 020 7534 1000    **F** 020 7534 1111    **w** ppluk.com

*Video Performance Limited*
*Address as PPL*
*T 020 7534 1400*
*F 020 7534 1414*
*Head of External Affairs* Colleen Hue
*Performer Registration Centre also at this address*
*T 020 7534 1234*
*F 020 7534 1383*
**E** *post@musmall.demon.co.uk*

## Radio Joint Audience Research (RAJAR)
Gainsborough House
81 Oxford St
London
W1D 2EU
**T** 020 7903 5350    **F** 020 7903 5351
**E** info@rajar.co.uk    **w** rajar.co.uk
*Managing Director* Jane O'Hara

## Scottish Music Information Centre Ltd
1 Bowmont Gardens
Glasgow
GL12 9LR
**T** 0141 334 6393    **F** 0141 337 1161
**E** info@smic.org.uk    **w** smic.org.uk
*Contact* Andrew Logan

*Exists to document and promote Scottish music.*
*Services include sale and hire of music, publishing*
*and promotion, comprehensive database, sound*
*archive and reference library*

## Society of European Songwriters & Composers
Gresham House
53 Clarendon Raod
Watford
Hertfordshire
WD1 1LA
**T** 01923 228870    **F** 01923 228872
**E** rightsw@sesac.co.uk
*Chairman* Wayne Bickerton

## South East Music Alliance
PO Box 91
Reigate
Surrey
RH2 0FG
**T** 01737 210848    **F** as telephone
**E** sema@dial.pipex.com
**w** dialspace.dial.pipex.com/sema
*Co-ordinator* Richard Coppen

## Student Radio Association
The Radio Academy
5 Market Place
London
W1N 7AH
**T** 020 7255 2010    **F** 020 7255 2029
**E** sra-exec@studentradio.org.uk
**w** studentradio.org.uk
*Chairman* Martin Dallaghan

## The Band Register
37 Rothschild Rd
London
W4 5HT
**w** bandreg.com
*Contact* Peter Whitehead

## The Radio Authority
Holbrook House
14 Great Queen St
London
WC2B 5DG
**T** 020 7430 2724    **F** 020 7405 7062
**E** info@radioauthority.org.uk
**w** radioauthority.org.uk
*Chief Press Officer* Julie McCaty

*Licenses and regulates all independent radio services*

## Umbrella
PO Box 763
London
SE24 9LL
**T** 020 8960 1871    **F** 020 8969 1694
*Contact* Brian Leafe

## Women in Music

7 Tavern St
Stowmarket
Suffolk
IP14 1PJ
**T** 01449 673990   **F** 01449 673994
**E** info@womeninmusic.org.uk
**W** womeninmusic.org.uk
*Administrator* Clare Adams


## Worshipful Company of Musicians

1st Floor
74–75 Watling St
London
EC4M 9BJ
**T** 020 7489 8888   **F** 020 7489 1614
**E** simonw@wcom.freeserve.co.uk
*Contact* Simon Waley

# 4

**Artist Management**

## 101 Management
35 Britannia Row
London
N1 8QH
**T** 020 7704 6708 **F** 020 7704 6709
**E** 101prod@dial.pipex.xom
*Managing Director* Cliff Whyte

## 11th Hour Arts
113 Cheesemans Rd
Star Rd
London
W14 9XH
**T** 020 7385 5447 **F** 020 7385 5446
*Contact* Debbie Golt

## 19 Management
Unit 32
Ransomes Dock
35–37 Parkgate Rd
London
SW11 4NP
**T** 020 7801 1919 **F** 020 7801 1920
*Managing Director* Simon Fuller

## 1905 Management
42a Rowley Rd
London
N15 3AX
**T** 020 8903 0360 **F** 020 8733 1301
**E** G1905@hotmail.com
*Contact* Graham Kelly

## 23/7
3rd Floor, 40 Langham St
London
W1N 5RG
**T** 020 7580 4088 **F** 020 7580 4098
**E** davecrompton@hotmail.com
*Contact* David Crompton

## 3cord Management
54 Portobello Rd
London
W11 3DL
**T** 020 7229 9218 **F** 020 7727 2275
**E** simon@3cord.net
*Contact* Simon Hicks

## 3rd Stone
PO Box 8
Corby
Northants
NN17 2XZ
T 01536 202295   F 01536 266246
E steve@adasam.demon.co.uk
W adasam.demon.co.uk
*Label Manager* Steve Kalidoski

## 406 Management
PO Box 10653
London
W5 4WR
T 020 8993 7441   F 020 8992 9993
E info@dorm.co.uk   W thedormgroup.com
*Contact* Dee O'Reilly

## 623 Management
24 Abbey St
Carlisle
Cumbria
CA3 8TX
T 01228 546622   F 01228 546633
E lbat623@aol.com
*Contact* L B Broyles

## 7hz
3 Harvard Rd
Isleworth
Middx
TW7 4PA
T 020 8847 3556   F 020 8232 8717
E julie@7hz.co.uk
*Contact* Julie Fletcher

*Specializes in record producers and singer/songwriters*
*Also Onion Music (publishers)*

## A Crosse The World Management
PO Box 23066
London
W11 3FR
T 07956 311810   E the@morrighan.com
W morrighan.com
*Contact* Jon Crosse

## A&G Management
PO Box 435
Huddersfield
HD4 5YD
T 01484 559099/07768 150156   F as first telephone
*Contact* Gladstone Shaw

## ABC Management
Alexandria House
6 Little Portland St
London
W1N 5AG
T 020 7907 1700   F 020 7907 1711
E email@globaltalentgroup.com
W globaltalentgroup.com
*Directors* David Forecast and Ashley Tabor

## Abstract Management
PO Box 777
Sheffield
South Yorkshire
S5 7YF
T 0114 261 7613   F 0114 261 9116
E alf@abstractmgt.freeserve.co.uk
*Contact* Alf Billingham

## ACA Music Management
7 North Parade
Bath
BA2 4DD
T 01225 428284   F 01225 400090
E aca_aba@freenet.co.uk   W acamusic.co.uk
*Contact* H Finegold

*Also ABA Booking and Release Records (same contact details)*

## Ace Eyed Management
2 Menelik Rd
London
NW2 3RP
T 020 7435 6116   F as telephone
E markalbert@bluemelon.co.uk
W bluemelon.co.uk
*Contact* Mark Albert

**Acker's International Jazz Agency**
53 Cambridge Mansions
Cambridge Rd
London
SW11 4RX
T 020 7978 5885   F 020 7978 5882
E pamela@ackersmusicagency.co.uk
W ackersmusicagency.co.uk
*Proprietor* Pamela F Sutton

*NB: personal management and exclusive agency for
Acker Bilk and his Paramount Jazz Band*

**Activ Management**
Unit 9
Mitre Bridge Trading Estate
Mitre Way
London
W10 6AU
W activ_recs.compuserve.com
*Contact* Paul Hallett

**Active Artistes Music Management**
8 Woodend
London
SE19 3NU
T 020 8653 5457   F 020 8771 4231
E george.graham@virginet.co.uk
*Contact* A Masker

**Active Music Management**
Suite 401
29 Margaret St
London
W1N 7LB
T 087 0120 7668   F 087 0120 9880
E marc@popstar.com
*Managing Director* Mark Winters

**Adrian Boss Promotions**
2 Elgin Avenue
London
W9 3QP
T 020 7286 1665   F 020 7286 1573
E adrain@adeboss.freeserve.co.uk
W adeboss.freeserve.co.uk
*Contact* Adrian Boss

**AEC Management**
PO Box 903
Sutton
Surrey
SM2 6BY
T 020 8642 1679   F 020 8642 5203
E aec.management@virgin.net
*Contact* Andy Cook

*Artistes, songwriters and producers*

**African Music Agency**
120 Kentish Town Rd
London
NW1 9PY
T 020 7267 1928   F as telephone
*Contact* D Lamptey

**AIR (Artistes' International Representation Ltd)**
Air House
Spennymoor
Co Durham
DL16 7SE
T 01388 814632   F 01388 812445
E air@agents-uk.com   W airagency.com
*Contact* Colin Pearson/John Wray

**Aisle Management**
9 Spedan Close
London
NW3 4XF
T 020 7431 9291   E aislerow@yahoo.com
*Contact* Alex Sexton

**Alan Bown Management**
71 Shaggy Calf Lane
Slough
Berks
SL2 5HN
T 01344 890001/01753 524227   F 01344 885323
E thealanbown@netscape.net
W thealanbown.co.uk
*Contact* Alan Bown

## Alan Seifert Management

1 Winterton House
24 Park Walk
London
SW10 0AQ
**T** 020 7795 0321/7565 0304   **F** as first telephone
*Contact* Alan Seifert

## Alan Whitehead Management

10 Deacons Close
Elstree
Herts
WD6 3HX
**T** 020 8953 8877/07957 358997   **F** 020 8207 0614
**E** alan_whitehead_uk@yahoo.com
*Managing Director* Alan Whitehead

## Alan Wood Agency

346 Gleadless Rd
Sheffield
South Yorkshire
S2 3AJ
**T** 0114 258 0338   **F** 0114 258 0638
**E** alan@alanwoodagency.co.uk
**W** alanwoodagency.co.uk
*Contact* Alan Wood

## Alchemy Management

PO Box 20426
London
SE17 1WS
**T** 020 7703 0200   **F** 020 7703 0355
**E** brian@alchemy1.demon.co.uk
*Managing Director* Brian Allen

## All Access

6 Chieveley Mews
London Rd
Sunnigdale
Berkshire
SL5 0UD
**T** 01344 626425   **F** 01344 621991
**E** swampprods@mcmail.com   **W** swamp.co.uk
*Director* Tristan Greatrex

## All Around The World

9–13 Penny St
Blackburn
Lancashire
BB1 6HJ
**T** 01254 264120   **F** 01254 693768
**E** matt@aatw.u-net.com
*Label Manager* Matt Cadman

## All Out Management

Dunbar House
13a British Row
Trowbridge
Wilts
BA14 8PB
**T** 07973 314237   **E** alloutmgmt@hotmail.com
*Contact* Mark or George

## All Seasons Management

Unit 1
Swallowfield Way
Hayes
Middlesex
UB3 1DO
**T** 020 8561 2552   **F** 020 8561 2113
**E** asf@btconnect.com
*Managing Director* Adam Porges

## Allan Wilson Enterprises

Queens House
Chapel Green Rd
Hindley
Wigan
Lancs
WN2 3LL
**T** 01942 258565/255158   **F** as second telephone
*Owner* Allan Wilson

## Alternative Route Management

68 Western Rd
Hove
East Sussex
BN43 5ZD
**E** garyh@mistral.co.uk   **W** alternativeroute.com
*Contact* Gary Hutchins

**Amber**
PO Box 1
Chipping Ongar
Essex
CM5 9HZ
T 01277 362916/01277 365046   F 01277 366736
*Contact* Paul Tage

**Andrew Flintham Productions**
29 Titlow Rd
Harleston
Norfolk
IP20 9DH
T 01379 853982   E andrew.flintham@talk21.com
*Contact* Andrew Flintham

*Chart-orientated dance music*

**Angels Tears Management**
20 Montague Rd
London
E8 2HW
T 020 7357 8292/07973 217878   F 020 7503 8034
E angelstears@appleonline.net   W angelstears.net
*Contact* Colin Jones

**Anger Management**
PO Box 6105
Birmingham
West Midlands
B43 6NZ
T 0121 357 3338/07941 139013   F 0121 580 2643
E anger.1965@virgin.net
*Contact* Carl Bedward

**Anglo-American Enterprises**
806 Keyes House
Dolphin Square
London
SW1V 3NB
T 020 7821 0254   F 020 7630 9475
*Managing Director* Bunny Lewis

**Apollo Management Ltd**
8 Apollo House
18 All Saints Rd
London
W11 1HH
T 020 7460 9207   F 020 7460 9209
*Managing Director* Giles Cooper

**ARC Management Ltd**
2 Beulah Rd
London
SW19 3SB
T 020 8255 7775   F 020 8255 7776
E sir.harry@lineone.net
*Contact* Sir Harry

**Archangel Management Ltd**
174 Camden High St
London
NW1 0NE
T 07887 552468/020 7267 3939   F 020 7482 1955

**Ardent Music**
59 Westbere Rd
London
NW2 3SP
T 020 7435 7706   F 020 7435 7712
E admin@ardentmusic.co.uk
*Contact* Ian Blackaby or Alexandra Bryant

*Classical crossover artists, singer/songwriters,*
*ex-major label artists now with own labels*
*Roster: Caroline Lavelle, Crash Test Dummies,*
*Cowboy Junkies, Dear Janes, Mouth Music,*
*Snowpony, Helicopter Girl*

**Arketek Management**
53 Edge St
Nutgrove
St Helens
Merseyside
WA9 5JX
T 0151 430 6290   E alan@arketek.co.uk
*Contact* Alan Ferreira

*Recording and publishing contracts for original*
*artists, music for film and TV*

**Art & Music Corporation**
Munro House
High Close
Rawdon
Leeds
West Yorkshire
LS19 6HF
T 0113 250 3338   F 0113 250 7343
E esc@a-m-c.demon.co.uk
*Managing Director* Stewart Coxhead

## Arthur Fuxache Help

Drivers Cottage
24 East Grinstead
Lingfield
Surrey
RH7 6EP
**T** 01342 833587  **E** watsonmacavity@aol.com
**W** pomdiddlyompom.com
*Contact* Arthur Fuxache

*Group management and live music promotion*

## Artist Development Organization

PO Box 1345
Ilford
Essex
IG4 5FX
**T** 07050 333555  **F** 07020 923292
**E** artdevorg.aol.com  **W** artistdevelopment.org
*Contact* M Levett

*Roster: Big Casino (DJ Remix/Production Team);
Karen D (pop/dance vocalist and songwriter);
Stevie A (MC)
Also promotional services (Q and A&R); Savannah
Entertainments also at this address. Contact: Freddie
Morrison*

## Artist Management Group Ltd/Qdos Entertainment

8 King St
London
WC2E 8HN
**T** 020 7240 5052  **F** 020 7240 4956
**E** pdale@qdosentertainment.plc.uk
**W** amg-group.co.uk
*Contact* Phil Dale

## Artist Rights Management

Northburgh House
10 Northburgh St
London
EC1V 0AT
**T** 020 7253 5860  **F** 020 7253 5850
**E** m21@m21.co.uk  **W** m21.co.uk
*Director* Jens Hills

## Artiste Promotions & Management

106 Trees Rd
Mount Merrion
Co Dublin
Ireland
**T** 00 353 1 278 9177  **F** 00 353 1 278 9198
**E** madelein@indigo.ie
*Director* Madeleine Seiler
Also The Headline Agency (same contact details)

## Asia Management

Plas Llecha
Llanhennock
Newport
Monmouthshire
NP6 1LU
**T** 01633 450603  **F** 01633 450666
**E** asia@globalnet.co.uk  **W** asiaworld.org

## Atlantic Crossing Artists

Unit 3, 33 Sinclair Gardens
London
W14 0AU
**T** 020 7603 2244/07730 160077  **F** 020 7602 4579
**E** atlanticcrossingartists@yahoo.com
**W** atlanticcrossingartists.freeservers.com
*Contact* Mark McAish

*Part of 2Big Music International, as is RDL/
TeleRyngg/Savant Records (artists and CD
promotion). Contact* Rhela St John
*(teleryngg2@onlineTV.com)*

## Atomic Management

32 Neal St
London
WC2H 9PS
**T** 020 7379 3010
*Contact* Mick Newton

## ATS Casting Ltd

26 St Michael's Rd
Headingley
Leeds
West Yorkshire
LS6 3AW
**T** 0113 230 4334  **F** 0113 275 6422
*Booker* Stanley Joseph

## Automatic Management
Eden House
59 Fulham High St
London
SW6 3JJ
**T** 020 7384 3022   **F** 020 7384 3033
**E** auto@automan.co.uk
*Managing Director* Jerry Smith

## Avalon Records
PO Box 929
Ferndown
Dorset
BH22 9YF
**T** 01202 896397   **F** as telephone
**E** galahad@lds.co.uk
**w** tios.cs.utwente.nl/-schudel/galahad
*Manager* Stuart Nicholson

## B&H Management
PO Box 65
Northwood
Middlesex
HA6 2GT
**T** 01923 826166/07885 200408   **F** 01923 826167
**E** simon@shooter-1.demon.co.uk
*Contact* Simon Harrison

*Also the largest session fixing agency in Europe*

## Backlash Music Management – Scotland
54 Carlton Place
Glasgow
G5 9TW
**T** 0141 418 0053   **F** 0141 418 0054
**E** info@backlash.co.uk
*Contact* Steve Gilmour

*Also at: 206 Kendall Place, London,*
*W1H 3AH*
*Tel: 020 7468 0202*
*Fax: 020 7468 0303*

## Backyard Management
164 New Cavendish St
London
W1M 7FJ
**T** 020 7580 8881   **F** 020 7580 8882
**E** backyard@bogo.co.uk
*Contact* Gil Goldberg

## Bad Habits Entertainment Group Ltd
PO Box 69
Daventry
Northamptonshire
NN1 4ZY
**T** 07000 243243/0870 7463153   **F** 01327 312545
**E** info@badhabitsentgroup.com
**w** badhabits-ent.com
*Contact* Steve Osborne

## Bajonor Ltd
Bajonor House
2 Bridge St
Peel
Isle Of Man
IM5 1NB
**T** 01624 844134/01624 844136   **F** 01624 844135
**w** rwcc.com
*Contact* Candy Atcheson

## Balcony Jump Management
24 Bradmore Park Rd
London
W6 0DT
**T** 020 8741 7000   **F** 020 8741 1700
**E** info@balconyjump.co.uk   **w** balconyjump.co.uk
*Managing Director* Tim Paton

## Bandana Management
Third Floor
11 Elvaston Place
London
SW7 5QG
**T** 020 7584 1111   **F** 020 7584 7722
**E** brian@bandana.fsnet.co.uk
*Contact* Brian Lane or Julia Gibbs

*Roster: A-Ha, A\* Teens, Espen Lind, Briskeby,*
*E-Type, Lisa Miskousky*

## Bang 'em Out
Prioryfield House
20–21 Canon St
Taunton
Somerset
TA1 1SW
**T** 01823 323363/0774 713 2149   **F** 01823 271072
*Contact* Kevin Locke

## Barn Dance and Line Dance Agency
62 Beechwood Rd
South Croydon
Surrey
CR2 0AA
T 020 8657 2813   F 020 8651 6080
*Contact* Derek Jones

## Barry Clayman Corporation Ltd
134 Wigmore St
London
W1H 0LD
T 020 7486 1222   F 020 7935 6276

## Barry Collings Entertainments
21a Clifftown Rd
Southend-On-Sea
Essex
SS1 1AB
T 01702 330005   F 01702 333309
E bcollent@aol.com   W barrycollings.co.uk
*Managing Director* Barry Collings

## Barry Dye Entertainments
PO Box 888
Ipswich
Suffolk
IP1 6BU
T 01473 744287/07831 700799   F 01473 745442
*Proprietor* Barry Dye

## Barter Management
3c Arden Rd
London
W13
T 020 8566 7220
*Managing Director* Harry Barter

## Bastard Management
22 Charmouth House
Dorset Rd
London
SW8 1EU
T 020 7582 5532   F as telephone
E bastardmgt@hotmail.com
*Manager* Alex Holland
*Artists: Nucleus Roots, The Embezzlers, DJ Badley*
*Also label Dreadymix Productions*

## Bazaar Music Management
61 Westgate
Mansfield
Nottingham
NG18 1RU
T 07973 322776/07973 772385
*Contact* David Knowles

## BB Promotions
119 Beech Crescent
Netley View
Hythe
Southampton
Hampshire
SO45 3QE
T 01703 207877
*Manager* Doug Bailey

*Specialists in small promotion shows for artists with
tour support and debut singles (van, PA, lighting and
crew available for hire)*

## BDA
Office 2, Toll Bar Business Park
Newchurch Rd
Stacksteads
Bacup
Lancs
OL13 0NA
T 01706 877771   F 01706 877551
E brian.durkin@btinternet.com
*Managing Director* Brian Durkin

*Entertainment, leisure and conference consultants*

## Bernard Lee Management
1 Heathside Place
Epsom Downs
Surrey
KT18 5TX
T 01737 354777   F as telephone
*Managing Director* Bernard Lee

## Big Bear Music
PO Box 944
Birmingham
B16 8UT
T 0121 454 7020   F 0121 454 9996
E bigbearmusic@compuserve.com
W bigbearmusic.com
*Managing Director* Jim Simpson

**Big Brother Management**
2nd Floor
15 Pratt Mews
London
NW1 0AD
T 020 7681 9222/020 7681 9223
F 020 7681 9224
E bigbrother@bigbromgt.freeserve.co.uk
*Contact* Geoff Wener

**Big Brother Management**
PO Box 1288
Gerrards Cross
Buckinghamshire
SL9 9YB
T 01753 890635    F 01753 892879
*Contact* Richard Allen

**Big Fish Music**
17 Stanlake Villas
London
W12 7EX
T 020 8743 5301    F 020 8740 8580
E bigfish@music-village.com
W music-village.com
*Director* John Carnell

**Big Life Management**
67–69 Chalton St
London
NW1 1HY
T 020 7554 2100    F 020 7554 2154
E biglife@biglife.co.uk    W biglife.co.uk
*Managing Director* Jazz Summers
*Contact* Jazz Summers or Tim Parry

**Big M Productions**
Big M House
1 Stevenage Rd
Knebworth
Hertfordshire
SG3 6AN
T 01438 814433    F 01438 815252
E bigm@bigmgroup.co.uk
W bigmgroup.u-net.com
*Managing Director* Joyce Wilde

**Billy Russell Management**
Binny Estate
Ecclesmachan
Edinburgh
EH52 6NL
T 01506 858885    F 01506 858155
E kitemusic@aol.com    W kitemusic.com
*Contact* Billy Russell

*Also Kite Music Ltd (publishers, same contact details)*

**Bish Management**
23 Carvery Rd
Leigh-on-Sea
Essex
SS9 2NN
T 01702 471871    F 01702 480873
E bish@bishmanagement.com
*Contacts* Stuart Bishop and Toni Pearson

**Bizarre Management**
29 Halifax Rd
Enfield
Middlesex
EN2 0PP
T 020 8351 0872    F as telephone
E matthias@siefert.freeserve.co.uk
*Contact* Matthias Siefert

**Bjorn Again Management**
PO Box 4058
London
W9 3ZT
T 020 8960 5862    F 020 8964 2474
E jtm@bjornagain.com    W bjornagain.com
*Contact* John Tyrrell or Rod Leissle

**BKO Productions**
The Old Truman Brewery
91 Brick Lane
London
E1 6ON
T 020 7377 9373    F 020 7377 6523
E byron@b-k-o.demon.co.uk
*Contact* Byron Orme

**Black Magic Management**
296 Earls Court Rd
London
SW5 9BA

**T** 020 7565 0806
**F** as telephone or 020 7244 0916
**E** blackmagicrecords@talk21.com
**W** blackmagicrecords.com
*Managing Director* Mataya Clifford

## Blacklist Entertainment Ltd
The Old Church Hall
67 Studdridge St
London
SW6 3TD
**T** 020 7610 6618    **F** 020 7736 9949
*Managing Director* Clive Black
*General Manager* Paul Mitchell

## Blackmail Management & Production
60 Cleveland Rd
New Malden
Surrey
KT3 3QJ
**T** 020 8942 9511/07770 233740
**F** as first telephone    **E** phnt@aol.com
*Contact* Pete Hinton

## Blaylock Management
39 Leyton Rd
Harpenden
Herts
AL5 2JB
**T** 01582 715098
*Managing Director* David Blaylock

## Blue August Management
35 Mansted Gardens
Romford
Essex
RM6 4ED
**T** 020 8590 2524    **F** as telephone
*Contact* John McDonald

## Blue Cherry Ltd
The Penthouse
20 Rupert St
London
W1V 7FN
**T** 020 7287 6261    **F** 020 7287 6210
*Contact* Gavin Myall

## Blue Movement
63 Dockland St
Royal Docks
London
E16 2JE
**T** 020 7476 7766
*Head of A&R* Simon Holt

## Blue Stack Music/Blue Stack Records
52 Abbott Avenue
London
SW20 8SQ
**T** 020 8540 3350    **F** as telephone
**E** bluestack@hotmail.com
**W** countrymusic.org.uk/heartfield
*Contact* Angela Williams

*Management and label for country-rock band
Heartfield and their songwriter Tony O'Leary*

## Blueprint Management
134 Lots Rd
London
SW10 0RJ
**T** 020 7351 4333/020 7352 9093
*Director* John Glover

## Bodo Music Co
186 Ashley Rd
Hale
Altrincham
Cheshire
WA15 9SF
**T** 07939 521 465    **F** 0161 928 8136
*Managing Director* F L Marshall

*Roster: Sabbamangalang, Green Zoo
Jazz and soul*

## Bond Management Ltd
Studio 75
Prospect Quay
Point Pleasant
London
SW18 1PS
**T** 020 8877 9250/020 8877 3335    **F** 020 8877 1337
**E** bondmgmt@dial.pipex.com
*Contact* Jon Barlow or Leonard Lowy

*Dance/pop specialists*

## Book Of Dreams Ltd

73 Couchmore
Esher
Surrey
KT10 9AX
**T** 020 8398 0255    **F** 020 8398 9022
**E** hpe@bookofdreamsmusic.com
**W** bookofdreamsmusic.com
*Managing Director* Harry Paton Evans
*Publishing Director* David Barnes

*Management and marketing consultancy working in
Europe, Japan and USA, providing complete career
service to clients through all media*

## BPR

36 Como St
Romford
Essex
RM7 7DR
**T** 01708 725330    **F** 01708 725322
**E** bprmusic@compuserve.com
*Contact* Ina Dittke, Brian Theobald, Vicki
Horrigan or Nick Eve

*Also agency, concert and tour promotion*

## Brandwood Communications

19 Longmeadow Grove
St Lawrence Court
Manchester
M34 2DA
**T** 0161 336 9300
*Contact* Derek Brandwood

## Brashreign Management

Foxley House
Rickling Green
Essex
CB11 3YD
**T** 07956 254542    **E** brashreign@aol.com
**W** brashreign.com
*Contact* Jonathan Rich

*Guitar-based melodic rock/indie (The Harbingers,
Colin Tyrer)*

## Brave Management

39a Trevelyan Rd
London
SW17 9LR
**T** 020 8672 2212    **F** 020 8672 0664
**E** netty_brave@dial.pipex.com
*Contact* Netty Walker

## Braw Music Management

78 Pentland Terrace
Edinburgh
Lothian
EH10 6HF
**T** 0131 445 3317    **F** 0131 445 4719
**E** braw@elvis.presence.co.uk
*Contact* Kenny MacDonald

## Brian Gannon Management

PO Box 106
Rochdale
Lancashire
OL16 4HW
**T** 01706 860400    **F** 01706 860406
**E** brian@entertainment-net.com
**W** entertainment-net.com
*Managing Director* Brian Gannon

## Brian Yeates Associates

Home Farm House
Canwell
Sutton Coldfield
West Midlands
B75 5SH
**T** 0121 323 2200    **F** 0121 323 2313
**E** info@brianyeates.co.uk    **W** brianyeates.co.uk
*Contact* Ashley Yeates

## Bridge

Cavendish House
423 New Kings Rd
London
SW6 4RN
**T** 020 7384 8029    **F** 020 7384 8027
**E** kate.bartlett@thebridge.uk.net
*Contact* Kate Bartlett

*Artist management and international consultancy for
production and management companies globally*

## Bright Music Ltd

PO Box 4536
Henley-On-Thames
Berkshire
RG9 3YD
**T** 01189 401780    **F** 07070 622034
**E** m-bright@dircon.co.uk
*Contact* Martin Wyatt

## Brilliant Artistes

253 Camberwell New Rd
London
SE5 0TH
**T** 020 7277 0088    **F** 020 7277 0099
**E** brilliant@dial.pipex.com
**W** obsolete.com/brilliant
*Contact* Jeanette Gibberson

## Brotherhood Of Man Management

Westfield
75 Burkes Rd
Beaconsfield
Bucks
HP9 1PP
**T** 01494 673073/01932 854900
**F** 01494 680920/01932 854661
**E** agency@brotherhoodofman.co.uk
**W** brotherhoodofman.co.uk

*NB: management for 1976 Eurovision winners
Brotherhood of Man*

## Brown McLeod

51 Clarkegrove Rd
Sheffield
South Yorkshire
S10 2NH
**T** 0114 268 5665    **F** 0114 268 4161
**E** entsuk@aol.com
*Contact* John Roddison

## BTM

PO Box 6003
Birmingham
West Midlands
B45 0AR
**T** 0121 477 9553    **F** 0121 693 2954
**E** barry@btm-gotham.demon.co.uk
*Contact* Barry Tomes

## Bullitproof Management

22a Lambolle Place
London
NW3 4PG
**T** 020 7691 4837/07711 629255    **F** 020 7209 0019
**E** diid.bullit@virgin.net
*Director* Diid Osman

## CA Management

Air Studios
Lyndhurst Rd
London
NW3 5NG
**T** 020 7794 0660    **F** 020 7916 2784
**E** adam@camanagement.demon.co.uk
*Managing Director* Adam Sharp

## Caleche Studios

175 Roundhay Rd
Leeds
LS8 5AN
**T** 0113 219 4929    **F** 0113 249 4941
*Managing Director* Leslie Coleman

## Cambrian Entertainments International

Trefeglwys
Newtown
Powys
SY17 5PU
**T** 01686 430411    **F** 01686 430331
**E** mbd (or info)@cambrianents.co.uk
**W** cambrianents.co.uk
*Managing Director* Michael Breese-Davies
*Contact* Michael or Robin Breese-Davies

*Specialist in summer seasons UK and cruising
worldwide*

## Caromac Music Management

Unit 207
Ducie House
Ducie St
Manchester
M1 2JW
**T** 0161 237 3403/0161 236 5324    **F** 0161 236 4268
**E** caroline.elleray@bmg.co.uk
*Contact* Caroline Elleray

**CCC/Crucial Chemystry Communications**
PO Box 10
London
N1 3RJ
**T** 020 7267 7893/020 7241 2183
**F** 020 7267 8793/020 7241 6233
**E** ccc@cyborganic.net   **w** teagarden.org
*Contact* Grant T Garden

**CEC Management**
4 Warren Mews
London
W1P 5DJ
**T** 020 7388 6500   **F** 020 7388 6522
**E** cec@cecmanagement.freeserve.co.uk
*Contact* Peter Felstead

**Chantelle Music**
3a Ashfield Parade
London
N14 5EH
**T** 020 8886 6236
*Managing Director* Riss Chantelle

**Charles Salt Management**
Leacroft
Cheriton Cross
Cheriton Bishop
Exeter
Devon
EX6 6JH
**T** 01647 25402/07867 788729
**E** charlie@supanet.com   **w** lizardsun-music.co.uk
*Contact* Charles Salt

*See also Skindependent (record company, same
contact details)*

**Charmenko**
46 Spenser Rd
London
SE24 0NR
**T** 020 7274 6618   **F** 020 7737 4712
**E** charmenko@atlas.co.uk   **w** charm.demon.co.uk
*Contacts* Nick Hobbs and Crayola

**Cherry Moon Ltd**
PO Box 666
Newtownards
County Down
BT22 2FJ
**T** 028 9084 2123/077 70 757666
**E** cherrymoon@cherrymoon.net
**w** cherrymoon.net
*Contact* Maurice Jay

*Also record label (same contact details)*

**Chester Hopkins International**
PO Box 1492
London
W6 9PD
**T** 020 8741 9910   **F** 020 8741 9914
*Managing Director* Adrian Hopkins

**Choir Connexion & London Community
Gospel Choir**
9 Greenwood Drive
London
E4 9HL
**T** 020 8531 5562   **F** 020 8523 4159
**E** groovking@aol.com   **w** lcgc.org.uk
*Contact* Bazil Meade or Yvonne White

**Chris Hillman Management**
PO Box 3037
Wokingham
Berkshire
RG40 4GR
**T** 0118 932 8320   **F** 0118 932 8237
**E** magickeye@magickeye.com   **w** magickeye.com
*Contact* Chris Hillman

**Clarion/Seven Muses**
47 Whitehall Park
London
N19 3TW
**T** 020 7272 4413/ 5125/8586   **F** 020 7281 9687
**E** admin@c7m.co.uk   **w** c7m.co.uk
*Partners* Nicholas Curry and Caroline Oakes

*NB: classical only. Personal management of a small
list of international artists and ensembles (no solo
singers)*

## Clive Banks Ltd
1 Glenthorne Mews
115a Glenthorne Rd
London
W6 0LJ
**T** 020 8748 5036   **F** 020 8748 3356
**E** mail@clivebanks.com   **w** clivebanks.com
*Contact* Caroline Stewart or Sharon Wheeler

## CMC Management
11 Birchlands Avenue
London
SW12 8ND
**T** 020 8333 5553/07802 627790
**F** as first telephone
**E** cmc@cmcmgmt.demon.co.uk
*Managing Director* Chris Molloy

## CMO Management (International) Ltd
Unit 32
Ransomes Dock
35–37 Parkgate Rd
London
SW11 4NP
**T** 020 7228 4000   **F** 020 7924 1608
*Managing Director* Chris Morrison

## Comet Records
First Floor
5 Cope St
Temple Bar
Dublin 12
Ireland
**T** 00 353 1 672 8001   **F** 00 353 1 671 8592/672 8005
**E** gforce@indigo.ie
**w** comet-records.com
*Contact* Brian O'Kelly

## Concentrated Management
Le Tone House
270 Watford Way
London
NW4 4UJ
**T** 020 8203 1988   **F** 020 8203 778
**E** concentrated.man@virgin.net
*Contact* Kieron Lyons

## Congo Music Ltd
17a Craven Park Rd
London
NW10 8SE
**T** 020 8961 5461   **F** as telephone
**E** congomusic@hotmail.com
**w** musiclinks.com/congo
*Managing Director* Byron Lye-Fook

*Also publishers, label and production, specializing in soul, reggae, jazz, blues and hiphop*

## Consortium
PO Box 1345
Ilford
Essex
IG4 5FX
**T** 07050 333555   **F** 07020 923292
**E** melevett@aol.com
**w** consortiumproductions.com
*Contacts* K Danzig, M Levett

## Contrast Management
c/o 308 Queens Rd
London
SE14 5JN
**T** 020 7252 8152/07958 639 692
**E** contrastman@hotmail.com
*Contact* Jacqui Norton

## Cool Badge Artists Management
96 Ferme Park Rd
London
N8 9SD
**T** 020 8374 3810/020 8372 5430   **F** 020 8374 3812
**E** russell&leigh@coolbadge.demon.co.uk
*Contact* Leigh McAlea

## Counterfeit Company
10 Barley Mow Passage
London
W4 4PH
**T** 020 8994 8397   **F** 020 8742 7684
**E** bbeatles@atlas.co.uk   **w** bootlegbeatles.com
*Contact* Raj Patel

**Crackteam Management**
Norden
2 Hillhead Rd
Newtonhill
Stonehaven
Kincardie and Deeside
AB39 3TS
T 01569 730962   F as telephone
*Managing Director* Doug Stone

**Craig Huxley Management**
13 Christchurch Rd
London
N8 9QL
T 020 8374 9133   F 020 8292 1205
E chuxleychm@aol.com
*Proprietor* Craig Huxley

*Roster: Genelab, AK47*

**Craig Williams Management**
6 Berkeley Crescent
Clifton
Bristol
BS8 1HA
T 0117 929 2393/07785 118724   F 0117 929 2696
E craigg.williams@virgin.net
*Contact* Craig Williams

**Crashed Music**
162 Church Rd
East Wall
Dublin 3
Ireland
T 00 353 1 888 1188   F 00 353 1 856 1122
E info@crashedmusic.com   W crashedmusic.com
*Managing Directors* Shay and Ian Hennessy

**Crisp Productions**
PO Box 979
Sheffield
South Yorkshire
S8 8YW
T 0114 261 1649   F as telephone
E dc@cprod.win-uk.net
*Contact* Darren Crisp

**Cromwell Management**
4–5 High St
Huntingdon
Cambridgeshire
PE18 6TE
T 01480 435600   F 01480 356250
E tricvic@lineone.net   W jazzmanagement.ic24.net
*Managing Partner* Vic Gibbons

*Jazz and blues artistes (management, agency, PR, promotion, publicity and media relations)*

**Cross Border Media**
10 Deer Park
Ashbourne
Co. Meath
Ireland
T 00 353 1 835 3471   F 00 353 1 835 0720
*Contact* Oliver Sweeney

**Crosstown Music**
Alexandra House
Earlsfort Terrace
Dublin 2
Ireland
T 00 353 1 676 1523/662 5728   F 00 353 1 661 562
E oliverw@iol.ie
*Contact* Oliver Walsh

**CRS Music Management**
PO Box 13459
London
W14 9FF
T 020 7460 0813   F 020 7460 8466
E campbellsmith@compuserve.com
*Contact* Campbell Smith

**Cruisin' Music Management**
Charlton Farm Studios
Hemmington
Bath
BA3 5XS
T 01373 834161   F 01373 834164
E sil@cruisin.co.uk   W cruisin.co.uk
*Contact* Sil Willcox

*Roster includes The Stranglers, Rachel Stamp, Headbound*

## Da Capo Music Management

30 Bentinck St
Kelvingrove
Glasgow
Strathclyde
G3 7TU
T 0141 334 5099   F 0141 339 0271
E byoung3752@aol.com
*Director* Brian Young

## Dark Blues Management Ltd

Unit 4, Hampton Hill Business Park
219 High St
Hampton Hill
Middx
TW12 1NP
T 020 8614 5950   F 020 8614 5958
*Contact* Trish Lusted (Operations Manager)

*All forms of live entertainment*

## Darrin Robson Management

319 City Rd
London
EC1V 1LJ
T 020 7278 1150/07802 481840   F 020 7278 1157
E info@fantasticplastic.co.uk
W fantasticplastic.co.uk
*Contact* Darrin Robson

## Dave Seamer Entertainments

46 Magdalen Rd
Oxford
OX4 1RB
T 01865 240054   F as telephone
E dave@daveseamer.co.uk   W daveseamer.co.uk
*Managing Director* Dave Seamer

## Dave Woolf Ltd

4th Floor
180–182 Tottenham Court Rd
London
W1P 9LE
T 020 7436 5529   F 020 7637 8776
E dwoolf@dircon.co.uk/annag@dircon.co.uk
*Contact* Dave Woolf

*Music PR and management (eg Jamiroquai, Beverley
Knight, Courtney Pine)*

## David Aspden Management

The Coach House
Capel Leyse
South Holmwood
Dorking
Surrey
RH5 4LJ
T 01306 712120   F 01306 713241
E d.aspden@virgin.net
*Contact* David Aspden

## David Curtis Management

Priors
Tye Green
Elsenham
Bishop Stortford
Hertfordshire
CM22 6DY
T 01279 813240/01279 815593   F 01279 815895
E procentral@aol.com
*Contact* David Curtis

## David Dorrell Management

Anglo House
2 Clerkenwell Green
London
EC1R ODE
E dorrell@dircon.co.uk
*Contact* Sam Whittaker

## David Morgan Management

192d Brooklands Rd
Weybridge
Surrey
KT13 ORJ
T 01932 855337   F 01932 851245/020 8232 8160
E dmmgmt@aol.com
*Managing Director* David Morgan

## Dazed Management

Onward House
11 Uxbridge St
London
W8 7TQ
T 020 7221 4275   F 020 7229 6893
*Contact* Debi McGrath

## DCM International

Suite 3
294–296 Nether St
Finchley
London
N3 1RJ
**T** 020 8343 0848   **F** 020 8343 0747
*Contact* Kelly Isaacs

## DD Productions

38 Johnston Terrace
London
NW2 6QJ
**T** 020 8450 0069   **F** 020 8450 0079
**E** ddproductions@easynet.co.uk
**W** duranduran.com
*Contact* Emma Anderson

*NB: DD Productions exists solely to look after Duran Duran, and does not take on other artists*

## Decadent Management

Unit 6
Frobisher House
89 Lillie Rd
London
SW6N 1UD
**T** 020 7610 2112   **F** 020 7610 2262
*Managing Director* Richard Holley

## Dee O'Reilly Management

PO Box 10653
London
W5 4WR
**T** 020 8993 7441   **F** 020 8992 9993
**E** info@dorm.co.uk   **W** thedormgroup.com
*Contact* David O'Reilly

*Pop and rock artists*

## Deluxe Management

PO Box 5753
Nottingham
NG2 7WN
**T** 0115 914 1429   **F** 0115 914 4889
**E** info@deluxeaudio.com
*Contact* Nick Gordon Brown

## Denis Vaughan Management

P.O. Box 28286
London
N21 3WT
**T** 020 7486 5353   **F** 01372 742448
**E** dvaughanmusic@dial.pipex.com
*Contact* Denis Vaughan

*Roster includes: Chaka Khan, Johnny Cash, Chuck Berry, Run D.M.C., Take Six, Rose Royce, Gipsy Kings, 10 c.c., Petula Clark*

## Dennis Heaney Promotions

Whitehall
Ashgrove Rd
Newry
Co Down
BT34 1QN
**T** 028 3026 8658   **F** 028 3026 66673
**E** dheaney@hotmail.com   **W** susanmccann.com
*Director* Dennis Heaney

*Main Artist: Susan McCann*

## Derek Boulton Management

76 Carlisle Mansions
Carlisle Place
London
SW1P 1HZ
**T** 020 7828 6533   **F** 020 7828 1271
*Contact* Derek Boulton

## Deutsch-Englische Freundschaft

31 Ansleigh Place
London
W11 4BW
**T** 020 7328 2922   **F** 020 7328 2322
**E** def2@globalnet.co.uk
*Contact* Eric Harle

## Diamond Sounds Music Management

The Fox And Punchbowl
Burfield Rd
Old Windsor
Berks
SL4 2RD
**T** 01753 855420   **F** as telephone
**E** samueldsm@aol.com
*Contact* Julie Samuel

**Direct Heat Management**
PO Box 1345
Worthing
West Sussex
BN14 7FB
T 01903 202426    F 01903 202426
E management@happyvibes.co.uk
w happyvibes.co.uk
*Contact* Mike Pailthorpe

*Specializing in dance, house, disco, garage, R&B and hiphop*
*Roster includes Geri Blam, Shelley, The Feel Foundation*

**Diverse Media Management (DMM)**
PO Box 3
South Croydon
Surrey
CR2 0YW
T 0707 123 3333    E dmm@diverse-media.com

*DMM also stands for Dance Music Management, the company's speciality*
*Also publishing and record label*

**Divine Management**
1 Cowcross St
London
EC1M 6DR
T 020 7490 7271    F 020 7490 7273
E divine@dial.pipex.com
*Contact* Natalie de Pace

**DJT**
PO Box 229
Sheffield
South Yorkshire
S1 1LY
T 0114 250 9775    F 0114 258 3164
E dtaylor@djtmanagement.freeserve.co.uk
*Director* David Taylor

*Manage Babybird*

**Doug Smith Associates**
PO Box 1151
London
W3 8ZJ
T 020 8993 8436    F 020 8896 1778

E doug (or eve)@dougsmithassociates.com
w dougsmithassociates.com
*Partners* Eve Carr and Doug Smith

**Dream Of Oswald**
Park House
Warren Row
Berkshire
RG10 8QS
T 07071 223951    F 07071 223952
*Contact* Ginni Hogarth

**Dreamscape**
30 Fitzjohns Avenue
London
NW3 5NB
T 010 7431 8060/07961 732239    F 010 7289 8883
E dreamscape25@hotmail.com
*Managing Director* Adam C Lamb

**Driven Music Management**
11 Clanricarde Gardens
London
W2 4JJ
T 020 7604 4928    F as telephone
E ross@drivenmusic.net
*Contact* Ross Foster

**Duty Free Artist Management**
63b Clerkenwell Rd
London
EC1M 5PT
T 020 7250 3409    F 020 7250 1046
E dj@dutyfreerecordings.co.uk
*Contact* Dale Thompson

**DV8 Media & Entertainment Ltd**
228 Canalot Studios
222 Kensal Rd
London
W10 5BN
T 020 8960 4030    F 020 8960 4095
E info@dv8media.net    w dv8media.net
*Contact* Danny Viala

## Easy Street Management

15 Grand Union Crescent
London
E8 4TR
**T** 020 7684 6044/07836 642652    **F** as first telephone
*Managing Director* Johnny Mac

## Eclectic Management

96 College Rd
London
NW10 5HL
**T** 020 8960 0086/07973 714923    **F** as first telephone
**E** ncairncross@mistral.co.uk
**W** mistral.co.uk/ncairncross/first.htm
*Contact* Nicola Cairncross

## Eclipse-PJM

41 Pullman Court
London
SW2 4ST
**T** 020 8671 5365/07798 651691
**F** as first telephone    **E** eclipse-pjm@btinternet.com
*Managing Director* Paul Johnson

## EG Management Ltd

61a Kings Rd
London
SW3 4NT
**T** 020 7730 2162    **F** 020 7730 1330
**E** sam.alder@egmusic.demon.co.uk
*Contact* Sam Alder

## EGO Management

36 Boughton Hall Drive
Chester
CH3 5QQ
**T** 01244 341295
*Managing Director* Neil Evington

## ELA Management

'Argentum'
2 Queen Caroline St
London
W6 9DX
**T** 020 8323 8014    **F** 020 8323 8080
*Contact* John Giacobbi

## EMAN8 Management

The Bomb
45 Bridlesmith Gate
Nottingham
NG1 2GN
**T** 0115 950 5553    **F** 0115 950 5554
**E** emma@emna8.com
*Contact* Emma-Clare Davies

*Also at 1 Ravens Court, 129 Marlborough Rd,*
*London,*
*N22 4NL.*
**T** *020 8889 1802*    **F** *020 8889 1802*
**E** *chris@eman8.com*
*Contact* Chris Organ

## Emkay Entertainments

Nobel House
Regent Centre
Blackness Rd
Linlithgow
Lothian
EH49 7HU
**T** 01506 845555    **F** 01506 845566
*Proprietor* Mike Kean

## Empire Management

3 Greek St
London
W1V 5LA
**T** 020 7529 9840    **F** 020 7287 4682
**E** empire@psilink.co.uk
*Contact* Neale Easterby or Richard Ramse

## ESP Music Management

83 Lilac Avenue
Framwellgate Moor
Durham
DH1 5JD
**T** 0191 384 4637    **F** 0191 234 2496
**E** jfinni5330@aol.com
*Contact* Jon Finnigan

## Essential Artistes Management

Dance Attic Studios
368 North End Rd
London
SW6 1LY
**T** 020 7385 2460/07958 900332    **F** 020 7610 0995
**E** essltd@aol.com
*Contact* Alex Oram

**ESSP**
The Sound House
PO Box 37b
Molesey
Surrey
KT8 2YR
**T** 020 8979 9997    **F** as telephone
*Contact* Dave Tuffnell

**ETC Management**
37 Buspace Studios
Conlan St
London
W10 5AP
**T** 020 8969 1600    **E** etcoosmr@aol.com
*Managing Director* Nigel Templeman

**Etude Promotions**
Horseshoe Business Park
Upper Lye Lane
Bricket Wood
St Albans
Herts
AL5 3TA
**T** 01923 893333    **F** 01923 894911
**E** celticmoon@skynow.co.uk
*Director* Joe Palmer

**European Arts & Media**
Administrator's office
Avenue House
St. Julian's Avenue
St. Peter Port
Guernsey
GY1 1WA
**T** 01481 716318
*Contact* John M Glauser

**Excellent Management**
50a Waldron Rd
London
SW18 3TD
**T** 020 8947 2224    **F** 020 8945 6545
**E** mark.modernwood@virgin.net
*Contact* Mark Wood

**Exclusive Management**
46 Chiltern Avenue
Macclesfield
Cheshire
SK11 8QW
**T** 01625 618114/07774 784254    **F** as first telephone
**E** pellis8426@aol.com
*Manager* Phil Ellis

**Expression Management**
3d Park Mews
213 Kilburn Lane
London
W10 4BQ
**T** 020 8960 5801    **F** 020 8960 5802
**E** expression@dial.pipex.com
*Contact* Vicki Lanes

**F&G Management**
Unit A105
326 Kensal Rd
London
W10 5BZ
**T** 020 8964 1917    **F** 020 8960 9971
**E** fgmanagement@hotmail.com
*Contact* Gavino Prunas or Roisin Potter

**Face Two Face Promotions & Management**
56 Oswald St
Glasgow
G1 4PL
**T** 0141 221 7871    **F** 0141 221 7875
*Contact* Sally Franklin

**Farguard Ltd**
21 Broughton Rd
Banbury
Oxon
OX16 9QB
**T** 01295 264436    **F** 01295 266411
**E** farguard@dial.pipex.com

*Hard rock and heavy metal specialists*

**Fat Cat Management**
P.O. Box 3400
Brighton
BN1 4WG
**T** 020 7716 3416    **F** 020 7716 3401

**E** info@fat-cat.co.uk
*Contacts*: Dave Cawley, Alex Knight

### FBI
Routenburn House
Routenburn Rd
Largs
Strathclyde
KA30 8SQ
**T** 01475 673392/0795 729 2054
**F** as first telephone    **E** wbrown8152@aol.com
*Contact* Willie Brown

### Feedback Communications
The Court
Long Sutton
Hook
Hampshire
RG29 1TA
**T** 01256 862865    **F** 01256 862182
**E** internet@crapola.com    **W** crapola.com
*Contact* Keir Jens-Smith

### Firebird Music
Kyrle House Studios
Edde Cross St
Ross-on-Wye
Herefordshire
HR9 7BZ
**T** 01989 562336    **F** 01989 566337
**E** pmartin@firebirdmusic.com    **W** firebird.com
*Chief Executive Officer* Peter Martin

*Principally production company/studio with own
label, management and pr/promo/design
Eurasian fusion, pop, r&b, dance*

### Firebrand Management
Suite 1.3
12 Rickett St
London
SW6 1RU
**T** 020 7381 2375/07885 282165    **F** 020 7386 5528
**E** firebrand@globalnet.co.uk
*Contact* Mark Vernon

*Artists and producers managed include John Cale, B
J Cole, Rob Ellis, Bobby Valentino and Dimitri
Tikovoi*

### Firehouse Communications & Promotions
Second Floor
Mercantile Chambers
53 Bothwell St
Glasgow
G2 6TS
**T** 0141 249 9888/07797 0392188    **F** 0141 249 9890
**E** louise@firehorse-agency.demon.co.uk
**W** urbanvibes.co.uk/firehorse

### First Avenue Management
The Courtyard
42 Colwith Rd
London
W6 9EY
**T** 020 8741 1419    **F** 020 8741 3289
**E** oliver@first-avenue.co.uk    **W** firstavenue.net
*Contact* Oliver Smallman

*Also label First Avenue Records and publishing First
Avenue Music (same contact details)*

### First Column Management Ltd
The Metway
55 Canning St
Brighton
East Sussex
BN2 2EF
**T** 01273 688359    **F** 01273 624884
**E** fcm@btinternet.com
*Managing Director* Phil Nelson

*Roster includes The Levellers, The 45s and The Milk
and Honey Band*

### First Move Entertainments Ltd
137 Shooters Hill Rd
London
SE3 8UQ
**T** 020 8305 2077    **F** 020 8853 3323
**E** firstmoves@aol.com
*Contact* Bruce MacIlwaine

### First Step Management
96 George St
Mansfield
Notts
NG19 6SB
**T** 01623 642778    **F** as telephone
**E** first.step@talk21.com    **W** theearlofsound.co.uk

*Contact* David Butcher

*Also First Step Records (same contact details)*

## First Time Management
Sovereign House
12 Trewartha Rd
Praa Sands
Penzance
Cornwall
TR20 9ST
**T** 01736 762826/07721 449477    **F** 01736 763328
**E** panamus@aol.com    **W** songwriters-guild.co.uk
*Managing Director* Roderick G Jones

## Firstars
1 Water Lane
London
NW1 8NZ
**T** 020 7267 1101    **F** 020 7267 7071/7466
*Contact* Steve Tannett

## Flamencovision
PO Box 508
London
N3 3SY
**T** 020 8346 4500    **F** 020 8346 2488
**E** hvmartin@dircon.co.uk    **W** flamencovision.com

## Flamingo Record Management
Toad House
Imberhorne Lane
East Grinstead
West Sussex
RH19 1QY
**T** 01342 317943    **F** as telephone
**E** ed@badgerflamingoanimation.com
**W** badgerflamingoanimation.com
*Managing Director* Ed Palmieri

*Roster: The Ets, Nose, Blush*

## Flashchoice
46 Broomwood Rd
London
SW11 6HT
**T** 020 7228 1161    **F** 020 7350 1983
*Contact* Griff Fender

## Flick Productions
PO Box 888
Penzance
Cornwall
TR20 8ZP
**T** 01736 788798    **F** 01736 787898
**E** info@flickpro.demon.co.uk
*Contact* Mark Shaw

*Also promotion and agency*

## Float Your Boat Management
5 Ralphs Retreat
Hazlemere
High Wycombe
Bucks
HP15 7DU
**T** 07958 415784    **E** melinda@zore.com
*Contact* Melinda Lawler

## Fluke
Pan West
326 Kensal Rd
London
W10 5BZ
**T** 020 8960 2252    **F** 020 8960 3227
**E** julian@fluke.demon.co.uk
*Manager* Julian Nugent

## Flying Music Co Ltd
FM House
110 Clarendon Rd
London
W11 2HR
**T** 020 7221 7799    **F** 020 7221 5016
**E** info@flyingmusic.com    **W** flyingmusic.com
*Contacts* Derek Nicol, Paul Walden

## Formidable Management
4th Floor, 40 Langham St
London
W1W 7AS
**T** 020 7323 4410    **F** 020 7323 4180
**E** carl@formidable-mgmt.com
*Contact* Carl Marcantonio

**Fortunes Fading Music**
Pepys Court
84 The Chase
London
SW4 0NF
T 020 7720 7266   F 020 7720 7255
E info@media.ftech.co.uk
*Contact* Peter Pritchard

**Frank McAweaney**
41 Dovercourt Rd
London
SE22 8SS
T 020 8693 8426   F 020 8693 8802
*Contact* Frank McAweaney

**Freedom Management**
218 Canalot Studios
222 Kensal Rd
London
W10 5BN
T 020 8960 443/01273 748599
F 020 8960 9889/01273 748599
E freedom@frdm.demon.co.uk
*Contact* Graham Hicks
*Directors* Martyn Barter, Keith Webb

*Management for artists, producers and writers*
*Roster includes Future Sound of London, Luca*
*Santucci, Eliot Kennedy, Tim Lever, Mike Percy,*
*Anthony Gorry, Jewels & Stone*

**Freedom Songs**
PO Box 272
London
N20 0BY
T 020 8368 0340   F 020 8361 3370
E john@jt-management.demon.co.uk
*Managing Director* John Taylor

**Freeway Music Group**
Federation House
85–87 Wellington St
Luton
Bedfordshire
LU1 5AF
T 01582 457503   F 01582 412215

**Fresh Management**
Unit 4
Grand Union Centre
West Row
London
W10 5AS
T 020 7221 9300   F 020 7221 0088
*Director* Dave Morgan

**Freshwater Management**
PO Box 54
Northaw
Herts
EN6 4PY
T 01707 664141   F 01707 661431
E fresh@fresh2000.freeserve.co.uk
*Contact* Brian Freshwater

**Friars Management Ltd**
33 Alexander Rd
Aylesbury
Bucks
HP20 2NR
T 01296 434731   F 01296 422530
E davidayles@aol.com
*Contact* David R Stopps

**Fruit**
The Saga Centre
326 Kensal Rd
London
W10 5BZ
T 020 8964 8448   F 020 8964 0323
E fruit.management@virgin.net
*Contact* Caroline Killoury

*Bands and producers managed include Portishead,*
*The Wiseguys, Mekon, 23 Skidoo and Nick Faber*

**Fume Productions Ltd**
Unit 53
Canalot Studios
222 Kensal Studios
London
W10 5BN
T 020 8964 5441   F 020 8964 3593
E fumemusic@aol.com
*Contact* Seamus Morley

## Fundamental Ltd
1 Davenport Mews
London
W12 8NG
T 020 8354 4900   F 020 8354 4901
E info@fundamental.co.uk   W fundamental.co.uk
*Contact* Tim Prior

## Fuse
Unit 220
Canalot Studios
222 Kensal Rd
London
W10 5BN
T 020 8964 4778   F 020 8968 4861
E fuse@sol.co.uk
*Contact* John MacLennan

## Future Management
PO Box 183
Chelmsford
Essex
CM2 9XN
T 01245 601910   F 01245 601048
E futuremgt@aol.com
W futuremanagement.co.uk
*Contact* Joe Ferrari

## Future Music
77 Bronson Rd
London
SW20 8DZ
T 020 8944 1868/020 8876 9966   F 020 8876 9336
E reuben@macxperts.co.uk
*Contact* Reuben Pearson

## Future Studios International
PO Box 10
London
N1 3RJ
T 020 7241 2183   F 020 7241 6233
*Contact* Michelle L Goldberg

## Futurescope Management Ltd
10 Bourlet Close
London
W1P 7PJ
T 020 7436 5633   F 020 7436 5607
E nick@futurescope.net
*Managing Director* Nick East

## Gailforce Management Ltd
24 Ives St
London
SW3 2ND
T 020 7584 5977   F 020 7838 0351
E gail@gailforcemanagement.co.uk
*Managing Director* Gail Colson

*Roster past and present, guided by Gail Colson's eclectic tastes, includes Peter Hammill, Peter Gabriel, Morrissey, Terrence Trent D'Arby, Nigel Kennedy and The Pretenders*

## Game Records (UK)
PO Box 11583
London
W13 0WP
T 020 8357 2337/0132 731 2505
F 020 8566 7215/0132 731 2545
E info@badhabitsent-group.com
W badhabitsent-group.com
*Contact* John Rushton

## Garry Brown Associates (Int)
27 Downs Side
Cheam
Surrey
SM2 7EH
T 020 8643 3991/020 8643 8375   F 020 8770 7241
E gbaltd@compuserve.com
*Managing Director* Garry Brown

## Gb2 Management
Merryhay House
Ilton Business Park
Ilton
Ilminster
Somerset
TA19 9DU
T 01460 554550   F 01460 53395
E gbsquared@demon.co.uk
*Contact* Ronnie Gleeson

## GBH Management
Unit 6
Frobisher House
89 Lillie Rd
London
SW6N 1UD
T 020 7610 2112   F 020 7610 2262
*Contact* Richard Holley

## Gem Organisation
Suite 309
Canalot Studios
222 Kensal Rd
London
W10 5BN
**T** 020 7565 9001   **F** 020 7565 9002
**E** gemorg@originalgem.demon.co.uk
*Contact* D Gorbun

## Gems
Firs Cottage
5 Firs Close
London
SE23 1BB
**T** 020 8291 7052   **F** 020 8699 2279
**E** genica.pigfish@virgin.net
*Managing Director* Nicky Howard-Kemp

## Generation Management
PO Box 6328
London
N2 0UN
**T** 020 8444 9841   **F** 020 8442 1973
**E** woolfman@compuserve.com
*Contact* Damian Baetens

## Genius Management
89a High Rd
London
N22 6BB
**T** 020 8881 6969   **F** 020 8888 1685
**E** genius@brmmusic.com   **W** brmmusic.com
*Contact* Bruce Ruffin or Phillip Rose

## Georgina Ivor Associates (Classical)
28 Old Devonshire Rd
London
SW12 9RB
**T** 020 8673 7179   **F** 020 8675 8058
**E** givor@aol.com   **W** members.aol.com/givor
*Contact* Georgina Ivor

*Small international artist agency dealing solely with classical musicians*

## Gerry Bron Management
17 Priory Rd
London
NW6 4NN
**T** 020 7209 2766   **F** 020 7813 2766
**E** gerrybron@easynet.co.uk   **W** gerrybron.com
*Contact* Gerry Bron

## Global Talent Management
97 Harley St
London
W1N 1DF
**T** 020 7487 4877   **F** 020 7487 5600
**E** email@globaltalentgroup.com
**W** globaltalentgroup.com
*Directors* David Forecast, Ashley Tabor

## Globeshine
101 Chamberlayne Rd
London
NW10 3ND
**T** 020 8960 8466   **F** 020 8968 5892
**E** b.hallin@virgin.net
*Managing Director* Brian Hallin

## Gloucester Entertainment Agency
Little Haven
Elmore Lane
Quedgeley
Gloucestershire
GL2 3NW
**T** 01452 721966   **F** 01452 722489
*Managing Director* Norman R Broady

## Goldpush Management Ltd
29 Beethoven St
London
W10 4LJ
**T** 020 8969 0299/07785 778342   **F** 020 8968 1047
**E** razgold@btinternet.com
*Contact* Raz Gold

## GR Management
974 Pollokshaws Rd
Shawlands
Glasgow
Strathclyde
G41 2HA
**T** 0141 632 1111   **F** 0141 649 0042

**E** gr@dial.pipex.com
*Admin Manager* Alan Connell

## Graham Stokes Music Ltd
10 Bourlet Close
London
W1P 7PJ
**T** 020 7436 4367   **F** 020 7637 1620
**E** gbstokes@aol.com
*Contact* Graham Stokes

## Grapedime Music
28 Hurst Crescent
Barrowby
Grantham
Lincs
NG32 1TE
**T** 01476 560241   **F** as telephone
**E** grapedime@pjbray.globalnet.co.uk

*Roster: Delivered, Paradox, Emanon, Foxglove*
*See also Grapedime Music (publishing)*

## Grosvenor Productions
Midlands & Western Office
The Limes
Brockley
Bristol
BS19 3BB
**T** 01275 463222   **F** 01275 462252
*Contact* Gordon Poole

## Guru Management
512 London Rd
Sheffield
South Yorkshire
S2 4HP
**T** 0114 255 3586   **F** 0114 255 1434
**E** rlsb@globalnet.co.uk
*Contact* Jak Lewis

## Hal Carter Organization
101 Hazelwood Lane
London
N13 5HQ
**T** 020 8886 2801   **F** 020 8882 7380
**E** mal.hco@ic24.net
*General Manager* Hal Carter

## Hall Or Nothing Management
3 Greek St
London
W1D 4DA
**T** 020 7439 3777   **F** 020 7439 3800
**E** martin (or lizzie)@hallornothing.com
**w** hallornothing.com
*Contact* Martin Hall

## Halo Management
88 Church Lane
London
N2 0TB
**T** 020 8444 0049   **F** 020 8883 5453
*Contact* Mike Maslen

*Roster includes Medicine Hat, Slinky Minx*

## Handle Artists Management Ltd
4 Gees Court
London
W1U 1JD
**T** 020 7569 9399   **F** 020 7569 9388
**E** david@handle-artists.co.uk
*Contact* David Walker

*Management for Status Quo and Barclay James Harvest*

## Harmony Entertainment
9 Shorland Oaks
Warfield
Berkshire
RG42 2JZ
**T** 020 8751 6060
*Managing Director* MDB Dixon

## Harold Holt
31 Sinclair Rd
London
W14 0NS
**T** 020 7603 4600   **F** 020 7603 0019
**E** info@holt.co.uk   **w** ds.dial.pipex.com/silvius/holt/
*Marketing Manager* Jonathan Fleming

*Classical artists only*

## Harrison Curtis Solicitors
40 Great Portland St
London
W1N 5AH
T 020 7637 3333   F 020 7637 3334
E mail@harrisoncurtis.co.uk
*Contact* Nora Mullally

## Harry Monk Ltd
37 Farringdon Rd
London
EC1M 3JB
T 020 7691 0088   F 020 7691 0081
E john@harrymonk.net   w harrymonk.net
*Contact* John Carver

## Harvey Lisberg Associates
Kennedy House
31 Stamford St
Altrincham
Cheshire
WA14 1ES
T 0161 941 4560   F 0161 941 4199
E harveylisberg@aol.com
*Contact* Harvey Lisberg

## Head On Management Ltd
1st Floor
16 Chalk Farm Rd
London
NW1 8AG
T 020 7267 9123   F 020 7267 9122
E gun@head-on.demon.co.uk
*Contact* Steve Baker

## Headquarters Publicity
4 The Hamlet
The Bank
Marlcliff
Bidford on Avon
Warwickshire
B50 4NT
T 01789 778482   F as telephone
E johntully@thehamlet6.freeserve.co.uk
*Managing Director* Mr J Tully

*NB: Lookalike bands*

## Headrow Management
Unit 1
Union Bridge Mill
Roker Lane
Pudsey
West Yorkshire
LS28 9LE
T 0113 255 9905   F 0113 255 9903
*Contact* Steve Mulhaire

## Heavenly Management
47 Frith St
London
W1V 5TE
T 020 7494 2998   F 020 7437 3317
E email@heavenlymanagement.com
w heavenlymanagement.com
*Contact* Martin Kelly or Andrew Walsh

*Roster: Saint Etienne, Starsailor, Andrew Weatherall*

## Henderson Management
51 Promenade North
Cleveleys
Blackpool
Lancashire
FY5 1LN
T 01253 863386/07770 588252   F 01253 867799
E agents@henderson-management.co.uk
w henderson-management.co.uk
*Contact* John Henderson

## Holier Than Thou
Norton Hall
Broadmarston Lane
Mickleton
Gloucestershire
GL55 6SQ
T 01386 438931   F 01386 438847
E httrecord@aol.com
w holierthanhourecords.com
*Director* David Begg

*Also label (same contact details)*

## Holland-Ford's
103 Lydyett Lane
Barnton
Northwich
Cheshire
CW8 4JT

**T** 01606 76960
*Managing Director* Bob Holland-Ford

## HQ
PO Box 37
Ashbourne
Derbyshire
DE6 2ZU
**T** 024 7641 0388/07711 817475
**F** 020 7641 6615/024 7633 0193
*Contact* Roger Lomas

## Hutt Russell Organisation
PO Box 64
Cirencester
Gloucestershire
GL7 5YD
**T** 01285 644622    **F** 01285 642291
**E** shows@huttrussellorg.com
**w** huttrussellorg.com
*Directors* Steven Hutt and Dudley Russell

## I&T Management
4a Murderdean Rd
Newtongrange
Edinburgh
Lothian
EH22 4PD
**T** 0131 654 0888    **F** as telephone
**E** appalusi@hotmail.com
*Contact* Ian Robertson, Tony Cochrane

## Ian Carlile Management
70 Cross Oak Rd
Berkhamstead
Herts
HP4 3HZ
**T** 01422 877485    **F** 01422 873019
**E** icmanagement@compuserve.com
*Contact* Ian Carlile

## Ian Grant Management
PO Box 107
South Godstone
Redhill
Surrey
RH9 8YS
**T** 01342 892074/01342 892178    **F** 01342 893411
**E** ig@igma.demon.co.uk    **w** bigcountry.co.uk
*Managing Director* Ian Grant

## ICE Group
3 St Andrews St
Lincoln
Lincolnshire
LN5 7NE
**T** 01522 539883    **F** 01522 528964
*Managing Director* Steve Hawkins

## Idle Hands
PO Box 129
Stevenage
Hertfordshire
SG1 2DN
**T** 01438 311633/340244    **F** 01438 724777
**E** pwa1734347@aol.com
*Contact* Paul Walker

## IE Music Ltd
111 Frithville Gardens
London
W12 7JG
**T** 020 8600 3400    **F** 020 8600 3401
**E** info@iemusic.co.uk
*Contact* David Enthoven

*Roster: Robbie Williams, Horrace Andy, One Giant
Leap, Archive, Sia*

## Ignition Management
54 Linhope St
London
NW1 6HL
**T** 020 7298 6000    **F** 020 7258 0962
**E** mail@ignition-man.co.uk

## Immoral Management
PO Box 2643
Reading
Berkshire
RG5 4GF
**T** 0118 969 9269    **F** 0118 969 9264
**E** jpsproductions@msn.com
*Contact* John Saunderson

## In Demand Management
Top Floor
233 Cowgate
Edinburgh
EH1 1JQ
**T** 0131 225 5062    **F** 0131 622 7358

E craigw@indemand.co.uk    w indemand.co.uk
*Director* Craig Wood

### Inner City Unit
Cadillac Ranch
Pencraig Uchaf
Llanwinio
Cwm Bach
Whitland
Dyfed
SA34 0DT
T 01994 484466    F 01994 484294
*Manager* C Augustino

### Instinct Management
10 Nightingale Lane
London
SW12 8TB
T 020 7240 1909/020 8675 9233    F 020 7240 1992
E geoff@instinct-mgt.demon.co.uk
*Director* Geoff Smith

### Interactive PSL
54 Ufton Rd
London
N1 4HH
T 020 7241 1144    F 020 7241 1244
*Contact* John Fairs

### Interceptor Enterprises
1st Floor
98 White Lion St
London
N1 9PF
T 020 7278 8001    F 020 7713 6298
E info@interceptor.co.uk
*Contact* Charlie Charlton

*Current roster: Fifth Amendment, Mandalay, Suede
Demos of great songs welcome*

### International Artistes Ltd
Mezzanine Floor
235 Regent St
London
W1R 8AX
T 020 7439 8401/0161 833 9838
F 020 7409 2070/0161 832 7480
E intartltd@aol.com    w ial.com
*Managing Director* Mr S Littlewood

*Also at: 2nd Floor, Television House, 10–12 Mount
Street, Manchester, M2 5FA*

### International Management Division Ltd
16 The Talina Centre
Bagleys Lane
London
SW6 2BW
T 020 7371 0995    F 020 7371 0993
E rachel@imd.demon.co.uk    w imd-info.com
*Managing Director* Rachel Birchwood-Gordon

*NB: DJ management*

### Interzone Management
Interzone House
74–77 Magdalen Rd
Oxford
OX4 1RE
T 01865 205600    F 01865 205700
E info@rotator.co.uk    w rotator.co.uk
*Contact* Richard Cotton

*International artist management*

### IRC2 London Ltd
2nd Floor, 12 Mercer St
London
WC2H 9QD
T 020 7240 8848    F 020 7240 8864
E irc2london@aol.com
*Contact* Lenny Zakatek

### Irene Knight
10 Clatterfield Gardens
Westcliff-on-Sea
Essex
SS0 0AX
T 01702 341983

### Ishka Management
14 Church St
Twickenham
Middx
TW1 3NJ
T 020 8744 2777/07740 643015    F 020 8891 1895
E ishka@dircon.co.uk
*Contact* Nina Jackson

*NB: producer management*

*Producers managed: Tom Rixton, Robin Guthrie, Simon Raymonde, Lincoln Fong, Kenny Paterson, Nigel Luby, Paul 'PK' Kendall, Joby Talbot (arranger), Mitsuo Tate*

## IZ Management
60 Beethoven St
London
W10 4LG
**T** 020 8964 0464   **F** 020 8969 5231
**E** izm@dircon.co.uk
*Director* John Wadlow

## J Management
55 Loudoun Rd
London
NW8 0DL
**T** 020 7604 3633   **F** 020 7604 3639
**E** j@jamjah.co.uk
*Contact* John Arnison

## Jackie Davidson Management
The Business Village
Gardiner House
3–9 Broomhill Rd
London
SW18 4JQ
**T** 020 8870 8744   **F** 020 8874 1578
**E** jackiedvn@aol.com/octaviag@aol.com
**W** hardzone.co.uk
*Contacts*: Jackie Davidson and Octavia Green

*Roster includes singer/songwriter Alistair Tennant (Westlife, Boyzone etc), songwriter Wayne Hector (eg Westlife's 'Flying Without Wings'), writer/producer Mickey P*

## Jam X Management
22a Lambolle Place
London
NW3 4PG
**T** 020 7813 0833   **F** 020 7209 0019
**E** jamx@easynet.co.uk
*Directors* Julian Able and Diid Osman

*Roster includes Contempo, Hell Is For Heroes, Stingray*

## Jamdown Ltd
Research House
Fraser Rd
Perivale
Middlesex
UB6 7AQ
**T** 020 8930 1070   **F** 020 8930 1073
**E** jamdownmusic@compuserve.com
*Managing Director* Othman Mukhlis

*Roster includes John Themis (writer for S Club 7, Boy George etc), Andy Morris (writer/producer for Lisa Stansfield, Dionne Warwick)*

## Jamie Spencer
57d Hatton Garden
London
EC1N 2HP
**T** 020 7831 3111   **F** 020 7831 9991
**E** jamie@eastcentralone.com
*Contact* Jo Donnelly

## JBS Management
Apartment 11
Dean Meadow
Newton-le-Willows
Lancs
WA12 9PX
**T** 01925 291159/07951 429434   **F** as first telephone
**E** jayuk3@hotmail.com
*Contact* John Sheffield

*Specialists in pop chart artists with full consultant service for dynamic up-and-coming acts aimed at the teen market*

## JC Music
5 Heathfield Gardens
London
W4 4JU
**T** 020 8995 0989   **F** 020 8995 0878
**E** jcmusic@dial.pipex.com
*Managing Director* John Campbell

## JDS Management
PO Box 9846
London
W13 9WR
*Contact* John de Souza

**Jef Hanlon Management Ltd**
1 York St
London
W1V 6PA
T 020 7487 2558    F 020 7487 2584
E jhanlon@agents-uk.com
*Contact* Jef Hanlon

**Jelly Deal Music**
21 Lockwood Crescent
Woodingdean
Brighton
East Sussex
BN2 6UH
T 01273 306825    F as telephone
*Contact* John Mogridge

**Jelly Street Music Ltd**
Chester Terrace
358 Chester Rd
Manchester
M16 9EZ
T 0161 872 6006    F 0161 872 6468
E kevkinsella@aol.com
*Managing Director* Kevin Patrick Kinsella

**Jellyset**
40 Riverview Gardens
London
SW13 8QZ
T 020 8563 0256    F 020 8563 0356
E mail@jellyset.demon.co.uk
*Contact* Abigail Lulham

**JFD Management**
Unit 9
Acklam Workshops
10 Acklam Rd
London
W10 5QZ
T 020 8968 7159    F 020 8960 0298
E jfdmanagement@pavilion.co.uk
*Contact* Ella Macpherson

**Jive Entertainment Services**
4 Pasteur Courtyard
Whittle Rd
Phoenix Parkway
Corby

Northants
NN17 3DD
T 01536 406406    F 01536 400082
*Managing Director* Dave Bartram

**JKM Management**
9 Richmond Rd
Lee-on-the-Solent
Hampshire
PO13 9NT
T 02392 525190/07775 511532    F 01625 619961
E jkm@musicchoice.co.uk

**Joe Bangay Enterprises**
River House
Riverwoods
Marlow
Buckinghamshire
SL7 1OU
T 01628 486193/07860 812529    F 01628 890239
E joebangay@joe-bangay.com    W joe-bangay.com
*Director* William Bangay

*Also Joe Bangay Photography (contact Joe Bangay, same details as above) specializing in photographing and styling bands and artists*

**Joe Brown Productions**
PO Box 272
London
N20 0BY
T 020 8368 0340    F 020 8361 3370
E john@jt-management.demon.co.uk
*Managing Director* John Taylor

**John Martin Promotions Ltd**
290 Hartfield Rd
London
SW19 3SG
T 020 8786 3620    F 020 8786 3621
*Contact* John Martin

**John Miles Organization**
Cadbury Camp Lane
Clapton-in-Gordano
Bristol
BS20 7SB
T 01275 854675/856770    F 01275 810186
*Managing Director* John Miles

## John Taylor Management

PO Box 272
London
N20 0BY
**T** 020 8368 0340    **F** 020 8361 3370
**E** john@jt-management.demon.co.uk
*Managing Director* John Taylor

## John Williams Management

PO Box 423
Chiselhurst
Kent
BR7 5TU
**T** 020 8295 3639    **F** 020 8295 3641
**E** jrwilliams@lineone.net
*Contact* John Williams

*Sole representative of Helen Shapiro and the 'Humph*
*'n' Helen' show with Humphrey Lyttelton, and agency*
*for Elaine Delmar, Craig Douglas and Terry Lightfoot*

## Jon Caine & Co

72 Tib St
Manchester
M4 1LG
**T** 0161 907 3602/07860 481041    **F** 0161 907 3604
**E** joncaine@aol.com

## Jon Sexton Management (JSM)

14 Lambton Place
London
W11 2SH
**T** 020 7482 4345/03706 15930    **F** 020 7482 4350
**E** copasetik1@aol.com    **w** copasetik.com
*Contact* Jon Sexton

## JPR Management

Unit 4 E&F
Westpoint
33–34 Warple Way
London
W3 0RG
**T** 020 8749 8874    **F** 020 8749 8774
**E** info@jprmanagement.co.uk
**w** jprmanagement.co.uk
*Contact* John Reid

## JPS Productions

PO Box 2643
Reading
Berks
RG5 4GF
**T** 0118 969 9269    **F** 0118 969 9264
**E** johnjpsuk@aol.com
*Contact* John Saunderson

## Jukes Productions

PO Box 13995
London
W9 2FL
**T** 020 7286 9532    **F** 020 7286 4739
**E** jukes@easynet.co.uk    **w** jukesproductions.co.uk
*Contact* Geoff Jukes or Amanda Hon

## Just Another Management Co

9 Gladwyn Rd
London
SW15 1JY
**T** 020 8780 5129    **F** 020 8788 1727
**E** justmusic@justmusic.co.uk    **w** justmusic.co.uk
*Director* John Benedict

## Justin Perry Management

PO Box 20242
London
NW1 7FL
**T** 020 7485 1113    **E** proofsongs@mailbox.xo.uk

## KAL Management

95 Gloucester Rd
Hampton
Middlesex
TW12 2UW
**T** 020 8783 0039    **F** 020 8979 6487
**E** kaplan222@aol.com    **w** kalmanagement.com

## Kamara Artist Management (UK)

81 Carlton Rd
Boston
Lincolnshire
PE21 8LH
**T** 07976 553624
*Contact* Chris Kamara

## Keith Harris Music
204 Courthouse Rd
Maidenhead
Berkshire
SL6 6HU
**T** 01628 674422  **F** 01628 631379
**E** keithharris1@compuserve.com
*Managing Director* Keith Harris

## Kevin King Management
16A Limetrees
Llangattock
Crickhowell
Powys
NP8 1LB
**T** 01873 810142  **F** 01973 811557  **E** silvergb@aol.com
*Contact* Kevin King

## Kickstart Management
10 Park House
140 Battersea Park Rd
London
SW11 4NB
**T** 020 7498 9696  **F** 020 7498 2064
**E** cms@cmsi.demon.co.uk
*Contact* Ken Middleton

*Genres: pop, dance, rock, country, etc*
*See also Kickstart Music (publishing)*

## Kinky Samosa Management
55 Albert St
Windsor
Berks
SL4 5BT
**T** 01753 771649  **E** steve@kinkysamosa.com
**W** kinkysamosa.com
*Contact* Steve Hughes

## Kitchenware Management
7 The Stables
St Thomas St
Newcastle upon Tyne
Tyne and Wear
NE1 4LE
**T** 0191 230 1970  **F** 0191 232 0262
**E** k&p@kware.demon.co.uk
*Managing Director* Keith Armstrong

*Lighthouse Family*
*(lighthousefamily.wildcardrecords.co.uk)*

*Prefab Sprout (prefabsprout.com)*

## KMO
Unit 7
39 Ivanhoe Rd
Liverpool
L17 8XF
**T** 0151 728 8905  **F** as telephone
**E** kmo7@btinternet.com
**W** geocities.com/emcsquareduk/
*Contact* Mick Moss

*No boy/girl band wannabees, shoe-gazers, stupid egos*
*Also record production company (same contact*
*details but use name Mix Moss)*

## KRT Productions
Hawkstone
Jacks Lane
Barton
Torquay
Devon
TQ2 8QX
**T** 01803 311534  **F** 01803 322152
*Contact* Kim Turner

## KSO Records
37 Trinity Rd
London
W2 8JJ
**T** 07956 120837
*Contact* Izzet al Hussein

## Kudos Management
Crown Studios
16–18 Crown Rd
Twickenham
Middlesex
TW1 3EE
**T** 020 8891 4233  **F** 020 8891 2339
**E** kudos@camino.co.uk
*Managing Director* Billy Budis

## Lakota Management
PO Box 4704
Ballsbridge
Dublin 4
Ireland
**T** 00 353 1 283 9071  **W** lakotarecords.com
*Contact* Conor Brooks

## Latin Arts Services

PO Box 14303
London
SE23 4SH
**T** 07000 472572   **F** as telephone
**E** latinarts@artquest.co.uk   **w** latinartsgroup.com

*Specialists in Latin-American entertainment, in a company that includes HMP (publishers), LAS Records UK (label), WAI World Artists Index (free-net index) and Mundo Graphics (graphic design)*

## Laurie Jay Enterprises

32 Willesden Lane
London
NW6 7ST
**T** 020 7625 0231   **F** 020 7372 5439
*Managing Director* Laurie Jay

## Leah Management

PO Box 54
Hyde
Cheshire
SK16 5JF
**T** 0161 339 5507/07973 724499   **F** 0870 164 1848
**E** jleah@siddibouard.demon.co.uk
*Contact* John Leah

## Leap Artist Management

33 Green Walk
London
NW4 2AL
**T** 020 8202 4120   **F** as telephone
**E** leap@gideonbenaim.com
*Contact* Gideon Benaim

## Lebor Artist Management & John Boy Productions

2 Kent House
96 Greencroft Gardens
London
NW6 3PH
**T** 020 7624 6167   **F** 020 7419 7920
*Contact* Jeremy Lebor

## Left Bank Organization

1st Floor, 13a Hillgate St
London
W8 7SP

**T** 020 7221 9050   **F** 020 7551 9060
**E** annickb@bank.com
*Contact* Lewis Kovac

## Legendary Artists

13 Ladbroke Walk
London
W11 3PW
**T** 020 7221 1522   **F** as telephone
*Contact* Eileen Treacy

## Lena Davis, John Bishop Associates

Cotton's Farmhouse
Whiston Rd
Cogenhoe
Northants
NN7 1NL
**T** 01604 891487   **F** 01604 890405
*Managing Director* Lena Davis

*Personal Management and PR*

## Les Hart (Southampton Entertainments)

1st Floor
225 High St
Eastleigh
Hants
SO50 5LX
**T** 023 8061 8311/023 8061 4889   **F** 023 8061 1090
*Contact* Rod Watts or Ian Hammond

*Specializing in bands, groups, DJs, cabarets*

## Liaison and Promotion Company

124 Great Portland St
London
W1N 5PG
**T** 020 7636 2345   **F** 020 7580 0045
**E** select.lp@blueprint.uk.com
*Director* Clifford Gee

## Lifetime Management

18 St George's Rd
St Margaret's
Twickenham
Middlesex
TW1 1QR
**T** 020 8892 4810   **F** 020 8744 0413
*Contact* Graeme Perkins

## Like No Other Music Ltd

PO Box 21335
London
WC2H 8QH
**T** 020 7379 0999   **F** 020 7379 3399
**E** mark@like-no-other.com   **W** like-no-other.com
*Contact* Mark Lambert-Stewart

## Line-Up PMC

9a Tankerville Place
Newcastle-upon-Tyne
Tyne and Wear
NE22 3AT
**T** 0191 281 6449   **F** 0191 212 0913
**E** c.a.murtagh@btinternet.com
**W** on-line-records.co.uk
*Managing Director* Christopher Murtagh

*Promotions, management, festivals, events, stadiums, audio/visual production and record label*

## Lintern Rees Organization

Unit 2, The Quarry
Kewstoke Rd
Worle
Weston-Super-Mare
BS22 9LS
**T** 01934 521222/521333
**E** davidrees@liveentertainments.com
**W** liveentertainments.com
*Contact* David Rees or Ken Lintern

*A package is useful in the first instance (picture, tape or CD, biography, video) to assess suitability*

## Lionheart Music

20 Grasmere Avenue
London
SW15 3RB
**T** 020 8546 4047   **F** 020 8546 0468
*Contact* Richard Gillinson

## Little Red Roster

PO Box 727
High Wycombe
Bucks
HP13 5ZB
**T** 01494 463766   **F** 01494 442667
*Contact* Simon Redgate

## Lock

The Coachhouse
Mansion Farm
Liverton Hill
Sandway
Maidstone
Kent
ME17 2NJ
**T** 01622 8583000   **F** as telephone
**E** info@eddielock.com
*Managing Director* Eddie Lock

*Specialists in dance music (eg Africka Bambaataa vs Carpe Diem's 'Got To Get Up', Santos' 'Camels'*

## LOE Entertainment

LOE House
159 Broadhurst Gardens
London
NW6 3AU
**T** 020 7328 6100   **F** 020 7624 6384
**E** mags@loe.demon.co.uk
*Creative Manager* Madeleine Swift

## Long Term Management

Suite B
2 Tunstall Rd
London
SW9 8DA
**T** 020 7733 5400   **F** 020 7734 4449
**E** paulette@longterm.freeserve.co.uk
*Contact* Paulette Long

## Loose

PO Box 67
Runcorn
Cheshire
WA7 4NL
**T** 01928 566261   **E** jaki.florek@virgin.com
*Contact* Jaki Florek

## Loose Management

Unit 205
5–10 Eastman Rd
London
W3 7YG
**T** 020 8749 9330   **F** 020 8749 2230
**E** tom@loosemusic.com
*Contact* Tom Bridgewater

## Louis Walsh Management

24 Courtney House
Appian Way
Dublin 6
Ireland
**T** 00 353 1 668 0309/0902   **F** 00 353 1 668 0721
**E** louiewalsh@eircom.net
*Contact* Louis Walsh

*Represents Westlife, Ronan Keating, Samantha Mumba, Omero Mumba, Lulu.*

## Luna Park Management

Suffolk House
1–8 Whitefield Place
London
W1P 5SF
**T** 020 7813 5555   **F** 020 7813 4567
**E** mail@lunarpark.co.uk
*Contact* Russell Vaught

## M2 Management

1 Parkway
London
NW1 7PH
**T** 020 7916 7970   **F** 020 7916 7958
*Contact* Mac or Steve

## Mainstreet Management

Studio 733
The Big Peg
120 Vyse St
Birmingham
B18 6NF
**T** 0121 688 5885   **F** 0121 688 4884
**E** trelogg@aol.com

## Major Entertainments

6c Standbridge Lane
Sandal
Wakefield
West Yorkshire
WF2 7DY
**T** 01924 254350   **F** 01924 259414
*Managing Director* Toby Major

## Major Players International

87 Bromley Common
Bromley
Kent
BR2 9RN
**T** 020 8289 1277   **F** 020 8289 0887
*Contact* Dave Hunt

## Make Music Management

PO Box 27170
London
W12 7WX
**T** 020 8746 2796/07956 386767   **w** makemusic.com
*Contact* Dominic Brownlow

*Mainly deals in alternative, guitar music, indie*

## Making Waves

45 Underwood St
London
N1 7LG
**T** 020 7490 0944   **F** 020 7490 1026
**E** info@makingwaves.co.uk
*Contact* Matt Williams

## Mal Spence Management

Cherry Tree Lodge
Copmanthorpe
York
YO23 3SH
**T** 01904 703764   **F** 01904 702312
**E** (name)@demon.co.uk
**w** thedandys.demon.co.uk
*Contact* Mal Spence or Richard Oaten

## Malcolm Feld Agency

Malina House
Sandforth Rd
Liverpool
Merseyside
L12 1JY
**T** 0151 259 6565   **F** 0151 259 5006
**E** malcolm@malcolmfeld.co.uk
**w** malcolmfeld.co.uk
*Managing Director* Malcolm Feld

*Management, agency, promotions, production*

## Mama Knows Best Management

530 Fulham Rd
London
SW6 5NR
T 020 7731 3555   E jon@mrib.co.uk

## Management Company

PO Box 150
Chsterfield
Derbyshire
S41 0YT
T 01246 236667   F as telephone
E tony@tonyhedley.com   W onlinepop.co.uk
*Contact* Tony Hedley

## Management Connection

3 Haversham Lodge
2–4 Melrose Avenue
London
NW2 4JS
T 020 8450 8882   F 020 8208 4219
E schevin@globalnet.co.uk
W thepublicityconnection.com
*Contact* Sharon Chevin
(sharon@thepublicityconnection.com)

## Management FXU

The Vibe Bar
91 Brick Lane
London
E1 8QN
T 020 7377 1516   F 020 7377 9949
E markbeder@hotmail.com
*Managing Director* Mark Beder

## MAP Management

208 Huyton Lane
Huyton
Liverpool
Merseyside
L36 1TQ
T 0151 489 6142   F as telephone
*Contact* Mike Walker

## Marble Floor Entertainment Ltd

72 New Bond St
London
W1S 1RR
T 020 7326 1390   F 020 7326 1390

E info@marblefloor-ent.com
*Contact* Daniel Kotey

*Represent songwriters, performers and producers for genres such as R'N'B, Hip Hop, Soul, Garage and Dance. Production services also offered*

## Marco Polo

23 Station Rd
Hayling Island
Hampshire
PO11 0EA
T 023 9246 1934   F 023 9246 1935
E markopolo@compuserve.com
*Director* Mark Ringwood

## Mark Hadley Management

25a Bridgnorth Avenue
Wombourne
Staffordshire
WV5 0AD
T 01902 896209   F as telephone
*Contact* Mark Hadley

## Mark II Management

18 Mountview Court
Green Lanes
London
N8 0SG
T 020 8374 2702   F 020 8374 2742   W ukb.com/mark-ii

## Marlene Ross Management

1 York St
Aberdeen
Grampian
AB11 5DL
T 01224 573100   F 01224 572598
*Contact* Marlene Ross

*Also Runrig Management*

## Marshall Arts

Leader House
6 Erskine Rd
London
NW2 7DL
T 020 7586 3831   F 020 7586 1422
E info@marshall.arts.co.uk   W marshall-arts.co.uk
*Contact* Barrie Marshall

## Marsupial Management Ltd

PO Box 5594
Thatcham
Berks
RG18 9YH
**T** 01488 657200    **F** 01488 657222
**E** marsupial@btinternet.com
*Contact* John Brand

## Martin Coull Management

6 New St
Edinburgh
EH8 8BH
**T** 0131 557 5330    **F** as telephone
**E** marticoull@aol.com    **W** peatbog-faeries.com
*Contact* Martin Coull

## Matinee Sound & Vision

132–134 Oxford Rd
Reading
Berkshire
RG1 7NL
**T** 0118 958 4934    **F** 0118 959 4936
*Managing Director* Chris Broderick

## Matrix Management

Christchurch Hall
67 Studdridge St
London
SW6 3TD
**T** 020 7731 3053    **F** 020 7371 8613
*Contact* Sarah Partridge

## Matthew Tullah Management

301 Firs Lane
London
N13 5QH
**T** 020 8807 0343    **F** 020 8807 3800
**E** matttullah@compuserve.com
**W** ourworld.compuserve.com/homepages/
matttullah

*Cabaret and corporate event management.*

## Maverick Music

20 Lavender Avenue
Mitcham
Surrey
CR4 3HH
**T** 020 8395 7556    **E** mavman@caleinet.co.uk

## Maximum Music

9 Heathmans Rd
London
SW6 4TJ
**T** 020 7731 1112    **F** 020 7731 1113
**E** nickgraham@maximummusic.demon.co.uk
*Contact* Nicky Graham

## Mayfair Management

PO Box 2311
Romford
Essex
RM5 2DZ
**T** 01992 763777    **F** 01992 763463
*Contact* Dan Donnelly

## McLeod Holden Enterprises Ltd

Priory House
1133 Hessle High Rd
Hull
East Yorkshire
HU4 6SB
**T** 01482 5656444    **F** 01482 353635
**E** petermcleod@mcleod-holden.com
**W** mcleod-holden.com
*Contact* Peter McLeod

## MCM

3rd Floor, 40 Langham St
London
W1N 5RG
**T** 020 7580 4088    **F** 020 7580 4098
**E** mcmemail@aol.com

*Contact* Meredith Cork

## MDMA

1a, 1 Adelaide Mansions
Hove
Sussex
BN3 2FD
**T** 01273 321602    **F** as telephone
**E** ricmdma@aol.com
*Contact* Rick French

## Me One Artist Management

52a Turnham Green Terrace
London
W4 1QP

**T** 020 8742 3579    **F** 020 8747 1699
*Contact* Pat Meagher

## Medium Productions
74 St Lawrence Rd
Upminster
Essex
RM14 2UW
**T** 07939 080524    **F** 01708 640291
**E** info@medium.productions.co.uk
**W** mediumproductions.co.uk
*Contact* Debi Zornes

*Also artist-owned record label (Steve Jansen, Richard Barbieri and Mick Karn)*

## Meek Music Management
7–11 Kensington High St
London
W8 5NP
**T** 020 7411 3111/020 7937 7220    **F** 020 7937 2579
*Contact* James Meek

## Mel Bush Organization Ltd
5 Stratfield Saye
20–22 Wellington Rd
Bournemouth
Dorset
BH8 8JN
**T** 01202 293093    **F** 01202 293080
**E** mbobmth@aol.com
*Managing Director* Mel Bush

## Mel Tyler Management
18 Buckinham Rd
Steeple Claydon
Bucks
MK18 2QB
**T** 01296 738474/07702 272100    **F** as first telephone
*Managing Director* Mel Tyler

## Menace Management
2 Park Rd
Radlett
Hertfordshire
WD7 8EQ
**T** 01923 853789/854789    **F** 01923 853318
**E** dennis@menacemusic.demon.co.uk
*Director* Dennis Collopy

## Merlin Group
40 Balcombe St
London
NW1 6ND
**T** 020 7723 7331    **F** 020 7723 0732
*Contact* Ray Santilli

## Metro Artist Management Ltd
26 Astwood Mews
London
SW7 4DE
**T** 020 7565 9100    **F** 020 7565 9101
**E** dolanmap@aol.com
*Contact* Mike Dolan

## Michael McDonagh Management
The Studio, 3c Wilson St
London
N21 1BP
**T** 020 8447 8882    **F** 020 8882 7679

## Midi Management Ltd
The Old Barn
Jenkins Lane
Great Halingbury
Essex
CM22 7QL
**T** 01279 759068/759067    **F** 01279 759069
**E** info@midi-management.com
*Contact* Mike Champion or Angie Potter

*Roster: Prodigy, Manchild*

## Mike & Margaret Storey Entertainments
Cliffe End Business Park
Dale St
Longwood
Huddersfield
West Yorkshire
HD3 4TG
**T** 01484 657054/657055    **F** as second telephone
*Contact* Mike Storey

## Misappropriate Management
The Sunday School
Rotary St
London
SE1 6LG
**T** 020 7620 3009    **F** 020 7928 9439
*Contact* Tony Smith

## Missing Link
25 Victoria Rd
London
NW7 4SA
**T** 020 8201 1031   **F** as telephone
**E** m.link@aol.com
*Managing Director* Laurence Bard

## Mission Impossible Management (MIM)
4 Belle Vue Gardens
Brighton
East Sussex
BN2 2AA
**T** 01273 677476   **F** 01273 677071
**E** tim_mim@pavilion.co.uk
**W** pavilion.co.uk/users/tim_mim
*Manager* Tim Collins

## MJM Entertainment
PO Box 453
Richmond
Surrey
TW10 6GW
**T** 020 8332 7474   **F** 020 8255 4279
**E** mjm@dircon.co.uk
*Contact* Jan Simmonds

## MLM
23 Thames St
Hampton
Middlesex
TW12 2EW
**T** 020 8783 1005   **F** 020 8783 1168
**E** mlm@hotmail.com
*Contact* Mike Leonard

## Mobile Management
31 Theobalds Rd
London
WC1X 8SP
**T** 020 7430 0444   **F** 020 7405 4391
*Contact* C Striker

## Modernwood Management
Cambridge House
Card Hill
Forest Row
East Sussex
RH18 5BA
**T** 01342 822619/020 8947 2224   **F** 020 8946 6545
**E** mickey.modernwood@virgin.net
*Contact* Mickey Modern or Mark Wood

*Roster: Dum Dums, Nik Kershaw, Frou Frou, Fahan Hassan, Mike Clarke, Mickey Lister, Jethro and Kelia*

## Moksha Management Ltd
PO Box 102
London
E15 2HH
**T** 020 8555 5423   **F** 020 8519 6834
**E** charles@moksha.demon.co.uk
*Managing Director* Charles Cosh

## Mole Management
1 Pauntley House
Pauntley St
London
N19 3TG
**T** 020 7281 8683/07973 386279   **F** as first telephone
*Contact* Grishma Jashapara

## Mondo Management/iht records
Unit 2d, Clapham North Arts Centre
26–32 Voltaire Rd
London
SW4 6DH
**T** 020 7720 7411   **F** 020 7720 8095
**W** davidgray.com and loopz.co.uk/orbital
*Contact* Rob Holden, Bernadette Barrett or Chris Norton

*Roster: David Gray and Orbital*
*Also label (same contact details)*

## Moneypenny Management
35 Britannia Row
London
N1 8QH
**T** 020 7704 8080   **F** 020 7704 8999
**E** doobwan@dial.pipex.com
*Managing Director* Nigel Morton

## MPC Entertainment
MPC House
15–16 Maple Mews
London
NW6 5UZ
**T** 020 7624 1184   **F** 020 7624 4220

**E** mpc@mpce.com  **w** mpce.com
*Chief Executive* Michael Cohen
*Contact* Nigel Forsyth

*NB: radio and club DJs, TV presenters, voice over artists and sporting celebrities*

### MRM Productions
5 Kirby St
London
EC1N 8TS
**T** 020 7404 5016  **F** 020 7404 6226
*Contact* Martin Patton or Richard Lowe

### Mrs Casey's Music
PO Box 296
Aylesbury
Bucks
HP19 3TL
**T** 01296 394411/433669  **F** 01296 392300
**w** mrscasey.co.uk
*Managing Director* Steve Heap

### Muirhead Management
202 Fulham Rd
London
SW10 9PJ
**T** 020 7351 5167  **F** 020 7352 1514
**E** muirhead_management@compuserve.com
*Chief Executive* Dennis Muirhead

### Multiplay Music Management
Maple Farm
56 High St
Harrold
Bedford
MK43 7DA
**T** 01234 720785  **F** 01234 720664
**E** multiplaymusic@maplefarm.demon.co.uk
**w** multiplaymusic.com
*Contact* Kevin White

### MumboJumbo Management
2a–6a Southam St
London
W10 5PH
**T** 020 8960 3253  **F** 020 8968 5111
**E** ian@mumbojumbo.co.uk
**w** mumbojumbo.co.uk
*Contact* Ian Clifford

### Music Design Company Management
23 New Mount St
Manchester
M4 4DE
**T** 0161 953 4114  **F** 0161 954 4001
*Contact* Lawrence Jones

### Music Group
60–62 Canalot Studios
222 Kensal Rd
London
W10 5BN
**T** 020 8969 5500  **F** 020 8969 0055
**E** info@themusicgroup.co.uk
*Managing Director* Debbie Lysaght

### Music Media Management
1st Floor, 754 Fulham Rd
London
SW6 5SH
**T** 020 7384 2232
*Contact* Alison Thomas

### NBM
43d Ferme Park Rd
London N4 4EB
**T** 020 8342 9220  **F** 020 8340 4721
**E** nbengali@lineone.net
*Contact* Neville Bengali

*Roster: Perry Blake, Jason Rowe (artists) and Rick Carter (producer)*

### Negus-Fancey Co
78 Portland Rd
London
W11 4LQ
**T** 020 7727 2063  **F** 020 7229 4188
*Contact* Charles Negus-Fancey

### NEM Productions (UK)
Priory House
55 Lawe Rd
South Shields
Tyne and Wear
NE33 2AL
**T** 0191 427 6207  **F** 0191 427 6323
**E** dave@nemproductions.com
**w** nemproductions.com
*Contact* Dave Smith

## New Vision Arts Management
Empire House Penthouse Suite
175 Piccadilly
London
W1V 9DB
**T** 0870 444 2506  **F** 07000 785 845
**E** info@newvisionarts.com  **w** newvisionarts.com
*Contact* Chris Nathaniel

## Nigel Martin-Smith Management
4th Floor, 54 Princess St
Manchester
M1 6HS
**T** 0161 237 9237  **F** 0161 236 7557

## Nita Anderson Entertainments
165 Wolverhampton Rd
Sedgley
Dudley
West Midlands
DY3 1QR
**T** 01902 882211/681224  **F** 01902 883356
**E** n900496952@blueyonder.co.uk
**w** nitaanderson.co.uk
*Managing Director* Juanita Anderson

## Noel Gay Artists
22–25 Dean St
London
W1V
**T** 020 7836 3941  **F** 020 7287 1816

## Noise 'n' Music Management
10 Glenhill Close
London
N3 2JS
**T** 020 8349 3330  **F** as telephone
*Contact* Martina Scholderle

## Noise Management Ltd
1st Floor, Unit a
16–24 Brewery Rd
London
N7 9NH
**T** 020 7700 2662  **F** 020 7700 2882
**E** roy@bsimerch.com/roger@noisemgt.com
*Contact* Roy Jenkins or Roger Hunt

*Represents Brutal Deluxe (Dream Catcher Records)*

## North and South
PO Box 1099 (Chart Moves)
London
SE5 9HT
**T** 020 7326 4824  **F** 020 7580 8485
**E** gamesmaster@chartmoves.com
**w** chartmoves.com
*Contact* Dave Klein

## Northern Music
Cheapside Chambers
43 Cheapside
Bradford
West Yorkshire
BD1 4HP
**T** 01274 306361  **F** 01274 730097
**E** mailman@ntnmusic.demon.co.uk
**w** northernmusic.freeserve.co.uk
*Contact* Andy Farrow or Vicky Langham

## Norwich Artistes
Bryden
115 Holt Rd
Norwich
Norfolk
NR6 6UA
**T** 01603 407101  **F** 01603 405314
**E** brian@norwichartistes.co.uk
**w** norwichartistes.co.uk
*Managing Director* Brian Russell

*Entertainment consultants and agency*

## NOW Music
15 Tabbs Lane
Scholes
Cleckheaton
West Yorkshire
BD19 6DY
**T** 01274 851365  **F** 01274 874329/865495
**E** nowmusic@now-music.com  **w** now-music.com
*Assistant Manager* John Wagstaff

## Nowhere Records/Publishing/Management
70 Nova Rd
Croydon
Surrey
CR0 2TL
**T** 020 8680 1848

**E** nowhererecords@netscapeonline.co.uk
**W** deletedrecordings.com
*Contact* Michael Wild

*Internet label plus publishing and management*

### NSE Entertainments
Minster Cottage
Sincox Lane
Broomers Corner
Shipley, nr Horsham
West Sussex
RH13 8PS
**T** 01403 741321
*Managing Director* Ian Long

### NUR Entertainment
Unit 50a
Canalot Studios
222 Kensal Rd
London
W10 5BN
**T** 020 8960 1800    **F** 020 8960 1802
*Managing Director* Trenton Harrison

### NVB Entertainments
80 Holywell Rd
Studham
Dunstable
Beds
LU6 2PD
**T** 01582 873623/873416    **F** 01582 873618
*Managing Directors*: H Harrison and Mrs Y Farrell

### Offside Management
Unit 9, 1st Floor
16–24 Brewery Rd
London
N7 9NH
**T** 020 7700 2662    **F** 020 7700 2882
**E** andy@bsimerch.com
*Contact* Andy Allen

### OMC Management
Oxford Music Central
2nd Floor, 65 George St
Oxford
OX1 2BE
**T** 01865 798 791    **F** 01865 798 792

**E** omcmanagement@oxfordmusic.net
*Contact* Dave Newton

### On the Verge Consultancy
22 Herbert St
Glasgow
G20 6NB
**T** 0141 337 1199    **F** 0141 357 0655
**E** otverge766@aol.com
*Contact* Robin Morton

### One Fifteen
The Gallery
28–30 Wood Wharf
Horseferry
London
SE10 9BT
**T** 020 8293 0999    **F** 020 8293 9525
**E** post@onefifteen.com    **W** onefifteen.com
*Contact* Paul Loasby

*All genres considered (SAE for demo return)*

### Opal
3 Pembridge Mews
London
W11 3EQ
**T** 020 7727 4153    **F** 020 7221 4901
*Managing Director* Anthea Norman-Taylor

### Opium (Arts) Ltd
49 Portland Rd
London
W11 4LJ
**T** 020 7229 5080    **F** 020 7229 4841
*Managing Director* Richard Chadwick

*Roster: David Sylvian, John Paul Jones, Michael Brook, Bill Nelson*

### OPL Management
4 The Limes
North End Way
London
NW3 7HG
**T** 020 8209 0025
*Contact* Sabina or Jez

*Also Atlantic Hire Services (PA, lights, recording and DJ equipment at best rates, same contact details)*

## Optimum Music Management Ltd

The Custard Factory
Studio 010/011
Gibb St
Digbeth
Birmingham
B9 4AR
**T** 0121 244 5151   **F** 0121 244 5159
**E** mail@optimummanagement.co.uk
**W** optimummanagement.co.uk
*Contact* F Johns or Jo Green

## Orb Management

1 Cowcross St
London
EC1M 6DR
**T** 020 7490 8990   **F** 020 7490 8987
*Contact* Alex Nightingale

## Orgasmatron Ltd

Flat 14
22 Red Lion St
London
WC1R 4PS
**T** 020 7404 9555   **F** 020 7900 6244
**E** info@orgasmatron.co.uk   **W** guychambers.com
*Contact* Dylan Chambers

## Ornadel Management

PO Box 16203
London
W3 8ZQ
**T** 020 8995 0027   **F** 020 8995 0097
**E** guy@ornadel.com
*Contact* Guy Ornadel

## Out There Management

37 York Rise
London
NW5 1SP
**T** 020 7267 1333   **F** 020 7267 1313
**E** tav@outthere.co.uk
*Contact* Stephen Taverner or Martha Parava

## Outside Organization Ltd

Queens House
180–182 Tottenham Court Rd
London
W1P 9LE
**T** 020 7436 3633   **F** 020 7436 3632
**W** outside-org.co.uk
*Contact* Alan Edwards

*Roster: Elton John, Beverley Knight, David Bowie, Spice Girls, All Saints, Boyzone etc*

## Oxygen Music Management

33–45 Parr St
Liverpool
Merseyside
L1 4JN
**T** 0151 707 1050   **F** 0151 709 4090
**E** oxygenmusic@btinternet.com
*Contact* Pete Byrne

*Acts for Echo and the Bunnymen, producer Ken Nelson and film composer John Murphy*

## P/M Management

2 Downsbury Studios
40 Steeles Rd
London
NW3 4SA
**T** 020 7586 3005   **F** 020 7681 0772
**E** jp@jonnypgood.freeserve.co.uk
*Contacts* Jonny Paul (mobile: 07980 555220) or Darren Michaelson (mobile: 07973 624443)

## P3 Music

PO Box 8403
Maybole

KA19 7YB
**T** 01655 750549   **F** 01655 750548
**E** james@p3music.com   **W** p3music.com
*Contact* James Taylor or Alison Burns

*Also agency, label, publishing and consultancy*

## Pachuco Management

Priestlands
Letchmore Heath
Hertfordshire
WD2 8EW
**T** 01923 854334/07802 657414   **F** 01923 857884
*Contact* Graham Carpenter

## Parachute Music

86 Birmingham Rd
Lichfield
Staffs
WS13 6PJ
**T** 01543 253576/07885 341745   **F** 01543 253576
**E** parachute.music@virgin.net
*Managing Director* Mervyn Spence

## Paradigm

Clarence House
36 Clarence St
Liverpool
Merseyside
L3 5TN
**T** 0151 708 6669   **F** as telephone
**E** paraprod@btinternet.com
**W** btinternet.com/-paraprod
*Contact* Andy Williams

## Park Promotions

PO Box 651
Oxford
OX2 9RB
**T** 01865 241717   **F** 01865 204556
**E** parkrecords@cwcom.net   **W** parkrecords.com
*Contact* John Dagnell

## Parliament Management

PO Box 6328
London
N2 0UN
**T** 020 8444 9841   **F** 020 8442 1973
**E** woolfman@compuserve.com
*Contact* Damian Baetons

## Part Rock Management Ltd

10 Bridge Avenue
Maidenhead
Berks
SL6 1RR
**T** 01628 626663   **F** 01628 780452
**E** partrock@msn.com
*Contact* Stewart Young

## Patrick Garvey Management Ltd

Top Floor
59 Lansdowne Place
Hove
East Sussex
BN3 1FL
**T** 01273 206623   **F** 01273 208484
**E** patrick or andrea@patrickgarvey.com
**W** patrickgarvey.com
*Managing Director* Patrick Garvey
*Director* Andrea McDermott

*Management of artists, principally conductors, plus
orchestral touring and recording projects worldwide*

## Paul Barrett (Rock 'N' Roll Enterprises)

16 Grove Place
Penarth
South Glamorgan
CF6 2LD
**T** 029 2070 4279   **F** 029 2070 9989
**E** barrett.rocknroll@amserve.net
*Managing Director* Paul Barrett
*Production* Ray Thompson
*Equipment/tech* Mike King
*Driver* Malcolm Batt

*Only represents pre-Beatles rock 'n' roll acts*

## Perfect Management Co

The Croft
25 Felltop
Blackhill Consett
Co Durham
DH8 8TR
**T** 01207 507068/07967 946231   **F** as first telephone
*Contact* Darren Eager

## Perfect World Network

PO Box 5
Sidcup
Kent
D14 6ZW
**T** 020 8300 5510   **F** 020 8300 6503
*Contact* Kevin Parkinson

## Pet Shop Boys Partnership
c/o The Mitch Clark Company
PO Box LB 791
London
W1A 9LB
**T** 020 7405 5131    **F** 020 7831 1578
**E** pspb@dircon.co.uk    **W** petshopboys.co.uk
*Contact* Mitch Clark

## Peter Haines Management
Montfort
The Avenue
Kingston, Lewes
East Sussex
BN7 3LL
**T** 01273 475846
**E** peter@uktourist.freeserve.co.uk
**W** recordbusiness.com
*Contact* Peter Haines

## PEZ Promotions
15 Sutherland House
137–139 Queenstown Rd
London
SW8 3RJ
**T** 020 7978 1503    **F** 020 7978 1502
**E** pez.promotions@virgin.net
*Contact* Perry Morgan

## PHAB
High Notes
Sheerwater Avenue
Woodham
Surrey
KT15 3DS
**T** 019323 48174    **F** 019323 40921
*Managing Director* Philip Bailey

## Philthy Rich Management
26 Greenend Rd
London
W4 1AJ
**T** 020 8354 0060    **F** 020 8354 0061
**E** richard@philthyrich.co.uk

## Pilot Management
222 Canalot Studios
22 Kensal Rd
London
W10 5BN
**T** 020 7565 2277    **F** 020 7565 2228
**E** amanda.fairhurst@virgin.net
*Contact* Amanda Fairhurst

## PJ Music
156a High St
London Colney
Hertfordshire
AL2 1QF
**T** 01727 827107/07860 902361    **F** as first telephone
**E** p.j.music@ukonline.co.uk
*Director* Paul J Bowrey

*Band development, production, management, consultancy*
*Rock, pop, dance*

## Pleasure Point Management and PR
1 St Paul's Court
Moreton-in-the-Marsh
Gloucestershire
GL56 0ET
**T** 01608 651802    **F** 01608 652814
**E** robbeden@madasafish.com
*Contact* Robb Eden

## Plus Music Management
36 Follingham Court
Drysdale Place
London
N1 6LZ
**T** 020 7684 8594    **F** 020 7684 8740
*Contact* D Chisholm

*Soul, pop, r&b, funk, house*

## Point
132 Royal College St
London
NW1 0TA
**T** 020 7424 9410    **F** 020 7424 9401
**E** pointmanagement@hotmail.com
*Managing Director* Chris Poole

## Pool Productions Ltd
3rd Floor, 9 Carnaby St
London
W1V 1PG
**T** 020 7437 1958   **F** 020 7437 3852
*Managing Director* Tony Hall

## Popcorp (Pop Corporation Ltd)
27 Advance House
109 Ladbroke Grove
London
W11 1PG
**T** 020 7792 3502   **F** 020 7229 5195
**E** popcorp@aol.com
*Contact* Pete Jones

## Poppy Artists
14a Hornsey Rise
London
N19 3SB
**T** 020 7482 5036   **F** 020 7482 5037
**E** poppy@poptel.org
*Contact* Kris Hoffmann

## PopWorks
420 Beaux-Arts Building
Manor Gardens
London
N7 6JW
**T** 020 7281 1928/07778 599232   **F** 020 7281 7380
**E** popworks1@yahoo.com
*Contact* Linda Duff

*Singer/songwriters welcome!*

## Portass & Carter
The Music Shop
26 Bridge Rd
Sutton Bridge
Spalding
Lincs
PE12 9UA
**T** 01406 350407/350266
*Managing Director* Nigel Portass

*Music shop first and foremost, plus tuition etc*

## Positive Management
23 Thornbury Rd
Isleworth
Middlesex
TW7 4LQ
**T** 020 8560 9557/07889 155533
**F** as first telephone
**E** positive-mgmt@easynet.co.uk
**W** positive-mgmt.com
*Contact* Meira Shore

*Positive represents Terry Collier, DJ Martin Morales, Lorna Brown, Inspiration Junkies and Mikey Benn (producer)*

## Potential Development
18 Sparkle St
Manchester
M1 2NA
**T** 0161 273 3435   **F** 0161 273 3695
**E** mailbox@pd-uk.com
*Contact* Gary McClarnan

## Power Artist Management
29 Riversdale Rd
Thames Ditton
Surrey
KT7 0QN
**T** 020 8398 5236/5732   **F** 020 8398 7901
*Managing Director* Barry Evans

## Powerhaus Management/Barclays Entertainments
Unit 5
Willtell Works
Upper St John St
Lichfield
Staffs
WS14 9ET
**T** 01543 303200   **F** 01543 303201
**E** mouse@pcdirect.fsnet.co.uk
**W** barclaysentertainment.co.uk
*Contact* Ray Mott or Rick Renaro

*Powerhaus represents pop/rock artists, Barclays is for bands, strippers, comedians, magicians etc*

**Premier Artist Management**
494 Archway Rd
London
N6 4NA
T 020 8340 5151   F 020 8340 5159
*Contact* Carl Pengelly

**Premiere**
Suite 4
Delme Court
Maytree Rd
Fareham
Hants
PO16 0HX
T 01329 238449   F 01329 233088
E premiere@agents-uk.com   W premiere.org.uk
*Contact* Del Mitchell

**Principle Management**
30–32 Sir John Rogerson's Quay
Dublin 2
Ireland
T 00 353 1 677 7330   F 00 353 1 677 7276
*Managing Director* Paul McGuinness

**Pro-Rock Management**
Caxton House
Caxton Avenue
Blackpool
Lancashire
FY2 9AP
T 01253 508670/591169
*Managing Director* R Sharples

**Prodmix Artist Management**
98 Edith Grove
London
SW10 0NH
T 020 7565 0324/07768 877426   F 020 7565 2797
E karen@prodmix.com   W prodmix.com
*Contact* Karen Goldie

*DJs and producers including Cirillo, Gareth Cooke,*
*Joe T Vannelli, Matt White, Pasta Boys and Severino*

**Product Exchange Ltd**
45 Mount Ash Rd
London
SE26 6LY
T 020 8699 5835   F as telephone

E product.exchange@virgin.net
*Director* Frank Rodgers

**Proper Management Ltd**
Electra House
93a Rivington St
London
EC2A 3AY
T 020 7613 4600   F 020 7613 4611
E tim@propermanagement.demon.co.uk
*Managing Director* Tim Abbot

**Prophet Music**
147 Drummond St
London
NW1 2PB
T 020 7383 5003   F 020 7383 5004
E info@prophetmusic.co.uk
W prophetmusic.co.uk
*Directors* Jonathan Brigden and Theresa
Bampton-Clare

*Artist management, session fixing, project*
*management, music supervision*

**Prospect Management**
Arlette House
143 Wardour St
London
W1V 3TB
T 020 7439 1919   F 020 7437 1791
E pmsl@thumbcandy.co.uk
*Contact* Jonathan Brigden

**Prostar Management**
106 Hillcrest Avenue
Dereham
Norfolk
NR19 1TD
T 01362 692078   F 01362 696600
*Contact* Malcolm Cook

**Protocol Management**
23a Benwell Rd
London
N7 7BW
T 020 7686 0044   F 020 7686 0050
E info@flintworks.com   W flintworks.com
*Contact* David Richardson

## PS! Management

PO Box 22626
London
N15 3WW
**T** 020 8211 0272   **F** as telephone
*Contact* Nick Carpenter

## Psycho Management Company

111 Clarence Rd
London
SW19 8QB
**T** 020 8540 8122   **F** 020 8715 2827
**E** agents@psycho.co.uk   **W** psycho.co.uk
*Director* J Mabley

## Pure Acts

17 Great Percy St
London
WC1X 9RD
**T** 020 7833 8855   **F** 020 7833 8856
**E** pureinc@dircon.co.uk   **W** pureacts.com
*Contact* Steve Fargnoli or Michael Hatton

## Purple Room Ltd

89a Leathwaite Rd
London
SW11 6RN
**T** 020 7924 1904   **F** 020 7738 1764
**E** thepurpleroom@music-room.com
**W** music-room.com
*Managing Director* S Hirani

## PVA Ltd

2 High St
Westbury-on-Trym
Bristol
BS9 3DU
**T** 0117 950 4504   **F** 0117 959 1786
**E** enquiries@pva.ltd.uk   **W** pva.ltd.uk
*Contact* Pat Vincent or John Hutchinson
*Managing Director* Pat Vincent

## PVA Management Ltd

Hallow Park
Worcester
WR2 6PG
**T** 01905 640663   **F** 01905 641842   **E** pva@pva.co.uk
*Contact* Lisa Ventura-Whiting or Cary Taylor

## Quail

39 Golders Gardens
London
NW11 9BS
**T** 020 8458 1178   **F** 020 8905 5191
*Contact* Jim Roland

## Quest Management

250 York Rd
London
SW11 3SJ
**T** 020 7716 3406   **F** 020 7223 3408
**E** scott@quest-management.com
*Contact* Scott Rodger

## Quinlan Rd (UK)

Unit 1
75–87 Agincourt Rd
London
NW3 2NT
**T** 020 7428 0946   **F** 020 7267 9488/9288
**E** postmaster@quinlanroad.com
**W** quinlanroad.com
*Contact* Ian Blackaby

## Quintessential Music

PO Box 546
Bromley
Kent
BR2 0RS
**T** 020 8402 1984   **F** 020 8325 0708
*Contact* Quincey

## R and M Entertainment

The Chrysalis Building
Bramley Rd
London
W10 6SP
**T** 020 7221 2213   **F** 020 7229 2510
**E** roye@chrysalis.co.uk
*Contact* Roy Eldridge

## R&B Productions

1a Raynham Terrace
London
N18 2JN
**T** 020 8884 3499/07956 117213
*Contact* Brian Knivett

**Rainbow Disco Shop**
44 Uxbridge Rd
London
W12 0NF
T 020 8965 2826   F 020 8965 2991
*Contact* M Thomas

**Rat Management**
34 Kempton Avenue
Hornchurch
Essex
RM12 6ED
T 01708 507028/641044
*Contact* Robert Cole or Trevor Barham

**Ravishing Management**
63 Keyham Lane
Leicester
Leics
LE5 1FH
T 0116 276 7952
*Managing Director* Ravinder Jandu

**Raw Talent Ltd**
55 Loudoun Rd
London
NW8 0DL
T 020 8744 1210   F as telephone
*Contact* Big Andy

**Raymond Coffer Management**
PO Box 595
Bushey
Herts
WD2 1PZ
T 020 8420 4430   F 020 8950 7617
E raymond@coffermichaelson.demon.co.uk
*Director* Raymond Coffer

**Razzmatazz Management**
Crofters
East Park Lane
Newchapel
Surrey
RH7 6HS
T 01342 835359   F 01342 835433
E mcgrogan@tinyworld.co.uk
*Director* Jill Shirley

**RDPR Music Management**
155 Potton Rd
Biggleswade
Beds
SG18 0ED
T 01767 317618/01453 832876
*Contact* Rachel Dunlop

**Reactor Management**
10 Fox House
Maysoule Rd
London
SW11 2BX
T 020 7738 1543/07956 198726
F as first telephone   E reactorlive@hotmail.com
W reactorlive.com
*Contact* Steve Japp

**Real Time Management**
1–2 Ramillies St
London
W1V 1DF
T 020 8287 7766   E charliei@realtimeinfo.co.uk
W realtimeinfo.co.uk
*Contact* Charlie Inskip

**Reckless**
122a Highbury Rd
Kings Heath
Birmingham
West Midlands
B14 7QP
T 0121 443 2186
E boblamb@recklessltd.freeserve.co.uk
*Managing Director* Bob Lamb

**Red Dog Management**
PO Box 22626
London
N15 3WW
T 020 8809 7008   F as telephone
*Contact* Jo Johnson

**Red Parrot Management**
Unit B114
Faircharm Studios
8–10 Creekside
London
SE8 3DX
T 020 8469 3541   F 020 8469 3542

**E** red.parrot@virgin.net   **W** mezzmusic.com
*Contact* John Cecchini

*Also agency (contact Andria Law) and labels (contact Andy Penny: Beak Recordings, Caged Records and Red Parrot Recordings)*
*Mainly dance music and culture*

## Retaliate First Management
68 Dalling Rd
London
W6 0JA
**T** 020 8741 3808   **F** 020 8741 5469
**E** mgmt@retaliatefirst.co.uk   **W** retaliatefirst.co.uk
*Contact* Steve Lowes

## Richard Martin Management
18 Ambrose Place
Worthing
West Sussex
BN11 1PZ
**T** 01903 823456   **F** 01903 823847
**E** ric@ricmartinagency.com
**W** ricmartinagency.com
*Managing Director* Richard Martin

*Management for Hot Chocolate*

## Richard Thompson
224 Chiltern Heights
White Lion Rd
Amersham
Bucks
HP7 9RY
**T** 01494 766371/00 1 323 874 9559
**F** as first telephone   **E** gravespms@aol.com
*Contact* Donnie Graves

## Richly Comic Artist Management
Unit 2
Stable Barn
New Yatt Rd
Witney
Oxon
OX2 6TA
**T** 01993 706632   **F** 01993 706689
**E** joel@richlycomic.com   **W** richlycomic.com
*Contact* Joel Harrison

*Roster includes Six Ray Sun and The Jokers*
*All types of music considered*

## Richman Management Ltd
Unit 133, Canalot Studios
222 Kensal Rd
London
W10 5BN
**T** 020 8964 4904
*Contact* Richard Shipman

## Richmond Management
The Coach House
Swinhope Hall
Swinhope
Market Rasen
Lincs
LN8 6HT
**T** 01472 399011   **F** 01472 399025
*Managing Director* Bernard Theobald

## Ricochet
5 Old Garden House
The Lanterns
Bridge Lane
London
SW11 3AD
**T** 020 7924 2255   **F** 020 7738 1881
*Managing Director* Stephen King

## Rideout Management
Lillie House
1a Conduit St
Leicester
Leics
LE2 0JN
**T** 0116 223 0318   **F** 0116 223 0302
*Contact* Darren Nockles

## Riot Club Management
Unit 4 27a Spring Grove Rd
Hounslow
Middlesex
TW3 4BE
**T** 020 8572 8809   **E** riotclub@currantbun.com

## Rise Management Ltd
Unit 37, 249–251 Kensall Rd
London
W10 5DB
**T** 020 8964 4722   **F** 020 8968 1929
**E** info@risemanagement.co.uk
*Contact* Tom Haxell

*Managing Directors* Dianne Wagg and David Jaynes

## Riverman Management
Top Floor, George House
Brecon Rd
London
W6 8PY
T 020 7381 4000  F 020 7381 9666
E info@generous.co.uk
*Contact* David McLean

## RLM (Richard Law Management)
58 Marylands Rd
London
W9 2DR
T 020 7286 1706  F 020 7266 1293
E richard.law00@virginnet.co.uk
*Contact* Richard Law

## Roger Boden Management
2 Gawsworth Rd
Macclesfield
Cheshire
SK11 8UE
T 01625 420163  F 01625 420168
E rogerboden@cottagegroup.co.uk
W cottagegroup.co.uk
*Managing Director* Roger Boden

## Roger Forrester Management
18 Harley House
London
NW1 5HE
T 020 7486 8056  F 020 7487 5663
*Managing Director* Roger Forrester

## Ron Winter Management Ltd
The Studio
Lynton Rd
London
N8 8SL
T 020 8347 5220  F 020 8347 5221
*Managing Director* Ron Winter

## Rose Rouge International
Aws Group
Aws House
Trinity Square
St. Peter Port
Guernsey
GY1 1LX
T 01481 728294  F 01481 714118
E aws@gtonline.net  W awsgroup.co.uk
*Director* Steve Free

*Also publishers and record company*

## Roy Massey Management
40 Salisbury Drive
Cannock
Staffs
WS12 5YP
T 01543 277431  F 01543 277431
E info@roymassey.co.uk  W roymassey.co.uk
*Contact* Roy Massey

## RPM Management
Pierce Entertainment Ltd
Pierce House
London Apollo Complex
Queen Caroline St
London
W6 9QU
T 020 8741 5557  F 020 8741 5888
E marlene-rpm@pierce-entertainment.com
W pierce-entertainment.com
*Contact* Marlene Gaynor

## Safe Management
St Ann's House
Guildford Rd
Lightwater
Surrey
GU18 5RA
T 01276 476676  F 01276 451109
E chris@safemanagement.co.uk
*Contact* Chris Herbert

## Saffa Music Ltd
8 Botteville Rd
Birmingham
B27 7YD
T 0121 708 1349  F 0121 707 6428
*Contact* Geoff Pearce

## SAFI Sounds Management & Promotion
CIK Kirklees Media Centre
7 Northumberland St
Huddersfield
West Yorkshire
HD1 1RL
T 01484 654894   F 01484 450239
*Contact* Sarah Hutton

## Sanctuary Music (Overseas)
1st Floor Suite
The Colonnades
82 Bishops Bridge Rd
London
W2 6BB
T 020 7602 6351
*Contact* Rod Smallwood

## Sandcastle Productions
PO Box 13533
London
E7 0SG
T 020 8534 8500   F 07070 718613
*Senior Partner* Simon Law

## Satellite Artists
34 Salisbury St
London
NW8 8QE
T 020 7402 9111   F 020 7723 3064
E satellite_artists@hotmail.com
*Director* Eliot Cohen

## Satori Management
2nd Floor
6 Salem Rd
London
W2 4BU
T 020 7221 5439   F 020 7229 9410
*Contact* Alex Satore

## Schofield Hughes Management
Schofield Hughes House
Cliffe Hill
Stapleford
Notts
NG9 7HD
T 0115 949 9007   F 0115 949 7360
E pete@schofield-hughes.co.uk
w schofield-hughes.co.uk

## Schoolhouse Management
The Cork House
104 Constitution St
Edinburgh
Lothian
EH6 6AW
T 0131 554 6656   F 0131 554 4405
E schoolhousemanagement@hotmail.com
*Managing Director* Bruce Findlay

## Seaview Music
28 Mawson Rd
Cambridge
CB1 2EA
T 01223 508431   F 01223 508449
E seaview@dial.pipex.com   w seaviewmusic.co.uk
*Manager* Alison Page

*NB: classical music specialist*

## Seb Shelton Management
13 Lynton Rd
London
N8 8SR
T 020 8341 9636   F as telephone
*Contact* Seb Shelton

## Sensible Events
90–96 Brewery Rd
London
N7 9NT
T 020 7700 9900   F 020 7700 7845
E andrewzweck@aol.com
*Contact* Andrew Zweck

*One-stop service for the creation and production of
entertainment, TV and sporting events with musical
content, from product launch to pop festival*

## Serious Artist Management Ltd
PO Box 13143
London
N6 5BG
T 020 8731 7300   F 020 8458 0045
E sam@seriousworld.com   w seriousworld.com
*Contact* Sam O'Riordan

## Seven Music Promotions Ltd

PO Box 2042
Luton
Beds
LU3 2EP
**T** 01582 457745   **F** 01582 411077
**E** j.waller@virgin.net   **w** rhythmmasters.com
*Managing Director* Jonathan M Walle.r

*Roster includes Rhythm Masters, Punk Chic, Tripple A*

## Seven Publishing and Management (7PM)

PO Box 2272
Rottingdean
Brighton
BN2 8XD
**T** 01273 304681   **F** 01273 308120
**E** seven-webster@beeb.net
Contact: Seven Webster

*See also under Publishers, and Jackpot Records (same contact details)*

## SGM

4th Floor, 40 Langham St
London
W1N 5RG
**T** 020 7323 4410   **F** 020 7323 4180
**E** simon.gunning@btinternet.com
*Contact* Simon Gunning

## Shalit Management

Cambridge Theatre
Seven Dials
London
WC2H 9HU
**T** 020 7379 3282   **F** 020 7379 3238
*Managing Director* Jonathan Shalit

## Shark Records

23 Rollscourt Avenue
London
SE24 0EA
**T** 020 7737 4580   **F** 020 7274 5103
**E** mellor@orbanix.fsbusiness.co.uk
*Contact* M H Mellor

## Shavian Enterprises Ltd

14 Devonshire Place
London
W1G 6HX
**T** 020 7935 6909   **F** 020 7224 6256
**E** info@sandieshaw.com   **w** sandieshaw.com
*Director* Louise Voss
*Contact* Louise Voss or Sandie Shaw

## Show Business Entertainment

The Bungalow
Chatsworth Avenue
Long Eaton
Notts
NG10 2FL
**T** 0115 973 5445   **F** 0115 946 1831
*Managing Director* Kim Holmes

## Showcase Management International

33 Mandarin Place
Grove
Oxon
OX12 0QH
**T** 01235 767171/771577   **F** as second telephone
**E** smi2@risdon.fsbusiness.co.uk
*Co-Presidents* Jane and Val Risdon
*Contact* Dave Wareham (Vice President, Special Projects, UK)

*Roster: Treana, Tag, Ignorance, Lucy, Blackout
Also Everday Productions and Miggins Music (same contact details)
Label (Asia): Brite Records/SMI Asia
US office (tel: 001 818 399 2344)*

## Shurwood Management

Tote Hill Cottage
Stedham
Midhurst
West Sussex
GU29 0PY
**T** 01730 817400   **F** 01730 815846
*Contact* Shurley Selwood

## Sick Dear Management

138a Chiswick High Rd
London
W4 1PU
**T** 020 8994 9007   **F** 020 8995 1051
*Contact* Rob Gunch

**Silent Records Ltd**
40 St Peters Rd
London
W6 9BD
**T** 020 8563 8884   **F** 020 8741 9174
**E** info@silentrecords.com   **w** silentrecords.com
*Contact* Julian Close

**Silentway Management Ltd**
Unit 61b, Pall Mall Deposit
124–128 Barlby Rd
London
W10 6BL
**T** 020 8969 2498   **F** 020 8969 2506
**E** silentway@aol.com   **w** simplyred.com
*Contact* Ian Grenfell

*Represents Simply Red and Stina Nordenstam*

**Silk Management**
The Sunset Suite
23 New Mount St
Manchester
M4 4DE
**T** 0161 953 4045   **F** 0161 953 4235
**E** lee.stanley@mcr1.poptel.org.uk
*Directors* Rose Marley and Lee Stanley

**Simon Davies Management**
1–3 Ashland House
Ashland Place
London
W1M 3JF
**T** 020 7935 1588   **F** 020 7487 3016
**E** 100441.2547@compuserve.com
*Managing Director* Simon Davies

**Simon Hart**
21 Westcombe Drive
Barnet
Herts
EN5 2BE
**T** 07713 515989   **E** simonhart@btinternet.com
**w** shart.freewire.co.uk
*Contact* Simon Hart

*Folk/rock management and mail-order music*

**Simon Lawlor Management**
17 Russell Close
London
W4 3NW
**T** 020 8995 4907/020 8742 8917
**F** as second telephone   **E** lawlor@dial.pipex.com
*Contact* Simon Lawlor

**Sincere Management**
Flat B, 6 Bravington Rd
London
W9 3AH
**T** 020 8960 4438   **F** 020 8968 8458
**E** sinman@compuserve.com
*Contact* Peter Jenner

*Roster: Billy Bragg, Eddi Reader, Michael Franti/
Spearhead*

**Six07 Music Ltd**
65 Barnsbury St
London
N1 1EJ
**T** 020 7607 2706   **F** 020 7607 8007
**E** info@607music.com   **w** 607music.com
*Directors* Vojkan Brankovic, Lee Haynes, Ian
Robinson, Ritu Singh

**Slapback Management**
27 Sherbourne Drive
Maidenhead
Berks
SL6 3EP
**T** 01628 675999   **F** 01628 676985
**E** slapback5@cs.com
*Contact* Keith Rowe

**Sleeping Giant Music**
34 Great James St
London
WC1N 3HB
**T** 020 7405 3786   **F** 020 7405 5245
**E** stjames2@dircon.co.uk
*Group chairman* Keith C Thomas
*A&R Director* Christian Baldock

*Group also includes St James Music, Prestige Elite
Records, Prestige Video Collection,
Music Avenue UK Ltd*

## Small World

4 Taylors Yard
67 Alderbrook Rd
London
SW12 8AD
T 020 8772 0600    F 020 8772 0700
*Contact* Tina Matthews

## Solar Management Ltd

42–48 Chalbert St
London
NW8 7BU
T 020 7722 4175    F 020 7722 4072
E info@solarmanagement.co.uk
W solarmanagement.co.uk
*Manager* Carol Crabtree

## Sonar Music + Media

PO Box 14553
London
W12 9ZR
T 020 8746 1984/07973 756862
F as first telephone    E info.sonar@virgin.net
*Contact* Gerard Grech

## Soul Children Management

8 Dark Lane
Bradfield
Reading
Berks
PG7 6DD
T 0118 974 4904    F 0118 974 4900
*Contact* Tim Kendall

## Sound & Vision Management Ltd

34 Salisbury St
London
NW8 8QE
T 020 7402 9111    F 020 7723 3064
*Director* Eliot M Cohen

## Sound Image

Unit 2b
Banquay Trading Estate
Slutchers Lane
Warrington
Cheshire
WA1 1PJ
T 01925 445742    F as telephone
*Contact* Steve Millington

## Sound Pets

Unit 13
Imperial Studios
Imperial Rd
London
SW6 2AG
T 020 7610 6969    F 020 7731 4358
E robinhill@soundpets.freeserve.co.uk
*Managing Director* Robin Hill

## Soundcakes

PO Box 562
London
N10 3LJ
T 020 7281 0018    F 020 7272 9609
*Contact* Raymond Bell
*Artists* World of Leather, Sara Davis

## Soundtrack Ltd

46b Cricklewood Lane
London
NW2 1HD
T 020 8208 2082/07973 835940    F 020 8208 0898
*Contact* Michael Lewis

## Soundtrack Music Associates Ltd

2 Kimberley Rd
London
NW6 7SG
T 020 7328 8211    F 020 7328 1444
E info@soundtrackcwm.co.uk
*Director* Olav Wyper

## Southside Management

20 Cromwell Mews
London
SW7 2JY
T 020 7225 1919    F 020 7823 7091
*Contact* Bob Johnson

## Sphinx Management And Entertainment Agency Ltd

2 Unity Place
Westgate
Rotherham
South Yorkshire
S60 1AR
T 01709 820379/820370    F 01709 369990
E tonyfrench@sphinx47.freeserve.co.uk
*Director* Anthony French

## Splinter Management
Terminal Studios
Lamb Walk
London
SE1 3TT
**T** 020 7357 8416   **F** 020 7357 8437

## Split Management
13 Sandys Rd
Worcester
Worcs
WR1 3HE
**T** 01905 29809/07970 793811   **F** 01905 613023
**E** split.music@virgin.net   **w** splitmusic.com
*Managing Director* Chris Warren

## SR Management Ltd
4 Monkton House
130a Haverstock Hill
London
NW3 2AU
**T** 020 7722 4373/07767 404748
**F** as first telephone   **E** srmgmt@aol.com
*Director* Sarah Rosenfield

## Stamina Management
47 Prout Grove
London
NW10 1PU
**T** 020 8450 5789   **F** 020 8450 0150
*Managing Director* Peter Gage

## Stan Green Management
PO Box 4
Dartmouth
Devon
TQ6 0YD
**T** 01803 770046   **F** 01803 770075
**E** sgm@clara.co.uk   **w** keithfloyd.co.uk
*Managing Director* Stan Green

## Star-Write Management
PO Box 16715
London
NW4 1WN
**T** 020 8203 5062   **F** 020 8202 3746
**E** de55@dial.pipex.com
*Director* John Lisners

## Stash Entertainment
1st Floor, 51 Hoxton Square
London
N1 6PB
**T** 020 7684 8170   **F** 020 7684 8175
**E** info@stashuk.com   **w** stashuk.com
*Contact* Danny Olayemi

## Stephen Budd Management
109b Regents Park Rd
London
NW1 8UR
**T** 020 7616 3303   **F** 020 7916 3302
**E** info@record-producers.com
**w** record-producers.com
*Managing Director* Stephen Budd

*Management of 35 of the leading UK and US
producers, mixers, songwriters and remixers*

## Stephen Wells Management
9 Woodchurch Rd
London
NW6 3PL
**T** 020 7372 5488   **F** as telephone
*Contact* Stephen Wells

*Development of bands and singers, career guidance,
both legal and artistic, working mainly in the rock
and pop fields*

## Steve Allen Entertainments
60 Broadway
Peterborough
Cambridgeshire
PE1 1SU
**T** 01733 569589   **F** 01733 561854
**E** steve@sallenent.co.uk   **w** sallenent.co.uk
*Contact* Steve Allen

## Steve Draper Entertainments
2 The Coppice
Beardwood Manor
Blackburn
Lancashire
BB2 7BQ
**T** 01254 679005   **F** as telephone
**E** steve@stevedraperents.fsbusiness.co.uk
**w** stevedraper.co.uk and comedians.org.uk
*Contacts* Steve Draper, Tracey Kendall

*NB: specializes in comedians, sporting dinners, male and female exotic dancers*

## Steve Harrison Management
2 Witton Walk
Northwich
Cheshire
CW9 5AT
**T** 01606 46444
*Managing Director* Steve Harrison

## Steve Weltman Management
91 Manor Rd South
Hinchley Wood
Esher
Surrey
KT10 0QB
**T** 020 8398 4144/07957 367214   **F** 020 8398 4244
**E** sweltman@ukgateway.net
*Contact* Steve Weltman

## Stevo Management
4 Denmark St
London
WC2H 8LP
**T** 020 7836 9995   **F** 020 7836 9909
**E** info@somebizarre.com   **w** somebizarre.com
*Director* Stevo

*Also Some Bizarre Records (same contact details)*

## Stingray Enterprises
Research House
Fraser Rd
Perivale
Middlesex
UB6 7AQ
**T** 020 8930 0132   **F** 020 8933 1694
**w** stingrayrecords.co.uk
*Contact* Ray McLeod

## Streetfeat Management
26 Bradmore Park Rd
London
W6 0DT
**T** 020 8846 9984   **F** 020 8846 9345
*Managing Directors* Colin Schaverien and Simon Napier-Bell

## Strike Back Management
271 Royal College St
London
NW1 9LU
**T** 020 7482 0115   **F** 020 7267 1169
**E** maurice@baconempire.com
*Managing Director* Maurice Bacon

*Artists managed: Mediaeval Babes*

## Sublime
65 Overdale Rd
London
W5 4TU
**T** 020 8840 2042   **F** 020 8840 5001
**E** info@sublimemusic.co.uk
**w** sublimemusic.co.uk
*Contact* Patrick Spinks

## Substance Management
25 Temple St
Brighton
East Sussex
BN1 3BH
**T** 01273 328700
*Contact* Dave Harper

## Sugar Management
49 Kensal Rd
London
W10 5DB
**T** 020 8964 4722   **F** 020 8968 1929
*Contact* Paul Hitchman

## Sugarcane Music
32 Blackmore Avenue
Southall
Middlesex
UB1 3ES
**T** 020 8574 2130   **F** as telephone
*Contact* Astrid Pringsheim

## Sunflower Management
PO Box 11732
London
N2 8AA
**T** 020 8446 0122
*Contact* Bruce Fisher

## SuperVision Management Ltd
109b Regents Park Rd
London
NW1 8UR
**T** 020 7916 3303   **F** 020 7916 3302
**E** paulcraig@record-producers.com
*Contact* Paul Craig

## Susan Read Management
PO Box 12
Little Milton
Oxford
OX44 7QJ
**T** 01844 278612   **F** 01844 278611
**E** susan-read@msn.com

*Business administration and project management for
established artists*

## Swamp Music
PO Box 94
Derby
Derbyshire
DE22 1XA
**T** 01332 332336/07702 564804   **F** as first telephone
**E** chrishall@swampmusic.demon.co.uk
*Managing Director* Chris Hall

## Sylvantone Promotions
17 Allerton Grange Way
Leeds
West Yorkshire
LS17 6LP
**T** 0113 268 7788   **F** 0113 266 0220
**E** tonygoodacre@hotmail.com
**W** countrymusic.org.uk/tony-goodacre/index
*Proprietor* Tony Goodacre

*Country music specialists*

## SYME International Management
81 Park Rd
Wath-upon-Dearne
Rotherham
South Yorkshire
S63 7LE
**T** 01709 877920   **F** 01709 873119/0870 1640589
**E** syme@csi.com
*Director* Martin E Looby

## Tantara Management
299 Camberwell New Rd
London
SE5 0TF
**T** 020 7701 3001   **F** 020 7703 7799
**E** tantara@imperialgardens.co.uk
*Contact* Raymond Stevenson

## Taurus Records (UK)
128 Anerley Rd
London
SE20 8DL
**T** 020 8778 2019
*Contact* Shola Adedayo

## Telegram Productions
Unit 3
6 Erskine Rd
London
NW3 3AJ
**T** 07768 807604   **E** tpl@telegram.co.uk
*Managing Director* Will Ashurst

## Telerynng UK
132 Chase Way
London
N14 5DH
**T** 07091 001209   **F** 020 8361 3757
**E** ldonessien@aol.com
*Contact* E Bell

## Temple Records
Shillinghill
Temple
Midlothian
EH23 4SH
**T** 01875 830328   **F** 01875 830392
**E** robin@templerecords.demon.co.uk
**W** rootsworld.com/temple
*Managing Director* Robin Morton

## Tender Prey
Studio 4
Ivebury Court
325 Latimer Rd
London
W10 6RA
**T** 020 8964 5417   **F** 020 8964 5418
**E** rayner@tenderprey.com   **W** nickcave.com
*Manager* Rayner Jesson

## Terrataktix
Monticello
Wellington Hill
High Beach
Loughton
Essex
IG10 4AH
**T** 020 8532 1654   **F** 020 8532 1656
**E** ania.e@btinternet.com
*Managing Director* Peter Edwards

## Terry Blamey Management
PO Box 13196
London
SW6 4NF
**T** 020 7371 7627   **F** 020 7731 7578
**E** info@terryblamey.com
*Contact* Allison MacGregor

*Artist managed: Kylie Minogue*

## Theobald Dickson Productions
The Coach House
Swinhope Hall
Swinhope
Market Rasen
Lincolnshire
LN8 6HT
**T** 01472 399011   **F** 01472 399025
*Managing Director* Bernard Theobald

## Timebomb
1st Floor
26 Stokes Croft
Bristol
BS1 3QD
**T** 0117 909 6607   **F** 0117 909 6606
**E** management@timebomb.globalnet.co.uk
**w** timebombmusic.co.uk
*Contact* Stephen Earl

## Tip Management
Unit 16
Acklam Rd Workshops
10 Acklam Rd
London
W10 5QZ
**T** 020 8960 5534   **F** 020 8960 5538
**E** tip@online.rednet.co.uk   **w** tip.co.uk
*Contact* Richard Bloor

## TKO Management
PO Box 130
Hove
East Sussex
BN3 6QU
**T** 01273 550088   **F** 01273 540969
**E** tkoadam@tkogroup.com   **w** mistral.co.uk/tko
*Contact* Adam Clavering

## TMR Management
PO Box 3775
London
SE18 QR
**T** 020 8316 4690   **F** as telephone
**E** marc@wufog.freeserve.co.uk
**w** wufog.freeserve.co.uk
*Managing Director* Marc Bell

## Tom Doherty Artist Management
Longfield House
Bury Avenue
Ruislip
Middlesex
HA4 7RT
**T** 01895 625397   **F** 01895 477522
**E** tomplastic@compuserve.com

## Toni Medcalf Management
1st Floor, 40 Langham St
London
W1A 5RG
**T** 020 7636 9090   **F** 020 7636 9091
**E** toni.medcalf@virgin.net

## Tony Bramwell
9 Brooking Barn
Ashprington
Totnes
Devon
TQ9 7UL
**T** 01803 732137   **F** as telephone
**E** bramwell@netlineuk.net

## Tony Denton Promotions Ltd
19 South Molton Lane
London
W1Y 1AQ
**T** 020 7629 4666   **F** 020 7629 4777
**E** mail@tdpromo.com   **w** tdpromo.com
*Contact* Tony Denton

**Too Hoots**
PO Box 202
Aylesbury
Bucks
HP20 1YL
T 01296 415580
*Contact* Ian Sloane or Richard Rye

**Top Draw Artist & Management**
Cary Point
Babbacombe Downs
Torquay
Devon
TQ1 3LU
T 01803 322233    F 01803 322244
E matpro@btinternet.com
*Contact* Colin Matthews

**Top Talent Agency**
Yester Rd
Chiselhurst
Kent
BR7 5HN
T 020 8467 0808    F as telephone
*Managing Director* John Day

**Tortured Artists Ltd**
Unit G
44 St Paul's Crescent
London
NW1 9TN
T 020 7284 0434    F 020 7267 6015
E torture@truelove.co.uk    w truelove.co.uk
*Contact* John Truelove

*Specialize in techno and house artists
Roster includes Chris Liberator, DAVE the
Drummer, The Source*

**Toshack, Keegan, One-Nil Management**
104 Brookdale Rd
Liverpool
Merseyside
L15 3JF
T 0151 709 3995/734 2314
*Contact* Philip Hayes

**Total Concept Management (TCM)**
29 Morton Grove
Dewsbury
West Yorkshire
WF12 9RA
T 01924 438295/07887 083678    F 01924 525378

**Touched Productions**
4 Varley House
County St
London
SE1 6AL
T 020 7403 5451    F 020 7403 5446
E toucheduk@aol.com    w touched.co.uk
*Contact* Armorel Weston

*Specialists in hybrid of folk, rock and jazz, songwriter
based*

**Tracy-Carter Management**
WT House
Pilling
Preston
Lancashire
PR3 6SJ
T 01253 790682    F 01253 790686/790157
E tcm@dial.pipex.com
*Director* William Tracy-Carter

**Triad Management**
173 Hills Rd
Cambridge
CB2 2RJ
T 01223 503107/07801 259801    F 01223 515974
E skybiz.cam@skybiz.com
*Contact* Trina Dolenz

**Trinifold Management**
12 Oval Rd
London
NW1 7DH
T 020 7419 4300    F 020 7419 4325
E trinuk@globalnet.co.uk
*Contact* Bill Curbishley or Robert Rosenberg

**TSD Records**
14 Coneycroft
Dunnington
York
North Yorkshire
YO1 5RL
T 01904 489337    F as telephone
E trevor@tsd-records.demon.co.uk
*Contact* T Dawton

**Twenty First Artists**
1 Blythe Rd
London
W14 0HG
T 020 7348 4800    F 020 7348 4801
*Creative Director* Derek Mackillop

**Ubik Management**
PO Box 26335
London
N8 9ZA
T 020 8340 8050    F 020 8340 8060
E ubik.management@virgin.net
*Contact* Stewart Pettey

**Ultimate Music Management**
49 Highlands Rd
Horsham
West Sussex
RH13 5LS
T 020 7371 0995    F 020 7371 0993
E ultimate@dial.pipex.com
w ultimate-music.co.uk
*Contact* Paul Wells

**Unicorn Entertainments**
21 Brookfield Cottages
Lymm
Cheshire
WA13 0DH
T 01925 757702    F 01925 757703
*Contact* Richard M Condo

**Upland Live Management**
71 Lansdowne Rd
Purley
Surrey
CR8 2PD
T 020 8645 0013    E flamingofleece@yahoo.com
w geocities.com/flamingofleece

*Contact* Alvin LeDup

*An ensemble of eclectic, high-quality low-fi acts*
*Scrummy Records: Andy Callen, Flamingo Fleece*
*Low Quality Accident label: Prairie Dogs of Abilene*
*'A punk organization with tunes'*

**Urban Management**
7a Middle St
Brighton
East Sussex
BN1 1AL
T 01903 877700/07831 651857
*Contact* Nick Sellors

**Value Added Talent Management (VAT)**
1–2 Purley Place
London
N1 1QA
T 020 7704 9720    F 020 7226 6135
*Managing Director* Dan Silver

**Vashti**
PO Box 1400
Maidenhead
Berks
SL6 1GU
T 01628 620082/620083    F 01628 637066
*Managing Director* Chris Robinson

**Verge Management**
Henry A Crosbie Business Centre
Ossory Rd
Dublin 3
Ireland
T 00 353 1 856 0526    F 00 353 1 856 0527
E colm.mcgrath@verge.ie    w verge.ie
*Contact* Colm McGrath

**Vern Allen Management**
Marvern
4 Newhayes Close
Exeter
Devon
EX2 9JJ
T 01392 273305/07850 331632    F 01392 426421
E vern@vernallen.co.uk    w vernallen.co.uk
*Contact* Vernon Winteridge

*Specialists in tribute and function bands*

**Vine Gate Music**
4 Vine Gate
Parsonage Lane
Farnham Common
Bucks
SL2 3NX
T 01753 643696   F 01753 642259
E vinegate@clara.net   W salenajones.co.uk
*Contact* Tony Puxley

*Label and management services and promotion for international jazz singer Salena Jones*

**Violation Management**
2 Malvern Rd
Luton
Beds
LU1 1LQ
T 01767 651552/07768 667076   F 01767 651228
E dicky_boy@msn.com
*Contact* Dick Meredith

**Vision Promotions**
10 Gottfried Mews
off Fortess Rd
London
NW5 2HN
T 020 7482 6622   F 020 7482 5599
E visionpromotions@madasafish.com
W visionmusic.co.uk
Head of Promotions: Rob Dallison

*Promotion service for labels and artists, mainly dance music in all genres*

**Voltage Music Management**
30a Woodstock Grove
London
W12 8LE
T 020 8743 4238   F 020 8746 1413
E voltage@dial.pipex.com
*Contact* Colin R Davey

**VROE**
Lanhearne
Meaver Rd
Mullion
Helston
Cornwall
TR12 7DN
T 01326 240662   F as telephone
*Managing Director* Andrew Reeve

**W G Stonebridge Artist Management**
The Chapel
57 St Dionis Rd
London
SW6 4UB
T 020 7731 2100   F 020 7371 7722
E gooner@netcomuk.co.uk
*Contact* Bill Stonebridge

**Wally Dent Entertainments**
121a Woodlands Avenue
West Byfleet
Surrey
KT14 6AS
T 01932 347885/351444   F 01932 336229
E wallydent@hotmail.com
*Managing Director* Wally Dent

**War Zones and Associates**
33 Kersley Rd
London
N16 0NT
T 020 7249 2894   F 020 7254 3729
E wz33@aol.com
*Contact* Richard Hermitage

**Websongs**
Portland House
164 New Cavendish St
London
W1M 7FJ
T 020 7323 5793   F 020 7323 5794
E rob.hatschek@websongs.co.uk
W websongs.co.uk
*Contact* Rob Hatschek

**Wedge Music**
63 Grosvenor St
London
W1X 9DA
**T** 020 7493 7831    **F** 020 7491 3028
*Contact* Tony Gordon


**Whatever Next! Management**
c/o Flat C, 87 Saltram Crescent
London
W9 3SS
**T** 020 8960 9310    **F** as telephone
**E** mandy@whatnext.freeserve.co.uk
*Contact* Mandy Freedman


**White Tiger Management**
19 Albert Bridge Rd
London
SW11 4PX
**T** 020 7207 4072/4073    **F** 020 7207 4074
**E** white.tiger@virgin.net
*Contact* Paul White


**Whitenoise Management Ltd**
8 Southam St
London
W10 5PH
**T** 020 8964 0020    **F** 020 8964 0021
**E** chrisb@white-noise.co.uk
*Managing Director* Chris Butler


**Wicked Wolf Management**
52 Wardour St
London
W1V 3HL
**T** 020 7437 0329    **F** 020 7494 4747
**E** shay@wickedwolf.co.uk
*Chief Executive Officer* Seamus Murphy

*See also Marshmallow Records*


**Wild Amazon (Personal Management)**
Norden
2 Hillhead Rd
Newtonhill
Stonehaven
Kincardine and Deeside
AB39 3TS
**T** 01569 730962    **F** as telephone
*Managing Director* Doug Stone


**Wild Honey Management**
1st Floor, Concorde House
81 Margaret St
Brighton
East Sussex
BN2 1TS
**T** 01273 818802    **F** 01273 818803
**E** jimtracey@aol.com    **W** wildhoney.co.uk
*Contact* Jim Tracey


**Wildlife Entertainment Ltd**
Unit F
21 Heathmans Rd
London
SW6 4TJ
**T** 020 7371 7008    **F** 020 7371 7708
**E** wildlife@dircon.co.uk
*Contact* Ian McAndrew or Colin Lester


**Wink Leisure Enterprises**
39 Blake Avenue
Wath upon Deame
Rotherham
South Yorkshire
S63 6NT
**T** 01709 872864    **F** 01709 873916
*Proprietor* John Winstanley


**WKS**
Quadrant House (Air St entrance)
80–82 Regent St
London
W1R 5PA
**T** 020 7304 4646    **F** 020 7304 4647
**E** pmoore@kingstonsmith.co.uk
**W** kingstonsmith.co.uk
*Contact* Paul Moore


**WS Management**
1 St Edmunds Avenue
Ruislip
Middlesex
HA4 7XW
**T** 01895 639701    **F** 01895 678766
**E** bill@wsmgt.demon.co.uk    **W** wsmgt.co.uk
*Contact* William L Smith

*Roster includes Stevie 'Vann' Lange*

## Wyze Management

34 Maple St
London
W1 5GD
T 07000 9993 100   F 07000 9993 200
*Contact* Kate Ross

## X-Dream Ltd

Stones
Wickham St Pauls
Halstead
Essex
CO9 2PS
T 01787 269089   F 01787 269029
*Contact* Alistair Gosling

## XL Talent Partnership

Reverb House
Bennett St
London
W4 2AH
T 020 8747 0660   F 020 8747 0880
*Contact* Ian Wright

## Yellow Balloon Productions Ltd

Freshwater House
Outdowns
Effingham
Surrey
KT24 5QR
T 01483 281500/281501   F 01483 281502
E yellowbal@aol.com
*Contact* Mike Smith, Sally Thomas or Daryl Smith

*Popular to punk. Also TV theme writers and publishers through sister company Mike Music Roster includes Karen Noble, Cleve 'M', Jay Taylor etc*

## Young Producers Stable

101 Chamberlayne Rd
London
NW10 3ND
T 020 8960 8466   F 020 8968 5892
*Managing Director* Brian Hallin

## Z Management

PO Box 19734
London
SW15 2WU
T 020 8874 3337/07956 912696   F 020 8874 3599

## Zero Degrees Management

PO Box 21967
London
SW16 6WW
T 020 8769 3455   F 020 8769 7770
*Contact* Neil Cranston

## AB Entertainments
Unit 2, The Quarry
Kewstoke Rd
Worle
Weston-Super-Mare
BS2 9LS
T 01934 522222/07050 277053
*Contact* Ken Lintern

## ABA Booking
7 North Parade
Bath
BA2 4DD
T 01225 428284    F 01225 400090
E aca_aba@freenet.co.uk
*Contact* H Finegold

*Also ACA Music Management and Release Records*
*(same contact details)*
*Jazz/swing, rock, pop/covers, blues and country*

## ABS Agency
2 Elgin Avenue
London
W9 3QP
T 020 7289 1160    F 020 7289 1162
E nigel@absagency.u-net.com
*Contact* Nigel Kerr

*All styles of music, contemporary, blues and world*

## Acker's International Jazz Agency
53 Cambridge Mansions
Cambridge Rd
London
SW11 4RX
T 020 7978 5885    F 020 7978 5882
E pamela@ackersmusicagency.co.uk
W ackersmusicagency.co.uk
*Contact* Pamela Sutton

*NB: personal management and exclusive agency for*
*Mr Acker Bilk and his Paramount Jazz Band*
*Also non-exclusive agents eg for Humphrey Lyttelton,*
*Kenny Ball and Chris Barber*

### African Caribbean Asian Entertainment Agency

Stars Building
10 Silverhill Close
Nottingham
NG8 6QL
**T** 0115 951 9864   **F** 0115 951 9874
**E** acts@african-caribbean-ents.com
*Contact* Mr L I Sackey

*Agency, distributor, manufacturer, producer*

### Agency Group Ltd

370 City Rd
London
EC1V 5QA
**T** 020 7278 3331   **F** 020 7837 4672

*Roster of over 400 acts including Barenaked Ladies,*
*Catatonia, Foo Fighters, Pink Floyd, Status Quo,*
*Alice Deejay, Bloodhound Gang, Eiffel 65*
*Offices in London, New York, Toronto, Amsterdam,*
*Copenhagen and Los Angeles*

### AIR Ltd

AIR House
Spennymoor
Co Durham
DL16 7SE
**T** 01388 814632   **F** 01388 812445
**E** air@agents-uk.com   **w** airagency.com
*Contact Name* Colin Pearson/John Wray

*Agents and Promoters*

### Arcadia Music Agency

1 Felday Glade
Holmbury St Mary
Surrey
RH5 6PG
**T** 01306 730040   **E** arcadia@musi.co.uk
**w** musi.co.uk
*Contact* Max Rankin

*Runs online sourcing service for working musicians*
*and entertainers for commercial and social functions,*
*offering free website presence*
*Approaches welcome from suitable artists with an*
*e-mail address*

### Asgard Promotions

125 Parkway
London
NW1 7PS
**T** 020 7387 5090   **F** 020 7387 8740
**E** info@asgard-uk.com
*Managing Directors* Paul Fenn and Paul Charles

*Contemporary agency with roster ranging from Tom*
*Waits to Ocean Colour Scene, Emmylou Harris to*
*Ray Davies*

### Avenue Artistes Ltd

8 Winn Rd
Southampton
Hampshire
SO17 1EN
**T** 01703 551000   **F** 01703 905703

### Barn Dance and Line Dance Agency

62 Beechwood Rd
South Croydon
Surrey
CR2 0AA
**T** 020 8657 2813   **F** 020 8651 6080
**E** barndanceagency@btinternet.com
**w** barn-dance.co.uk
*Contact* Derek Jones

*Also Barn Dance Publications Ltd, suppliers of*
*country dance books, videos, CDs and cassettes (same*
*contact details)*

### Barry Collings Entertainments

21a Clifftown Rd
Southend-on-Sea
Essex
SS1 1AB
**T** 01702 330005   **F** 01702 333309
**E** bcollent@aol.com   **w** barrycollings.co.uk
*Contact* Barry Collings

*Began in 1964, first as manager, then as agent*
*Roster includes Abba tributes, Alvin Stardust, Cliff*
*Bennett, Dave Berry, Edwin Starr, Geno*
*Washington, Mud and Suzi Quatro*

## Barry Dye Entertainments
PO Box 888
Ipswich
Suffolk
IP1 6BU
T 01473 744287/07831 700799    F 01473 745442
E barrydye@aol.com

## Barry Peller
14 West St
Beighton
Sheffield
S20 1EP
T 0114 247 2365    F 0114 247 2156
E barry@pellerartistes.com    w pellerartistes.com
*Contact* Barry Peller

*UK's leading supplier of tribute acts to the corporate market*

## Bechhofer Agency
51 Barnton Park View
Edinburgh
EH4 6HH
T 0131 339 4083    F 0131 339 9261
E agency@bechhofer.demon.co.uk
*Contact* Frank Bechhofer

*Sole British representation for a roster of folk and folk related artists*

## Big Bear Music
PO Box 944
Birmingham
West Midlands
B16 8UT
T 0121 454 7020    F 0121 454 9996
E bigbearmusic@compuserve.com
w bigbearmusic.com
*Contact* Jim Simpson

*Part of Big Bear Music Group (management, agency, jazz festival organizers, British Jazz Awards, publishing and magazine)*

## Bite Agency
Suite 207A
The Saga Centre
326 Kensal Rd
London
W10 5BZ

## Celtic Artists – Aisling Entertainments
95 Carshalton Park Rd
Carshalton Beeches
Surrey
SM5 3SJ
T 020 8647 3084    F 020 8395 3560
E keirajennings@cwcom.net
*Contact* Keira Jennings

## Club Jamin
44 Lupton St
London
NW5
T 020 7482 5042    F 020 7482 5042
*Contact* Lee Hudson

*Specialists in African, reggae, ragga, hiphop, Latin, jazz and blues*

## Complete Entertainment Services
PO Box 112
Seaford
East Sussex
BN25 2DQ
T 01323 492266    F 01323 492234
E chrisbray@completeentertainment.co.uk
w completeentertainment.co.uk
*Contact* Chris Bray

*Full member of the National Entertainment Agents Council*

## Concert Clinic Ltd
35 Britannia Row
London
N1 8QH
T 020 7704 8000    F 020 7704 8999
E info@concertclinic.com    w concertclinic.com
*Contact* Rob Challice or Clive Underhill-Smith

## Concorde International Artistes

101 Shepherds Bush Rd
London
W6 7LP
T 020 7602 8822   F 020 7603 2352
E cia@cia.uk.com
*Contact* Solomon Parker or Paul Fitzgerald

*Also band management*

## Continental Drifts

Hatherley Mews
London
E17 4QP
T 020 8509 3353   F 020 8509 9531
E demojury@continentaldrifts.co.uk
W continentaldrifts.uk.com
*Contact* Chris Tofu

*UK's largest agency dealing with unsigned acts, and
organizer of the Firestarter stage at festivals featuring
new bands
Also circus acts, comedy, kids performers etc
Plus British Underground, an association of
independent labels*

## Creeme Entertainments

East Lynne, Harper Green Rd
Doe Hey, Farnworth
Bolton
Lancashire
BL4 7HT
T 01204 793441/793018   F 01204 792655
E info@creeme.co.uk   W creeme.co.uk
*Contact* Tom Ivers, Lynne Ivers or Anthony

*Quality entertainment for clubs and cabaret,
corporate events and private functions*

## Crown Entertainments

103 Bromley Common
Bromley
Kent
BR2 9RN
T 020 8464 0454   F 020 8290 4038
E info@crownentertainments.co.uk
W crownentertainments.co.uk
*Contact* David Nash

*Specialists in functions, cover bands, tributes and
self-contained solos and duos*

## Dave Seamer Entertainments

46 Magdalen Rd
Oxford
OX4 1RB
T 01865 240054   F 01865 240054
E dave@daveseamer.co.uk   W daveseamer.co.uk
*Contact* Dave Seamer

## DCM International (Dance Crazy Management)

Suite 3
294–296 Nether St
London
N3 1RJ
T 020 8343 0848   F 020 8343 0747
E dancecm@aol.com   W dancecrazy.co.uk

*Specialize in all forms of commercial recording,
dance artistes and singers
UK and overseas for clubs, pubs, corporate events,
festivals and concerts
DJs, lookalikes, tributes and speciality acts*

## Denis Vaughan

PO Box 28286
London
N21 3WT
T 020 7486 5353   F 01372 742448
E dvaughanmusic@dial.pipex.com
*Contact* Denis Vaughan

*NB: Works with established artists as impresario, eg
Chuck Berry, Demis Roussos, Nana Mouskouri etc*

## Dinosaur Promotions/Pulse (The Agency)

5 Heyburn Crescent
Westport Gardens
Stoke-on-Trent
Staffs
ST6 4DL
T 01782 824051   F 01782 761752
E alan@dinoprom.com
songs@dinosaurmusic.co.uk
W dinoprom.com and dinosaurmusic.co.uk
*Contact* Alan E Dutton

*Suppliers of all kinds of entertainers and
entertainment*

## Emkay Entertainments

Regent Centre
Linlithgow
West Lothian
EH49 7HU
T 01506 845555   F 01506 845566
E emkay@cwcom.net
*Contact* Mike Kean

*Also artiste management*

## Essential Music Distributions

Stars Building
10 Silverhill Close
Nottingham
NG8 6QL
T 0115 951 9864   F 0115 951 9874
*Contact* Elaine Sackey

## F&G Management & Booking

Unit A105
326 Kensal Rd
London
W10 5BZ
T 020 8964 1917/020 8960 9562   F 020 8960 9971
E roisinp@btclick.com
*Contact* Roisin Potter

## Flick Productions

PO Box 888
Penzance
Cornwall
TR20 8ZP
T 01736 788798   F 01736 787898
E info@flickpro.demon.co.uk
*Contact* Mark Shaw

*Also management and promotion*

## Fruit Pie Music Agency

The Shop
443 Streatham High Rd
London
SW16 3PH
T 020 8679 9289   F 020 8679 9775
E info@fruitpiemusic.com   w fruitpiemusic.com
*Contact* Kumar

*Specialists in tribute and covers bands, but also
general entertainment*

## Gordon Poole Agency Ltd

The Limes
Brockley
Bristol
BS48 3BB
T 01275 463222   F 01275 462252
E agents@gordonpoole.com   w gordonpoole.com
*Contact* Gordon Poole

*Established in the 1960s, and provides all types of
musicians and bands throughout the world for
corporate, hotel, public and private events*

## Groove Company

39 Meadow Way
Old Windsor
Berks
SL4 2NX
T 01753 866518
E groovco@groovyred.screaming.net
w groovecompany.co.uk
*Contact* Tracey Askem

*Provides live music/musicians for any occasion
Original and cover bands
Also Alker & Askem Arrangements, a musical
arranging/transcription service for cabaret singers,
bands etc*

## Hal Carter Organization

101 Hazelwood Lane
London
N13 5HQ
T 020 8886 2801   F 020 8882 7380
E artists@halcarterorg.com   w halcarterorg.com
*Contact* Malcolm Cook and Abbie Carter

*1960s and 70s artists
The Illegal Eagles, Rumours of Fleetwood Mac, The
Carpenters' Story and Blondie Goes to Hollywood
Occasional co-promotion of shows and tours, artist
management and festival bookings*

## Headline Agency

106 Trees Rd
Mount Merrion
Co. Dublin
Ireland
T 00 353 1 278 9177   F 00 353 1 278 9198
E madelein@indigo.ie
*Director* Madeleine Seiler

*Also Artiste Promotions & Management (same contact details)*

## Henderson Management Agency
51 Promenade North
Cleveleys
Blackpool
Lancs
FY5 1LN
**T** 01253 863386/07770 58852   **F** 01253 867799
**E** agents@henderson-management.co.uk
**W** henderson-management.co.uk
*Contact* John Henderson

*Tributes, named 60s – 90s bands, dance, soul and party bands, cover bands, lookalikes etc*

## Hilton International Entertainments/GBA (Int)
27 Downs Side
Cheam
Surrey
SM2 7EH
**T** 020 8643 3991/020 8643 8375   **F** 020 8770 7241
**E** gbaltd@compuserve.com
*Contact* A G Brown

*Suppliers to major shipping lines and hotel groups*

## Hinc Inc Ltd
PO Box 7
Ware
Herts
SG12 9UD
**T** 01920 467780   **F** 01920 466077
**E** hincdom@ntlworld.com
*Contact* Mike Hinc

## International Artistes Ltd
2nd Floor, Television House
10–12 Mount St
Manchester
M2 5FA
**T** 0161 833 9838   **F** 0161 832 7480
**E** intartltd@aol.com   **W** i-a-l.com
*Managing Director* Stuart Littlewood

*Also at Mezzanine Floor, 235 Regent Street, London W1R 8AX (phone: 020 7439 8401; fax: 020 7409 2070)*

## International Talent Booking
3rd Floor, 27a Floral St
London
WC2E 9DQ
**T** 020 7379 1313   **F** 020 7379 1744

## John Boddy Agency
10 Southfield Gardens
Twickenham
Middx
TW1 4SZ
**T** 020 8892 0133/020 8891 3809   **F** 020 8892 4283
**E** email@johnboddyagency.co.uk
*Contact* John Boddy

*International entertainment consultants, artiste representation, production services*

## John Martin Promotions
3 Manor Park
Staines
Middx
TW18 4XF
**T** 01784 456324   **F** 01784 454433
**E** johnmartinpromotions@talk21.com
*Contact* John Martin

## John Miles Organization
Cadbury Camp Lane
Clapton in Gordano
Bristol
BS20 7SB
**T** 01275 854675/856770   **F** 01275 810186
**E** john@johnmiles.org.uk

## Kennedy Street Enterprises Ltd
Kennedy House
31 Stamford St
Altrincham
Cheshire
WA14 1ES
**T** 0161 941 5151   **F** 0161 928 9491
**E** kse@kennedystreet.com
*Contact* Danny Betesh, Jim Colson or Stuart Owen

*Mainly concert promoters (eg Van Morrison, Meatloaf, B B King etc)*

## Label Spinners/UK Booking Agency

Box No.1, 404 Footscray Rd
London
SE9 3TU
**T** 020 8857 8775/020 8355 9700   **F** 020 8857 8775
**E** spinners@dircon.co.uk/
info@ukbookingagency.co.uk
**w** labelspinners.co.uk/ukbookingagency.co.uk
*Contact* Steve Goddard

*Label Spinners works across the board, including
aircraft charter, stage, sound and lights, marquees etc
Also record label, A&R and management
UK booking also deals in less 'musical' acts (variety,
hypnotists, comics etc)*

## Leighton-Pope Organization (Artist Agency)

8 Glenthorne Mews
115a Glenthorne Rd
London
W6 0LJ
**T** 020 8741 4453   **F** 020 8741 4289
**E** andrew@l-po.com/carl@l-po.com
*Contact* Carl or Andrew Leighton-Pope

## Limelight Entertainment

23 Westbury Avenue
Droitwich Spa
Worcs
WR9 0RT
**T** 01905 796816   **F** 01905 798449
*Contact* John Nash

*Cover acts from 1960s to 90s and themed evenings (eg
Bavarian, Irish, Medieval)*

## Mike & Margaret Storey Entertainments

Cliffe End Business Park
Dale St
Longwood
Huddersfield
West Yorks
HD3 4TG
**T** 01484 657054/657055   **F** 01484 657055
*Contact* Mike Storey

*Specialists in country music*

## Mike Malley Entertainments

10 Holly Park Gardens
London
N3 3NJ
**T** 020 8346 4109/020 8346 4293   **F** 020 8346 1104
**E** mikemall@globalnet.co.uk   **w** ukstars.co.uk
*Contact* Mike Malley

*NB: new bands only with major deal
Interested in good cover bands, particularly with
female vocalists*

## Miracle Prestige International

1 Water Lane
London
NW1 8NZ
**T** 020 7267 5599   **F** 020 7267 5155
**E** agents@mpi-agency.co.uk   **w** mpi-agency.com
*Contact* Phil Banfield

*Roster of dance, alternative, DJ and mainstream acts
including Bentley Rhythm Ace, The Freestylers, The
Human League, Jools Holland, Ruby Turner, Sting
and Supertramp*

## Mission Control Agency

50 City Business Centre
Lower Rd
London
SE16 2XB
**T** 020 7252 3001   **F** 020 7252 2225
**E** agents@mission-control.co.uk
**w** mission-control.co.uk
*Contact* Guy Anderson

*Agents for pop and dance music groups worldwide*

## Mrs Casey Music

PO Box 296
Aylesbury
Bucks
HP19 3TL
**T** 01296 394411   **F** 01296 392300
**E** mcm@mrscasey.co.uk   **w** mrscasey.co.uk

## NDS Management Services
The Barn
South Cottage
Barns Green
Horsham
West Sussex
RH13 7PR
**T** 01403 730230    **F** 01403 730430
**E** sales@ndsm.co.uk    **W** ndsm.co.uk
*Contact* Neale Francis

*Corporate and private functions, dance bands and tributes, classical and ethnic bands/musicans*

## New Music Enterprises
Meredale
Reach Lane
Heath and Reach
Leighton Buzzard
Beds
LU7 0AL
**T** 01525 237700    **F** 01525 237700
**E** pauldavis@newmusic28.freeserve.co.uk
**W** lcf.uk.net
*Contact* Paul Davis

*NB: Specialists in Christian music*

## Nita Anderson Agency
165 Wolverhampton Rd
Sedgley
nr Dudley
West Midlands
DY3 1QR
**T** 01902 882211    **F** 01902 883356
**E** na004a6952@blueyonder.co.uk
**W** nitaanderson.co.uk
*Contact* Juanita Anderson

## Norman Jackson Entertainment Agency
2 Dawlish Rd
London
E10 6QD
**T** 020 8556 3222    **F** 020 8556 3223
*Contact* Ray Gould

*Bands of all types (ballroom, jazz, ethnic, pop, classical, cockney, olde-tyme, disco, c&w, barn dance, Latin etc)*

## P3 Music
PO Box 8403
Maybole
KA19 7YB
**T** 01655 750549    **F** 01655 750548
**E** james@p3music.com    **W** p3music.com
*Contact* James Taylor or Alison Burns

*Also record company, publishing, management and consultancy*

## Paul Barrett (Rock 'n' Roll Enterprises)
16 Grove Place
Penarth
S Glamorgan
CF6 2LD
**T** 029 2070 4279    **F** 029 2070 9989
**E** barrett.rocknroll@amserve.net
*Contact* Paul Barrett

*NB: Only handles pre-Beatles rock 'n' roll music and performers, UK and American*
*Roster includes The Jets, Matchbox, Crazy Cavan & The Rhythm Rockers and The Rimshots*

## Portass & Carter Entertainment
26 Bridge Rd
Sutton Bridge
Lincs
PE12 9OA
Spalding
**T** 01406 350407/350266

## Premiere, The One Stop Entertainment Shop Ltd
Suite 4, Delme Court
Maytree Rd
Fareham
Hampshire
PO16 0HX
**T** 01329 238449    **F** 01329 238449
**E** premiere@agents-uk.com    **W** onestopents.com
*Contact* Del Mitchell

## Profile Artists Agency
Unit 101, J Block
Tower Bridge Business Complex
110 Clements Rd
London
SE16 4DG
**T** 020 7394 0012    **F** 020 7394 0094

**E** enquiry@profileagency.co.uk
**W** profileagency.co.uk
*Contact* Serena Parsons

*Dance music specialists (hiphop, house, garage, drum
'n' bass, breakbeat and jazz breaks)*


## Pure Energy Productions
PO Box 4265
Poole
Dorset
BH15 3YJ
**T** 01202 777724   **F** 01202 777726
**E** ian@pepuk.com   **W** pepuk.com
*Contact* Ian Walker


## PVA Ltd
2 High St
Westbury-on-Trym
Bristol
BS9 3DU
**T** 0117 950 4504   **F** 0117 959 1786
**E** enquiries@pva.ltd.uk   **W** pva.ltd.uk
*Contact* Pat Vincent or John Hutchinson


## Red Parrot Agency
Unit 20, Phoenix House
86 Fulham High St
London
SW6 3LF
**T** 020 7736 9676   **F** 020 7736 3726
**E** red.parrot@virgin.net   **W** mezzmusic.com
*Contact* Andria Law

*Also Red Parrot Management (contact John
Cecchini) and labels Beak Recordings, Caged Records
and Red Parrot Recordings (contact Andy Penny)
Mainly dance music and culture*


## Ridiculous Music Productions
Stars Building
10 Silverhill Close
Nottingham
NG8 6QL
**T** 0115 951 9864   **F** 0115 951 9874
**E** anr@ridiculous-music-productions.com
**W** ridiculous-music-productions.com
*Contact* Isaacs

## Ro-Lo Productions
35 Dillotford Avenue
Styvechale
Coventry
West Midlands
CV3 5DR
**T** 024 7641 0388/07711 817475   **F** 024 7641 6615
**E** roger.lomas@virgin.net
*Contact* Roger Lomas

*Ska specialist (The 2 Tone Collective, The Selecter,
Desmond Dekker) plus other bands like Roy Wood's
Army and The Fortunes*


## Second Wave Promotions
PO Box 385
Uxbridge
Middx
UB9 5DZ
**T** 01494 580951   **F** 01494 580952
**E** swprom@aol.com
*Contact* Glenn Povey

*Also concert promotion
Artists include Gong, Caravan, Hugh Cornwell*


## Serious Ltd
Chapel House
18 Hatton Place
London
EC1N 8RU
**T** 020 7405 9900   **F** 020 7405 9911
**E** david@serious.org.uk   **W** serious.org.uk
*Contact* David Jones

*NB: New music only (no tribute, pop, mainstream
etc) and first contact by mail, please*


## Solo Agency
55 Fulham High St
London
SW6 3JJ
**T** 020 7736 5925   **F** 020 7731 6921
**E** solo@solo.uk.com   **W** solo.uk.com

## South Yorkshire Musical Enterprises

81 Park Rd
Wath-upon-Dearne
Rotherham
South Yorks
S63 7LE
**T** 01709 877920  **F** 01709 873119/0870 1640589
**E** syme@csi.com

## Steve Allen Entertainments

60 Broadway
Peterborough
PE1 1SU
**T** 01733 569589  **F** 01733 561854
**E** steve@sallenent.co.uk  **W** sallenent.co.uk
*Contact* Steve Allen

*Specialists in corporate occasions, private parties and social events*

## Steve Draper Entertainments

2 The Coppice
Beardwood Manor
Blackburn
Lancs
BB2 7BQ
**T** 01254 679005  **F** 01254 679005
**E** steve.draper@access2.co.uk

## Swamp Music

PO Box 94
Derby
DE22 1XA
**T** 01332 332336/07702 564804  **F** 01332 332336
**E** chrishall@swampmusic.co.uk
**W** swampmusic.co.uk
*Contact* Chris Hall

*Specialists in cajun and zydeco*
*Both UK (R Cajun and the Zydeco Brothers, Bearcats, Zydecomotion) and Louisiana (Steve Riley and the Mamou Playboys, Sean Ardoin 'n' Zydekoll etc)*
*Also Bearcat Records*

## Timebomb

1st Floor, 26 Stokes Croft
Bristol
BS1 3QD
**T** 0117 909 8881  **F** 0117 909 8882

**E** agency@timebomb.globalnet.co.uk
**W** timebombmusic.co.uk
*Contact* Steve Symons

*Live bands and DJs*
*Roster includes The Bays, Fuzz Against Junk, Organic Audio and Unsung Heroes*

## Tony Bennell Entertainment Agency

10 Manor Way
Kidlington
Oxfordshire
OX5 2BD
**T** 01865 372645/07885 204274  **F** 01865 372645
**E** tonybennell@hotmail.com

## Tony Denton Promotions Ltd

19 South Molton Lane
London
W1K 5LE
**T** 020 7629 4666  **F** 020 7629 4777
**E** mail@tdpromo.com  **W** tdpromo.com
*Contact* Tony Denton

*Represents over 140 chart and classic artistes*

## Top Talent Agency

Yester Rd
Chiselhurst
Kent
BR7 5HN
**T** 020 8467 0808  **F** 020 8467 0808
*Contact* John Day

*Cabarets, shows, bands, after-dinner speakers, race nights*

## Total Concept Management (TCM)

PO Box 128
Dewsbury
West Yorks
WF12 9XS
**T** 01924 438295  **F** 01924 525378
**E** tcm.info@ntlworld.com

*Also artist management, eg The Inseminators*

## UK Steel Bands Agency

Stars Building
10 Silverhill Close
Nottingham
NG8 6QL
**T** 0115 976 2726    **F** 0115 951 9874
**E** bands@uk-steel-bands-agency.com
**W** uk-steel-bands-agency.com
*Contact* Mr L I Sackey

*Agency and steel band distributor*


## Value Added Talent Agency

1–2 Purley Place
London
N1 1QA
**T** 020 7704 9720    **F** 020 7226 6135
**E** vatlondon@aol.com

## !K7 Records/Rapster Records
1 Devonport Mews
London
W12 8NG
T 020 8762 9910   F 020 8762 9912
E katherine@studio-k7.com   W studio-k7.com
*Contact* Katherine Eykelenboom

## 10 Kilo
Unit 16
Acklam Rd Workshops
10 Acklam Rd
London
W10 5QZ
T 020 8960 5534   F 020 8960 5538
E tip@online.rednet.co.uk   W tip.co.uk
*Contact* Richard Bloor

## 100%love Records
PO Box 134
Horley
Surrey
RH6 0FT
T 01293 862459   F 01293 862913

## 101 Management
35 Britannia Row
London
N1 8QH
T 020 7704 6708   F 020 7704 6709
*Contact* Cliff Whyte

## 13th Moon Records
PO Box 416
Cardiff
CF11 6UU
T 029 2022 3479   F as telephone
E 13thmoon@asf-13thmoon.demon.co.uk
W asf-13thmoon.demon.co.uk
*Contact* Liz Howell

## 23rd Precinct Recordings
23 Bath St
Glasgow
G2 1HU
T 0141 332 9740/4806   F 0141 353 3039
E limbo@23rdprecinct-limbo.com
W 23rdprecinct-limbo.com
*A&R Director* Billy Kiltie

## 2B3 records

27 Solon Rd
London
SW2 5UU
**T** 020 7738 7144/7274 0782  **F** 020 7738 4399
*Contact* Neville Thomas

## 3 Beat Music Ltd

58 Wood St
Liverpool
L1 4AQ
**T** 0151 707 1669  **F** 0151 707 0227
**E** info@3beat.co.uk  **W** 3beat.co.uk
*Label Manager* Michelle Woolf
*Managing Director* Jon Barlow

*Dance specialist*

## 304 Records

75 School Rd
Moseley
Birmingham
B13 9TF
**T** 07980 886513  **F** 0121 551 9250

*Also Zenith Productions*
*Both specializing in reggae, soul, R&B, hiphop*
*See also Earth (recording studio)*

## 33 Records

33 Guildford St
Luton
Beds
LU1 2NQ
**T** 01582 419584/07850 207346  **F** 01582 459401
**E** 33jazz@compuserve.com  **W** 33jazz.com
*Contact* Paul Jolly

## 34 Salisbury Street

London
NW8 8QE
**T** 020 7402 9111  **F** 020 7723 3064
*Managing Director* Eliot Cohen

*Also Satellite Music Ltd (same details)*

## 3Beat

58 Wood St
Liverpool
L1 4AQ
**T** 0151 707 1669  **F** 0151 707 0227
**E** rob@3beat.co.uk  **W** 3beat.co.uk
*Contact* Rob Jay

*Dance music*
*See also Glow Records*

## 3D Recordings

Unit 9, Morrison Yard
551a High Rd
London
N17 6SB
**T** 020 8801 5878  **F** 020 8808 9885
**E** dave@roundway.com
*Contact* Dave Thompson

## 4 Liberty Records

Unit 16a
149 Roman Way
London
N7 8XE
**T** 020 7609 6005  **F** 020 7609 6008
**E** generalinfo@libertyrecords.com
**W** libertyrecords.com
*Contact* Tony Portelli (Managing Director); Doug
Cooper (Club Promotions Manager); Marina
Forsythe (Press & PR Manager); Paul Hamilton
(A&R Manager)

## 4AD

17–19 Alma Rd
London
SW18 1AA
**T** 020 8870 9724  **F** 020 8874 6600
**E** fourad@almaroad.co.uk  **W** 4ad.com
*Managing Director* Chris Sharp
*Head of A&R* Ed Horrox

*Independent record label, founded in 1980*
*Roster includes Kristin Hersh and Tanya Donelly,*
*The Breeders and Piano Magic*

## 500 Rekords

PO Box 9499
London
E5 0UG
**T** 020 7375 1500  **F** as telephone

**E** paul@500records.freeserve.co.uk
**W** 500records.co.uk
*Contact* Paul C

*Dance music specialists*

## 706 Records
202 Fulham Rd
London
SW10 9PJ
**T** 020 7351 5167   **F** 020 7352 1514
**E** muirhead_management@compuserve.com
*Chief Executive Officer* Dennis Muirhead

## A New Day
75 Wren Way
Farnborough
Hants
GU14 8TA
**T** 01252 540270   **F** 01252 372001
**E** davidrees1@compuserve.com
**W** anewdayrecords.co.uk
*Managing Director* Dave Rees

## A2 Records
Tudor House
Pinstone Way
Gerrards Cross
Buckinghamshire
SL9 7BJ
**T** 01753 893665/105140   **F** 01753 889888
**E** amp@assassination.co.uk   **W** assassination.co.uk
*Contact* Rupert Withers

## aardvarkrecords.co.uk
75 Alderwood Parc
Penryn
TR10 8RL
**T** 01326 376707/07974 694735   **F** as first telephone
**E** musicman@aardvarkrecords.co.uk
**W** aardvarkrecords.co.uk
*Contact* Andrew Reeve

*By exercising A&R control, marketing and
promotion, the Vark is an Internet record company
and not an online CD shop. We are currently
exploring ways of distributing through record shops*

## Absolute Records
Craig Gowan
Carr Bridge
Inverness-shire
PH23 3AX
**T** 01479 841771   **E** absolutemuse@hotmail.com
**W** absoluterecords.co.uk
*Contact* Stephen Richter

*Specializing in indie-pop*

## Abstract Sounds/Candlelight Records
10 Tiverton Rd
London
NW10 3HL
**T** 020 7286 1106   **F** 020 7289 8679
**E** abstract@btinternet.com
**W** abstractsounds.co.uk and candlelightrecords.co.uk
*Contact* Edward Christie

*Abstract is for indie rock and pop (also Northsouth
for dance, trance and world)
Candlelight is for metal and extreme metal*

## Abyss Music Ltd
PO Box 1511
Ascot
Berkshire
SL5 9XH
**T** 01344 874677   **F** 01344 622376
**E** 106175.611@compuserve.com
*Contact* Brian Long

## Academy Street Records
PO Box 11
Bathgate
Edinburgh
EH48 1RX
**T** 01506 636038/07785 222205   **F** 01506 633900
**E** mail@clubscene.co.uk   **W** clubscene.co.uk
*Managing Director* Bill Grainger

## Ace Eyed Records
2 Menelik Rd
London
NW2 3RP
**T** 020 7435 6116   **F** as telephone number
**E** steveglen@appleonline.net
**W** bluemelon.co.uk and barbaracartland.com
*Contact* Steven Glen

## Ace Records

42–50 Steele Rd
London
NW10 7AS
**T** 020 8453 1311   **F** 020 8961 8725
**E** info@acerecords.co.uk   **w** acerecords.co.uk
*Sales* Phil Stoker

*Re-issue specialists*

## Acid Jazz Records

Unit 1
The Cooperage
91–95 Brick Lane
London
E1 6QN
**T** 020 7247 6677/7078   **F** 020 7247 8244
**E** acid-jazz@acidjazz.co.uk   **w** acidjazz.co.uk
*Contact* Julia Browne

## ACL

PO Box 31
Potters Bar
Hertfordshire
EN6 1XR
**T** 01707 644706   **F** as telephone number
**E** wmd644706@aol.com
*Contact* David Thomas

## Acoustics Records

PO Box 350
Reading
Berkshire
RD6 7DQ
**T** 0118 926 8615   **F** 0118 935 3216
**E** mail@acousticsrecords.co.uk
**w** acousticsrecords.co.uk
*Managing Director* H A Jones

## AD Music Ltd

PO Box 3021
Littlehampton
West Sussex
BN16 2NX
**T** 01903 772577   **F** as telephone
**E** admin@admusic.ltd.uk   **w** admusic.ltd.uk
*Directors* Elaine Wright, David Wright and David
Mantripp

*Artists include ambient band Code Indigo, electronic*

*duo Enterphase, composer Robert de Fresnes and
gothic ambients Witchcraft*
*Fanzine: for subscription details, write to AD*

## Additive/Positiva Records

43 Brook Green
London
W6 7EF
**T** 020 7605 5157   **F** 020 7605 5186
**E** kevin.robinson@emimusic.com
*Managing Director* Kevin Robinson
*A&R Manager* Jason Ellis
*Label Manager* Sid Li

## ADSR Records

130 Ongar Rd
Brentwood
Essex
CM15 9DJ
**T** 01277 260550   **F** 01245 468802
**E** phil@adsrrecords.com   **w** adsrrecords.com
*Contact* Phil Wyard

*Dance label: progressive house, house, breakbeat,
leftfield*

## Alias Records UK

Suite 9
Horseshoe Business Park
Upper Lye Lane
Bricket Wood
St Albans
Hertfordshire
AL2 3TA
**T** 01923 893333   **F** 01923 894911
**E** celticmoon@skynow.co.uk
*Contact* Joe Palmer

## All Around The World

9–13 Penny St
Blackburn
Lancashire
BB1 6HJ
**T** 01254 264120   **F** 01254 693768
**E** matt@aatw.com   **w** aatw.com
*General Manager* Matt Cadman

## All Good Vinyl
14 Lambton Place
London
W11 2SH
**T** 020 7482 4345    **F** 020 7482 4350
*Managing Director and Head of A&R* Jon Sexton

## All Saints Records
179 Gloucester Place
London
NW1 6DX
**T** 020 7224 9292    **F** 020 7224 9060
**E** allsaints@easynet.co.uk
*Managing Director* Dominic Norman-Taylor

## Almafame Ltd
125 Shoreditch High St
London
E1 6JE
**T** 020 7729 7799    **F** 020 7729 6776
**E** almafame@aol.com    **W** almafame.co.uk
*Contact* Kevin Crace

## Almighty Records
PO Box 12173
London
N19 4SQ
**T** 020 7281 3212    **F** 020 7281 8002
**E** info@almightyrecords.com
**W** almightyrecords.com
*Contact* Alison Travis

## Almo Sounds
3 Heathmans Rd
London
SW6 4TJ
**T** 020 7731 6828    **F** 020 7736 1884    **W** almo.co.uk/
almo
*Contact* Fun Cheung
*A&R* Nick Page

## Altarus Inc
Eastern Dene
Bailbrook Lane
Bath
BA1 7AA
**T** 01225 852323    **F** 01225 852523
**E** 100775.2716@compuserve.com
*Manager* Alistair Hinton

## Amato Disco International
Units 13–14
Barley Shotts Business Park
246 Acklam Rd
London
W10 5YG
**T** 020 8964 3302    **F** 020 8964 3312
**E** info@amatodistribution.co.uk
**W** amatodistribution.co.uk
*A&R* Duane Dawson

## Amazing Feet
Interzone House
74–77 Magdalen Rd
Oxford
OX4 1RE
**T** 01865 205600    **F** 01865 205700
**E** info@rotator.co.uk    **W** rotator.co.uk
*Contact* Richard Cotton

*Independent label with long history in alternative music*

## Amazon Records Ltd
Suite 1
Canalot Studios
222 Kensal Rd
London
W10 5BN
**T** 020 7460 4006    **F** 020 7598 1184
**E** face@ndirect.co.uk
*Managing Director* Frank Sansom

*Dance music*

## Amber
PO Box 1
Chipping Ongar
Essex
CM5 9HZ
**T** 01277 362916/365046    **F** 01277 366736
*Contact* Paul Tage

## Ambition Records Ltd
PO Box 379
Hemel Hempstead
Herts
HP2 4GU
**T** 07801 256026    **F** 0870 056 7179
**E** info@ambition.uk.com    **W** ambition.uk.com
*Managing Director* Steve Dandy

## AMC Records
WT House
Pilling
Preston
Lancs
PR3 6SJ
**T** 01253 790682 **F** 01253 790686/790157
*Managing Director* William Tracy-Carter

## American Activities
29 St Michael's Rd
Leeds
LS6 3BG
**T** 0113 274 2106 **F** 0113 278 6291
**E** sales@bluescat.com **W** bluescat.com
*Contact* Dave Foster

## Amos Recordings
Unit 1
Union Bridge Tull
Roker Lane
Pudsey
West Yorkshire
LS28 9LE
**T** 0113 255 9905 **F** 0113 255 9903
**E** a-m-o-s@dial.pipex.com
*Contact* Chris Madden

## Anagram Records
Unit 17
Elysium Gate West
126–128 New Kings Rd
London
SW6 4LZ
**T** 020 7371 5844 **F** 020 7384 1854
**E** infonet@cred.demon.co.uk **W** cherryred.co.uk
*Contact* Adam Velasco or Iain McNay

## Andrew & Maurice Records
271 Royal College St
London
NW1 9LU
**T** 020 7482 0115 **F** 020 7267 1169
**E** maurice@baconempire.com
*Managing Director* Maurice Bacon

*Artists: Senser, Loadstar*

## Anew Records
162 Church Rd
East Wall
Dublin 3
Ireland
**T** 00 353 1 856 1011 **F** 00 353 1 856 1122
**E** shay@crashedmusic.com **W** crashedmusic.com
*Contact* Shay Hennessy or Paul Melrose

## Angel Air Records
PO Box 14
Stowmarket
Suffolk
IP14 4UD
**T** 01449 770138/770139 **F** 01449 770133
**E** enquiry@angelair.force9.co.uk
**W** angelair.force9.co.uk
*Contact* Peter Purnell

*NB: Rock and pop retro releases only*

## Antenna Recordings Corps Ltd
PO Box 17394
London
NW1 9ZA
**T** 020 7267 6785 **F** 020 7681 8034
**E** antenna@cableinet.co.uk
**W** wkwebs.cableinet.o.uk/antenna

## APL
Oddfellows Hall
London Rd
Chipping Norton
Oxon
OX7 5AR
**T** 01608 641592 **F** 01608 641969

## Apollo-Sound
32 Ellerdale Rd
London
NW3 6BB
**T** 020 7435 5255 **F** 020 7431 0621
**E** info@apollosound.com **W** apollosound.com
*Contact* H Herschmann

*Easy listening music from 1960s and 70s, test card music, latin-american, jazz, classical*

**Aquarius Records**
Unit 20
Buspace Studios
Conlan St
London
W10 5AP
T 020 7565 9111   F 020 7565 9222

**Ardent Music**
59 West Bere Rd
London
NW2 3SP
T 020 7435 7706/7712   F as telephone numbers
E admin@ardentmusic.co.uk

**Arista Records**
Cavendish House
423 New Kings Rd
London
SW6 4RN
T 020 7384 7700   F 020 7371 9324
E jodie.dalmeda@bmg.co.uk
*Managing Director* Ged Doherty
*Head of Press* Jodie Dalmeda

**Ariwa Sounds**
34 Whitehorse Lane
London
SE25 6RE
T 020 8653 7744/020 8771 1470   F 020 8771 1911
E info@ariwa.com   W ariwa.com

**ARK 21/Pagan Records**
1 Water Lane
London
NW1 8NZ
T 020 7267 1101   F 020 7267 7466
E ark21records@aol.com   W ark21.com
*Label Manager* Mark Haddon

**Arrival Records**
39 Leyton Rd
Harpenden
Herts
AL5 2JB
T 01582 715098
*Managing Director* David Blaylock

**Artful Records**
3 Hansard Mews
London
W14 8BJ
T 020 8968 1231   F 020 8968 1162
E info@artfulrecords.co.uk   W artfulrecords.co.uk
*Managing Director* John Lennard

**Artificial Records**
17 Russell Close
London
W4 2NU
T 020 8742 8917   F 020 8995 4907
*Contact* Simon Lawlor

**Artist Development Organization**
PO Box 1345
Ilford
Essex
IG4 5FX
T 07050 333555   F 07020 923292
W artistdevelopment.org
*Contact* M Irving

**Artist Record Company (ARC)**
1 North Worple Way
London
SW14 8QG
T 020 8876 2533   F 020 8878 4229
E artistrec@aol.com   W arcarc.com
*Director of Promotions* Geraldine Perry

**Ash International Touch**
13 Osward Rd
London
SW17 7SS
T 020 8767 2368   F 020 8682 3414
E touch@touch.demon.co.uk
W touch.demon.co.uk and ashinternational.com
*Contact* Michael Harding

**Astor Place Jazz**
1a Hearne Rd
Strand on the Green
London
W4 3NJ
T 020 8995 6229   F 020 8742 8469
*International Director* Jon Sharp
*Business Affairs* Alan Johnson

## Astralwerks

Kensal House
553–579 Harrow Rd
London
W10 4RH
**T** 020 8964 6220   **F** 020 8964 6221
**w** astralwerks.com
*Contact* John Pavely

## ASV

1 Lochaline St
London
W6 9SJ
**T** 020 8741 2807   **F** 020 8741 8477
**E** info@asv.co.uk   **w** asv.co.uk
*Managing Director* Richard Harrison

*Specialists in rare classical repertoire, vintage jazz
and nostalgia
Five labels include Gaudeamus (authentic
performances of Early Music), White Line (light
classics) and Quicksilver (budget classical)*

## Atlas Records

Lynwood House
13 Hitchin Rd
Stevenage
Herts
SG1 3BJ
**T** 01438 729770   **F** 01438 317511
**E** celticmoon@skynow.co.uk
*Contact* Tony Wells

## Attaboy Records

65 Duke St
London
W1M 5DH
**T** 020 7408 0683   **F** 020 7499 0485
**E** emelvinyl@aol.com
*Contact* Mike Loveday

## AU Records

Suite 4
108 Prospect Quay
Point Pleasant
London
SW18 1PR
**T** 020 8877 0887   **F** 020 8877 0687

## Aura Records

Liverpool Rd
London
W5 5NZ
**T** 020 8579 4333   **F** as telephone number
*Managing Director* Aaron Six

## Autograph

19 Longmeadow Grove
St Lawrence Court
Manchester
M34 2DA
**T** 0161 336 9300   **F** as telephone number
*Managing Director* Derek Brandwood

## Automatic Records

Unit 129
The Canalot Centre
222 Kensal Rd
London
W10 5BN
**T** 020 8964 8890   **F** 020 8960 5741
**E** mail@automaticrecords.co.uk
**w** automaticrecords.co.uk
*Contact* Glenn Mack

*Progressive house and trance
Also Transient Records Ltd for trance and psychedelic
trance (Glenn Mack at glenn@transient.com, website:
transient.com)*

## Autonomy

43 Brook Green
London
W6 7EF
**T** 020 7605 5381   **F** 020 7605 5569
**w** autonomyrecords.co.uk

## Avalanche

17 West Nicolson St
Edinburgh
EH8 9DA
**T** 0131 668 2374   **F** 0131 668 3234
*Managing Director* Kevin Buckle

## Avalon Records

PO Box 929
Ferndown
Dorset
BH22 9YF
**T** 01202 896397   **F** as telephone number
**E** galahad@lds.co.uk   **w** galahadonline.com
*Manager* Stuart Nicholson

## Avid

10 Metro Centre
Dwight Rd
Tolpits Lane
Watford
Herts
WD18 9UF
**T** 01923 281281   **F** 01923 281200
**E** info@avidgroup.co.uk   **w** avidgroup.co.uk
*Contact* Richard Lim or Clive Hudson

*Specializing in jazz, nostalgia and classical music*

## Awesome Records

59 Moore Park Rd
London
SW6 2HH
**T** 020 7731 0022   **F** 020 7731 1715
*Contact* Falcon Stuart

## Azuli Records

25 D'Arblay St
London
W15 3FH
**T** 020 7287 1932   **F** 020 7439 2490
**E** info@azuli.com   **w** azuli.com
*Contact* Simon Marks

## Babel

18 West Hill Park
London
N6 6ND
**T** 020 8348 8638   **E** babel@easynet.co.uk
**w** babel.offworld.co

## Back 2 Basic Recordings Ltd

PO Box 41
Tipton
West Midlands
DY4 7YT
**T** 0121 520 1150/07958 900126   **F** 0121 520 2150
**E** contact@back2basicsrecords.co.uk
*Contact* Jason Ball

## Backs Recording Company

St Mary's Works
St Mary's Plain
Norwich
Norfolk
NR3 3AF
**T** 01603 624290/626221   **F** 01603 619999
**E** backs@cwcom.net
*Managing Director* Jonathan Appel

## Bad Habits

PO Box 111
London
W13 0ZH
**T** 020 8357 2337/07000 243243
**F** 020 8566 7215/0132 731 2545
**E** info@badhabitsent-group.com
**w** badhabitsent-group.com
*Contact* John S Rushton

## Bad Magic Records

Office 2, 9 Thorpe Close
London
W10 5XL
**T** 020 8969 1144   **F** 020 8969 1155
**E** voodoo@bad-magic.com   **w** bad-magic.com
*Contact* Dan Gregory or Kishan Patel
*Managing Director* Mark Jones

## Badlands

11 St George's Place
Cheltenham
Gloucs
GL50 3LA
**T** 01242 227724   **F** 01242 227393
**E** badlands@cityscape.co.uk
*Contact* Philip Jump

## Baktabak Records

Network House
29–39 Stirling Rd
London
W3 8DJ
**T** 020 8993 5966   **F** 020 8993 1396
**E** tabak@arab.co.uk
*Director* Chris Leaning

## Bandleader Records

9 Gillingham St
London
SW1V 1HN
**T** 020 7233 7801　**F** 020 7233 7802
**E** janice@modernpublicity.co.uk
*Contact* Janice Cameron

## Bare Tunes

9 Warren Mews
London
W1P 5DJ
**T** 020 7388 5300　**F** 020 7388 5399
**w** nuderecords.com
*Contact* Saul Galpern

## Barely Breaking Even Records

8b Langton Rd
London
NW2 6QA
**T** 020 8830 6885　**F** 020 8830 5972
**E** peter@bbemusic.demon.co.uk
**w** bbemusic.com
*Contact* Peter Adarkwah or Lee Bright

*Music compilations, original artists and spoken word*
*Rock, jazz, funk, disco, hiphop, latin and dance*

## Basilica

PO Box 16671
London
W8 6ZY
**E** incoming@freakapuss.co.uk　**w** freakapuss.co.uk
*Contact* Suzana Gulin

*Specializes in acoustic, beat, hiphop, drum 'n' bass*
*Main artists: Zarjaz, Star Spike, Top Hoodlum*
*Programme*

## BBC Music

Room 116–17
East Wing
Bush House
Strand
London
WC2B 4PH
**T** 020 7557 1023　**F** 020 7557 1052
**E** alan.taylor.bbc.co.uk
*Head of Marketing* Alan Taylor

## Bearcat Records

PO Box 94
Derby
DE22 1XA
**T** 01332 332336/07702 564804　**F** as first telephone
**E** chrishall@swampmusic.demon.co.uk
*Contact* Chris Hall

*See also Swamp Music (agency)*

## Beat Goes On Records

PO Box 22
Bury St Edmunds
Suffolk
IP28 6XQ
**T** 01284 724406/762137　**F** 01284 762245/762433
**E** contact.mike.bgo@dial.pipex.com
**w** bgo-records.com
*Chairman and CEO* Mike Gott

*Owned by Andy Gray of leading independent*
*retailers Andy's Records*
*Specializes in re-releases including Man, The*
*Groundhogs, B B King and Steppenwolf*

## Beatnik Records

1 Beechwood Avenue
Chorlton
Manchester
M21 8UA
**T** 0161 374 3645
*Contact* Carl Emery

*Work with pioneering musicians promoting the*
*abstract, weird and funky side of electronica*

## Beechwood Music Ltd

Littleton House
Littleton Rd
Ashford
Middx
TW15 1UU
**T** 01784 423214　**F** 01784 251245　**w** beechwoodmusic.co.uk
*Contact* Tim Millington

## Beechwood Records

62 Beechwood Rd
Croydon
CR2 0AA
**T** 020 8657 2813　**F** 020 8651 6080
*Director* Derek Jones

## Beggars Banquet Records
17–19 Alma Rd
London
SW18 1AA
**T** 020 8870 9912  **F** 020 8871 1766
**E** beggars@almaroad.co.uk  **w** beggars.com
*Label Head* Roger Trust

## Bella Union
The Boathouse
Ranelagh Drive
Twickenham
Middx
TW1 1QZ
**T** 020 8891 1611  **F** 020 8891 1895
*Contact* Fiona Glyn-Jones

## Beyond Muisc
1st Floor, 13a Hillgate St
London
W8 7SP
**T** 020 7221 9050  **F** 020 7221 9060
**E** annickb@lbank.com
*Contact* Lewis Kovac

## Biddulph Recordings
34 St George St
Hanover Square
London
W1R 0ND
**T** 020 7408 2458  **F** 020 7495 6501/1428
**E** giorgio.cuppini@btinternet.com
*Contact* Giorgio Cuppini

## Big Bear Records
PO Box 944
Birmingham
B16 8UT
**T** 0121 454 7020  **F** 0121 454 9996
**E** bigbearmusic@compuserve.com
**w** bigbearmusic.com
*Managing Director* Jim Simpson

*Promoter of Birmingham International Jazz Festival*
*(Contact details as above)*

## Big Cat (UK) Records
PO Box 3074
London
W11 4GY
**T** 020 7610 4662  **F** 020 7602 9427
**E** cats@big-cat.co.uk
*Label Manager* Tim Vaas

## Big Chill
PO Box 7378
London
N4 3RH
**T** 020 7688 8080  **F** 020 7688 8082
**E** info@bigchill.net  **w** bigchill.net
*Contact* Katrina Larkin; Peter Larkin (Directors)

*Also Big Chill Events*

## Big Dada
Winchester Wharf
Clink St
London
SE1 9DG
**T** 020 7357 7180  **F** 020 7357 7197
**E** will@ninjatune.net  **w** ninjatune.net/bigdada/
*Contact* Will Ashton

## Big Fish Music
5 Astrop Mews
London
W6 7HR
**T** 020 8746 4040  **F** 020 8746 4060
**E** bigfish@music-village.com
**w** bonzairecords.com/music-village.com
*Director* John Carnell
*Head of Music* Natalie Martin
*Label Manager* Justin Deighton

*Umbrella dance company, incorporating labels UK*
*Bonzai, Product DeLuxe, Five AM, Acetate Ltd,*
*Superstition UK*
*Also management of Sunscreem*

## Big Idea Records
6 Northend Gardens
Kingswood
Bristol
BS15 1UA
**T** 0117 967 2282  **F** as telephone
**E** ply501@netscapeonline.co.uk
**w** members.netscapeonline.co.uk/ptrmchls/

*Managing Director* Peter Michaels

*Independent label established 1999, also Chuckle*
*Music Publishing*
*Label available for releases by other parties: see*
*website for procedures and fees*

## Big Moon Records
PO Box 347
Weybridge
Surrey
KT13 9WZ
T 01932 859472    F 01932 889802
E info@tzuke.com    W tzuke.com
*Managing Director* Paul Muggleton

*NB: sole artist label for Judie Tzuke*

## Big Noise Muzik
32 Magpie Hill Lane
Bromley
Kent
BR2 8ER
T 020 8462 3624    F 020 8462 0062
*Contact* Nigel Williams

## Big Onion Records
Unit 9
Morrison Yard
551a High Rd
London
N17 6SB
T 020 8801 5878    F 020 8808 9885
E dave@roundway.com
*Contact* Dave Thompson

## Birdland Records
39 Clitterhouse Crescent
London
NW2 1DB
T 020 8458 1020    F as telephone
*Managing Director* Mike Carr

## Bitch Records
129 Canalot Studios
222 Kensal Rd
London
W10 5BN
T 020 8964 9020    F 020 8960 5741

E bitch@bitchrecords.com    W bitchrecords.com
*Contact* Russel Coultart

*Specialist in hard house music*

## BKO Productions
The Old Truman Brewery
91 Brick Lane
London
E1 6ON
T 020 7377 9373    F 020 7377 6523
E byron@b-k-o.demon.co.uk
*Contact* Byron Orme

## Black Magic Records
296 Earls Court Rd
London
SW5 9BA
T 020 7565 0806
F as telephone or 020 7244 0916
E blackmagicrecords@talk21.com
W blackmagicrecords.com
*Managing Director* Mataya Clifford

## Black Mountain Records
1 Squire Court
The Marina
Swansea
SA1 3XB
T 01792 301500    F as telephone
E info@welshchairs.co.uk
*Director* Mike Evans

## Black on Black Records
1st Floor, 44a Charlotte Rd
London
EC2A 3PD
T 020 7613 0404    F 020 7729 8160
E bob@on-black.demon.co.uk
*Managing Director* Bob Jones

## Blackmoon Records (UK) Ltd
PO Box 14535
London
N17 0WG
T 020 8376 1650    F 020 8376 8622
E p-ingram@blackmoon.netlineuk.net
*Contact* Phil Ingram

**Blakamix International Records**
Garvey House
42 Margetts Rd
Bedford
Beds
MK42 8DS
**T** 01234 856164/302115   **F** 01234 854344
**E** blakamix@aol.com
*Contact* Dennis Bedeau

**Blaster!**
77 Nightingale Shott
Egham
TW20 9SU
**T** 01784 741613   **F** 01784 741529
**E** martinw@netcomuk.co.uk
*Contact* Martin Whitehead

*Indie pop and rock*
*Also The Subway Organization: same details*

**Blue Banana Records**
2 Menelik Rd
London
NW2 3RP
**T** 020 7435 6116   **F** as telephone
**E** m.albert@bluemelon.co.uk   **w** bluemelon.co.uk
*Contact* Mark Albert

**Blue Crystal Music Ltd**
Yew Tree Studios
Stone St
Stanford North
Kent
TN25 6DH
**T** 01303 814880   **F** 01303 814884
**E** relax@bluecrystalmusic.demon.co.uk
**w** welcome.to/blue-crystal-music
*Contact* Geoff Milner

**Blue Melon**
2 Menelik Rd
London
NW2 3RP
**T** 020 7435 6116   **F** as telephone
**E** steveglen@appleonline.net
**w** bluemelon.co.uk and barbaracartland.com
*Contact* Steven Glen

*Also Blue Planet Records*

**Blue Movement**
63 Dockland St
Royal Docks
London
E16 2JE
**T** 020 7476 7766   **F** 020 7511 5303
*Director* Mr Tora March

**Blue Room Co-op, The**
84 Walton Rd
East Molesey
Surrey
KT8 0DL
**T** 020 8979 8809/0024   **F** as first telephone
**E** theblueroom@btinternet.com
*Contact* Greg Belson

**BlueRoom Released**
6c Littlehampton Rd
Worthing
West Sussex
BN13 1QE
**T** 01903 260033   **F** 01903 261133
**E** info@blueroom.co.uk and rrowles@melt2000.com
**w** melt2000.com
*Contact* Roy Rowles
*Label Manager* Silvio Bukbardis

**BMG Commercial Division**
Bedford House
69–79 Fulham High St
London
SW6 3JW
**T** 020 7384 7672   **F** 020 7973 0345
**E** ray.jenks@bmg.co.uk
*Commercial Director* Ray Jenks
*Catalogue Manager* Linda Nevill
*Licensing Manager* Paul Robinson

**BMG Entertainment International UK & Ireland**
Bedford House
69–79 Fulham High St
London
SW6 3JW
**T** 020 7384 7500   **F** 020 7371 9298
**E** (firstname.surname)@bmg.co.uk
*Chairman* Hasse Breitholtz
*Vice President, Media* Nigel Sweeney
*Vice President, A&R and Marketing* Nick Stewart

## BMG Entertainment UK & Ireland Ltd
Bedford House
69–79 Fulham High St
London
SW6 3JW
**T** 020 7384 7961   **F** 020 7384 8146
**E** (firstname.surname)@bmg.co.uk
**W** click2music.co.uk
*Vice President, Media* Nigel Sweeney

## BMG Ireland
Grafton Buildings
34 Grafton St
Dublin 2
Ireland
**T** 00 353 1 677 9006   **F** 00 353 1 677 9204   **W** bmg.ie
*Managing Director* Freddie Middleton

## BMP (UK) Ltd
303 Riverbank House
1 Putney Bridge Approach
London
SW6 3JD
**T** 020 7371 0022   **F** 020 7371 0099
**E** ripe@compuserve.com
*Managing Director* Jurgen Damm

## Bolshi
PO Box 2423
London
W1A 5XY
**T** 020 7323 3888   **F** 020 7636 3551
**E** sarah@biglife.co.uk   **W** bolshi.com
*Contact* Sarah Francis

## Bonaire Records
2 Menelik Rd
London
NW2 3RP
**T** 020 7435 6116   **F** as telephone
**E** m.albert@bluemelon.co.uk   **W** bluemelon.co.uk
*Contact* Mark Albert

## Boom Bang Records Ltd
9 Thorpe Close
Portobello Rd
London
W10 5XL
**T** 020 8960 1195   **F** as telephone

**E** boombang@headroomstudios.co.uk
*Contact* Ralph P Ruppert

## Bootleg Records
Westminster House
6 Westminster Rd
Manchester
M35 9LQ
**T** 0161 681 4414   **F** as telephone

*Also at Prince of Wales Building, 2nd Floor*
*67 Piccadilly, Manchester*
*M1 9PL*
*Tel/fax: 0161 236 0606*

## Bounce Music
42 Edith Grove
London
SW10 0NJ
**T** 020 7460 1866   **F** 020 7376 4591
*Contact* Andy Taylor

## Breakbeat Science
PO Box 699
London
SW10 0LS
**T** 020 7460 8967   **F** 020 7565 0871
**E** whoever@deviant.co.uk   **W** deviant.co.uk
*Managing Director* Rob Deacon

## Breakin' Loose
32 Quadrant House
Burrell St
London
SE1 0UW
**T** 020 7633 9576/07721 065618
*Managing Director* Steve Bingham

## Brewhouse Music
Breeds Farm
57 High St
Wicken
nr Ely
Cambs
CB7 5XR
**T** 01353 720309   **F** 01353 723364
*Contact* Eric Cowell

## British Underground

UoW
Watford Rd
Northwick Park
Harrow
Middx
HA1 3TP
**T** 020 8509 3353
**E** christofu@continentaldrifts.uk.com
**W** britishunderground.net
*Contact* Chris or Mel at the above, or Crispin (020 7911 5901, *crispin.p@virgin.net*)

*Part of the Continental Drifts agency, this is a huge association of independent labels ranging from Suddendef (drum 'n' bass) to Nervous (rockabilly). Check the website for full details*

## BRM Music Publishing Ltd

89a High Rd
London
N22 6BB
**T** 020 8881 6969    **F** 020 8888 1685
**E** info@brmmusic.com    **W** brmmusic.com
*Contact* Bruce Ruffin

## Broadley Records

Broadley House
48 Broadley Terrace
London
NW1 6LG
**T** 020 7258 0324    **F** 020 7724 2361
**E** ellis@broadleystudios.com
**W** broadleystudios.com
*Managing Director* Ellis Elias

## Broken Records

PO Box 4416
London
SW19 8XR
**T** 01984 623968    **E** fans@davebarb.demon.co.uk
**W** davebarb.demon.co.uk
*Contact* John Marshall

*NB: Founded in 1981 solely to issue the recordings of keyboard/vocal duo Dave Stewart and Barbara Gaskin
No approaches please from other acts*

## Bronze Records

Great Linford Manor
Great Linford
Milton Keynes
Bucks
MK14 5AX
**T** 01908 667 432    **F** 01908 668 164
*Contact* Sue Dawson

## Brothers Records Ltd

The Music Village
118 Osiers Rd
London
SW18 1NI
**T** 020 8870 0011    **F** 020 8870 2101
**E** info@the-brothers.co.uk
*Directors* Ian Titchener, Nick Titchener
*General Manager* Jo Underwood

## BSC Records

23 Corbyn St
London
N4 3BY
**T** 020 7281 1313
*Contact* Andreas Monoyos

*Production and re-mixing by Ruff 'n' Tumble*

## Bubbles Recordings

Glen House
200–208 Tottenham Court Rd
London
W1P 9LA
**T** 020 7573 4531    **F** 020 7631 3667

## Bubblin Blu

61 Ellesmere Rd
London
E3 5QU
**T** 020 8980 0742    **F** 020 8980 7760
**E** amanda_02m@hotmail.com    **W** 02m.co.uk
*Contact* Amanda Miller

## Bulldog Records

PO Box 130
Hove
East Sussex
BN3 6QU
**T** 01273 550088    **F** 01273 540969

**E** tkoadam@tkogroup.com
*Contact* Adam Clavering


**Burning Ice Records**
PO Box 48
Dorking
Surrey
RH4 1YE
**T** 01306 877692   **E** tim@objayda.co.uk
**W** objayda.co.uk
*Contact* Tim Howe

*Distribution through Avid/BMG*


**Bushranger Records**
86 Rayleigh Rd
Hutton
Essex
CM13 1BH
**T** 01277 222095   **F** kathlist@aol.com
*Contact* Kathy Lister


**Buzz Records**
14 Corsiehill Rd
Perth
Perthshire
PH2 7BZ
**T** 01738 638140/0771 220 7635   **F** as first telephone
**E** dave@radiotones.com   **W** radiotones.com
*Managing Director* Dave Arcari

*Alternative roots and blues*


**Buzz To It Records**
27 Britton St
London
EC1M 5NQ
**T** 020 7251 2376   **F** 020 7490 0474
*Contact* Michael Bukowski


**BXR Records UK**
Unit 1, Pepys Court
84–86 The Chase
London
SW4 0NF
**T** 020 7720 7266   **F** 020 7720 7255
**E** mark@nukleuz.co.uk   **W** nukleuz.com
*Contact* Mark Wilson


**Caged Records**
Unit 20
Phoenix House
86 Fulham High St
London
SW6 3LF
**T** 020 7736 9676   **F** 020 7736 3726
**E** caged@redparrot.co.uk
*Contact* Hayes R Hickman


**Cala Records Ltd**
17 Shakespeare Gardens
London
N2 9LJ
**T** 020 8883 7306   **F** 020 8365 3388
**E** music@calarecords.com   **W** calarecords.com
*Contact* Geoffrey Simon

*Also Cala Music Publishing, a division of Cala Records Ltd*


**Caleche Studios**
175 Roundhay Rd
Leeds
LS8 5AN
**T** 0113 219 4929   **F** 0113 249 4941
*Managing Director* Leslie Coleman


**Camino Records**
Crown Studios
16–18 Crown Rd
Twickenham
Middx
TW1 3EE
**T** 020 8891 4233   **F** 020 8891 2339
**E** mail@camino.co.uk   **W** camino.co.uk

*Artists: Steve Hackett, Ian McDonald, David Poe, Chester Thompson*


**Campion Records**
1st and 2nd Floors
7 High St
Cheadle
Cheshire
SK8 1AX
**T** 0161 491 6655   **F** 0161 491 6688
**E** dimus@aol.com   **W** dimusic.co.uk
*Contact* Alan Wilson

*Classical label owned by Disc Imports Ltd*

## Candid Productions Ltd

16 Castelnau
London
SW13 9RU
T 020 8741 3608    F 020 8563 0013
E candid_records@compuserve.com
W candidrecords.com
*Managing Director*(A&R): Alan Bates

*Labels: Candid, Choice, Big City, Why Not, Celebrity*
*Jazz, Blues, R&B, Latin*
*Inaugurated in New York City, 1960*

## Candor Records

Petham
Canterbury
Kent
CT4 5QU
T 01227 700516    F 01227 700128
*Managing Director* Chris Dors

## Candy Records

249 Kensal Rd
London
W10 5DB
T 020 8964 4722    F 020 8968 1929
*Contact* Paul Hitchman

## Carbon Dioxide Records

50 Watson Rd
Leicester
Leics
LE4 6RY
T 0116 261 3146
*Contact* Andrew Thompson or Lyn Muller

## Cargo Records

17 Heathmans Rd
London
SW6 4TJ
T 020 7731 5125    F 020 7731 3866
E info@cargoik.demon.co.uk
*Managing Director* Philip Hill

## Cargogold Productions

39 Clitterhouse Crescent
London
NW2 1DD
T 020 8458 1020    F as telephone

E mike@mikecarr.co.uk    W mikecarr.co.uk
*Managing Director* Mike Carr

*Also Cargogold Productions, Birdland Records and*
*Cargo Music Publishing*
*Jazz musical director in bebop, blues and soul fields*

## Caritas Records

28 Dalrymple Crescent
Edinburgh
EH9 2NX
T 0131 667 3633    F as telephone
E caritas-records@caritas-music.co.uk
W caritas-music.co.uk
*Director* Katharine H Douglas

## Carlton Home Entertainment

The Waterfront
Elstree Rd
Elstree
Herts
WD6 3BS
T 020 8207 6207    F 020 8207 5789
*A&R* Norman Joplin

## Celtic Music

24 Mercer Row
Louth
Lincs
LN11 9JJ
T 01507 606371    F 01507 603283
*Commercial Affairs Director* Neil Sharpley

*Specializing in folk, blues, country and world music*
*Roster includes Black Crow, Making Waves, New*
*Country, Alba, Leader, Sweet Folk All*

## Celtic Music

Dublin Rd
Monasterevin
County Kildare
Ireland
T 00 353 45 525009/0116 275 1752
F 00 353 50 262086    E hazel@iol.ie
*Contact* John Kelly

## Centaur Discs
40–42 Brantwood Avenue
Dundee
DD3 6EW
**T** 01382 776595 **F** 01382 736702 **E** cdser@aol.com
*Managing Director* David Shoesmith

*Primarily synthesizer new age/progressive rock music*

## Certificate Eighteen
PO Box 4029
London
SW15 2XR
**T** 020 7924 1333/07850 116508 **F** 020 7924 1833
**E** info@certificate18.com **w** certificate18.com
*Contact* Paul Arnold

*Drum 'n' bass, electronica, break beat, freestyle*

## Champion Records
181 High St
London
NW10 4TE
**T** 020 8961 5202/7442 **F** 020 8965 3948/8961 6665
**E** mel@championrecords.co.uk
**w** championrecords.co.uk
*Contact* Mel Medalie

*Also Cheeky Records Ltd*

## Chantel Records
3a Ashfield Parade
London
N14 5EH
**T** 020 8886 6236
*Managing Director* Riss Chantelle

## Charly Records (UK) Ltd
13 Bridge Wharf Rd
Church Rd
Isleworth
Middx
TW7 6BS
**T** 020 8232 1300 **F** 020 8232 1301
**E** samantha.richards@charly.co.uk
*Director* Samantha Richards
*A&R* John O'Toole

## Chemikal Underground Records
PO Box 3609
Glasgow
G42 9TP
**T** 0141 550 1919 **F** 0141 550 1918
**E** underground@chemical.demon.co.uk
*Contact* Andrew Savage

## Cherry Moon Ltd
PO Box 666
Newtownards
Co. Down
BT22 2FJ
**T** 028 9084 2123/077 70 757666
**E** cherrymoon@cherrymoon.net
**w** cherrymoon.net
*Contact* Maurice Jay

*Also artist management (same contact details)*

## Cherry Red Records
Unit 17
Elysium Gate West
126–128 New Kings Rd
London
SW6 4LZ
**T** 020 7371 5844 **F** 020 7384 1854
**E** infonet@cred.demon.co.uk **w** cherryred.co.uk
*Contact* Adam Velasco or Iain McNay

## Chestnut Records
17 Greened Rd
Boxmoor
Hemel Hempstead
Herts
HP1 1QW
**T** 020 8960 1127 **F** 020 8964 9449
**E** pprpublicity@pprpublicity.force9.co.uk
*Contact* Ben Raudnitz

## Christabel Records
PO Box 232
Harrow
Middlesex
HA1 2NN
**T** 020 8907 6030 **F** 020 8909 1030
**E** christabel@jmht.org

**Chrome Dreams**
PO Box 230
New Malden
Surrey
KT3 6YY
**T** 020 8715 9781    **F** 020 8241 1426
**E** andywalker@chromedreams.co.uk
*Contact* Paula Gillespie

**Chute Records**
PO Box 211
Dundee
DD1 9PH
**T** 01382 228067/07941 286555    **F** as first telephone
**E** sparesnare@hotmail.com    **W** sparesnare.co.uk
*Manager* Jan D Burnett

*Originally set up as vehicle for the band Spare Snare, now continues to release their product and other eclectic combos*

**Circle Sound Services**
Circle House
14 Waveney Close
Bicester
Oxon
OX6 8GP
**T** 01869 240051    **F** as telephone
*Managing Director* John Willett

**Circulation Recordings Ltd**
Building 34W
The Lingfield Estate
McMullen Rd
Darlington
Durham
DL1 1YU
**T** 01325 365553/483683
**F** as first telephone or 255252
**E** circrecds1@aol.com
**W** members.aol.com/circrecds1
*Contact* Martyn Alderdice
*Managing Director* Graeme Robinson

**City Slang Records**
Suite 209
Bon Marche Centre
241–251 Ferndale Rd
London
SW9 8BJ
**T** 020 7733 9700/07958 655308    **F** 020 7733 9060

**E** ww@cityslang.demon.co.uk    **W** cityslang.com
*Contact* Wyndham Wallace

**CKS Records Instrumental Music**
426b Greenford Rd
Greenford
Middlesex
UB6 8SG
**T** 0881 444003    **F** 020 8575 7531

**Claddagh Records Ltd**
Dame House
Dame St
Dublin 2
Ireland
**T** 00 353 1 677 8943    **F** 00 353 1 679 3664
**E** claddagh@crl.ie    **W** indigo.ie/claddagh
*Co-Manager* Jane Bolton

*Distributor, label, mail order and retailer specializing in Irish traditional music and spoken word, with a shop in Temple Bar, Dublin*

**Claudio Records Ltd**
Studio 17
The Promenade
Peacehaven
East Sussex
BN10 8PU
**T** 01273 580250    **F** 01273 583530
**E** info@claudio-records.ltd.uk
**W** claudio-records.ltd.uk
*Contact* Colin Attwell

*Classical, contemporary, bohemian, demo recordings and concert recitals*

**Clay Records**
Regent House
1 Pratt Mews
London
NW1 0AD
**T** 020 7267 6899    **F** 020 7267 6746
*Managing Director* Colin Newman

## Clear

PO Box 11509
London
W14 9FT
**T** 020 7386 7865   **E** clear.london@easynet.co.uk
*Contact* Hal Udell

## Cleveland City

52a Clifton St
Chapel Ash
Wolverhampton
West Midlands
WV3 0QT
**T** 01902 838500   **F** 01902 839500
*Contact* Mike Evans

## Cloud Nine Records

3 Prowse Place
London
NW1 9PH
**T** 020 7482 5500   **F** 020 7482 2385
**E** cnr@silvascreen.co.uk   **w** deewiz.demon.co.uk
*Managing Director* David Wishart

## Clubscene

PO Box 11
Bathgate
Lothian
EH48 1RX
**T** 01506 636038/07785 222205   **F** 01506 633900
**E** mail@clubscene.co.uk   **w** clubscene.co.uk
*Managing Director* Bill Grainger

## Cola Records Ltd

33c Warwick Avenue
London
W9 2PR
**T** 020 7289 4848   **F** as telephone
**E** marcus@colarecords.demon.co.uk
*A&R/Licensing* Marcus Fergusson

*Specialists in dance, particularly funky house, trance, garage etc*
*Licences on a per-single basis*
*Has represented, for example, Klatsch, Lee Marrow, Anthony and Georgio, Perfect State, Kevin Edge and Antoine Clamaran*

## Colortone Record Company

Prospect Farm
West Marsh
Canterbury
Kent
CT3 2LS
**T** 01304 812815   **F** as telephone
*Contact* Mr S Jackson

## Colossus Records

Lower Ground Floor
5–6 Hoxton Square
London
N1 6NU
**T** 020 7739 8783   **F** 020 7729 5867

## Columbia Records

10 Great Marlborough St
London
W1V 2LP
**T** 020 7911 8200   **F** 020 7911 8783
*Managing Director* Blair McDonald
*Int A&R Manager* Oliver Behzadi
*Marketing Manager* Jo Headland
*A&R Manager* Matt Ross
*Head of Press* Carl Fysh

## Commercial Recordings

12 Lisnagleer Rd
Dungannon
Co. Tyrone
BT70 3LN
**T** 028 8776 1195
**E** commercialrecordings@telinco.co.uk
**w** commercialrecordings.com

*Recording Irish music, songs and comedy*

## Communique Records

Longfield House
Bury Avenue
Ruislip
Middlesex
HA4 7RT
**T** 01895 477522   **F** as telephone
**E** tomdoherty@supanet.com
*Managing Director* Tom Doherty

*Rock, metal, alternative metal, extreme metal*

## Compact Organization, The

PO Box 562
London
N10 3BR
**T** 020 7482 5036   **F** 020 7482 5037
**E** poppy@poptel.org

## Complete Record Company Ltd, The

2 Prescott Place
London
SW4 6BT
**T** 020 7498 9666   **F** 020 7498 1828
*Managing Director* Jeremy Elliott

## Concept Marketing and Distribution Ltd

3 Blackhorse Lane
London
E17 6DS
**T** 020 8498 4800   **F** 020 8498 4849
**E** sales@concept-marketing.co.uk
*Managing Director* Patricia Fox

## Confetti Records

PO Box 11541
London
N15 4DW
**T** 020 8801 6760   **F** 020 8808 4413

## Confidential Records

127 Dewsbury Rd
Ossett
Wakefield
West Yorkshire
WF5 9PA
**T** 01924 277508   **F** as telephone
**E** confidential@usound.freeserve.co.uk
**W** usound.freeserve.co.uk/conrec.htm
*Contact* Nev Barker

## Congo Music Ltd

17a Craven Park Rd
London
W10 8SE
**T** 020 8961 5461   **F** as telephone
**E** congomusic@hotmail.com   **W** musiclinks.com/
congo
*Managing Director* Byron Lye-Fook

## Connoisseur Collection Ltd

2–3 Fitzroy Mews
London
W1T 6DF
**T** 020 7383 7773   **F** 020 7383 7724
**E** info@connoisseurcollection.co.uk
**W** connoisseurcollection.co.uk
*Managing Director* Bob Fisher
*Sales Manager* Andrew Carden
*General Manager* Claire Higgins

*NB: Catalogue and re-issue only in mid-price CD
format, no contemporary recordings*

## Cooking Vinyl

10 Allied Way
London
W3 0RQ
**T** 020 8600 9200/8743 7534   **F** 020 8743 7448
**E** info@cookingvinyl.demon.co.uk
**W** cookingvinyl.com
*Managing Director* Martin Goldschmidt
*Marketing & A&R* Rob Collins
*Promotions Manager* Paddy Forwood

## Cool Badge Recordings

96 Ferme Park Rd
London
N8 9SD
**T** 020 8374 3810/8372 5430   **F** 020 8374 3812
**E** russell&leigh@coolbadge.demon.co.uk
*Contact* Russell Yates

## Copasetik Recordings Ltd

14 Lambton Place
London
W11 2SH
**T** 020 7482 4345   **F** 020 7482 4350
**E** copasetik1@aol.com   **W** copasetik.com
*Managing Director and Head of A&R* John Sexton

*Also Creamy Groove Machine Recordings*

## Copper Records

2 Barony St
Edinburgh
EH3 6PE
**T** 0131 558 8895   **F** as telephone
**E** vic@copper.co.uk   **W** copper.co.uk
*Contact* Mike Galloway

## Corban Recordings
PO Box 2
Glasgow
G44 3LB
**T** 0141 637 5277   **E** alcorban@hotmail.com
**W** corbanrecordings.com
*Contact* Alastair

*Specializing in Scottish folk music, traditional and contemporary, features the recorded works of Alastair McDonald, Peter Morrison and the Scottish jazz ensemble, Clan Macjazz*

## Courtyard Music
22 The Nursery
Sutton Courtenay
Oxon
OX14 4UA
**T** 01235 845800   **F** 01235 847692
**E** andy@cyard.com and john@cyard.com
**W** cyard.com
*Contact* Andy Ross or John Bennett
Also Microbe (Email: andy@cyard.com, Website: microbe.cyard.com), blackplastic.com, medalworld.com

## Crackle! Records
PO Box 7
Otley
Leeds
West Yorkshire
LS21 1YB
**E** crackle@thecafe.co.uk

## Crapola Records
PO Box 808
Hook
Hampshire
RG29 1UF
**T** 01256 862865   **F** 01256 862182
**E** internet@crapolarecords.com
**W** crapolarecords.com
*Contact* Keir Jens-Smith

## Crashed Records
162 Church Rd
East Wall
Dublin
Ireland
**T** 00 353 1 888 1188   **F** 00 353 1 856 1122
**E** info@crashedmusic.com   **W** crashedmusic.com
*Contact* Shay Hennessy or Ian Hennessy

## Creation Records
109x Regents Park Rd
London
NW1 8UR
**T** 020 7722 8866   **F** 020 7722 3443
**E** info@creation.co.uk   **W** creation.co.uk
*Head of Communications* Andy Saunders
*Managing Director* Mark Taylor

## Creative Dialogue Ltd
24 Highbury Grove
London
N5 2DQ
**T** 020 7359 7122   **E** info@creativedialogue.co.uk
**W** creativedialogue.co.uk
*Contact* Ian Dean

*Music production company offering music writing and recording projects with artists from concept to delivery in classical, film and pop, development of recording and music technology in surround sound through to DVD surround mastering music supervision for film*

## Creature Music
57d Hatton Garden
London
EC1N 2HP
**T** 020 7831 3111   **F** 020 7831 9991
**E** manfred@eastcentralone.com
**W** manfredmann.co.uk
*Contact* Steve Fernie

## Creole Records Ltd
The Chilterns
France Hill Drive
Camberley
Surrey
GU15 3QA
**T** 01276 686077   **F** 01276 686055
**E** creole@clara.net
*Directors* Bruce and Sue White

## Critical Mass
Unit 2a Queens Studios
121 Salusbury Rd
London
NW6 6RG
**T** 020 7372 4474   **F** 020 7372 4484/7328 4447
**E** alex@newstate.co.uk
*Contact* Alex Payne

**Crocodile Music**
7 Goodge Place
London
W1P 1FL
**T** 020 7580 0080    **F** 020 7580 0560
**E** malcolm@crocodilemusicstudios.co.uk
**W** crocodilemusic.com
*Contact* Malcolm Ironton

**Cross Border Media**
10 Deer Park
Ashbourne
Co. Meath
Ireland
**T** 00 353 1 835 3471    **F** 00 353 1 835 0720
**E** cbm@iol.ie    **W** aranmusic.com
*Contact* Oliver Sweeney

**Cube Records**
Onward House
11 Uxbridge St
London
W8 7QT
**T** 020 7221 4275    **F** 020 7229 6893
*Contact* Simon Platz

**Culburnie Records Ltd**
PO Box 13350
Jedburgh
TD8 6YA
**T** 01450 860727    **F** 01450 860612
**E** ukinfo@culburnie.com    **W** culburnie.com

**Cultural Foundation**
Dale Head
Rosedale
North Yorkshire
YO18 8RL
**T** 01751 417147
*Contact* Peter Bell

**Culture Press UK**
74–75 Warren St
London
W1P 5PA
**T** 020 7387 3344/5550    **F** 020 7388 2756
**E** zep@sternsmusic.com
*Contact* Zep

**Curveball Recordings**
4th Floor, 40 Langham St
London
W1N 5RG
**F** 020 7323 4180
*Contact* Rob Jefferson

**Cutting Edge Music**
20 Accommodation Rd
London
NW11 8EP
**T** 020 8455 5560    **E** cemltd@aol.com
*Contact* Beverley King

**Cyberdisk**
PO Box 12916
London
N12 9WA
**E** dgreener@dircon.co.uk
*Contact* Terry Cassidy

**Cycle Records**
PO Box 2793
London
NW1 7SJ
**T** 01923 444440    **F** as telephone
**E** info@cycle-records.demon.co.uk
**W** cycle-records.demon.co.uk
*A&R* Neil Armstrong

**Cyclo Music**
1c Spasholt Rd
London
N19 4EL
**T** 020 8348 0985    **F** 020 8348 1139
**E** cyclo@dircon.co.uk
*Contact* Philipp Marchal

**Cyclops**
33a Tolworth Park Rd
Tolworth
Surrey
KT6 7RL
**T** 020 8339 9965    **F** 020 8399 0070
**E** postmaster@gft-cyclops.co.uk
**W** gft-cyclops.co.uk
*Contact* Malcolm Parker

*NB: progressive rock only*

**Da Doo Ron Ron Records**
5 Mayfield Court
Victoria Rd
Freshfield
Liverpool
L37 7JL
T 01704 834105    F as telephone
E ronellis50@hotmail.com
*Managing Director* Ron Ellis

**Dance 2 Recordings Ltd**
9 Woodbridge Rd
Guildford
Surrey
GU1 4PU
T 01483 451003/451002    F as first telephone
E jon@aspectrecords.co.uktobie@aspectrecords.co.uk
W aspectrecords.co.uk
*Contact* Jon Skinner

*House and garage specialists*
*Also Aspect Records (drum 'n' bass) and Perspective*
*Records (drum 'n' bass)*

**Dance Off Records**
299 Camberwell New Rd
London
SE5 0TF
T 020 7703 1001    F 020 7703 7799
E danceoff@imperialgardens.co.uk
*Contact* Raymond Stevenson

*Also Southside Collective Records (same address and*
*telephone. E-mail: southside@imperialgardens.co.uk.*
*Website: southside-collective.co.uk)*

**Danceline**
8 Stoney Lane
Rathcoole
Co Dublin
Ireland
T 00 353 1 627 1900    F 00 353 1 627 4404
*Managing Director* Eddie Joyce

**Dangerous Records**
Sandwell Manor
Totnes
Devon
TQ9 7LN
T 01803 867850    F as telephone
*Managing Director* Dennis Smith

**Dark Beat Records**
Unit 8a
Mostyn Hall
Friargate
Penrith
Cumbria
CA11 7XR
T 01768 483724/07778 180766    F 01768 483748
E darkbeat@compuserve.com
W ourworld.compuserve.com/homepages/darkbeat
*Contact* Glenn Wilson

**Darker Than Blue Ltd**
Aizlewood Mill
Nursery St
Sheffield
South Yorkshire
S3 8GG
T 0114 233 3024/282 3116    F as telephones
W purplepeople.co.uk and englishelectric.net
*Managing Director* Simon Robinson

*Labels: Purple Records (CD re-issues), English*
*Electric (contemporary CD releases)*

**Data Records**
28 Silksby St
Coventry
West Midlands
CB3 5FX
T 024 7650 5946/07880 816388
F as first telephone    E dave@dainrecords.com
W datarecords.com
*Contact* Dave Harris

**db records**
PO Box 19318
London
W4 1DS
T 020 8747 9911    F 020 8742 2443
E david@dbrecords.co.uk    W dbrecords.co.uk
*Contact* David Bates, Chris Hughes or Tom Friend

**Dead Earnest**
PO Box 6921
Dundee
DD4 8YN
T 01382 776595    E andygee@dial.pipex.com
W dialspace.dial.pipex.com/andygee
*Contact* Andy Garibaldi

*Ambient, space-rock, post-rock*
*Roster: Krel, Mooch, Doug Snyder and Bob*
*Thompson, Spacehead*

### Dead Happy Records/Vibezone
3b Castledown Avenue
Hastings
East Sussex
TN34 3RJ
**T** 01424 434778   **E** vibezone@excite.com
*Director* David Arnold

*Dead Happy is indie rock/alternative, Vibezone is*
*ambient dance*
*Cassette demos welcome, SAE essential*

### Debonair Records & Tapes
Eaton House
39 Lower Richmond Rd
London
SW15 1ET
**T** 020 8788 4557   **F** 020 8780 9711
**E** eatonmus@aol.com
*Managing Director* Terry Oates

### Decca Music Group, The
347–353 Chiswick High Rd
London
W4 4HS
**T** 020 8747 8787   **F** 020 8742 5585
**W** universalclassics.com and deccaclassics.com
*Head of Media and Artist Relations* Sophie Jeffries

*Mainly classical music with labels Decca, Philips,*
*Decca (black label) and decca broadway*
*Crossover and soundtracks*

### Decca UK
22 St Peters Square
London
W6 9NW
**T** 020 8910 5000   **F** 020 8910 5411

### Deceptive Records
The Sunday School
Rotary St
London
SE1 6LG
**T** 020 7620 3009   **F** 020 7928 9439

**E** deceptive@bluff.demon.co.uk
**W** deceptive.co.uk
*Contact* Tony Smith

### Deconstruction
Bedford House
69–79 Fulham High St
London
SW6 3JW
**T** 020 7384 2298   **F** 020 7371 8165
**E** info@deconstruction.co.uk
**W** deconstruction.co.uk
*Contact* Amand Eastwood

### Defected Records Ltd
PO Box 2862
London
W1V 5QE
**T** 020 7439 9995   **F** 020 7439 4545
**E** defected@defected.co.uk   **W** defected.co.uk
*Contact* Simon Dunmore (A&R Director)
*A&R Manager* Seamus Haji

*Also Defected Management (Artists), Ground Floor,*
*25 Heathman's Road, London*
SW6
*(Contact: Will Stoppard, 020 7371 7223)*

### Defunkt Records
1 Constance St
Knott Hill
Manchester
M15 4PS
**T** 0161 236 6616/07973 344606   **F** 0161 228 2399
*Contact* Mike Kirwin

### Dejamus Productions
Suite 11
Accurist House
44 Baker St
London
W1M 1DH
**T** 020 7486 5838   **F** 020 7487 2634
*Managing Director* Stephen James

## Delerium Records

PO Box 1288
Gerrards Cross
Buck
SL9 9YB
**T** 01753 890635   **F** 01753 892879   **w** delerium.co.uk
*Contact* Richard Allen or Ivor Trueman

## Delta Music plc

222 Cray Avenue
Orpington
Kent
BR5 3EZ
**T** 01689 888888   **F** 01689 888800/888894
**E** info@deltamusic.co.uk
*Managing Director* Laurie Adams

## Delta Records plc

222 Cray Avenue
Orpington
Kent
BR5 3PZ
**T** 01689 888888   **F** 01689 888800
**E** info@deltamusic.co.uk
*Managing Director* Laurie Adams

*Budget & low priced labels: Music Digital, Laserlight and Delta*
*High price classical label: Capriccio*

## Delux Audio

PO Box 5753
Nottingham
NG2 7WN
**T** 0115 914 1429   **F** 0115 914 4889
**E** info@deluxaudio.com
*Managing Director* Nick Gordon Brown

## Demi Monde Records

Foel Studio
Llanfair
Caereinionn
Powys
SW21 0DS
**T** 01938 810758   **F** as telephone
**E** demi.monde@dial.pipex.com
**w** demimonde.co.uk/demimonde
*Managing Director* Dave Anderson

## Demon Records Ltd

Marpol House
6 The Green
Richmond
Surrey
TW9 1PL
**T** 020 8948 0011   **E** demon@fbeat.demon.co.uk

## Dental Records

139 Whitfield St
London
W1P 5RY
**T** 020 7380 1000/07768 242057
**F** as first telephone   **E** neil@nuff.co.uk
*Producers* Neil Stainton and Vito Benito

*Also production company*

## DEP International

1 Andover St
Birmingham
West Midlands
B5 5RD
**T** 0121 633 4742   **F** 0121 643 4904

## Destiny Music Ltd

Iron Bridge House
3 Bridge Approach
London
NW1 8BD
**T** 020 7734 3251   **F** 020 7439 2391
**E** cpm@carlinmusic.co.uk
*Managing Director* Nick Farries

## Detour Records Ltd

PO Box 18
Midhurst
West Sussex
GU29 9YU
**T** 01730 815422/815935   **F** as first telephone
**E** detour@btinternet.com   **w** detour-records.co.uk
*Directors* Dizzy and Tania Holmes

*Specialists in Mod and 1977-influenced punk also operating a mail-order company*

## Deviant
PO Box 699
London
SW10 0LS
**T** 020 7460 8697   **F** 020 7565 0871
**E** (whoever)@deviant.co.uk   **w** deviant.co.uk
*Managing Director* Rob Deacon
*A&R Director* Seymore Banz

*Electronic music*
*Roster includes Paul Van Dyk, Animated, Ashtrax,*
*Witchman*

## Devinyl Records Ltd
Walnut Tree Cottage
Watercress Lane
Wingham Well
Canterbury
Kent
CT3 1NR
**T** 01227 728409   **F** as telephone
**E** devinylrecords@breathe.com
*Contact* Blair Hart

*License and develop artists. Also music video*
*production*

## Diamond Disque Music
33 Broadfield Rd
London
SE6 1ND
**T** 020 8244 7344/8488 3159
*Managing Director* Alf Sena

## Diamond Recordings
Millmead Business Centre
Millmead Rd
London
N17 9QU
**T** 020 8493 0420   **F** 020 8801 0719
**E** diamond@zirc.co.uk
*Contact* Roger Dopson

*Re-issue specialists*

## Different Drummer
PO Box 2571
Birmingham
B30 1DZ
**T** 0121 603 0033   **F** 0121 603 0060
**E** diffdrum@dircon.co.uk   **w** diffdrum.co.uk
*Contact* Richard Whittingham or Adam Regan

*Subsiduary label Leftfoot Recordings*

## Dinosaur Records Ltd
PO Box 1685
Stoke-on-Trent
Staffs
ST6 4RX
**T** 01782 839513   **F** as telephone
**E** records@dinosaurmusic.co.uk
**w** dinosaurmusic.co.uk
*Managing Director* Alan E Dutton

## Direct Heat Records
PO Box 1345
Worthing
East Sussex
BN14 7FB
**T** 01903 202426   **F** 01903 202426
**E** directheatrecords@happyvibes.co.uk
**w** happyvibes.co.uk
*Contact* Mike Pailthorpe

*Specializing in the funky side of dance music, house,*
*disco, garage, R&B etc*

## Discipline GM
PO Box 1533
Salisbury
Wilts
SP5 5ER
**T** 01722 780187   **F** 01722 78142
**E** info@disciplineglobalmobile.com
*Label Manager* David Singleton

## Discordant Records
PO Box 6050
London
SW6 2SQ
**T** 020 7343 5632   **F** 020 7343 5656
**E** rob@discordantrecords.co.uk
*Contact* Rob Jefferson

## Disky Communications Ltd
Connaught House
112–120 High Rd
Loughton
Essex
IG10 4HJ
**T** 020 8508 3723   **F** 020 8508 0432

**E** disky.uk@disky.nl
*Managing Director* Alan Byron

**Disorient**
44 Poland St
London
W1V 3DA
**T** 020 7434 4288    **F** 020 7439 1828

**Distance Records UK**
Unit 1
Torriano Mews
London
NW5 2RZ
**T** 020 7482 1492    **F** 020 7482 2848
**E** distance@dircon.co.uk
*Contact* Jean Karakos
*A&R Manager* Joe Stanley

**Distinct'ive Records**
1st Floor, Berners House
47–48 Berners St
London
W1T 3NF
**T** 020 7323 6610    **F** 020 7323 6413
**E** (firstname)@distinctiverecords.com
**W** distinctiverecords.com
*Head of A&R* Richard Ford
*Press* Leah Riches

*Also Distinct'ive Breaks and Ink Records
Roster includes Hybrid, Way Out West, Commie,
Chris Coco, Prophets of Sound*

**Divine Art Record Company, The**
31 Beach Rd
South Shields
Tyne & Wear
NE33 2QX
**T** 0191 456 1837    **F** 0191 455 2954
**E** info@divine-art.com    **W** divine-art.com
*Contact* Stephen Sutton

**DiY**
Square Centre
389–394 Alfred St North
Nottingham
NG3 1AA
**T** 0115 911 1096    **F** 0115 911 1098

**E** diyhar@globalnet.co.uk
*Managing Director* Harry

**DJZ Music**
PO Box 9846
London
W13 9WR
**E** john@djzmusic.com    **W** djzmusic.com
*Contact* John de Souza

**Dog-To-Dot Internet Music**
PO Box 250
Witney
Oxon
OX8 5DB
**E** us@dog-to-dot.co.uk

**Dolls House Records**
7a Burnbank Place
Glasgow
G20 6UH
**T** 0141 331 1444    **F** as telephone

**Dolphin Traders Ltd**
Unit 4
Great Ship St
Dublin 8
Ireland
**T** 00 353 1 478 3455    **F** 00 353 1 478 2143
**E** irishmus@iol.ie    **W** dolphin-dara.ie
*Contact* David Cashell

**Dome Records Ltd**
59 Glenthorne Rd
London
W6 0LJ
**T** 020 8748 4499    **F** 020 8748 6699
**E** info@domerecords.co.uk    **W** domerecords.co.uk
*Managing Director* Peter Robinson

**Domestique**
74 Caithness Place
Kirkcaldy
Fife
KY1 3EE
**T** 01592 651740
*Contact* Kenny Hutchinson

## Domino Recording Company

PO Box 4029
London
SW15 2XR
T 020 8875 1390   F 020 8875 1391
E info@dominorecordco.com
w dominorecordco.com and domino-mart.com
*Contact* Jacqui Rice

## Donut

111 The Business Design Centre
52 Upper St
London
N1 0OH
T 020 8288 6048   E donut@donut.demon.co.uk
*Contact* Rob Davis

## DOR

PO Box 1797
London
E1 4TX
T 020 7702 7842   F 020 7790 0764
E dor@dor.co.uk   w dor.co.uk
*Managing Director* Martin Parker

*Roster includes Moondogg, Apollon, Funkturn,
Doppler 20:20, Chemical Plant, Tasha Killer Pussies*

## Dorado Records

76 Brewer St
London
W1R 3PH
T 020 7287 1689   F 020 7287 1684
E info@dorado.net   w dorado.net
*Managing Director* Ollie Buckwell

## Dorigen Music

Units 31–32
Queensbrook
Bolton
BL1 4AY
T 01204 544105   F 01204 393710
E hi@uniquedist.ue-net.com
*Contact* James Waddicker

## Down By Law Records

PO Box 20242
London
NW1 7FL
T 020 7485 1113   E proofsongs@mailbox.xo.uk

*See also United Nations Recordings (label) and Proof
Songs (publisher)*

## Downboy Recordings

Chevron House
2a Benbow Rd
London
W6 0AG
T 020 8743 5544   E brian@downboy.demon.co.uk
*Managing Director* Brian Harris
*A&R* Simon Lee Marlin

## Dragon Records

5 Church St
Aylesbury
Bucks
HP20 2QP
T 01296 415333   F 01296 397092
E johnh@fosterwiggins.co.uk
*Contact* John Heydon

## Dragonfly Records

67–69 Chalton St
London
NW1 1HI
T 020 7554 2100   F 020 7554 2154
E dragonfly@dragonflyrecords.co.uk
w dragonflyrecords.com
*Label Manager/A&R* Darren Stubbs
*Marketing Manager/A&R* Murray Rose

## Dreamworks Records

8 St James Square
London
SW1Y 4JU
T 020 7747 4227   F 020 7747 4399
w dreamworksrecords.com
*A&R* Tim Carr

## Dressed To Kill/Metrodome

110 Park St
London
W1K 6NX
T 020 7408 2121   F 020 7409 1935
E dtk@metrodomegroup.com
w dressed2kill.co.uk
*Contact* George Kimpton

## Dukes Avenue Records
138a Chiswick High Rd
London
W4 1PU
**T** 020 8994 9007   **F** 020 8995 1051
**E** info@dukesavenue.co.uk   **W** dukesavenue.com
*Managing Director* Harry Bozadjian
*A&R* Edwick Chi
*Promotions* Neece Osbourne

*Specializing in hip-hop and R&B*
*See also Air Tank Studios*

## dumb/SULK trigg-er Records
PO Box 13220
Galashiels
TD1 2YF
*Contact* Roger Simian

## Dust 2 Dust
Tempo House
15 Falcon Rd
London
SW11 2PJ
**T** 020 7228 6821/07956 616693   **F** 020 7228 6972
**E** massimo@dust2dust.demon.co.uk
**W** dust2dust.demon.co.uk
*A&R* Massimo Bonaddio

## Duty Free Recordings
3rd Floor, 67 Farringdon Rd
London
EC1M 3JB
**T** 020 7831 9931   **F** 020 7831 9331
**E** info@dutyfreerecordings.co.uk
**W** dutyfreerecordings.co.uk
*Contact* Steffan Chandler

## Eagle Records/Spitfire Records
Eagle House
22 Armoury Way
London
SW18 1EZ
**T** 020 8870 5670   **F** 020 8875 0050
**E** sioux@eagle-rock.com   **W** eagle-rock.com
*Managing Director* Lindsay Brown

*Specialists in heritage rock, progressive rock, rhythm*
*and blues and jazz*

## Eagle Rock Entertainment
Eagle House
22 Armoury Way
London
SW18 1EZ
**T** 020 8870 5670   **F** 020 8874 2333
**E** mail@eagle-rock.com
*Managing Director* Geoff Kempin

## Ealing Records
Timperley House
11 St Albans Rd
Skircoat Green
Halifax
West Yorkshire
HX3 0AE
**T** 01422 367040
*Managing Director* Bill Byford

*Over 20 years' experience of producing film*
*soundtracks*
*Also specialize in blues and avant-garde jazz*
*Distribution deals throughout the world*

## Earache Records Ltd
Suite 1–3
Westminster Building
Theatre Square
Nottingham
Notts
NG1 6LG
**T** 0115 950 6400   **F** 0115 950 8585
**E** earache@earache.com
*Managing Director* Digby Pearson

## Earth Records Ltd
Unit 104a
The Old Gramophone Works
326 Kensal Rd
London
W10 5BZ
**T** 020 8968 4545   **F** 020 8968 3737
**E** sales@samplecraze.com   **W** samplecraze.com
*Contact* Philip Allen

*Producers of music samples for DJs, producers and*
*studios under the 'Samplecraze' banner*
*Specialists in re-mixing for dance genres*

## Earthworks

19 Finstock Rd
London
W10 6LT
T 020 8969 1387/7387 5550   F 020 7388 2756
E trevor@sternsmusic.com   w sternsmusic.com
*Contact* Trevor Herman

## East Central One

1 York St
London
W1U 6PA
T 020 7486 2248   F 020 7486 8515
E enquiries@eastcentralone.com
w eastcentralone.com
*Contact* Steve Fernie

*Also Creature Music Limited (primarily for Manfred Mann's Earth Band) and Cold Harbour Recording Company Limited (publisher)*

## East West Records

Electric Lighting Station
46 Kensington Court
London
W8 5DP
T 020 7938 2181   F 020 7937 6645
w eastwest.co.uk

## eastcentralfour

160 Clifford's Inn
Fetter Lane
London
EC4A 1BY
T 020 7242 1664   E mark@nutonic.co.uk
w eastcentralfour.com
*Contact* Mark Lewczynski

## Eastern Bloc

Unit 5, Central Buildings
Oldham St
Manchester
M1 1JQ
T 0161 228 6432   F 0161 228 6728
E info@easternblocrecords.co.uk
w easternblocrecords.co.uk

*Music stocked: UK house, import house, tech house, UK/euro/US techno, progressive house, electro, drum 'n' bass, psychedelic trance*

## Eastside Records (Dv8/IKG)

The Image Centre
33 Clementina Rd
London
E10 7PD
T 020 8539 9333   F 020 8539 9335
*Contact* Alexis Michaelides

## Easy Street Records

15 Grand Union Crescent
London
E8 4TR
T 020 7684 6044/07836 642652   F as first telephone
*President and General Manager* Johnny Mac
*Promotions* Laura Mac
*A&R* David Prince

## Easy!Tiger Records

Suite 209
Bon Marche Centre
241–251 Ferndale Rd
London
SW9 8BJ
T 020 7733 9700   F 020 7733 9060
*Contact* Wyndham Wallace

## Echo Label Ltd, The

The Chrysalis Building
13 Bramley Rd
London
W10 6SP
T 020 7229 1616   F 020 7465 6296/792 1299
E clairea@chrysalis.co.uk   w echo.co.uk
*Managing Director* Jeremy Lascelles
*General Manager* John Chuter

## Eclectic Records Ltd

6 Barclay Terrace
Bruntsfield
Edinburgh
EH10 4HP
T 0131 229 9299   F 0131 229 9298
E eclectic@btinternet.com
*Director* Gordon Stevenson

## Edel UK Records Ltd

12 Oval Rd
London
NW1 7DH
T 020 7482 4848   F 020 7482 4846

E *contactuk@edel.com*  **w** edel.co.uk
*Managing Director* Daniel Lycett
*Head of Press* Carolyn Norman
*Label Manager* Claire Horseman

## Edel UK Records Ltd

12 Oval Rd
London
NW1 7DU
**T** 020 7482 4848    **F** 020 7482 4846
**E** contact@edel.com    **w** edel.com
*Label Manager* Claire Horseman
*A&R* Clive Black
*Managing Director* Daniel Lycett

*Also labels Hollywood Records, Disney Records, West
2 Recordings, Religion Music, Club Tools*

## EG Records

61a Kings Rd
London
SW3 4NT
**T** 020 7730 2162    **F** 020 7730 1330
*Contact* Sam Alder

## Eighth Music Ltd

11 Glasgow Rd
London
N18 2EG
**T** 020 8482 6114/07956 994089
**F** as first telephone    **E** james@jazz-specialist.com
*Managing Director* James C Henriot

## Electric Melt

6c Littlehampton Rd
Worthing
West Sussex
BN13 1QE
**T** 01902 260033    **F** 01903 261133
*Label Manager* Patrick Horgan

## Elemental Records

250 York Rd
London
SW11 3SJ
**T** 020 7716 3400/3414    **F** 020 7716 3401
**E** elemental@indian.co.uk
**w** elemental.music.co.uk

## Ember Records Ltd

PO Box 130
Hove
East Sussex
BN3 6QU
**T** 01273 550088    **F** 01273 540969
**E** h.kruger@tkogroup.com
*Contact* Howard Kruger

*NB: Back catalogue and licensing only. No new
artists*

## Embryonic Records

Rear Basement
92–98 Bourne Terrace
London
W2 5TH
**T** 020 7289 8142
*Contact* Chris Thomas

## Emerald Music (Ireland) Ltd

120a Coach Rd
Templepatrick
Ballyclare
Co. Antrim
BT39 0HB
**T** 028 9443 2619    **F** 028 9443 2162
**E** info@emeraldmusic.co.uk
*Contact* George or Jean Doherty

## Emergency Broadcast System, The

PO Box 6131
London
W3 8ZR
**T** 020 8993 8436    **F** 020 8896 1778
**E** star_rat@hawkwind.com    **w** hawkwind.com
*Contact* Eve Carr

## EMI Records Group UK and Ireland

EMI House
43 Brook Green
London
W6 7EF
**T** 020 7605 5000    **F** 020 7605 5182
**E** alan.pell@emimusic.com    **w** emichrysalis.co.uk
*Head of A&R*(EMI/Chrysalis): Alan S Pell

## Emmellar Records
PO Box 1345
Ilford
Essex
IG4 5FX
**T** 07050 333555   **F** 07020 923292
**E** emmelleye@aol.com
*A&R* Wendy Kicks
*Label Manager* Paul Booth

## Emotif/Botchit & Scarper
PO Box 16047
London
NW1 7ZH
**T** 020 7729 8030   **F** 020 7729 8121
**E** botchit@styx.cerbernet.co.uk
**W** botchitand scarper.co.uk
*Contact* Martin Love

*Emotif and its sub-label Double Zero are for drum
'n' bass, Botchit & Scarper and its sub-label Botchit
Breaks for new-school breakbeat
See also Medley's Creek Music (publisher)*

## Energize UK
Unit 3
Hawthorne House
Fitzwilliam St
Parkgate
Rotherham
South Yorkshire
S62 6EP
**T** 01709 710022   **F** 01709 523141
**E** gary@mfeg.demon.co.uk   **W** musicfactory.co.uk
*Label Directors* Gary Simmons, Dave Kinghorn

## Entropica
c/o CCC
PO Box 10
London
N1 3RJ
**T** 020 7267 7897/7241 2183
**F** 020 7267 8797/7241 6233   **E** ccc@cyborganic.net
**W** entropica.com
*Contact* Grant T Garden

## Ephemoral Recordings
PO Box 6076
London
SW1V 4XD
**T** 020 7630 7461   **F** as telephone
**E** ephemoral@dial.pipex.com
*Managing Director* Kevin Waller

## Epic Head Records/Jadestone Productions
PO Box 183
Sheffield
South Yorks
S1 2XF
**T** 0114 273 1398/020 7932 4917
**E** ehead@jadestne.demon.co.uk

## Epic Records
10 Great Marlborough St
London
W1V 2LP
**T** 020 7911 8200   **F** 020 7911 8600
*Contact* Kim Machray
*A&R Director* Nick Mander
*Promos Director* Adrian Williams
*Head of Press* Iain Watt

## Epidemic Records
The Arches
2–3 Crosslee Steading
Ettrick Valley
Selkirk
TD7 5HT
**T** 01750 62289   **F** 01750 62307

## Escapade Records
Tempo House
15 Falcon Rd
London
SW11 2PJ
**T** 020 7228 6821   **F** 020 7228 6972
**E** post@rumour.demon.co.uk
**W** rumour.demon.co.uk
*Directors* David Brooker and Anne Plaxton

## ESSP
The Sound House
PO Box 37b
Molesey
Surrey
KT8 2YR
**T** 020 8979 9997   **F** as telephone
*Contact* Dave Tuffnell

## Europa Records

12 Southam St
London
W10 5PH
**T** 020 8960 3253 **F** 020 8968 5111
**E** info@europarecords.com **w** europarecords.com
*Contact* Jake Mansell

## European Artists & Entertainment

The Studio
Lynton Rd
London
N8 8SL
**T** 020 8347 5220 **F** 020 8347 5221
*Commercial Director* Mike Fay

*Also TMO Music Ltd (same details)*

## Eurozone Recordings

28a Academy St
Bathgate
Edinburgh
EH48 1DX
**T** 01506 636068/07785 222205 **F** 01506 633900
**E** mail@clubscene.co.uk **w** clubscene.co.uk
*Managing Director* Bill Grainger

## Evangeline Recorded Works Ltd

10 Hillary Rise
New Barnet
Herts
EN5 5AZ
**T** 020 8364 8248 **F** 020 8364 8288
**E** pete@evangeline.co.uk
*Contact* Pete Macklin

## EVE Records

PO Box 16102
London
SW16 2FP
**T** 020 8769 3456 **F** 020 8769 9779
**E** steven@everecords.com **w** everecords.com

## Eventide Music

PO Box 27
Baldock
Herts
SG7 6UH
**T** 01462 893995 **F** as telephone

**E** eventidmus@aol.com **w** members.aol.com/
eventidmus
*Managing Director* Kevin Kendle

## Everyday Records

PO Box 56
Westhoughton
Bolton
Lancs
BL5 2WW
**T** 07747 654659

*Specializing in commissioned works for stage, TV and film*
*Small company with in-house composers/songwriters*

## Excalibur Records

34 Salisbury St
London
NW8 8QL
**T** 020 7402 9111 **F** 020 7723 3064
**w** orcmedia.co.uk
*Managing Director* Eliot Cohen

## ExlusivRNB.com

PO Box 1345
Ilford
Essex
IG4 5FX
**T** 07050 333555 **F** 07020 923292
**E** melevett@aol.com **w** exclusivrnb.com
*Contact* Fat Freddie

## Exotica Records

49 Belvoir Rd
London
SE22 0QY
**T** 020 8299 2342 **F** 020 8693 9006
**E** jim@exoticarecords.co.uk
**w** exoticarecords.co.uk
*Contact* Jim Phelan

*Specialists in bizarre Beatle cover versions and football-related albums, particularly Manchester United, for example The Red Album, Cantona the Album, Georgie the Best Album*
*Also graphic design studio specializing in sleeves, particularly for the indie sector*

## Expansion Records

Skratch Music House
81 Crabtree Lane
London
SW6 6LW
**T** 020 7381 8315   **F** 020 7385 6785
**E** ralph@expansion-records.co.uk
**W** musiclinks.com/expansion
*Contact* Ralph Tee

*Also Passion Jazz (same details)*

## Experience Grooves Ltd

43 Canham Rd
London
W3 7SR
**T** 020 8749 8860   **F** 020 8742 9462
*Contact* Andy Howarth

*Also Imprint Recordings Ltd*

## Eye Q Records

100c Edith Grove
London
SW10 0NH
**T** 07092 076965   **F** 020 7351 3506
**E** feedback@eyeq.co.uk   **W** eyeq.co.uk
*Managing Director* Heinz Roth

## F-Hot Music

PO Box 3442
Tollesbury
Essex
CM9 8UQ
**T** 01621 869702   **F** as telephone
**E** bark@saltydogs.swinternet.co.uk
**W** saltydogs.swinternet.co.uk
*Contact* Dan Peachey

## F1 Records

PO Box 238
Cheltenham
Gloucs
GL52 6XT
**T** 01242 257238   **F** 01242 257192
**E** phil@fantazia.co.uk   **W** fantazia.co.uk
*A&R* Phil Roberts

## Fairy Cake Universe

35 Playfield Crescent
London
SE22 8QR
**T** 020 8299 1645   **F** 020 8299 1685
**E** aquamanda@skyfruit.demon.co.uk
*Contact* Amanda Greatorex

## Faith & Hope Records Ltd

23 New Mount St
Manchester
M4 4DE
**T** 0161 953 4090   **F** 0161 953 4095
**E** email@faithandhope.co.uk
**W** faithandhope.co.uk
*Directors* Neil Claxton and David Wood
*A&R and Label Manager* Amul Batra

*All types of pop music*

## Faith Music Corporation

PO Box 111
London
W13 0ZH
**T** 020 8357 2337/07000 243 243
**F** 020 8566 7215/0132 731 2545
**E** info@faith-music-corp.com
**W** faith-music=corp.com
*Contact* John Rushton

## Fantastic Plastic

319 City Rd
London
EC1V 1LJ
**T** 020 7278 1150   **F** 020 7278 1157
**E** info@fantasticplastic.co.uk
**W** fantasticplastic.co.uk
*Managing Director* Darrin Robson

## Fantazia Music

PO Box 238
Cheltenham
Gloucs
GL52 6XT
**T** 01242 257133   **F** 01242 257192
**E** charles@fantazia.co.uk   **W** fantazia.co.uk
*Press and Marketing* Charles Perkins

**Far Out Recordings**
The Studio
3a Osterley Rd
Isleworth
Middlesex
TW7 4PE
T 020 8758 1233    F 020 8758 1244
E farout@farout.co.uk    W farout.co.uk
*Contact* Nadia Audhali or Joe Davis
( joe@faroutrecordings.freeserve.co.uk)

*Brazilian jazz, experimental house and electronica*
*Subsidiary label: Solaria (dance music, electronic*
*jazz, future disco)*

**Fashion Records**
17 David's Rd
London
SE23 3EP
T 020 8291 6253    F 020 8291 1097
*Contact* Chris Lane or John MacGillivary
*Producer* Chris Lane

**Fast Western Ltd**
Bank Top Cottage
Meadow Lane
Millers Dale
Derbyshire
SK17 8SN
T 01298 872462    F 01298 872461
E fast.west@virgin.net
*Managing Director* Ric Lee

*Also publishing and production*
*Commercial music of all sorts*
*First approach by telephone, please*

**Fastforward Music Ltd**
Sorrel Horse House
1 Sorrel Horse Mews
Ipswich
Suffolk
IP4 1LN
T 01473 210555    F 01473 210500
E sales@fastforwardmusic.co.uk
*Managing Director* Neil Read

**Fat Cat records**
348 Old St
London
EC1V 9NQ
T 020 7729 7981    F 020 7729 7991
E fatcat@indian.co.uk    W fat-cat.co.uk
*Contact* Dave or Alex

**Fatt Boy**
125 Fonthill Rd
London
N4 3HH
T 020 7263 1600    F 020 7263 4999
E luk@fattboy.com
*Contact* Luke Coke

**FAYMUS Recordings**
PO Box 748
Luton
Beds
LU1 5ZA
T 01582 481222    F as telephone
E faymus@dial.pipex.com    W ds.dial.pipex.xom/
faymus
*Senior Partner* Dave Tong

**Faze Freak Records**
114 Lower Park Rd
Loughton
Essex
IG10 4NE
T 020 8508 4564/07831 430030
F as first telephone
E djone@howardmarks.freeserve.co.uk
*Contact* Marisa Mark

**Fearless Records**
PO Box 14996
London
SW17 9AR
T 020 8682 0243    F as telephone
E michael@life.freeserve.co.uk
*Contact* Michael Fuller

**Fellside Recordings Ltd**
PO Box 40
Workington
Cumbria
CA14 3GJ
T 01900 61556    F 01900 61585

**E** info@fellside.com   **W** fellside.com
*Contact* Paul Adams

*Three labels: Fellside specializes in folk and was founded in 1976, Lake Records is the UK's leading independent label for British trad jazz, and Smallfolk is for children's material (e.g Bagpuss)*

## Fiction Records

4 Tottenham Mews
London
W1T 4AB
**T** 020 7323 5555   **F** 020 7323 5323
**E** ita@fictionsongs.co.uk   **W** fictionsongs.com
*Managing Director* Ita Martin

## Fifty First Recordings

4–5 Hazlitt Mews
Hazlitt Rd
London
W14 0JZ
**T** 020 7751 1237   **F** 020 7751 1149
**E** woody@fiftyfirst.co.uk
*Project Manager* Woody

## Final Frontier Music

29 Roundwood Rd
Hastings
Sussex
TN37 7LD
**T** 01424 753792   **E** davidffroberts@aol.com
*Managing Director* David Roberts

*Instrumental music only*

## Finger Lickin' Records/VA Recordings

c/o Vinyl Addiction
6 Inverness St
London
NW1 7HJ
**T** 020 7482 1114   **F** 020 7681 6039
**E** fingerlickin@ukf.net
**W** fingerlickin.co.uk and vinyl-addiction.co.uk
*Managing Director* Justin Rushmore

## Fire Records

21a Maury Rd
London
N16 7BP
**T** 020 8806 9922   **F** 020 8806 8021

*A&R* Clive Solomon, Jon Eydmann
*Publishing A&R* Trevor Holden

## Firebird

Kyrle House Studios
Edde Cross St
Ross-on-Wye
Herefordshire
HR9 7BZ
**T** 01989 562336   **F** 01989 566337
**E** pmartin@firebirdmusic.com   **W** firebird.com
*Chief Executive Officer* Peter Martin

*Production company/studio with own label, management and pr/promo/design Eurasian fusion, pop, r&b, dance*

## First Avenue Records

The Courtyard
42 Colwith Rd
London
W6 9EY
**T** 020 8741 1419   **F** 020 8741 3289
**E** (name)@first-avenue.co.uk   **W** firstavenue.net
*Contact* Oliver Smallman

*Also First Avenue Management and publisher First Avenue Music (same Contact details)*

## First Frequency Ltd

12 Pepys Court
84 The Chase
London
SW4 0NF
**T** 020 7498 9666   **F** 020 7498 1828
*Managing Director* Jeremy Elliott

## First Night Records

2–3 Fitzroy Mews
London
W1P 5DQ
**T** 020 7383 7767   **F** 020 7383 3020
**E** information@first-night-records.com
**W** first-night-records,com
*Managing Director* John Craig

## First Step Records

96 George St
Mansfield
Notts
NG19 6SB
**T** 01623 642778    **F** as telephone
**E** first.step@talk21.com    **w** theearlofsound.co.uk
*Contact* David Butcher

*Also First Step Management (same contact details)*

## First Time Records

Sovereign House
12 Trewartha Rd
Praa Sands
Penzance
Cornwall
TR20 9ST
**T** 01736 762826/07721 449477    **F** 01736 763328
**E** panamus@aol.com    **w** panamamusic.co.uk
*Managing Director* Roderick G Jones

*Also Mohock Records, Pure Gold Records, Rainy Day Records (same contact details)*

## Flair Records

15 Tabbs Lane
Scholes
Cleckheaton
West Yorkshire
BD19 6DY
**T** 01274 851365    **F** 01274 874329/65495
**E** nowmusic@now-music.com    **w** now.music.com
*Contact* John Wagstaff

*Mainly pop music management*

## Flat Records

5 Doods Rd
Reigate
Surrey
RH2 0NT
**T** 01737 210848    **F** as telephone
**E** panther@dial.pipex.com
**w** netlink.co.uk/users/sonic/flat.htm
*Managing Director* Richard Coppen

## Flaw Recordings

87 Rickmansworth Rd
Pinner
Middx
HA5 3TJ
**T** 020 8866 9541    **F** as telephone
*Managing Director* Dean Thatcher

*Sister label: Screaming Target
Roster includes The Aloof*

## flexi:POP!

2 Daubeny Court
Draycot Place
Bristol
BS1 4RE
**T** 01275 464600

## Flick Productions

PO Box 888
Penzance
Cornwall
TR20 8ZP
**T** 01736 788798    **F** as telephone
**E** info@flickpro.demon.co.uk
*Managing Director* Mark Shaw

## Flo Records/Nation Records

19 All Saints Rd
London
W11 1HE
**T** 020 7792 8167    **F** 020 7792 2854
**E** aki@nationrecords.co.uk
**w** nationrecords.co.uk
*Managing Director* Aki Nawaz

*Creative and cutting edge music*

## Fluent Records

18 New Rd
Solihull
Birmingham
B29 6NA
**T** 0121 764 5078    **F** 0121 764 5080
**E** chester@kingadora.com    **w** fluentmusic.com
*Contact* Mark Chester

## Fluffy Bunny
20 Elderberry Rd
London
W5 4AN
T 020 8575 8753

## Flying Record Company, The
FM House
110 Clarendon Rd
London
W11 2HR
T 020 7221 7799   F 020 7221 5016
E info@flying music.co.uk   W flyingmusic.co.uk
*Contact* Paul Walden or Derek Nicol

*A division of The Flying Music Company Ltd*

## Flying Records UK
73 Albion Mews
off Galina Rd
London
W6 0XL
T 020 8741 7713/7719

## Flying Rhino Records
252 Belsize Rd
London
NW6 4BT
T 020 7624 8555   F 020 7624 8027
W flying-rhino.co.uk
*Contact* Cass Cutbush
*A&R* James Monro

## FM-Revolver Records
162 Goldthorn Hill
Penn
Wolverhampton
West Midlands
WV2 3JA
T 01902 345345   F 01902 345155
*Managing Director* Paul Birch

## Folksound Records
250 Earlsdon Avenue North
Coventry
West Midlands
CV5 6GX
T 02476 711935   F 02476 711191
E rootsrecs@btclick.com
*Managing Director* Graham Bradshaw

## Folktrax International
Heritage House
16 Brunswick Square
Gloucester
Gloucs
GL1 1UG
T 01452 415110/503643
E peter@folktrax.freeserve.co.uk   W folktrax.org
*Manager* Peter Kennedy

*Extensive international archive of field recordings*
*Unique reference library of oral traditions*

## Fony Records
Cambridge House
Card Hill
Forest Row
Surrey
RH18 5BA
T 01342 22619   F as telephone
E mickey_modernwood@compuserve.com
*Managing Director* Mickey Modern

## Food Records
9 Greenland St
London
NW1 0ND
T 020 7284 2554   F 020 7284 2560
W foodrecords.com
*Contact* Tasha Waithe
*Director* Andy Ross

## Forever Gold
69 Rivington St
London
EC2A 3AY
T 020 7613 1344/3911   F 020 7613 3319/3088
E forevergold@btinternet.com
W forevergold.co.uk
*Contact* John Tracy

*Nostalgia label specializing in 1930s–1950s*
*compilations*
*Also The Perennial Music Co Ltd (mail order*
*company, same contact details)*

## Formula One Records

71 Alan Moss Rd
Loughborough
Leics
LE11 5LR
T 01509 213632
*Managing Director* Ian Barker

*Specializing in rock*

## Foulplay Records

15 Church End
Liverpool
L24 4AX
T 07932 025055   E info@foulplayrecords.com
W foulplayrecords.com
*Contact* Lance Thomas

## Four D Recordings Lyd

Forum House
235 Regents Park Rd
London
N3 3LF
T 0956 623018/0777 556 8059   F 020 8349 1741
E info@fourdrecordings.com
W fourdrecordings.com
*Contact* Adam Davis

## Fox Records Ltd

62 Lake Rise
Romford
Essex
RM1 4EE
T 01708 760544   F 01708 760563
E foxrecords@talk21.com
*Promotion and Marketing* Colin Brewer

*Pop, rock, dance, house*
*Subsidiary company Fox Records Ltd (artist management)*

## FR Records

47 Clifton Grove
Leeds
West Yorks
LS9 6HD
T 0113 226 0416   E fuzzbird@mcmail.com
*Contact* John Parkes

*Small indie label*

## FreakStreet records

PO Box 6627
London
E1 2RF
T 020 7423 9993   F 020 7423 9996
E admin@12one.com   W 12one.com
*Director* Paul Kennedy

## Freek Records

PO Box 445
Camberley
Surrey
GU16 5YY
E pmorgan@globix.xom   W apexonline/freek.com
*Managing Director* Peter Morgan

## Freeway Music Group Ltd

Federation House
85–87 Wellington St
Luton
Beds
LU1 5AF
T 01582 457503   F 01582 412215
*Contact* Ken Wiltsher

## Fresh Ear Records

101 Chamberlayne Rd
London
NW10 3ND
T 020 8960 8466   F 020 8968 5892
E b.hallin@virgin.net
*Contact* Brian Hallin

## Fresh Records/Freskonova Records/Fresh Music

PO Box 4075
Pangbourne
Berks
RG8 7FV
T 0118 984 3468   F 0118 984 3463
E info@freshmusic.co.uk/info@freskonova.com
*Directors* Dave Morgan, Vicki Aspinall
*A&R/Production* Dave Morgan

*See also Fresh Songs (publishing)*

## Freskanova
7a Colville Terrace
London
W11 2BE
**T** 020 7221 9300   **F** 020 7221 0088
**E** freska@freshrecords.freeserve.co.uk
*Director* Vicky Aspinall

## Friction Burns Recordings
1a Kings Rd
Westcliff-on-Sea
Essex
SS0 8BH
**T** 01702 312015   **F** 01702 300634

## Fuel Records
18–20 Scrutton St
London
EC2A 4RJ
**T** 020 7392 2101   **F** 020 7392 2123
*Director* Richard Warren

## Full Cycle Records
Unit 23
Easton Business Centre
Felix Rd
Bristol
BS5 0HE
**T** 0117 941 5824   **F** 0117 941 5823
**E** info@fullcycle.co.uk   **w** fullcycle.co.uk
*Contact* Rebecca Hubbard

*Drum 'n' bass label started in 1993.*

## Fundamental Records Ltd
1 Devonport Mews
London
W12 8NG
**T** 020 8354 4900   **F** 020 8354 4901
**E** info@fundamental.co.uk   **w** fundamental.co.uk
*Director* Tim Prior
*A&R Director* Bernhard Griffiths
*A&R (R&B)* Everton Webb

## Funky Inc
206 Golden House
29 Great Pulteney St
London
W1R 3DD
**T** 020 7434 0711   **F** 020 7434 0710
**E** funkyinc@funkyinc.com   **w** funkyinc.com
*Contact* Brendan Donohoe

## Furious? Records
PO Box 40
Arundel
West Sussex
BN18 0UQ
**T** 01243 558444   **F** 01243 558455
**E** info@furiousrecords.co.uk   **w** delirious.co.uk
*Contact* Tony Patoto

## Fury Records
7–11 Minerva Rd
London
NW10 6HJ
**T** 020 8963 0352   **F** 020 8963 1170
**w** nervous.co.uk/furygtm

## Future Earth
59 Fitzwilliam St
Wath Upon Dearne
Rotherham
South Yorkshire
S63 7HG
**T** 01709 872875   **F** as telephone
**E** future_earth@csi.com
**w** ourworld.compuserve.com/homepages/
future_earth/
*Managing Director* David Moffitt

## Future Legends Records
PO Box 727
Kenley
Surrey
CR8 5YF
**T** 020 8668 0493   **F** as telephone
**E** mouse@mailbox.co.uk
**w** future.legend.records.freeservers.com
*Managing Director* Russell Brennan

## Future Music Records
10 Baddow Rd
Chelmsford
Essex
CM2 0DG
**T** 01245 353878   **F** 01245 352490
**E** ttaylor228@aol.com

## Future Sound & Vision (FSV)
2nd Floor, 35–37 Brent House
London
NW4 2EF
**T** 020 8203 9966   **F** 020 8203 4747
**E** simon.davis@diamondtime.co.uk
**w** fsvconnect.com
*Contact* Simon Davis

## Future Underground Nation
80 Monks Rd
Exeter
Devon
EX4 7BE
**T** 01392 490064   **F** 01392 420580
**E** fun@fun-1.com   **w** fun-1.com
*Contact* Biff

## FX Promotions
Promotions House
46 Grenville Rd
London
N19 4EH
**T** 020 7281 8363   **F** 020 7281 7663
**E** (name)@fxpromotions.demon.co.uk
**w** fxpromotions.demon.co.uk

## FXU Records
The Brewery
91 Brick Lane
London
E1 6QN
**T** 020 7377 1516   **F** 020 7377 9949
**E** markbeder@hotmail.com
*Managing Director* Mark Beder

## Gable Records
16 Pendle Court
Astley Bridge
Bolton
Lancs
BL1 6PY
**T** 01204 596648
*Proprietor* Len Goodwin

## Galactic Disco Music
Red Corner Door
17 Barons Court Rd
London
W14 9DP
**T** 020 7386 8760   **F** 020 7381 8014
**E** galactic@globalinternet.co.uk
**w** hospitalrecords.com
*Contact* Tony Colman

## GAS Records
10 St John's Square
Glastonbury
Somerset
BA6 9LJ
**T** 01458 833040   **F** 01458 833958
**E** jonny@planetgong.co.uk   **w** planetgong.co.uk
*Contact* Jonny Greene

## Gator Records
56 Oswald St
Glasgow
G1 4PL
**T** 0141 221 7871   **F** 0141 221 7875
*Managing Director* Robert Fields

## Gecko Recordings Ltd
PO Box 853
Wallington
Surrey
SM6 8UL
**T** 020 8773 0605   **F** as telephone
**E** info@geckorecordings.com
**w** geckorecordings.com
*Managing Director* Andy Neville

*See also Triple XXX Recordings at same address*

## Gemini Entertainments Group
Satril House
3 Blackburn Rd
London
NW6 1RZ
**T** 020 7328 8283   **F** 020 7328 9037
**E** hho@dial.pipex.xom
**w** dspace.dial.pipex.com/hho/
*Product Manager* John Morton

## Genetic Recordings
PO Box 10815
London
W4 5WZ
**T** 020 8783 1005  **F** 020 8783 1168
**E** genetic@imperial-design.demon.co.uk
*Managing Director* Mike Leonard
*General Manager* Andrew Wills

## Genius Records Ltd
89a High Rd
London
N22 6BB
**T** 020 8881 6969  **F** 020 8888 1685
**E** genius@brmmusic.com  **w** brmmusic.com
*Managing Director* Bruce Ruffin
*A&R* Simon Kay

## Giant Electric Pea
PO Box 24
Bishops Waltham
Hampshire
SO32 1XJ
**T** 01489 891815  **F** as telephone
**E** gepuk@email.msn.com
*Contact* Martin Orford

*Specializing in progressive/symphonic rock*
*Releases include IQ, John Wetton, Spocks Beard,*
*Jadis, Threshold*

## Gimell Records
PO Box 197
Beckley
Oxford
OX3 9YJ
**T** 01865 358282  **F** 08700 568880
**E** info@gimell.com  **w** gimell.com
*Managing Director* Steve Smith

*NB: only deals with The Tallis Scholars, no demos*
*please*

## Ginga Recording Company
54 Carlton Place
Glasgow
G5 9TW
**T** 0141 418 0053  **F** 0141 418 0054
*Creative Director* Steve Gilmour
*PR* Joolz MacCaskill

## Gipsy Records
The Studio
Lynton Rd
London
N8 85L
**T** 020 8347 5220  **F** 020 8347 5221

## Glasgow Records Ltd
Lovat House
Gavell Rd
Glasgow
G65 9BS
**T** 01236 826555  **F** 01236 825560
**E** info@glasgowrecords.com

## Glass Gramophone Company Ltd, The
Lower Farm Barns
Bainton Rd
Bucknell
Oxon
OX6 9LT
**T** 01869 325052  **F** 01869 325072
**E** clarity@pastperfect.com  **w** pastperfect.com
*Managing Director* Michael Daly

*Specializing in re-mastered original recordings from*
*the 1920s–1940s*
*Ranging from classic jazz, swing and blues to*
*nostalgia and movie songs*
*Free catalogue available*

## Global Beat Records
49 Darley St
Bradford
West Yorkshire
BD1 3HN
**T** 01274 770094
*Directors* Drew Prophet, Jamie Prophet

## Global Harmony Records
Devonshire House
223 Upper Richmond Rd
London
SW15 6SQ
**T** 020 8780 0612  **F** 020 8789 8668
**E** christian@cdpool.co.uk  **w** globalharmony.co.uk
*Contact* Christian Larsson

## Global Records

171 Southgate Rd
London
N1 3LE
**T** 020 7704 8542 **F** 020 7704 2028
**E** peterknightjr@compuserve.com
*Contact* Peter Knight Jr

## Global Talent (Records)

Alexandra House
6 Little Portland St
London
W1N 5AG
**T** 020 7907 1700 **F** 020 7907 1711
**E** email@globaltalentgroup.com
**w** globaltalentgroup.com
*Directors* David Forecast and Ashley Tabor

## Glow Records

9–10 Slater St
Liverpool
Merseyside
L1 4AQ
**T** 0151 707 1669 **F** 0151 707 0227
**E** rob@3beat.co.uk **w** glowrecords.co.uk
*Contact* Rob Jay

*Dance music*
*See also 3Beat*

## GMG

PO Box 3376
London
NW3 7SH
**T** 020 8455 3439 **F** 020 8455 0507
**E** gmgmusic@dircon.co.uk
*General Manager* Ray McCarville

## Go Ahead Music Ltd

Kerchesters
Waterhouse Lane
Kingswood
Surrey
KT20 6HT
**T** 01737 833713 **F** 01737 833812
**E** ian@goahead.co.uk **w** amphonic.co.uk
*Managing Director* Ian Dale

## Go Beat

Fulham Palace
Bishops Avenue
London
SW6 6EA
**T** 020 7800 4400 **F** 020 7800 4401
**E** gobeat@btinternet.com **w** gobeatrecords.com
*Contact* Ferdy Unger-Hamilton

## Go Crazy Music

50 Jail Lane
Biggin Hill
Kent
TN16 3SA
**T** 01959 573806 **F** 01959 574910
*Director* Daz Shields

## Go-Go Girl

PO Box 8931
London
SW16 2ZA
**T** 07957 436333 **E** rick@gogogirl.demon.co.uk
*Contact* Rick Lucas

## Gobbywobble Records

Head Office
14 The Malt House
The Drays
Long Melford
Sudbury
Suffolk
CO10 9TP
**T** 01787 372968 **F** 01787 237837
**E** dean@gobbywobble.com **w** gobbywobble.com
*Managing Director* Dean Shaw
*Heads of Artist Relations* Sonia Robinson and Sarah Hall

*Caters for all types of new and up-and-coming talent*

## Gold n' Delicious

The Place
28 Bryan St
Hanley
Stoke-on-Trent
Staffs
ST1 5AF
**T** 01782 284433/07976 366798 **F** 01782 207526
*Contact* Les Hemstock

## Good Groove Recording Ltd

Unit 217, Buspace Studios
Conlan St
London
W10 5AP
**T** 020 7565 0050   **F** 020 7565 0049
**E** (first name)@goodgroove.co.uk
*Contact* Gary Davies

## Good Looking Records

84 Queens Rd
Watford
Herts
WD17 2LA
**T** 01923 690700   **F** 01923 249495
**E** glo@glouk.com   **w** glo.uk.com

*Independent dance label mainly specializing in drum
'n' bass etc
Subsidiary labels: Cookin, Earth, Nexu, Looking
Good, Ascendant Grooves, 720, Blue Vinyl, Deep
Rooted
Further e-mail addresses: apex@glo.uk.com
(touring), catie@glo.uk.com (press) and
sarah@glo.uk.com (A&R)*

## Gorgeous Music Ltd

Suite D
67 Abbey Rd
St Johns Wood
London
NW8 0AE
**T** 020 7604 3080   **F** 020 7604 3789
**E** davix@gorgeousmusic.net   **w** gorgeousmusic.net
*A&R Directors*: Victoria Elliott and David Ross

*Specializing in all aspects of pop, and linked as part
of the Davix Group incorporating Bullet Records,
Fabulous Productions (TV/film) and Davix
Management*

## Gosh Records

55 Fulham High St
London
SW6 3JJ
**F** 07070 622034   **E** smile@dircon.co.uk

## Gotham Records

PO Box 6003
Birmingham
West Midlands
B45 0AR
**T** 0121 477 9553   **F** 0121 693 2924
**E** barry@btm-gotham.demon.co.uk
*Contact* Barry Tomes

## Graduate Records

St Swithun's Institute
The Trinity
Worcester
Worcs
WR1 2PN
**T** 01905 20882   **F** as telephone
**E** david_wirr@compuserve.com
**w** davevale.demon.co.uk/graduate
*Managing Director* David Wirr

## Grand Central Records Ltd

c/o Fat City Record Shop
20 Oldham St
Manchester
M1 1JN
**T** 0161 245 2002   **F** 0161 245 2003
**E** info@grandcentralrecords.co.uk
**w** grandcentralrecords.co.uk
*Label Manager* Eliza Tyrrell

*Hip-hop and soul-influenced music*

## Grand Prix Productions

21 Fairways Avenue
Harrogate
North Yorkshire
HG2 7EH
**T** 01423 884478/0140 083086   **F** 01423 881248
*Contact* Jon Starkey

## Grand Records

107a High St
Canvey Island
Essex
SS8 7RF
**T** 01268 694888   **F** 01268 695009
**E** grandrecords@aol.com   **w** drfeelgood.de
*Contact* Ann Adley
*Owner* Chris Fenwick

*NB: label for Dr Feelgood*

## Grand Royal Records

PO Box 90
Edenbridge
Kent
TN8 6ZE
T 01732 865330   F 01732 867850
E shrimpy@globalnet.co.uk   W grandroyal.com
*Managing Director* Dave Cronen

## Grapevine Label (Ireland)

5–6 Lombard St East
Westland Row
Dublin
Ireland
T 00 353 1 672 7277   F 00 353 1 677 9386
E grape@iol.ie
*Contact* Peter Kenny

## Grapevine Label (UK)

33–35 Wembley Hill Rd
Wembley
Middlesex
HA9 8RT
T 020 8733 1300   F 020 8782 4707
E paddy@rmgplc.com   W rmg.com
*Contact* Paddy Prendergast

## Grasmere Records

59 Marlpit Lane
Coulsdon
Surrey
CR5 2HF
T 020 8666 0201   F 020 8667 0037
*Managing Director* Bob Barratt

*Established 1984*
*Subsidiary label: Langdale*
*Roster includes Phil Kelsall, The Yetties, Houghton Weavers*

## Greensleeves Records Ltd

Unit 14, Metro Centre
St John's Rd
Isleworth
Middx
TW7 6NJ
T 020 8758 0564   F 020 8758 0811
E mail@greensleeves.net   W greensleeves.net
A&R: Chris Cracknell
*Operations* Clive Dickenson
*Sales* Oliver Geywitz

*Promotion* Caroline Pead

*Specialists in reggae, established for more than 25 years*

## Greentrax Recordings Ltd

Cockenzie Business Centre
Edinburgh Rd
Cockenzie
East Lothian
EH32 0XL
T 01875 815888   F 01875 813545
E greentrax@aol.com   W greentrax.com
*Managing Director* Ian D Green

*Orders: 01875 814155*

## Groovin' Records

PO Box 39
Hoylake
Merseyside
CH47 2HP
T 0151 632 6156/07855 945297   F as first telephone
E al@groovinrecords.com   W groovinrecords.com
*Contact* Al Willard Peterson

*Independent Internet-based label promoting rhythm-and-blues and funk-and-blues from Merseyside and the Northwest*
*See also Mayday Music (publisher)*

## Grosvenor Records

16 Grosvenor Rd
Handsworth Wood
Birmingham
West Midlands
B20 3NP
T 0121 356 9636   F as telephone
*Contact* John R Taylor

## Gull Records

21c Heathmans Rd
London
SW6 4TJ
T 020 7731 9321   F 020 7731 9314
E gull@darah.co.uk
*Managing Director* Irene Howells

## Gut Records

Byron House
112a Shirland Rd
London
W9 2EQ
**T** 020 7266 0777   **F** 020 7266 7734
**E** info@gut-intermedia.com
**W** gutrecords.com
*Contact* Debbie Myers (020 7266 7722)
*Managing Director* Caroline Lewis
*A&R Manager* James O'Driscoll

## Halo Records

10 Lambton Place
London
W11 2SH
**T** 020 7313 9779   **F** 020 7727 9770
**E** chris@halorecords.co.uk
*Managing Director* Chris Wiggs

## Hammerhead Music

Sebek
St Clement
Jersey
Channel Islands
JE2 6QF
**T** 01534 856545   **F** 01534 856232   **E** hammer@itl.net
*Contact* Mike Hamon

## Hands On Records

3 Lambton Place
London
W11 2SH
**T** 020 7221 7872   **F** 020 7221 7195
**E** handson@channel.co.uk   **W** horuk.co.uk
*Directors* Susie Rogers and Sandra Turnbull

## Handspun Records Ltd

45 Pembridge Rd
London
W11 3HG
**T** 020 7727 6306   **F** 020 7792 2523
*Contact* Anthony Cooper

*Roster includes Vortex, BTKA, Have a Nice Day*

## Harbourtown Records

PO Box 25
Ulverston
Cumbria
LA12 7UN
**T** 01229 588290   **F** as telephone
**E** records@hartown.demon.co.uk
**W** harbourtownrecords.com
*Managing Director* Gordon Jones

*Specializing in folk and roots*

## Hard Discs

3 Chester Place
Green Lane
Northwood
Middx
HA6 2XX
**T** 01923 822124   **F** 01923 827284
**E** jon_harddiscs@hotmail.com   **W** harddiscs.com
*Managing Director* Jon Williams

## Hard Hands

2nd Floor, 6 Pembridge Rd
London
W11 3HL
**T** 020 7243 6200   **F** 020 7243 0893
**E** hard_hands@hotmail.com
*Contact* Lisa Horan or Jean Coffey

## Haven Records

St Mary's Works
St Mary's Plain
Norwich
Norfolk
NR3 3AF
**T** 01603 624290/626221   **F** 01603 619999
**E** backs@cwcom.net
*Contact* Derek Chapman or Boo Hewerdine

## Hazel Records

Dublin Rd
Monasterevin
County Kildare
Ireland
**T** 00 353 45 525009/0116 275 1752
**F** 00 353 45 525810   **E** hazel@iol.ie
*Contact* John Kelly

**Headphone Records**
618a Finchley Rd
London
NW11 7RR
**T** 020 8201 9499    **F** 020 8201 8803
*Director* Alan Fox

**Headrow Management**
Unit 1
Union Bridge Mill
Roker Lane
Pudsey
West Yorkshire
LS28 9LE
**T** 0113 255 9905    **F** 0113 255 9903
*Contact* Steve Mulhaire or Chris Madden

**Headscope**
St End Lane
Broadoak
Heathfield
East Sussex
TN21 8TU
**T** 01435 863994    **F** 01435 867027    **W** rongeesin.com

*No demos*
*No sales mail*

**Headstone**
PO Box 3
Shepshed
Leicester
LE12 9RU
**T** 01509 504798    **F** 01509 651213
*Managing Director* Colin Spencer

**Headzone Ltd**
43 Canham Rd
London
W3 7SR
**T** 020 8749 8860    **F** 020 8742 9462
*Contact* Andy Howarth

**Heat Recordings**
Unit 8, The Shaftesbury Centre
85 Barlby Rd
London
W10 6BN
**T** 020 8969 2912    **F** 020 8969 2551

**E** info@heatrecordings.com
**W** heatrecordings.com
*Contact* Alex Payne

*Also labels Critical Mass, Urban Heat and Nu-Tone*

**Heaven Records**
100 Bridle Rd
Burton Joyce
Nottingham
NG14 5FP
**T** 0115 931 3184/962 6755
*A&R Manager* Mark Randall

**Heavenly Recordings**
47 Frith St
London
W1D 4SE
**T** 020 7494 2998    **F** 020 7437 3317
**E** email@heavenlyrecordings.com
**W** heavenlyrecordings.com
*Contact* Martin Kelly or Jeff Barrett

**Helicopter Records**
14 Spencer Hill
London
SW19 7QP
**T** 020 8944 6072    **F** as telephone
*Production Executive* Dominic Houston

**Hengest Records**
81 Park Rd
Wath-upon-Dearne
Rotherham
South Yorkshire
S63 7LE
**T** 01709 877920    **F** 01709 873119/0870 1640589
**E** hrecords@csi.com
*Director* Martin E Looby

**Heritage Records**
Chapel Mews
Crewe Rd
Alsager
Staffs
ST7 2HA
**T** 01270 883779    **F** 01270 883847
*Contact* John Young

**Hi-Note Music**
PO Box 26
Windsor
Berks
SL4 2YX
**T** 01784 432868    **F** 01784 477702
**E** enquiry@hi-note.com    **W** hi-note.com
*Contact* Graham Brook

*Labels: Background; Aftermath; English Garden;
Headline*
*Also Independent Artist Distribution – promotion,
sales and distribution for bands with self-produced
and -pressed CDs.*

**Hiatus Music**
PO Box 10815
London
W4 5WZ
**T** 020 8783 1005    **F** 020 8783 1168
**E** hiatus@imperial-design.demon.co.uk
*Contact* Andrew Wills

**Higher Ground**
10 Great Marlborough St
London
W1V 2LP
**T** 020 7911 8869    **F** 020 7911 8879
**E** mail@higherground.co.uk
**W** higherground.co.uk
*Managing Director* Mick Clark
*Label Manager* Mark Conway

**Higher State**
95–99 North St
London
SW4 0HF
**T** 020 7627 5656/5699    **F** 020 7627 5757
**E** info@higherstate.co.uk/info@99north.co.uk
**W** higherstate.co.uk and 99north.co.uk
*Contact* Jamie Pierce

*Subsidiary companies: 99 North, 99 Degrees
House and garage label*

**Highlight Records**
160 Montrose Avenue
Luton
Beds
LU3 1HT
**T** 01582 753246    **F** 01582 619093

**E** highlightreco@hotmail.com
*Managing Director* Michael Robinson

**Hitmakers**
39–41 Romsey Rd
Winchester
Hants
SO22 5BE
**T** 01962 774096

**Hocus Pocus**
9 Willcocks Close
Chessington
Surrey
KT9 1HG
**T** 020 8391 4201    **F** 020 8397 6262
**E** hocuspocus.music@virgin.net

**Holier Than Thou**
Norton Hall
Broadmarston Lane
Mickleton
Gloucestershire
GL55 6SQ
**T** 01386 438931    **F** 01386 438847
**E** httrecord@aol.com
**W** holierthanthourecords.com
*Director* David Begg

*Also artist management (same contact details)*

**Hooj Choons**
49–51 Lonsdale Rd
London N
W6 6RA
**T** 020 7328 7787    **F** 020 7328 7727
**E** info@hoojchoons.co.uk    **W** hoojchoons.co.uk
*General Manager* Anna Luget

**Hook-Bellboy Records**
PO Box 32043
London
NW1 9GE
**T** 020 7267 1447    **F** 020 7267 1448
**E** stuart@hookrecordings.com
**W** hookrecordings.com
*Contact* Stuart Emslie
*Directors* Stuart Emslie and Chris Cowie

*Dance (techno, eclectic and progressive house)*

*Roster includes Chris Cowie, Christopher Lawrence, Frankie Bones, Sandra Collins and Transa*

## Horatio Nelson
76 Carlisle Mansions
Carlisle Place
London
SW1P 1HZ
T 020 7828 6533    F 020 7828 1271
*Managing Director* Derek Boulton

## Hospital Records
Red Corner Door
17 Barons Court Rd
London
W14 9DP
T 020 7386 8760    F 020 7381 8014
E info@hospitalrecords.com
w hospitalrecords.com
*Contact* Chris Goss

## Hot House Records
311 Gray's Inn Rd
London
WC1X 8PX
T 020 7278 0703    F 020 7833 2218
E hh@molejazz.co.uk    w molejazz.co.uk
*Managing Director* Peter Fincham

## Hot Records
PO Box 333
Brighton
East Sussex
BN1 2EH
T 01903 779443    F 01903 779442
E hotrecords@pavilion.co.uk
*Contact* Andrew Bowles

## HRL
Bray Film Studios
Down Place
Water Oakley
Windsor
Berks
SL4 5UG
T 01628 622111
*A&R Co-ordinator* Paul Wallace

## HTD Records
Unit 10
Kent House
Old Bexley Business Park
19 Bourne Rd
Bexley
Kent
DA5 1LR
T 01322 557355    F 01322 522878
E mholmes822@aol.com    w htdrecords.com
*Managing Director* Barry Riddington

## Hudson Records Co Ltd
2nd Floor
11–20 Capper St
London
WC1E 6JA
T 020 7631 3600    F 020 7631 3700
E info@hudsonmusic.co.uk
w hudsonmusic.co.uk
*Contact* W De Wolfe

## Hue Records
44 Ballyshannon Rd
Dublin 5
Ireland
T 00 353 1 847 6314    F 00 353 1 676 0310
E hue@iol.ie    w dojo.ie/hue
*Manager* Roger Lee

## Human Condition Records
120a West Granton Rd
Edinburgh
EH5 1PF
T 0131 551 6632    F as telephone
E jamie@humancondition.co.uk
w humancondition.co.uk
*Contact* Jamie Watson

*Rock, indie, country, folk etc*

## Hurdy Gurdy
Park House
Warren Row
Berks
RG10 8QS
T 07071 223951    F 07071 223952
E monkey@dreamofoswald.co.uk
*Contact* Keith James

**HurraH Ltd**
Unit 4
27a Spring Grove Rd
Hounslow
Middx
TW3 4BE
T 020 8570 8100    F 020 8563 0396
E lee@hurrah.co.uk
*Contact* Lee Farrow

**Hut Recordings**
Kensal House
553–579 Harrow Rd
London
W10 4RH
T 020 8964 6107    F a&r: 020 8964 6109
W raft.vmg.co.uk

**Hwyl**
2 The Square
Yapham
York
YO42 1PJ
T 01759 304514
W angelfire.com/myband/hwylnofio
*Contact* Julia Parry

*Contemporary instrumental music, post-rock,*
*experimental, contemporary jazz, ambient, published*
*through Hwyl Publishing*
*Roster includes Hwyl-Nofio (post-rock), Steve Parry*
*(ambient/noise), Fredrik Soegaard (experimental*
*guitar), Balazs Major ( jazz percussion), Trevor*
*Stainsby (ambient), Sandor Szabo (infinite guitar)*

**Hydrogen Dukebox**
89 Borough High St
London
SE1 1NL
T 020 7357 9799    F 020 7357 9750
E hydrogen@dukebox.demon.co.uk
W hydrogendukebox.com
*Contact* Matthew Lee

**Hype Records**
Unit 5
Willtell Works
Upper St John St
Lichfield
Staffs
WS14 9ET
T 01543 303200    F 01543 303201
E hype@fsnet.co.uk

**I Life Records**
PO Box 14996
London
SW17 0AR
T 020 8682 0243    F as telephone
E michael@ilife.freeserve.co.uk
*Contact* Michael Fuller

**I&B Records (Irish Music) Ltd**
2a Wrentham Avenue
London
NW10 3HA
T 020 8960 9169/9160    F 020 8968 7332
*Contact* Martin McDonald

**I-Anka**
PO Box 197
London
W10 5FA
T 020 8968 6221    F 020 8964 2844
*Managing Director* J Punford

**IDNY Records**
Top Floor
233 Cowgate
Edinburgh
EH1 1JQ
T 0131 225 5062    F 0131 622 7358
E craig@indemand.co.uk    W indemand.co.uk

**Ignition**
54 Linhope St
London
NW1 6HL
T 020 7298 6000    F 020 7258 0962
W ignition-man.co.uk

## Illicit Recordings
12 Southam St
London
W10 5PH
**T** 020 8960 3253  **F** 020 8968 5111
**E** info@illicitrecordings.com
**W** illicitrecordings.com
*Contact* Ian Clifford

## Imagemaker Sound & Vision
PO Box 69
Launceston
Cornwall
PL15 7YA
**T** 01566 86308  **F** as telephone
*Contact* Olive Lister

## Imaginary Music
7 Ruxley Close
Wootton Bassett
Wiltshire
SN4 7LB
**T** 01793 853922  **F** as telephone
**E** halls@dialin.net  **W** collective.co.uk/gphall
*Contact* G P Hall

## Immaterial Records
First Floor
2 Elgin Avenue
London
W9 3QP
**T** 020 7286 1400/07973 676160
**F** as first telephone  **E** bwi.bij@btinternet.com
*Contact* Bijal Dodhia

## Immoral Recordings
PO Box 2643
Reading
Berks
RG5 4GF
**T** 0118 969 9269  **F** 0118 969 9264
**E** jpsproductions@msn.com
*Contact* John Saunderson

## Imprint
PO Box 1797
London
E1 4TX
**T** 020 7702 7842  **F** 020 7790 0764
**E** imprint@dor.co.uk
*Contact* Martin Parker

## In Demand Records
233 Cowgate
Edinburgh
EH1 1JQ
**T** 0131 225 5062  **F** 0131 622 7358
**E** craigw@indemand.co.uk  **W** indemand.co.uk
*Director* Craig Wood

## In The City Ltd
8 Brewery Yard
Deva Centre
Trinity Way
Salford
M3 7BB
**T** 0161 839 3930  **F** 0161 839 3940
**E** info@inthecity.co.uk  **W** inthecity.co.uk
*Contact* Anthony Wilson or Yvette Livsey

*In The City is an International Music Convention,
running for 9 years, but it also holds a competition
for unsigned bands
Anthony Wilson was formerly boss of Factory
Records*

## Incentive/IDJ
PO Box 20153
London
W10 5FG
**T** 020 8960 4538  **F** 020 8968 0167
**E** incentive@incentivemusic.co.uk
**W** incentivemusic.com
*Managing Director* Nick Halkes
*A&R* Craig Dimech, Simon Patterson
*Label Co-ordinator* Patriisah Roberts
*General Manager* Will Nicol
*Marketing & Promotions* Anthony Hamer-Hodges

*Independent dance music label putting emphasis on
quality rather than genre*

## Incredible
10 Great Marlborough St
London
W1V 2LP
**T** 020 7911 8859

## Independiente Ltd
The Drill Hall
3 Heathfield Terrace
London
W4 4JE
**T** 020 8747 8111   **F** 020 8747 8113/8995 5907
**E** inde@independiente.co.uk
*Chairman* Andy Macdonald
*Senior A&R Director* Dave Gilmour

## Indigo Records
Regent House
1 Pratt Mews
London
NW1 0AD
**T** 020 7267 6899   **F** 020 7267 6746
**E** del@trojan-records.com   **w** trojan-records.com
*Contact* Del Taylor

## Infectious Records Ltd
1 Shorrolds Rd
London
SW6 7TR
**T** 020 7343 5678   **F** 020 7343 5656/5657
**E** feedback@infectious-records.co.uk
**w** infectiousuk.com
*General Manager* Nigel Adams

*Indie rock music*
*Roster: Ash, My Vitriol, Seafood, Gerling*

## Inferno Records
Fox Studios
32–36 Telford Way
London
W3 7XS
**T** 020 8742 9300   **F** 020 8742 9097
**E** enquiries@infernorecords.co.uk
**w** infernorecords.co.uk
*Managing Director* Steve Long
*A&R* Pat Travers

*Independent dance label*

## Infinity Records
PO Box 82
Shepperton
Middx
TW17 0TL
**T** 01932 562384/07966 285576

**E** infinity@alice-temple.demon.co.uk
*Contact* Ian Ford

## Influential Recordings/Influential Films
PO Box 402
Manchester
M60 4AU
**T** 07050 395708   **w** influential.net
*Contact* Mike Swindells

## Innocent
Kensal House
553–579 Harrow Rd
London
W10 4RH
**T** 020 8962 5800   **F** 020 8962 5801
*Managing Director* Hugh Goldsmith
*Label Manager* Justine Cavanagh

## Instant Hit
20 Dunbar Rd
Frimley
Surrey
GU16 5UZ
**T** 01252 837556   **F** 01252 834298
*General Manager* Jon Monks

## Instant Karma
36 Sackville St
London
W1X 1DB
**T** 020 7851 0900   **F** 020 7851 0901
**E** zen@instantkarma.co.uk
*Chairman* Rob Dickins
*Assistant* Fiona Porter
*A&R* Carrie Booth, Amy Crowley, Giles Martin,
Paul Toogood

## Interactive Music
Alexandra House
Earlsfort Terrace
Dublin 2
Ireland
**T** 00 353 1676 1523/1477   **F** 00 353 1 661 8562/4854
**E** suriya@interactive-music.com
**w** interactive-music.com
*Contact* Suriya Moodliar or Oliver Walsh

*Also distribution company (Cooking Vinyl, ECM,*
*Ministry of Sound, Rough Trade etc)*

**Internal Bass Records Ltd**
PO Box 445
Chobham
Woking
Surrey
GU24 8YQ
E info@internalbass.com  w internalbass.com
*A&R* Chino Lopez

**Intersound Media Services (IMS)**
Nomis Studios
45–53 Sinclair Rd
London
W14 0NS
T 020 7602 6351  F 020 7300 6569
E imsworld@aol.com
*Managing Director* Alan Bellman

**Invisible Hands Music**
PO Box 243
Epsom
Surrey
KT19 8YJ
T 01372 739137  F 01372 739173
E biz_aff@invisiblehands.co.uk
w invisiblehands.co.uk
*Operations Manager* John Shepherd

**Irksome**
124 New Bond St
London
W1Y 9AE
T 020 7836 9995
*Director* Stevo

**It Records/Really Useful Records**
22 Tower St
London
WC2H 9NS
T 020 7240 0880  F 020 7240 8922
E info@itrecords.com  w reallyuseful.com
*Managing Director* Tris Penna
*General Manager* Tracey Connolly
*A&R* Bob Stanley, Paul Tucker
*Recordings Manager* Emma Wood

**Jackpot Records**
PO Box 2272
Rottingdean
Brighton
BN2 8XD
T 01273 304681  F 01273 308120
E seven-webster@beeb,net
*Contact* Seven Webster

*See also Seven Publishing & Management (7PM), same contact details*

**Jam-It UK Recordings**
12b Reachview Close
London
NW1 0TY
T 020 7209 2564  F 020 7209 2906
E jamituk@yahoo.com
*Contact* Hugh Bernard

**Jasmine Records**
Unit 8
Forest Hill Trading Estate
London
SE23 2LX
T 020 8291 6777  F 020 8291 0081
E jasmine@zoo.co.uk
*Contact* Carl Hazeldine

*Also Hasmick Promotions*

**Jastoy Arts**
PO Box 1257
London
E5 0UD
T 07956 398152/020 8986 1984
E toyin (or jason)@jastoy.co.uk  w jastoy.co.uk
*Contact* J Halliday or T Agbetu

*Also Leap of Faith Records, Unyque Artists, Intrigue, EP Records (same contact details)*

**Javelin**
Satril House
3 Blackburn Rd
London
NW6 1RZ
T 020 7328 8283  F 020 7328 9037
E hho@dial.pipex.com
w dspace.dial.pipex.com/hho/
*Creative Director* Mark Arthurwerry

## Jazz Fudge Recordings Ltd
PO Box 535a
Surbiton
Surrey
KT6 7WJ
**T** 020 7326 0606   **F** 020 7326 1585
**E** mail@jazzfudge.co.uk   **w** jazzfudge.co.uk
*Managing Director* Simon Rose

*Specializes in all forms of hiphop*

## JBO
The Saga Centre
1st Floor, 326 Kensal Rd
London
W10 5BZ
**T** 020 8960 4495   **F** 020 8960 3256   **w** jbo.co.uk
*Contact* Lucy Farthing

## Jealous Records
15 Pratt Mews
London
NW1 0AD
**T** 020 7916 0191   **F** 020 7916 4407
**E** jealous@skyrock.co.uk   **w** jealous.co.uk

## Jeepster Recordings Ltd
217 Canalot Production Studios
222 Kensal Rd
London
W10 5BN
**T** 020 8964 9432   **F** 020 8964 8600
**E** a-and-r@jeepster.co.uk   **w** jeepster.co.uk
*Contact* Mark Jones

## Jelly Street Records
Chester Terrace
358 Chester Rd
Cornbrook
Manchester
M16 9EZ
**T** 0161 872 6006   **F** 0161 872 6488
*Managing Director* Kevin Kinsella

## Jester Records
PO Box 9093
Sutton
Surrey
SM2 6BY
**T** 020 8642 1679   **F** 020 8642 5203

*Contact* Andy Cook

## JFM Records
11 Alexander House
Tiller Rd
London
E14 8PT
**T** 020 7987 8596   **F** as telephone
*Contact* Julius Pemberton Maynard

## JML (Jazz Monkey Ltd)
PO Box 695
Watford
Herts
WD18 7TQ
**T** 07941 121822   **F** 01923 227827
**E** info@jazzmonkey.co.uk   **w** jazzmonkey.co.uk
*Contact* Karalyne Chalmers

## Joint Effort
241a East Barnet Rd
East Barnet
Herts
EN4 8SS
**T** 020 8449 0766   **F** as telephone
*Label Manager* Angelique Ekart

## JPH Records
9 Green Lane
Little Common
Bexhill-on-Sea
East Sussex
TN39 4PH
**T** jphy@clara.net   **F** jphy.clara.net
*Contact* Joseph P Haughey

## JSP Records
PO Box 1584
London
N3 3PS
**T** 020 8346 8663   **F** 020 8346 8848
**E** john@jsprecords.com   **w** jsprecords.com
*Managing Director* John Stedman

## Juice Records

PO Box 1
Stanford-le-Hope
Essex
SS17 8LT
**T** 01375 677332  **F** 01375 642111
**E** hilltop@dircon.co.uk  **w** juice-records.co.uk
*Joint Owner/Producer* Darren Hickey

## Jungle Records

Old Dairy Mews
62 Chalk Farm Mews
London
NW1 8AN
**T** 020 7267 0171  **F** 020 7267 0912
**w** jungle-records.com

*Alternative rock and indie music including new and
catalogue punk, grunge etc
Subsidiary labels: Mint, Fall Out, Middle Earth etc
Distributor for Mortarhate*

## Junior Recordings Ltd

The Saga Centre
326 Kensal Rd
London
W10 5BZ
**T** 020 8960 4495  **F** 020 8960 3256
**w** junior-records.com
*Contact* Paul Byrne

## Just Create Records

20 Station Rd
Eckington
Sheffield
South Yorkshire
S21 4FX
**T** 01246 432507/07785 232176  **F** as first telephone
**E** richardcory@lineone.net
*Contact* Richard Cory

## K-Tel Entertainment (UK)

K-Tel House
12 Fairway House
Greenford
Middx
UB6 8PW
**T** 020 8747 7550  **F** 020 8575 2264
**E** janie@k-tel-uk.com  **w** k-tel-uk.com
*General Manager* Janie Webber

## Kabuki

1st Floor, 46 Buckingham Rd
Brighton
East Sussex
BN1 3RQ
**T** 01273 748344  **F** as telephone
**E** email@kabuki.co.uk  **w** kabuki.co.uk

## Kahuna Cuts

79 Parkway
London
NW1 7PP
**T** 020 7482 7166  **F** 020 7482 7286
**E** dog@bestest.co.uk
*Contact* John Best

*Also Mako Records*

## Kamera Shy Records

PO Box 6003
Birmingham
B45 0AR
**T** 0121 477 9553  **F** 0121 693 2954
**E** barry@btm-gotham.demon.co.uk
**w** btm-gotham.demon.co.uk
*Contact* Barry Tomes

## Kamikaze Records

42 Granville Rd
Parkstone
Poole
Dorset
BH1Z 3BS
**T** 07971 480482/01202 383183

## Karon Productions

20 Radstone Court
Hillview Rd
Woking
Surrey
GU22 7NB
**T** 01483 755153
*Managing Director* Ron Roker

*Karon is a popular music genre dance and R&B
label; it also has library/background music and is
linked to several programmers and re-mixers*

## KBS Records

Norden
2 Hillhead Rd
Newtonhill
Stonehaven
Kincardine and Deeside
AB39 2TS
**T** 01569 730962   **F** as telephone
*Managing Director* Doug Stone

## Keda Records

The Sight and Sound Centre
Priory Way
Southall
Middx
UB2 5EB
**T** 020 8843 1546   **F** 020 8574 4243
**E** kuljit@compuserve.com   **w** keda.co.uk
*Contact* Kuljit Bhamra

*Bhangra label (also 24-track studio, pre-production and management)*

## Keg Records

35 Dearney Rd
Warmley
Bristol
BS16 9JB
**T** 0117 904 4480   **F** as telephone
**E** enerchiuk@aol.com   **w** enerchiuk.com
*Contact* Alan Britton

## Keystone Records Ltd

PO Box 10653
London
W5 4WR
**T** 020 8993 7441   **F** 020 8992 9993
**E** keystone@dorm.co.uk   **w** thedormgroup.com
*Contact* John O'Reilly

## Kickin Music Ltd

Unit 1, Acklam Workshops
10 Acklam Rd
London
W10 5QZ
**T** 020 8964 3300   **F** 020 8964 4400
**E** info@kickinmusic.com   **w** kickinmusic.com
*Managing Director* Peter Harris

*An umbrella of labels including Kickin Records, Kickin Underground, Stoned Asia Records, Slip 'n'*

*Slide, Slip 'n' Slide Blue, Hardleaders, Fragmented, Pandemonium, Conqueror, Basement 282, Downlow, Well Equipped*
*House, drum 'n' bass, techno, downtempo, jazzy beats, reggae, garage, soul*
*See also Haripa Music (same contact details)*

## Kinetix

The Black Office
DC Warehouse
Unit 6
Industrial Park
Maple Cross
Herts
WD3 2AS
**T** 01494 549000
*Chairman* J Sharp

## Kinetix

Spire Ark
Hall Farm
West Clayton
Chorleywood
Herts
WD3 5EX
**T** 01923 285281   **F** 01923 285286   **w** kinetix.ltd.uk
*Contact (and Managing Director)* Jon Sharp

*Cutting edge electronic dance label, releasing techno, trance, chillout, dub, leftfield and house*

## King Street Records (UK)

96 College Rd
London
NW10 5HL
**T** 020 8960 0086/07973 714923
**E** ncairncross@mistral.co.uk
*Contact* Nicola Cairncross

## Kingdom Records Ltd

Clarendon House
Shenley Rd
Borehamwood
Herts
WD6 1AG
**T** 020 8207 7006   **F** 020 8207 5460
**E** kingdomrec@aol.com
*Managing Director* Terry King

*Also: Killerwatt Records*

**Kingsize Records**
28 Lyom Rd
Hersham
Surrey
KT12 3PU
**T** 01932 700400   **F** 01932 702144
**E** info@kingsize.co.uk
*Contact* Richard Crowmains

**Kingsway Music**
Lottbridge Rd
Eastbourne
East Sussex
BN23 6NT
**T** 01323 437708   **F** 01323 411970
**E** music@kingsway.co.uk   **w** worship.co.uk
*Head of Music* Stuart Townend

**Kite Records**
Binny Estate
Ecclesman
Edinburgh
EH52 6NL
**T** 01506 858885   **F** 01506 858155
**E** kitemusic@aol.com   **w** kitemusic.com
*Managing Director* Billy Russell

**Kitty Kitty Corp**
The Litter Box
PO Box 3801
London
NW1 9BX
**T** 020 7729 6006   **F** 020 7729 0775
**E** sean@mutante-inc.demon.co.uk
**w** quickspace.mcmail.com

**KOCH International**
Charlotte House
87 Little Ealing Lane
London
W5 4EH
**T** 020 8832 1800/1818   **F** 020 8832 1813/1808
*Managing Director* Rashmi Patani
*Sales and Marketing Manager* Simon Carver
*Label Manager* Michael K Jones

**KRL**
9 Watt Rd
Hillington
Glasgow
G52 4RY
**T** 0141 882 9060/9986   **F** 0141 883 3686
**E** krl@krl.co.uk   **w** krl.co.uk/bulk

**Krypton Records**
31 Fife St
St James
Northampton
NN5 5BH
**T** 01604 752800   **F** as telephone
**E** rock-n-roll@the-jets.freeserve.co.uk
**w** the-jets.freeserve.co.uk
*Contact* Ray Cotton

**Kudos Records**
79 Fortess Rd
London
NW5 1AG
**T** 020 7482 4555   **F** 020 7482 4551
**E** kudos@kudos.demon.co.uk
**w** kudosrecords.co.uk
*Directors* Danny Ryan and Mike Hazell

**L&D International Ltd**
2nd Floor, Foframe House
35–37 Brent St
London
NW4 2EF
**T** 020 8203 9966   **F** 020 8203 4747
**E** hasfa@ldinternational.co.uk
*Contact* Hasfa Abubacker

**L&R Records**
Foxhollow
West End
Nailsea
Somerset
BS19 2DB
**T** 01934 521333
*Managing Directors*: David Rees and Ken Lintern

## Labrador Records

9 Overline House
Station Way
Crawley
West Sussex
RH10 1JA
**T** 01293 402040   **F** 01293 402050
**E** unsigned@labradorrecords.com
**W** labradorrecords.com
*Managing Director* Nick Coquet

## Lager Records

14 Shott Lane
Letchworth
Herts
SG6 1SE
**T** 01462 636799/07767 268714
**E** lager.prod@mailcity.com
*Contact* Steve Knight

## Lakota Records

PO Box 4704
Ballsbridge
Dublin 4
Ireland
**T** 00 353 1 283 9071   **E** lakota@indigo.ie
**W** lakotarecords.com
*A&R* Conor Brooks

## Lammas Records

34 Carlisle Avenue
St Albans
Herts
AL3 5LU
**T** 01727 851553   **F** as telephone
**E** enquiries@lammas.co.uk
**W** lammas.co.uk or lammasrecords.com
*Contact* Lance Andrews or Nicholas Crickmay
*Proprietor* Lance Andrews

*Specialists in cathedral choirs and choirs of similar
standing
Also CDs of organ music
Particular interest in treble soloists*

## LAS Records UK

PO Box 14303
London
SE26 4ZH
**T** 07000 472572   **F** as telephone
**E** latinarts@artquest.co.uk   **W** latinartsgroup.com

*Part of Latin Arts Group, specializing in Latin
American entertainment, that includes HMP
(publisher), WAI World Artists Index (free-net
index), Mundo Graphics (graphic design) and Latin
Arts Services (management/agency)*

## Late Night Vinyl

1 Orchard Rd
Reigate
Surrey
RH2 0PA
**T** 01737 244666
*Managing Director* Mike Sammes

## Latest Recording Company, The

PO Box 3636
London
N12 5EE
**T** 07050 055167   **F** 0870 741 5252
**E** atlanticcrossingartists@yahoo.com
**W** atlanticcrossingartists.freeserve.com
*Contact* Richard Struple

## Laurel Records

233 Portobello Rd
London
W11 1LT
**T** 020 7221 5566   **F** 020 7221 6655
*Contact* Howard Gough

## Leaf Label, The

Suite 219
Bon Marche Building
241 Ferndale Rd
London
SW9 8BJ
**T** 020 7733 1818   **F** 020 7733 5818
**E** leaf@posteverything.com
**W** posteverything.com/leaf
*Contact* Tony Morley

*Specialists in leftfield electronica, with a roster
including 310, Susumu Yokota, Manitoba and
Eardrum
Also operates a press office, No.9, whose clients
include 23 Skidoo, Fridge, Fourtet and Pole, and a
mail-order company Posteverything (same contact
details)*

## Leopard Records

23 Thrayle House
Stockwell Rd
London
SW9 0XU
**T** 020 7564 8476    **F** as telephone
*Managing Director* Errol Jones

## Like No Other

PO Box 21335
London
WC2H 8QH
**T** 020 7379 0999    **F** 020 7379 3399
**E** mark@like-no-other.com    **W** like-no-other.com
*Contact* Mark Lambert Stewart

## Linn Records

257 Drakemire Drive
Castlemilk
Glasgow
G45 9SZ
**T** 0141 303 5027/5026/5029    **F** 0141 631 1485
**E** records@linn.co.uk    **W** linnrecords.com
*Label Manager* Philip Hobbs
*Press and Marketing* Jennie Gardner

## Lioneagle

4 Hunters Meadow
Great Shefford
Berks
RG17 7EQ
**T** 01488 648768    **F** 01488 648033
**E** geo@lionhart.demon.co.uk
**W** reeltime.music.co.uk

## Liquid

The Workstation
15 Paternoster Row
Sheffield
South Yorkshire
S1 2BX
**T** 0114 281 2128    **F** 0114 279 6522

## Lismor Recordings

27–29 Carnoustie Place
Scotland St
Glasgow
G5 8PH
**T** 0141 420 1881    **F** 0141 420 1892

**E** lismor@lismor.com    **W** lismor.com
*Director* Ronnie Simpson

*Also Iona Records*

## Little Piece of Jamaica

55 Finsbury Park Rd
London
N4 2JY
**T** 020 7359 0788    **F** 020 7226 2168
**E** paulhuelpoj@yahoo.co.uk
*Managing Director* Paul Hue

## Little Red Roster Records

PO Box 727
High Wycombe
Bucks
HP13 5ZB
**T** 01494 463766    **F** 01494 442667
*Contact* Simon Redgate

## Livid Records

Suite C
88 Caister Mews
London
SW12 8QW
**T** 020 8673 3140    **F** as telephone
**E** leslie_f_primo@yahoo.com
*Label Manager* Leslie Fitzgerald

## Loaded/Skint Records

PO Box 174
Brighton
East Sussex
BN1 4BA
**T** 01273 738527    **F** 01273 208766
**E** mail@loaded-records.com/mail@skint.net
**W** loaded-records.com and skint.net
*Directors* Tim Jeffery and J C Reid

*NB: dance music only*

## Locked On

679 Holloway Rd
London
N19 5SE
**T** 020 7263 4660    **F** 020 7263 9669/5590
**E** lockedon@puregroove.co.uk
**W** puregroove.co.uk
*A&R* Andy Lewis

## Lockjaw Records

1 Oaklands
Cradley
Malvern
Worcs
WR13 5LA
**T** 01886 880035    **F** 01886 880135
**E** info@lockjawrecords.co.uk
**W** lockjawrecords.co.uk
*Business Affairs Manager* Jack Turner
(e-mail: management@lockjawrecords.co.uk)
*A&R and Tour Booker* Ben Turner
(e-mail: ben@lockjawrecords.co.uk)
*Administration and Accounts* Jim Turner
(e-mail: jim@lockjawrecords.co.uk)
*Distribution and Publicity* Sam Turner
(e-mail: *sam@lockjawrecords.co.uk*)

*Also publicity, management and booking network*

## Lodge Records

Ballinclea Lodge
Ballinclea Rd
Killiney
Co Dublin
Ireland
**T** 00353 1 285 0851    **F** as telephone
**E** patalodge@man.com
*Managing Director* Pat Dempsey

## LOE Records

LOE House
159 Broadhurst Gardens
London
NW6 3AU
**T** 020 7328 6100    **F** 020 7624 6384
**E** mags@loeg.demon.co.uk
*Creative Manager* Madeleine Swift

## Logic Records UK Ltd

1st Floor
34–35 Berwick St
London
W1V 3RF
**T** 020 7434 2193    **F** 020 7287 4555
**W** logicrecords.co.uk
*General Manager* Barry Evangeli
*Product Manager* Mark Shade

## London Records

57–63 Old Church St
London
SW3 5BS
**T** 020 7761 6000    **F** 020 7761 6062
**W** londonrecords.co.uk
*Managing Director* Laurie Cokell
*Head of A&R*(London) Mark Lewis
*Head of Press* Eugene Manzi

## Loose

PO Box 67
Runcorn
Cheshire
WA7 4NL
**T** 01928 566261    **E** jaki.florek@virgin.com
*Contact* Jaki Florek

## Loose Recordings

5–10 Eastman Rd
London
W3 7YG
**T** 020 8749 9330    **F** 020 8749 2230
**E** tom@loosemusic.com
*Contact* Tom Bridgewater

## Loose Records

The BEST Building
Wigton
Cumbria
CA7 9PZ
**T** 016973 45422    **F** as telephone

## Loose Tie Records

61 Queen's Drive
London
N4 2BG
**T** 020 8802 5984    **F** 020 8809 7436
**E** paul@paulrodriguezmus.demon.co.uk
*Contact* Paul Rodriguez

*Also Amalie Records and No Tiez*

## Loriana Music

30a Tudor Drive
Gidea Park
Romford
Essex
RM2 5LH
**T** 01708 750185/07751 450362    **F** as first telephone

**E** info@lorianamusic.com  **W** lorianamusic.com
*Director* Jean-Louis Fargier

*Ambient, chillout, chilled house, film theme music, easy listening*
*Also music production*


## Love This International Ltd
Hundred House
100 Union St
London
SE1 0NL
**T** 020 7928 4444   **F** 020 7401 3697


## Luna Park
Suffolk House
1–8 Whitfield Place
London
W1P 5SF
**T** 020 7813 5555   **F** 020 7813 4567
**E** mail@lunapark.co.uk
*Contact* Neil Armstrong


## Lunar Recordings
138 Vartry Rd
London
N15 6HA
**T** 020 8800 1934
*A&R* Neal Handley


## Lunar Records
5–6 Lombard St
Dublin 2
Ireland
**T** 00 353 1 677 4229/9762   **F** 00 353 1 671 0421
**E** lunar@indigo.ie
*Managing Director* Brian Molloy

*See also Briar Music (same contact details)*


## M21
Northburgh House
10 Northburgh St
London
EC1V 0AT
**T** 020 7253 5860   **F** 020 7253 5850
**E** m21@m21.co.uk   **W** m21.co.uk
*Managing Director* Adrian Faiers


## Macmeanmna
Quay Brae
Portree
Isle of Skye
IV51 9DB
**T** 01478 612990   **F** 01478 613263
**E** acormack@dircon.co.uk
*Partner* Arthur Cormack


## Madacy Entertainment Group (GB) Ltd
Unit 12
Brunswick Industrial Park
Brunswick Way
New Southgate
London
N11 1HX
**T** 020 8361 2163   **F** 020 8361 0741
**E** madacyuk@aol.com
*Manager* Karen Moran


## Maestro Records
PO Box 85B
East Molesey
Surrey
KT8 9EJ
**T** 020 8398 9018   **F** 020 8398 9744
**E** maestro.uk@virgin.net
*Contact* Tommy Sanderson


## Magick Eye Records
PO Box 3037
Wokingham
Berks
RG40 4GR
**T** 0118 932 8320   **F** 0118 932 8237
**E** magickeye@magickeye.com   **W** magickeye.com
*Managing Director* Chris Hillman


## Magmasters
20 St Anne's Court
London
W1V 3AW
**T** 020 7437 8273   **F** 020 7494 1281
**W** theframe.com/services/magmasters.html
*Contact* Cliff Norman

**Majic Music**
PO Box 66
Manchester
M12 4XJ
T 0161 225 9991    F as telephone
E info@majicmusic.co.uk    w majicmusic.co.uk
*Contact* Mike Coppock

*Specializing in 'moody' dance, trance, euro*
*Always interested in new singers*

**Mako Music**
55 Tunis Rd
London
W12 7EY
T 020 8746 2796/07956 386767
*Contact* Dominic Brownlow

**Malaco Records**
4 Warren Mews
London
W1P 5DJ
T 020 7388 6500    F 020 7388 6522
*Managing Director* Peter J Felstead

**Mammoth**
36b Notting Hill Gate
London
W11 3JQ
T 020 7221 0989

**Manic Records**
55 The Crescent
South Shore
Blackpool
Lancs
FY4 1EQ
T 01253 349219    F 01253 752025
*Contact* Phil Holmes

**MAP Records**
27 Abercorn Place
London
NW8 9DX
T 07774 267373    F 020 7624 7219
E hkhan@greycoat.co.uk

**Maple Label, The**
PO Box 12
Chilton
Ferryhill
Co. Durham
DL17 0YZ
T 01388 720553

**Marble Bar**
The Boathouse
Lower Mall
London
W6 9DJ
T 020 8563 7555    F 020 8563 7999

**Market Square Records**
Market House
Market Square
Winslow
Bucks
MK18 3AF
T 01296 715228    F 01296 715486
E peter@marketsquarerecords.co.uk
w marketsquarerecords.co.uk
*Contact* Peter Muir

*Specializing in quality folk/roots and rock catalogue*

**Marshmallow Records Ltd**
52 Wardour St
London
W1V 3HL
T 020 7437 0329    F 020 7494 4747
E info@marshmallowrecords.com
*Contact* Seamus Murphy (Chief Executive Officer)

*Also Wicked Wolf Management*

**Masquerade Music Ltd**
The Studio
Lynton Rd
London
N8 8SL
T 020 8347 5220    F 020 8347 5221
*General Manager* Ken Starkey

**Mastertone Multimedia Ltd**
8 Temple Square
Aylesbury
Bucks
HP20 2QH
**T** 01296 334454   **F** 01296 334464
*Managing Director* Nigel French

**Matador Records Ltd**
14 St Marks Road
London
W11 1RQ
**T** 020 7792 3210   **F** 020 7229 4138
**E** matador.netcomuk.com.uk
**W** matador,recs.com
*Contact* Mike Holdsworth

**Matiz Music Ltd**
86 Fulwich Rd
Dartford
Kent
DA1 1UT
**T** 01322 289459   **F** as telephone
**E** glenn.payne@btinternet.com
*Contact* Glenn A Payne

**Matsuri Productions**
Room 221
Panther House
38 Mount Pleasant
London
WC1X 0AP
**T** 020 7419 4747   **F** 020 7419 4746
**E** matsuri@matsuri.demon.co.uk
**W** matsuri-productions.com
*Label Manager* Richard Palk

**Maximum Reality Records**
Flat 4/3
James Court
493 Lawnmarket
Edinburgh
EH1 2PB
**T** 0131 225 5570
*Managing Director* Roderick Habeshaw

**MC Rex**
7 Northington St
London
WC1N 2JF
**T** 020 7404 2647   **F** as telephone
*Contact* Kevin de Las Casas

**MCI**
4th Floor, Holden House
57 Rathbone Place
London
W1T 1JU
**T** 020 7396 8899   **F** 020 7470 6655
**E** info@mcimusic.co.uk   **W** vci.co.uk
*Managing Director* Ian Foster

**Media Records Ltd**
Unit 1, Pepys Court
84–86 The Chase
London
SW4 0NF
**T** 020 7720 7266   **F** 020 7720 7255
**E** peter (or laura).pritchard@mediarec.co.uk
**W** nukleuz.com
*Contact* Peter or Laura Pritchard

*See also Nukleuz Records, BXR Records UK*

**Medium Productions**
74 St Lawrence Rd
Upminster
Essex
RM14 2UW
**F** 01708 640291
**E** info@mediumproductions.co.uk
**W** mediumproductions.co.uk
*Contact* Debi Zornes

*Artist owned (Steve Jansen, Richard Barbieri, Mick Karn)*

**MEGA Hit Records (UK)**
PO Box 56
Boston
Lincs
PE22 8JL
**T** 07970 512967   **F** as telephone
**E** chriskamara@megahitrecordsuk.freeserve.co.uk
**W** megahitrecords.co.uk
*Contact* Chris Kamara

## Melankolic

12 Pembridge Rd
London
W11 3HL
**T** 020 7727 6320   **F** 020 7727 6319
**E** office@melankolic.co.uk
*Label Manager* Niki Fyson

## Melcot Music

PO Box 2404
New Milton
Hants
BH25 7XZ
**T** 01425 611924   **F** as telephone
**E** carol@melcot.com   **W** melcot.com
*Contact* Tudor Williams

*Producer of organ CDs (mainly classical)*
*Sole artist: Carol Williams*

## Melon Records UK

23 Thames St
Hampton
Middx
TW12 EW
**T** 020 8783 1005   **F** 020 8783 1168
**E** mlm@hotmail.com
*Managing Director* Michael Leonard
*General Manager* Andrew Wills

## MELT 2000

6C Littlehampton Rd
Worthing
West Sussex
BN13 1QE
**T** 01903 260033   **F** 01903 261133
**E** info@melt2000.com   **W** melt2000.com
*Director/Chairman* Robert Trunz

## Memnon Entertainment Ltd/Prettybwoy Records

c/o Gray & Co
Habib House, 3rd Floor
9 Stevenson Square
Piccadilly
Manchester
M1 1DB
**T** 0161 237 3360/07711 269939   **F** 0161 236 6717
**E** grayco@grayand.co.uk
*Contact* Rudi Kidd

## Memoir Records

PO Box 66
Pinner
Middx
HA5 2SA
**T** 020 8866 4865   **F** 020 8866 7804
**W** memoir.demon.co.uk
*Managing Director* G Gray

## Mercury

Chancellors House
72 Chancellors Rd
London
W6 9QB
**T** 020 8910 5678   **F** 020 8910 5896
*Managing Director* Howard Berman
*General Manager* Jonathan Green
*A&R Director* David Rose
*Director of Press* Anita Mackie

## Meridian Records

PO Box 317
London
SE9 4SF
**T** 020 8857 3213   **F** 020 8857 0731
**E** meridian-records@supanet.com
*Managing Director* John Shuttleworth

## Meringue Productions Ltd

37 Church St
Twickenham
Middx
TW1 3NR
**T** 020 8744 2277   **F** 020 8744 9333
**E** enquiries@meringue.co.uk   **W** meringue.co.uk
*Contact* Lynn Earnshaw

## Merlin Group, The

40 Balcombe St
London
NW1 6ND
**T** 020 7723 9216/7616 8100   **F** 020 7723 0732
*Contact* Ray Santilli

## Messy Productions Ltd

Unit 3
134 Bermondsey Wall East
London
SE16 4TT

T 020 7394 1706/07956 226779
F as first telephone    E messypro@msn.com

## Metalheadz
Unit 52 Canalot Studios
222 Kensal Rd
London
W10 2BN
T 020 8964 0898    F 020 8964 0890
E label@metalheadz.co.uk    w metalheadz.co.uk
*Contact* Jo Hines

## Metro Entertainment Group
26 Astwood Mews
London
SW7 4DE
T 020 7565 9100    F 020 7565 9101
E dolan@aol.com
*Managing Director* Mike Dolan

## Metro Groove Records
PO Box 6076
London
SW1V 4XD
T 020 7630 7461    F as telephone
E ephemoral@dial.pipex.com
*Managing Director* Paul Zawierka

## Metromedia Communications International (UK)
322 Gatestone Rd
London
SE19 3AT
T 020 8319 3553 x22/8563 3550    F 020 8653 5355
E mazmusic@mm.com    w metromedia.com
*Managing Director* Orlando R Mazzoli

## Michele International
Michele House
The Acorn Centre
Roebuck Rd
Hainault
Essex
IG6 3TU
T 020 8500 1819/8559 8918
F 020 8500 1745/8559 9800
E michele_int@compuserve.com
*Contact* Janine Denoff

## Millennium Records Ltd
9 Thorpe Close
Portobello Rd
London
W10 5XL
T 020 8964 9495    F 020 8964 9497
E millennium@yr2000.demon.co.uk
w millenniumrecords.com
*Contact* Ben Recknagel

## Ministry of Sound Recordings
103 Gaunt St
London
SE1 6DP
T 020 7378 6528    F 020 7403 5348
E club@ministryofsound.co.uk
w ministryofsound.co.uk
*Managing Director* Matt Jagger
*Label Manager* Ewan Grant
*Head of A&R* Clare Gage

## Minority One
Unit 10
Kent House
Old Bexley Business Park
19 Bourne Rd
Bexley
Kent
DA5 1LR
T 01322 557355    F 01322 522878
E mholmes822@aol.com    w htdrecords.com

## Mint Records
8 Market Court
Kilsyth
Glasgow
G65 0BJ
T 01236 821890    E mintrecords@yahoo.com
w mintrecords.com
*Contact* Damian Beattie

*Roster includes Manganese and Oldsolar*

## Mo Wax Labels Ltd
1 Codrington Mews
London
W11 2EM
T 020 875 6266    E mowax@almaroad.co.uk
w mowax.com
*Managing Director* James Lavelle

*Sub labels: Major Force West, Vecta, Mo Wax*
*Asscociated (art-based projects)*

### Mo's Music Machine
Unit 11
Forest Business Park
South Access Rd
London
E17 8BA
**T** 020 8520 7264   **F** 020 8509 1472/8520 9130
**E** info@mosmusic.co.uk   **W** mosmusic.co.uk
*Production & Manufacture* James Orfeur
*Distribution* Gary Kay
*Licensing* Ronny Anderson

*Specializing in production, manufacture and*
*distribution of dance music*

### Mobius Records
120a Coach Rd
Templepatrick
Ballyclare
Co. Antrim
BT39 0HB
**T** 028 9443 2619   **F** 028 9443 2162
**E** sales@mobiusrecords.com
**W** mobiusrecords.com
*Contact* George Doherty

*Also The Modern Group, same details*

### Mogul Records
24 Pepper St
London
SE1 0EB
**T** 020 7928 9777   **F** 020 7928 9222
*Managing Director* Guy Rippon

### Mohock Records
Sovereign House
12 Trewartha Rd
Praa Sands
Penzance
Cornwall
TR20 9ST
**T** 01736 762826/07721 449477   **F** 01736 763328
**E** panamus@aol.com   **W** panamamusic.co.uk
*Managing Director* Roderick G Jones

*Also First Time Records, Pure Gold Records, Rainy*
*Day Records (same contact details)*

### Moken Music
110 High St
Hythe
Kent
CT21 5LE
**T** 01303 267876   **F** 01303 261013
*Contact* Mike Eakins

### Moksha Recordings Ltd
PO Box 102
London
E15 2HH
**T** 020 85555423   **F** 020 8519 8834
**E** recordings@moksha.demon.co.uk
*Contact* Charles Cosh

### Mondo Management/iht records
Unit 2d, Clapham North Arts Centre
26–32 Voltaire Rd
London
SW4 6DH
**T** 020 7720 7411   **F** 020 7720 8095
**W** davidgray.com and loopz.co.uk/orbital
*Contact* Rob Holden, Bernadette Barrett or Chris
Norton

*Roster: David Gray and Orbital*
*Also artist management (same contact details)*

### Monkey Records
9 Mornington Rd
Radlett
Herts
WD7 7BL
**T** 01923 852888   **F** 01923 852678
**E** simon@monkeyrecords.com
**W** monkeyrecords.com
*Contact* Simon Hill

### MonRe Records
2 St Richards Court
Ashburnham Rd
Richmond
Surrey
TW10 7NS
**T** 020 8940 3680   **F** as telephone
**E** marlon.gruss@galactica.co.uk
**W** newklassical.com
*Managing Director* Marlon Gruss

## Moody Food Records

PO Box 516
Newcastle-under-Lyme
Staffs
ST5 0BD
**T** 01782 623666   **F** as telephone
*Contact* Emma Brown

## Mook Records

PO Box 155
Leeds
West Yorkshire
LS7 2XN
**T** 0113 216 3365/230 4008   **E** mookdiscs@aol.com
**W** members.aol.com/mookdiscs
*Contact* Phil Mayne

## Mooncrest Records

1 Pratt Mews
London
NW1 0AD
**T** 020 7267 6899   **F** 020 7267 6746
**W** trojan-records.com
*Contact* Frank Lea

## More Protein

City House
72–80 Leather Lane
London
EC1N 7TR
**T** 020 7242 9730   **F** 020 7242 9731
**E** bel.mp@virgin.net
*Contact* Bel

*Combines indie-pop label Things To Come (AKA,
Fake, Serum), dance label Gross Natural Product
(Kinky Roland, Boogie Macs) and Third World Disco*

## Mother Records

32 Sir John Rogerson's Quay
Dublin 2
Ireland
**T** 00 353 1671 1141   **F** 00 353 1 671 1802

## Mother Records

72–80 Black Lion Lane
London
W6 9BE
**T** 020 8910 4900   **F** 020 8910 4901
*Managing Director* Malcolm Dunbar

## Mother Tongue Records

9 Warren Mews
London
W1T 6AU
**T** 020 7388 6500   **F** 020 7388 6522
**E** julian@takats.com
*Contact* Julian de Takats

## Mother's Little Helper Records

2 Menelik Rd
London
NW2 3RP
**T** 020 7435 6116   **F** as telephone
**E** markalbert@bluemelon.co.uk
**W** bluemelon.co.uk
*Contact* Mark Albert

## Motiv8 Records/Movin' House Records

55 Dixon Avenue
Crosshill
Glasgow
G42 8EG
**T** 0141 423 2192   **F** as telephone
*Contact* John Keenan

## Mouse Records

28 Breamore Rd
Seven Kings
Essex
IG3 9NB
**T** 020 8590 6356
*Contact* Dave Clarke

*Roster includes Noel Redding Band, Shut Up Frank,
The Dream Machine, The Devas*

## Moving Shadow Ltd

2nd Floor, 17 St Anne's Court
London
W1V 3AW
**T** 020 7734 6770   **F** 020 7734 6771
**E** info@movingshadow.com
**W** movingshadow.com
*Contact* Rob Playford

## Mr Bongo

44 Poland St
London
W1V 3DA
**T** 020 7434 4288   **F** 020 7439 1828

## Mr Modos Ltd
137 Arundel St
Sheffield
South Yorkshire
S1 2NU
**T** 0114 249 4014   **F** 0114 249 4016
**E** mrmodo@lodestone.force9.co.uk

## MRR
6 Berkeley Crescent
Clifton
Bristol
BS8 1HA
**T** 0117 929 2393/973 4881
**F** 0117 929 2696/973 4881
**E** craig.williams@virgin.net
*Contact* Craig Williams

## Multiply Records
The Studio
5 King Edward Mews
Byfield Gardens
London
SW13 9HP
**T** 020 8846 9946   **F** 020 8741 5584
**E** info@multiply.co.uk   **w** multiply.co.uk
*Contact* Ceri Pierson
*Managing Director* Mike Hall
*Head of A&R* Moussa Clarke

## MumboJumbo Records
Office 2
9 Thorpe Close
London
W10 5XL
**T** 020 8960 3253   **F** 020 8964 5954
*Contact* Ian Clifford

## Murder Music
Monticello
Wellington Hill
High Beach
Loughton
Essex
IG10 4AH
**T** 020 8532 1654   **F** 020 8532 1656
**E** ania.e@btinternet.com
*Managing Director* Peter Edwards

## Murgatroid Independent Recording Company
The Foundry
Edward St
Limerick
Ireland
**T** 00 353 61 410566   **F** 00 353 61 401310
**E** mur@indigo.ie
*Contact* Pearse or Edel

## Mush Mouth Records
85 Swains Lane
London
N6 6PJ
**T** 020 7379 0000   **F** mark@like-no-other.com
**w** like-no-other.com
*Contact* Mark-Lambert Stewart

## Mushroom Records
1 Shorrolds Rd
London
SW6 7TR
**T** 020 7343 5678   **F** 020 7343 5656
**E** waz@mushroom-records.co.uk
**w** mushroomuk.com
*General Manager* Wez

*Also the Infectious and Perfecto labels*

## Mushroom Records (UK) Ltd
1 Shorrolds Rd
London
SW6 7TR
**T** 020 7343 5678   **F** 020 7343 5656
**E** feedback@mushroom-records.co.uk
**w** mushroomuk.com
*Managing Director* Korda Marshall
*General Manager* Wez

## Music 4 Music Records
c/o DV8 Mecia & Entertainment Ltd
228 Canalot Studios
222 Kensal Rd
London
W10 5BN
**T** 020 8960 4030   **F** 020 8960 4095
**E** info@dv8media.net
*Contact* Danny Viala

## Music & Elsewhere

6 Farm Court
Farm Rd
Frimley
Camberley
Surrey
GU16 8TJ
**T** 01276 502706
**E** magic@uwunderground.fsnet.co.uk
**W** music-elsewhere.hypermart.net

## Music Box Productions

Whitehall
Ashgrove Rd
Newry
Co. Down
BT34 1QN
**T** 028 3026 8658    **F** 028 3026 6673
**E** dheaney@hotmail.com    **W** susanmccann.com
*Contact* Dennis Heaney

## Music City Ltd

122 New Cross Rd
London
SE14 5BA
**T** 020 7277 9657    **F** 0870 757 2004
**E** info@musiccity.co.uk    **W** musiccity.co.uk
*Contact* Brian Harmon (label), Myles Bradley
(recording), Chris Raw (rehearsals)
*Directors* Jim Woodward and Jono Ryan

*Label, studio, rehearsals, hire, editing, CD burning, shop and café*

## Music Factory Mastermix

Hawthorne House
Fitzwilliam St
Parkgate
Rotherham
South Yorkshire
S62 6EP
**T** 01709 710022    **F** 01709 523141
**E** andy@mfeg.demon.co.uk    **W** musicfactory.co.uk
*Director* Andy Pickles

## Music For Nations

333 Latimer Rd
London
W10 6RA
**T** 020 8964 9344    **F** 020 8964 5460
**E** mfn@music-for-nations.co.uk
**W** music-for-nations.co.uk
*Managing Director* Andy Black

*Rock and metal specialists*

## Music From Another Room Ltd

The Penthouse
20 Bulstrode St
London
W1M 5FR
**T** 020 7224 4442    **F** 020 7224 3167
**W** music-from-another-room.co.uk

## Music Fusion Ltd

Head Office
Bajonor House
2 Bridge St
Peel
Isle of Man
IM5 1NB
**T** 01624 844134/844136    **F** 01624 844135
**W** rwcc.com
*Contact* Candy Atcheson

*Dealing with Rick Wakeman Recordings*

## Music Like Dirt

12 Kenneth Court
173 Kennington Rd
London
SE11 6SS
**T** 020 7582 6959    **F** 020 7793 0285
**E** patrick@musiclikedirt.demon.co.uk
*Contact* Patrick Meads

## Music Masters Ltd

Orchard End
Upper Oddington
Moreton-in-the-Marsh
Gloucs
GL56 0XH
**T** 014951 870701    **F** 014951 870702
*Managing Director* Michael John

## Music Media Ltd

PO Box 2154
Hove
East Sussex
BN3 6RG
**T** 01273 235043   **F** as telephone
**E** musicmedia@mistral.co.uk   **w** mistral.co.uk/tko
*Contact* Howard Kruger

*NB: Back catalogue and licensing only. No new artists*

## Music Of Life Records

Liscombe Park
Soulbury
Beds
LU7 0JL
**T** 01296 689066   **F** 01296 689067
**E** chris@musicoflife.com   **w** musicoflife.com
*Managing Director* Chris France

## Music Release

Brewmasters House
91 Brick Lane
London
E1 6QN
**T** 020 7375 2332   **F** 020 7375 2442
*A&R* Gary Dedman

## Musketeer Records

56 Castle Bank
Stafford
Staffs
ST16 1DW
**T** 01785 258746   **F** 01785 255367
*Managing Director* Paul Halliwell

## Mute Records

429 Harrow Rd
London
W10 4RE
**T** 020 8964 2001   **F** 020 8968 4977
**E** info@mutehq.co.uk   **w** mute.com
*Managing Director* Daniel Miller

*Also Partisan Recordings, Novamute, Blast First, 13th Hour, The Grey Area*

## MVM Records

35 Alma Rd
Reigate
Surrey
RH2 0DN
**T** 01737 224151
*Managing Director* Maryetta Midgley

## Mystic Records

Keeley House
22–30 Keeley Rd
Croydon
Surrey
CR0 1TE
**T** 020 8686 7171   **F** 020 8680 5895
**E** mystic-records@msn.com
**w** mysticrecords.co.uk
*Contact* R Barrs James

## Nachural Records

PO Box 2656
Smethwick
Warley
West Mids
B66 4JF
**T** 0121 558 2264   **F** 0121 429 1122/558 2331
**E** ninder.johal@nachural.co.uk   **w** nachural.co.uk
*Proprietor* Ninder Johal

## Nation Records Ltd

19 All Saints Rd
London
W11 1HE
**T** 020 7792 8167   **F** 020 7792 2854
**E** aki@nationrecs.demon.co.uk
**w** nationrecs.demon.co.uk
*Managing Director* Aki Nawaz

## Natural Grooves

3 Tannsfeld Rd
London
SE26 5DQ
**T** 020 8488 3677   **F** 020 8473 6539
**E** naturalgrooves@hotmail.com
**w** naturalgrooves.com
*Contact* Jonathan Sharif

*Soul, folk, hiphop, jazz, breakbeat, electro, house, garage etc*
*See also Between The Grooves (music magazine)*

## Natural Records Ltd
PO Box 272
London
N20 0BY
T 020 8368 0340   F 020 8361 3370
E natural@jt-management.demon.co.uk
*Contact* John Taylor

## Natural Records Ltd
Riverside Studios
7 Mill Rd
Clarkston
Glasgow
G76 8BJ
T 0141 644 5572   F 0141 644 4421
E natural@jt-management.demon.co.uk
*Contact* Duncan Cameron

## Neat Records
71 High St East
Wallsend
Tyne & Wear
NE28 7RJ
T 0191 262 4999   F 0191 263 7082/240 2580
E cjess@hotmail.com   W neatrecords.com
*Managing Director* Jess Cox

*Subsidiary labels Edgy Records, Eldethorn Records,*
*Neat Metal Records*
*The oldest hard rock labels, established 1979,*
*specializing in new and re-issue product by name acts*

## Nemesis Records
41 South King St
Manchester
M2 6DE
T 0161 832 8080   F 0161 832 1613
*Managing Director* Nigel Martin-Smith

## Nervous Records
7–11 Minerva Rd
London
NW10 6HJ
T 020 8963 0352   F 020 8963 1170
E nervous@compuserve.com   W nervous.co.uk
*Managing Director* Roy Williams

## Nettwerk Productions UK
Lincoln House
32–34 York Way
London
N1 9AB
T 020 7837 2755   F 020 7837 3955
E gary@tora-co.demon.co.uk
*Director* Gary Levermore

## New Age Music LTD
17 Priory Raod
London
NW6 4NN
T 020 7209 2766   F 020 7813 2766
E gerrybron@easynet.co.uk   W gerrybron.com
*Contact* Gerry Bron

## New Dawn Records
1–2, 191 Greenhead St
Glasgow
G40 1HX
T 0141 554 6475   F as telephone
E newdawnrecords@talk21.com
W belles.demon.co.uk
*Contact* John Delday

*Also Urbanelite Productions*
*Specializing in hiphop, rap*
*No unsolicited material to be sent, contact before*
*sending anything*

## New Leaf Records
9 Church Rd
Conington
Peterborough
Cambs
PE7 3QJ
T 01487 830778   E indie500@madasafish.com/
awclifton@supanet.com
W leavesmusic.co.uk and indie500.co.uk
*Proprietor* Andrew Clifton

## New Millennium Communications
3rd Floor, Clifton Centre
110 Clifton St
London
EC2A 4HT
T 020 7729 0100   F 020 7729 4379/4409
E music@n-m-c.co.uk

## New Music Enterprises
Meredale
Reach Lane
Heath and Reach
Leighton Buzzard
Beds
LU7 0AL
**T** 01525 237700   **F** as telephone
**E** pauldavis@newmusic28.freeserve.co.uk
*Proprietor* Paul Davis

*Specializing in gospel music*
*Roster includes Wes Davis, George Hamilton IV,*
*Judy Leigh, Kingsfold Choral Society, Jerry Arhelger*
*etc*

## New State Entertainment
Unit 2a Queens Studios
121 Salusbury Rd
London
NW6 6RG
**T** 020 7372 4474   **F** 020 7372 4484/7328 4447
**E** info@newstate.co.uk   **w** newstate.co.uk
*Contact* Tom Parkinson or Tim Binns

## New World Music
The Barn
St Andrews
Beccles
Suffolk
NR34 8NG
**T** 01986 781682/642 (Retail)   **F** 01986 781645
**E** info@newworldmusic.co.uk
**w** newworldmusic.com
*Managing Director* Jeff Stewart
*Director of Marketing* Phil Nind

*Handles a large range of music, including New Age,*
*Ambient, World and Ethnic through its label and*
*distributed labels such as World Music Network,*
*Royal Guide, Domo (Kitaro)*

## NGM Records
North Glasgow College
110 Flemington St
Glasgow
G21 4BX
**T** 0141 558 6440/9001 x249   **F** 0141 558 9905
*Co-ordinator* Keith Baird

## Nice 'n' Ripe Records
FX Promotions
Promotions House
46 Grenville Rd
London
N19 4EH
**T** 020 7281 8363   **F** 020 7281 7663
**E** nicenripe@fxpromotions.demon.co.uk
**w** fxpromotions.demon.co.uk/nicenripe
*Managing Director* George Power
*Head of A&R* James Clyne

*UK garage/2-step and disco house*
*Other labels: City Dub Traxx, Deep Trouble, FX*
*Reecordings, G.O.D. Limited, Large Joints, Strickly*
*Dubz, U.S.L. (United Sounds of London)*

## Nightbreed Recordings
PO Box 6242
Nottingham
NG1 5HY
**T** 0115 910 1908   **F** 0115 910 0810
**E** richard@nightbrd.demon.co.uk
**w** nightbrd.demon.co.uk
*Contact* Richard Chambers

*Specializing in gothic, industrial, alternative music*
*Also extensive music mail-order service*

## Nikt Records
Cadillac Ranch
Pencraig Uchaf
Cwm Bach
Whitland
Dyfed
SA34 0DT
**T** 01994 484466   **F** as telephone
*Contact* Nik Turner

## Nimbus Records Ltd
Wyastone Leys
Monmouth
Gwent
NP25 3SR
**T** 01600 890007   **F** 01600 892119
**E** carl.wade@nimbus.ltd.uk   **w** nimbus.ltd.uk
*Managing Director* Adrian Farmer
*A&R* Dominic Fyfe

## Ninja Tune

Winchester Wharf
Clink St
London
SE1 9DG
**T** 020 7357 7180    **F** 020 7357 7197
**E** ninja@ninjatune.net    **W** ninjatune.net
*Contact* Peter Quicke

## NMC Recordings Ltd

4th Floor, 18–20 Southwark St
London
SE1 1TJ
**T** 020 7403 9445    **F** 020 7403 9446
**E** nmc@nmcrec.co.uk    **W** nmcrec.co.uk
*Administrator* Hannah Vlcek

*Independent label specializing in contemporary
British classical music*

## No Logo Records

26 Dovedale Avenue
Prestwich
Manchester
M25 0BU
**T** 0161 795 8545
*Proprietor* Avril Eventhal

## No U Turn Records

Safestore
5–10 Eastman Rd
London
W3 7YG
**T** 020 8746 0998    **F** 020 87432362
**E** tarek (or nico)@nouturn.fsnet.co.uk
*Contact* Tarek Gjonnes
*Managing Director* Nick Sykes

*Drum 'n' bass music
Susidiary labels: Turn U On Records, Saigon
Records, Nu Black Records, 1210
Recording studio available for hire*

## Noir Records

124 Great Portland St
London
W1N 5PG
**T** 020 7636 2345    **F** 020 7580 0045
*Director* Gary Davison

## Noise UK

Lincoln House
32–34 York Way
London
N1 9AB
**T** 020 7837 2755    **F** 020 7837 3955
**E** gary@toraco.demon.co.uk
*Director* Gary Levermore

## Noisebox Records

135–137 King St
Norwich
Norfolk
NR1 1QH
**T** 01603 767726/07767 660207    **F** 01603 767746
**E** info@noisebox.co.uk    **W** noisebox.co.uk
*Contact* Pete Morgan

*Record label from 1992 to 2001
From 2001, manufacturers of CDs/vinyl*

## Nomad Rush

67 West St
Dunstable
Beds
LU6 1ST
**T** 01582 605222    **F** 01582 690906
**E** nomadrush@cix.co.uk    **W** nomadrush.co.uk

## Northern Sky Music

The Imperial Centre
Suites 116–117
Grange Rd
Darlington
Co. Durham
DL1 5NQ
**T** 01325 467000    **F** 01325 351170
**E** afullheadofsteam@gofree.co.uk
**W** afullheadofsteam.co.uk
*Contact* Ian Luck

## Northwestside

Cavendish House
423 New Kings Rd
London
SW9 4RN
**T** 020 7384 7500    **F** 020 7371 9298
**E** (firstname.surname)@bmg.co.uk
*Managing Director* Nick Raphael

**Now and Then**
Unit 23
Empress Industrial Estate
Anderton St
Ince
Wigan
Lancs WN2 2BG
**T** 01942 206040   **F** as telephone
**W** nowandthen.co.uk
*Label Manager* Mark Ashton

**NOW Music**
15 Tabbs Lane
Scholes
Cleckheaton
West Yorkshire
BD19 6DY
**T** 01274 851365   **F** 01274 874329/865495
**E** nowmusic@now-music.com
**W** now-music.com
*Head of A&R* John Wagstaff

*Mainly pop music management*
*See also Flair Records*

**Nubian Records**
148 Ashley Rd
Montpelier
Bristol
BS6 5PA
**T** 0117 941 1998/942 1870   **F** 0117 941 3758
*Director* Alfredo Vasquez

**Nucamp Records**
Office 2, 9 Thorpe Close
London
W10 5XL
**T** 020 8969 1144   **F** 020 8969 1155
**E** carryon@nucamp.co.uk
*Contact* Alivin Collis
*Managing Director* Mark Jones

**Nude Records**
5 Warren Mews
London
W1T 6AU
**T** 020 7388 5300   **F** 020 7388 5399
**E** nude@nuderecords.com   **W** nuderecords.com
*Managing Director* Saul Galpern
*General Manager* Vanessa Sanders
*A&R* Ben James

**Nukleuz Records**
Unit 1, Pepys Court
84–86 The Chase
London
SW4 0NF
**T** 020 7720 7266   **F** 020 7720 7255
**E** ed@nukleuz.co.uk   **W** nukleuz.com
*Contact* Ed Jenkins

*See also Media Records Ltd, BXR Records UK*

**Numa Records**
86 Staines Rd
Wraybury
Middx
TW19 5AA
**T** 01784 483589   **F** 01784 483211
**E** tonywebb@numan.co.uk   **W** numan.co.uk/
*Managing Director* Tony Webb

**Nuphonic Records**
5a Chapel Place
Rivington St
London
EC2A 3DQ
**T** 020 7739 8757   **F** 020 7739 8761

**NYJO Records**
11 Victor Rd
Harrow
Middx
HA2 6PT
**T** 020 8863 2717   **F** 020 8863 8685
**E** bill.ashton@virgin.net   **W** nyjo.org.uk
*Director* Bill Ashton

*Specialist jazz label*

**Nyrangongo Records**
113 Cheesemans Terrace
Star Rd
London
W14 9XH
**T** 020 7385 5447   **F** as telephone
*Contact* Debbie Golt

*World, dance and global specialist*

## O2 Records
29 Faversham Rd
London
SE6 4XE
T 020 8314 1899
*Contact* Nick Phillips

## Ocean Records (UK) Ltd
PO Box 8392
London
SW7 5XP
F 020 7681 1011    E info@oceanrecords.com
W oceanrecords.com
*Managing Director* James Fletcher

## Ochre Records
PO Box 155
Cheltenham
Gloucs
GL51 0YS
T 01242 514332    F as telephone
E ochre@talbot.force9.co.uk    W ochre.co.uk
*Contact* Talbot

*Experimental and electronic music (eg Sonic Boom's
Experimental Audio Research, Skyray, Windy &
Carl, Bunnymen guitarist Will Sergeant's Glide
project, Stylus, The Land of Nod, 90 Degrees South
and Longstone)*

## Ogun Records
61–71 Collier St
London
N1 9BE
T 020 7278 7391    F 020 7278 7394
*Managing Director* Hazel Miller

## Oh Eye Records
97 Albert St
Edinburgh
EH7 5LY
T 0131 554 9861    F as telephone
E oheye.records@virgin.net
W oheye-records.co.uk
*Contact* Yvette Fugue or Pat Coll

*Roster: Reachout, STS, Nutty Prof
Hiphop music*

## Old Bridge Music
PO Box 7
Ilkley
West Yorkshire
LS29 9RY
T 01943 602203    F as telephone
E mail@oldbridgemusic.com
W oldbridgemusic.com
*Partner* Chris Newman

## On The Corner Records
33 Enterprise Centre
Cranborne Rd
Potters Bar
Herts
EN6 3DQ
T 01707 851500    F 01707 852248
E jem@otc-records.com    W otc-records.com
*Contact* Jeremy Price

## On-Line Records & Publishing
9a Tankerville Place
Newcastle-upon-Tyne
Tyne and Wear
NE2 3AT
T 0191 281 6449    F 0191 212 0913
E c.a.murtagh@btinternet.com
W on-line-records.co.uk
*Managing Director* Christopher Murtagh

## One Little Indian Records
34 Trinity Crescent
London
SW17 7AE
T 020 8772 7600    F 020 8772 7601
E genneaht@indian.co.uk    W indian.co.uk
*Managing Director* Derek Birkett
*Label Co-ordinator* Glenneah Turner

## One Step Music Ltd
Independent House
54 Larkshall Rd
London
E4 6PD
T 020 8523 9000    F 020 8523 8888
E andybailey@independentmusicgroup.com
*Contact* Andy Bailey

## Oompa-Loompa Records
119 Walcot St
Bath
BA1 5BW
**T** 01225 465439

## Opaque
2nd Floor, 29 Prince's St
London
W1R 7RG
**T** 020 7734 9964   **F** 020 7734 1197
**E** harvey@fujint.co.uk
*Managing Director* Mitsuya Fujimoto

## Opaz Records
293–295 Mare St
London
E8 1EJ
**T** 020 8986 8066   **F** 020 8533 7978

## Orangewood Records
39 Church Rd
Chavey Down
Ascot
Berks
SL5 8RR
**T** 01344 883261   **F** 01344 89116
**E** tony-duckworth@msn.com

## Org Records
Suite 212
The Old Gramophone Works
326 Kensal Rd
London
W10 5BZ
**T** 020 8964 3066   **F** 020 8964 5626
**E** organ@organart.demon.co.uk
*Contact* Sean Worrall

## Origin Music
20 Haunch of Venison Yard
London
W1Y 1AF
**T** 020 7491 2480   **F** 020 7495 2935
*Contact* Adam Phillips

## Other Records
Unit F 32–34
Gordon House Rd
London
NW5 1LP
**T** 020 7485 7474

## Out of the Loop Recordings
3e Beehive Mill
Jersey St
Manchester
M4 6JG
**T** 0161 278 1938   **F** as telephone
**W** outofthelooprecordings.com
*Contact* Hamish Anderson

## Outcaste Records
Queens House
1 Leicester Place
Leicester Square
London
WC2H 7BP
**T** 020 7434 2000/7432 3224   **F** 020 7432 3225
**E** paul.outcaste@mvillage.co.uk   **W** outcaste.com
*Contact* Paul Franklyn

## Outdigo Records
OMC
Suite 1 2nd Floor
65 George St
Oxford
OX1 2BE
**T** 01865 798791   **F** 01865 798792
**E** outdigo@oxfordmusic.net
*Contact* Dave Newton

## Outlaw Records
Unit 222
Canalot Studios
222 Kensal Rd
London
W10 5BN
**T** 020 7565 2229   **F** 020 7565 2228
*Contact* Amanda Fairhurst

## Outlet Recording Company Ltd

15–21 Gordon St
Belfast
Co. Antrim
BT1 2LG
T 028 9032 2826    F 028 9033 2671
E mail@outlet-music.com    w outlet-music.com
*Sales and Marketing Manager* Neill Duffy

## Oval Records

326 Brixton Rd
London
SW9 7AA
T 020 7622 0111    E cgillett@oval.demon.co.uk
w oval.demon.co.uk
*Directors* Charlie Gillett and Gordon Nelki

*From Kilburn and the Highroads, Paul Hardcastle
and Lene Lovich in the past to Touch and Go and
Dreamcatcher currently*

## OVC

88 Berkeley Court
Baker St
London
NW1 5ND
T 020 7402 9111    F 020 7723 3064
*Contact* Joanne Goldring-Cohen

## Owl Records

1 Stanaway Drive
Dublin 12
Ireland
T 00 353 1 455 7750    F 00 353 1 455 7782
E owl@eircom.net    w owlrecords.com
*Managing Director* Reg Keating

## OxRecs Digital

Magdalen Farm Cottage
Standlake
Witney
Oxon
OX8 7RN
T 01865 300347    F as telephone
E info@oxrecs.com    w oxrecs.com
*Studio Manager* Bernard Martin

## P3 Music

PO Box 8403
Maybole
KA19 7YB
T 01655 750549    F 01655 750548
E james@p3music.com    w p3music.com
*Contact* James Taylor or Alison Burns

*Also agency, publishing, management and
consultancy*

## Pagan Records

1 Water Lane
London
NW1 8NZ
T 020 7267 1101    F 020 7267 7466
E paganrecs@aol.com    w paganrecords.com
*A&R Director* Richard Breeden

## Palm Pictures

8 Kensington Park Rd
London
W11 3PU
T 020 7229 3000    F 020 7221 9988
w palmpictures.com
*Managing Director* Suzette Newman

## Papillon Records/The Hit Label

The Chrysalis Building
13 Bramley Rd
London
W10 6SP
T 020 7221 2213    F 020 7229 2510
E roye@chysalis.co.uk    w papillonrecords.co.uk
*Contact* Roy Eldridge or Mike Andrews

## Parachute Music

86 Birmingham Rd
Lichfield
Staffs
WS13 6PJ
T 01543 253576/07885 341745    F as first telephone
E parachute.music@virgin.net
w ourworld.compuserve.com/homepages/
parachute_music/
*Contact* Mervyn Spence

## Paradigm Shift Recording Ltd
42 Anstey St
Easton
Bristol
BS5 6DQ
**T** 0117 939 5255/07976 524951　**F** as first telephone
**E** paradigmshift@bristolsound.co.uk
**W** paradigmshiftrecords.co.uk
*Contact* Sean Hockey

*Specializing in cutting edge techno and psy trance*

## Paradox Records
The Warehouse
Elysium Place
London
SW6 4JY
**T** 020 7705 4266　**F** 020 7705 4248

## Parallel
The Blue Building
42–46 St Luke's Mews
London
W11 1DG
**T** 020 7221 5101　**F** 020 7221 3374
*Label Manager* Anthony Lewis

## Park Records
PO Box 651
Oxford
Oxon
OX2 9RB
**T** 01865 241717　**F** 01865 204556
**E** parkrecords@cwcom.net　**W** parkrecords.com
*Managing Director* John Dagnell

## Parlophone
EMI House
43 Brook Green
London
W6 7EF
**T** 020 7605 5000　**F** 020 7605 5050
**W** parlophone.co.uk
*Managing Director* Keith Wozencroft
*A&R Director* Miles Leonard
*Director of Press* Murray Chalmers

## Pasadena Records
Priors
Tye Green
Elsenham
Bishop's Stortford
Herts
CM22 6DY
**T** 01279 813240/815593　**F** 01279 815895
**E** procentral@aol.com
*Contact* David Curtis

## Past & Present Records
33–37 Hatherley Mews
London
E17 4QP
**T** 020 8521 2211　**F** 020 8521 6911
**E** spencer@megaworld.co.uk
*Label Manager* Spencer Kelly

## Past Perfect
Lower Farm Barns
Bainton Rd
Bucknell
Oxon
OX6 9LT
**T** 01869 325052　**F** 01869 325072
**E** clarity@pastperfect.com　**W** pastperfect.com
*Managing Director* Michael Daly

*Specializing in re-mastered original recordings from
the 1920s–1940s*
*Ranging from jazz, swing and blues to nostalgia and
movie songs*
*Free catalogue available*
*See also The Glass Gramophone Company Ltd*

## Pavilion Records Ltd
Sparrows Green
Wadhurst
East Sussex
TN5 6SJ
**T** 0189 278 3591　**F** 0189 278 4156
**E** pearl@pavilionrecords.com
**W** pavilionrecords.com
*Managing Director* John Waite

*Labels include Pearl, Opal and Topaz*
*Established 1968*
*Classical, jazz, nostalgia, drama, documentary,
comedy, light music, popular music to 1950, opera,
musicals, cabaret*
*Distributed worldwide*

## Peaceville Records

PO Box 101
Cleckheaton
West Yorkshire
BD19 4YF
**T** 01274 878101    **F** 01274 874313
**E** hammy@peaceville.com    **W** peaceville.com
*Contact* Hammy

## People Music

The Basement
The Saga Centre
326 Kensal Rd
London
W10 5BZ
**T** 020 8969 9333/8960 2444    **F** 020 8960 7010
**E** people@globaluk.demon.co.uk
*Contact* Mike Slocombe

## Perfect Sounds Recording Co, The

The Croft
25 Felltop
Blackhill
Consett
Co. Durham
DH8 8TR
**T** 01207 507068/07967 946231    **F** 01207 507068
*Contact* Darren Eager

## Perfect World Recordings

PO Box 5
Sidcup
Kent
DA14 6ZW
**T** 020 8300 5510    **F** 020 8300 6503
*Contact* Kevin Parkinson

## Perpetual

Unit 228
Canalot Studios
222 Kensal Rd
London
W10 5BN
**T** 020 8960 3067    **F** 020 8960 9751

## Pet Sounds

Unit 13
Imperial Studios
Imperial Rd
London
SW6 2AG
**T** 020 7610 6969    **F** 020 7610 6622
**E** robin.hill@soundpets.freeserve.co.uk
*Contact* Robin Hill

## PHAB Records

High Notes
Sheerwater Avenue
Woodham
Weybridge
Surrey
KT15 3DS
**T** 019323 48174    **F** 019323 40921
*Contact* Phil H A Bailey

## Phantasm Records/Psychic Deli Records

Unit B140–141
Riverside Business Centre
Bendon Valley
London
SW18 4UQ
**T** 020 8870 4484    **F** 020 8870 4483
**E** john@phantasm-uk.demon.co.uk
**W** phantasm-uk.demon.co.uk
*Contact* John Ford

*Specializing in psychedelic trance*

## Pharm Recordings Ltd

Waltonbank Farm
Stafford Rd
Eccleshall
Staffs
ST21 6JT
**T** 01785 282848    **F** 01785 282842
**E** admin@pharm.co.uk    **W** pharm.co.uk/label

## Phenomina Music

PO Box 12905
London
NW3 2WX
**T** 020 7813 0589    **F** 020 7813 0557
**E** ikeleo@netscape.net
*Contact* Ike Leo

## Phonomenon
Unit 123c Canalot Studios
222 Kensal Rd
London
W10 5BN
**T** 020 8960 3875　**F** 020 8960 7646
**E** nicola@stip.demon.co.uk　**w** stip.demon.co.uk
*Label Manager* Nicola Meighan
*Managing Director* Hein van der Ree

## Phuture Trax Records
2nd Floor, 125 Fonthill Rd
London
N4 3HH
**T** 020 7263 1600　**F** 020 7263 4999
**E** welcome@phuturetrax.enterprise-plc.com
*Contact* Paul Ruiz

## Piano
PO Box 50
Houghton-le-Spring
Tyne & Wear
DH4 5YP
**T** 0191 512 1103　**F** 0191 512 1104
**E** info@voiceprint.co.uk
**w** voiceprint.co.uk/piano

## PIAS Recordings (Play It Again Sam)
338a Ladbroke Grove
London
W10 5AH
**T** 020 8324 2500　**F** 020 8324 0010
**E** pias@piasrecordings.com　**w** pias.com
*General Manager* Pete Dodge

## Pickled Egg Records
19 College Records
Leicester
LE2 0JF
**T** 0116 210 4718　**E** nigelt@uk.uu.net
**w** pickled-egg.co.uk
*Contact* Nigel Turner

*NB: eclectic music only*

## Pinnacle Labels
333 Latimer Rd
London
W10 6RA
**T** 020 8964 9544　**F** 020 8964 5460
*Contact* Sue Armstrong

## Pioneer Entertainment Europe
Pioneer House
Holly Bush Hill
Stoke Poges
Slough
SL2 4QP
**T** 01753 789611/789650　**F** 01753 789647/789646
**E** diego_pedrini@peu.pioneer.co.uk
*Sales and Marketing* Diego Pedrini

## Pip Records
29 North End Rd
London
NW11 7RI
**T** 020 8455 4707
*Managing Director* Ian Cameron

## Piranha Records
PO Box 16715
London
NW4 1WN
**T** 020 8203 5062　**F** 020 8202 3746
**E** de55@dial.pipex.com
*Director* John Lisners

*Also Star-Write Music (same details)*
*See also Star-Write Publishing*

## Pisces Productions
20 Middle Row
London
W10 5AT
**T** 020 8964 4555　**F** 020 8964 4666
**E** hq@pisces.uk.vom　**w** pisces.uk.com
*Managing Director* Morgan Khan

## Planet Organization, The
107 Central Avenue
Welling
Kent
DA16 3BG
*Contact* Trevor Porter

## Planet Records
11 Newmarket St
Colne
Lancs
BB8 9BJ
**T** 01282 866317　**F** as telephone

E mel@ripped.demon.co.uk
w ripped.demon.co.uk
*Contact* Adrian Melling


## Planet Reggae Records
PO Box 1017
Leicester
LE3 6BY
T 0116 231 3352    F 0116 231 3354
w planetreggae.com
*Contact* Maz Karia

*Also Planet Ska Records*


## Plankton Records
PO 13533
London
E7 0SG
T 020 8534 8500    F 07070 718613
*Senoir Partner* Simon Law


## Plastic Head Records Ltd
Unit 15
Bushell Business Estate
Hither Croft
Wallingford
Oxon
OX10 9DD
T 01491 825029    F 01491 826320/824144
E plastichead@compuserve.com
w plastichead.co.uk
*Director* Steve Beatty


## Platipus Records Ltd
Unit GM
Copper House
2 Michael Rd
London
SW6 2AD
T 020 7731 4004    F 020 7731 0008
E platipus@platipus.com    w platipus.com
*Label Manager* Paul Glancy
*A&R Manager* Rick Phillips
*Label Assistant and Website Coordinator* Vip Rama

## Play It Again
2 Merchants Court
Rownham Mead
Hotwells
Bristol
BS8 4YF
T 0117 927 3822    F as telephone
E play@cablenet.co.uk    w auracle.com/pia
*Managing Director* Geoff Leonard


## Playpen Records
1 York St
London
W1H 1PZ
T 020 7487 2558    F 020 7487 2584
*Contact* Terry O'Brien


## Plaza Records
PO Box 726
London
NW11 7XQ
T 020 8455 7965/8458 6200    F as telephones
w etoile.co.uk/poto/poto.html
*Managing Director* Roberto Danova


## Pleasure
110 Ducie House
Ducie St
Manchester
M1 2JW
T 0161 279 1255    F 0161 228 7513
E info@pleasuremusic.net    w pleasuremusic.net
*Label Manager* Pete Robinson


## Plum Projects
8 Perseverance Place
Richmond
Surrey
TW9 2PN
T 020 8288 0531    F 0870 0548334
E info@plumprojects.com    w plumprojects.com
*Contact* Sl!m

*Progressive dance*


## Pogo/RTL
White House Farm
Shropshire
TF9 4HA
T 01630 647374    F 01630 647612

*Copyright Manager* Catherine Lematt

*See also Pogo Music (publishing)*

## Pollytone Records
PO Box 124
Ruislip
Middx
HA4 9BB
**T** 01895 638584/07721 501750   **F** 01895 624793
**E** val@pollyton.demon.co.uk   **W** pollytone.com
*Contact* Val Bird

## Polo Records
23 Powis Gardens
London
NW11 8HH
**T** 020 8455 2469   **F** 020 8965 3948
*Managing Director* Mel Medalie

## Polydor Associated Labels/Polydor UK
Black Lion House
72–80 Black Lion Lane
London
W6 9BE
**T** 020 8910 4800
*Managing Director* Lucian Grainge
*Director of Press* Selina Webb

## Poppy Records
**E** poppy@poptel.org   **W** poppyrecords.com
*Contact* Kris Hoffmann

*Also Tweed Records*
*Contact only by e-mail*

## Pork Recordings
PO Box 18
Kingston-upon-Hull
East Yorkshire
HU1 3YU
**T** 01482 441455   **F** as telephone
**E** pork@pork.co.uk   **W** pork.co.uk
*Managing Director* Dave and Mark Brennand

## Pose Records
3 Bammf Rd
Alyth
Blairgowrie
Perthshire
PH11 8DZ
**T** 01828 633337   **F** 01828 633330
*Head of A&R* Alan Key

## Positiva
43 Brook Green
London
W6 7EF
**T** 020 7605 5157   **F** 020 7605 5186
**W** positivarecords.com
*Managing Director* Kevin Robinson
*A&R Manager* Jason Ellis
*Label Manager* Sid Li
*Label Assistant* Chris Rodwell

*Dance label*

## Pow!
Unit 11
Impress House
Mansell Rd
London
W3 7QH
**T** 020 8932 3033   **F** 020 8932 3032
*Director* Paul Gotel

## Power Records
29 Riversdale Rd
Thames Ditton
Surrey
KT7 0QN
**T** 020 8398 5236/5732   **F** 020 8398 7901
*Managing Director* Barry Evans

## PRD Labels Ltd
50b Canalot Studios
222 Kensal Rd
London
W10 5BN
**T** 020 8968 4661   **F** 020 8964 5104
**E** mike@prdlab.demon.co.uk
*Contact* Angie Goulding

**Preaching Diva Ltd**
PO Box 19544
London
SW11 1FF
E preaching_diva@hotmail.com
*Managing Director* Nigel Karan

**Precious Organization, The**
The Townhouse
1 Park Gate
Glasgow
G3 6DL
T 0141 353 2255    F 0141 353 3545
*Contact* Eliot Davis

**Premium Music**
Studio 4
108 Prospect Quay
Point Pleasant
London
SW18 1PR
T 020 8877 0887    F 020 8877 0687

**President Records Ltd**
Units 6–7, 11 Wyfold Rd
Fulham
London
SW6 6SE
T 020 7385 7700    F 020 7385 3402
w president-records.co.uk
*Managing Director* David Kassner

**Primate Recordings**
340 Athlon Rd
Alperton
Middx
HA0 1BX
T 020 8601 2200    F 020 8601 2262
E music@primedistribution.co.uk
w primedistribution.co.uk
*Contact* John Warwick

*Also Primevil, Primary Recordings, Premier Sounds,*
*Primal Rhythms, Sweet Life Recordings (same*
*contact details)*
*Primate Recordings, Primevil: Trance music*
*Primary Recordings: Deep house*
*Premier Sounds: Commercial Dance*
*Primal Rhythms: DJ mix CDs*
*Sweet Life Recordings: UK garage*

**Priory Records**
Unit 9b
Upper Winbury Courtyard
Wingrave
Bucks
HP22 4LW
T 01296 682255    F 01296 682275
E sales@priory.org.uk    w priory.org.uk
*Managing Director* Neil Collier

**Prism Leisure Corporation plc**
1 Dundee Way
Enfield
Middx
EN3 7SX
T 020 8804 8100    F 020 8805 8001
E music@prismleisure.com    w prismleisure.com
*Sales Director* Simon Checketts
*Licensing* Steve Brink

*Mid-price and budget label*

**Production House**
1 Herbert Gardens
London
NW10 3BX
T 020 8968 8870    F 020 8960 0719
*Contact* Raj Malkani

**Proper Records Ltd**
The Powerhouse
Cricket Lane
Beckenham
Kent
BR3 1LW
T 020 8676 5180    F 020 8676 5193
E malc@proper.uk.com    w proper.uk.com
*Managing Director* Malcolm Mills

**Props Records Ltd**
7 Croxley Rd
London
W9 3HH
T 020 8960 1115    F 020 8962 0359
E martin.lascelles@virgin.net    w props.co.uk
*Director* Martin Lascelles

## Protected Records Ltd

Toad House
Imberhorne Lane
East Grinstead
West Sussex
RH19 1QY
**T** 01342 317943    **F** as telephone
**E** ed@protectedrecords.com
**W** protectedrecords.com
*Managing Director* Ed Palmieri

*Roster: The ETs, Nose, Blush*

## Provocateur Records

Friendly Hall
31 Fordwich Rd
Fordwich
Kent
CT2 0BW
**T** 01227 711008    **F** 01227 712021
**E** info@provocateurrecords.co.uk
**W** provocateurrecords.co.uk
*Contact* Jane Lindsey

## Pukka Records

107 Mortlake High St
London
SW14 8HQ
**T** 020 8878 7888    **F** 020 8878 7886
*Managing Director* Jeremy Marsh
*A&R Co-ordinator* Lisa Tillyard

## Pulse Records

Suite 1
Regency House
Regent Rd
Liverpool
Merseyside
L5 9TB
**T** 0151 298 1100    **F** 0151 298 2810
**E** info@pulse-records.co.uk
**W** pulse-records.co.uk
*Managing Directors* Rob and Alan Fennah

## Pure Gold Records

Sovereign House
12 Trewartha Rd
Praa Sands
Penzance
Cornwall
TR20 9ST

**T** 01736 762826/07721 449477    **F** 01736 763328
**E** panamus@aol.com    **W** panamamusic.co.uk
*Managing Director* Roderick G Jones

*Also Mohock Records, First Time Records, Rainy Day Records (same contact details)*

## Pure Impact

63a Bruce Grove
London
N17 6RN
**T** 020 8808 4554    **F** 020 8365 0143
*Contact* Karen-Joy Langley

## Pussyfoot Records

6 Denmark St
London
WC2H 8LP
**T** 020 7240 1700    **E** matasyfoot.co.uk
**W** pussyfoot.co.uk
*Contact* Mat Anthony

## Quail Records

29 Golders Gardens
London
NW11 9BS
**T** 020 8458 1178    **F** 020 8905 5191
*Contact* Jim Roland

## Quartz Records

PO Box 6912
Birmingham
West Midlands
B27 7BB
**T** 0121 770 8544/07990 532745
**F** as first telephone    **E** quartzrecords@lineone.net

## Quench Recordings

Po Box 2311
Romford
Essex
RM5 2DZ
**T** 01992 763777    **F** 01992 763463
**E** quench@subbase.com    **W** subbase.com
*Contact* Dan Donnelly

## Quinlan Road

1 Heathgate Place
Unit 1, 75–87 Agincourt Rd
London
NW3 2NT
**T** 020 7428 0946/7267 0093
**F** 020 7267 9488/7428 0971
**E** postmaster@quinlan.demon.co.uk
**W** quinlanroad.com
*Contact* Karen Shook

*'Eclectic Celtic' singer/composer Loreena McKennitt's own label*

## Qzone Ltd

21c Heathmans Rd
London
SW6 4TJ
**T** 020 7731 9313    **F** 020 7731 9314
**E** (firstname).(lastname)@qzoneuk.com
*Contact:*Nicki L'Amy

## R&B Division

34 Salisbury St
London
NW8 8QE
**T** 020 7402 9111    **F** 020 7723 3064
*Managing Director* Eliot Cohen

## Radioactive

5–7 Mandeville Place
London
W1M 5LB
**T** 020 7535 3512    **F** 020 7535 3712
**E** raduk@dircon.co.uk    **W** radioactive.net
*Manager* Beverley Hollanders

## Rainbow Quartz

33a Upper Grosvenor Rd
Tunbridge Wells
Kent
TN1 2DX
**T** 01634 305577/00 1 212 977 6777
**E** rainbowqtz@aol.com

## Rainy Day Records

Sovereign House
12 Trewartha Rd
Praa Sands
Penzance
Cornwall
TR20 9ST
**T** 01736 762826/07721 449477    **F** 01736 763328
**E** panamus@aol.com    **W** panamamusic.co.uk
*Managing Director* Roderick G Jones

*Also Mohock Records, Pure Gold Records, First Time Records (same contact details)*

## Ram Records Ltd

PO Box 70
Hornchurch
Essex
RM11 3NR
**T** 01708 445851    **F** 01708 441270
**E** info@ramrecords.co.uk
*Contact* Scott Bourne

## Rampage The Label

7–11 Kensington High St
London
W8 5NP
**T** 07000 726724    **F** 0000 726732
**E** dee@rampagesound.com
**W** rampagesound.com
*Contact* Mike Anthony

## Rampant Art

62–64 Murray St
Hartlepool
Cleveland
TS26 8PL
**T** 01429 860110
*Contact* Graham Palmer

## Random House

20 Vauxhall Bridge Rd
London
SW1V 2SA
**T** 020 7840 8400    **F** 020 7233 6129

**Range Records**
7 Garrick St
London
WC2E 9AR
T 020 7240 1628    F 020 7497 9242
E valentine@bandleader.co.uk
W bandleader.co.uk
*Managing Director* Tony Byworth

**Rapid 9547**
281 Walworth Rd
London
SE17 3RP
T 020 7708 0003    F 020 7708 1152
*Managing Director* Bernie Simons

**Raw Fish Records**
Room D12
The Arden Centre
Sale Rd
Northendon
Manchester
M23 0DD
T 0161 957 1792/1795    F 0161 957 1742/1732
E p.ellis@ccm.ac.uk    W ccm.ac.uk/rawfish
*Label Manager* Phil Ellis

**Razorhead Productions**
The Loft
40 Antrobus Rd
London
W4 5HZ
T 020 8742 3815    F as telephone
E pgoufc@aol.com
*Contact* Pete Gardiner

*Specialist in catalogue representation, licensing and
synchronization*

**RCM Music Operations**
Operations House
Po Box 2267
London
NW10 5TQ
T 07958 571103    F 0870 0554837
E roger@rcmmusic.demon.co.uk
W rcmmusic.demon.co.uk
*Operations Manager* Roger Brown

**RDL Records**
132 Chase Way
London
N14 5DH
T 020 8655 2614    F 020 8361 3757
E ldonessien@aol.com
*Director* C Jacques

**React Music Ltd**
138b West Hill
London
SW15 2UE
T 020 8780 0305    F 020 8788 2889/8780 3368
E mailbox@react-music.co.uk
W react-music.co.uk
*Managing Director* Thomas Foley

*Dance, chill out, world music*
*Subsidiary labels: Industry, Recharge, Dope or Plastic*

**Real Recordings**
35 Greenfield Rd
Great Barr
Birmingham
B43 5AR
T 0121 358 5346    F as telephone
*Managing Director* Malcolm Bell

**Real World Records**
Mill Lane
Box
Corsham
Wilts
SN13 8PL
T 01225 743188    F 01225 743787
E amanda.jones@realworld.co.uk
W realworld.on.net
*Label Manager* Amanda Jones

**Receiver Records**
Regent House
1 Pratt Mews
London
NW1 0AD
T 020 7267 6899    F 020 7267 6746
W trojan-records.com
*Contact* Frank Lea

## Recognition

31 Silver St
Bradford-on-Avon
Wilts
BA15 1JX
T 01225 864422/868007    F 01225 864466
E sue@recognition.freeserve.co.uk
*Contact* Andy Richmond

*See also Recognition Records Ltd*
*Also distribution*

## Recognition Records Ltd

Suite 6, Piccadilly House
London Rd
Bath
BA1 6PL
T 01225 448438    F 01225 448439
E sue.richmonderdltd.com
W recognition-distribution.com
*Managing Director* Andy Richmond
*Managing Director* Sue Richmond
*Senior A&R Director* Sir Harry
*General Manager (Distribution)* Wilf Mann

*Roster includes Errol Brown, FAB!, Ruff Driverz*
*Also distribution*

## Record Label, The

The Old Schoolhouse
138 Lower Mortlake Rd
Richmond
Surrey
TW9 2JZ
T 020 8332 7245    F 020 8332 7631
E info@recordlabel.co.uk    W recordlabel.co.uk
*Contact* Matt Nicholson

## Red Head Records

95 Gloucester Rd
Hampton
Middx
TW12 2UW
T 020 8783 0039/7490 7744    F 020 8979 6487
*Contact* Kaplan Kaye or Danny Brittain

## Red Hot Records

105 Emlyn Rd
London
W12 9TG
T 020 8749 3730    E redhotrecs@aol.com
*Contact* Brian Leafe

## Red Lightnin'

The White House
42 The St
North Lopham
Diss
Norfolk
IP22 2LU
T 01379 687693    F 01379 687559
E peter@redlightnin.com    W redlightnin.com
*Contact* Pete Shertser

*Specializing in blues*
*Also film, TV, advertising etc*

## Red Parrot Recordings

Unit B114
Faircharm Studios
8–10 Creekside
London
SE8 3DX
T 020 8469 3541    F 020 8469 3542
E red.parrot@virgin.net    W mezzmusic.com
*Contact* Andy Penny

*Two other labels: Beak Recordings and Caged*
*Records*
*Also Red Parrot Management (contact John*
*Cecchini) and Red Parrot Agency (contact Andria*
*Law)*
*Mainly dance music and culture*

## Red Sky Records

PO Box 27
Stroud
Gloucs
GL6 0YQ
T 01453 836877    F as telephone
E info@redskyrecords.co.uk
W redskyrecords.co.uk
*Managing Director* Johnny Coppin

## Reel Track Records

PO Box 1099 (Chart Moves)
London
SE5 9HT
T 020 7326 4824    F 020 7580 8485
E gamesmaster@chartmoves.com
W chartmoves.com
*A&R Manager* Dave Mombasa

## Reggae Retro Records (UK) Ltd
PO Box 8154
Birmingham
B11 3LA
**T** 0121 684 9023/07971 691260   **F** 0121 684 9024
**E** rretro@clara.net

## Rel Records Ltd
86 Causewayside
Edinburgh
EH9 1PY
**T** 0131 668 3366   **F** 0131 662 4463
**E** rel@relrecords.co.uk   **W** relrecords.co.uk
*Managing Director* Neil Ross

## Related Recordings
PO Box 89
Slough
Berks
SL1 8NA
**T** 01628 667124   **F** 01628 669783/667057
**E** info@dmcworld.demon.co.uk
**W** stressrecords.com
*Label Manager* Nick Darby

## Release Records
7 North Parade
Bath
BA2 4DD
**T** 01225 428284   **F** 01225 400090
**E** aca_aba@freenet.co.uk
*Contact* H Finegold

*Also ABA Booking and ACA Music Management
(same contact details)*

## Remote Records
25 Elysium Gate
126–128 New Kings Rd
London
SW6 4LZ
**T** 020 7731 1991   **F** as telephone
*Chief Executive Officer* Denis O'Regan
*A&R Director* Clive Black

## Renk Records
Shore Business Centre
Shore Rd
London
E9 7TA
**T** 020 8986 0314   **F** 020 8533 1899
*Managing Director* Junior Hart

## Rephlex
PO Box 2676
London
N11 1AZ
**T** 020 8368 5903   **F** 020 8361 2811
**E** help@rephlex.com   **W** rephlex.com
*Contact* Matthew Prigg

## Resolution Productions
Mission Studios WCI
Crab Lane
Warrington
WA2 0DB
**T** 01925 494208/494494   **F** 01925 816077
**E** g.blazey@warr.ac.uk
*Contact* Gareth Blazey (Course Leader); Russell
Dyson (Lecturer); Andy Nixon (Technician)

*Part of BA in Commerical Music Production
(Media) Degree*

## Resurgence
PO Box 50
Houghton-le-Spring
Tyne & Wear
DH4 5YP
**T** 0191 512 1103   **F** 0191 512 1104
**E** info@voiceprint.co.uk   **W** voiceprint.co.uk
*Contact* Anne Marie Hill

## Retch Records
49 Rose Crescent
Southport
Merseyside
PR8 3RZ
**T** 01704 577835/07951 201407
**E** retchrecords@netscapeonline.co.uk
**W** sites.netscape.net/retchrecordsh
*Owner* M Hines

*Mainly punk rock
Roster includes Blitzkrieg, Parasites, The Varukers,
Airbomb*

## Reverb Records Ltd/D&D Recordings

Reverb House
Bennett St
London
W4 2AH
**T** 020 8747 0660/07831 320837   **F** 020 8747 0880
**E** markreverb@hotmail.com/
marklusty@reverbxl.com
*Contact* Mark Lusty

*Specializing in garage, house, jazz, acid jazz, dance*

## Reverberations

27 Wallorton Gardens
London
SW14 8DX
**T** 020 8876 4589   **F** 020 8392 1422
**E** reverberations@mailcity.com
*Contact* Asad Rizvi

## Revolver Music

152 Goldthorn Hill
Penn
Wolverhampton
West Midlands
WV2 3JA
**T** 01902 345345   **F** 01902 345155
*Managing Director* Paul Birch

## Rhiannon Records

20 Montague Rd
London
E8 2HW
**T** 020 7275 8292/07973 217878   **F** 020 7503 8034
**E** info@rhiannonrecords.co.uk
**W** rhiannonrecords.co.uk
*Contact* Colin Jones

*See also Rhiannon Music Ltd (publishing)*

## Rhythm Syndicate Records

5 Cobble Yard
Napier St
Cambridge
CB1 1HP
**T** 01223 323264/328822   **F** 01223 362212
**E** rhythmsyndicate@breathe.co.uk
*Contact* Sammie Cullip

## Rhythmbeat Records

PO Box 589
London
SE6 4PU
**T** 020 8690 6515   **F** as telephone
*Contact* P & R Mac

## Ribble Records

Bramley Meade Hall
Whalley
Clitheroe
Lancashire
**T** 01254 823001   **F** 01254 823938
*Contact* Leon Hardman

## Richly Comic Records

Unit 2 Stable Barn
New Yatt Rd
Witney
Oxon
OX29 6TA
**T** 01993 706632   **F** 01993 706689
**E** w.furlong@richlycomic.com   **W** richlycomic.com
*Head of A&R* Windyke Furlong

*Previous releases include The Klyrz, The Jokers and Momyenng*

## Riddle Records

Cadillac Ranch
Pencraig Uchat
Cwm Bach
Whitland
Dyfed
SA34 0DT
**T** 01994 484466   **F** 01994 484294
*Contact* M Menendes

## Rideg Records

1 York St
Aberdeen
AB11 5DL
**T** 01224 573100   **F** 01224 572598

## Rideout Records

Lillie House
1a Conduit St
Leicester
LE2 0JN
**T** 0116 223 0318   **F** 0116 223 0302

**E** rideout@stayfree.co.uk   **w** cathybonner.com
*Contact* Darren Knockles

### Right Recordings
177 High St
Harlesden
London
NW10 4TE
**T** 020 8961 3889   **F** 020 8961 4620
**E** right@supanet.com
*Managing Director* David Landau

### Righteous Recording Company, The
Unit 229
Canalot Studios
222 Kensal Rd
London
W10 5BN
**T** 020 7436 4436   **E** richard@richman.demon.co.uk
*Contact* Richard Shipman

### Rita Records
PO Box 11014
London
N4 2YE
**T** 020 8888 5564   **F** 020 8888 5568
**E** ritarecords@demon.co.uk
**w** sweet-candy.net/music/rita
*Managing Director* Howard Williams

### Riverhorse Records Ltd
115 Eastbourne Mews
London
W2 6LQ
**T** 0171 262 2882   **F** 0171 262 1661
**E** theherd@riverhorse.com
*Managing Director* Robin Godfrey-Cass
*General Manager* Hillary Shaw

### Riviera Record Co
Old Apple Trees
Northgate
Crawley
West Sussex
RH10 2AE
**T** 01293 616033   **E** henryturtle@btconnect.com
**w** henryturtle.co.uk
*Contact* Tina Bartle

### RMG (Ritz Music Group plc)
33–35 Wembley Hill Rd
Wembley
Middx
HA9 8RT
**T** 020 8733 1300   **F** 020 8903 5859   **w** rmgplc.com
*Contact* Paddy Prendergast

### RMG (Ritz Music Group) Ireland
5–6 Lombard St East
Dublin 2
Ireland
**T** 00 353 1 677 9046/672 7277   **F** 00 353 1 677 9386
**E** grape@aiol.ie   **w** rmgplc.com
*General Manager* Peter Kenny

### Roadrunner Records
Suites W&T
Tech West House
Warple Way
London
W3 0UL
**T** 020 8749 2984   **F** 020 8749 2523
**E** rrguest@roadrunnerrecords.co.uk
**w** roadrunnerrecords.co.uk
*General Manager* Mark Palmer

### Robin Records
Priory House
1133 Hessle High Rd
Kingston-upon-Hull
East Yorkshire
HU4 6SB
**T** 01482 565444   **F** 01482 353635
**E** robin.carew@mcleod-holden.com
*Contact* Robin Carew

### Rockin' Rodent Recordings
PO Box 835
Westcliff-on-Sea
Essex
SS0 0SQ
**E** 3geezers@thehamsters.co.uk
**w** thehamsters.co.uk

*NB: label for The Hamsters blues band*

## Rogue Records Ltd

PO Box 337
London
N4 1TW
**T** 020 8340 9651   **F** 020 8348 5626
**E** rogue@froots.demon.co.uk
*Managing Director* Ian Anderson

## Rollercoaster Records

Rock House
London Rd
St Mary's
Chalford
Gloucs
GL6 8PU
**T** 01453 886252   **F** 01453 885361
**E** rollerrec@aol.com

*Re-issue label*

## Ron Winter Productions

The Studio
Lynton Rd
London
N8 8SL
**T** 020 8347 5220   **F** 020 8347 5221
*Commercial Director* Mike Fay

## Ronco/Temple

3 The Old Power Station
121 Mortlake High St
London
SW14 8SN
**T** 020 8876 7111   **F** 020 8878 0331
*General Manager* Gill Massey

## Rooster Records

33 Park Chase
Wembley
Middx
HA9 8EQ
**T** 020 8902 5523   **F** as telephone
*Managing Director* Eddie Stevens

## Rose Rouge International

Aws Group
Aws House
Trinity Square
St. Peter Port
Guernsey
GY1 1LX
**T** 01481 728294   **F** 01481 714118
**E** aws@gtonline.net   **W** awsgroup.co.uk
*Director* Steve Free

*Also publishers and artist management*

## Ross Records

29 Main St
Turriff
Aberdeenshire
AB53 4AB
**T** 01888 562403/568899   **F** 01888 568890
**E** aross16168@aol.com
*Managing Director* Gibson Ross

## Rotator

Interzone House
74–77 Magdalen Rd
Oxford
OX4 1RE
**T** 01865 205600   **F** 01865 205700
**E** info@rotator.co.uk   **W** rotator.co.uk
*Contact* Richard Cotton

## Rough Trade Records

250 York Rd
London
SW11 3SJ
**T** 020 7716 3400   **F** 020 7716 3401
**E** mailman@roughtrade.music.co.uk
**W** roughtrade.music.co.uk

## Round Tower Music

48 Downside Heights
Skerries
Co. Dublin
Ireland
**T** 00 353 1 849 0644
**E** chudson@roundtower.com   **W** roundtower.com
*Director* Clive Hudson

## RP Media Ltd
Kingsway House
134–140 Church Rd
Hove
East Sussex
BN3 2DL
**T** 01273 220700   **F** 01273 220800/321932
**E** rp_media@compuserve.com   **w** rpmedia.co.uk
*Contact* David Paramor

## RPM Records Ltd
Aizlewood Mill
Nursery St
Sheffield
South Yorkshire
S3 8GG
**T** 01142 333024   **F** as telephone
**w** rpmrecords.co.uk
*Managing Director* Simon Robinson

## RTL Records
Whitehouse Farm
Shropshire
TF9 4HA
**T** 01630 647374   **F** 01630 647612
*Head A&R* Tanya Woof

*Send C/D & M/D cassettes or videos (P.A.L)*

## Rubicon Records
59 Park View Rd
London
NW10 1AJ
**T** 020 8450 5154   **F** 020 8452 0187
**w** rubiconrecords.co.uk
*Contact* Graham Le Fevre

## Rumour Records
Tempo House
15 Falcon Rd
London
SW11 2PJ
**T** 020 7228 6821   **F** 020 7228 6972
**E** post@rumour.demon.co.uk
**w** rumour.demon.co.uk
*Directors* David Brooker, Anne Plaxton
*Label Manager* Oscar Engles

*Specialist in all dance music genres*
*Subsidiary labels: Klone, Stonegroove, Treat,*
*Escapade, Tempo Toons, Dust 2 Dust*

## Rykodisc Ltd
78 Stanley Gardens
London
W3 7SZ
**T** 020 8746 1234   **F** 020 8746 2129
**E** rykoeuro@rykodisc.com   **w** rykodisc.com
*Managing Director* Ian Moss

## Sain (Recordiau) Cyf.
Canolfan Sain
Llandwrog
Caernarfon
Gwynedd
LL54 5TG
**T** 01286 831 111   **F** 01286 831 497
**E** music@sain.wales.com   **w** sain.wales.com
*Managing Director* Dafydd Iwan

*Organization incorporates Stiwdio Sain (recording*
*studio), Cyhoeddiadau Sain (music publishing) and*
*Fideo Sain (Video, CD and CD Rom authoring and*
*duplication)*
*Labels: Sain, Crai, Cambrian, Gwynfryn, Tryfan*
*Founded in 1969, Sain specializes in Welsh music,*
*from classical to rock, traditional and contemporary*
*Best known for choral, folk and harp music and*
*Welsh language singing*

## Sanctuary Records
Sanctuary House
45–53 Sinclair Rd
London
W14 0NS
**T** 020 7602 6351   **F** 020 7603 5941
**E** info@sanctuaryrecords.co.uk
**w** sanctuarygroup.com

## Sanctuary Records Group Ltd
A29 Barwell Business Park
Leatherhead Rd
Chessington
Surrey
KT9 2NY
**T** 020 8974 1021   **F** 020 8974 2674/2880
**E** customerservices@sanctuarygroup.com
**w** sanctuaryrecordsgroup.co.uk
*Chief Executive Officer* Joe Cokell
*Commercial Operating Officer* Roger Semon
*Distributor* Pinnacle

## Sangraal

PO Box 979
Sheffield
South Yorkshire
s8 8yw
**T** 0114 274 5895   **F** as telephone
**E** dc@cprod.win-uk.net
*Contact* Darren Crisp

## Savant

132 Chase Way
London
N14 5DH
**T** 020 8655 2614   **F** 020 8361 3757
**E** ldonessien@aol.com
*Contact* R Struple

## Savoy Records

PO Box 271
Purley
Surrey
CR8 4YL
**T** 01737 554 739   **F** 01737 556 737
**E** admin@savoymusic.com   **W** savoymusic.com
*Contact* Wendy Smith

## Saxology Records

49e St Paul's Rd
London
N1 2LT
**T** 020 7354 2595/7930 4284   **F** 020 7354 5094/
7930 2322   **E** 106500.325@compuserve.com
**W** users.dircon.co.uk/paulcarm/saxology
*Managing Director* Mike Tanousis

## Saydisc Records

The Barton
Inglestone Common
Badminton
Gloucs
GL9 1BX
**T** 01454 299 858   **F** as telephone
**E** saydisc@aol.com   **W** saydisc.com
*Managing Director* Gef Lucena

*Traditional, world, early music*

## SBS Records

PO Box 37
Blackwood
Gwent
NP12 2YQ
**T** 01494 201116/07711 984651   **F** 01495 201190
**E** enquiry@sbsrecords.co.uk   **W** sbsrecords.co.uk
*Contact* Glenn Powell

## Scarlet Records

Unit 64
Millmean Industrial Estate
Millmead Rd
London
N17 9QU
**T** 020 8365 0800   **F** 020 8885 6030
**E** info@scarletrecording.co.uk
**W** scarletrecording.co.uk
*Contact* Liz Lenten

## Scenario Records

PO Box 6971
London
W10
**T** 020 8969 4062   **F** as telephone
**E** edscenario@hotmail.com
*Label Manager and A&R* Ed Pitt

*Specialist music area: hip hop*

## Science Friction

PO Box 979
Sheffield
South Yorkshire S8 8YW
**T** 0114 261 1649   **F** as telephone
**E** dc@cprod.win-uk.net
*Contact* Darren Crisp

## Scotdisc – BGS Productions Ltd

Newtown St
Kilsyth
Glasgow
G65 0JX
**T** 01236 821081   **F** 01236 826900
**E** nscott@scotdisc.co.uk   **W** scotdisc.co.uk
*Director's Assistant* Yvonne McKay

## Scratch Records
Hatch Farm Studios
Unit 16, Hatch Farm
Chertsey Rd
Addlestone
Surrey
KT15 2EH
**T** 01932 828715   **F** 01932 828717/829938
**E** 101476.1233@compuserve.com
*Director* Brian Adams

## Screaming Target Recordings
66c Chalk Farm Rd
London
NW1 8AN
**T** 020 7485 1444   **F** 020 7485 4404

## Scrummy Records
71 Lansdowne Rd
Purley
Surrey
CR8 2PD
**T** 020 8645 0013   **E** flamingofleece@yahoo.com
**W** geocities.com/flamingofleece
*Contact* Alvin LeDup

*An ensemble of eclectic, high-quality low-fi acts*
*Scrummy Records: Andy Callen, Flamingo Fleece*
*Low Quality Accident label: Prairie Dogs of Abilene*
*'A punk organization with tunes'*

## See For Miles Records
PO Box 328
Maidenhead
Berks
SL6 2NE
**T** 01784 247176   **F** 01784 241168
**E** es95@dial.pipex.com   **W** seeformiles.co.uk
*Managing Director* Colin Miles

*Specialist re-issue company*
*1940s–1980s music released*
*Established 1981*

## Sequel Records
A29 Barwell Business Park
Leatherhead Rd
Chessington
Surrey
KT9 2NY
**T** 020 8974 1021   **F** 020 8974 3700

**E** info@castlecom.com   **W** castlecom.com
*Label Manager* John Reed

## Serengeti Records
43a Old Woking Rd
West Byfleet
Surrey
KT14 6LG
**T** 01932 351925   **F** 01932 336431
**E** serengeti_records@msn.com
*General Manager* Martin Howell

## Serious Records Ltd
PO Box 13900
London
N6 5BG
**T** 020 8381 4805   **F** 020 8458 1465
**E** records@seriousworld.com
**W** seriousworld.com

## Seriously Groovy
3rd Floor, 28 D'Arblay St
London
W1V 3FH
**T** 020 7439 1947   **F** 020 7734 7540
**E** seriousgrv@aol.com
**W** members.sol.com/seriousgrv/
*Managing Director* Dave Holmes

## Setanta Records
174 Camden Rd
London
NW1 9HJ
**T** 020 7284 4877   **F** 020 7284 3577
**E** keith@setantarecords.com
**W** setantarecords.com
*Contact* Keith Cullen

## Seventh Wave
5c Prince of Wales Drive
London
SW11 4SB
**T** 020 7924 3425   **E** seventhwave@mcmail.com
*Managing Director* David Izen

## Shade Factor Productions Ltd
4g Cleveland Square
London
W2 6DH
F 020 7402 6477 E 020 7402 7144
*Managing Director* Ann Symonds

## Shake Recordings
Ashburton House
Send
Woking
Surrey
GU23 7AD
T 07976 939415

## Shamtown Records
13 St Mary's Terrace
Taylor's Hill
Galway
Ireland
T 00 353 91 521309/565368    F 00 353 91 526341
E sawdoc@eircom.net    w sawdoctors.com
*Contact* Ollie Jennings

## Shaping the Invisible
Howard St
Oxford
OX4 3AY
T 07585 498800    F 01865 722552
E charlie@bsdr.com
*Contact* Charlie Seaward

## Shark Records
23 Rollscourt Avenue
London
SE24 0EA
T 020 7737 4580    F 020 7274 5703
*Managing Director* M H Mellor

## Sharma Productions
12 Telford House
Tiverton St
London
SE1 6NY
T 020 7407 4921/07956 887 162
E leo294@dircon.co.uk
*Contact* Phillip Leo

## Sharp End Records Ltd
Grafton House
2–3 Golden Square
London
W1R 3AD
T 020 7439 8442    F 020 7439 1814
E sharpend2@aol.com
*Contact* Robert Lemon

## Sharpe Music
9a Irish St
Dungannon
Co. Tyrone
BT70 1DB
T 028 8772 4621    F 028 8775 2195
E sharpemusic@email.com
w sharpemusicireland.com

*Distribution of major Irish labels*
*See also Commercial Recordings*

## Shattered Records
PO Box 612
Belfast
BT1 6DT
T general@shatteredrecords.com
F shatteredrecords.com
*Co-Managing Director* Christopher P Kamar

## Sheepfold
37 South Rd
Bishop's Stortford
Herts
CM23 3JQ
T 01297 659155/01920 462210    F 01920 461187
*Contact* Paul Burrell

## Sheer Bravado Records
East Garth
Far Lane
Waddington
Lincs
LN5 9QG
T 01522 72837
*Managing Director* Vince Ford

## Shifty Disco Ltd
OMC Suite 1
Floor 2, 65 George St
Oxford
OX1 2BE
**T** 01865 798791   **F** 01865 798792
**E** info@shiftydisco.co.uk   **W** shiftydisco.co.uk
*Contact* Andy Clyde

## Shima Uma
Bret Court
Bretton Industrial Estate
Saville Town
Dewsbury
West Yorkshire
WF12 0BB
**T** 01924 464646   **F** 01924 464666
**E** qc@post.almac.co.uk
*Contact* Jon Crabtree

## Shinkansen Recordings
PO Box 14274
London
SE11 6ZG
**T** 020 7582 2877   **F** 020 7582 3342
**E** shink@dircon.co.uk   **W** shink.dircon.co.uk
*Contact* Matt Haynes

## Shock Records
PO Box 5242
Brinklow
Milton Keynes
MK7 8YR
**T** 01908 639908   **F** 01908 378072
**E** graham@shockrecords.co.uk
**W** shockrecords.co.uk
*Contact* Graham Young

## Sick Slut Recordings
Brewmasters House
91 Brick Lane
London
E1 6QN
**T** 020 7375 2332   **F** 020 7375 2442
*A&R* Gary Dedman

## Silent Groove Records
Unit 37
Swingfield House
Templecombe Rd
London
E9 7LX
**T** 020 7525 5848   **F** as telephone
**E** info@silentgroove.com   **W** silentgroove.com

## Silva Screen Records
3 Prowse Place
London
NW1 9PH
**T** 020 7428 5500   **F** 020 7482 2385
**E** info@silvascreen.co.uk
*Managing Director* Reynold da Silva

## Silver Planet Recordings
PO Box 23038
London
W11 2WH
**T** 020 8964 8802   **F** 020 8964 3551
**E** recordings@silverplanet.freeserve.co.uk
**W** silverplanetrecordings.com
*A&R Manager* Dave Conway
*Legal and Business Affairs* Henriette Amiel
*Promotions* Nick Cave
*Management* Dave Conway and Henriette Amiel

*Progressive house ( James Holden, Timo Maas' Mad Dogs, Main Element, King of Spin, Chimera & Sadie Glutz)*
*Subsidiaries: Easyaccess Recordings (progressive house), Planet Breakz (breakz), Blue Planet Recordings (electronica)*
*Also Silver Planet Management ( James Holden, Gwill Morris, King of Spin)*

## Silverwood Music Group
Crickhowell
Powys
NP8 1LB
**T** 01873 810142   **F** 01873 811557   **E** silvergb@aol.com
*Managing Director* Kevin Holland King

## Silverword Music Group
16 Limetrees
Llangattock
Crickhowell
Powys
NP8 1LB
**T** 01873 810142/07798 915060   **F** 01873 811557
**E** silvergb@aol.com
*Contact* Kevin Holland King

## Simply Vinyl Ltd/Simply 12 Ltd
65 Duke St
London
W1M 5DH
**T** 020 7408 0683/8521 2626   **F** 020 7499 0485
**E** info@simplyvinyl.com   **w** simplyvinyl.com
*Managing Director* Mike Loveday
*Head of A&R* Ian Dewhirst
*Label Manager* Mike Morrison
*Administration and Enquiries* Lisa Rodgers

*Simply Vinyl Ltd: Specializing in the re-issue of
albums on 180 gm vinyl LPs
Simply 12 Ltd: Specializing in classic 12" singles from
the 70s–90s*

## Siren Music Ltd
37 Colwyn Rd
Hartlepool
Cleveland
TS26 9AS
**T** 01429 424603   **F** as telephone
**E** dave@revival-music.demon.co.uk
**w** siren-music.demon.co.uk
*Directors* Pete Duncan and Dave Hill

## Sixo7 Music Ltd
65 Barnsbury St
London
N1 1EJ
**T** 020 7607 2706   **F** 020 7607 8007
**E** info@607music.com   **w** 607music.com
*Directors* Vojkan Brankovic, Lee Haynes, Ian
Robinson, Ritu Singh

*Internet and traditional record label*

## Skindependent
Leacroft
Cheriton Cross
Cheriton Bishop
Exeter
Devon
EX6 6JH
**T** 01647 24502/07867 788729
**E** charlie@supanet.com   **w** lizardsun-music.co.uk
*Contact* Charles Salt

*See also Charles Salt Management (same contact details)*

## Skinny Malinky
Unit 36, Buspace Studios
Conlan St
London
W10 5AP
**T** 020 8969 1600   **E** etc@smr.aol.com
*Managing Director* Joel Brandon

## Slalom Recordings
1 Mill Cottage
Midford
Bath
BA2 7DE
**T** 01225 840715   **F** as telephone

## SLAM Productions
3 Thesiger Rd
Abingdon
Oxon
OX14 2DX
**T** 01235 529012   **F** as telephone
**E** slamprods@aol.com   **w** members.aol.com/
slamprods
*Contact* George Haslam

*Specializing in modern jazz
Artists from USA, UK, Europe and Argentina*

## Slamm Records
Unit 107
1st Floor, 146 Curtain Rd
London
EC2A 3AR
**T** 020 8300 5510

## Slate Records

PO Box 173
New Malden
Surrey
KT3 3YR
**T** 020 8949 7730   **F** 020 8949 7798
**E** johnosb1@aol.com
*Contact* John Osborne

## Smitten Frenzy Ltd

The Old Truman's Brewery
91 Brick Lane
London
E1 6QN
**T** 020 7377 5155   **F** 020 7377 5559
**E** steves@smitten.ndirect.co.uk
*Contact* Steven Smith

## Snapper Music

3 The Coda Centre
189 Munster Rd
London
SW6 6AW
**T** 020 7610 0330   **F** 020 7386 7006
**E** sales@snappermusic.co.uk
**W** snappermusic.com
*Chief Executive Officer* Jon Beecher
*A&R Director* Dougie Dudgeon

## Solent Records

PO Box 22
Newport
Isle of Wight
PO30 1LZ
**T** 01983 524110   **F** 0870 164 0388
**E** solrec@solentrecords.co.uk
**W** solentrecords.co.uk
*Contact* John Waterman

*Mainly mainstream music from artists based in the south of England*

## Soma Quality Recordings

2nd Floor, 22 Jamaica St
Glasgow
G1 4DD
**T** 0141 572 1477   **F** 0141 572 1478
**E** info@somarecords.com   **W** somarecords.com
*Managing Director* Dave Clarke

## Sonar Records

82 London Rd
Coventry
West Midlands
CV1 2JT
**T** 024 7622 0749   **F** 024 7625 7255
*Label Manager* Jon Lord

## Songlife Records

15 St John's Church Rd
Folkestone
Kent
CT19 5BQ
**T** 01303 257714/257285   **E** songlife@btinternet.com
*Managing Director* V Woodward

## Songlines Ltd

PO Box 20206
London
NW1 7FF
**T** 020 7284 3970   **F** 020 7485 0511
**E** doug@songline.demon.co.uk
*Managing Director* Doug D'Arcy

## Sony Music Entertainment (UK) Ltd

10 Great Marlborough St
London
W1V 2LP
**T** 020 7911 8200   **F** 020 7911 8600
*Chairman/Chief Executive Officer* Paul Burger

*Also Sony Soho Square (S2): same address*

## Sorted Records

The Durham Ox
Bowling Green St
Leicester
LE1 6AS
**T** 0116 225 42793   **W** dspace.dial.pipex.xom/town/estate/nigel.t/sorted.h
*Contact* Dave Dixey

## Soul Jazz Records Ltd

12 Ingestre Place
London
W1F 0JF
**T** 020 7734 3341   **F** 020 7494 1035
**E** mailorder@soundsoftheuniverse.com
**W** soundsoftheuniverse.com
*Contact* Angela Scott

## Soul Rooms, The
22 Jamaica St
Glasgow
G1 4QD
**T** 0141 572 0068    **F** 0141 572 0069
*Contact* JoJo Gould

## Sound and Media
Unit 3
Wells Place
Gatton Park Business Centre
Battlebridge Lane
Redhill
Surrey
RH1 3DR
**T** 01737 644445/644443    **F** 01737 646213/644310
**E** philw@soundandmedia.co.uk
*Managing Director* Phil Worsfold
*Sales Manager* Paul Chantry
*Procurement Director* Oliver Lamberti

## Sound Culture
PO Box 656
Belfast
BT9 5HX
**T** 028 90 299844/028 90 299845    **F** 028 90 299846
**E** gsheppard@ntlworld.com
*Managing Director* Gerard Sheppard

*Also event promoter and artist management*

## Sound Entertainment Ltd
The Music Village
Osiers Rd
London
SW18 1NL
**T** 020 8874 8444    **F** 020 8874 0337
**E** info@soundentertainment.co.uk
**W** soundentertainment.co.uk
*Contact* Bob Nolan

*Also deal in audiobooks (mainly comedy on CD and cassette)*

## Sound Moves (UK) Ltd
Unit 6
Armadale Rd
Feltham
Middx
TW14 0LW
**T** 020 8831 0500    **F** 020 8831 0520

**E** ballpark@soundmoves.co.uk
*Contact* Martin Corr

## Soundclash
Unit 1
Union Bridge Mill
Roker Lane
Pudsey
West Yorkshire
LS28 9LE
**T** 0113 255 9905    **F** 0113 255 9903
**E** a-m-o-s@dial.pipex.com
*Contact* Moose

## Soundclash
28 St Benedicts St
Norwich
Norfolk
NR2 4AQ
**T** 01603 761004    **F** 01603 762248
**E** soundclash@btinternet.com
**W** soundclash.cwc.net
*Managing Director* Paul Mills

## Soundscape Music
34 Edward Rd
Farnham
Surrey
GU9 8NP
**T** 01252 721096    **F** 01252 733909
**E** bobholroyd@soundscapemusic.co.uk
**W** soundscapemusic.co.uk
*Contact* Bob Holroyd

*Specializing in ambient, world and dance music*

## Soundtrack Music Records
25 Ives St
London
SW3 2ND
**T** 020 7590 2800    **F** 020 7823 7086
**E** info@soundtrackcom.co.uk
*Contact* Olav Wyper

## Soundwaves

The Old Dairy
Charles St
Droylsden
Greater Manchester
M43 6HD
**T** 0161 370 6908   **F** 0161 371 8207

## SoundWorld

2 Rosslyn Hill
London
NW3 1PH
**T** 020 8909 9639   **F** 020 7433 1775
*Contact* Troy Banarzi

## Soup Records

50a Canalot Studios
222 Kensal Rd
London
W10 5BN
**T** 020 8960 6969   **F** 020 8960 0505
**E** alistair@souprecords.com   **W** souprecords.com

## Source Records

113–117 Farringdon Rd
London
EC1R 3BX
**T** 020 7841 0150   **F** 020 7833 9702
**E** info@aloneinlondon.net   **W** sourcelab.net
*Managing Director* Philippe Ascoli

*Roster includes Kings of Convenience, Gemma
Hayes, Luca, Simian etc*

## Southbound Records Ltd

9 Wadley Rd
London
E11 1JF
**T** 020 8556 3575   **F** 020 8532 8614
**E** jeffrey@southboundrecords.com
**W** southboundrecords.com
*Managing Director* Jeffrey Strothers

## Southside Collective Records

299 Camberwell New Rd
London
SE5 0TF
**T** 020 7703 1001   **F** 020 7703 7799
**E** southside@imperialgardens.co.uk

## Sovereign Music

The Coach House
345 Jockey Rd
Sutton Coldfield
West Midlands
B73 5XD
**T** 0121 321 2212   **F** 0121 355 8929
*Contact* Mike Gibbs

## Space Age Recording

PO Box 8
Corby
Northants
NN17 2XZ
**T** 01536 202295   **F** 01536 266246
**E** steve@adasam.demon.co.uk
**W** adasam.demon.co.uk
*Label Manager* Steve Kalidoski

*Also Them's Good Records (same details)*
*Also 3rd Stone (same details)*

## Spacefunk Recordings

12 Southam St
London
W10 5PH
**T** 020 8960 3253   **F** 020 8968 5111
**E** info@spacefunk.com   **W** spacefunk.com

## Spectrum Music

1 Sussex Place
London
W6 9XS
**T** 020 8910 5000   **F** 020 8910 5039
**E** silvia.montello@music.com
*Senior Product Manager* Silvia Montello

## Sperm Records

The Sperm Bank
28–30 Wood Wharf
Horseferry Place
London
SE10 9BT
**T** 020 8293 3345   **E** andy@yumyum.demon.co.uk
**W** sperm.demon.co.uk
*Label Manager* Andy Chatterley

## Spin It Records

13 High Rd
Willesden Green
London
NW10 2TE
T 020 8459 0761   F 020 8459 7464
E sales@spinitrecords.co.uk   W spinitrecords.co.uk
Contact P J Wagstaff

Chart, R&B, mail-order, accessories, house and
garage, promos

## Splash Records

29 Manor House
Marylebone Rd
London
NW1 5NP
T 020 7723 7177   F 020 7262 0775/7724 6295
E splashrecords.uk@btinternet.com
Contact Chas Peate

## Split Records

13 Sandys Rd
Barbourne
Worcester
WR1 3HE
T 01905 29809   F 01905 613023
E split.music@virgin.net   W splitmusic.com
Head of A&R Chris Warren

## Sprawl

63 Windmill Rd
Brentford
Middx
TW8 0QQ
T 020 8568 3145   F as telephone
E douglas@benfo.demon.co.uk
W dfuse.com/sprawl
Contact Douglas Benford

## Spring Recordings

Dargan House
Duncairn Terrace
Bray
Co. Wicklow
Ireland
T 00 353 1 286 8175   F 00 353 1 286 1514
E atrisk@iol.ie   W mrspring.net
Contact Mr Spring or Sean Brennan

## Springthyme Records

Balmalcolm House
Balmalcolm
Cupar
Fife
KY15 7TJ
T 01337 830773   F 01337 831773
E music@springthyme.co.uk
W springthyme.co.uk
Director Peter Shepheard

Specialists in Scottish folk and ytraditional music

## Square Biz Records

65a Beresford Rd
London
N5 2HR
T 020 7354 0841   F 020 7503 6457
E sujiro.gray@btinternet.com
Managing Director J Gray

## Square Root

Fernbank Studios
Bonnings Lane
Barrington
Ilminster
Somerset
TA10 0JN
T 01460 55747   F 01460 53396
E gb2@gbsquared.demon.co.uk
Contact Ronnie Gleeson

## Squashed Frog Records

2A Downing St
Ashton-under-Lyne
OL7 9LR
T 0161 292 9493   F 0161 344 1673
E pincer@pincermetal.com   W pincermetal.com
Managing Director D Murphy

Rock and heavy metal music
Squashed Frog Records is the home of metal band
Pincer

## Sraffito Records

Le Tone House
270 Watford Way
London
NW4 4UJ
T 020 8203 1988   F 020 8203 7178
A&R Danny Marshall

## SSU Records

Sunnyside House
22 Grand Union Centre
West Row
London
W10 5AS
**T** 01708 473473   **F** 01708 473540
**W** sunnysideup.co.uk/ssu/
*A&R Director* K Young

## State Art

The Basement
3 Eaton Place
Brighton
East Sussex
BN2 1EH
**T** 01273 572090   **F** as telephone
**E** stateart@tinyonline.co.uk
**W** mexone.50megs.com
*Contact* Paul Mex

*Esoteric alternative music label*

## State Records

6 Kenrick Place
London
W1U 6HD
**T** 020 7486 9878   **F** 020 7486 9934
**E** recordings@staterecords.co.uk
**W** staterecords.co.uk
*Managing Director* Wayne Bickerton

## Steel Trax Recordings

Steel House
17–19 Westfield Terrace
Sheffield
South Yorkshire
S1 4GH
**T** 0114 272 0349/07702 627017   **F** as first telephone
*Contact* Keith Watkins

## Steppin' Out Music Ltd

PO Box 130
Hove
East Sussex
BN3 6QU
**T** 01273 550088   **F** 01273 540969   **W** mistral.co.uk/
tko
*Contact* Howard Kruger

*NB: Back catalogue and licensing only. No new artists*

## Steralized Decay Productions

PO Box 16
Barrow-in-Furness
Cumbria
LA14 3GH
**T** 01924 473625   **F** goblin@sardu.demon.co.uk

## Stern's Records

74–75 Warren St
London
W1P 5PA
**T** 020 7387 5550   **F** 020 7388 2756
**E** info@sternsmusic.com   **W** sternsmusic.com
*Managing Director* Don Bay
*A&R* Trevor Herman

## Sticky Music

PO Box 176
Glasgow
G11 5YS
**T** 01698 207230   **F** 0141 576 4753
**E** charlie@stickymusic.co.uk   **W** stickymusic.co.uk
*Contact* Charlie Irvine

*Also Sticky Kids, cassettes for the under 5s*

## Stiff Records

42–46 St Luke's Mews
London
W11 1DG
**T** 020 7221 5101   **F** 020 7221 3374
*Contact* Paul Bedford

## Stig (Europe)

Stig House
19 York Rd
Chorlton
Greater Manchester
M21 9HP
**T** 0161 860 4753/020 8568 1641   **F** 0161 862 9602

**Stillwater Records**
PO Box 19
Ulverston
Cumbria
LA12 9TF
**T** 01229 581766   **F** as telephone
*Managing Director* J G Livingstone

**Stranded Records**
24/3 Loganlea Drive
Edinburgh
EH7 6LG
**T** 0131 661 8326
*Managing Director* L A Nicol

**Strange Fruit Records**
333 Latimer Rd
London
W10 6RA
**T** 020 8964 9544   **F** 020 8964 5460
**E** sfm@strange-fruit-music.co.uk
*Label Manager* Sue Armstrong

**Strathan Media Productions**
32 Strathan
Lochinver
Sutherland
IV27 4LR
**T** 01571 844747   **F** 01571 844769
*Director* Karen Brimm

**Stream Records (Disabled Artists' Specialists)**
77a Hindmans Rd
London
SE22 9NQ
**T** 020 8299 2998   **F** 020 8693 0349
**W** colloquim.co.uk/thewilderness.stream
*Co-ordinator* Genie Cosmas

**Streamline Music Ltd**
40 Sciennes
Edinburgh
EH9 1NH
**T** 0131 668 3366   **F** 0131 662 4462
*Contact* Gordon Campbell

**Street Culture Records**
PO Box 262
Chatham
Kent
ME4 6DF
**T** 01634 814119   **F** 01494 433191
**E** mailbox@streetculture.com
**W** streetculture.com
*Contact* Chris Bloomfield

**Streetfighter Records**
Unit 222
Canalot Studios
222 Kensal Rd
London
W10 5BN
**T** 020 7565 2229   **F** 020 7565 2228
*Contact* Frankie Foncett

**Stress Recordings**
PO Box 89
Slough
Berks
SL1 8NA
**T** 01628 667124   **F** 01628 669783/667057
**E** info@dmcworld.demon.co.uk
**W** stressrecords.com
*Label Manager* Nick Darby

**Strike Back Records**
271 Royal College St
London
NW1 9LU
**T** 020 7482 0115   **F** 020 7267 1169
**E** maurice@baconempire.com
*Managing Director* Maurice Bacon

**Stringbean International Records**
Unit 19
2nd Floor, 2–8 Fountayne Rd
London
N15 4QL
**T** 020 8885 3020   **F** as telephone
**E** stringbeaninternational.records@btinternet.com
*Contact* Fitzroy Bailey

## Structure Recordings

PO Box 26273
London
W3 6FN
T 0870 207 7720   F 0870 208 8820
E sound@structure.co.uk   W structure.co.uk
*Contact* Olly Groves

*See also XS Music (same contact details)*

## Strut

2 Hargrave Place
London
N7 0BP
T 020 7485 7855   F 020 7284 1151
E info@strut.co.uk   W strut.co.uk
*Managing Director* Quinton Scott

*Specializing in back catalogue dance music, quality
soul, funk, disco, afrobeat compilations and single
artist retrospectives
Subsidiary: Afrostrut, for African funk catalogue*

## Sublime Recordings

65 Overdale Rd
London
W5 4TU
T 020 8840 2042   F 020 8840 5001
E info@sublimemusic.co.uk
W sublimemusic.co.uk

## Subsymphonic

143 West Vale
Neston
South Wirral
Cheshire
CH64 0TJ
T 0151 336 6657   E andy@subsymphonic.com
W subsymphonic.com
*Contact* Andy Williams

## Subversive Records

16 Chalk Farm Rd
London
NW1 8AG
T 020 7209 2626   F 020 7209 0202
E daniel@subversiverecords.co.uk
W subversiverecords.co.uk
*Contact* Daniel Pope

## Subway Organization, The

100b Huddleston Rd
London
N7 0EG
T 020 7272 6894   F as telephone
E martinw@netcomuk.co.uk
*Contact* Martin Whitehead

## Sugar Records

249 Kensal Rd
London
W10 5DB
T 020 8964 4722   F 020 8968 1929
W sugar-records.demon.co.uk
*Contact* Paul Hitchman

## Summer of Love Records

Piglet Productions
PO Box 3126
London
NW3 1LY
T 020 7431 6286   F 020 7431 6295
W gbdirect.co.uk/ents/fab-gere
*Contact* Mike Southon

## Summerhouse Records

PO Box 34601
London
E17 6GA
T 020 8520 2650   F 01909 500880
E office@summerhouserecordsltd.co.uk
W summerhouserecordsltd.co.uk
*Contact* William Jones

## Sunflower Records

PO Box 11732
London
N2 8AA
T 020 8435 9468/7482 5555
*Contact* Bruce Fisher

## Survival Records

PO Box 888
Maidenhead
Berks
SL6 2YQ
T 01628 788700   F 01628 788950
E survivalrecords@globalnet.co.uk
W capercaillie.co.uk
*A&R* David Rome

## Suspended State Records

5 Doverfield Rd
London
SW2 5NE
**T** 020 8671 2310   **F** as telephone
**E** jon@suspendedstate.freeserve.co.uk
**W** mp3.com/whailguru
*Contact* Jon Izbell

## SVA Records

Unit 37
Swingfield House
Templecombe Rd
London
E9 7LX
**T** 020 7525 5848   **F** as telephone
**E** info@svarecords.com   **W** svarecords.com

## Sweet FA Records Ltd

Chester Terrace
358 Chester Rd
Manchester
M16 9EZ
**T** 0161 872 6006   **F** 0161 972 6468
*A&R Director* Nathan Neill Conroy

## Sylvantone Records

17 Allerton Grange Way
Leeds
West Yorkshire
LS17 6LP
**T** 0113 268 7788   **F** 0113 266 0220
**E** tonygoodacre (or sylvantone)@hotmail.com
**W** countrymusic.org.uk/tony-goodacre/index
*Proprietor* Tony Goodacre

*Country music specialist*

## SYME International Records

81 Park Rd
Wath-upon-Dearne
Rotherham
South Yorkshire
S63 7LE
**T** 01709 877920   **F** 01709 873119/0870 1640589
**E** syme@csi.com
*Director* Martin E Looby

## Symposium Records

110 Derwent Avenue
East Barnet
Herts
EN4 8LZ
**T** 020 8368 8667   **F** as telephone
**E** symposium@cwcom.net
**W** symposiumrecords.co.uk

*Classical specialist in the re-issue of carefully
engineered important historical and rare recordings
dating from the late 19th and early 20th centuries*

## Tailormade Music Ltd

27 Howard Business Park
Howard Close
Waltham Abbey
Essex
EN9 1XE
**T** 01992 763222   **F** 01992 763463
*Directors* Edward Short, Dan Donnelly

## Tanty Records

PO Box 557
Harrow
Middx
HA2 8QE
**T** 020 8864 4394/07802 463154   **F** 020 8933 1027
**E** kelvin.r@tantyrecord.com   **W** tantyrecord.com
*Label Manager* Kelvin Richard

## Tara Music Company Ltd

8 Herbert Lane
Dublin 2
Ireland
**T** 00 353 1 678 7871   **F** 00 353 1 678 7873
**E** info@taramusic.com   **W** taramusic.com
*Managing Director* John Cook

## Taste Media Ltd

1 Prince of Wales Passage
117 Hampstead Rd
London
NW1 3EF
**T** 020 7388 8635   **F** 020 7387 0233
**E** sjpdodgy@easynet.co.uk   **W** sjpdodgy.co.uk
*Proprietor* Safta Jaffery

## Taste the Music
12 Kenneth Court
173 Kennington Rd
London
SE11 6SS
**T** 020 7582 6959   **F** 020 7793 0285
**E** tastethemusic@musiclikedirt.demon.co.uk
*Contact* Patrick Meads

## Taurus Records (UK)
128 and a half Anerley Rd
London
SE20 8DL
**T** 020 8778 2019   **F** as telephone
*Contact* Shola Adedayo

## Telstar Records Ltd
107 Mortlake High St
London
SW14 8HQ
**T** 020 8878 7888   **F** 020 8878 7886
**E** information@telstar.co.uk   **W** telstar.co.uk
*Managing Director*, Record Labels: Jeremy Marsh

## Tema International
151 Nork Way
Banstead
Surrey
SM7 1HR
**T** 01737 219607   **F** 01737 219609
**E** music@tema-intl.demon.co.uk
**W** tema-intl.demon.co.uk
*Contact* Tony Evans

## Temple Records
Shillinghill
Temple
Midlothain
EH23 4SH
**T** 01875 830328   **F** 01875 830392
**E** robin@templerecords.demon.co.uk
**W** rootsworld.com/temple
*Managing Director* Robin Morton

## That's Entertainment Records Ltd
107 Kentish Town Rd
London
NW1 8PB
**T** 020 7485 9593   **F** 020 7485 2282

**E** john@jayrecords.com   **W** jayrecords.com
*Contact* John Yap

*Also Jay Productions Ltd*

## Theobald Dickson Productions
The Coach House
Swinhope Hall
Swinhope
Market Rasen
Lincs
LN8 6HT
**T** 01472 399011   **F** 01472 399025
*Contact* Bernard Theobald

## This Way Up
22 St Peters Square
London
W6 9NW
**T** 020 8910 3283   **F** 020 8910 3293
*Contact* David Bedford

## Thunderbird Records
9 Park End St
Oxford
OX1 1HH
**T** 01865 204066   **F** 01865 204099
**E** mark@thunderbird.co.uk   **W** thunderbird.co.uk
*Managing Director* Mark Stratford

## Tidalwave Direct
Unit 83
Millmead Business Centre
Millmead Rd
London
N17 9QU
**T** 020 8493 8848/8808 6565   **F** 020 8493 8858
*Contact* Roger Greenidge

## Tidy Trax
Room 909
Fitzwilliam St
Parkgate
Rotherham
South Yorkshire
S62 6EP
**T** 020 8874 7877/01709 521801   **F** 020 8870 8170/
01709 523141   **E** simon@tidytrax.yahoo.com
**W** tidytrax.co.uk
*Director* Andy Pickles

*Label Manager* Simon Paul

## Timbre Ltd
PO Box 3698
London
NW2 6ZA
**T** 0709 202 1943   **F** as telephone
**E** info@timbre.co.uk   **W** timbre.co.uk
*Contact* Diane M Hinds

## Timbuktu Music Ltd
99c Talbot Rd
London
W11 2AT
**T** 020 7471 3656   **F** 020 7471 3630
**E** mark.bond@vsmusic.com
*General Manager* Mark Bond

## Time Universal Recordings/Univista Records
14 Jesmond Avenue
Wembley
Middx
HA9 6EA
**T** 020 8902 9023   **F** as telephone
**W** timeuniversal.co.uk and univesta.co.uk
*Contact* David Mclaverty

*Soulful/vocal garage, some R&B*

## Timewarp Records
80 St John's Hill
London
SW11 1SF
**T** 020 7738 9488   **F** 020 7738 2278
**E** timewarp@dircon.co.uk
**W** tunes.co.uk/timewarp
*Contact* Bill Shannon

## TKO Magnum Music
Magnum Distribution Centre
Pilot Trading Estate
West Wycombe Rd
High Wycombe
Bucks
HP12 3AB
**T** 01494 450606   **F** 01494 450230
**E** music@tkomagnum.co.uk   **W** tkomagnum.co.uk
*Joint Chief Executive* Nigel Molden

*See also Magnum Distribution (distribution company)*

## TMR Records
PO Box 3775
London
SE18 3QR
**T** 020 8316 4690   **F** as telephone
**E** marc@wufog.freeserve.co.uk
**W** wufog.freeserve.co.uk
*Managing Director* Marc Bell
*Contact* Marc Bell or Neelu Berry

## Toff Records – Pendragon
Fairfields
Ascot Rd
Warfield
Berks
RG42 6HS
**T** 01344 884704   **F** 01344 893693
**E** toff@pndragon.demon.co.uk   **W** toffrecords.com
*General Manager* Nick Barrett

*Specializing in progressive rock; main artist Pendragon*

## Tommy Boy
3rd Floor, 151 Freston Rd
London
W10 6TH
**T** 020 7313 8300   **F** 020 7792 9519
**E** richard.chamberlain@tommyboy.com
**W** tommyboy.com
*Managing Director* Richard Chamberlain
*Press* Sandra Scott

## Tony Bramwell Records
9 Brooking Barn
Ashprington
nr Totnes
Devon
TQ9 7UL
**T** 01803 732137   **F** as telephone
**E** bramwell@netlineuk.net

**Tony Savage Records**
21 Eaton Rd
Margate
Kent
CT9 1BX
**T** 01843 220765
*Contact* T & M Savage

**Too Much Records**
2nd Floor, 29 Prince's St
London
W1R 7RG
**T** 020 7734 9964    **F** 020 7734 1197
**E** harvey@fujint.co.uk
*Label Manager* Harvey Leonard

**Too Pure**
3a Highbury Crescent
London
N5 1RN
**T** 020 7609 2415    **F** 020 7609 9244
**E** toopure@toopure.demon.co.uk    **W** toopure.com
*Managing Director* Nick West

**Topic Records**
50 Stroud Green Rd
London
N4 3EF
**T** 020 7263 1240    **F** 020 7281 5671
*Managing Director* Tony Engle

**TOV (Trouble on Vinyl) Music Group**
120 Wandsworth Rd
London
SW8 2LB
**T** 020 7498 3888    **F** 020 7207 1221
**E** info@tovmusic.com    **W** tovmusic.com
*Managing Director*s: Clayton Hines and Mark Hill

*Specializing in underground drum 'n' bass*

**Transient Records**
Unit 129, The Canalot Centre
222 Kensal Rd
London
W10 5BN
**T** 020 8964 8890    **F** 020 8960 5741
**E** mail@transient.com    **W** transient.com
*Contact* Russel Coultart
*A&R* Glenn Mack

*Established 1994*
*Specializing in progressive and psychedelic trance*
*Roster inlcudes Astral Projection, Cosmosis*

**Transmission Recordings Ltd**
Bedford House
88 Berkeley Gardens
London
W8 4AP
**T** 020 7243 2921    **F** 020 7243 2894
**E** notting@netcomuk.co.uk
*Contact* Peter Chalcraft

**Treasure Island Recordings Ltd**
2 St Mobui Drive
Glasnevin
Dublin 9
Ireland
**T** 00 353 1 284 6336    **F** 00 353 1 280 0743
**E** treasureislanddiscs@tinet    **W** treasureisland.ie
*Contact* Robert Stephenson

**Trial Records**
Unity House
19a Hunts Hill
Glemsford
Suffolk
CO10 7RL
**T** 01787 881887    **F** as telephone
*Contact* Stephen Guy-Clarke

**Triple A Multimedia Group Ltd/Triple A Records Ltd**
GMC Studio
Hollingbourne
Kent
ME17 1UG
**T** 01622 880599    **F** 01622 880020
**E** records@triple-a.uk.com    **W** triple-a.uk.com
*Contact* Terry Armstrong

*Comprising seven media-related companies revolving*
*around the Armstrong Multimedia Arts Academy.*
*Each company is student-driven*

## Triple Earth Records

PO Box 240
Wembley
Middx
HA0 4FX
**T** 020 8922 7216　**E** iain@triple-earth.co.uk
*Managing Director* Iain Scott

*Preferred music: African, Latin, Asian, world*


## Triple XXX Recordings

PO Box 853
Wallington
Surrey
SM6 8UL
**T** 020 8773 0605　**F** as telephone
**E** info@triplexxx.co.uk　**w** triplexxx.co.uk
*Managing Director* Andy Neville

*Trance, progressive, hard house*
*See also Gecko Recordings Ltd at same address*


## Tripoli Trax

679 Holloway Rd
London
N19 5SE
**T** 020 7263 4660　**F** 020 7263 9669
**E** info@puregroove.co.uk　**w** puregroove.co.uk
*Managing Director* Tarik Nashnush
*A&R* Steve Thomas

*House label established in 1994*
*Roster includes Knuckleheadz, Mark Kavanagh,*
*Steve Thomas*
*Other affiliated labels: Locked On, Y2K*


## Trojan Recordings

Regent House
1 Pratt Mews
London
NW1 0AD
**T** 020 7267 6899　**F** 020 7267 6746
**w** trojan-records.com
*Contact* Frank Lea


## Tropical Fish

1 Pauntley House
Pauntley St
London
N19 3TG
**T** 020 7281 8683/07973 386 2/9　**F** as first telephone
*Contact* Grishma Jashapara


## Truelove Records

Unit G
44 St Paul's Crescent
London
NW1 9TN
**T** 020 7284 0434　**F** 020 7267 6015
**E** tlc@truelove.co.uk　**w** truelove.co.uk

*A collective of dance labels (house, trance and*
*techno) including TeC, Its Fabulous!, Kingpin, TLC*
*and (online only) Stay Up Forever, Cluster,*
*Maximum Minimum, Low Rent Operator,*
*Hydraulix, Yolk, 4x4, R.A.W., Blackout Audio*


## TSD Records

14 Coneycroft
Dunnington
York
YO19 5RL
**T** 01904 489337　**E** tsd-records@demon.co.uk
*Managing Director* T Dawton


## Tuff Twins Recordings

494 Archway Rd
London
N6 4NA
**T** 020 8340 5151　**F** 020 8340 5159
**E** carlpengelly@ukonline.co.uk
*Contact* Carl Pengelly


## Tumi Music

6 Westmoreland Station Rd
Bath
BA2 3HQ
**T** 01225 464736　**F** 01225 444870
**E** tumi.music@ndirect.co.uk　**w** tumidirect.com
*Contact* Peter Walmsley or Mo Fini


## TW Records

7 Argyle St
Bath
BA2 4BA
**T** 01225 331521
*Managing Director* Jenni Nicholson


## Tweed Records

14a Hornsey Rise
London
N19 3SB
**T** 020 7281 0018　**F** 020 7272 9609

**E** poppy@mailbox.co.uk   **W** poppy.com.uk
*General Manager* Tot Taylor


## Twenty Stone Blatt Records
Punk Rock HQ
PO Box 14911
Grangemouth
FK3 8WA
**E** briantsbb@hotmail.com


## Tylis Corporation Ltd
18 Buckingham Rd
Steeple Claydon
Bucks
MK18 2QB
**T** 01296 738474   **F** as telephone
*Managing Director* Mel Tyler


## UFG Records
1 Constance St
Knott Hill
Manchester
M15 4PS
**T** 0161 236 6616/07973 344 606   **F** 0161 228 2399
*Contact* Mike Kirwin


## UK Bonzai
5 Astrop Mews
London
W6 7HR
**T** 020 8746 4070   **F** 020 8746 4060
**E** bonzai@music-village.com
**W** bonzairecords.com
*Contact* Natalie Martin

*Also see Big Fish Music*


## Ultimate Dilemma
The Truman Brewery
91 Brick Lane
London
E1 6QN
**T** 020 7426 0268   **F** 020 7426 0269
**E** info@ultimate-dilemma.com
**W** ultimate-dilemma.com
*Managing Director* Max Lousada


## Undiscovered Recordings
41b British Grove South
London
W4 2PU
**T** 020 8748 1729   **F** as telephone
*Contact* A Bernado


## Unicorn-Kanchana Records
PO Box 339
London
W8 7SJ
**T** 020 7727 3881   **F** 020 7243 1701
*Contact* Nigel Brandt


## Union Records
5 Pelham Close
London
SE5 8LW
**T** 020 7733 0754   **F** as telephone
*Contact* Mike Lettman


## Union Square Music
Unit 2
Grand Union Office Park
Packet Boat Lane
Cowley
Uxbridge
UB8 2GH
**T** 01895 458515   **F** 01895 458516
**E** info@unionsquaremusic.co.uk
**W** unionsquaremusic.co.uk
*Managing Director* Peter Stack

*Specializing in re-issues and compilations*


## Unique Corp Ltd
15 Shaftesbury Centre
85 Barlby Rd
London
W10 6BN
**T** 020 8964 9333   **F** 020 8964 9888
**E** alanbellman@aol.com   **W** uniquecorp.co.uk
*Managing Director* Alan Bellman


## United Dance Recordings
PO Box 2851
Chelmsford
Essex
CM2 7QW
**T** 01245 322294

## United Nations Recordings

PO Box 20242
London
NW1 7FL
**T** 020 7485 1113    **E** proofsongs@mailbox.xo.uk

*See also Down By Law Records (label) and Proof
Songs (publisher)*

## Universal Egg

The Cottage
15 Overbury Rd
London
N15 6RH
**T** 020 8880 1926    **F** 020 8802 3100
**E** zt@wobblyweb.com    **W** wobblyweb.com
*Managing Director* Neil Perch

## Universal Records (Ireland)

9 Whitefriars
Aungier St
Dublin 2
Ireland
**T** 00 353 1 475 7700    **F** 00 353 1 475 7860
**E** dave.pennefather@umusic.com
*Deputy Managing Director* Dave Pennefather

## Universal/Island Records

22 St Peter's Square
London
W6 9NW
**T** 020 8910 3333    **F** 020 8748 0998
*Managing Director* Marc Marot

## Univista Records

14 Jesmond Avenue
Wembley
Middx
HA9 6EA
**T** 020 8902 9023    **F** as telephone    **W** univista.co.uk
*Contact* David Mclaverty

*Soulful vocal garage, some R&B*
*Also Time Universal Music (same contact details)*

## Unyque Artists

PO Box 1257
London
E5 0UD
**T** 020 8986 1984/07956 390206    **F** 020 8986 7451

**E** jastoy@compuserve.com
*Managing Director* Tee

## Upbeat Recordings Ltd

Sutton Business Centre
Restmor Way
Wallington
Surrey
SM6 7AH
**T** 020 8773 1223/8647 5275    **F** 020 8669 6752
**E** info@upbeat.co.uk    **W** upbeat.co.uk
*Managing Director and Executive Producer* Liz
Biddle

## Urban Collective Records

The Ready Rooms
Bedford St
Bere Alston
Devon
PL20 7DL
**T** urbancol@mail.znet.co.uk    **F** urbancol.com
*Contact* Peter Miller

## Urban Hero Records

505 Bristol Rd
Selly Oak
Birmingham
B29 6AU
**T** 0121 414 0240    **F** 0121 471 2070/3060
*A&R Managers* Phil Dockerty and Adam Presdee

## Urbcom

Studio 2
PO Box 13805
London
NW1 9WY
**T** 020 8768 7272    **F** 020 8768 9562
**E** urbcom@netlineuk.net
*A&R* J Van Hookens

## Usk Recordings

26 Caterham Rd
London
SE13 5AR
**T** 020 7274 5610/8318 2031    **F** 020 7737 0063
**E** info@uskrecordings.com    **W** uskrecordings.com
*Contact* Rosemary Lindsay

## Uxbridge Street
Onward House
11 Uxbridge St
London
W8 7TQ
**T** 020 7221 4275    **F** 020 7229 6893
*Contact* Pedro

## V2 Music Group Ltd
131–133 Holland Park Avenue
London
W11 4UT
**T** 020 7471 3000    **F** 020 7603 4796
**w** v2music.com
*Contact* Polly Birkbeck
*Chief Executive Officer* Jeremy Pearce
*General Manager* David Steele
*Head of Promotions* Neil Ashby

*Also V2 Records Ltd (same address/telephone)*

## Valentine Music Group, The
7 Garrick St
London
WC2E 9AR
**T** 020 7240 1628    **F** 020 7497 9242
**E** valentine@bandleader.co.uk
**w** bandleader.co.uk
*Managing Director* John Nice

## Vanity Label, The
PO Box 1071
Faringdon
Oxon
SN7 7XW
**T** 07721 618489    **F** 01793 784135
**E** perkins@satellite7.com    **w** satellite7.com
*Contact* Matt Perkins

## Veesik Records
Havelock Cottage
Back Charlotte Lane
Lerwick
Shetland
ZE1 0JD
**T** 01595 696622    **F** as telephone
**E** alan@veesikrecords.co.uk
**w** veesikrecords.co.uk
*Managing Director* Alan Longmuir

*Primarily the music of Shetland, from traditional to rock*
*See also Shetland Music Distribution Ltd*

## Verjam Records
Metro House
Northgate
Chichester
West Sussex
PO19 1BE
**T** 0870 1598694    **E** verjam.music@earlands.co.uk
*Contact* Roger James Verner

## Vicarage Records
PO Box 3115
Brighton
East Sussex
BN1 3SF
**T** 07971 839606/586001    **E** vicarage.records@virgin.net
*Contact* Nick Flint

## Viktor Records
Unit 213, The Saga Centre
326 Kensal Rd
London
W10 5BZ
**T** 020 8969 3370    **F** 020 8969 3374
**E** cs@streetfeat.demon.co.uk
*Contact* Colin Schaverien
*Managing Directors* Colin Schaverien, Simon Napier-Bell
*General Manager* Vicki Bannister

*Also Streetfeat Management*

## Vine Gate Music
4 Vine Gate
Parsonage Lane
Farnham Common
Bucks
SL2 3NX
**T** 01753 643696    **F** 01753 642259
**E** tonypuxley@vinegate.clara.net
**w** salenajones.co.uk
*Contact* Tony Puxley

## Vinyl Japan

98 Camden Rd
London
NW1 9EA
**T** 020 7284 0359   **F** 020 7267 5186
**E** office@vinyljapan.demon.co.uk
**W** vinyljapan.demon.co.uk
*Label Manager* John Whitfield

## Vinyl Solution

231 Portobello Rd
London
W11 1LT
**T** 020 7792 9791/07958 342494   **F** 020 7792 9871
**E** lilith@dircon.co.uk
*Contact* Julie Weir

*Also Visible Noise (same details)*

## Viper Records Ltd

45–53 Sinclair Rd
London
W14 0NS
**T** 020 7300 6561   **F** 020 7300 6560
**E** haydn@viperrecords.com
**W** sanctuarygroup.com
*Managing Director* John Williams

## Virgin Records

Kensal House
553–579 Harrow Rd
London
W10 4RH
**T** 020 8964 6000   **F** 020 8968 6533
**E** vrlpress@vmg.co.uk   **W** vmg.co.uk
*Media Director* Steve Morton
*Chairman and Chief Executive Officer* Ken Berry
*President, Virgin UK* Paul Conroy
*Senior A&R Director* David Boyd

## Virgo Records

208 Huyton Lane
Huyton
Merseyside
L36 1TQ
**T** 0151 489 6142   **F** as telephone
**E** mike@virgo-music.demon.co.uk
*Managing Director* Mike Walker

## Visible Noise

231 Portobello Rd
London
W11 1LT
**T** 020 7792 9791/07958 342494   **F** 020 7792 9871
**E** julie@visiblenoise.com   **W** visiblenoise.com
*A&R Manager* Julie Weir

*Specialists in metal, crossover and guitar-based genres*
*Roster includes Kill II This, Lostprophets and Kilkus*
*Linked to UK cult black metal label Cacophonous*

## Vision Discs

PO Box 92
Gloucester
Gloucs
GL4 8HW
**T** 01452 814321   **F** 01452 812106
*Managing Director* Vic Coppersmith-Heaven

## Vital Spark Records

1 Waterloo
Breakish
Isle of Skye
IV42 8QE
**T** 01471 822484/07768 031060   **F** 01471 822952
**E** chris@vitalspark.demon.co.uk
**W** surf.to/chrisrainbow
*Managing Director* Chris Harley

## Viva! Records

7a Colville Terrace
London
W11 2BE
**T** 020 7221 9300   **F** 020 7221 0088
*Director* Dave Morgan

## Vivid Records

Kingston Hill Centre
Kingston-upon-Thames
Surrey
KT2 7LB
**T** 020 8547 8169/8549 0014   **F** 020 8547 7337/8167
**E** info@vividrecords.com   **W** vividrecords.com
*Label Manager* Keith Wilson

## Voice of Shade

46 Spenser Rd
London
SE24 0NR
**T** 020 7274 6618   **F** 020 7737 4712
**E** vox@charm.demon.co.uk
*Label Manager* Crayola

## Voiceprint

PO Box 50
Houghton-le-Spring
Tyne & Wear
DH4 5YP
**T** 0191 512 1103   **F** 0191 512 1104/584 6792
**E** info@voiceprint.co.uk   **w** voiceprint.co.uk
*Label Manager* Rob Ayling

*Also distribution company*

## Voltone International Recordings

PO Box 12594
London
NW2 5WL
**T** 020 8357 4362   **F** 020 8357 2310
**E** paul@voltone.com   **w** voltone.com/
*Label Manager* Paul Caff

## Voluptuous Records

4th Floor, 40 Langham St
London
W1W 7AS
**T** 020 7323 4410   **F** 020 7323 4180
**E** carl@formidable-mgmt.com
*Contact* Carl Marcantonio

## Vulcan Entertainment

20 St Anne's Court
London
W1V 3AW
**T** 020 7437 8273   **F** 020 7734 1215
*Contact* Liz Reeves

## VX Recordings

PO Box 7888
London
SW19 1TN
**T** 020 8542 7278   **F** as telephone
**E** sales@v-x.co.uk   **w** v-x.co.uk/music
*Contact* John Pepper

## Wall of Sound Recordings

Office 2, 9 Thorpe Close
London
W10 5XL
**T** 020 8969 1144   **F** 020 8969 1155
**E** general@wallofsound.uk.com
**w** wallofsound.net
*Managing Director* Mark Jones

## Walt Disney Records

3 Queen Caroline St
London
W6 9PE
**T** 020 8222 1222   **F** 020 8222 1163
*Label Director* Patrick Wilson

## Ward Industries Ltd

Providence Rd
Brooks Rd
Raunds
Northants
NN9 6NS
**T** 01933 624963   **F** 01933 625458
**E** wardind1@aol.com
*Managing Director* Paul Cherrington

*Specializing in folk music*
*Main artist: Pamela Ward*

## Warner Music (Ireland)

Alexandra House
Earlsfort Centre
Earlsfort Terrace
Dublin 2
Ireland
**T** 00 353 1 676 2022   **F** 00 353 1 676 2602
*Contact* Dennis Woods

## Warner Music (UK)

The Warner Building
28 Kensington Church St
London
W8 4EP
**T** 020 7937 8844   **F** 020 7938 3901
**E** wmuk@wmintl.com   **w** warnermusic.co.uk
*Chairman* Nick Phillips

**Warp Records**
Spectrum House
32–34 Gordon House Rd
London
NW5 1LP
**T** 020 7284 8350   **F** 020 7284 8360
**E** info@warprecords.com   **W** warprecords.com
*Managing Directors*: Rob Mitchell and Steve
Beckett

*Roster includes Aphex Twin, Boards of Canada*
*See website before sending demo*


**Waveform Records**
27 Henniker Mews
London
SW3 6BL
**T** 020 8968 1001/07860 391902   **F** 020 8968 3201
**E** tonybyrne@compuserve.com
*Managing Director* Tony Byrne


**Way Out West Records**
16c Bolton Road
Chiswick
London
W4 3TB
**T** 020 8995 2462   **F** 020 8995 2462
**E** 100441.2547@compuserve.com
**W** wowrecords.co.uk
*Managing Director* Simon Davies


**We Love You Records**
Office 2, 9 Thorpe Close
London
W10 5XL
**T** 020 8969 1144   **F** 020 8969 1155
**E** darling@weloveyou.uk.com   **W** weloveyou.co.uk
*Contact* Jo Hillier
*Managing Director* Mark Jones


**WEA Records**
The Warner Building
28 Kensington Church St
London
W8 4EP
**T** 020 7937 8844   **F** 020 7937 6645/7938 3563
**W** wea.co.uk
*Managing Director* Moira Bellas
*Senior A&R Manager* Mike Peden
*Director of Press* Barbara Charone

**Weird and Wonderful**
Hiltongrove Business Centre
Hatherley Mews
London
E17 4QP
**T** 020 8921 2424   **F** 020 8521 4343
**E** guy@hiltongrove.com   **W** hiltongrove.com
*Contact* Guy Davis


**West 4 Tapes & Records**
105 Stocks Lane
Bracklesham Bay
West Sussex
PO20 8NV
**T** 01243 671238
*Managing Director* Kenneth G Roe


**Whipcord**
77 Whipcord Lane
Chester
CH1 4DG
**T** 07997 445565   **E** adam@whipcord-records.co.uk


**Whippet Records**
PO Box 72
York
YO31 1YU
**T** 01904 410038/423060   **F** as telephones
**E** wp@whiskypriests.co.uk   **W** whiskypriests.co.uk
*Managing Director* G Miller

*Roster: The Whisky Priests, Mad Dogs and*
*Englishmen*


**Whirlie Records**
14 Broughton Place
Edinburgh
EH1 3RX
**T** 0131 557 9099   **F** 0131 557 6519
*Contact* George Brown


**Whole Nine Yards, The**
PO Box 212
East Molesey
Surrey
KT8 9YN
**T** 01932 701643   **F** 01932 843072
**W** whole9yards.freeserve.co.uk
*Label Manager* Mark Pember

**Wide-Eyed Music**
24a Camden Rd
London
NW1 9DP
T 020 7482 5277   F 020 7267 3430
*Contact* Vid Lakhani

**Wienerworld Ltd**
Unit B2 Livingstone Court
55–63 Peel Rd
Wealdstone
Harrow
Middx
HA3 7QT
T 020 8427 2777   F 020 8427 0660
E wworld@wienerworld.com   W wienerworld.com
*Contact* Anthony Broza

*The leading independent music video and DVD
label, from rock to soul, country to reggae, hiphop to
R&B and garage to pop*

**Wiiija Records**
17–19 Alma Rd
London
SW18 1AA
T 020 8875 6300   F 020 8874 6600
E wiiija@almaroad.co.uk   W wiiija.com
*Label Head* Gary Walker

*Started in 1988 by Rough Trade (at
W11 1JA) with releases by Terminal Cheesecake,
Bastard Kestrel, Silverfish etc, moving on to the riot
grrrl movement, notably the label's stars Cornershop*

**Wild Abandon Ltd**
16 Pembridge place
London
W2 4XB
T 020 7792 5600   F as telephone
E gooner46@aol.com
*Director* Nigel Grainge

**Wildstar Records**
107 Mortlake High St
London
SW14 8HQ
T 020 8878 7888   F 020 8878 7886
E information@telstar.co.uk   W telstar.co.uk
*Managing Director* Jeremy Marsh

**Windsong in Concert**
33 Latimer Rd
London
W10 6RA
T 020 8964 9544   F 020 8964 5460
*Label Manager* Sue Armstrong

**Wing an' a Prayer**
21 Bowsprit Point
London
E14 8NT
T 020 7515 9289
*Contact* Andrew Skortis

**Wire Editions, The**
45–46 Poland St
London
W1F 7NA
T 020 7439 6422   F 020 7287 4767
E info@thewire.co.uk   W thewire.co.uk
*Contact* Tony Herrington

**Wizzard Records**
Cottons Farmhouse
Whiston Rd
Cogenhoe
Northants
NN7 1NL
T 01604 891487   F 01604 890405

**Wooded Hill Recordings**
Lister House
117 Milton Rd
Weston-super-Mare
Somt
BS23 2UX
T 01934 644309   F 01934 644402
E cliffd@globalnet.co.uk
*Contact* Cliff Dane

*A mid-price label specializing in folk and roots music
Includes subsidiary label Pier Music*

**Woodworm Records**
PO Box 37
Banbury
Oxon
OX16 8YN
F 01869 337142   W fairportconvention.co.uk
*Contact* Dave Pegg

**Word (UK) Music**
9 Holdom Avenue
Bletchley
Milton Keynes
Bucks
MK1 1QR
T 01908 648440    F 01908 648592
w wordonline.co.uk

**Workers Playtime**
64 Mountgrove Rd
London
N5 2LT
T 020 7359 2223    E info@workersplaytime.co.uk
w workersplaytime.co.uk
*Contact* Bill Gilliam

**Working Class Records Ltd**
28a High St
Ewell
Surrey
KT17 1RW
T 020 8786 8888    F 020 8786 8178
*Contact* Ian Wills

**World Circuit Records**
106 Cleveland St
London
W1P 5DP
T 020 7383 4907    F 020 7383 4908
E post@worldcircuit.co.uk    w worldcircuit.co.uk
*General Manager* Guy Morris

*Specializing in music from Cuba and West Africa*
*Voted label of the year 2000*
*Roster includes Orlando 'Cachaito' Lopez, Ibrahim*
*Ferrer and Ali Farka Toure*

**World Domination Productions Ltd**
PO Box 20426
London
SE17 1WS
T 020 7703 0200    F 020 7703 0355
E brian@alchemy1.demon.co.uk
*Contact* Brian Allen

**Wow Recording**
PO Box 3906
London
NW1 6BZ
T 020 8207 5909/7724 2471    F 020 8207 4058/
7724 6245

**Wrench Records**
BCM Box 4049
London
WC1N 3XX
F 020 7607 9580    E mail@wrench.org
w wrench.org
*Contact* Charlie Chainsaw

*NB: punk only!*

**Wrong Recordings**
27 Wallorton Gardens
London
SW14 8DX
F 020 8392 1422    E wrongans@mailcity.com
*Contact* Asad Rizvi

*London-based label specializing in deep and dark*
*tech-house*

**WSM (Warner Strategic Marketing)**
The Warner Building
28 Kensington Church St
London
W8 4EP
T 020 7368 2500    F 020 7368 2773

**WYZE Recordings**
34 Maple St
London
W1 5GD
T 07000 9993 100    F 07000 9993 200
E wyzeuk@aol.com
*Contact* Kate Ross

*Specialist dance management and production*
*company*

**X-traudio Music**
57 Muswell Hill
London
N10 3PN
T 020 8372 9182
*Managing Director* Stirling Cash

**X:treme Records**
1st Floor, 87 Wardour St
London
W1V 3TF
T 020 7437 1442    F 020 7437 1770
E xtremerecords@btconnect.com
W xtremerecords.com
*Contact* Tony Farrell

**Xenophile Records**
c/o 26 Milward Crescent
Hastings
East Sussex
TN34 3RU
T 01424 713904    F 01424 461224
E johncrosby@pressproms.demon.co.uk
*Contact* John Crosby

**XL Recordings Ltd**
1 Codrington Mews
London
W11 2EH
T 020 8870 7511    F 020 8871 4871
E jessicamackey@almaroad.co.uk
W xl@xlrecordings.com
*Label Co-ordinator* Jessica Mackey
*Managing Director* Richard Russell
*Director of A&R* Nick Worthington

**XS Music**
PO Box 26273
London
W3 6FN
T 0870 207 7720    F 0870 208 8820
E records@xs-music.com
*Chair* Jim Braithwaite
*Managing Director* Olly Groves

*See also Structure Recordings (same contact details)*

**Xsf Recordings**
39 Berwick St
London
W1F 8RU
T 020 7287 2496    F 020 7437 6255
E records@xsfrecord.com    W xsfrecord.com
*Label Manager* J Carlos Zaghis

**xtc uk**
PO Box 1797
London
E1 4TX
T 020 7702 7842    F 020 7790 0764
*Managing Director* Martin Picton

**Xtravaganza**
Unit 3d West Point
36–37 Warple Way
London
W3 0RG
T 020 8740 9700    F 020 8749 4738
*Contact* Alex Gold

**Y'Off!**
9f Arcinston House
All Saints Avenue
Margate
Kent
CT9 1XR
*Contact* Frank Foy

*Also TV & film music, songwriting*

**Yardbird Suite Records**
Unit 1, Union Bridge Mill
Roker Lane
Pudsey
West Yorkshire
LS28 9LE
T 0113 255 9905/230 2113    F 0113 255 9903
*Contact* Steve Mulhaire or Gip Dammone

**Year 3 Thousand**
11 Stainer St
London
SE1 9RL
T 020 7407 2744/07957 136199    F 020 7407 2544
E year3thousand@bigfoot.com
W jump.to/year3thousand
*Managing Director* Zachary Williams

**Yellow Balloon Records**
Freshwater House
Outdowns
Effingham
Surrey
KT24 5QR
T 01483 281500/281501    F 01483 281502

**E** yellowbal@aol.com
*Head of A&R* Daryl Smith

**York Ambisonic**
PO Box 66
Lancaster
Lancs
LA2 6HS
**T** 01524 823020 **F** 01524 824420
*Contact* Brendan Hearne

**Yoshiko Records**
Great Westwood
Old House Lane
Kings Langley
Herts
WD4 9AD
**T** 01923 261545 **F** 01923 261546
**E** info@yoshiko.box.co.uk
*Managing Director* Yoshiko Ouchi

**Yum Yum Records**
HMS President (1918)
nr Blackfriars Bridge
Victoria Embankment
London
EC4Y 0HJ
**T** 020 7583 0236 **F** 020 7583 7221
**E** musicbiz.info@dial.pipex.com
*General Manager* Zaffar Zaidi

**Z Records**
PO Box 58
Skelmersdale
WN8 8FN
**T** 01695 559882/0151 525 0099 **F** 01695 722398
**E** info.records@virgin.net **W** zrecords.net
*Contact* Mark Alger

*NB: deal only with the hard rock spectrum*

**Zane Records**
162 Castle Hill
Reading
Berks
RG1 7RP
**T** 0118 957 4567 **F** 0118 956 1261
**E** info@zanerecords.com **W** zanerecords.com
*Managing Director* Peter Thompson

*Specializing in roots music, mostly American blues, soul, cajun, R&B and singer/songwriters*

**Zeall.com Ltd**
47 Gap Rd
Wimbledon
London
SW19 8JE
**T** 020 8543 8994 **F** 020 8540 0392
**E** zeall@agendamedia.co.uk **W** zeall.com
*Directors* Steve Crickmer and Dave McGeachie

**Zerga Records Company Ltd, The**
PO Box 103
Pinner
Middx
HA5 3FR
**T** 020 8868 7408 **F** as telephone
**E** nicholasdicker@zerga.freeserve.co.uk
*Managing Director* Nicholas Dicker

**Zeus Records Ltd**
Gloucester House
68 Gloucester Rd
New Barnet
Herts
EN5 1NB
**T** 020 8441 7441 **F** 020 8441 7461
**E** info@zeusrecords.com **W** zeusrecords.com
*Contact* Ash White or D E King

**Zip Dog Records**
PO Box 3
Chesham
Bucks
HP5 1YL
**T** 020 8948 2320 **F** as telephone
**E** zipdog@compuserve.com **W** zipdog.com
*Contact* Stu Lambert

**Zircon Recordings**
Millmead Business Centre
Millmead Rd
London
N17 9QU
**T** 020 8493 0420 **F** 020 8801 0719
**E** zircon@zirc.demon.co.uk
*Contact* Roger Dopson

## Zok Records
106–114 Borough High St
London
SE1 1LB
**T** 020 7407 7604   **F** 020 7378 0200
*Contact* Mr Wheatley

## Zomba Records Ltd
Zomba House
165–167 Willesden High Rd
London
NW10 2SG
**T** 020 8459 8899   **F** 020 8451 3900
**E** postmaster@zomba.co.uk   **W** zomba.co.uk
*Directors* Clive Calder, Nick Howe, Steve Jenkins
*General Manager* Tina Wisby
*A&R* Scott MacLachlan, Dave Wibberley
*Head of Press and PR* Peter Berry

## Zone 6 Records Ltd
PO Box 6489
Birmingham
B42 7FD
**T** 0121 244 7386   **F** 0121 604 4754
**E** zone.6@virgin.net
*Contact* Jake Grants-George

## Zopf Records
2 Hippodrome Place
London
W11 4NG
**T** 020 7221 2361   **F** 020 7792 7855
**E** thetable@penguincafe.com   **W** penguincafe.com
*General Manager* Sallie Berriff

## ZTT Records
The Blue Building
42–46 St Luke's Mews
London
W11 1DG
**T** 020 7221 5101   **F** 020 7221 3374   **W** ztt.com
*Label Manager* Claire Moon
*A&R* Rob Adamson

## ZYX Records UK
11 Cambridge Court
210 Shepherds Bush Rd
London
W6 7NJ
**T** 020 7371 6969   **F** 020 7371 6688/6677

**E** lauren.lorenzo@zyxrecords.freeserve.co.uk
**W** zyx.de
*General Manager* Lauren Lorenzo

### A&R Music Publishing Ltd

2 Beulah Rd
London
SW19 3SB
T 020 8255 7775    F 020 8255 7776
E sir.harry@lineone.net
*Contact* Sir Harry

### Abyss Music

PO Box 1511
Ascot
Berks
SL5 9XH
T 01344 874677    F 01344 622376
*Contact* Brian Long

### Accolade Music

250 Earlsdon Avenue North
Coventry
West Midlands
CV5 6GX
T 02476 711935    F 02476 711191
*Managing Director* Graham Bradshaw

*Also Oblivion Music (same details)*

### Ace Eyed

2 Menelik Rd
London
NW2 3RP
T 020 7435 6116    F as telephone
E markalbert@bluemelon.co.uk
W bluemelon.co.uk and barbaracartland.com
*Contact* Mark Albert

### Acuff-Rose Music Ltd

25 James St
London
W1U 1AA
T 020 7486 2525    F 020 7486 2424
E tpeters@acuffroseltd.com
*General Manager* Tony Peters

### AD-Chorel Music

40 Sciennes
Edinburgh
EH9 1NH
T 0131 668 3366    F 0131 662 4463
E rel@relrecords.co.uk    W relrecords.co.uk
*Managing Director* Neil Ross

**Adtrax Ltd**
21 Cherbury Gardens
Booterstown
Co. Dublin
Ireland
**T** 00 353 1 283 5941   **E** picket@iol.ie
*Managing Director* Deke O'Brien

**AEI Music Ltd**
Forest Lodge
Westerham Rd
Keston
Kent
BR2 6HE
**T** 01689 882200   **F** 01689 882208
**W** aeimusic.com and aei.co.uk
*Music Programming and Broadcast Director* Andrew
Griffiths

**Ainm Music Publishers**
5–6 Lombard St East
Dublin 2
Ireland
**T** 00 353 1 677 8701   **F** as telephone
**E** fstubbs@ainm-music.com   **W** ainm-music.com
*Chief Executive Officer* Frank Stubbs

*Irish traditional and Irish dancing music*

**Air-Edel Associates**
18 Rodmarton St
London
W1H 3FW
**T** 020 7486 6466   **F** 020 7224 0344
**E** kelliott@air-edel.co.uk
*Contact* Karen Elliott

*Composer agent specializing in film, TV,
commercials and multi-media, publisher, music
supervision, research and clearance*

**Alarcon Music Ltd**
The Old Truman Brewery
91 Brick Lane
London
E1 6QN
**T** 020 7377 9373   **F** 020 7377 6523
**E** byron@b-k-o.demon.co.uk
*Contact* Byron Orme

**Albert J & Son (UK) Ltd**
8–10 Colebrooke Place
London
N1 8JD
**T** 020 7704 8888   **F** 020 7704 2244
**E** info@albertmusic.co.uk   **W** albertmusic.co.uk
*Contact* Sue Crawshaw

**All Around the World Music**
Munro House
High Close
Rawdon
West Yorkshire
LS19 6HF
**T** 01132 503338   **F** 01132 507343/01254 693768
**E** stewart@a-m-c.demon.co.uk
*Contact* Stewart Coxhead

**All Good Music (AGM)**
14 Lambton Place
London
NW1 8LH
**T** 020 7482 4345   **F** as telephone
*Managing Director and Head of A&R* Jon Sexton

**All Media Music Ltd**
61 Queen's Drive
London
N4 2BG
**T** 020 8802 5984   **F** 020 8809 7436
*Contact* Paul Rodriguez

**Alpadon Music**
Shendoah
Manor Park
Chislehurst
Kent
BR7 5QD
**T** 020 8295 0310   **F** 020 8295 0311
**E** don@dpap.demon.co.uk
*Managing Director* Don Percival

**Aluna Music Group**
31a The Parade
Claygate
Surrey
KT10 0PD
**T** 01372 465477   **F** as telephone
**E** Petergiles@alunamusic.com   **W** alunamusic.com
*Contact* Peter Giles

**Amazing Feet Publishing**
PO Box 2000
Oxford
OX1 2XX
**T** 01865 205600    **F** 01865 205700
**E** info@rotator.co.uk
*Contact* Richard Cotton

**Ambassador Music**
22 Denmark St
London
WC2H 8NA
**T** 020 7836 5996/7240 5349    **F** 020 7379 5205
**E** music@mautoglade.fsbusiness.co.uk
*Managing Director* Lee Pincus

**AMCO Music Publishing**
2 Gawsworth Rd
Macclesfield
Cheshire
SK11 8UE
**T** 01625 420163    **F** 01625 420168
**E** rogerboden@cottagegroup.co.uk
**W** cottagegroup.co.uk
*Managing Director* Roger Boden

**Amokshasong**
PO Box 102
London
E15 2HH
**T** 020 8555 5423    **F** 020 8519 6834
**E** amoksha@moksha.demon.co.uk
*Contact* Charles Cosh

**Ampersand Music**
33 Old Market St
Thetford
Norfolk
IP24 2EQ
**T** 01842 752697
*Managing Director* John Crisp

**Amphonic Music**
Kerchesters
Waterhouse Lane
Kingswood
Surrey
KT20 6HT
**T** 01737 832837    **F** 01737 833812
**E** ian@amphonic.co.uk    **W** amphonic.com

*Managing Director* Ian Dale

*Specialist in all types of production music, with own library*
*Demos with SAE accepted for consideration*

**Angel Sword Productions Ltd**
Little Barn
Plaistow Rd
Loxwood
West Sussex
RH14 0SX
**T** 01403 753564    **F** as telephone
**E** jonn@jonnsavannah.co.uk
**W** jonnsavannah.co.uk
*Contact* Jonn Savannah

**Anglia Music Company**
39 Tadorne Rd
Tadworth
Surrey
KT20 5TF
**T** 01737 812922    **F** as telephone
*Director and Company Secretary* Norma Camby

**Angus Publications**
14 Graham Terrace
London
SW1 8JH
**T** 07850 845280    **F** 020 7730 3368
**E** billpuppetmartin@ic24.net
*Contact* Bill Martin

*Former writing partner of Phil Coulter*
*Writer of many hits including 'Puppet on a String' and 'Congratulations'*

**April Music Ltd**
1st Floor, 754 Fulham Rd
London
SW6 5SH
**T** 020 7384 2232    **F** 020 7384 2272
*Contact* James Arlon

**Archway Music**
11 Mercatoria
St Leonards
East Sussex
TN38 0EB
**T** 01424 423636    **E** j.c.hamill@themail.co.uk

**w** clairehamill.co.uk
*Contact* Claire Hamill

## Arena Music Company
Unit 16
Hatch Farm
Chertsey Rd
Addlestone Moor
Addlestone
Surrey
KT15 2EH
**T** 01932 828715    **F** 01932 828717
*Managing Director* Brian Adams

## Aristocrat Music Ltd
Clarendon House
Shenley Rd
Borehamwood
Herts
WD6 1AG
**T** 020 8207 7006    **F** 020 8207 5460
*Managing Director* Terry King

## Ariwa Music
34 Whitehouse Lane
London
SE25 6RE
**T** 020 8653 7744/8771 1470    **F** 020 8771 1911
**E** info@ariwa.com    **w** ariwa.com
*Contact* Neil Fraser

## Arpeggio Music
Bell Farm House
Eton Wick
Windsor
Berks
SL4 6LII
**T** 01753 864910/884810
*Managing Director* Beverley Campion

## Artfield
5 Grosvenor Square
London
W1K 4AF
**T** 020 7499 9941    **F** 020 7499 9010
**E** artfield@dial.pipex.com    **w** artfieldmusic.com
*Managing Director* B B Cooper

*Film and TV themes, musical theatre, jazz, pop, rock, classical, ethnic*

## Ashley Mark Publishing Company
1–2 Vance Court
Trans Britannia Enterprise Park
Blaydon on Tyne
Tyne & Wear
NE21 5NH
**T** 0191 414 9000    **F** 0191 414 9001
**E** mail@ashleymark.co.uk    **w** fretsonly.com
*Managing Director* Maurice J Summerfield

*Also see Classical Guitar Magazine*

## Associated Music International Ltd
34 Salisbury St
London
NW8 8QE
**T** 020 7402 9111    **F** 020 7723 3064
**E** eliot@amimedia.co.uk    **w** amimedia.co.uk
*Managing Director* Eliot Cohen

*Also Satellite Music Ltd (same details)*
*Music library*

## Asterisk Music
Rock House
London Rd
St Mary's
Chalford
Gloucs
GL6 8PU
**T** 01453 886252    **F** 01453 885361
**E** rollerrec@aol.com
*Contact* John Beecher

*NB: Catalogue, not current material*

## Astwood Music Ltd
26 Astwood Mews
London
SW7 4DE
**T** 020 7565 9100    **F** 020 7565 9101
**E** dolanma@aol.com
*Contact* Mike Dolan

## Atlantic Seven Productions/Music Library Ltd
52 Lancaster Rd
London
N4 4PR
**T** 020 7263 4435    **F** 020 7436 9233/8374 9774
**E** musicproduction(or musiclibrary)@atlanticseven.com
*Contact* Patrick Shart

*Also publishing company Djanik Music and music productions/music consultant company Victory Entertainment Ltd (same contact details)*

## AudioMass
111 The Business Design Centre
52 Upper St
London
N1 0QH
T 020 7288 6048
*Contact* Robert Davis

## Automatic Songs Ltd
Unit 129
The Canalot Centre
222 Kensal Rd
London
W10 5BN
T 020 8964 8890    F 020 8960 5741
E autosong@transient.com
*Contact* Russel Coultart

*NB: dance music tracks only*

## Aviation Music Ltd
1 Pratt Mews
London
NW1 0AD
T 020 7267 6899    F 020 7267 6746
E partners@newman-and.co.uk
*Contact* Colin Newman

*Also Barn Publishing (Slade) Ltd, Morgan Music Co Ltd, New Town Sound Ltd, Panache Music, Russell Street Music Ltd, Maxwood Music Ltd, B&C Music Publishing Ltd and Whild John Music Ltd (same details)*

## B&H Productions
295 Regent St
London
W1R 8JH
T 020 7291 7222    F 020 7436 5675
E media@boosey.com    w boosey.com/media
*Contact* Chris Dobbs

## Bacon Empire Publishing Ltd
271 Royal College St
London
NW1 9LU
T 020 7482 0115    F 020 7267 1169
E maurice@baconempire.com
*Managing Director* Maurice Bacon

## Bad Habits Music Publishing
PO Box 111
London
W13 0ZH
T 020 8357 2337/07000 740 243    F 020 8566 7215/
0132 731 2545
E publishing@badhabitsent-group.com
w badhabitsent-group.com
*Contact* John S Rushton

## Baerenreiter
Burnt Mill
Elizabeth Way
Harlow
Essex
CM20 2HX
T 01279 828930    F 01279 828931
E baerenreiter@dial.pipex.com
w baerenreiter.com
*Contact* Christopher Jackson

## Bandleader Music
7 Garrick St
London
WC2E 9AR
T 020 7240 1628    F 020 7497 9242
E valentine@bandleader.co.uk
w valentinemusic.co.uk
*Managing Director* John Nice

*Publishers of military and wind band music
Part of Valentine Music Group*

## Banks Music Publications
The Old Forge
Sand Hutton
York
North Yorkshire
YO41 1LB
T 01904 468472    F 01904 468679
E banksramsay@cwcom.net
w banksmusicpublications.cwc.net
*Contact* Margaret Silver

**Bardis Music**
Glenageary Office Park
Glenageary
Co. Dublin
Ireland
**T** 00 353 1 285 8711    **F** 00 353 1 285 8928
**E** bardis@iol.ie
**W** homepages.iol.ie/bardis/index2.htm
*Managing Director* Peter Bardon

**Bare Tunes**
9 Warren Mews
London
W1P 5DJ
**T** 020 7387 6220    **F** 020 7388 8947
**E** bare.tunes@virgin.net
*Managing Director* Saul Galpern
*A&R* Vanessa Sanders

**Barking Green Music**
1 Star St
London
W2 1QD
**T** 020 7258 0093    **F** 020 7402 9238
**E** peter@playwrite.uk.com
*Contact* Peter Stretton

**Basement Music**
20 Cyprus Gardens
London
N3 1SP
**T** 020 8922 4908    **F** as telephone
**E** basementmusic@btintenret.com
*Contact* John Cefai

**Bathtub Music**
7 Argyle St
Bath
BA2 4BA
**T** 01225 331521
*Managing Director* Jenni Nicholson

**BBC Music Publishing (BBC Worldwide Ltd)**
BBC Bush House
PO Box 76
Strand
London
WC2B 4PH
**T** 020 7557 1330    **F** 020 7557 1339

**E** mike.cobb@bbc.co.uk
*Head of Music Publishing* Mike Cobb

**Beaney Ltd**
PO Box 445
Chobham
Surrey
GU24 YQ
**E** groove@internalbass.com    **W** internalbass.com

**Bearsongs**
PO Box 944
Birmingham
B16 8UT
**T** 0121 454 7020    **F** 0121 454 9996
**E** bigbearmusic@compuserve.com
**W** bigbearmusic.com
*Managing Director* Jim Simpson

**Beat That Music Ltd**
Independent House
54 Larkshall Rd
London
E4 6PD
**T** 020 8523 9000    **F** 020 8523 8888
**E** erich@independentmusicgroup.com
*Managing Director* Ellis Rich

*Also International Music Network Ltd, JSE Music
Publishing Ltd, Music 1 Ltd, R&E Music, Rolf Baierle
Music and Supreme Songs (same details)*

**Beechwood Music Ltd**
Littleton House
Littleton Rd
Ashford
Middx
TW15 1UU
**T** 01784 423214    **F** 01784 251245
**W** beechwoodmusic.co.uk
*Contact* Tim Millington

**Beijing**
105 Emlyn Rd
London
W12 9TG
**T** 020 8233 2877    **F** 020 8233 2879
**E** brianleafe@aol.com
*Owner* Brian Leafe

## Belsize Music

29 Manor House
Marylebone Rd
London
NW1 5NP
**T** 020 7723 7177   **F** 020 7262 0775/7724 6295
**E** belsizemmusic.uk@btinternet.com
*Contact* Chas Peate

## Big City Triumph Music

3 St Andrews St
Lincoln
LN5 7NE
**T** 01522 539883   **F** 01522 528964
*Managing Director* Steve Hawkins

## Big Life Music/Big Life Management

67–69 Chalton St
London
NW1 1HY
**T** 020 7554 2100   **F** 020 7554 2154
**E** biglife@biglife.co.uk   **w** biglife.co.uk
*Managing Directors* Jazz Summers and Tim Parry

## Big Picture Music

118–120 Wardour St
London
W1F 0TU
**T** 020 7494 0011   **F** 020 7494 0111
**E** big.picture@boosey.com   **w** booseymedia.com
*Contact* Abigail Rossi

*Part of the BooseyMedia Group*

## Big Shot Music Ltd

PO Box 14535
London
N17 0WG
**T** 020 8376 1650   **F** 020 8376 8622
**E** info@p-ingram.supanet.com

*All musical styles*

## Biswas Music/Digger Music

24 Pepper St
London
SE1 0EB
**T** 020 7928 9777   **F** 020 7928 9222
*Managing Director* Guy Rippon

## Blaster! Music

77 Nightingale Shott
Egham
TW20 9SU
**T** 01784 741613   **F** 01784 741529
**E** martinw@netcomuk.co.uk
*Contact* Martin Whitehead

*Specialists in indie pop and rock*

## Blow Up Songs (Publishing)

24 Pancras Rd
London
NW1 2TB
**T** 020 7837 0099   **F** 020 7837 1166
**E** webmaster@blowup.demon.co.uk
*Contact* Paul Tunkin

## Blue August Music Ltd

35 Manstead Gardens
Romford
Essex
RM6 4ED
**T** 020 8590 2524   **F** as telephone
*Contact* John McDonald

## Blue Melon Music Publishing

2 Menelik Rd
London
NW2 3RP
**T** 020 7435 6116   **F** as telephone
**E** steveglen@appleonline.net   **w** bluemelon.co.uk
*Contact* Steven Glen

*Also Blue Planet Music and Paradise Line Music
(same details)*

## Blue River

Dublin Rd
Monasterevin
Co. Kildare
Ireland
**T** 00 353 45 525009   **F** 00 353 45 525810
**E** hazelmusic@tinet.ie
*Contact* John Kelly

## BMG Music Publishing Ltd
Bedford House
69–79 Fulham High St
London
SW6 3JW
T 020 7384 7600   F 020 7384 8167
*A&R MD* Paul Curran
*Director of A&R* Ian Ramage
*Marketing Manager* Annie Woolf

*Also BMG Music Publishing International (Fax: 020 7384 8162)*

## BMG Production Music
Bedford House
69–79 Fulham High St
London
SW6 3JW
T 020 7384 8188   F 020 7384 2744
E production.music@bmg.co.uk
W bmgprodmusic.com
*Head of Sales and Marketing* Mark Poole

## BMG Manchester
Unit 207
Ducie House
Ducie St
Manchester
M1 2JW
T 0161 236 5324   F 0161 236 4268
E caroline.elleray@bmg.co.uk
*Contact* Caroline Elleray

## BMP (Broken Music Publishing)
Riverbank House
1 Putney Bridge Approach
London
SW6 3JD
T 020 7371 0022   F 020 7371 0099
E ripe@compuserve.com
*Managing Director* Jurgen Dramm

## Bocu Music Ltd
1 Wyndham Yard
Wyndham Place
London
W1H 2QF
T 020 7402 7433
*Directors* Carole Broughton and John Spalding

*Also Prestige Music Ltd (same details)*
*NB: no unsolicited material*

## Bonskeid Music (Castlesound Studios)
44 Beauchamp Rd
Edinburgh
EH16 6LU
T 0131 666 1024   F as telephone
E info@castlesound.co.uk   W castlesound.co.uk

*Fully equipped professional recording studio with Neve 72-channel console, 48-track Radar II Hard Disk, 24-track Studer 2" analogue etc*

## Boomerang Music Publishing Co Ltd
54 Carlton Place
Glasgow
G5 9TB
T 0141 418 0053   F 0141 418 0054
*Contact* Frank Shapiro or Steve Gilmour

## BooseyMedia
295 Regent St
London
W1B 2JH
T 020 7291 7222   F 020 7436 5675
E booseymedia@boosey.com   W booseymedia.com
*Contact* Abigail Rossi

*See also Big Picture Music*
*Part of the Boosey & Hawkes Group, leading classical music publishers*
*BooseyMedia commissions and produces music for radio, film, new media and TV*

## Bop Top Music Publishing
65 Ash Tree Rd
Crumpsall
Manchester
M8 5SA
T 0161 795 9018/6467

## Boulevard Music Publishing
16 Limetrees
Llangattock
Crickhowell
Powys
NP8 1LB
T 01873 810142   F 01873 811557   E boulegb@aol.com
*Contact* Kevin Holland King

## Bourne Music
Suite C, 1st Floor
Standbrook House
2–5 Old Bond St
London
W1X 3TB
T 020 7493 6412    F 020 7493 6583
*Contact* Maxine Harrison

## Tony Bramwell
9 Brooking Barn
Asprington
nr Totnes
Devon
TQ9 7UL
T 01803 732137    F as telephone
E bramwell@netlineuk.net

## Brand New Music Ltd
20 Rydens Park
Walton-on-Thames
Surrey
KT12 3DP
T 01932 221727    F as telephone
*Managing Director* Mike Vernon

## Breakin' Loose
32 Quadrant House
Burrell St
London
SE1 0UW
T 020 7633 9576/07721 065618
W thefoundations.co.uk
*Managing Director* Steve Bingham

## Kitty Brewster Songs
Norden
2 Hillhead Rd
Newtonhill
Stonehaven
Kincardine & Deeside
AB39 3TS
T 01569 730962    F as telephone
*Managing Director* Doug Stone

## Briar Music
5–6 Lombard St
Dublin 2
Ireland
T 00 353 1 677 4229/9762    F 00 353 1 671 0421

E lunar@indigo.ie
*Managing Director* Brian Molloy (founding
Director of Today FM, Ireland's only national
commercial radio station)

*Also Squirrel Music, Lunar Records and Westland
Studios (same contact details)*

## Bright Music Ltd
PO Box 4536
Henley-on-Thames
RG9 3YD
T 01189 401780    F 07070 622034
E m-bright@dircon.co.uk
*Managing Director* Martin Wyatt

## Brightly Music
231 Lower Clapton Rd
London
E5 8EG
T 020 8533 7994/07973 616342    F 020 8986 4035
E abrightly@yahoo.com    W chimesbar.com

## Britton Music
The Powder Keg
Chesley Hill
Wick
Bristol
BS15 5NE
T 0117 904 1389
*Contact* Alan Britton

## BRM Music Publishing Ltd
89a High Rd
London
N22 6BB
T 020 8881 6969    F 020 8888 1685
E info@brmmusic.com    W brmmusic.com
*Contact* Bruce Ruffin

## Broadley Music (Int)
Broadley House
48 Broadley Terrace
London
NW1 6LG
T 020 7258 0324    F 020 7724 2361
E ellis@broadleystudios.com
W broadleystudios.com
*Managing Director* Ellis Elias

*Also Broadley Music Library (same details – General Manager* Manny Elias)

**Brothers Records Ltd**
The Music Village
11b Osiers Rd
London
SW18 1NL
**T** 020 8870 0011   **F** 020 8870 2101
**E** info@the-brothers.co.uk
*Director*s Ian Titchener and Nick Titchener
*General Manager* Jo Underwood

**Broughton Park Music**
Kennedy House
31 Stamford St
Altrincham
Cheshire
WA14 1ES
**T** 0161 941 4560   **F** 0161 941 4199
**E** harveylisberg@aol.com
*Contact* Harvey Lisberg

*Also Music Trunk Publishing Company Ltd (same details)*

**BTW Music**
106 Westpole Avenue
Cockfosters
Herts
EN4 0BB
**T** 020 8449 6110   **F** as telephone
*Partner* John Borthwick

**Bill Buckley Music**
Saunders
Wood & Co
The White House
140a Tachbrook St
London
SW1V 2NE
**T** 020 7821 0455   **F** 020 7821 6196
*Contact* Nigel J Wood

**Bucks Music Group**
Onward House
11 Uxbridge St
London
W8 7TQ
**T** 020 7221 4275   **F** 020 7229 6893
**E** info@bucksmusicgroup.co.uk
**W** bucksmusicgroup.com
*Director* Simon Platz

**Budding Music**
'Leigh'
Brompton Ralph
Taunton
Somerset
TA4 2SF
**T** 01984 623968   **F** 01984 62311
*Contact* John Marshall

**Bug Music Ltd**
31 Milson Rd
London
W14 0LJ
**T** 020 7602 0727   **F** 020 7603 7483
**E** info@bugmusic.co.uk   **W** bugmusic.com
*Managing Director* Mark Anders

*Specialists in administration of a songwriter's catalogue, enabling the writer to retain ownership*
*Many styles of music represented*
*Creative departments for pitching songs as covers, film and TV, ads etc*

**Bugle Songs Ltd**
1 Water Lane
London
NW1 8NZ
**T** 020 7267 1101   **F** 020 7267 8879
*Contact* Andy Graham

**Bulk Music Ltd**
9 Watt Rd
Hillington Park
Hillington
Glasgow
G52 4RY
**T** 0141 882 9060/9986   **F** 0141 883 3686
**E** krl@krl.co.uk   **W** krl.co.uk/bulk
*Managing Director* Gus McDonald

**Bull-Sheet Music**
18 The Bramblings
London
E4 6LU
**T** 020 8529 5807   **F** as telephone
*Managing Director* Irene Bull

## Bullseye Music
AIR House
Spennymoor
Co. Durham
DL16 7SE
**T** 01388 814632   **F** 01388 812445
**E** air@agents-uk.com   **w** airagency.com
*Contact* John Wray

## Burning Petals Music Ltd
Greyhound House
George St
Richmond
Surrey
TW9 1HY
**T** 020 7691 7620   **F** 020 7691 7621
**E** richard@burning-petals.com
**w** burning-petals.com
*Contact* Richard Jay

*World music specialists*

## Bushranger Music
86 Rayleigh Rd
Hutton
Brentwood
Essex
CM13 1BH
**T** 01277 222095   **E** kathlist@aol.com
*Managing Director* Kathy Lister

## Campbell Connolly & Co
8–9 Frith St
London
W1V 5TZ
**T** 020 7434 0066   **F** 020 7439 2848
**E** chris.butler@musicsales.co.uk
**w** musicsales.co.uk
*Contact* Chris Butler

## Candid Music
16 Castelnau
London
SW13 9RU
**T** 020 8741 3608   **F** 020 8563 0013
**E** candid_records@compuserve.com
**w** candidrecords.com
*Contact* Nieves Pascua-Bates

*Jazz, blues, film, R&B, Latin*

## Candle
44 Southern Row
London
W10 5AN
**T** 020 8960 0111/07860 912192   **F** 020 8968 7008
**E** mail@candle.org.uk   **w** candle.org.uk
*Contact* Tony Satchell

*All styles of commissioned music for TV, radio and cinema commercials, TV and film music, CD Rom and website music, video animatics and off-line digital editing*
*Composers/ Producers: Charlie Spencer, Philip Thurston, Ian Ritchie, John Thomas*
*Studios with ProTools etc*

## Cara Music
The Studio
3c Wilson St
London
N21 1BP
**T** 020 8447 8882   **F** 020 882 7679
*Director* Michael McDonagh

## Cargo Music Publishing
39 Clitterhouse Crescent
London
NW2 1DB
**T** 020 8548 1020   **F** as telephone
*Managing Director* Mike Carr

## Caritas Music Publishing
28 Dalrymple Crescent
Edinburgh
EH9 2NX
**T** 0131 667 3633   **F** as telephone
**E** caritas@caritas-music.co.uk   **w** caritas-music.co.uk
*Proprietor* Katharine H Douglas

*Also labels Caritas, Caritas Classics and Caritas Media Music*

## Carlin Music Corporation
Iron Bridge House
3 Bridge Approach
London
NW1 8BD
**T** 020 7734 3251   **F** 020 7439 2391
**E** (firstname)(lastname)@carlinmusic.com
**w** carlinmusic.com
*Managing Director* David Japp

## Carnaby Music

78 Portland Rd
London
W11 4LQ
**T** 020 7727 2063  **F** 020 7229 4188
*Director* Charles Negus-Fancey

*Also Glissando Music (same details)*

## Castle Hill Music

2 Laurel Bank
Lowestwood
Huddersfield
Yorkshire
HD7 4ER
or
PO Box 7
Huddersfield
HD7 4YA
**T** 01484 846333  **F** as telephone
**E** hotleadrec@lineone.net  **W** fimusic.co.uk
*Managing Director* Ian R Smith

*Soul, reggae, indie pop, Europop, country, rock,
R&B, bluegrass, MOR, adult contemporary, blues
Associate companies: Reggae Giant (UK), Bobbysox
Music Int'l (USA)*

## Cavendish Music Ltd

295 Regent St
London
W1R 8JH
**T** 020 7291 7222  **F** 020 7436 5675
**E** cavendish@boosey.com  **W** booseymedia.com
*Contact* Ann Dawson, Abigail Rossi, Mike Shaw

## Celtic Moon Label, The

Suite 9
Horseshoe Business Park
Upper Lyne Lane
Bricket Wood
St Albans
Herts
AL2 3TA
**T** 01923 893333  **F** 01923 894911
**E** celtic.moon@virgin.net
*Director* Joe Palmer

## Frank Chacksfield Music

8–9 Frith St
London
W1V 5TZ
**T** 020 7434 0066  **F** 020 7439 2848
*Managing Director* Robert Wise

## Champion Music

181 High St
London
NW10 4TE
**T** 020 8961 5202/7442  **F** 020 8961 6665/8965 3948
**E** info@championrecords.co.uk
**W** championrecords.co.uk
*Managing Director* Mel Medalie

## Chantelle Music

3a Ashfield Parade
London
N14 5EH
**T** 020 8886 6236
*Managing Director* Riss Chantelle

## Charisma Music Publishing Co Ltd

25 Ives St
London
SW3 ND
**T** 020 7590 2600  **F** 020 7584 5774
*Managing Director* Jon Crawley

## Charly Publishing Ltd

Suite 379
37 Store St
London
WC1E 7BS
**T** 07050 136143  **F** 07050 136144
*Contact* Jan Friedmann

## Chart Music Company Ltd

Island Cottage
Rod Eyot
Wargrave Rd
Henley-on-Thames
Oxon
RG9 3JD
**T** 01491 412946  **F** 01491 574361
**E** 101363.1404@compuserve.com
*Director* J W Farmer

## Chelsea Music Publishing Co Ltd

124 Great Portland St
London
W1N 5PG
T 020 7580 0044   F 020 7580 0045
E eddie@chelseamusicpublishing.com
W chelseamusicpublishing.com
*Managing Director* Eddie Levy

*Pop, jazz, dance, MOR*


## Cherrysongs Music Publishing

50 Cumbrian Way
Millbrook
Southampton
Hants
SO16 4AU
T 023 8078 0627   F 023 8052 8342
*Owner* Jeff Cherrington


## Chester Music

8–9 Frith St
London
W1V 5TZ
T 020 7434 0066   F 020 7287 6329
E music@musicsales.co.uk   W musicsales.co.uk
*Managing Director* J T C Rushton


## Chestnut Music

Wishanger Lane
Churt
Farnham
Surrey
GU10 2QJ
T 01252 794253   F 01252 792642
E keynote@dial.pipex.com
*Managing Director* Tim Wheatley


## Chisholm Songs

36 Follingham Court
Drysdale Place
London
N1 6LZ
T 020 7684 8594   F 020 7684 8740
*Contact* Desmond Chisholm


## Christabel Music

32 High Ash Drive
Alwoodley
Leeds
West Yorkshire
LS17 8RA
T 0113 268 5528   F 0113 266 5954
*Contact* Jeff Christie


## Christel Music Ltd

Fleet House
173 Haydons Rd
London
SW19 8TB
T 020 8241 6351   F 020 8241 6450
E christel@cableinet.co.uk
W wkweb4.cableinet.co.uk/abcde/lnson.htm
*Contact* Dennis Sinnott


## Chrome Dreams

PO Box 230
New Malden
Surrey
KT3 6YY
T 020 8715 9781   F 020 8241 1426
E rob@chromedreams.co.uk
W chromedreams.co.uk
*Contact* Rob Johnstone


## Chrysalis Music Ltd

The Chrysalis Building
13 Bramley Rd
London
W10 6SP
T 020 7221 2213   F 020 7465 6178 (a&r)
E clairea@chrysalis.co.uk   W chrysalis.co.uk
*Managing Director* Jeremy Lascelles
*General Manager* Catherine Bell
*General Manager, A&R* Paul Kinder


## Chuckle Music

6 Northend Gardens
Kingswood
Bristol
BS15 1UA
T 0117 983 7586   F as telephone
E peter@records22.freeserve.co.uk
*Managing Director* Peter Michaels

## CLM

153 Vauxhall St
The Barbican
Plymouth
Devon
PL4 0DF
**T** 01752 667100  **F** 01752 224281
**E** robhancock@lineone.net
*Partner* Rob Hancock

## Club Jamin

44 Lupton St
London
NW5 2HT
**T** 020 7482 5042/7607 6459  **F** as first telephone
*Contact* Lee Hudson

## CMA Publications

10 Avenue Rd
Kingston
Surrey
KT1 2RB
**T** 020 8541 0857  **F** 020 8974 8120
**E** grp@cma-publications.co.uk
**w** cma-publications.co.uk
*General Manager* Geraldine Russell-Price

*Instrumental music: orchestral, wind band, wind &*
*brass ensembles*

## Cold Harbour Recording Company

1 York St
London
W1U 6PA
**T** 020 7486 2248  **F** 020 7486 8515
**E** chrc@eatcentralone.com
*Contact* Steve Fernie

*Also east central one (label) and Creature Music*
*Limited (label for Manfred Mann's Earth Band):*
*same Contact details*

## Barry Collings Entertainments

21a Clifftown Rd
Southend-on-Sea
Essex
SS1 1AB
**T** 01702 330005  **F** 01702 333309
**E** bcollnet@aol.com
*Contact* Barry Collings

## Come Again Music

48 Broadley Terrace
London
NW1 6LG
**T** 020 7258 0324  **F** 020 7724 2361
**E** manny@broadleystudios.com
**w** broadleystudios.com
*General Manager* Manny Elias

## Complete Music

3rd Floor, Bishops Park House
25–29 Fulham High St
London
SW6 3JH
**T** 020 7731 8595  **F** 020 7371 5665
**E** complete@complete.ftech.co.uk
**w** complete-music.co.uk
*Managing Director* Martin Costello

## Concord Partnership, The

5 Bushey Close
Old Barn Lane
Kenley
Surrey
CR8 5AU
**T** 020 8660 4766/3914  **F** 020 8668 5273
**E** concordptnrship@aol.com

*Holding company for The Concord Music Hire*
*Library (Contact: Ray Lee/tel: 020 8660 4766/fax:020*
*8668 5273/e-mail:concordmusichire@aol.com),*
*Maecenas Music Ltd (Contact: Maggie Barton/tel:*
*020 8660 3914/fax: 020 8668 5273/e-mail:*
*maecenasmusicltd@aol.com), Maecenas*
*Contemporary Composers Contact: Giles*
*Easterbrook/tel, fax: as Concord/e-mail:*
*maecenascontemp@aol.com), and Camford Summer*
*School of Music (Contact: Malcolm Binney/tel, fax:*
*as Concord/e-mail: camfordsummersch@aol.com)*

## Confetti Publishing

PO Box 11541
London
NW1 4DW
**T** 020 8801 6760  **F** 020 8808 4413

## Congo Music Ltd

17a Craven Park Rd
London
NW10 8SE
**T** 020 8961 5461  **F** as telephone

E congomusic@hotmail.com
w musiclinks.com/congo
*Managing Director* Byron Lye-Fook

## Connect 2 Music Ltd
20 Woodlands Rd
Bushey
Herts
WD2 2LR
T 01923 244673   F 01923 244693
E info@connectmusic.com   w connectmusic.com
*Managing Director* Barry Blue

*Specialists in production music and commissions for
film, TV and media worldwide*

## Paul Cooke Music/88interactive.com
6 Cheyne Walk
Hornsea
East Yorkshire
HU18 1BX
T 01964 533982/07971 841995   F 01964 536022
E paul@88interactive.com   w 88interactive.com
*Secretary* Sue Cooke

*Mainly audio-visual distribution via the Internet and
the production of electronic music using computers*

## Copasetik Music Ltd
14 Lambton Place
London
W11 2SH
T 020 7482 4345/03706 15930   F 020 7482 4350
E copasetik1@aol.com   w copasetik.com
*Managing Director and Head of A&R* Jon Sexton

*Also Creamy Groove Machine Music (same details)*

## Cordella Music Ltd
Croakers Hatch
Manor Rd
Chilworth
Hants
SO16 7JE
T 08450 616616/07831 456348   F 02380 768929
E barryupton@cordellamusic.co.uk
w cordellamusic.co.uk
*Contact* Barry Upton

## Cramer Music
23 Garrick St
London
WC2E 9RY
T 020 7240 1612   F 020 7240 2639
*Managing Director* Peter Maxwell

## Crashed Music
162 Church Rd
East Wall
Dublin 3
Ireland
T 00 353 1 856 1011   F 00 353 1 856 1122
E shay@crashedmusic.com   w crashedmusic.com
*Managing Director* Shay Hennessy

## Creole Music Ltd
The Chilterns
France Hill Drive
Camberley
Surrey
GU15 3QA
T 01276 686077   F 01276 686055
E creole@clara.net
*Director* Bruce White

## Cruz Music
21b Heathmans Rd
London
SW6 4TJ
T 020 7736 1777   F 020 7736 1555
E darah@dial.pipex.com
*Contact* David Howells

## CTV Music
The Television Centre
St Helier
Jersey
Channel Islands
JE1 3ZD
T 01534 816816   F 01534 816778
E broadcast@channeltv.co.uk   w channeltv.co.uk
*Contact* Gordon de Ste. Croix

## David Cunningham Music
Minton House
263 Hartshill Rd
Hartshill
Stoke on Trent
Staffs
ST4 7NQ
**T** 01782 410237    **F** as telephone
*Contact* David Cunningham

## Cutting Edge Music (Holdings)
43–45 Beak St
London
W1R 3LE
**T** 0207 439 2119    **F** 0207 439 2169
*Chief Executive Officer* Phillip Moross
*General Manager* John Boughtwood

## Cwmni Cyhoeddi Gwynn Cyf
Y Gerlan
Heol y Dwr
Penygroes
Caernarfon
Gwynedd
LL54 6LR
**T** 01286 881797    **F** 01286 882634
**w** gwynn.co.uk
*Contact* Wendy Jones

## Cyhoeddiadau Sain
Canolfan Sain
Llandwrog
Caernarfon
Gwynedd
LL54 5TG
**T** 01286 831111    **F** 01286 831497
**E** music@sain.wales.com    **w** sain.wales.com
*Contact* Dafydd Iwan

## Daisy Music
Onward House
11 Uxbridge St
London
W8 7TQ
**T** 020 7221 4275    **F** 020 7229 6893
*General Manager* Debi McGrath

## Danceline
8 Stoney Lane
Rathcoole
Co. Dublin
Ireland
**T** 00 353 1 458 0578    **F** 00 353 1 627 4404
*Managing Director* Eddie Joyce

## Darah Music
21c Heathmans Rd
London
SW6 4TY
**T** 020 7731 9313    **F** 020 7731 9314
**F** david.howells@darah.co.uk
*Contact* David Howells

## Dazed Music
Onward House
11 Uxbridge St
London
W8 7TQ
**T** 020 7221 4275    **F** 020 7229 6893
*Contact* Liz Gallacher or Debi McGrath

## DB Publishing Ltd
89a Leathwaite Rd
London
SW11 6RN
**T** 020 7924 1904
*Managing Director* Alastair Nicholas

*Small publisher attached to studio and production unit, interested in chart and dance material with cross-over potential*

## db Records
PO Box 19318
London
W4 1DS
**T** 020 8747 9911    **F** 020 8742 2443
**E** david@dbrecords.co.uk    **w** dbrecords.co.uk
*Contact* David Bates, Chris Hughes or Tom Friend
*Chairman* David Bates

## Decentric Music
12 Tideway Yard
125 Mortlake High St
London
SW14 8SN
**T** 020 8977 4616    **F** as telephone

*Contact* James Bedbrook

## Deceptive Music

The Sunday School
Rotary St
London
SE1 6LG
**T** 020 7620 3009   **F** 020 7928 9439
*Contact* Tony Smith

## Deconstruction Songs

Bedford House
69–79 Fulham High St
London
SW6 3JW
**T** 020 7384 7971   **F** 020 7384 8056
**E** fozia.shahabmg.co.uk
*Managing Director* Mike Sefton

## Dejamus Ltd

Suite 11, Accurist House
44 Baker St
London
W1U 7AZ
**T** 020 7486 5838   **F** 020 7487 2634
**E** dejamus@dejamus.co.uk
*Chairman* Stephen James
*Copyright Manager* Linda Watts

## Depotsound

12 Raddington Rd
London
W10 5TG
**T** 020 8968 1717   **F** 020 8968 0177
*Head of Finance and Business Affairs* Maxine Tate

*Music for TV and film*

## Diamond Publishing Group Ltd

45 St Mary's Rd
London
W5 5RQ
**T** 020 8579 1082   **F** 020 8566 2024

## Digger Music

34 Great James St
London
WC1N 3HB
**T** 020 7404 1422   **F** 020 7242 2555

**E** tills@globalnet.co.uk
*Contact* Tilly Rutherford

## Digital Pressure.com Inc

Peer House
12 Lower Pembroke St
Dublin 2
Ireland
**T** 00 353 1 662 9337   **F** 00 353 1 662 9339
**E** darragh@digitalpressure.com
**w** digitalpressure.com
*Vice President, Europe* Darragh M Kettle

*See also Peermusic (Ireland)*

## Dinosaur Music Publishing

PO Box 1685
Stoke-on-Trent
ST6 4RX
**T** 01782 839513   **F** as telephone
**E** songs@dinosaurmusic.co.uk
**w** dinosaurmusic.co.uk
*Managing Director* Alan E Dutton

## Diverse Music Ltd

95 Hawkesfield Rd
London
SE23 2TN
**T** 020 8291 3687   **F** 020 8699 1438
**E** diversemusicltd@compuserve.com
*Contact* Diana Graham

*Also Grapevine Music Ltd and Monument Music Ltd (same Contact details)*

## Dolphin Traders

Unit 4
Great Ship St
Dublin 8
Ireland
**T** 00 353 1 478 3455   **F** 00 353 1 478 2143
**E** irishmus@aol.ie   **w** dolphin-dara.ie
*Contact* David Cashell

*Contemporary and Irish traditional music*

**DOR Encryption**
PO Box 1797
London
E1 4TX
T 020 7702 7842  F 020 7790 0764
E encryption@dor.co.uk
*Managing Director* Martin Parker


**Double Entrée Music**
130 Pembroke Rd
Seven Kings
Ilford
Essex
IG3 8PF
T 020 8252 6891
*Partner* Steve Bryant


**Dream of Oswald Publishing Ltd**
Park House
Warren Row
Berks
RG10 8QS
T 07071 223951  F 07071 223952
E monkey@dreamofoswald.demon.co.uk
*Contact* Steve James


**Earache Songs UK Ltd**
PO Box 144
Notts
NG3 4GE
T 0115 950 6400  F 0115 950 8585
E earache@earache.com  w earache.com
*Managing Director* Digby Pearson


**Earth Music Publishing**
Unit 104a
The Old Gramophone Works
326 Kensal Rd
London
W10 5BZ
T 020 8968 4545  F 020 8968 3737
*Contact* Philip Allen


**Eaton Music**
8 West Eaton Place
London
SW1X 8LS
T 020 7235 9046  F 020 7235 7193
E eatonmus@aol.com
*Managing Director* Terry Oates


**Edel Publishing**
12 Oval Rd
London
NW1 7DH
T 020 7482 4848  F 020 7482 4846  w edel.co.uk
*Contact* David Hockman


**Editions Penguin Café Ltd**
144 Camden High St
London
NW1 0NE
T 020 7543 7500  F 020 7543 7643
E sperry@penguincafe.com  w penguincafe.com
*Contact* Sharon Perry


**EG Music Ltd**
61a Kings Rd
London
SW3 4NT
T 020 7730 2162  F 020 7730 1330
*Contact* Sam Alder


**William Elkin Music Services**
Station Rd Industrial Estate
Salthouse
Norwich
Norfolk
NR13 6NS
T 01603 721302  F 01603 721801
E sales@elkinmusic.demon.co.uk
w elkinmusic.co.uk
*Contact* Richard Elkin

*International suppliers of printed music from all
publishers worldwide
Specialists in choral music*


**Emerson Edition Ltd**
Windmill Farm
Ampleforth
North Yorkshire
YO62 4HF
T 01439 788324  F 01439 788715
E juneemerson@compuserve.com
*Contact* June Emerson

*NB: specialist publisher of music for wind
instruments
Part of June Emerson Wind Music (specialist music
suppliers)*

## EMI Music Publishing

127 Charing Cross Rd
London
WC2H QEA
**T** 020 7434 2131   **F** 020 7434 3531

*Also EMI Music Publishing Continental Europe
(same details except Fax: 020 7287 5254)*

## Endomorph Music Publishing

29 St Michael's Rd
Leeds
West Yorkshire
LS6 3BG
**T** 0113 274 2106   **F** 0113 278 6291
**E** hotshot@peternet.co.uk/sales@bluescat.com
**W** bluescat.com
*Contact* D Foster

## English West Coast Music

The Old Bakehouse
150 High St
Honiton
Devon
EX14 1JX
**T** 01404 42234/07767 865360   **F** 01404 45346/
07767 869029   **E** publishing@ewcm.co.uk
**W** ewcm.co.uk
*Contact* Julie Dent

## Ela Music

'Argentum'
2 Queen Caroline St
London
W6 9DX
**T** 020 8323 8014   **F** 020 8323 8080
*Contact* John Giacobbi

## Eschenbach Editions

28 Dalrymple Crescent
Edinburgh
EH9 2NX
**T** 0131 667 3633   **F** as telephone
**E** eschenbach@caritas-music.co.uk
**W** caritas-music.co.uk
*Managing Director* James Douglas

## Esquire Music Company

185a Newmarket Rd
Norwich
Norfolk
NR4 6AP
**T** 01603 451139
*Managing Director* Peter Newbrook

*NB: jazz music only*

## Essex Music Group, The

Suite 207, Plaza 535
Kings Rd
London
SW10 0SZ
**T** 020 7823 3773   **F** 020 7351 3615
**E** bharris@essexmusic.demon.co.uk
*Contact* Bob Harris
*Managing Director* Frank D Richmond

*NB: no new material currently required*

## ESSP

The Sound House
PO Box 37b
Molesey
Surrey
KT8 2YR
**T** 020 8979 9997   **F** as telephone
*Contact* David Tuffnell

## Euston Music

2–3 Fitzroy Mews
London
W1P 5DQ
**T** 020 7383 7043   **F** 020 7383 3020
*Contact* John Craig

## Evil Boy Music

11 Stourton Rd
Quinton
Birmingham
B32 1QY
**T** 0121 422 7220/01462 117233   **F** as first telephone

## Evita Music

Elsinore House
77 Fulham Palace Rd
London
W6 8JA
**T** 020 8741 8686   **F** as telephone
*Director* R Alexander

## Express Music (London) Ltd

Prospect Farm
West Marsh
Canterbury
Kent
CT3 2LS
**T** 01304 812815   **F** as telephone
*Managing Director* Siggy Jackson

## Faber Music

3 Queen Square
London
WC1N 3AU
**T** 020 7833 7900   **F** 020 7833 7939
**E** information@fabermusic.com
**W** fabermusic.com
*Contact* Sophie Donat

*NB: publisher of serious, educational and recreational music*

## Fairwood Music Ltd

72 Marylebone Lane
London
W1U 2PL
**T** 020 7487 5044   **F** 020 7935 2270
**E** pbrown@westury.music.co.uk
*General Manager* Paul Brown

## Faith Music Corporation

PO Box 111
London
W13 0ZH
**T** 020 8357 2337/07000 243 243   **F** 020 8566 7215/
0132 731 2545   **E** info@faith-music-corp.com
**W** faith-music-corp.com
*Contact* John Rushton

## Famous Music Publishing

Bedford House
69–79 Fulham High St
London
SW6 3JW
**T** 020 7736 7543   **F** 020 7471 4812
**E** luke.famousmusic@bigfoot.com
*Managing Director* Dominic Walker
*A&R* Luke McGrellis

## Fanfare Music

The Chrysalis Building
13 Bramley Rd
London
W10 6SP
**T** 020 7465 6203   **F** 020 7465 6318
**E** peterk@chrysalis.co.uk   **W** chrysalis.co.uk
*Contact* Peter Knight Jr

## Fashion Music

17 Davids Rd
London
SE23 3EP
**T** 020 8291 6253   **F** 020 8291 1097
*Producer* Chris Lane

## Fast Western

Bank Top Cottage
Meadow Lane
Millers Dale
Derby
SK17 8SN
**T** 01298 872462   **F** 01298 872461
**E** fast.west@virgin.net
*Managing Director* Ric Lee

## Fastforward Music Publishing Ltd

Sorrel Horse House
1 Sorrel Horse Mews
Ipswich
Suffolk
IP4 1LN
**T** 01473 210555   **F** 01473 210500
**E** sales@fastforwardmusic.co.uk
*Contact* Neil Read

**Favoured Nations Music Ltd**
20 Woodland Rd
Bushey
Herts
WD2 2LR
T 01923 244673    F 01923 244693
E connect2music@btinternet.com
W connectmusic.com
*Managing Director* Barry Blue


**Fenman Music**
Fenman Cottage
13 Lower Green
Tewin
Welwyn
Herts
AL6 0LB
T 01438 714909    F as telephone
*Managing Director* Paul Griggs


**Fentone Music**
Fleming Rd
Earlstrees
Corby
Northants
NN17 4SN
T 01536 260981/0800 616415
F 01536 401075/0800 616415
E music@fentone.com    W fentone.com
*Contact* Iain Fenton


**FI Music**
2 Laurel Bank
Lowestwood
Huddersfield
Yorkshire
HD7 4ER
or
PO Box 7
Huddersfield
HD7 4YA
T 01484 846333    F as telephone and 01924 257795
E hotleadrec@lineone.net/fimusic@lineone.net
W fimusic.co.uk
*Contact* Ian R Smith or Frannie Haywood

*Cabaret, folk, pop, adult contemporary, jazz, ballads*


**Fiction Songs**
4 Tottenham Mews
London
W1P 9PJ
T 020 7323 5555    F 020 7323 5323
*Professional Manager* Kate Dale


**John Fiddy Music**
Fruit Farm House
Foxton
Cambs
CB2 6RT
T 01763 208610/01763 208142    F 01763 208241
E johnfiddymusic@dial.pipex.com
*Manager* Glynne Fiddy


**Final Frontier Music**
29 Roundwood Rd
Hastings
East Sussex
TN37 7LD
T 01424 753792    E dffroberts@aol.com
*Contact* David Roberts


**Firebird Music**
Kyrle House Studios
Edde Cross St
Ross-on-Wye
Hereford
HR9 7BZ
T 01989 762269    F 01989 566337
E pmartin@firebirdmusic.com    W firebird.com
*Chief Executive Officer* Peter Martin

*Primarily a production company/studio with in-house label, publishing, management and PR/ promo design*


**Fireworks Music**
Snake Ranch Studios
8 Berwick St
London
W1F 0PH
T 020 292 0000    F 020 292 0016
E fwx@fireworksmusic.co.uk
W fireworksmusic.co.uk
*Contact* Claire Griffin

## First Avenue Music

The Courtyard
42 Colwith Rd
London
W6 9EY
**T** 020 8741 1419   **F** 020 8741 3289
**E** (name)@first-avenue.co.uk   **w** firstavenue.net
*Contact* Oliver Smallman

*Also First Avenue Management and First Avenue Records (same contact details)*

## First Time Music (Publishing) UK

Sovereign House
12 Trewartha Rd
Praa Sands
Penzance
Cornwall
TR20 9ST
**T** 01736 762826/07721 449477   **F** 01736 763328
**E** panamus@aol.com   **w** panamamusic.co.uk
*Managing Director* Roderick G Jones

## FJR Music

1 Herbert Gardens
London
NW10 3BX
**T** 020 8968 8870   **F** 020 960 0719
*Contact* Raj Malkani

## Flying Music Company Ltd, The

FM House
110 Clarendon Rd
London
W11 2HR
**T** 020 7221 7799   **F** 020 7221 5016
**E** info@flyingmusic.co.uk   **w** flyingmusic.com
*Contact* Andy Sharrocks (Production Manager)
*Production Assistant* David Parker

## Focus Music (Publishing) Ltd

4 Pilgrims Lane
London
NW3 1SL
**T** 020 7453 8266   **F** 020 7435 1505
**E** info@focusmusic.com   **w** focusmusic.com
*Managing Director* Paul Greedus

## Folktrax & Soundpost Publications

Heritage House
16 Brunswick Square
Gloucester
GL1 1UG
**T** 01452 415110   **F** 01452 503643
**E** peter@folktrax.freeserve.co.uk   **w** folktrax.org
*Managing Director* Peter Kennedy

*Publisher of over 300 CDs of international traditions*

## Fortissimo Music

78 Portland Rd
London
W11 4LQ
**T** 020 7727 2063   **F** 020 7229 4188

## Fortunes Fading Music

Pepys Court
84 The Chase
London
SW4 0NF
**T** 020 7720 7266   **F** 020 7720 7255
**E** ptp.producer@virgin.net
*Contact* Peter Pritchard

## Four Seasons Music

Killarney House
Bray
Co. Wicklow
Ireland
**T** 00 353 1 286 9944   **F** 00 353 1 286 9945
**E** coulter@indigo.ie   **w** philcoulter.com
*Contact* Phil Coulter

*Specialists in acoustic, new age and celtic music
Also record production*

## 4 Tunes Music Ltd

Unit 9
Morrison Yard
551a High Rd
London
N17 6SB
**T** 020 8801 5878   **F** 020 8808 9885
**E** dave@roundway.com
*Contact* Dave Thompson

## 4 Vending Music
22 Coronet St
London
N1 6HD
**T** 020 7729 6633   **F** 020 7729 6613
**E** rwbold@aol.com
*Managing Director* Richard Barclay

## FreakStreet Music Ltd
PO Box 6627
London
E1 2RF
**T** 020 7423 9993   **F** 020 7423 9996
**E** admin@12one.com   **W** 12one.com
*Managing Director* Paul Kennedy

## Freedom Songs Ltd
PO Box 272
London
N20 0BY
**T** 020 8368 0340   **F** 020 8361 3370
**E** freedom@jt-management.demon.co.uk
*Managing Director* John Taylor

## Freeway Music Group
Federation House
85–87 Wellington St
Luton
Beds
LU1 5AF
**T** 01582 457503   **F** 01582 412215
*Contact* Ken Wiltsher

## Fresh Songs
PO Box 4075
Pangbourne
Berks
RG8 7FV
**T** 0118 984 3468   **F** 0118 984 3463
**E** info@freshmusic.co.uk/info@freskanova.com
*Directors* Dave Morgan and Vicki Aspinall
*A&R/Production* Dave Morgan

*See also Fresh Records, Freskanova Records, Fresh
Music (same contact details)*

## Friendly Overtures
Walkers Cottage
Aston Lane
Henley-on-Thames
Oxon
RG9 3EJ
**T** 01491 574457   **F** as telephone
*Creative Director* Michael Batory

*Specialists in contemporary folk music*

## Full Flavour Music
56 Glenthorne Rd
London
W6 0LJ
**T** 020 8748 4499   **F** 020 8748 6699

## Fume Music Ltd
Unit 53, Canalot
222 Kensal Rd
London
W10 5BN
**T** 020 8964 5441   **F** 020 8964 3593
**E** fumemusic@aol.com
*Contact* Seamus Morley

## Fundamental Music Ltd
1 Devenport Mews
London
W12 8NG
**T** 020 8354 4900   **F** 020 8354 4901
**E** info@fundamental.co.uk   **W** fundamental.co.uk
*Contact* Tim Prior

## Funtastik Music
43 Seaforth Gardens
Stoneleigh
Surrey
KT19 0LR
**T** 020 8393 1970   **F** 020 8393 2428
*Contact* John Burns

## Future Earth Music Publishing
59 Fitzwilliam St
Wath Upon Dearne
Rotherham
South Yorkshire
S63 7HG
**T** 01709 872875   **E** music@future-earth.co.uk

**w** future-earth.co.uk
*Managing Director* David Moffitt

**Fyne Music**
2 Chester Avenue
Southport
Merseyside
PR9 7ET
**T** 01704 224666   **F** as telephone
*Contact* Lou Fyne

**Galaxi Promotions Ltd**
67 West St
Dunstable
Beds
LU6 1ST
**T** 01582 605222   **F** 01582 690906
**E** nomadrush@cix.co.uk
**w** galaxi.co.uk and popromos.com

**Game Records (UK)**
PO 11583
London
W13 0WP
**T** 07000 243 243
**E** game@badhabitsent-group.com
**w** badhabitsent-group.com
*Contact* John Rushton

**Garron Music**
Newtown St
Kilsyth
Glasgow
G65 0JX
**T** 01236 821081/825843   **F** 01236 826900/825683
**E** nscott@scotdisc.co.uk
*Contact* W B Garden

**Gas Music Publishing**
2nd Floor, 65 George St
Oxford
OX1 2BE
**T** 01865 798 791   **F** 01865 798 792
**E** gasmusic@oxfordmusic.net
*Contact* Dave Newton

**Noel Gay Music**
c/o Music Sales Ltd
8/9 Frith St
London
W1V 5TZ
**T** 020 7434 0066   **F** 020 7439 2848
*Contact* David Carroll

**GB2 Publishing**
Fernbank Studio
Bonnings Lane
Barrington
Ilminster
Somerset
TA19 0JN
**T** 01460 55450   **F** 01460 53395
**E** gb2@gbsquared.demon.co.uk
*Contact* Ronnie Gleeson

**GDR Music Publishing Ltd**
2 Beaconsfield St
Darlington
Co. Durham
DL3 6ER
**T** 01325 483683   **F** 01325 255252
**E** gdrmusic@aol.com
**w** members.aol.com/circrecds1/gdrmusic
*Contact* Graeme Robinson

**Gee Music Group Ltd**
7 Fleetsbridge Business Centre
Upton Rd
Poole
Dorset
BH17 7AF
**T** 01202 686368   **F** 01202 686363
**E** enquiries@musicgifts.co.uk   **w** musicgifts.co.uk

*Consists of Music Forte, an orchestral sheet music
catalogue of over 6000 titles, and Music Gifts
Company, selling giftware with a musical theme*

**Genetic Music**
PO Box 10815
London
W4 5WZ
**T** 020 8783 1005   **F** 020 8783 1168
*Managing Director* Mike Leonard

## Ghost Music Ltd

PO Box 272
London
N20 0BY
**T** 020 8368 0340   **F** 020 8361 3370
**E** ghost@jt-management.demon.co.uk
*Contact* John Taylor

## Fay Gibbs Music Services

Warwick Lodge
37 Telford Avenue
London
SW2 4XL
**T** 020 8671 9699   **F** 020 8674 8558
**E** faygibbs@fgmusicservice.demon.co.uk
**w** fgmusicservice.co.uk
*Managing Director* Fay Gibbs

*Administration and royalty collection*

## Gill Music

40 Highfield Park Rd
Bredbury
Stockport
Cheshire
SK6 2PG
**T** 0161 494 2098
*Contact* Gill Cragen

*Also label agency and management*
*Please write in first instance*
*In-house writing: pop, ballads, C&W, R&B*

## Steve Glen Music

2 Menelik Rd
London
NW2 3RP
**T** 020 7435 6116   **F** as telephone
**E** steveglen@appleonline.net
**w** bluemelon.co.uk and barbaracartland.com
*Contact* Steven Glen

## Global Force t/a Comet Records

1st Floor, 5 Cope St
Temple Bar
Dublin 2
Ireland
**T** 00 353 1 672 8001/671 8592   **F** 00 353 1 672 8005
**E** comet@indigo.ie
*Contact* Brian O'Kelly

## Global Chrysalis Music Publishing Co Ltd

The Chrysalis Building
13 Bramley Rd
London
W10 6SP
**T** 020 7465 6203   **F** 020 7465 6318
**E** peterk@chrysalis.co.uk   **w** chrysalis.co.uk
*Contact* Peter Knight Jr

*Also Klynch Music (same details)*

## Global Talent Publishing

Alexandra House
6 Little Portland St
London
W1N 5AG
**T** 020 7907 1700   **F** 020 7907 1711
**E** email@globaltalentgroup.com
**w** globaltalentgroup.com
*Contact* Miller Williams
*Directors* David Forecast, Ashley Tabor

## Go Crazy Music

50 Jail Lane
Biggin Hill
Kent
TN16 3SA
**T** 01959 573806   **F** 01959 574910
*Director* Daz Shields

## Golden Apple Productions

8–9 Frith St
London
W1V 5TZ
**T** 020 7434 0066   **F** 020 7287 6329
**E** music@musicsales.co.uk   **w** musicsales.co.uk
*Contact* James Rushton

## Good Groove Songs Ltd

Unit 217, Buspace Studios
Conlan St
London
W10 5AP
**T** 020 7565 0050   **F** 020 7565 0049
**E** (first name)@goodgroove.co.uk
*Contact* Gary Davies

## Good Move Music
27 Spedan Close
London
NW3 7XF
**T** 020 7435 5302    **F** 020 7435 7152
*Managing Director* Philip Simmonds

## Grade One Music Ltd
34 Salisbury St
London
NW8 8QE
**T** 020 7402 9111    **F** 020 7723 3064
*Managing Director* Eliot Cohen

## Graduate Music
St Swithun's Institute
The Trinity
Worcester
WR1 2PN
**T** 01905 20882    **F** as telephone
**E** david_virr@compuserve.com
**W** davevale.demon.co.uk/graduate/
*Managing Director* David Virr

## Grand Central Music Publishing Ltd
3rd Floor, Habib House
9 Stevenson Square
Piccadilly
Manchester
M1 1DB
**T** 0161 200 1255    **F** 0161 236 6717
**E** rachel@grandcentralrecords.co.uk
*Contact* Rachel Wood

## Grapedime Music
28 Hurst Crescent
Barrowby
Grantham
Lincs
NG32 1TE
**T** 01476 560241    **F** as telephone
**E** grapedime@pjbray.globalnet.co.uk

*Rock and pop*
*Also management (Delivered, Paradox, Emanon, Foxglove)*

## Grapevine Music Ltd
95 Hawkesfield Rd
London
SE23 2TN
**T** 020 8291 3687    **F** 020 8699 1438
**E** diversemusicltd@compuserve.com
*Contact* Diana Graham

*Also Diverse Music Ltd and Monument Music Ltd (same contact details)*

## Grass Roots Music Publishing
29 Love Lane
Rayleigh
Essex
SS6 7DL
**T** 01268 747077
*Managing Director* Gerald Mahlowe

*A one-man operation working with new talent*

## Green Park Music
32 Queensdale Rd
London
W11 4SA
**T** 020 7602 1124    **F** 020 7602 0704
**E** musidiscuk@btinternet.com
*Contact* Francois Grandchamp

## Greensleeves Publishing Ltd
Unit 14, Metro centre
St John's Rd
Isleworth
Middx
TW7 6NJ
**T** 020 8758 0564    **F** 020 8758 0811
**E** mail@greensleeves.net    **W** greensleeves.net
*Managing Director* Chris Sedgwick
*Administration* Claire Ram

## Grin Music
138b West Hill
London
SW15 2UE
**T** 020 8780 2564    **F** 020 8788 2889
*Copyright Manager* Patrick Davis

## G&M Brand Publications

PO Box 367
Aylesbury
Bucks
HP22 4LJ
**T** 01296 682220 **F** 01296 681989
**E** g&mbrand@rsmith.co.uk
*Managing Director* Michael Brand


## G2 Music

The Powerhouse
70 Chiswick High Rd
London
W4 1SY
**T** 020 8742 3366/07711 669392 **F** 020 8950 1294
**E** rod@g2-music.co.uk **W** g2-music.co.uk
*Contact* Rod Gammons


## Gull Songs

21c Heathmans Rd
London
SW6 4TJ
**T** 020 7731 9321 **F** 020 7731 9314
**E** gull@darah.co.uk
*Managing Director* Irene Howells


## Gut Music

Byron House
112a Shirland Rd
London
W9 2EQ
**T** 020 7266 0777 **F** 020 7266 7734
*Chairman* Guy Holmes
*Managing Director* Caroline Lewis
*A&R* Simon De Winter, Uche Uchendu


## Gwynn Publishing

Heol-y-dwr
Pen-y-groes
Caernarfon
Gwynedd
LL54 6LR
**T** 01286 881797 **F** 01286 882634
**E** gwynn@sain.wales.com
*Contact* Wendy Jones


## Habana Music

PO Box 370
Newquay
Cornwall
TR8 5YZ
**T** 01637 831011 **F** 01637 831037
**E** habanaco@aol.com
*Contact* Rod Buckle, Di Melbourne or Alan Whaley

*Also Gazell Music, Eyeball Music and Alligator Music*
*NB: sub-publishers only, representing other national and international catalogues*


## Halcyon Music

11 Howitt Rd
London
NW3 4LT
**T** 07000 783633 **F** 07000 783634
*Managing Director* Alan Williams


## Tony Hall Group of Companies

3rd Floor, 9 Carnaby St
London
W1V 1PG
**T** 020 7437 1958/1959 **F** 020 7437 3852
*Managing Director* Tony Hall


## Halo Management UK Ltd

The Dog House
1 St Edmunds Avenue
Ruislip
Middlesex
HA4 7XW
**T** 01895 639 701 **F** 01895 678 766
**E** halo@wsmgt.co.uk **W** wsmgt.co.uk
*Contact* William L. Smith


## Hammer Film Music

Elstree Studios
Shenley Rd
Borehamwood
Herts
WD6 1JG
**T** 020 8207 4011 **F** 020 8905 1127
*Contact* Graham Skeggs

## Haripa Music

Unit 1, Acklam Workshops
10 Acklam Rd
London
W10 5QZ
T 020 8964 3300   F 020 8964 4400
E info@kickin.co.uk   W kickinmusic.com
*Contact* Peter Harris

## Hatton & Rose Publishers

46 Northcourt Avenue
Reading
Berks
RG2 7HQ
T 0118 987 4938   F as telephone
*Contact* Graham Hatton

## Havasong Music

c/o 169 Cecil Rd
Rochester
Kent
ME1 2HW
T 01634 815613
*Partner* J M Hirst-Amos

## Head Music Ltd

2 Munro Terrace
London
SW10 0DL
T 020 7376 4456   F 020 7351 5569
*Contact* John Curd

## Heaven Music

PO Box 92
Gloucester
GL4 8HW
T 01452 814321   F 01452 812106
*Managing Director* Vic Coppersmith-Heaven

## Heavenly Songs

47 Frith St
London
W1D 4SE
T 020 7494 2998   F 020 7437 3317
*Contact* Jeff Barrett

## Heavy Truth Music Publishing

PO Box 8
Corby
Northants
NN17 2XZ
T 01536 202295   F 01536 266246
E steve@adasam.demon.co.uk
W adasam.demon.co.uk
*Label Manager* Steve Kalidoski

## Hello Cutie

Cadillac Ranch
Pencraig Uchaf
Cwm Bach
Whitland
Dyfed
SA34 0DT
T 01994 484466   F 01994 484294
*Contact* Helios Steelgrave

## HHO Publishing

Satril House
3 Blackburn Rd
London
NW6 1RZ
T 020 7328 8283   F 020 7328 9037
E licensing@hho.co.uk
*Contact* Sue Pilina

## Hit & Run Music (Publishing) Ltd

25 Ives St
London
SW3 2ND
T 020 7590 2600   F 020 7584 5774
*Managing Director* Jon Crawley
*Creative & International Director* Michelle de Vries

## Hornall Bros Music

1st Floor, 754 Fulham Rd
London
SW6 5SH
T 020 7736 7891   F 020 7736 9377
E stuart@hobro.co.uk   W hobro.co.uk
*Contact* Stuart Hornall

**Jatta Howell Services**
13 Boleyn Drive
West Molesey
Surrey
KT8 1RE
**T** 020 8873 3373    **E** jattapinstripe.net

**Howlin' Music Ltd**
114 Lower Park Rd
Loughton
Essex
IG10 4NE
**T** 020 8508 4564/07831 430080
**F** as first telephone
**E** djone@howardmarks.freeserve.co.uk
*General Manager* Marisa Marks
*A&R* Howard Marks

**HQ**
4 The Hamlet
The Bank
Marlcliff
Bidford on Avon
Warwickshire
B50 4NT
**T** 01789 778482    **F** as telephone
**E** thehamlet@freeserve.co.uk
*Contact* John Tully

**Hugely Music Publishing**
202 Fulham Rd
London
SW10 9PJ
**T** 020 7351 5167    **F** 020 7352 1514
**E** muirhead_management@compuserve.com
*Chairman* Hugh Padgham

**HMP (Hugo Music Publishing)**
PO Box 14303
London
SE26 4ZH
**T** 07000 472572    **F** as telephone
**E** latinarts@artquest.co.uk    **W** latinartsgroup.com

*Part of Latin Arts Services, specializing in
Latin-American entertainment, that includes LAS
Records UK (label), WAI World Artists Index
(free-net index), Mundo Graphics (graphic design)
and Latin Arts Services (management/agency)*

**Hurley Music Productions Ltd**
7 Saint Andrew St
Dublin 2
Ireland
**T** 00 353 1 677 7377    **F** as telephone
*Contact* Liam or Avril Hurley

*Specializing in record production, radio and TV
advertisements and film music*

**Hyde Park Music**
110 Westbourne Terrace Mews
London
W2 6QG
**T** 020 7402 8419
*Chairman* Tony Hiller

**I Life Music**
PO Box 14996
London
SW17 9WD
**T** 020 8682 0243    **F** as telephone
**E** michael@ilife.freeserve.co.uk
*Contact* Michael Fuller

**In The Frame Music**
42 Winsford Gardens
Westcliff on Sea
Essex
SS0 0ED
**T** 01702 390353    **F** 01702 390355
*Contact* Will Birch

*Also Off the Peg Songs (same details)
NB: no unsolicited demos*

**Inception Music Publishing**
323 Middle Rd
Gendros
Swansea
SA5 8EW
**T** 01792 589296    **F** 01792 581500
**E** paulscottwkf@talk21.com
*Contact* Paul Scott

## Independent Music Group

Independent House
54 Larkshall Rd
London
E4 6PD
**T** 020 8523 9000    **F** 020 8523 8888
**E** erich@independentmusicgroup.com
*Chairman* Ellis Rich

*Also International Music Network and JSE Music Publishing (same details)*

## Inky Blackness Ltd

51 Rossendale Way
London
NW1 0XB
**T** 07958 520580    **E** inky@inkyblackness.co.uk
**w** inkyblackness.co.uk
*Contact* Ian Tregoning

*Publishers of Tokamak, Jon Ryman, Magnetic North, Interloper and Stranger*

## International Music Publications (IMP)

Griffin House
161 Hammersmith Rd
London
W6 8BS
**T** 020 8222 9222    **F** 020 8222 9263
**E** imp-info@warnerchappell.com
*Contact* Richard Martin

*A Warner Bros Publications company*

## International Songwriters' Music

PO Box 46
Limerick City
Ireland
**T** 00 353 61 228837/020 7486 5353
**F** 00 353 61 229464/020 7486 2094
**E** jliddane@songwriter.iol.ie    **w** songwriter.co.uk
*Managing Director* James D Liddane

## Invisible Hands Music

PO Box 243
Epsom
Surrey
KT19 8YJ
**T** 01372 739137    **F** 01372 739173

**E** info@invisiblehands.co.uk
**w** invisiblehands.co.uk
*Contact* John Shepherd

## IQ Music

Commercial House
52 Perrymount Rd
Haywards Heath
West Sussex
RH16 3DT
**T** 01444 452857    **F** 01444 451739
**E** iq.music@virgin.net
*Director* Kathie Iqbal

## Isa Music

27–29 Carnoustie Place
Scotland St
Glasgow
G5 8PH
**T** 0141 420 1881    **F** 0141 420 1892
**E** info@isa-music.com    **w** isa-music.com
*Business Manager* Bob McDowall

## Jam Publishing

Suite 16, The Linnen House
253 Kilburn Lane
London
W10 4BQ
**T** 020 8962 6702    **F** 020 8964 8556
**E** jammin@tba.co.uk
*Joint Managing Director* Andrew Cleary

## Jamdown Music Ltd

Research House
Fraser Rd
Perrivale
Middx
UB6 7AQ
**T** 020 8930 1070    **F** 020 8930 1073
**E** jamdownmusic@compuserve.com
*Managing Director* Othman Mukhlis

## Jammy Music Publishers

The Beeches
244 Anniesland Rd
Glasgow
G13 1XA
**T** 0141 954 1873    **F** 0141 954 6341
**E** jammymusic@compuserve.com
*Managing Director* John MacCalman

**Jelly Street Music Ltd**
Chester Terrace
358 Chester Rd
Manchester
M16 9EZ
**T** 0161 872 6006    **F** 0161 872 6468
*Managing Director* Kevin Kinsella Snr

**Jenjo Music Publishing**
68 Wharton Avenue
Sheffield
South Yorkshire
S26 3SA
**T** 0114 287 9882    **F** as telephone
*Contact* Mike Ward

**Jester Song Ltd**
78 Gladstone Rd
London
SW19 1QT
**T** 020 8543 4056    **F** 020 8542 8225
**E** jestersong@msn.com
*Contact* Roland B Rogers

*Mainly music publishing and music services*

**JHT Music**
The Music Village
11b Osiers Rd
London
SW18 1NL
**T** 020 8870 0011    **F** 020 8870 2101
**E** nick@keepcalm.demon.co.uk
*Directors* Ian Titchener and Nick Titchener
*General Manager* Jo Underwood

**Jonsongs Music**
3 Farrers Pace
Croydon
Surrey
CRO 5HB
**T** 020 8654 5829    **F** 020 8654 4682
**E** john.johnson@vopak.com
*Contact* Patricia Bancroft

**David Julius Publishing**
11 Alexander House
Tiller Rd
London
E14 8PT
**T** 020 7987 8596    **F** as telephone
*Contact* David Maynard

**Just Create Music**
20 Station Rd
Eckington
Sheffield
South Yorkshire
S21 4FX
**T** 01246 432507/07785 232176    **F** as first telephone
**E** richardcory@limeone.net
*Contact* Richard Cory

**Just Publishing**
9 Gladwyn Rd
London
SW15 1JY
**T** 020 8780 5129    **F** 020 8788 1727
**E** j.benedict@vigin.net    **W** justmusic.co.uk
*Contact* John Benedict

**Kaleidoscope Music**
89–91 Bayham St
London
NW1 0AG
**T** 020 7284 3354    **F** 020 7916 9984
**E** ross@kaleidoscope-music.com
**W** kaleidoscope-music.com
*Contact* Ross Fitzsimons

**Alfred A Kalmus**
38 Eldon Way
Paddock Wood
Tonbridge
Kent
TN12 6BE
**T** 01892 833422    **F** 01892 836038
*Managing Director* John Palmer

**Kamara Music Publishing**
PO Box 56
Boston
Lincs
PE22 8JL
**T** 07976 553624

E chriskamara@megahitrecordsuk.freeserve.co.uk
*Contact* Chris Dunn

## Karon Productions
20 Radstone Court
Hillview Rd
Woking
Surrey
GU22 7NB
T 01483 755153
*Managing Director* Ron Roker

## Kassner Associated Publishers Ltd
Units 6–7, 11 Wyfold Rd
London
SW6 6SE
T 020 7385 7700    F 020 7385 3402
E dkassner@kassner-music.co.uk
W president-records.co.uk
*Managing Director* David Kassner

## Kaplan Kaye Music
95 Gloucester Rd
Hampton
Middx
TW12 2UW
T 020 8783 0039    F 020 8979 6487
E kaplan222@aol.com
*Contact* Kaplan Kaye

## Keep Calm Music
The Music Village
11b Osiers Rd
London
SW18 1NL
T 020 8870 0011    F 020 8870 2101
E carl@keepcalm.demon.co.uk
*Directors* Colin Peter and Carl Ward

## Kennedy Music
1–3 Ashland House
Ashland Place
London
W1M 3JF
T 020 7935 9856    F 020 7487 3015
*Contact* William Kennedy

## Kickstart Music
10 Park House
140 Battersea Park Rd
London
SW11 4NB
T 020 7498 9696    F 020 7498 2064
E cms@cmsi.demon.co.uk
*Contact* Frank Clark

*Specialists in pop, rock, dance, R&B, country and blues*
*All submissions welcome*
*See also Kickstart Management*

## Kevin King Music Publishing
16 Limetrees
Llangattock
Crickhowell
Powys
NP8 1LB
T 01873 810142    F 01873 811557    E silvergb@aol.com
*Managing Director* Kevin King

## Kingsway Music
Lottbridge Drove
Eastbourne
East Sussex
BN23 6NT
T 01323 437708    F 01323 411970
E music@kingsway.co.uk    W worship.co.uk
*Head of Music* Stuart Townend

## Kirklees Music
Unit 12, Rook Lane Mills
Law St
Dudley Hill
Bradford
West Yorkshire
BD4 9NF
T 01274 689984    F 01274 680122
E sales@kirkleesmusic.co.uk
W kirkleesmusic.co.uk
*Contact* D W Horsfield

*Classical, solo, hymns, Christmas, small ensemble, wind band, educational etc*
*Also mail order music (tel/fax: 01484 722855) at 609 Bradford Road, Bailiff Bridge, Brighouse, West Yorks*
HD6 4DN

## Kite Music Ltd

Binny Estate
Ecclesmachan
Edinburgh
EH52 6NL
**T** 01506 858885    **F** 01506 858155
**E** kitemusic@aol.com    **w** kitemusic.com
*Managing Director* Billy Russell

*Also Billy Russell Management (same contact details)*

## KPM Music

127 Charing Cross Rd
London
WC2H 0EA
**T** 020 7412 9111    **F** 020 7413 0061
**E** kpm@kpm.co.uk
*Creative Manager* Elaine Van Der Schoot

## Kristannar Music

33 Park Chase
Wembley
Middx
HA9 8EQ
**T** 020 8902 5523    **F** as telephone
*Managing Director* Eddie Stevens

## Lantern Music/Music For Films

34 Batchelor St
London
N1 0EG
**T** 020 7278 4288
*Contact* Rob Gold

*Lantern publishes film and TV music and songs, while Music For Films represents feature film and TV composers, also offering a music supervision and consultancy service for producers and directors*

## Dick Leahy Music

1 Star St
London
W2 1QD
**T** 020 7258 0093    **F** 020 7402 9238
*Contact* Peter Stretton

## Lee Music Publishing

White House Farm
Shropshire
TF9 4HA
**T** 01630 647374    **F** 01630 647612
*Copyright Manager* Catherine Lematt

*Also Lematt Music (same details), which is also a distributor*

## Leosong Copyright Service

Independent House
54 Larkshall Rd
London
E4 6PD
**T** 020 8523 9000    **F** 020 8523 8888
**E** jmatthews@independentmusicgroup.com
*General Manager* John Matthews

## Light Fantastic Publishing

8 Berwick St
London
W1V 3RG
**T** 020 7292 0000    **F** 020 7292 0010
**E** ko@easynet.co.uk
*Contact* Ko Barclay

## Lightman Music

353 St Margaret's Rd
St Margaret's
Twickenham
Middx
TW1 1PW
**T** 020 8891 3293    **F** 020 8744 0811
**E** richard@lightman.demon.co.uk
*Contact* Richard Lightman

## Like No Other Music Ltd

28 Denmark St
London
WC2H 8QH
**T** 020 7379 0999    **F** 020 7379 3399
**E** mark@like-no-other.com    **w** like-no-other.com
*Contact* Mark Lambert Stewart

## Lindsay Music

23 Hitchin St
Biggleswade
Beds
SG18 8AX
**T** 01767 316521   **F** 01767 317221
**E** sales@lindsaymusic.co.uk
**W** lindsaymusic.co.uk
*Partner* C Lindsay Douglas

*Also retailers*
*House composer: Douglas Coombes*

## Line-Up PMC (inc. On-Line Records)

9a Tankerville Place
Newcastle-upon-Tyne
Tyne and Wear
NE2 3AT
**T** 0191 281 6449   **F** 0191 212 0913
**E** c.a.murtagh@btinternet.com
**W** on-line-records.co.uk
*Managing Director* Christopher Murtagh

## Link Music

PO Box 184
Ashford
Kent
TN24 0ZS
**T** 01233 660206   **F** 01233 660550
*General Manager* Sonia Bailey

## Lionheart Music

20 Grasmere Avenue
London
SW15 3RB
**T** 020 8546 4047   **F** 020 8546 0468
*Managing Director* Richard Gillinson

## Lock 'n' S

The Coachhouse
Mansion Farm
Liverton Hill
Sandway
Maidstone
Kent
ME17 2NJ
**T** 01622 858300   **F** as telephone
**E** info@eddielock.com
*Contact* Eddie Lock

## LOE Music

LOE House
159 Broadhurst Gardens
London
NW6 3AU
**T** 020 7328 6100   **F** 020 7624 6384
**E** kato@loeg.demon.co.uk
*Managing Director* Hiroshi Kato

## Logo Songs

22 Denmark St
London
WC2H 8NA
**T** 020 7836 5996/7240 5249   **F** 020 7379 5205
**E** music@mautoglade.fsbusiness.co.uk
*Managing Director* Geoffrey Hannington

## Lomond Music

32 Bankton Park
Kingskettle
Fife
KY15 7PY
**T** 01337 83074   **F** 01337 830653
**E** bruce.fraser@zetnet.co.uk   **W** lomondmusic.com

## London Orchestrations

PO Box 423
Wallington
Surrey
SM6 9SZ
**T** 020 8773 8319   **E** dt@londorch.demon.co.uk
*Contact* Dave Tanner

## London Publishing House

22 Denmark St
London
WC2 8NA
**T** 020 7836 5996/7240 5349   **F** 020 7379 5205
**E** music@mautoglade.fsbusiness.co.uk
*Managing Director* Rudi Slezak

## Long Term Music

Suite B
2 Tunstall Rd
London
SW9 8DA
**T** 020 7733 5406   **F** 020 7733 4449
**E** paulette@longterm.freeserve.co.uk
*Contact* Paulette Long

## Longbeach Music
Brunswick Studios
7 Westbourne Grove Mews
London
W11 2RU
**T** 020 7727 8636    **F** 020 7229 4061
*Contact* Simon Watson

## Loose Music
The BEST Building
Wigton
Cumbria
CA7 9PZ
**T** 01697 345422    **F** as telephone
*Director* Simon James

## Low Music
192d Brooklands Rd
Weybridge
Surrey
KT13 0RJ
**T** 01932 855337    **F** 020 8232 8160
*Managing Director* David Morgan

## Lowspeak Music
54–56 Compton St
London
EC1V 0JE
**T** 020 7251 5448    **F** 020 7250 3442

## Luna Park
Suffolk House
1–8 Whitfield Place
London
W1P 5SF
**T** 020 7813 5555    **F** 020 7813 4567
**E** mail@lunarpark.co.uk
*Contact* Russell Vaught

## Lupus Music
1 Star St
London
W2 1QD
**T** 020 7706 7304    **F** 020 7706 8197
**E** morrison@powernet.co.uk
*Managing Director* Bryan Morrison

## Lynwood Music
2 Church St
West Hagley
Stourbridge
West Mids
DY9 0NA
**T** 01562 886625    **F** as telephone
**E** downlyn@globalnet.co.uk
**W** users.globalnet.co.uk/downlyn/index.html
*Managing Director* Rosemary Cooper

*NB: Selected British and European composers of the 20th and 21st centuries*

## M Corporation, The
The Market Place
Ringwood
Hants
BH24 7SZ
**T** 01425 470007    **F** 01425 480569
**E** mm@m-corp.com    **W** m-corp.com

## Machola Music
21c Heathmans Rd
London
SW6 4TJ
**T** 020 7731 9313    **F** 020 7731 9314
**E** machola@qzoneuk.com
*Contact* Nicki L'Amy or David Howells

## Maecenas Music
5 Bushie Close
Old Barn Lane
Kenley
Surrey
CR8 5AU
**T** 020 8660 4766/3914    **F** 020 8668 5273
*Sales Manager* Alan Kirk

## Magick Eye
PO Box 3037
Wokingham
Berks
RG40 4GR
**T** 0118 932 8320    **F** 0118 932 8237
**E** magickeye@magickeye.com    **W** magickeye.com
*Managing Director* Chris Hillman

## Maid Music

28 York Rd
Bury St Edmunds
Suffolk
IP33 3EG
**T** 01284 750058    **F** as telephone
**E** mabsalom@aol.com
*Owner* Mary Bird

## Maingrove Enterprises Publishing

45 Brook Rd
Shanklin
Isle of Wight
PO37 7LD
**T** 01983 866601/53364    **F** 01983 533570
**E** chambe2697@aol.com
*Managing Director* Martin Chambers

## MAP Publishing

27 Abercorn Place
London
NW8 9DX
**T** 07774 267373    **F** 020 7624 7219
**E** hkhan@greycoat.co.uk
*Managing Director* Anthony Pringle

## George Martin Music Ltd

Air Studios
Lyndhurst Rd
London
NW3 5NG
**T** 020 7794 0660    **F** 020 7916 2784
**E** info@georgemartinmusic.com
**W** georgemartinmusic.com
*Chairman* George Martin
*A&R* Adam Sharp and Giles Martin

## Matinee Sound and Vision

132–134 Oxford Rd
Reading
Berks
RG1 7NL
**T** 0118 958 4934    **F** 0118 959 4936
**E** info@matinee.co.uk    **W** matinee.co.uk
*Managing Director* Chris Broderick

## Mautoglade Music

22 Denmark St
London
WC2H 8NA
**T** 020 7836 5996/7240 5349    **F** 020 7379 5205
**E** music@mautoglade.fsbusiness.co.uk
*Managing Director* Frank Coachworth

## Maxwood Music

1 Pratt Mews
London
NW1 0AD
**T** 020 7267 6899    **F** 020 7267 6746
**E** *partners@newman-and.co.uk*
*Contact* Colin Newman

## Mayday Music

PO Box 39
Hoylake
Merseyside
CH47 2HP
**T** 0151 632 6156/07855 945297    **F** as first telephone
**E** al@groovinrecords.com    **W** groovinrecords.com
*Contact* Al Willard Peterson

*See also Groovin' Records*

## Mcasso Music Publishing

9 Carnaby St
London
W1V 1PG
**T** 020 7734 3664    **F** 020 7439 2375
**E** music@mcasso.com    **W** mcasso.com
*Contact* Chris Laurie

## McGuinness Whelan

30–32 Sir John Rogerson's Quay
Dublin 2
Ireland
**T** 00 353 1 677 7330    **F** 00 353 1 677 7276
**E** mcgw@numb.ie    **W** billwhelan.com
*Managing Director* Barbara Galavan

## MCI Music Publishing Ltd

72–74 Dean St
London
W1V 5HB
**T** 020 7396 8899    **F** 020 7470 6659
**E** info@mcimusic.co.uk
*Managing Director* David White

## Medley's Creek Music

PO Box 16047
London
NW1 7ZH
**T** 020 7729 8030 **F** 020 7729 8121
**E** botchit@styx.cerbernet.co.uk
**W** botchitandscarper.co.uk
*Contact* Martin Love

*See also Emotif and Botchit & Scarper (labels)*

## Melody Lauren Music

Unit B2 Livingstone Court
55–63 Peel Rd
Wealdstone
Harrow
Middx
HA3 7QT
**T** 020 8427 2777 **F** 020 8427 0660
**E** wworld@wienerworld.com **W** wienerworld.com
*Managing Director* Anthony Broza

## Melody With Energy

Unit 5, Willtell Works
Upper St John St
Lichfield
Staffs
WS14 9ET
**T** 01543 303200 **F** 01543 303201

## Men From The North Ltd

71 High St East
Wallsend
Tyne and Wear
NE28 7RJ
**T** 0191 262 4999 **F** 0191 263 7082/240 2580
**E** cjess@hotmail.com **W** neatrecrods.com
*Managing Director* Jess Cox

## Menace Music

2 Park Rd
Radlett
Herts
WD7 8EQ
**T** 01923 853789/854789 **F** 01923 853318
**E** dennis@menacemusic.demon.co.uk
*Managing Director* Dennis Collopy

## Meringue Productions Ltd

64 Cole Park Rd
Twickenham
Middx
TW1 1HU
**T** 020 8744 2277 **F** 020 8744 9333
**E** meringue@meringue.co.uk
*Contact* Lynn Earnshaw

## Merlin Group, The

40 Balcombe St
London
NW1 6ND
**T** 020 7616 8100 **F** 020 7723 0732
*Contact* Ray Santilli

## Metcom Music Ltd

26 Astwood Mews
London
SW7 4DE
**T** 020 7565 9100 **F** 020 7565 9101
**E** dolanmap@aol.com
*Managing Director* Mike Dolan

## Mike Music Ltd

Freshwater House
Outdowns
Effingham
Surrey
KT24 5QR
**T** 01483 281500/281501 **F** 01483 281502
**E** mikemultd@aol.com
*Managing Director* Mike Smth
*PA* Sally Thomas
*Head of A&R* Daryl Smith

*Mike Music is administered by Global/Chrysalis Ltd*

## Mikosa Music

9–10 Regent Square
London
WC1H 8HZ
**T** 020 7837 9648 **F** as telephone
*Contact* Mike Osapanin

**Millennium Songs Ltd**
9 Thorpe Close
Portobello Rd
London
W10 5XL
T 020 8964 9495   F 020 8964 9497
E millennium@yr2000.demon.co.uk
*Managing Director* Ben Recknagel

**Minaret Music**
59 Glenthorne Rd
London
W6 0LJ
T 020 8748 4499   F 020 8748 6699
E minaretmusic@dial.pipex.com
*Managing Director* Peter Robinson

**Minder Music Ltd**
18 Pindock Mews
London
W9 2PY
T 020 7289 7281   F 020 7289 2648
E songs@mindermusic.com   W mindermusic.com
*Directors* John Fogarty and Beth Clough
*Copyright and Royalties* Fran Young
*A&R* S Boy

**Ministry of Sound Music Group**
103 Gaunt St
London
SE1 6DP
T 020 7378 6528   F 020 7403 5348
W ministryofsound.com
*Chief Executive Officer* Matt Jagger
*Head of A&R* Ben Cook

**Miriamusic**
1 Glanleam Rd
Stanmore
Middx
HA7 4NW
T 020 8954 2025   F as telephone
*Managing Director* Zack Laurence

**Mix Music (UK)**
3 Progress Business Centre
Whittle Parkway
Burnham
Bucks
SL1 6DQ
T 01628 667124   F 01628 605246/669783
E info@dmcworld.demon.co.uk
*Business Affairs Manager* Jeremy Butson

**Moggie Music Ltd**
101 Hazelwood Lane
London
N13 5HQ
T 020 8886 2801   F 020 8882 7380
E moggie@halcarterorg.com
*Contact* Hal or Abbie Carter

*Always open to good-quality commercial
songs*

**4AD Music Ltd**
17–19 Alma Rd
London
SW18 1AA
T 020 8871 2121/020 8870 9912   F 020 8871 2745
*Managing Director* Andy Heath

**Moncur Street Music Ltd**
PO Box 16114
London
SW3 4WG
T 020 7349 9909/020 7351 0272   F 020 7376 8532
E 106712.447@compuserve.com
W moncurstreet.uk.com
*Contact* Jonathan Simon

**Monument Music Ltd**
95 Hawkesfield Rd
London
SE23 2TN
T 020 8291 3687   F 020 8699 1438
E diversemusicltd@compuserve.com
*Contact* Diana Graham

*Also Diverse Music Ltd and Grapevine Music Ltd
(same contact details)*

## Bryan Morrison Music

1 Star St
London
W2 1QD
**T** 020 7706 7304    **F** 020 7706 8167
**E** morrison@powernet.co.uk
**W** cyberconcerts.com
*Managing Director* Bryan Morrison

*Also Suburban Base Music, Lupus Music, Morrison Evans Music, Morrison Budd Music, Cyberconcerts (same contact details)*

## Morrison Leahy Music

1 Star St
London
W2 1QD
**T** 020 7258 0093    **F** 020 7402 9238
*Contact* Peter Stretton

## Moss Music

7 Dennis Rd
Corfe Mullen
Wimborne
Dorset
BH21 3NF
**T** 01202 695965    **F** as telephone
*Director* Peter Moss

*Also production, music arranging and preparation*

## Mostyn Music

8 Milvil Court
Milvil Rd
Lee-on-the-Solent
Hants
PO13 9LY
**T** 02392 550566    **F** as telephone
**E** tony@mostynmusic.com    **W** mostynmusic.com
*Managing Director* Tony Cresswell

*Specialists in music for junior brass bands, wind bands, junior orchestra and classroom music*

## Moving Shadow Music

2nd Floor
17 St Anne's Court
London
W1V 3AW
**T** 020 7734 6770    **F** 020 7734 6771

**E** info@movingshadow.com
**W** movingshadow.com
*Managing Director* Rob Playford

## Mozo Music

PO Box 3383
London
NW1 0NN
**T** 020 8348 2233    **F** 020 8348 2234
**E** zoomrecrods@zoom.co.uk
*Contact* David Wesson

## MP Music

78 Portland Rd
London
W11 4LQ
**T** 020 7727 2063    **F** 020 7229 4188
*Manager* Cathy Negus-Fancey

## Mr And Mrs Music

3 Warwick Way
London
SW1V 1QU
**T** 020 7976 6021    **F** 020 7976 6431
*Director* Les Burgess

## MSM & LGB Music

Gilbert House
406 Roding Lane South
Woodford Green
Essex
IG8 8EY
**T** 020 8551 1282    **F** 020 8550 8377
*Managing Directors* Mrs ML Wright and Mr MD Jackson

## M21

Northborough House
10 Northborough St
London
EC1V 0AT
**T** 020 7253 5860    **F** 020 7253 5850
**E** m21@m21.co.uk    **W** m21.co.uk
*Director* Adrian Faiers

## Muirhead Music Publishing

202 Fulham Rd
London
SW10 9PJ
**T** 020 7351 5167   **F** 020 7352 1514
**E** muirhead_management@compuserve.com
*Chief Executive Officer* Dennis Muirhead

## Multiplay Music

Maple Farm
56 High St
Harrold
Beds
MK43 7DA
**T** 01234 720785   **F** 01234 720664
**E** multiplaymusic@maplefarm.demon.co.uk
**W** multiplaymusic.com
*Contact* Kevin White

## Mummer Music

38 Grovelands Rd
London
N13 4RH
**T** 020 8350 0613   **F** as telephone
**E** jim@j.cook21.freeserve.co.uk
*Contact* Jim Cook

*Also legal and business affairs, and music consultant*

## Munnycroft

21c Heathmans Rd
London
SW6 4TJ
**T** 020 7731 9321   **F** 020 7731 9314
**E** munnycroft@darah.co.uk
*Managing Director* Irene Howells

## Murder Music

Monticello
Wellington Hill
High Beach
Loughton
Essex
IG10 4AH
**T** 020 8532 1654   **F** 020 8532 1656
**E** ania.e@btinternet.com
*Managing Director* Peter Edwards

## Murfin Music International

Old Smithy Recording Studio
1 Post Office Lane
Kempsey
Worcs
WR5 3NS
**T** 01905 820659   **F** 01905 820015
**E** muff.murfin@virgin.net
*Managing Director* Muff Murfin

*Also Happy Face Music (same details)*

## Murray Music

24 Woodhouse Lodge
Woodhouse Eaves
Northwood
Middx
HA6 3NF
**T** 01923 829083
*Contact* Stuart Reid; *Partner* Patricia Reid

*Country Music*

## Mushroom Music

1 Shorrolds Rd
London
SW6 7TR
**T** 020 7343 5678   **F** 020 7343 5656
**W** mushroomuk.com

## Music & Elsewhere (Mmatterial)

6 Farm Court
Farm Rd
Frimley
Camberley
Surrey
GU16 5TJ
**T** 01276 684209
*Managing Director* Mick Magic

## Music Exchange (Manchester) Ltd

Claverton Rd
Wythenshawe
Greater Manchester
M23 9ZA
**T** 0161 946 1234   **F** 0161 946 1195
**E** mail@music-exchange.co.uk
**W** music-exchange.co.uk
*Contact* John O'Brien
*Director* Tony Osborn

*Publisher and distributor, also selling music by all publishers worldwide (classical, popular and examination scores)*

## Music Factor Ltd, The

61 Queen's Drive
London
N4 2BG
**T** 020 8802 5984   **F** 020 8809 7436
**E** themusicfactor@paulrodriguezmus.demon.co.uk
*Contact* Paul Rodriguez

## Music House (International) Ltd

2nd Floor, 143 Charing Cross Rd
London
WC2H 0EE
**T** 020 7434 9678   **F** 020 7434 1470
**E** enquiries@musichouse.co.uk
**W** musichouse.co.uk
*General Manager* Simon James

*NB: production music library*

## Music Like Dirt

12 Kenneth Court
173 Kennington Rd
London
SE11 6SS
**T** 020 7582 6959   **F** 020 7793 0285
**E** patrick@musiclikedirt.co.uk
*Contact* Patrick Meads

## Music Sales Ltd

8–9 Frith St
London
W1V 5TZ
**T** 020 7434 0066   **F** 020 7439 2848
**E** chris.butler@musicsales.co.uk
**W** internetmusicshop.com
*Contact* Chris Butler
*Managing Director* Robert Wise

*Music Sales is a worldwide company involved in copyright ownership and exploitation, sheet music publishing, book publishing, music retailing and e-commerce*

## Musicare Ltd

60 Huntstown Wood
Clonsilla
Dublin 15
Ireland
**T** 00 353 1 820 6483   **F** 00 353 1 820 5626
*Contact* Brian Barker

## Mute Song

Lawford House
429 Harrow Rd
London
W10 4RE
**T** 020 8964 2001   **F** 020 8968 6983
**E** dmcginnis@mutehq.co.uk
*Creative Licensing* David McGinnis
*General Manager* Andrew King

## Neon Productions Ltd

Studio One
19 Marine Crescent
Kinning Park
Glasgow
G51 1HD
**T** 0141 429 6366   **F** 0141 429 6377
**E** neon.productions@dial.pipex.xom
**W** go2neon.com
*Contact* Stephanie Pordage

## Nervous Publishing

7–11 Minerva Rd
London
NW10 6HJ
**T** 020 8963 0352   **F** 020 8963 1170
**E** 100613.3456@compuserve.com   **W** nervous.co.uk
*Managing Director* Roy Williams

*Also Zorch Music (same details)*

## New Age Music Ltd

17 Priory Rd
London
NW6 4NN
**T** 020 7209 2766   **F** 020 7813 2766
**E** gerrybron@easynet.co.uk   **W** gerrybron.com
*Contact* Gerry Bron

*Also artist management*

## New Music Enterprises

Meredale
Reach Lane
Heath and Reach
Leighton Buzzard
Beds
LU7 0AL
**T** 01525 237700   **F** as telephone
**E** pauldavis@newmusic28.freeserve.co.uk
**w** lcf.uk.net
*Proprietor* Paul Davis

*Specialists in gospel music*

## Niles Productions/Nucool Records/Nucool Studio

34 Beaumont Rd
London
W4 5AP
**T** 020 8248 2157   **F** 020 8248 2154
**E** smiles@richardniles.demon.co.uk   **w** 1212.com/a/niles/richard
*Managing Director* Richard Niles

*Publisher, producer, composer, arranger and owner of the Nucool label and studio*

## 19 Music

Unit 33, Ransomes Dock
35–37 Parkgate Rd
London
SW11 4NP
**T** 020 7801 1919   **F** 020 7801 1920/7738 1819
*Contact* Joanne McCormack

## No Known Cure Publishing

190 Harwich Rd
Colchester
Essex
CO4 3DE
**T** 01206 865813
*Managing Director* T F McCarthy

## Noise of Shade

46 Spenser Rd
London
SE24 0NR
**T** 020 7274 6618   **F** 020 7737 4712
**E** charmenko@atlas.co.uk   **w** charm.demon.co.uk
*Contact* Nick Hobbs

## North Star Music Publishing Ltd

PO Box 868
Cambridge
CB1 6SJ
**T** 01223 890908   **F** 01223 890471
**E** nsminfo@aol.com   **w** northstarmusic.co.uk
*Contact* Grahame Maclean

## Northern Light Music

Suite 222
Glenfield Park
Lomeshaye
Nelson
Lancs
BB9 7DR
**T** 01282 611547   **F** 01282 718901
*Contact* Andrew Hall

## Notation Music

1st Floor, 37 Cantelowes Rd
London
NW1 9XU
**T** 020 7485 4466
*Contact* Ana Turner

## Notting Hill Music (UK) Ltd

Bedford House
8b Berkeley Gardens
London
W8 4AP
**T** 020 7243 2921   **F** 020 7243 2894
**E** notting@netcomuk.co.uk
*Managing Director* David Loader
*Chair* Andy McQueen

## Novello & Company

8–9 Frith St
London
W1V 5TZ
**T** 020 7434 0066   **F** 020 7287 6329
**E** music@musicsales.co.uk   **w** musicsales.co.uk

## Obelisk Music

32 Ellerdale Rd
London
NW3 6BB
**T** 020 7435 5255   **F** 020 7431 0621
*Contact* H Herschmann

## Odd On Music

21 Nottingham Place
London
W1M 3FF
**T** 020 7487 5373   **F** 020 7487 2769
*Contact* Roger Lahaye

## Old Bridge Music

PO Box 7
Ilkley
West Yorkshire
LS29 9RY
**T** 01943 602203   **F** as telephone
**E** obm@compuserve.com   **W** oldbridgemusic.com
*Partner* Chris Newman

## 100%love Music

PO Box 134
Horley
Surrey
RH6 0FT
**T** 01293 862459   **F** 01293 862913

## Onion Music

3 Harvard Rd
Isleworth
Middx
TW7 4PA
**T** 020 8847 3556   **F** 020 8232 8717
**E** julie@onionmusic.co.uk
*Contact* Julie Fletcher

*Any style as long as it's good*
*Also 7hz (management company with same contact details)*

## Online Music

Unit 18, Croydon House
1 Peall Rd
Croydon
Surrey
CRO 3EX
**T** 020 8287 8595/07802 813008
**E** onlinerecs@cableinet.co.uk
**W** onlinestudios.co.uk
*Contact* Dave Ivy

## Opal Music

3 Pembridge Mews
London
W11 3EQ
**T** 020 7727 8656   **F** 020 7221 4909
*Director* Anthea Norman-Taylor

## 141099 Songs Ltd

21 Denmark St
London
WC2H 8NA
**T** 020 7240 7696   **F** 020 9379 3398/7240 8976
*Contact* Dennis Sinnott

## Orestes Music Publishing

PO Box 10653
London
W5 4WR
**T** 020 8993 7441   **F** 020 8992 9993
**E** orestes@dorm.co.uk   **W** orestesmusic.com
*Contact* David O'Reilly

## Origin Music

Le Tone House
270 Watford Way
London
NW4 4UJ
**T** 020 8203 1988   **F** 020 8203 7178
**E** origin.pub@virgin.net
*Contact* Kieron Lyons

## Oxford University Press

Great Clarendon St
Oxford
Oxfordshire
OX2 6DP
**T** 01865 556767   **F** 01865 267749
*Contact* Suzy Gooch

## P3 Music

PO Box 8403
Maybole
KA19 7YB
**T** 01655 750549   **F** 01655 750548
**E** james@p3music.com   **W** p3music.com
*Contact* James Taylor or Alison Burns

*Also agency, label, management and consultancy*

### Larry Page Productions Ltd
9 Roehampton Court
Queens Ride
London
SW13 0HU
**T** 020 8878 3384/07850 303001   **F** 020 8392 9149
*Managing Director* Larry Page

### Palan Music Publishing Ltd
Greenland Place
115–123 Bayham St
London
NW1 0AG
**T** 020 7446 7444   **F** 020 7446 7447
**E** chrig@palan.com   **W** palan.com
*Contact* Chris Gray

### Panama Music (Library)
Sovereign House
12 Trewartha Rd
Praa Sands
Penzance
Cornwall
TR20 9ST
**T** 01736 762826/07721 449477   **F** 01736 763328
**E** pananus@aol.com   **W** panamamusic.co.uk
*Managing Director* Roderick Jones
*Copyright and Royalties* Carole Jones
*Prod Dir* Colin Eade
*Business Affairs* Anne Eade

### Panganai Music
296 Earls Court Rd
London
SW5 9BA
**T** 020 7565 0806   **F** 020 7565 0806/020 7244 0916
**E** blackmagicrecords@talk21.com
**W** blackmagicrecords.com
*Managing Director* Mataya Clifford

### Parachute Music Ltd
86 Birmingham Rd
Lichfield
Staffordshire
WS13 6PJ
**T** 01543 253576/07585 341745   **F** as first telephone
**E** 106454.2770@compuserve.com
**W** ourworld.compuserve.com/homepages/
parachute_music_mjs_pro
*Managing Director* Mervyn Spence

### Paradigm Music
143 West Vale
Neston
South Wirral
Cheshire
CH64 0TJ
**T** 0151 336 6657   **F** as telephone
**E** andy@subsymphonic.com
**W** subsymphonic.com
*Contact* Andy Williams

### Parliament Music
PO Box 6328
London
N2 0UN
**T** 020 8444 9841   **F** 020 8442 1973
**E** woolfman@compuserve.com
*Contact* David Woolfson

### Partisan Songs
c/o Terminal Studios
4–10 Lamb Walk
London
SE3 3TT
**T** 020 7357 8416   **F** 020 7357 8437
*Managing Director* Caroline Butler

*Specialist drum 'n' bass label*

### Patterdale Music Ltd
59 Marlpit Lane
Coulsdon
Surrey
CR5 2HF
**T** 020 8666 0201   **F** 020 8667 0037
*Managing Director* Bob Barratt

### PED Publishing
PO Box 2311
Romford
Essex
RM5 2DZ
**T** 01992 763777   **F** 01992 763463
*Contact* Dan Donnelly

## Peermusic (Ireland)

Peer House
12 Lower Pembroke St
Dublin 2
Ireland
**T** 00 353 1 662 9337    **F** 00 353 1 662 9339
**E** dublin@peermusic.com    **w** peermusic.com
*Managing Director* Darragh M Kettle

*See also Digital Pressure.com Inc*

## Peermusic (UK)

Peer House
8–14 Verulam St
London
WC1X 8LZ
**T** 020 7404 7200    **F** 020 7404 7004
**E** peersears@peermusic.com    **w** peermusic.com
*European Vice President* Nigel Elderton

## Pequuliar Publishing

111 Clarence Rd
London
SW19 8QB
**T** 020 8540 8122    **F** 020 8715 2827
*Director* John Mabley

## Perfect Songs

The Blue Building
42–46 St Luke's Mews
London
W11 1DG
**T** 020 7221 5101    **F** 020 7221 3374
**E** liam@perfectsongs.com
*Contact* Liam Teeling

## Petal Music

PO Box 46
Radlett
Herts
WD7 7JE
**T** 020 7434 9678    **F** 01923 852776
**E** bigal@globalnet.co.uk
**w** users.globalnet.co.uk/-bigal/home/htm
*Contact* Alan Hawkshaw

## Peters Edition

10–12 Baches St
London
N1 6DN
**T** 020 7553 4000/020 7553 4020    **F** 020 7490 4921
**E** sales@uk.edition-peters.com
**w** edition-peters.com

*NB: classical music publisher*
*Peters Edition has been publishing music for over 200*
*years and offers comprehensive range of sheet music*
*including Grade & Piano Anthologies and music for*
*the 'A' Level syllabus*
*Free catalogue and information available on request*

## PHAB Music

High Notes
Sheerwater Avenue
Woodham
Surrey
KT15 3DS
**T** 01932 348174    **F** 01932 340921
*Managing Director* Philip HA Bailey

## Phantom Publishing

59 Moore Park Rd
London
SW6 2HH
**T** 020 7731 0022    **F** 020 7731 1715
*Managing Director* Falcon Stuart

## Pisces Publishing

20 Middle Row
London
W10 5AT
**T** 020 8964 4555    **F** 020 8964 4666
**E** hq@pisces.uk.com    **w** pisces.uk.com
*Managing Director* Morgan Khan

## Playpus Music

PO Box 5594
Thatcham
Berkshire
RG18 9YH
**T** 01488 657200    **F** 01488 657222
*Contact* John Brand

## Playbox Music Ltd
101 Chamberlayne Rd
London
NW10 3ND
**T** 020 8960 8466   **F** 020 8968 0804
**E** clive@csatelltapes.demon.co.uk
*Managing Director* Clive Stanhope

## Plus Music Publishing
36 Follingham Court
Drysdale Place
London
N1 6LZ
**T** 020 7684 8594   **F** 020 7684 8740
*Contact* Mr D Chisholm

*Soul, pop, r&b, funk, house*

## Pluto Music
Hulgrave Hall
Tiverton
Tarporley
Cheshire
CW6 9UQ
**T** 01829 732427/07973 861777   **F** 01829 733802
**E** info@plutomusic.com
*Managing Director* Keith Hopwood

## Pogo Music
White House Farm
Shropshire
TF9 4HA
**T** 01630 647374   **F** 01630 647612
*Copyright Manager* Catherine Lematt

*Also RTL Music*
*Pogo and RTL are also record companies*

## Popsongs Ltd
27 Advance House
109 Ladbroke Grove
London
W11 1PG
**T** 020 7792 3502   **F** 020 7229 5195
**E** popcorp@aol.com
*Contact* Pete Jones

## POW! Music
Unit 11, Impress House
Mansell Rd
London
W3 7QH
**T** 020 8932 3044   **F** 020 8932 3032
**E** info@powmusic.co.uk
*Contact* Keith Neill

## Power Music
29 Riversdale Rd
Thames Ditton
Surrey
KT7 0QN
**T** 020 8398 5236/5732   **F** 020 8398 7901
*Managing Director* Barry Evans

## Power Music Company
1 Station Rd
Harecroft
Wilsden
Bradford
West Yorkshire
BD15 0BS
**T** 01535 272905   **F** 01535 273520
**E** power music@btinternet.com
**W** btinternet.com/power.music
*Managing Director* James Power

*Educational music, instrumental trios, quartets, jazz solos and string ensembles*

## Precious Music Co.
The Townhouse
1 Park Gate
Glasgow
G3 6DL
**T** 0141 353 2255   **F** 0141 353 3545

## Premium Music
Unit 1, The Stableyard
16a Balham Hill
London
SW12 9EB
**T** 020 8673 2525   **F** 020 8673 2625
**E** info@premium.softnet.co.uk

## Prime Music Publishing Ltd
340 Athlon Rd
Alperton
Middx
HA0 1BX
**T** 020 8601 2200 **F** 020 8601 2262
**E** max@primedistribution.co.uk
*Contact* Max Mackie

## Primrose Music Publishing Ltd
1 Leitrim House
36 Worple Rd
London
SW19 4EQ
**T** 020 7736 5520 **F** 020 8946 3392
**E** jestersong@msn.com **W** primrosemusic.com
*Director* Roland B Rogers

*Music library providing production music for all media, 'from the gavotte to garage'*

## Proof Songs
PO Box 20242
London
NW1 7FL
**T** 020 7485 1113 **E** proofsongs@mailbox.xo.uk

*Specialists in dance music*

## Proper Music Publishing
PO Box 89
Bromley
Kent
BR2 0ZU
**T** 020 8699 8100
*Contact* Malcolm Mills

## PSI-Pumphouse Songs Inc
The Brewery
91 Brick Lane
London
E1 6GN
**T** 020 7377 1516 **E** markbeder@hotmail.com
*Managing Director* Mark Beder

## Published By Patrick
18 Pindock Mews
London
W9 2PY
**T** 020 7289 7281 **F** 020 7289 2648

**E** songs@mindermusic.com **W** mindermusic.com
*Director* John Fogarty

*See also Minder Music Ltd*

## Pure Groove Music
679 Holloway Rd
London
N19 5SE
**T** 020 7263 4660 x23 **F** 020 7263 9669
**E** mickshiner@puregroove.co.uk
**W** puregroove.co.uk
*Contact* Mick Shiner

## Purple Patch Music
144 Camden High St
London
NW1 0NE
**T** 020 7543 7500 **F** 020 7543 7643
**E** sperry@purplepatch.com **W** purplepatch.com
*Contact* Sharon Perry

## PXM Publishing
45 Mount Ash Rd
London
SE26 6LY
**T** 020 8699 5835 **F** as telephone
**E** pxm.publishing@virgin.net
**W** pxmpublishing.com
*Administration* Carolyne Rodgers

## QD Music
35b Marryat Square
Wyfold Rd
London
SW6 6UA
**T** 020 7381 5529/07956 858814
**F** as first telephone
**E** info@qdmusic.demon.co.uk
**W** qdmusic.demon.co.uk
*Contact* Drew Todd

## Quaife Music Publishing
9 Carroll Hill
Loughton
Essex
IG10 1NL
**T** 020 8508 3639 **F** 0870 401 6885
**E** qmusic@carrollhill.freeserve.co.uk
*Contact* A E Quaife

*NB: deals exclusively with the work of Peter O'Donnell*

### Radio Music Britain

Unit 9, Elsinore House
77 Fulham Palace Rd
London
W6 8JA
**T** 020 8741 8686   **F** 020 8741 8646
*Director* R Alexander

### RAK Publishing

42–48 Charlbert St
London
NW8 7BU
**T** 020 7586 2012   **F** 020 7722 5823
**E** trisha@rakstudios.co.uk/
rakpublishing@ukmax.com   **W** rakstudios.co.uk
*Managing Director* Mickie Most

### Rapid Publishing

26 Rochester Mews
London
NW1 9JB
**T** 020 7267 2249   **F** 020 7267 4277
*Contact* Felly Munga

### Raw Talent Music Ltd

55 Loudon Rd
London
NW8 0DL
**T** 020 8744 1210   **F** as telephone
*Contact* A Neville

### Real World Music Ltd

Box Mill
Mill Lane
Box
Wilts
SN13 8PL
**T** 01225 743188   **F** 01225 744369
**E** publishing@realworld.co.uk
**W** realworld.on.net/publishing/index
*Contact* Rob Bozas

*World music publishing company specializing in films, TV and advertising*

### Really Useful Group

22 Tower St
London
WC2H 9NS
**T** 020 7240 0880   **F** 020 7240 1204
**E** robinsond@reallyuseful.co.uk
**W** reallyuseful.com
*Contact* David Robinson

*NB: Specialists in music theatre*

### Really Wicked Publishing

Unit 10, Kent House
Old Bexley Business Park
19 Bourne Rd
Bexley
Kent
DA5 1LR
**T** 01322 657355   **E** mholmes822@aol.com
**W** htdrecords.com
*Contact* Barry Riddington

### Rebecca Music

Terwick Place
Rogate
Petersfield
Hampshire
GU31 5PY
**T** 01730 821644   **F** 01730 821597
**E** donna@lesreed.com   **W** lesreed.com
*Directors* Donna Reed and Les Reed OBE

### Red Bus Music International/Library

34 Salisbury St
London
NW8 8QE
**T** 020 7402 9111   **F** 020 7723 3064
*Contact* Eliot Cohen

### Redrock Music

The Weald
58 Hillside Rd
Northwood
Middx
HA6 1QB
**T** 01923 825997
*Contact* Mrs M Pitts

## Reverb Music Ltd
Reverb House
Bennett St
London
W4 2AH
**T** 020 8747 0660   **F** 020 8747 0880
**E** ian.wright@reverbxl.com   **W** reverbxl.com
*Managing Director* Ian Wright

## Revolver Music Publishing
152 Goldthorn Hill
Penn
Wolverhampton
West Midlands
WV2 3JA
**T** 01902 345345   **F** 01902 345155

## Rhiannon Music Ltd
20 Montague Rd
London
E8 2HW
**T** 020 7275 8292   **F** 020 7503 8034
**E** info@rhiannonrecords.co.uk
**W** rhiannonrecords.co.uk
*Contact* Colin Jones

*See also Rhiannon Records*

## Rich Mountain Music
PO Box 19
Ulverston
Cumbria
LA12 9TF
**T** 01229 581766   **F** as telephone
*Managing Director* J G Livingstone

## Rickim Music Publishing Company
Big M House
1 Stevenage Rd
Knebworth
Herts
SG3 6AN
**T** 01438 814433   **F** 01438 815252
**E** rickim@bigmgroup.co.uk
**W** bigmgroup.u-net.com
*General Manager* Joyce Wilde

## G Ricordi & Co (London) Ltd
Bedford House
69–79 Fulham High St
London
SW6 3JW
**T** 020 7384 8195   **F** 020 7371 7270
**E** miranda.jackson@bmg.co.uk
*Contact* Miranda Jackson

*Affiliate of BMG Music Publishing UK*

## Riff Raff Records/Riff Raff Management
99 Peerless Drive
Harefield
Middx
UB9 6JF
**T** 01895 825424   **F** 01895 820246
**E** roy@riffraffmanagement.com
*Contact* Roy Jackson

*Songwriters and Producer Management
Artist Record Company*

## Rita (Publishing) Ltd
41 Culverhay
Ashtead
Surrey
KT21 1PP
**T** 01372 276293   **F** 01372 276328
**E** thebestmusicis@ritapublishing.com
**W** ritapublishing.com
*Contact* Ralph Norton

## Rive Droite Music
Home Park House
Hampton Court Rd
Kingston upon Thames
Surrey
KT1 4AE
**T** 020 8977 0666   **F** 020 8977 0660
**E** pzauriew@rivedroitemusic.com   **W** 13bis.com
*Contact* Phillipe Zauriew

## Riverhorse Songs Ltd
115 Eastbourne Mews
London
W2 6LQ
**T** 020 7262 2882   **F** 020 7262 1661
**E** theherd@riverhorserecords.com
**W** riverhorserecords.com
*Managing Director* Robin Godfrey-Cass

*General Manager* Angela O'Connor
*Creative Manager* Darran Bennett

## RMO Music
37 Phillip Close
Carshalton
Surrey
SM5 2FE
*Managing Director* Reg McLean

## Roberton Publications
The Windmill
Wendover
Aylesbury
Buckinghamshire
HP22 6JJ
T 01296 623107    F 01296 696536
W impulse-music.co.uk/roberton and gbdf.co.uk
*Managing Partner* Kenneth Roberton

*Sacred and secular music for mixed voice choirs,
music for children's and female voices, part songs and
arrangement for male voice choirs, songs for solo
voice, instrumental music*

## Robin Song Music (UK)
Hammersley Lodge
Hammersley Lane
Penn
Buckinghamshire
HP10 8HE
T 0149 481 6987    F 0149 481 5524
E mike@collierassociate.demon.co.uk
*Managing Director* Mike Collier

*Leading independent publisher, formerly promoter
and co-producer of such artists as Sam Cooke and
The Isley Bros in the US, The Hollies, Herman's
Hermits and Georgie Fame in the UK before
discovering Duran Duran*

## Paul Rodriguez Music Ltd
61 Queen's Drive
London
N4 2BG
T 020 8802 5984    F 020 8809 7436
E paul@paulrodriguezmus.demon.co.uk
*Contact* Paul Rodriguez

## Rokstone Music Ltd
21a Heathmans Rd
London
SW6 4TJ
T 020 7736 1555    F 020 7731 9314
E mail@darah.co.uk
*Contact* David Howells

## Rondor Music (London) Ltd
3 Heathmans Rd
London
SW6 4TJ
T 020 7731 4161    F 020 7736 1880
E r.thomas@rondor.co.uk
*Managing Director* Richard Thomas

## Rosehill Music Publishing Company Ltd
Suite 7, Pegasus House
Haddenham Business Park
Haddenham
Bucks
HP17 LL
T 01844 290798    F 01844 290757
E sales@rosehillmusic.com    W rosehillmusic.com
*Managing Director* Peter Wilson

*Specialists in music for brass bands, wind bands and
brass soloists/ensembles*

## Rose Rouge International
Aws Group
Aws House
Trinity Square
St Peter Port
Guernsey
GY1 1LX
T 01481 728294    F 01481 714118
E aws@gtonline.net    W awsgroup.co.uk
*Director* Steve Free

*Also record company and artist management*

## Rough Trade Publishing Ltd
81 Wallingford Rd
Goring
Reading
Berkshire
RG8 0HL
T 01491 873612    F 01491 872744
E info@rough-trade.com    W rough-trade.com
*A&R* Matt Wilkinson

## MRM (Mark Rowles Music)

Cedar House
Vine Lane
Hillingdon
Middx
UB10 0BX
**T** 01895 251515 **F** 01895 251616
**E** mail@mrmltd.co.uk
*Managing Director* Mark Rowles

*Also radio documentary specialist*

## RP Media Publishing Ltd

Kingsway House
134–140 Church Rd
Hove
East Sussex
BH3 2DL
**T** 01273 220700 **F** 01273 220800
**E** rp_media@compuserve.com
*Contact* David Paramor

## Rubicon Music

59 Park View Rd
London
NW10 1AJ
**T** 020 8450 5154 **F** 020 8452 0187
**W** rubisonrecords.co.uk
*Contact* Graham Le Fevre

## Rufus Music

The Cooperage
91–95 Brick Lane
London
E1 6QN
**T** 020 7247 6677 **F** 020 7247 8244
*Contact* Mark Blanch

## Rumour Records

Tempo House
15 Falcon Rd
London
SW11 2PJ
**T** 020 7228 6821 **F** 020 7228 6972
**E** post@rumour.demon.co.uk
**W** rumour.demon.co.uk
*Directors* David Brooker and Anne Plaxton

*Specialist in all dance music genres*

## Rykomusic Ltd

329 Latimer Rd
London
W10 6RA
**T** 020 8960 3311 **F** 020 8960 4334
**E** paul.lambden@rykodisc.co.uk
*General Manager* Paul Lambden

## St James Music

34 Great James St
London
WC1N 3HB
**T** 020 7405 3786/3798 **F** 020 7405 5245/
020 7404 7043 **E** stjames2@dircon.co.uk
*Managing Director* Keith C Thomas
*A&R Director* Christian Baldock

*Also Sleeping Giant Music International, Prestige
Records Ltd, Prestige Video Collection and Music
Avenue UK Ltd (same details)*

## Salvin Music Ltd

3rd Floor
9 Carnaby St
London
W1V 1PG
**T** 020 7437 1958/1959 **F** 020 7437 3852
*Managing Director* Tony Hall

## Sanctuary Publishing

1st Floor Suite
The Collonades
82 Bishops Bridge Rd
London
W2 6BB
**T** 020 7602 6351

## Sanctuary Music Publishing

Sanctuary House
45–53 Sinclair Rd
London
W14 0NS
**T** 020 7300 1866 **F** 020 7300 1864
**E** jamie.arlon@sanctuarygroup.com
**W** sanctuarygroup.com
*Contact* James Arlon

*Representing songwriters who write and produce for
major artists, and singer/songwriters and artists for
soundtrack and commercial music
Owns April Music Ltd*

## SANE
78 Barnards Hill
Marlow
Bucks
SL7 2NZ
**T** 01628 473991/0836 342256
**E** stuart@snewton.fsbusiness.co.uk
*Contact* Stuart Newton

*Also songwriter and producer management and consultancy, with 25 years of independent and corporate publishing experience*

## Sarah Music
Cherry Tree Lodge
Copmanthorpe
York
North Yorks
YO23 3SH
**T** 01904 703764    **F** 01904 702312
**E** (user name)@demon.co.uk
**W** thedandys.demon.co.uk
*Contact* Mal Spence

## Scamp Music
Sovereign House
12 Trewartha Rd
Praa Sands
Penzance
Cornwall
TR20 9ST
**T** 01736 762826/07721 449477    **F** 01736 763328
**E** panamus@aol.com    **W** panamamusic.co.uk
*Managing Director* Roderick G Jones

## Schauer & May
Simrock House
220 The Vale
London
NW11 8HZ
**T** 020 8731 6665    **F** 020 8731 6667

*Also Richard Schauer (same details)*

## School-Sheet Music
18 The Bramblings
London
E4 6LU
**T** 020 8529 5807    **F** as telephone
*Managing Director* David Bull

## Schott & Co Ltd
48 Great Marlborough St
London
W1F 7BB
**T** 020 7437 1246    **F** 020 7437 0263
**E** marketing@schott-music.co.uk
**W** schott-music.com
*Contact* Judith Webb

## SCO Music
29 Oakroyd Avenue
Potters Bar
Herts
EN6 2EL
**T** 01707 651439    **F** as telephone
**E** constantine@steveconstantine.freeserve.co.uk
*Contact* Steve Constantine

## Scotty's Sound Studio
Newtown St
Kilsyth
Glasgow
Strathclyde
G6S 0JX
**T** 01236 823291/825843    **F** 01236 826900
**E** nscott@scotdisc.co.uk    **W** scotdisc.co.uk
*Director* Bill Garden

## Sea Dream Music
PO Box 13533
London
E7 0SG
**T** 020 8534 8500    **F** 07070 718613
*Snr Partner* Simon Law

## SEBEK
Georgetown Park
St Clement
Jersey
Channel Islands
JE2 6QF
**T** 020 7431 9565/01534 856545    **F** 020 7431 1563
**E** hammer@itl.net
*Contact* Bob Miller

## See For Miles Music
Unit 10, Littleton House
Littleton Rd
Ashford
Middx
TW15 1UU
**T** 01784 247176   **F** 01784 241168
**E** es95@dial.pipex.com   **W** seeformiles.co.uk
*Director* Colin Miles

## Selectus Music
145 Uxendon Hill
Wembley
Middx
HA9 9SH
**T** 020 8904 1900
*Contact* Lee Gopthal

## Seriously Groovy Music Ltd
3rd Floor
28 D'Arblay St
London
W1V 3FH
**T** 020 7439 1947   **F** 020 7734 7540
**E** seriousgrv@aol.com
**W** members.aol.com/seriousgrv/
*Director* Dave Holmes

## Seven Publishing & Management (7PM)
PO Box 2272
Rottingdean
Brighton
BN2 8XD
**T** 01273 304681   **F** 01273 308120
**E** seven-webster@beeb.net
*Contact* Seven Webster

*See also under Management, and Jackpot Records
(same contact details)*

## SGO Music Publishing Ltd
PO Box 26022
London
SW10 0FY
**T** 07071 226822   **F** 07071 225119
**E** sgomusic@aol.com   **W** sgomusic.co.uk
*Chief Executive* Stuart Ongley

## Shake Up Music
Ickenham Manor
Ickenham
Uxbridge
Middx
UB10 8QT
**T** 01895 672994   **F** 01895 633264
**E** mail@shakeupmusic.co.uk
*Contact* Joanna Tizard

*Speciality: Production Library Music*

## Shalit Music
Cambridge Theatre
Seven Dials
London
WC2H 9HU
**T** 020 7379 3282   **F** 020 7379 3238
*Managing Director* Jonathan Shalit

## Shanna Music Ltd/Connect 2 Music Ltd
PO Box 31
Bushey
Herts
WD23 2LR
**T** 01923 244673   **F** 01923 244693
**E** info@connectmusic.com   **W** connectmusic.com
*Chief Executive Officer* Barry Blue

*Shanna deals with commercial tracks, Connect 2 is a
production music library servicing the media, TV/
film and video companies*

## Sharp End Music Group
Grafton House
2–3 Golden Square
London
W1F 9HR
**T** 020 7439 8442   **F** 020 7439 1814
**E** sharpend2@aol.com
*Directors* Robert Lemon and Ron McCreight

*Also PR, promotion and label*

## Sherlock Holmes Music
2 Pride Court
80 White Lion St
London
N1 9PF
**T** 020 7278 8860   **F** 020 7278 6852
*Contact* Ian Volke

## Silva Screen Music (Publishers) Ltd
3 Prowse Place
London
NW1 9PH
**T** 020 7428 5500    **F** 020 7482 2385
**E** info@silvascreen.co.uk    **W** silvascreen.co.uk
*Managing Director* Reynold D'Silva

## Alan Simmons Music
PO Box 7
Scissett
Huddersfield
West Yorkshire
HD8 9YZ
**T** 01924 848888
**E** mail@alansimmonsmusic.com
**W** alansimmonsmusic.com
*Managing Director* Alan Simmons

*Specialist in music for schools and choirs*
*Catalogues available on request*

## Single Minded Music Publishing
Suite 16, The Linen House
253 Kilburn Lane
London
W10 4BQ
**T** 0181 968 1001/07860 391902    **F** 0181 968 3210
**E** tonybyrne@compuserve.com
**W** singleminded.com
*Managing Director* Tony Byrne

## SJ Music
23 Leys Rd
Cambridge
Cambridgeshire
CB4 2AP
**T** 01223 314771    **F** 01223 560353
**W** printed-music.com/sjmusic
*Contact* Judith Rattenbury

*Less well-known string chamber music for various*
*combinations of instruments, mainly 18thC and 19thC*

## Skratch Music Publishing
Skratch Music House
81 Crabtree Lane
London
SW6 6LW
**T** 020 7381 8315    **F** 020 7385 6785

**E** colin.smith@skratchmusic.co.uk
**W** passion-music.co.uk
*Publishing Manager* Colin Smith

## SLNB
143 Westmead Rd
Sutton
Surrey
SM1 4JP
**T** 020 8395 3045    **F** 020 8395 3046
**E** smal143@tesco.net
*Contact* Steve McIntosh

## Smith Maynard International
72 Rushton Rd
Desborough
Northamptonshire
NN14 2QD
**T** 01536 760402    **F** 01536 416068
*Contact* G Smith

## Solent Songs
PO Box 22
Newport
Isle Of Wight
PO30 1LZ
**T** 01983 524110    **F** 0870 164 0388
**E** songs@solentrecords.co.uk
**W** solentrecords.co.uk

## Sonar Music
82 London Rd
Coventry
West Midlands
CV1 2JT
**T** 0204 7622 0749    **F** 0204 7625 7255
**E** caryl@aol.com
*A&R Manager* Jon Lord

## Songlife Music
36 Radnor Park Rd
Folkestone
Kent
CT19 5AU
**T** 01303 256959    **E** vernon@songlife.co.uk
**W** songlife.co.uk
*Contact* D or V Woodward
*Managing Director* D Woodward

*Also production company, writing and production, library production and re-mixes*

## Songlines Ltd
PO Box 20206
London
NW1 7FF
**T** 020 7284 3970    **F** 020 7485 0511
**E** doug@songlines.demon.co.uk
*Contact* Doug D'Arcy

## Songmatic Music Publishing
14a Hornsey Rise
London
N19 3SB
**T** 020 7281 0018    **F** 020 7272 9609
*General Manager* Kris Hoffmann

## Songs In The Key Of Knife
Red Corner Door
17 Barons Court Rd
London
W14 9DP
**T** 020 7386 8760    **F** 020 7381 8014
**E** galactic@globalnet.co.uk
*Contact* Tony Coleman

## Songstream Music
Nestlingdown
Chapel Hill
Porthowan
Truro
Cornwall
TR4 8AS
**T** 01209 890606
*Managing Director* R Bourne

*Songs supplied for TV, drama, new age, gospel, dance, trance, thrash, rap, garage, house, new reggae, ballads*
*Songs written to order for established artists*

## Songwaves
2nd Floor
Halfmoon Chambers
Bigg Market
Newcastle-Upon-Tyne
NE1 1UW
**T** 0191 233 0599

## Sonic Arts Network
The Jerwood Space
171 Union St
London
SE1 0LN
**T** 020 7928 7337    **F** 020 7928 7338
**E** phil@sonicartsnetwork.org
**W** sonicartsnetwork.org
*Contact* Phil Hallett

## Sony/ATV Music Publishing
13 Great Marlborough St
London
W1V 2LP
**T** 020 7911 8200    **F** 020 7911 8600
**E** charlie_pinder@uk.sonymusic.com
*Managing Director* Charlie Pinder

## Southbound Publishing Ltd
9 Wadley Rd
Leytonstone
London
E11 1JF
**T** 020 8556 3575    **F** 020 8532 8614
**E** publishing@southboundrecords.com
**W** southboundrecords.com
*Managing Director* Jeffrey Stothers

## Sovereign Music UK/Sovereign Lifestyle Music
PO Box 356
Leighton Buzzard
Beds
LU7 3WP
**T** 01525 385578    **F** 01525 372743
**E** sovereignm@aol.com
*Managing Director* Robert Lamont

*NB: Christian Praise and Worship only*

## Space City Music
77 Blythe Rd
London
W14 0HP
**T** 020 7371 4000    **F** 020 7371 4001
**E** spacecity@btinternet.com
*Contact* Amanada Alexander

## Sparta-Florida Music Group
8–9 Frith St
London
W1V 5TZ
T 020 7434 0066   F 020 7439 2848
E music@musicsales.co.uk   W musicsales.co.uk

## Spectrum Music4 Yarcombe
Adelaide Rd
Surbiton
Surrey
KT6 4LN
T 020 8399 7043   F 020 8390 3463
E smd.music@virgin.net
*Contact* Al Dickinson

## Springthyme Music
Balmalcolm House
Balmalcolm
Cupar
Fife
KY15 7TJ
T 01337 830773   F 01337 831773
E music@springthyme.co.uk
*Director* Peter Shepheard

## St Anne's Music
Kennedy House
1 Stamford St
Altrincham
Cheshire
WA14 1ES
T 0161 941 5151   F 0161 928 9491
*Contact* Danny Betesh or Anthony Addis

## St Margaret's Music
6 Highgate
St Margaret's Rd
Altrincham
Cheshire
WA14 2AP
T 0161 941 4560   F 0161 941 4199
*Contact* Philip Lisberg

## Stainer & Bell Ltd
PO Box 110
Victoria House
23 Gruneisen Rd
London
N3 1DZ
T 020 8343 3303   F 020 8343 3024
E post@stainer.co.uk   W stainer.co.uk

*Specialists in early music and hymnody*
*Publishers of Musica Britannica etc*
*Hire library includes Vaughan Williams, Elgar,*
*Holst, Delibes and contemporary composers*

## Stanza Music
11 Victor Rd
Harrow
Middx
HA2 6PT
T 020 8863 2717   F 020 8863 8685
E bill.ashton@virgin.net   W nyjo.org.uk
*Director* Bill Ashton

*Specialists in jazz and big band music*
*Catalogue available*

## Star-Write Publishing
PO Box 16715
London
NW4 1WN
T 020 8203 5062   F 020 8202 3746
E de55@dial.pipex.com
*Director* John Lisners

*Also Piranha Records (drum 'n' bass), Star-Write*
*Music (recording company), Star-Write*
*Management and Star-Write Legal and Business*
*Affairs*
*Dance music*

## State Music/Odyssey Music
20 Watford Rd
Radlett
Herts
WD7 8LE
T 01923 857792   F 01923 858052
*Managing Director* Wayne Bickerton

## Steelworks Songs

218 Canalot Studios
222 Kensal Rd
London
NW10 5BN
**T** 020 8960 4443　**F** 020 8960 9889
**E** freedom@frdm.co.uk
*Contact* Martyn Barter or Graham Hicks

## Steppin' Publishing

4 Murderdean Rd
Newtongrange
Edinburgh
EH22 4PD
**T** 0131 654 1888　**F** 0131 654 2888
**E** 100616.373@compuserve.com　**w** steppinout.com
*Contact* Ian Robertson

## Sticky Music

PO Box 176
Glasgow
G11 5YJ
**F** 0141 576 8431
**E** enquiries@stickymusic.co.uk
**w** stickymusic.co.uk

*Also record company*
*NB: no unsolicited demos*

## Stickysongs

Great Oaks Granary
Kennel Lane
Windlesham
Surrey
GU20 6AA
**T** 01276 479255　**F** as telephone
*Managing Director* Peter Gosling

## Stip Publishing

Unit 123c Canalot Studios
222 Kensal Rd
London
W10 5BN
**T** 020 8960 3857　**F** 020 8960 7646
**E** nicola@stip.demon.co.uk　**w** stip.demon.co.uk
*Contact* Nicola Meighan
*Managing Director* Hein van der Ree

## Stix & Keys

15 Sutherland House
137–139 Queenstown Rd
London
SW8 3RJ
**T** 020 7978 1503　**F** 020 7978 1502
*Contact* Perry Morgan

## Street Corner Music

21c Heathmans Rd
London
SW6 4TJ
**T** 020 7731 9321　**F** 020 7731 9314
**E** gull@darah.co.uk
*Managing Director* Irene Howells

## Strongsongs Publishing

The Studio
5 King Edward Mews
Byfeld Gardens
London
SW13 9HP
**T** 020 8846 9946　**F** 020 8741 5584
**E** strongsongs@telstar.co.uk　**w** telstar.co.uk
*Managing Director* Anna Jolley
*Senior A&R Manager* Fiona Huston
*A&R Manager* Angus Blair
*Business Affairs Director* Charlie Wale
*Film and TV* Marion McCormack

## Strung Out Songs

Henley Wood
Henley Lane
Box
Corsham
Wilts
SN13 8BZ
**T** 07966 452686　**F** 01225 743158
**E** rob@bozasco.demon.co.uk
*Contact* Rob Bozas

## Studio G

Ridgway House
Great Brington
Northampton
NN7 4JA
**T** 01604 770551/770776　**F** 01604 770022
**E** library@studiog.co.uk　**w** studiog.co.uk
*Managing Director* John Gale

*Specialists in the supply of production music library material*

### Stylex Music
PO Box 1257
London
E5 0UD
**T** 020 7293 7286   **E** jastoy@hotmail.com
*Managing Director* T Agbetu

### Sublime Music Publishing
65 Overdale Rd
London
W5 4TU
**T** 020 8840 2042   **F** 020 8840 5001
**E** info@sublimemusic.co.uk
**W** sublimemusic.co.uk
*Contact* Patrick Spinks

### Sugar Music
249 Kensal Rd
London
W10 5DB
**T** 020 8964 4722   **F** 020 8968 1929
*Contact* Paul Hitchman

### Sugarcane Music
32 Blackmore Avenue
Southall
Middx
UB1 3ES
**T** 020 8574 2130   **F** as telephone
*Contact* Astrid Pringsheim

### Sunnyside Music Ltd
Unit 7, Dovers Corner Industrial Estate
Rainham
Essex
RM13 8QT
**T** 01708 554000   **F** 10708 559999
*Managing Director* Alan Marcus

### Survival Music
PO Box 888
Maidenhead
Berks
SL6 2YQ
**T** 01628 788700   **F** 01628 788950

**E** survivalrecords@globalnet.co.uk
**W** capercaillie.co.uk
*Director* Anne-Marie Heighway

### Swan Island Music Publishing Ltd
100 New Kings Rd
London
SW6 4LX
**T** 020 7384 3005/7731 8199   **F** 020 7384 3025
**E** xpressswan@aol.com
*Contact* Berni Dollman

### Swanyard Music
12–27 Swan Yard
London
N1 1SD
**T** 020 7354 3737   **F** 020 7226 2581
*Contact* Tim Horne

### Sweet 'n' Sour Songs
2–3 Fitzroy Mews
London
W1P 5DQ
**T** 020 7383 7767   **F** 020 7383 3020
*Managing Director* John Craig

### Sylvantone Music
17 Allerton Grange Way
Leeds
West Yorkshire
LS17 6LP
**T** 0113 268 7788   **F** 0113 266 0220
**E** tonygoodacre@hotmail.com
**W** countrymusic.org.uk/tony-goodacre/index
*Proprietor* Tony Goodacre

*Specialists in country music*

### SYME Music Publishing
81 Park Rd
Wath-upon-Dearne
Rotherham
South Yorkshire
S63 7LE
**T** 01709 878072   **F** 01709 873119/0870 1640589
**E** hrecords@csi.com
*Managing Director* Martin E Looby

**Tabitha Music Ltd**
39 Cordery Rd
Exeter
Devon
EX2 9DJ
T 01392 499889   F 01392 498068
E graham@tabithamusic.fsnet.co.uk
*Managing Director* Graham Sclater

*Established 1975*


**Tairona Songs Ltd**
PO Box 102
London
E15 2HH
T 020 8555 5423   F 020 8519 6834
E tairona@moksha.demon.co.uk
*Managing Director* Charles Cosh


**Taste Music**
1 Prince of Wales Passage
117 Hampstead Rd
London
NW1 3EF
T 020 7388 8635   F 020 7387 0233
E sipdodgy@easynet.co.uk   w sipdodgy.co.uk
*Managing Director* S Jaffrey


**Taste the Music**
12 Kenneth Court
172 Kennington Rd
London
SE11 6SS
T 020 7582 6959   F 020 7793 0285
*Contact* Patrick Meads


**Tema International**
151 Nork Way
Banstead
Surrey
SM7 1HR
T 01737 219607   F 01737 29609
E music@tema-intl.demon.co.uk
w temamusic.com
*Contact* Tony Evans


**Thames Music**
445 Russell Court
Woburn Place
London
WC1H 0NJ
T 020 7837 6240   F 020 7833 4043
*Managing Director* C W Adams


**Three 4 Music**
Queens House
180–182 Tottenham Court Rd
London
W1P 9LE
T 020 7436 3633   F 020 7436 3632
*Contacts* Alan Edwards, Dave Woolf or Sacha
Skarbek


**Three Saints Music**
241 Union St
Middlesbrough
Cleveland
TS1 4EF
T 01642 211741
*Contact* Paul Mooney


**3MV Music Publishing**
81–83 Weston St
London
SE1 3RS
T 020 7378 8866   F 020 7378 8855
E guyv@theknowledge.com   w 3mvmusic.com
*Managing Director* Guy Van Steene


**Tilt Music**
26a Red Lion St
London
WC1R 4PS
T 020 7242 0349   F 020 7242 0348
*Contact* Tim Smith


**Timbuktu Music**
99c Talbot Rd
London
W11 2AT
T 020 7471 3656   F 020 7471 3630
*Contact* Mark Bond

## Time Universal Music
14 Jesmond Avenue
Wembley
Middx
HA9 6EA
**T** 020 8902 9023 **F** as telephone
**W** timeuniversal.com
*Contact* David Mclaverty

*Also Univista Records (same Contactdetails, plus
website: univista.co.uk)*
*Soulful vocal garage, some R&B*

## Tin Pan Alley Music
The Chrysalis Building
13 Bramley Rd
London
W10 6SP
**T** 020 7704 8541 **F** 020 7465 6318
**E** peterk@chrysalis.co.uk **W** chrysalis.co.uk
*Contact* Peter Knight Jr

## TKO Publishing/Songs For Today
PO Box 130
Hove
East Sussex
BN3 6QU
**T** 01273 550088 **F** 01273 540969
**E** jskruger@tkogroup.com/
publishing@tkogroup.com
**W** mistral.co.uk/tko

*Jazz and blues/soul songs mainly for mood library
usage*
*NB: no unsolicited pop demos*

## TMC Publishing
PO Box 150
Chesterfield
Derbyshire
S40 0YT
**T** 01246 236667 **F** as telephone
**E** tony@tonyhedley.com **W** onlinepop.co.uk

## TMR Publishing
PO Box 3775
London
SE18 3QR
**T** 020 8316 4690 **F** as telephone

**E** marc@wufog.freeserve.co.uk
**W** wufog.freeserve.co.uk
*Contact* Marc Bell

## TNR Music
13 Sandys Rd
Worcester
WR1 3HE
**T** 020 8343 9971/01905 29809 **F** 01905 613023
**E** split.music@virgin.net
*Contact* Chris Warren

## Tonecolor Music
Prospect Farm
Westmarsh
Kent
TN27 0AU
**T** 01304 812815 **F** as telephone
*Managing Director* S Jackson

## Tooti Frooti
120 Crouch Hill
London
N8 9DY
**T** 020 8347 5366 **F** 020 8347 5364
*Managing Director* Richard Jakubowski

## Topic Records
50 Stroud Green Rd
London
N4 3ES
**T** 020 7263 1240 **F** 020 7281 5671
**E** info@topicdirect.co.uk
*Managing Director* Tony Engle

## Toybox International Ltd
2nd Floor, 12 Mercer St
London
WC2H 9QD
**T** 020 7240 8848 **F** 020 7240 8864
**E** toyboxint@aol.com
*Contact* Lenny Zakatek

## Trackdown Music

Ickenham Manor
Ickenham
Uxbridge
Middx
UB10 8QT
**T** 01895 621655   **F** 01895 633264
**E** mail@trackdownmusic.co.uk
*Contact* Joanna Tizard

*Speciality: TV and Film Music*


## Tracksuit Publishing

PO Box 1099 (Chart Moves)
London
SE5 9HT
**T** 020 7326 4824   **F** 020 7580 8485
**E** gamesmaster@chartmoves.com
**W** chartmoves.com
*Managing Director* Dave Klein


## Treasure Island Publishing

Bartor Studio
Harbour Rd
Dalkey
Co. Dublin
Ireland
**T** 00 353 1 284 6336   **F** as telephone
**W** treasureisland.ie
*Contact* Robert Stephenson


## Trial Publishing

Unity House
19a Hunts Hill
Glemsford
Suffolk
CO10 7RL
**T** 01787 881887   **F** as telephone


## Triple Earth Music

24–25 Foley St
London
W1P 7LA
**T** 020 7636 5442   **F** 020 7636 5443
**E** iain@triple-earth.co.uk
*Managing Director* Iain Scott


## Truelove Music

Unit G
4 St Paul's Crescent
London
NW1 9TN
**T** 020 7284 0434   **F** 020 7267 6015
**E** tlm@truelove.co.uk   **W** truelove.co.uk
*Contact* John Truelove

*Specialists in house and techno (also management)*
*Roster includes Dave Clarke, Chris Liberator, DAVE*
*the Drummer, Rachel Auburn, OD404*


## True Trax

Rosevale Business Park
Newcastle-under-Lyme
Staffs
ST5 7QT
**T** 01782 566566   **F** 01782 580008
*Contact* Jed Taylor


## UFG Publishing

1 Constance St
Knott Mill
Manchester
M15 4PS
**T** 0161 236 6616/07973 344 606   **F** 0161 228 2399
*Contact* Mike Kirwin


## Ultimate Musical Publishing Co Ltd

271 Royal College St
London
NW1 9LU
**T** 020 7482 0115   **F** 020 7267 1169
**E** maurice@baconempire.com
*Managing Director* Maurice Bacon


## Union Records

5 Pelham Close
London
SE5 8LW
**T** 020 7733 0754   **F** as telephone
*Contact* Michael Lettman


## United Music Publishers

42 Rivington St
London
EC2A 3BN
**T** 020 7729 4700   **F** 020 7739 6549

**E** info@ump.co.uk   **w** ump.co.uk
*Promotions Manager* Russell Tandy

*British contemporary classical music, and UK agent for all major French classical music publishers*

### Universal Music Publishing Ltd

Elsinore House
77 Fulham Palace Rd
London
W6 8JA
**T** 020 8752 2600   **F** 020 8752 2601
**E** firstname.surname@umusic.com
*Managing Director and Executive Vice President, Europe* Paul Connolly
*Deputy Managing Director* Mike McCormack
*Vice President of International* Kim Frankiewicz
*A&R* Stephen Jones, Tony Garvey, Jamie Campbell, Willi Morrison, Hugo Bedford, Daryl Watts, Ruth Rothwell

### USE Music

Flat 4, 15 Nevern Place
London
SW5
**T** 020 7243 3509   **E** usemusic@hotmail.com
*Contact* Max

### Utopia Music

Utopia Village
7 Chalcot Rd
London
NW1 8LH
**T** 020 7586 3434   **F** 020 7586 3438
*Managing Director* Phil Wainman

### Valentine Music Group

7 Garrick St
London
WC2E 9AR
**T** 020 7240 1628   **F** 020 7497 9242
**E** valentine@bandleader.co.uk
**w** valentinemusic.co.uk
*Managing Director* John Nice

*NB: Publishers and producers of military and organ videos*

### Valley Music

Elsinore House
77 Fulham Palace Rd
London
W6 8JA
**T** 020 8741 8686   **F** 020 8741 8646
*Contact* R Alexander

### Vanderbeek & Imrie Ltd

15 Marvig
Lochs
Isle of Lewis
HS2 9QP
**T** 01851 880216   **F** as telephone
**E** mapamundi@aol.com

### Vanessa Music Co

35 Tower Way
Dunkeswell
Devon
EX14 4XH
**T** 01404 891598
*Managing Director* Don Todd, B.mus

*Light music, including all compositions by Rikki Caine*
*Also DTP Radio Productions*

### Denis Vaughan Music

Bond St House
14 Clifford St
London
W1X 2JD
**T** 020 7486 5353   **F** 01372 742448
*Managing Director* Denis Vaughan

### Verulam Music Co

1 Wyndham Yard
Wyndham Place
London
W1H 1AR
**T** 020 7402 7433
*Director* Carole Broughton

*NB: no unsolicited material*

## Very Positive Music

Kirklees Media Centre
7 Northumberland St
Huddersfield
West Yorkshire
HD1 1RL
**T** 01484 452013   **F** 01484 435861
**E** bssstud@architechs.com
*Contact* Chris Ellis

## Village Productions

4 Midas Business Centre
Wantz Rd
Dagenham
Essex
RM10 8PS
**T** 020 8984 0322   **F** 020 8593 0198
**E** village@btconnect.com
*Managing Director* Tony Atkins

## Vinyl Japan (UK) Ltd

98 Camden Rd
London
NW1 9EA
**T** 020 7284 0359   **F** 020 7267 5186
**E** office@vinyljapan.com   **W** vinyljapan.com
*Contact* John Whitfield

*Mainly re-issues, rockabilly and hard core punk*

## Vital Spark Music

1 Waterloo
Breakish
Isle of Skye
IV42 8QE
**T** 01471 822484/07768 031060   **F** 01471 822952
**E** chris@vitalspark.demon.co.uk
*Managing Director* Chris Harley

*Also record production*

## VROE Music

Lanhearne Vegetarian/Vegan B&B
Meaver Rd
Mullion
Helston
Cornwall
TR12 7DN
**T** 01326 240662   **F** as telephone
*Contact* Andrew Reeve

## V2 Music Publishing Ltd

99c Talbot Rd
London
W11 2AT
**T** 020 7471 3000   **F** 020 7471 3610   **W** v2music.com

## Waif Productions

1 North Worple Way
London
SW14 8QG
**T** 020 8876 2533   **F** 020 8878 4229
**E** artistrec@aol.com   **W** arcarc.com
*General Manager* Marie Hourihan

## Walk on the Wild Side

4th Floor, 40 Langham St
London
W1N 5RG
**T** 020 7323 4410   **F** 020 7323 4180
*Managing Director* Dave Massey

## Wall of Sound Music

Office 3, 9 Thorpe Close
London
W10 5XL
**T** 020 8969 1144   **F** 020 8969 1155

## Wam Music Ltd

Broadley House
48 Broadley Terrace
London
NW1 6LG
**T** 020 7258 0324   **F** 020 7724 2361
**E** ellis@broadleystudios.com
**W** broadleystudios.com
*Managing Director* Ellis Elias

## Warlock Music Ltd

329 Latimer Rd
London
W10 6RA
**T** 020 8960 3311   **F** 020 8960 4334
**E** paul.lambden@rykodisc.co.uk
*General Manager* Paul Lambden

## Warner/Chappell Music Ltd

Griffin House
161 Hammersmith Rd
London
W6 8BS
**T** 020 8563 5800   **F** 020 8563 5801
**W** warnerchappell.com
*Managing Director* Richard Manners
*Director of A&R* Alison Donald
*A&R:* Mike Sault, Kehinde Olarinmoye, David
Donald, Declan Morrell
*Film & TV* Ian Neil

## Watermills Music

5–6 Lombard St East
Dublin 2
Ireland
**T** 00 353 1 677 9046   **F** 00 353 1 677 9386
*Contact* Michael O'Riordan

## Jeff Wayne Music Group

8–9 Ivor Place
London
NW1 6BY
**T** 020 7724 2471   **F** 020 7724 6245
**E** jwmgroup@atlas.co.uk
*Contact* Jane Jones

## Websongs

Portland House
164 New Cavendish St
London
W1M 7FJ
**T** 020 7323 5793   **F** 020 7323 5794
**E** kip.trevor@websongs.co.uk
*Contact* Kip Trevor

## Bruce Welch Music

64 Stirling Court
Marshall St
London
W1F 9BD
**T** 020 7434 1839   **F** as telephone
**E** bwml@globalnet.co.uk
*Managing Director* Bruce Welch

## Westbury Music

Suite B, 2 Tunstall Rd
London
SW9 8ER
**T** 020 7733 5400   **F** 020 7733 4449
**E** westbury@connectfree.co.uk
*Managing Director* Caroline Robertson

*Also Contact: Jon Handle, Felix Hines, Paulette
Long, Kennedy Mensha*
*Probably the UK's largest independent publisher of
underground dance music: drum 'n' bass, hard
house, techno, garage, reggae, breakbeat, down
tempo, new jazz*

## Wicked Works Publishing

PO Box 727
Kenley
Surrey
CR8 5YF
**T** 020 8668 0493   **F** as telephone
**E** mouse@mailbox.co.uk
**W** future.legend.records.freeserve.com
*Contact* Russell Breyunan

## Wilson Editions

1st & 2nd Floors, 7 High St
Cheadle
Cheshire
SK8 1AX
**T** 0161 491 6655   **F** 0161 491 6688
**E** dimusic@aol.com   **W** dimusic.co.uk
*Contact* Alan Wilson

*Publishing arm of Disc Imports Ltd (classical)*

## Winchester Music

3 Sovereign Court
Graham St
Birmingham
B1 3JR
**T** 0121 233 9192   **F** 0121 233 0135
*Contact* Craig Blake Jones

## Windswept Music (London) Ltd

Hope House
40 St Peter's Rd
London
W6 9BD
**T** 020 8237 8400   **F** 020 8741 0825

**E** mail@windswept.co.uk   **w** windswept.co.uk
*Managing Director* Bob Grace
*Director* Peter McCamley
*Dance A&R* Justyn Williams
*Business Affairs* Paul Flynn

*All types of popular music*


## Wipe Out Music Ltd
PO Box 1NW
Newcastle upon Tyne
NE99 1NW
**T** 0191 266 3802   **F** 0191 266 6073
**E** wipeoutmusic@callnetuk.com
*Contact* John Esplen


## Wise Buddah Music Ltd
5 Little Portland St
London
W1N 5AG
**T** 020 7815 9639/07976 826702   **F** 020 7815 9640
**E** catherine.cloherty@wisebuddah.com
**w** wisebuddah.com
*Managing Director* Bill Padley


## WOMAD Music Ltd
Box Mill
Mill Lane
Box
Wilts
SN13 8PL
**T** 01225 743188   **F** 01225 744369
**E** publishing@realworld.co.uk
**w** realworld.on.net/publishing/index
*Contact* Annie Reed

*See also Real World Music Ltd*
*World music publishing company specializing in*
*films, TV and adverts*
*Also Real World Works (same Contactdetails)*


## WOT Music
Suite 3, 44 Mortimer St
London
W1N 7DG
**T** 020 7323 5901/07973 335557   **F** 020 7323 5903
*Contact* Jackie Thomas


## XS Music Publishing
PO Box 26273
London
W3 6FN
**T** 0870 207 7720   **F** 0870 208 8820
**E** music@xs-music.com   **w** xs-music.com
*Managing Director* Oliver Groves


## Yesterday's Music
Maple Farm
56 High St
Harrold
Bedford
MK43 7DA
**T** 01234 720785   **F** 01234 720664
**E** yesterdaysmusic@maplefarm.demon.co.uk
*Contact* Kevin White


## Yoshiko Publishing
Great Westwood
Old House Lane
Kings Langley
Herts
WD4 9AD
**T** 01923 261545   **F** 01923 261546
**E** info@yoshiko.bdx.co.uk
*Managing Director* Yoshiko Ouchi


## Your Music
39 Leyton Rd
Harpenden
Herts
AL5 2JB
**T** 01582 715098
*Managing Director* David Blaylock


## Zane Music
162 Castle Hill
Reading
Berks
RG1 7RP
**T** 0118 9574567   **F** 0118 9561261
**E** info@zaneproductions.demon.co.uk
*Managing Director* Peter Thompson

**Zomba Music Publishers**
Quadrant Business Centre
135 Salusbury Rd
London
NW6 6RJ
T 020 7604 2600    F 020 7604 2601
E (firstname).(last name)@zomba.co.uk
*Managing Director* Steven Howard
*A&R* Michael Morley, Daniel Payne
*Senior Creative Manager* Tim Smith
*Creative Manager* Anna Carpenter
*A&R Scout* Jay Greenwood
*Film & TV* Richard Kirstein

*Also Jive Records*

# 8

## Pressers and Duplicators

### A to Z Music Services
43–51 Wembley Hill Rd
Wembley
Middx
HA9 8AU
**T** 020 8903 0046  **F** 020 8782 4601/4602
**E** info@a2zmusic.co.uk  **W** atozmusic.com
*Sales Manager* Andy Higgins

### Accurate Sound
Melton Rd
Queniborough Industrial Estate
Queniborough
Leics
LE7 3FP
**T** 0116 260 2064  **F** 0116 260 0108
**E** paul@accuratesound.demon.co.uk
**W** accuratesound.co.uk
*Contact* Paul Komedera

### ACS (Audio & Computer Supplies Ltd)
The Studios
PO Box 37
Newbury
Berks
RG14 7YW
**T** 01635 552237/580448  **F** 01635 34179
*Contact* Wilber Craik

### Adrenalin Manufacturing
252–253 Argyll Avenue
Trading Estate
Slough
Berks
SL1 4HA
**T** 01753 523200
*Managing Director* Sue Owlett

### AGR Multimedia
Unit 7
River Park Business Park
33 River Rd
Barking
Essex
IG11 0EA
**T** 020 8594 9412/9410  **F** 020 8507 0681
**E** info@agrmultimedia.free-online.co.uk
*Contact* Production Department

## Alfasound Duplication Ltd
Old School House
1 Green Lane
Ashton On Mersey
Sale
Cheshire
M33 5PN
**T** 0161 905 1361   **F** 0161 282 1360
**E** garry-adl@btinternet.com
*Managing Director* Garry Bowen

## All Th@ Duplication
59 Sutherland Place
London
W2 5BY
**T** 020 7229 1779   **F** 020 7229 1526
**E** duplication@allthat.co.uk   **w** allthat.co.uk
*Contact* Darren Tai

## Alpha Recording and Marketing Company
Units 1 and 2
Forest Industrial Park
Forest Rd
Hainault
Essex
IG6 3HL
**T** 020 8500 1981   **F** 020 8501 1319
**E** armco@globalnet.co.uk
*Director* Jan Fonseca

*Cassettes only*

## Amato Distribution
Units 13–14
Barley Shotts Business Park
246 Acklam Rd
London
W10 5YG
**T** 020 8964 3302   **F** 020 8964 3312
**E** amato@easynet.co.uk
*Label Manager* Sharon Green

## Arioso/Timbre Ltd
PO Box 3698
London
NW2 6ZA
**T** 020 8450 0445   **F** 0709 217 9302
**E** neil@timbre.co.uk

## Audio Services Ltd (ASL)
6 Orsman Rd
London
N1 5QJ
**T** 020 7739 9672   **F** 020 7739 4070/7729 5948
**E** asl@audio-services.co.uk
*General Manager* Mel Gale
*Chairman* Steve Mason

*Black and coloured vinyl manufacture, CD, CD
Rom, DVD and cassette
Mastering, processing, reprographics and printing
across all formats
Complete music manufacturing for clients large and
small*

## Avid
10 Metro Centre
Dwight Rd
Tolpits Lane
Watford
Herts
WD18 9UF
**T** 01923 281281   **F** 01923 281200
**E** info@avidgroup.co.uk   **w** avidgroup.co.uk
*Contact* Richard Lim, Frank Pratt

*CD, video, DVD*

## AWL Compact Disc Company
356 Scraptoft Lane
Leicester
LE5 1PB
**T** 0116 241 3979   **F** 0116 243 3760
*Contact* Andrew Lipinski

## Brain Dead Studios
PO Box 3775
London
SE18 3QR
**T** 020 8316 4690   **F** as telephone
**E** marc@wufog.freeserve.co.uk
**w** wufog.freeserve.co.uk
*Contact* Marc Bell

## Canon Video (UK) Ltd
Main Drive
GEC Estate
East Lane
Wembley
Middx
HA9 7FF
T 020 8908 5784/5188   F 020 8385 0722
*Sales Director* Mike Seaman

*Video cassettes only*

## CD Industries
Units 7–10
Sovereign Park
Coronation Rd
London
NW10 7QP
T 020 8961 8898   F 020 8961 8688
E mayron@compuserve.com
*Contact* Ms. M E Tan

## CDA Compact Disc Ltd
5th Floor
Regal House
68 London Rd
Twickenham
Middx
TW1 4RJ
T 020 8744 2111   F 020 844 9700
*Contact* Ian Mackay

## CEEMA Productions Ltd
Cromer House
1 Caxton Way
Stevenage
Herts
SG1 2DF
T 01438 316888   F 01438 316999
E info@ceemaproductions.co.uk
W ceemaproductions.co.uk
*Director* Mark Andrews

*Management of CD, DVD, cassette and vinyl manufacturing*

## Chain Reaction
93 Harehills Lane
Chapel Allerton
Leeds
West Yorkshire
LS7 4HA
T 0113 225 2246   F as telephone

## Clear Sound And Vision Ltd
Clarendon House
117 George Lane
London
E18 1AN
T 020 8989 8777   F 020 8989 9777
E mail@c-s-v.co.uk   W c-s-v.co.uk
*Contact* Clive Robins

*Project management across all audio and video platforms, including design, associated print, packaging and manufacturing.*
*CD, CD Rom, DVD, cassette, video and vinyl*

## COPS
The Studio
Kent House Station Approach
Barnmead Rd
Beckenham
Kent
BR3 1JD
T 020 8778 8556   F 020 8676 9716
E musicmanufacture@cops.co.uk   W cops.co.uk
*Director* Elie Dahdi

*Quotes for manufacturing all formats, especially vinyl, available on-line. Website also includes package deal for novices, a guide to the music industry and free ads. In business 21 years*

## Cornmeer Services
2 Quadeast
Warne Rd
Weston-super-Mare
Somerset
BS23 3UU
T 01934 628219/0800 389 9094   F 01934 624630
E sales@cornmeer.co.uk   W cybercity.co.uk/
cornmeer/cornhp.htm
*Managing Director* Mark Cardwell

## Cottage Recording
2 Gawsworth Rd
Macclesfield
Cheshire
SK11 8UE
**T** 01625 420163/0467 813 533   **F** 01625 420168
**E** rogerboden@cottagegroup.co.uk
**w** cottagegroup.co.uk
*Contact* Roger Boden


## Cutgroove Ltd (Vinyl Pressing Agency)
43 Canham Rd
London
W3 7SR
**T** 020 8749 8860   **F** 020 8742 9462
**E** nikki_howarth@hotmail.com
*Contact* Mrs. Nikki Howarth


## CVB
179a Bilton Rd
Perrivale
Middx
UB6 7HQ
**T** 020 8991 2610/01453 886078   **F** 020 8997 0180/
01453 8866078   **E** cvbduplication@aol.com/
devonsent@aol.com
*Managing Director* Phil Stringer


## CYP Children's Audio
The Fairway
Bush Fair
Harlow
Essex
CM18 6LY
**T** 01279 444707   **F** 01279 445570
**E** gary@cypmusic.co.uk   **w** kidsmusic.co.uk
*Sales Manager* Gary Wilmot

*Specialists in the origination, marketing and
distribution of high-quality children's audio*


## Damont Audio Ltd
20 Blyth Rd
Hayes
Middx
UB3 1BY
**T** 020 8573 5122   **F** 020 8813 6692
**E** sales@damontaudio.com   **w** damontaudio.com
*Sales Manager* Malcolm Pearce
*Contact* Malcolm Pearce, Keith McGregor


## Disctronics
Southwater Business Park
Worthing Rd
Southwater
West Sussex
RH13 7YT
**T** 01403 739600   **F** 01403 733786
**E** sales@disctronics.co.uk   **w** disctronics.co.uk
*Contact* Sue Mackie (General Manager)
*Sales Executive* Dean Pearce

*One of the largest independent manufacturers, with
plants in France, Italy and Texas, offering full service
for CD, CD Rom, DVD etc*


## Diskxpress
7 Willow Court
Bourton Industrial Park
Bourton on the Water
Gloucs
GL54 2HQ
**T** 01451 820070   **F** 01451 820075
*General Manager* Dave Mitchell


## DOCdata (UK) Ltd
50 York Rd
London
SW11 3SJ
**T** 020 7801 2400   **F** 020 7801 0945
*Sales Director* John Barker


## DocData Ablex
Halesfield 14
Telford
Salop
TF7 4QR
London office:
Unit 2b
Walpole Court
London
W5 5ED
**T** 01952 680131/0208 799 5400
**F** 01952 583501/0208 799 5401
**E** mtatman@docdata.com/uksales@docdata.com
**w** ablex.co.uk
*Sales Director* Martine Tatman

*The largest CD and cassette manufacturer in the UK,
with over 30 years' experience
Design assistance where required
The UK subsidiary of DocData NV, which has*

*manufacturing facilities in Holland, France, Germany and the USA*

## Downsoft Ltd
Downsway House
Epsom Rd
Ashtead
Surrey
KT21 1LD
**T** 01372 272422    **F** 01372 276122
**E** work@downsoft.force9.co.uk    **w** downsoft.co.uk

*Blank CDs and audio cassettes*
*Cassettes wound to any length, duplicated CDs and cassettes from most formats, blank and printed labels and inserts*
*Also reel-to-reel, DAT, mini disc and video*
*Specialist in small runs with fast turnaround*

## Duplitape Recording Services
37 Shaw Rd
Heaton Moor
Stockport
Cheshire
SK4 4AG
**T** 0161 442 6910

*Cassettes only*

## East London Cassette Copying
54–56 Compton St
London
EC1V 0UE
**T** 020 7251 6630    **F** 020 7490 7426
**E** mark@elcc-ideal.co.uk    **w** elcc-ideal.co.uk

## EMI Manufacturing Services
EMI Compact Disc (UK)
Penny Lane
Swindon
Wilts
SN3 3LP
**T** 01793 567000    **F** 01793 567131
**E** bob.simpson (or deb.coleman)@emimusic.com
**w** ccgweb.com and emigroup.com
*Contact* Bob Coleman (tel: 01793 567134) or Deb Coleman (tel: 01793 567130)

## EMI Music Services (UK)
252–254 Blyth Rd
Gate 4
Hayes
Middx
UB3 1BW
**T** 020 8589 7800    **F** 020 8589 7823
**E** emily.bingham@emimusic.com
*Customer Development Manager* Emily Bingham
*Operations Manager* Antony Webster

*Vinyl only*

## EPS Productions
40 College Avenue
Mutley
Devon
PL4 7AN
**T** 01752 670831/0374 849 060
*Owner* Andy Wrigler

## Euro Compact Sound
Clock House
Spencers Close
Maidenhead
Berks
SL6 6LL
**T** 01628 632115    **F** 01628 632666
*Contact* Jane Hill

## Eurodisc Manufacturing Ltd
10–16 Tiller Rd
London
E14 8EX
**T** 020 7345 5172    **F** 020 7308 0007
**E** ediscsteve@aol.com
*Contact* Steve Pryor

## Fairview Music
Great Gutter Lane
Willerby
Hull
East Yorkshire
HU10 6DP
**T** 01482 653116    **F** 01482 654667
**E** keith@fairview-music.demon.co.uk
**w** fairview-studios.co.uk
*Partner* Keith Herd

### Fideo Sain
Canolfan Sain
Llandwrog
Caernarfon
Gwynedd
LL54 5TG
T 01286 831111   F 01286 831497
E music@sain.wales.com   w sain.wales.com
*Managing Director* Dafydd Iwan

*Video, CD and CD Rom authoring and duplication
Part of the Sain group (label, distribution, studios,
publishing: same contact details)*

### Filterbond Ltd
JBS Records Division
19 Sadlers Way
Hertford
SG14 2DZ
T 01992 500101   F as telephone
E jbsrecords.filterbondltd@virgin.net
*Managing Director* John B Schefel

*Also jbsRecords/Filterbond Ltd (Cassette ¼" reel and
RDAT only)*

### First Sound & Vision (CD & Cassette)
4–10 North Rd
London
N7 9HN
T 020 7865 3800   F 020 7865 3803   w fsv.co.uk
*Contact* Sales Team

### Forward Sound & Vision (Vinyl)
Sterling Industrial Estate
Rainham Rd South
Daggenham
Essex
RM10 8HP
T 020 8592 0242   F 020 8595 8182   w fsv.co.uk
*Contact* Paula Sadagos

*Vinyl only*

### Global Dance Distribution Ltd
The Basement
The Saga Centre
326 Kensal Rd
London
W10 5BZ
T 020 8969 9333   F 020 8960 7010

E globaldance@hotmail.com
w globaldance.co.uk/flipsiderecords.com
*Contact* Bettina Costanzo

### Grampian Records
Unit 4a
Airport Industrial Estate
Wick
Caithness
KW1 4QS
T 01955 605030   F 01955 604418
E gramprec@aol.com
*General Manager* John Hunter

### Ground Bass Productions
The Windsor Centre
Windsor St
London
N1 8QH
T 020 7288 1833   F 020 7288 1834
E productions@groundbass.com
w groundbass.com
*Contact* Dorian Smellie

### Hiltongrove
Hiltongrove Business Centre
Hatherley Mews
London
E17 4QP
T 020 8521 2424   F 020 8521 4343
E info@hiltongrove.com   w hiltongrove.com
*Managing Director* Guy Davis

### ICC Duplication
Unit 27
Hawthorn Rd Industrial Estate
Eastbourne
East Sussex
BN23 6QA
T 01323 647880   F 01323 643095
E info@iccduplication.co.uk
w iccduplication.co.uk
*Contact* Andy Thorpe

*One-stop media duplication: CD, cassette, video,
DVD*

## ICE Group

3 St Andrews St
Lincoln
LN5 7NE
T 01522 539883  F 01522 528964
*Managing Director* Steve Hawkins

## Icon

Chesnut Barn
Green Farm
Littlebury Green
Saffron Walden
Essex
CB11 4XB
T 01763 838493  F 01763 837142
E icon@dircon.co.uk
*Contact* Tash

## Impress Music Ltd

Unit 5c
Northfield Industrial Estate
Beresford Avenue
Wembley
Middx
HA0 1NW
T 020 8795 0101  F 020 8795 0303
E info@impressmusic-uk.com
W impressmusic-uk.com
*Contact* Alastair Bloom

*Complete CD Rom manufacturing and printing
service including brochures, CD booklets and inlays,
and special packaging
Also short-run CD burns from 10 units upwards*

## Isis Duplicating Company

Unit 11
Shaftesbury Industrial Centre
The Runnings
Cheltenham
Gloucs
GL51 9NH
T 01242 571818  F 01242 571315
*Sales Manager* Glyn Ellis Evans

## ITD Cassettes Ltd

Faraday Rd
Rabans Lane Industrial Area
Aylesbury
Bucks
HP19 8RY
T 01296 27211  F 01296 392019
E itdcassets@aol.com
*Managing Director* M A McLoughlin
*Chairman* Roy Jackson-Moore

## James Upton

98–138 Barford St
Birmingham
B5 6AP
T 0121 607 7300  F 0121 607 7400

## James Yorke Ltd

Unit M, 40–44 The Bramery
Alstone Lane
Cheltenham
Gloucs
GL51 8HE
T 01242 584222/07710 407636  F 01242 222445
E jill@jamesyorke.co.uk
*Managing Director* Ken Leeks

*Mastering from DAT, CD, Mini Disc
Basic editing
All masters checked in real time
Minimum order 500 per title
On-cassette printing and creation
All types of packing and fulfilment available*

## JTS

73 Digby Rd
London
E9 6HX
T 020 8965 3000  F 020 8986 7688

## Key Production

8 Jeffreys Place
London
NW1 9PP
T 020 7284 8800  F 020 7284 8844
E info@keyproduction.co.uk
*Sales Department:*Katy Rose

*Vinyl, DVD, CD and cassette pressers and
duplicators, plus printers of all connected paper parts*

## Keynote Audio Services
Wishanger Lane
Churt
Farnham
Surrey
GU10 2QJ
**T** 01252 794253   **F** 01252 792642
**E** admin@keynoteaudio.co.uk
**w** keynoteaudio.co.uk
*Director* Tim Wheatley

*Established 25 years*
*CD and cassette mastering and duplicating, full print*
*service*
*Free brochure on request*

## KG Engineering
Unit 6
Ipplepen Business Park
Edgelands Lane
Ipplepen
Newton Abbot
Devon
TQ12 5QG
**T** 01803 813833   **F** 01803 813141
**E** keithg@kg-digital.co.uk   **w** kg-digital.co.uk
*Contact* Keith Gould

## Line-Up PMC
9a Tankerville Place
Newcastle Upon Tyne
Tyne and Wear
NE2 3AT
**T** 0191 281 6449   **F** 0191 212 0913
**E** c.a.murtagh@btinternet.com
**w** on-line-records.co.uk
*Managing Director* Christopher Murtagh

*Promotions and marketing consultancy*
*Also festivals, events, artist management and*
*representation*
*Audio and visual production including On-Line*
*Records*

## Logicom Sound and Vision
Portland House
1 Portland Drive
Willen
Milton Keynes
MK15 9JW
**T** 01908 663848   **F** 01908 666654

**E** paul.evans@luk.net   **w** luk.net
*Contact* Paul Evans

## London Vinyl Pressing
Unit 32
Atlas Business Centre
Oxgate Lane
London
NW2 7HU
**T** 020 8452 5544   **F** 020 8450 6647
**E** xpressvinyl@compuserve.com.uk
*Contact* Sales Department

*Vinyl and CD*

## MacTrak Duplicating
3/2 Inveresk Industrial Estate
Musselburgh
Edinburgh
EH21 7UL
**T** 0131 665 5377   **F** 0131 653 6905
**E** mactrack@ednet.co.uk   **w** ednet.co.uk/mactrak
*Proprietor* M D MacGregor

## Magicwand Manufacturing
Littleton House
Littleton Rd
Ashford
Middx
TW15 1UU
**T** 01784 423214   **F** 01784 251267
**E** info@magicwand.co.uk
*Contacts* Rob McCartney, Jo Kemp

## Matinee Sound and Vision
132–134 Oxford Rd
Reading
Berks
RG1 7NL
**T** 0118 958 4934   **F** 0118 959 4936
*Contact* Chris Broderick

## Mayron Multimedia
Unit 7
Sovereign Park
Coronation Rd
London
NW10 7QE
**T** 020 8561 8898

## Modo Production Ltd

Ground Floor
25 Heathmans Rd
London
SW6 4TS
**T** 020 7384 1151  **F** 020 7384 1243
*Contact* Henry Lavelle

## Moving Image International

14 Cromwell Avenue
London
N6 5HL
**T** 01438 718541
*Contact* Guy Warren

## MPO Ireland Ltd

Blanchardstown Industrial Estate
Snugborough Rd
Blanchardstown
Dublin 15
Ireland
**T** 00 353 1 822 1363  **F** 00 353 1 806 6064
**E** ronan@mpo.ie
*Contact* Ronan Sweeney

## MPO UK Ltd

33 Acton Park Estate
The Vale
London
W3 7QE
**T** 020 8600 3900  **F** 020 8749 7057
**E** mpouk@aol.com  **w** mpo.fr
*Contact* Sales Department

## Music Media Manufacturers UK Ltd

Unit F11D
Parkhall Rd Trading Estate
40 Martell Rd
London
SE21 8EN
**T** 020 8265 6364  **F** 020 8265 6423
**E** mail@musicmedia-uk.com
**w** musicmedia-uk.com
*General Manager* Mike Spenser
*Production Manager* Brian Nadi
*Art Director* Zoran Simoneuvic

## Musicbase Music Pressing

Unit 12
Imperial Studios
3–11 Imperial Rd
London
SW6 2AG
**T** 020 7384 2626  **F** 020 7384 2622
**E** kelly@musicbase.demon.co.uk
*Director* Kelly Swain

## Nimbus Manufacturing (UK) Ltd

Llantarnam Park
Cwmbran
Gwent
NP44 3AD
**T** 01633 877121  **F** 01633 867131
*Contact* gcooper@nimbuscd.com

*London office: 020 7565 0008*
*Fax: 020 8968 0111*

## Offside Management

Unit 16–24, Brewery Rd
London
N7 9NH
**T** 020 7700 2662  **F** 020 7700 2882
**E** richard@bsimerch.com  **w** bsimerch.com
*Contact* Richard Cassar

## Online Studios

Unit 18
Croydon House
1 Peall Rd
Croydon
CRO 3EX
**T** 020 8287 8585/01802 813008
**E** onlinerecs@cableinet.co.uk
**w** onlinestudios.co.uk
*Contact* Rob Pearson

## Optical Disc Management Ltd

1b Apollo House
Calleva Park
Aldermaston
Berks
RG7 8DA
**T** 0118 981 3347  **F** 0118 981 3250
**E** shirleyr@pointgroup.co.uk
*Contact* Martin Daniell

## Pioneer LDCE
Pioneer House
Hollybush Hill
Stoke Poges
Slough
Bucks
SL2 4QP
**T** 01753 789611/789634   **F** 01753 789647
**E** diego_pedrini@peu.pioneer.co.uk
**W** ldce.pioneer.co.uk/pioneer2
*Sales Manager* Diego Pedrini

## PR Records
Hamilton House
Endeavour Way
London
SW19 8UH
**T** 020 8241 9000   **F** 020 8241 2227

## Prime CDs/Multimedia Ltd
7 St Marks Studios
Chillingworth Rd
London
N7 8QJ
**T** 020 7700 3060   **F** 020 7700 5544
**E** enquiries@primecds.com   **W** primecds.com
*Director* Phillip Staniforth

## Professional Magnetics Ltd
Cassette House
329 Hunslet Rd
Leeds
LS10 1NJ
**T** 0113 270 6066   **F** 0113 271 8106
**E** promags@aol.com   **W** promags.freeserve.co.uk
*Contact* Hilary

*Audio and video duplication, cassettes, CD, DVD etc*
*Also standards conversions NTSC, PAL, SECAM and*
*any other cassette and disc requirements*

## Propaganda
Symal House
423 Edgware Rd
London
NW9 0HU
**T** 020 8200 1000   **F** 020 8200 4929
**E** prop@sweet-concepts.co.uk
*Contact* Stephen Taylor

## Prosoft Logisitics
Unit 3
Space Way
Feltham
Middx
TW4 0TH
**T** 020 8890 8290   **F** 020 8890 7381
**E** terry@prosoftlogistics.ltd.uk
**W** prosoftlogisitics.ltd.uk/it
*Contact* Terry Loveday

## Quod Video Productions
7–11 York St
Broadstairs
Kent
CT10 1PD
**T** 01843 604200
*Proprietor* Keith Croft

*Video cassettes only*

## Rank Video Services
Phoenix Park
Great West Rd
Brentford
Middx
TW8 9PL
**T** 020 8568 4311   **F** 020 8847 4032
*Major Account Controller* Russ Bryan

*Video cassette and CD-ROM only*

## Real Recordings
19 Green Lane
Ashton-on-Mersey
Sale
Cheshire
M33 5PN
**T** 0161 973 1884   **F** 0161 905 2171
*Managing Director* David Greatbanks

*Audio cassette and CD*

## Reflex Media Services Ltd
Unit 5
Cirrus
Glebe Rd
Huntingdon
Cambs
PE29 7DL
**T** 01480 434333/412222   **F** 01480 411441

**E** sales@reflex-media.freeserve.co.uk
**W** reflex-media.co.uk
*Contact* John Garrad

## Replica
North Works
Hookstone Park
Harrowgate
North Yorkshire
HG2 7DB
**T** 01423 888979   **F** 01423 885761
**E** cbmbm@compuserve.co.uk
*Director* David Bulmer

## RMS Studios
43–45 Clifton Rd
London
SE25 6PX
**T** 020 8653 4965   **F** as telephone
*Duplicating Manager* Alan Jones

## RP Media Ltd
Kingsway House
134–140 Church Rd
Hove
East Sussex
BH3 2DL
**T** 01273 220700   **F** 01273 220800
**E** rp_media@compuserve.com
*Contact* David Paramor

## RPM (Repeat Performance Mastering)
Unit 6
Grand Union Centre
West Row
London
W10 5AS
**T** 020 8960 7222   **F** 020 8968 1378
**E** info@repeat-performance.co.uk
**W** repeat-performance.co.uk
*Managing Director* Robin Springall

## RTS Onestop Ltd
Unit M2
Albany Rd
Prescot
Merseyside
L34 2UP
**T** 0151 430 9001   **F** 0151 430 7441

**E** rts.onestop@virgin.net   **W** rtsonestop.co.uk
*Managing Director* John Fairclough

## Sanctuary Mastering and Duplication
Sanctuary House
45–53 Sinclair Rd
London
W14 0NS
**T** 020 7300 6575   **F** 020 7300 6600
**E** mastering@sanctuarystudios.co.uk
**W** sanctuarystudios.co.uk
*Contact* Mark or Peter

## SDC UK Ltd
29–31 Fairview Industrial Estate
Clayton Rd
Hayes
Middx
UB3 1AN
**T** 020 8581 9200   **F** 020 8581 9249
**E** lsa@sdcuk.com/dmc@sdcuk.com
**W** sdc-group.com
*Sales* Lisa Sawney, Daragh McDonogh

*Part of the SDC DanDisc group, offering DVD, CD,*
*CD Rom, video and cassette replication services*
*across Europe*
*Local sales teams offer a personalized service*

## Selecta Sound
PO Box 4137
Hornchurch
Essex
RM11 1GY
**T** 01708 453424   **F** 01708 455565
**E** john@selecta-sound.co.uk
**W** selecta-sound.co.uk
*Contact* John Smailes

*CD, MD, cassettes and DAT copies*
*Studio supplies blank cassettes and CD Roms*

## Silver Road Studios
2 Silver Rd
Wood Lane
London
W12 7SG
**T** 020 8746 2000   **F** 020 8746 0180
**E** enquiries@silver-road-studios.co.uk
**W** silver-road-studios.co.uk
*Studio manager* Samantha Leese

## SKM Europe

SKM House
Springfield Rd
Hayes
Middx
UB4 OTY
**T** 020 8573 0909　**F** 020 8573 9990
**E** sales@skmeurope.co.uk
*Sales Director* Steve Castle

*Cassettes Only*

## Sonopress (UK) Ltd

King's Hill Business Park
Darlaston Rd
Wednesbury
West Midlands
WS10 7SH
**T** 0121 502 7800　**F** 0121 502 7811
**E** info@sonopress.co.uk　**w** sonopress.uk
*Managing Director* Tim Bevan
*Sales Director* Anshu Bagga

## Sound & Video Services (UK)

Shentonfield Rd
Sharston Industrial Estate
Manchester
M22 4RW
**T** 0161 491 6660　**F** 0161 491 6669
**E** sales@svsmedia.com　**w** svsmedia.com
*Managing Director* Mike Glasspole

*Blank recording media distributor*
*Audio and video tape, discs and data media products*
*Brands: BASF, JVC, Maxell, Mitsui, Quantegy, Sony,*
*TDK, Verbatim and Fuji*

## Sound Discs Manufacturing Ltd

5 Barley Shorts Business Park
246 Acklam Rd
London
W10 5YG
**T** 020 8968 7080　**F** 020 8968 7475
**E** sound.discs@virgin.net　**w** sound-discs.co.uk
*Contact* Debbie & Karen

## Sound Performance

80 Blackheath Rd
London
SE10 8DA
**T** 020 8691 2121　**F** 020 8691 3144

**E** christian.v@soundperformance.co.uk
**w** soundperformance.co.uk

*One-Stop manufacturing, print and fulfilment*
*services for CD, CD Rom and cassettes*

## Sound Recording Technology

Audio House
Edison Rd
St Ives
Cambs
PE27 3LF
**T** 01480 461880　**F** 01480 496100
**E** srt@btinternet.com
**w** soundrecordingtechnology.co.uk
*Contact* Sarah Pownall

*CD mastering and pressing*
*CD Rom manufacture and authoring, music*
*recordings, post-production, digital audio editing,*
*video and encoding plus packaging and artwork*
*services*

## Sounds Good

12 Chiltern Enterprise Centre
Station Rd
Theale
Berks
RG7 4AA
**T** 0118 930 1700　**F** 0118 930 1709
**E** office@sounds-good.co.uk
**w** sounds-good.co.uk
*Director* Martin Maynard

*CD and CD Rom pressing and duplication, cassette*
*duplication, CD mastering, in-house design and*
*reprographics, with over 10 years of experience*
*Package deals for musicians*
*New mastering studio with the most accurate*
*monitoring in its class*

## Spool Multi Media (UK)

Unit 30
Deeside Industrial Park
Deeside
Flintshire
CH5 2NU
**T** 01244 280602　**F** 01244 288581
**E** admin@smmuk.demon.co.uk　**w** smmuk.co.uk
*Managing Director* Roy Varley
*Sales Director* Gill Allman

*CD, cassette, print, pack and distribution service*

**SRL Cassette Services**
47 High St
Pinner
Middx
HA5 5PJ
**T** 020 8868 5555   **F** 020 8866 5555
**E** srl@btinternet.com   **W** hello.2/srl
*Managing Director* John Bales

*Cassettes and videos only*


**Stanley Productions Ltd**
147 Wardour St
London
W1F 8WD
**T** 020 7439 0311   **F** 020 7437 2126
**E** slaes@stanleyproductions.co.uk
**W** stanleyproductions.co.uk
*Contact* Stanley Aarons /Sales


**Tape Duplication**
77 Barlow Rd
Stannington
Sheffield
South Yorkshire
S6 5HR
**T** 0114 233 0033   **F** as telephone
*Contact* Ian Stead

*Cassettes only*


**Tape To Tape**
19 Heathmans Rd
London
SW6 4TJ
**T** 020 7371 0978   **F** 020 7371 9360
**W** tapetotape.co.uk
*Contact* Simon Payne


**Tapemaster Ltd**
King George's Place
764 Eastern Avenue
Newbury Park
Ilford
Essex
IG2 7HU
**T** 020 8518 4202   **F** 020 8518 4203
**E** tapemaster@msn.com   **W** tapemaster.co.uk

*Manufacturers of CD and DVD cases and audio/
video cassettes*


**Tapestream Duplication Ltd**
Unit 4
Hampers Green Estate
Petworth
West Sussex
GU28 9NR
**T** 01798 344108   **F** 01798 342116
**E** colin@tapestream.demon.co.uk
**W** tapestream.co.uk

*Cassette and CD duplication, pre-production
mastering to exabyte*


**TC Video**
Wembley Commercial Centre
East Lane
Wembley
Middx
HA9 7UU
**T** 020 8904 6271   **F** 020 8904 0172
**E** marketing@tcvideo.co.uk   **W** tcvideo.co.uk
*Contact* Lissandra Xavier

*Everything regarding video, CD and DVD, from
production to duplication, packaging and
distribution, all under one roof*


**Technicolor Video Services (UK)**
Northfield Industrial Estate
Beresford Avenue
Wembley
Middx
HA0 1NW
**T** 020 8900 6531/1122   **F** 020 8903 6013
*Contact* Sales Department


**Thames Valley Video**
660 Ajax Avenue
Slough
Berks
SL1 4BG
**T** 01753 553131   **F** 01753 554505

*Videos only*


**The Metro Group**
53 Great Suffolk St
London
SE1 0DB
**T** 020 7928 2088/020 7439 3494   **F** 020 7261 0685/

020 7437 3782   E info@metrogroup.co.uk
*Marketing Director* Sue Alexander

*Video cassette and CD-ROM only*

### Think Tank
Unit 1
The Stable Yard
16a Balham Hill
London
SW12 9EB
T 020 8673 2525   F 020 8673 2625
E info@tank.softnet.co.uk
*Contact* Sales Department

### Touchstone Productions
TPL House
Beccles Business Park
Copland Way
Suffolk
NR34 7TL
T 01502 716056   F 01502 717124

*DAT and video only*

### Trend Studios
9 South Prince's St
Dublin 2
Ireland
T 00 353 1 671 3544   F 00 353 1 671 0042
E info@trendstudios.com   W trendstudios.com
*Contact* Anne Queally
*Managing Director* John D'Ardis

### Tribal Manufacturing Ltd
11 Hillgate Place
Balham Hill
London
SW12 9ER
T 020 8673 0610   F 020 8675 8652
E sales@tribal.co.uk   W tribal.co.uk
*Contact* Alison Wilson, Martin Gopthal

### TVi
142 Wardour St
London
W1V 3AV
T 020 7878 0000   F 020 7878 7800

*Videos only*

### TVP/TVi
2 Golden Square
London
W1R 3AD
T 020 7439 7138   F 020 7434 1907
E jaquiw@tvp.co.uk   W tvp.co.uk
*Group Sales and Marketing Manager* Jaqui Winston

### Unicorn Studios
PO Box 387
London
N22 6SF
T 020 889 0616
E unicorn@ampmusic.demon.co.uk
*Director* Mark Jenkins

### Universal Manufacturing & Logistics Ltd
Philips Rd
Blackburn
Lancs
BB1 5RZ
T 01254 505401/020 8910 5525   F 01254 505421/
020 8910 5526   E merrick.iszatt@umusic.com
W u-m-l.com
*Contact* Angela Kaye (Blackburn) or Merrick Iszatt
(London satellite office)

*Manufacturing arm of Universal Music
International
Pre-mastering, glass mastering, reprographics,
replication and packaging of all formats including
audio CDs, enhanced CDs and CD Extra, CD Text,
CD Rom inc. CD+G, DVD Rom and DVD Video
Minimum order 500 Audio CD, 100 CD Rom/DVD*

### Vanderquest
7 Latimer Rd
Teddington
Middx
TW11 8QA
T 020 8977 1743/020 8943 2818   F 020 8943 4812
*Contact* Nick Maingay

*Videos only*

## Vector Television

Vector House
Battersea Rd
Heaton Mersey Industrial Estate
Stockport
Cheshire
SK4 3EA
T 0161 432 9000   F 0161 443 1325
*Managing Director* Martin Tetlow

*Laserdisc only*

## Video Duplicating Company Ltd

VDC House
South Way
Wembley
Middx
HA9 0EH
T 020 8903 3345   F 020 8903 8691/020 8902 1716
E (name)@cd-systems.co.uk

## Videocopy

329 Hunslet Rd
Leeds
LS10 1NJ
T 0113 262 5650   F 0113 237 4008
E promags@aol.com   W promags.freeserve.co.uk
*Contact* Hilary

*Audio and video copying CD and cassette, inlays, labels,
standards conversions (PAL, NTSC, SECAM) etc*

## Vinyl Pressing

308 High St
London
E15 1AJ
T 020 8519 4260   F 020 8519 5187
*Managing Director* Terance Murphy

## Voyager Media Ltd

341 Brook St
Dundee
DD5 2DS
T 01382 527252   F 01382 527253
E voyager@sol.co.uk
W taynet.co.uk/users/voyager
*Sales Manager* Brad Sutherland

## Warren Recordings

59 Hendale Avenue
London
NW4 4LP
T 020 8203 0306   F as telephone
*Director* Stanley Warren

## WNE

Unit 7
Sovereign Centre
Lichfield Rd Industrial Estate
Tamworth
Staffs
B79 7XA
T 01827 310052   F 01827 60868

*Cassettes only*

### Absolute Marketing & Distribution
112 Beckenham Rd
Beckenham
Kent
BR3 4RH
**T** 020 8663 0301/07850 358438   **F** 020 8663 0302
**E** info@absolutemarketing.co.uk
**w** absolutemarketing.co.uk
*Contact* Henry Semmence

*Offers a sales, marketing, manufacturing and
distribution service to independent labels*

### ADA
36 Saturday Market Place
Beverley
East Yorkshire
HU17 9AG
**T** 01482 868024   **F** as telephone
*Contact* Jez Riley

### After Dark Distribution
Holborn Gate
1st Floor, 330 High Holborn
London
WC1V 7QT
**T** 020 7203 8366   **F** 020 7203 8409
**E** outletpromotions@compuserve.com
**w** outlet-promotions.com
*Contact* Glenn Wilson

*Also (same address) Outlet Promotions (PR and
marketing) plus the labels Darkbeat Records and
Infinity Records*

### Alphamagic
Unit 3
Westmoreland House
Scrubs Lane
London
NW10 6RE
**T** 020 8960 4777   **F** 020 8960 7266
**E** alphamagic@btinternet.com
*Contact* Dominic Thornton

*Dance music distributor and record label*

## Amato Distribution

Units 13–14
Barley Shotts Business Park
246 Acklam Rd
London
W10 5YG
**T** 020 8964 3302   **F** 020 8964 3312
**E** info@amatodistribution.co.uk
**W** amatodistribution.co.uk

*UK's leading dance music distributor*

## Apex Entertainment Group Ltd

Grove House
320 Kensal Rd
London
W10 5BZ
**T** 020 8968 1100   **F** 020 8968 1171
**E** harrymaloney@apex-music.co.uk
**W** apex-ent.com
*Managing Director* Harry Maloney
*Sales & Marketing Director* Wilf Mann (e-mail:
wilfmann@apex-music.co.uk)

## Arabesque Distribution

Network House
29–39 Stirling Rd
London
W3 8DJ
**T** 020 8992 7732/0098
**F** 020 8992 0340/020 8993 7906
**E** sales@arab.co.uk
*Sales Director* Greg Warrington

## ARC Music Productions International Ltd

PO Box 111
East Grinstead
West Sussex
RH19 4FZ
**T** 01342 328567   **F** 01342 315958
**E** info@arcmusic.co.uk   **W** arcmusic.co.uk

*World music label specializing in traditional and
ethnic music only*

## ARD (Artists Record Distribution)

Unit 20
Buspace Studios
Conlan St
London
W10 5AP
**T** 020 7565 9111   **F** 020 7565 9222
*Contact* Roy Aquarius

## Audio Book And Music Co Ltd

240 Centennial Park
Elstree Hill South
Elstree
Borehamwood
Herts
WD6 3DE
**T** 020 8236 2310   **F** 020 8236 2312
**E** abm@label.co.uk   **W** abmlabel.co.uk
*General Manager* Mark Lawton

## Avanti Records

Unit 11
Airlinks Industrial Estate
Spitfire Way
Heston
Middlesex
TW5 9NR
**T** 020 8848 9800   **F** 020 8756 1883
**E** avantirecords@aol.com
*Managing Director* Paul Weiss

*Export and import wholesaler*

## Avid

10 Metro Centre
Dwight Rd
Tolpits Lane
Watford
Herts
WD18 9UF
**T** 01923 281281   **F** 01923 281200
**E** info@avidgroup.co.uk   **W** avidgroup.co.uk
*Contact* Richard Lim, Clive Hudson, Andrew
Green or Paul Bouchard

### Backs Records

St Mary's Works
St Mary's Plain
Norwich
Norfolk
NR3 3AF
**T** 01603 624290/626221   **F** 01603 619999
**E** backs@cwcom.net
*Labels Manager* Derek Chapman

### Bad Habits

PO Box 111
London
W13 0ZH
**T** 020 8357 2337/07000 740 243   **F** 020 8566 7215
**E** info@badhabitsent-group.com
**W** badhabitsent-group.com
*Contact* John S Rushton

### BDS (Bertelsmann Distributions Services)

24 Crystal Drive
Sandwell Business Park
Warley
West Midlands
B66 1QG
**T** 0121 543 4000   **F** 0121 543 4399

### Beechwood Music Distribution

Littleton House
Littleton Rd
Ashford
Middlesex
TW15 1UU
**T** 01784 423214   **F** 01784 251245
**E** dan@b-m-d.co.uk
*Contact* Dan Pepperrell

### Beehive International Ltd

1 Warple Mews
Off Warple Way
London
W3 0RF
**T** 020 8742 9540   **F** 020 8749 1608/8455
**E** sales@beehiveint.co.uk/oliver@beehiveint.co.uk
*Directors* O. Comberti, R. Kent, A. Nazareth and S.
Sparks

### Brothers Distribution

Music Village
11b Osiers Rd
London
SW18 1NL
**T** 020 8870 0011   **F** 020 8870 2101
**E** info@the-brothers.co.uk
**W** brothersdistribution.com
*Contact* Nick Titchener

*Dance music specialists, offering full range of support
and marketing activities, label management,
third-party and international licensing, etc*

### Cadillac Jazz Distribution

63–71 Colliers St
London
N1 9BE
**T** 020 7278 7391   **F** 020 7278 7394
**E** hazel@cadillacjazz.com.uk
*Contact* Hazel Miller or John Jack

*Jazz specialists, also mail-order and record
production
Ogun Records, Cadillac Records and mail-order
Acorn Music*

### Cargo Records (UK) Ltd

17 Heathmans Rd
London
SW6 4TJ
**T** 020 7731 5125   **F** 020 7731 3866
**E** info@cargouk.demon.co.uk
**W** cargorecords.co.uk
*Managing Director* Philip Hill

### Caroline 2

56 Standard Rd
London
NW10 6ES
**T** 020 8961 2919   **F** 020 8961 1873
**E** c2.sales@uk.uumail.com
*General Manager and Sales Manager* Nik Podgorski

### Chandos Records

Chandos House
Commerce Way
Colchester
Essex
CO2 8HQ
**T** 01206 225200   **F** 01206 225201

**E** sales@chandos.net   **W** chandos.net
*Sales Manager* Ginny Cooper

## Changing World Distribution
Willow Croft
Wagg Drove
Huish Episcopi
Near Langport
Somerset
TA10 9ER
**T** 01458 250317/253838   **F** as first telephone
**E** enquiries@changing-world.com
**W** changing-world.com
*Contact* Susan Malleson

*CD distribution for ambient, dub, trance, drum 'n'*
*bass, chill out, world, world fusion, meditation*
*Also retail outlet at 7 High Street, Glastonbury,*
*Somerset (01458 831453)*

## Chart Records
5–6 Lombard St
East Westland Row
Dublin 2
Ireland
**T** 00 353 1 671 0237/677 9914   **F** 00 353 1 671 0237
**E** imw@iol.ie   **W** irishwarehouse.ie
*Managing Director* Noel Cusack

## Chrome Dreams
PO Box 230
New Malden
Surrey
KT3 6YY
**T** 020 8715 9781   **F** 020 8241 1426
**E** mail@chromedreams.co.uk
**W** chromedreams.co.uk
*Contact* Michele White

*Label/publisher specializing in music-related spoken*
*word CDs and books*

## Claddagh Records Ltd
Dame House
Dame St
Dublin 2
Ireland
**T** 00 353 1 677 8943   **F** 00 353 1 679 3664
**E** claddagh@crl.ie   **W** indigo.ie/claddagh
*Co-Manager* Jane Bolton

*Distributor, label, mail order and retailer specializing*
*in Irish traditional music and spoken word, with a*
*shop in Temple Bar, Dublin*

## Clubscene Independent Distribution
Unit 26, Coatbank Way
Coatbridge
Lanarkshire
ML5 3AG
**T** 01236 449557/07785 222205   **F** 01236 449577
**E** mail@clubscene.co.uk   **W** clubscene.co.uk
*Contact* Bill Grainger

## CM Distribution
North Works
Hook Stone Park
Harrogate
North Yorkshire
HG2 7DB
**T** 01423 888979   **F** 01423 885761
*Contacts* D R Bulmer or R Bulmer

## Complete Record Company Ltd, The
22 Prescott Place
London
SW4 6BT
**T** 020 7498 9666   **F** 020 7498 1828
**E** info@complete-record.co.uk
*Managing Director* Jeremy Elliott

## Confetti Distribution
PO Box 11541
London
N15 4DW
**T** 020 8801 6760   **F** 020 8808 4413

## Consortium, The
PO Box 1345
Ilford
Essex
IG4 5FX
**T** 07050 333555   **F** 07020 923292
**E** melevett@aol.com   **W** citeandsoundcard.com
*Contact* K Danzig or M Levett

## Contact(UK)
Research House
Fraser Rd
Greenford
Middx
UB6 7AQ
**T** 020 8997 5662/5663
**F** 020 8997 5664/8566 8093
**E** contactukltd@btinternet.com
**W** contactmusic.co.uk
*Contact* Michael Lo Bianco

*Specialists in vinyl 12" and albums to include DJ
promos, re-issue and special pressings, collectors'
items
Established in 1988 to fill the vinyl gap left by the
development of CDs*

## Copperplate Distribution
68 Belleville Rd
London
SW11 6PP
**T** 020 7585 0357    **F** as telephone

## Culture Press
74–75 Warren St
London
W1P 5PA
**T** 020 7387 3344/5550    **F** 020 7388 2756
**E** zep@sternsmusic.com
*Contact* Zep

## DA Tape & Records
56 Castle Bank
Stafford
ST16 1DW
**T** 01785 258746    **F** 01785 255367
*Managing Director* Paul Halliwell

## Delta Home Entertainment Ltd
222 Cray Avenue
Orpington
Kent
BR5 3PZ
**T** 01689 888888    **F** 01689 888800
**E** info@deltamusic.co.uk
*Product Manager* Neil Kellas

## Disc Imports Ltd
1st & 2nd Floors, 7 High St
Cheadle
Cheshire
SK8 1AX
**T** 0161 491 6655    **F** 0161 491 6688
**E** dimus@aol.com    **W** dimusic.co.uk
*Managing Director* Al Wilson

*Classical distributor*

## Digital Import Software Co
The Old Coach House
Windsor Crescent
Radyr
South Glamorgan
CF15 8AE
**T** 029 2084 3334    **F** 029 2084 2184
**E** digitaldisc@ision.co.uk
*Proprietor* Paul Karamouzis

*Import CD specialists*

## Disc Distribution
Unit 12
Brunswick Industrial Park
London
N11 1HX
**T** 020 8362 8111/8122 (sales)    **F** 020 8362 8119

## Discovery Records Ltd
Nursteed Rd
Devizes
Wilts
SN10 3DY
**T** 01380 728000    **F** 01380 720055
**E** discovery.records@virgin.net
*Managing Director* Mike Cox

*CD importers and distributors to retail trade, and
mail order, particularly lesser-known labels and
hard-to-find product from majors
Classical, world and jazz*

## Discus Export
48–50 Springfield Rd
Horsham
West Sussex
RH12 2PD
**T** 01403 217453    **F** 01403 242506

**E** discus@pncl.co.uk   **w** jones.co.uk/access/discus
*Director* Paul Shoebridge

## Downing Records
5 Mount Pleasant
Waterloo
Liverpool
Merseyside
L22 5AP
**T** 0151 920 8088   **F** 0151 920 1211
*Managing Director* Ron Downing

## Gordon Duncan
20 Newtown St
Kilsyth
Glasgow
G65 0LY
**T** 01236 827550   **F** 01236 827560
**E** gordon-duncan@solcd.uk

## EIS Global Fulfillment
Unit F, Tech West House
10 Warple Way
London
W3 0UE
**T** 020 8746 1199   **F** 020 8746 2002
**E** london@globalfulfillment.com
*Managing Director* Jimmy Devlin

## ELSE Distribution Ltd
Lombard House
Upper Bridge St
Canterbury
Kent
CT1 5NF
**T** 01227 780078/454533   **F** 01227 454532
*Managing Director* Janet Dawe

## EMI Distribution
Hermes Close
Tachbrook Park
Leamington Spa
Warks
CV34 6RP
**T** 01926 466300   **F** 01926 466392
*Operation Director* Kevin Paterson

## EMI Records (Ireland)
1 Ailesbury Rd
Dublin 4
Ireland
**T** 00 353 1 269 3344   **F** 00 353 1 269 6341
**E** (firstname).(lastname)@emimusic.com
**w** emirecords.ie
*Managing Director* Willie Kavanagh

## Entertainment Network, The
Rabans Lane
Aylesbury
Bucks
HP19 3BX
**T** 01296 426151   **F** 01296 391828
**E** gwen_pearce@ten-distribution.com
*Managing Director* Gwen Pearce

## Entertainment UK
243 Blyth Rd
Hayes
Middx
UB3 1DN
**T** 020 8848 7511   **F** 020 8754 6601
*Managing Director* Richard Cowan

## Essential Direct
Brewmaster House
91 Brick Lane
London
E1 6QL
**T** 020 7375 2332   **F** 020 7375 2442
**E** minkydedman@hotmail.com
**w** essentialdirect.co.uk
*Contact* Gary Dedman

*Also Essential Exports (same details)*

## ESSP
The Sound House
PO Box 37b
Molesey
Surrey
KT8 2YR
**T** 020 8979 9997   **F** as telephone
*Contact* David Tuffnell

## Excel Marketing Services Ltd
Becker Transport Building
Crompton Rd
Stevenage
Herts
SG1 2EE
T 01438 740301/01923 721004    F 01438 747434
E excelms@aol.com    W director: vinoth kumar

## Fat Cat International Ltd
20 Liddell Rd Estate
Maygrove Rd
London
NW6 2EW
T 020 7624 4335    F 020 7624 4866
E sales@fatcatint.demon.co.uk

*Wholesaler to CD and record retailers*

## Fat Shadow Records Ltd
Unit 23
Cygnus Business Centre
Dalmeyer Rd
London
NW10 2XA
T 020 8830 2233    F 020 8830 2244
E mikekirk@fatshad.co.uk
*Managing Director* Michael Kirkman

*Specialists in reggae and world music*

## Fearless Exports
144 Algernon Rd
London
SE13 7AW
T 020 8690 7658    F 020 8692 9258
E justin@fearlessexports.freeserve.co.uk
*Sales and Licensing Manager*: Justin Simpson

## Flute Worldwide
1 Campaspe Park
Fordbridge Rd
Sunbury-on-Thames
Middx
TW16 6AX
T 01932 769760    F 01932 780481
E info@fluteworldwide.co.uk
*Sales Director* Duncan Peel

## Flying Records UK
73 Albion Mews
off Galina Rd
London
W6 0XL
T 020 8741 7713/7719
*Contact* A Bernardo

## Fopp Ltd
Unit 27
Hurlbutt Rd
Heathcote Industrial Estate
Warwick
CV34 0NF
T 01926 888460    F 01926 883138
E andy.singh@fopp.co.uk    W fopp.com
*Warehouse Manager* Andrew Singh

## Global Dance Distribution Ltd
The Basement
The Saga Centre
326 Kensal Rd
London
W10 5BZ
T 020 8969 9333    F 020 8960 7010
E anyone@globaldance.co.uk
W globaldance.co.uk
*Contact* Bettina Costanzo

*Specialists in dance music*
*Also Flipside Records*

## Global Force
29 Weston Parkway Business Centre
Lower Ballymount Rd
Dublin 12
Ireland
T 00 353 1 450 7565
*Contact* Brian O'Kelly

## Golds
Gold House
69 Flempton Rd
London
E10 7NL
T 020 8539 3600    F 020 8539 2176
E golds@airtime.co.uk/golds@goldcat.co.uk
W goldcat.co.uk
*Managing Director* Barrie Gold

*Distributors and wholesalers (the largest independent*

*in the UK) dealing in audio, video, spoken word, DVD, games, accessories and CD Roms*

## Gospel Direct (Worldwide)
Samuel House
21 Arica Rd
London
SE4 2PY
**T** 020 7732 4548/7277 9858　**F** 020 7277 9488

## Greyhound Records
130a Plough Rd
London
SW11 2AA
**T** 020 7924 1166/254　**F** 020 7924 1471/4271
**E** sales@greyhound-records.com
**W** greyhound-records.com
*Managing Director* J R Wright
*Directors* Paul Callaghan, Tony Hickmott

## Hallmark Music & Entertainment
25–26 Ivor Place
London
NW1 6HR
**T** 020 7616 8100　**F** 020 7224 9309
**E** caroline@pointgroup.co.uk
*Managing Director* Marcall Tammaro
*Marketing Manager* Des De Silva

## Hermanex Ltd
Connaught House
112–120 High Rd
Loughton
Essex
IG10 4HJ
**T** 020 8508 3723　**F** 020 8508 0432
**E** uk@hermanex.nl
*Managing Director* Lee Harmer

*Europe's largest overstock and deletion specialist for audio, video and multimedia*

## Hot Records
PO Box 333
Brighton
East Sussex
BN1 2EH
**T** 01903 779443　**F** 01903 779442
**E** hotrecords@pavilion.co.uk　**W** hotrecords.com
*Contact* Andrew Bowles or Geraint Jones

## Hot Shot Records
29 St Michael's Rd
Leeds
West Yorkshire
LS6 3BG
**T** 0113 274 2106　**F** 0113 278 6291
**E** sales@bluescat.com　**W** bluescat.com
*Managing Director* Dave Foster

*Blues, r&b, gospel and jazz specialist*

## I&B Records (Irish Music) Ltd
2a Wrentham Avenue
London
NW10 3HA
**T** 020 8960 9160/9169　**F** 020 8968 7332
**E** sales@celticcorner.co.uk　**W** celticcorner.co.uk
*Contact* Martin McDonald

## Interaudio Direct Ltd
22 Jamaica St
Glasgow
G1 4QD
**T** 0141 572 0068　**F** 0141 572 0069
*Contact* Damian Beattie

## InterGroove Ltd
43 Canham Rd
off Warple Way
London
W3 7SR
**T** 020 8749 8860　**F** 020 8742 9462
**E** info@intergroove.co.uk　**W** intergroove.co.uk
*Contact* Andy Howarth

*Also Experience Grooves Ltd (record label) and Headzone Ltd (record label)*

## Javelin Distribution
Satril House
3 Blackburn Rd
London
NW6 1RZ
**T** 020 7328 8283　**F** 020 7328 9037
**E** sales@hho.co.uk　**W** hho.co.uk
*Head of Sales & Marketing* Sarah Black

## Jazz Music
Glenview
Moylegrove
Cardigan
Dyfed
SA43 3BW
**T** 01239 881278   **F** 01239 881296
**E** jazz.music@btinternet.com
*Contact* Jutta Greaves

## Jet Star Phonographics
155 Acton Lane
London
NW10 7QJ
**T** 020 8961 5818   **F** 020 8965 7008

## K-tel Entertainment (UK) Ltd
K-tel House
12 Fairway Drive
Greenford
Middx
UB6 8PW
**T** 020 8747 7550   **F** 020 8575 2264
**E** info@k-tel-uk.com   **W** k-tel-uk.com
*General Manager* Janie Webber
*CFO* Andrew Smith

## Kingdom Distribution
Clarendon House
Shenley Rd
Borehamwood
Herts
WD6 1AG
**T** 020 8207 7006   **F** 020 8207 5460
**E** kingdomrec@aol.com
*Managing Director* Terry King

## Koch International
Charlotte House
87 Little Ealing Lane
London
W5 4EH
**T** 020 8832 1800/1818 (orders)   **F** 020 8832 1813/1808 (orders)
*Managing Director* Rashmi Patani
*Sales & Marketing Manager* Simon Carver
*Label Manager* Michael K Jones

## KRD
Unit 114
Sherborne House
Sherborne St
Birmingham
B16 8JU
**T** 0121 248 2548   **F** 0121 248 2549
**E** krd1@supanet.com
*Managing Director* Pat Ward

## Kudos Records Ltd
79 Fortess Rd
London
NW5 1AG
**T** 020 7482 4555   **F** 020 7482 4551
**E** kudos@kudos.demon.co.uk
**W** kudosrecords.co.uk
*Director* Mike Hazell

## Lasgo Exports
Unit 2
Chapmans Park Industrial Estate
378–388 High Rd
London
NW10 2DY
**T** 020 8549 8800   **F** 020 8451 5555
**E** info@lasgo.co.uk
*Sales Manager* Paul Burrows

## Le Matt Music
Whitehouse Farm
Shropshire
TF9 4HA
**T** 01630 647374   **F** 01630 647612
*Contact* Xavier Lee

## Lightning Export
Unit 3–4
Northgate Business Centre
Crown Rd
Enfield
Middx
EN1 1TG
**T** 020 8805 5151   **F** 020 8805 5252
**E** lightning@lightningexport.co.uk   **W** startle.com
*Managing Director* Graham Lambdon
*Sales Manager* Bill Brightley

*UK's largest exporter, all labels, all genres*

## MAC Distribution Ltd

27–29 Carnoustie Place
Scotland St
Glasgow
G5 8PH
**T** 0141 429 0999   **F** 0141 429 4174
**E** macdist@cableol.co.uk
*Operations Manager* Derek Moir

## Magnum Distribution

Magnum House
High St
Lane End
Bucks
HP14 3JG
**T** 01494 882858   **F** 01494 882631
**E** music@tkomagnum.co.uk   **w** tkomagnum.co.uk
*Contact* Nigel Molden

*See also TKO Magnum Music (record company)*

## Media UK Distribution

Sovereign House
12 Trewartha Rd
Praa Sands
Penzance
Cornwall
TR20 9ST
**T** 01736 762 826/07721 449477   **F** 01736 763328
**E** panamus@aol.com   **w** panamamusic.co.uk
*Managing Director* Roderick G Jones

## Megaworld Ltd

33–37 Hatherley Mews
London
E17 4QP
**T** 020 8521 2211   **F** 020 8521 6911
**E** megaworld@btinternet.co.uk
**w** megaworld.co.uk
*Director* Nigel King

## M8 Magazine

11 Lynedoch Place
Glasgow
G3 6AV
**T** 0141 353 1118   **F** 0141 353 1448
**E** davidm8mag@aol.com   **w** m8magazine.com
*Contact* David Faulds

## MELT Distribution

MELT 2000 Ltd
6c Littlehampton Rd
Worthing
West Sussex
BN13 1QE
**T** 01903 260033   **F** 01903 261133
**E** rrowles@melt2000.com/
phorgan@melt2000.com   **w** melt2000.com
*Contacts*: Ray Rowles and Patrick Horgan

## Michele International

Michele House
The Acorn Centre
Roebuck Rd
Hainault
Essex
IG6 3TU
**T** 020 8500 1819/8559 8918   **F** 020 8500 1745/
8559 9800   **E** micheleint@btconnect.com
*Contact* Eileen Knight

## MIDI UK

457 Blackburn Rd
Bolton
Lancs
BL1 8NN
**T** 01204 307505/417375   **F** 01204 417374
**E** music@midiuk.u-net.com   **w** midiuk.u-net.com
*Contact* Keith Andrews

## Midland Records

Chase Rd
Brownhills
West Midlands
WS8 6JT
**T** 01543 378222/378225   **F** 01543 360988
*Managing Director* John Skidmore

## Millennium Distribution

Westgate House
149 Roman Way
Islington
N7 8XH
**T** 020 7967 9966   **F** 020 7700 7926
**E** enquiries@millenniumdistribution.co.uk
**w** millenniumdistribution.co.uk

### Mo's Music Machine

Unit 11
Forest Business Park
South Access Rd
London
E17 8BA
**T** 020 8520 7264/07785 696969   **F** 020 8520 9130/
8223 0351   **E** info@mosmusic.co.uk
**W** mosmusic.co.uk/mosmusic
*Managing Director* Morris Czechowicz

### Multiple Sounds Distribution

Unit 6
Woodgate Park
Whitelund Trading Estate
Morecambe
Lancs
LA4 5DG
**T** 01524 851177   **F** 01524 851188
**E** mike_hargreaves@compuserve.com
*Managing Director* Mike Hargreaves

### Music Express Wholesale Ltd

Sheepscar St South
Sheepscar
Leeds
West Yorkshire
LS7 1AD
**T** 0113 234 4112   **F** 0113 234 4113
**E** office@music-express.co.uk
*Contact* Christopher Lane

### Music Sales (Northern Ireland)

224b Shore Rd
Lower Greenisland
Carrickfergus
Co. Antrim
BT38 8TX
**T** 028 9086 5422   **F** 028 9086 2902
*Director* Eddie Graham

### Nervous

7–11 Minerva Rd
London
NW10 6HJ
**T** 020 8963 0352   **F** 020 8963 1170
**E** 100613.3456@compuserve.com   **W** nervous.co.uk
*Managing Director* Roy Williams

### New Note Distribution Ltd

Electron House
Cray Avenue
Orpington
Kent
BR5 3RJ
**T** 01689 877884   **F** 01689 877891
**E** mail@newnote.com   **W** newnote.com
*Joint Managing Director* Graham Griffiths

*UK distributor specializing in jazz, world music,
classical and blues*

### Nimbus Records Ltd

Wyastone Leys
Monmouth
NP25 3SR
**T** 01600 890007   **F** 01600 892119
**E** sales@nimbus.ltd.uk   **W** nimbus.ltd.uk
*Sales & Marketing Manager* Carl Wade

*Exclusive UK distributors for Nimbus, Meridian,
Delos, Dorian, Ivory Classics, Deux-Elles, Claudio,
Regent and Label M
Nimbus Records are also a classical recording
company with on-site studio*

### North West Music

10 Magnet Rd
GEC East Lane Estate
Wembley
Middx
HA9 7RG
**T** 020 8904 7700   **F** 020 8904 1999
**E** northwestmusic@compuserve.com
*Director* Gary Harries

### One For You UK Ltd

39 Lemur Drive
Cambridge
CB1 4XZ
**T** 01223 504620   **F** 01223 413360   **E** sale@ofy.net
**W** ofy.net
*Contact* Tjerk Sekeris

## One Nation Exports
Unit G11
Belgravia Workshops
159–163 Marlborough Rd
London
N19 4NP
**T** 020 7263 3100   **F** 020 7263 3002
**E** barry@onenation.co.uk
*Contact* Barry Milligan

## Outlet Distribution Ltd
15–21 Gordon St
Belfast
BT1 2LG
**T** 028 9032 2826   **F** 028 9033 2671
**w** outlet-music.com
*Sales & Marketing Manager* Neill Duffy

## OVC
88 Berkeley Court
Baker St
London
NW1 5ND
**T** 020 7402 9111   **F** 020 7723 3064
**E** joanne.ovc@virgin.net   **w** ovcmedia.co.uk
*Director* Joanne Goldring-Cohen

## Pendle Hawk Music Distribution
11 Newmarket St
Colne
Lancs
BB8 9BJ
**T** 01282 866317   **F** as telephone
**E** mel@ripped.demon.co.uk
**w** ripped.demon.co.uk
*Contact* Adrian Melling

## Pinnacle Imports
The Teardrop Centre
London Rd
Swanley
Kent
BR8 8TS
**T** 01322 619234   **F** 01322 619257
**E** team@pinnacle-imports.co.uk
*General Manager* Peter Barnett

## Pinnacle Records
Electron House
Cray Avenue
St Mary's Cray
Orpington
Kent
BR5 3RJ
**T** 01689 870622 (admin)   **F** 01689 878269
**w** pinnacle-records.co.uk
*Chairman* Steve Mason
*Managing Director* Tony Powell
*Head of Label Management* Susan Rush
*Marketing Manager* Simon Holland

*Also represents 3MV, Complete, New Note,
Shellshock, Kudos*

## Plastic Head Music Distribution Ltd
Unit 15
Bushell Business Estate
Hithercroft
Wallingford
Oxon
OX10 9DD
**T** 01491 825029   **F** 01491 826320 (admin)/826144
**E** plastichead@compuserve.com
**w** plastichead.co.uk
*Director* Steve Beatty

## David Powell Distribution Ltd
Brook House
182 Park Avenue
Riverside Business Park
London
NW10 7XH
**T** 020 8963 1717   **F** 020 8961 3910
**E** david@dpdist.com   **w** dpdist.com
*Managing Director* David Powell

## President Records Ltd
Units 6+7
11 Wyfold Rd
London
SW6 6SE
**T** 020 7385 7700   **F** 020 7385 3402
**E** hits@president-records.co.uk
**w** president-records.co.uk
*Managing Director* David Kassner

## Prime Distribution
340 Athhlon Rd
Alperton
Middx
HAO 1BX
**T** 020 8601 2200　**F** 020 8997 2292/8998 0322
**E** music@primedistribution.co.uk
**W** primedistribution.co.uk
*Contact* Clare Ireland

## Priory Records Ltd
3 Eden Court
Eden Way
Leighton Buzzard
Beds
LU7 4FY
**T** 01525 377566　**F** 01525 371477
**E** sales@priory.org.uk　**W** priory.org.uk
*Managing Director* N Collier

## Prism Leisure Corp plc
Unit 1
Dundee Way
Enfield
Middx
EN3 7SA
**T** 020 8804 8100　**F** 020 8805 8001
**E** simon@prismles.com
*Managing Director* Ivor Young
*Sales Director* Simon Checketts
*Licensing and Repertoire* Steve Brink

## Proper Music Distribution Ltd
The Powerhouse
Cricket Lane
Beckenham
Kent
BR3 1LW
**T** 020 8676 5100　**F** 020 8699 5111
*Managing Director* Malcolm Mills
*Director* Philip Harding
*Sales Director* Graham Jones
*Finance Director* John Glockler

## RDL Distribution
132 Chase Way
London
N14 5DH
**T** 07050 055167/07958 592526　**F** 0870 741 5252
**E** 2bigmusicintl@excite.com
*Contact* Colin Jaques

*Marketing, promotion and distribution*
*Also IE Music Websites (same address, email:*
*colinjaques@excite.com) for interactive e-commerce*
*websites and website publicity*

## Recognition Distribution Ltd
31 Silver St
Bradford-on-Avon
Wilts
BA15 1JX
**T** 01225 864422/868007　**F** 01225 864466
**E** sue@recognition1.freeserve.co.uk
*Contact* Andy Richmond

## Record Services
30–32 Sir John Rogerson Quay
Dublin 2
Ireland
**T** 00 353 1 671 4011/4317　**F** 00 353 1 671 4554
**E** rsirl@indigo.ie
*Managing Director* Brian Wynne
*Administration* Terry Wynne
*Distribution* Dennis Callanan

## Red Lightnin' (Distribution)
The White House
42, The St
North Lopham
Diss
Norfolk
IP22 2LU
**T** 01379 687693　**F** 01379 687559
**E** peter@redlightnin.com　**W** redlightnin.com
*Managing Director* Peter Shertser

*Distributes in-house blues label Red Lightnin'*

## Revolver Music
152 Goldthorn Hill
Penn
Wolverhampton
West Midlands
WV2 3JA
**T** 01902 345345　**F** 01902 345155/620671
**E** revolvermusic@compuserve.com
**W** revolver-records.com
*Managing Director* Paul Birch
*Head of Third Party Labels* Malcolm Bell

**RM Associates**
46 Great Marlborough St
London
W1F 7JW
**T** 020 7439 2637    **F** 020 7439 2316
**E** rma@rmassociates.co.uk
*Managing Director* Reiner Moritz

**RMG Distribution Ltd**
43–51 Wembley Hill Rd
Wembley
Middx
HA9 8AU
**T** 020 8903 0360    **F** 020 8782 4706
**E** graham@rmgplc.com    **w** rmgplc.com
*Managing Director* Nigel Reveler
*General Manager* Graham Kelly

**Rollercoaster Records**
Rock House
London Rd
St Mary's
Chalford
Gloucs
GL6 8PU
**T** 01453 886252    **F** 01453 885361
**E** info@rollercoasterrecords.com
**w** rollercoasterrecords.com
*Contact* John Beecher

*NB: manaufacturers and distributors of reissue
product only*

**Roots Records**
250 Earlsdon Avenue North
Coventry
West Midlands
CV5 6GX
**T** 024 7671 1935    **F** 024 7671 1191
**E** rootsrecs@btclick.com
*Managing Director* Graham Bradshaw

*Specialists in folk, roots and acoustic music
Worldwide mail-order and festival merchandising*

**Rose Records**
1b Ellington St
London
N7 8PP
**T** 020 7609 8288    **F** 020 7607 7851
*Managing Director* John Butcher

*NB: Distributors to public authority libraries only*

**Ross Records**
29 Main St
Turriff
Aberdeen
AB53 4AB
**T** 01888 562403/568899    **F** 01888 568890
**E** gibson@rossrecords.com    **w** rossrecords.com
*Managing Director* Gibson Ross

**RP Media**
Kingsway House
134–140 Church Rd
Hove
East Sussex
BN3 2DL
**T** 01273 220700    **F** 01273 220800
**E** rp_media@compuserve.com    **w** rpmedia.co.uk
*Contact* David Paramor

**Sain (Recordiau) Cyf**
Canolfan Sain
Llandwrog
Caenarfon
Gwynedd
LL54 5TG
**T** 01286 831111    **F** 01286 831497
**E** muisc@sain.wales.com    **w** sain.wales.com
*Contact* D Iwan

**Sales Office, The**
Unit 5
Fieldside Farm
Doddershall
Quainton
Aylesbury
Bucks
HP22 4DQ
**T** 01296 655908    **F** 01296 655909
**E** nigel@the sales office.demon.co.uk
*Contact* Nigel French

**Savoy Strict Tempo Distributors**
POBox 271
Purley
Surrey
CR8 4YL
**T** 01737 554 739    **F** 01737 556 737
*Contact* Wendy Smith

## Securicor Omega Express

Comewell House
North St
Horsham
West Sussex
RH12 1BQ
**T** 01403 264164    **F** 01403 255028
**E** mick.green@soe.securicor.co.uk
**w** securicor.com
*National Operations Manager* Mick Green (mobile: 07850 660661)

*The leading business-to-business parcel carrier in the UK with a range of same-day, next-day and European delivery services from a network of over 140 branches*

## Select Music & Video Distribution

34a Holmethorpe Avenue
Redhill
Surrey
RH1 2NN
**T** 01737 760020    **F** 01737 766316
**E** aanderson@selectmusic.co.uk
**w** selectmusic.co.uk
*Managing Director* Anthony Anderson

*Classical CD and DVD specialist offering full range of sales, marketing and distribution services, both domestic and export*

## Shellshock

23a Collingwood Rd
London
N15 4LD
**T** 020 8800 8110/8130    **F** 020 8800 8140/836 5054
**E** info@shellshock.co.uk
*Managing Director* Garreth Ryan

## Shetland Music Distribution Ltd

Griesta
Tingwall
Shetland
ZE2 9SB
**T** 01595 840670    **F** 01595 840671
**E** smd.ltd@zetnet.co.uk
**w** shetlandmusicdistribution.co.uk
*Directors* Alan Longmuir, Ronnie Jamieson, Debbie Scott

*See also Veesik Records*

## Silva Productions

3 Prowse Place
London
NW1 9PH
**T** 020 7428 5500    **F** 020 7482 2385
**E** info@silvascreen.co.uk    **w** silvascreen.co.uk
*Sales Manager* James Fitzpatrick
Also Silva Screen (same details)

## Silver Sounds CD Ltd

Unit 7
Peerglow Estate
Queensway
Ponders End
Enfield
Middx
EN3 4SB
**T** 020 8364 7711    **F** 020 8805 1135
**E** info@silversounds.co.uk    **w** dresscircle.co.uk
*Managing Director* Murray Allan

*Importers of CDs and books from around the world, supplying to all major retailers*

## Soul Trader

Unit 43
Abbey Business Centre
Ingate Place
London
SW8 3NS
**T** 020 7498 0732    **F** 020 7498 0737
*Managing Director* Marc Lessner

## Sound & Video Gems Ltd

Quakers Coppice
Crewe
Cheshire
CW1 6EY
**T** 01270 589321    **F** 01270 587438
*Managing Director* Michael Bates

## Sound and Media Ltd

Unit 3
Wells Place
Gatton Park Business Centre
New Battlebridge Lane
Redhill
Surrey
RH1 3DR
**T** 01737 644445/644443    **F** 01737 644310

**E** philw@soundandmedia.co.uk
**W** soundand media.com

*Part of Virgin group, distributor of major-label overstocks and deletions, plus budget, special interest and cult music/video*
*Complete management of sales campaign from conception to stock selection, stickering, bar-coding, shrink-wrapping and monitoring*

## Sound Entertainment Ltd
The Music Village
Osiers Rd
London
SW18 1NL
**T** 020 8874 8444   **F** 020 8874 0337
**E** info@soundentertainment.co.uk
**W** soundentertainment.co.uk
*Contact* Bob Nolan

*Records and distributes spoken word, especially comedy, as well as music*

## SRD
70 Lawrence Rd
London
N15 4EG
**T** 020 8802 3000/4444   **F** 020 8802 2222
**E** info@southern.com
*Managing Director* John Knight

## ST Holdings Ltd
Unit 2, Old Forge Rd
Ferndown Industrial Estate
Wimborne
Dorset
BH21 7RR
**T** 01202 8908898   **F** 01202 890886
**E** info@stholdings.co.uk   **W** stholdings.co.uk
*Contact* Chris Parkinson

## Startle Distribution
Unit 3–4
Northgate Business Centre
Crown Rd
Enfield
Middx
EN1 1TG
**T** 020 8805 8822/7788   **F** 020 8805 5225/9210
**E** sales@startle.co.uk   **W** startle.com
*Managing Director* Graham Lambdon

*Sales Manager* Nick Marley

*UK's leading independent wholesaler to independent stores and multiples*

## Steppin' Out Distribution
4–4a Murderdean Rd
Newtongrange
Edinburgh
EH22 4PD
**T** 0131 654 0888   **F** as telephone
*Contact* Ian Robertson

## Sterns Distribution
74 Warren St
London
W1P 5PA
**T** 020 7388 5533/7387 5550   **F** 020 788 2756
**E** ian@sternsmusic.com   **W** sternsmusic.com
*UK Sales Manager* Ian Thomas

*Specialists in African and world music*
*Retail outlet at Sterns African Record Centre, 293 Euston Road, London NW1 3AD*

## Stingray Enterprises
Research House
Fraser Rd
Perivale
Middx
UB6 7AQ
**T** 020 8930 0132   **F** 020 8933 1694

## Stream Records (Disabled Artists' Specialists)
77a Hindmans Rd
London
SE22 9NQ
**T** 020 8299 2998   **F** 020 8693 0349
**E** genie@cdboxset.co.uk
*Co-ordinator* Genie Cosmas

## Streets Ahead Ltd
Unit 21
Townsend Enterprise Park
Townsend St
Belfast
BT13 2ES
**T** 020 9032 3160   **F** as telephone
**E** paul.wyness@business.ntl.com
*Managing Director* Paul Wyness

*Distributors of all chart music, video and DVD. Also budget and Irish labels*

### Swift Record Distributors/Flyright Records
3 Wilton Rd
Bexhill-on-Sea
East Sussex
TN40 1HY
**T** 01424 220028   **F** 01424 213440
**E** swiftrd@btinternet.com
*Managing Director* Robin L Gosden

### Technicolor Distribution Services Ltd
Unit 8
Northfield Industrial Estate
Beresford Avenue
Wembley
Middx
HA0 1NW
**T** 020 8900 1122   **F** 020 8900 1658
*Managing Director* Paul Chesney

### Technicolor Distribution Services Ltd
Unit A, Swift Point
Cosford Lane
Valley Park
Rugby
CV21 1QN
**T** 01788 821122   **F** 01788 821141
**E** peter.branston@technicolor.com
*Managing Director* Peter Branston

### TEN (The Entertainment Network)
Rabans Lane
Aylesbury
Bucks
HP19 3BX
**T** 01296 426151   **F** 01296 481009
*Contact* Gwen Pearce

### Tent Music Entertainments
89a High Rd
London
N22 6BB
**T** 020 8889 0903   **F** 020 889 0310
**E** wscott@brmmusic.prestel.co.uk
*District Manager* Wayne Scott

### Thames Distributors Ltd
Unit 12
Millfarm Business Park
Millfield Rd
Hounslow
Middx
TW4 5PY
**T** 020 8898 2227   **F** 020 8898 2228
**E** thamesuk@aol.com   **W** move.to/thamesuk.com
*Director* Norman L Woolfson

### THE (Total Home Entertainment)
Unit 1
Rosevale Business Park
Newcastle
Staffs
ST5 7QT
**T** 01782 566566   **F** 01782 565400
**E** news@the.co.uk   **W** the.co.uk
*Managing Director* Dennis Ashton

*State-of-the-art distribution of music and video including product guidance, marketing support, stock management, distribution, invoicing, cash collection and account management. Also e-commerce from website design to product despatch*

### 3MV
City Network House
81–83 Weston St
London
SE1 3RS
**T** 020 7378 8866   **F** 020 7378 8855
**E** 3mvmw@theknowledge.com
**W** theknowledge.com
*Managing Director* Dave Trafford

### Timewarp Distribution
80 St John's Hill
London
SW11 1SF
**T** 020 7738 9488   **F** 020 7738 2278
**E** timewarp@dircon.co.uk   **W** tunes.co.uk
*Managing Director* Bill Shannon

### TKO Communications
PO Box 130
Hove
East Sussex
BN3 6QU
**T** 01273 550088   **F** 01273 540969

E jskruger@tkogroup.com   W mistral.co.uk/tko
*Managing Director* Jeffrey S Kruger

## Trojan Sales
Regent House
1 Pratt House
London
NW1 0AD
T 020 7267 6899   F 020 7267 6746
W trojan-records.com
*Contact* Frank Lea

## Twang (Wholesalers)
Lorne House
51 Lorne St
Reading
Berks
RG1 7YW
T 0118 950 8608   F 0118 957 4629

*Established 1974: distributors of budget CDs, cassettes, video and DVD*

## Under One Sun
The Old Truman Brewery
91 Brick Lane
London
E1 6QN
T 020 7377 2001   F 020 7377 2002
E underone@aol.com
*Contact* Vek McGuire

## Unique Records & Distribution
Units 31–32
Queensbrook
Spa Rd
Bolton
BL1 4AY
T 01204 544100   F 01204 393710
E hi@uniquedist.co.uk   W uniquedist.co.uk
*Contact* James Waddicker

## Universal Music Operations Ltd
Chippenham Drive
Kingston
Milton Keynes
Bucks
MK10 0AT
T 020 8910 1500/0870 590 0909   F 01908 452600

W umusic.com
*Distribution Director* Russell C Richards

## Urban Grooves Network
PO Box 445
Chobham
Surrey
GU24 8YQ
T 01276 485846   F 01276 857740
E sales@urbangrooves.net   W urbangrooves.net

*Soul, funk, jazz – urban grooves*

## Victoria Music Ltd
Unit 215
The Saga Centre
326 Kensal Rd
London
W10 5BZ
T 020 7565 8193   F 020 8960 3834
E vicmusic@dircon.co.uk   W victoria-music.com/
killabite.com
*Contact* Robert Jarvis

*Managers of 14 record labels all specializing in dance music*
*Manufacturing, licensing, new acts signed, pressing and distribution deals*
*Also Killa Bite Records and room-tone recordings*

## Vital Distribution
338a Ladbroke Grove
London
W10 5AH
T 020 8324 2400   F 020 8324 0001
E info@vitaluk.com
*London Managing Director* Peter Thompson

*Also Unit 6, Barton Hill Trading Estate, Herapath Street, Bristol BS5 9RD (Tel: 0117 988 3300/Fax: 0117 988 0600)*

## Vivante Music Ltd
Unit 4
60 High St
Hampton Wick
Surrey
KT1 4DB
T 020 8977 6600   F 020 8977 4445
E vivantelondon@compuserve.co.uk
*Contact* Steven Carr

## Wholesale Recordings

163–165 Lower Church Rd
Burgess Hill
West Sussex
RH15 9AA
T 01444 242476  F as telephone
*Contact* Ron Sains

## Wienerworld Ltd

Unit B2
Livingstone Court
55–63 Peel Rd
Wealdstone
Harrow
Middx
HA3 7QT
T 020 8427 2777  F 020 8427 0660
E wworld@wienerworld.com  w wienerworld.com
*Contact* Anthony Broza

## Windsong International

Electron House
Cray Avenue
St Mary Cray
Orpington
Kent
BR5 3RJ
T 01689 836969  F 01689 890392/890394
E sales@windsong.co.uk
*Managing Director* Dave Pegg

## Word (UK) Music

9 Holdom Avenue
Bletchley
Milton Keynes
Bucks
MK1 1QR
T 01908 364218  F 01908 648592
E shelleyn@wordonline.co.uk
w wordonline.co.uk
*Contact* Shelley Needham

## Worldwide Record Distributors (WRD)

282 Camden Rd
London
NW1 9AB
T 020 7267 6762/6763  F 020 7482 4029
E wrdmusik@aol.com
*Managing Director* S Johanson
*Sales and District Manager* Julian Kay

## Zander Exports

34 Sapcote Trading Centre
374 High Rd
London
NW10 2DJ
T 020 8451 5955  F 020 8451 4940/8459 5408
E zander@btinternet.com
*Director* John Yorke

## ZYX Records Ltd (Distribution)

Unit 11
Cambridge Court
210 Shepherds Bush Rd
London
W6 7NJ
T 020 7371 6969  F 020 7371 6688/6677
E lauren-lorenzo@zyxrecords.freeserve.co.uk
*Contact* Lauren Lorenzo

*Record and distribution company*

## Access All Areas

Inside Communications
Bank House
23 Warwick Rd
Coventry
West Midlands
CV1 2EW
**T** 024 7655 9590 **F** 024 7663 1185
**E** mike_gartside@mrn.co.uk **W** access.aa.co.uk
*Business Manager* Clair Whitecross
*Contact* Mike Gartside

## Arcadia

John Brown Publishing
The New Boathouse
136–142 Bramley Rd
London
W10 6SR
**T** 020 7565 3266 **F** 020 7565 3061
*Editor* Cathy FitzGerald
*Advertising Manager* Douglas McDonald

## Artistes & Agents

Richmond House Publishing Co Ltd
3 Richmond Buildings
Dean St
London
W1V 5AE
**T** 020 7437 9556 **F** 020 7287 3463
**E** sales@rhpco.co.uk **W** artistesandagents.co.uk
*Contact* Spencer Block
*Editor* Lee Rotbart

## Atomic

21 Asher Lane
Ruddington
Nottingham
NG11 6HS
**T** 0115 921 2985
*Editor* L A Kenton

## Attitude

Northern & Shell Tower
City Harbour
London
E14 9GL
**T** 020 7308 5090 **F** 020 7308 5075
**E** attitude@norshell.co.uk
*Editor* Adam Mattera
*Advertising Manager* Chris Dicey

## Audio Media

AM Publishing
Atlantica House
11 Station Rd
St Ives
Cambs
PE17 4BH
**T** 01480 461555   **F** 01480 461550
**E** mail@audiomedia.com   **W** audiomedia.com
*Editor* Paul MacDonald
*Advertising Manager* Ian Swain

## AV Magazine

19 Scarbrook Rd
Croydon
CR9 1LX
**T** 020 8565 4224   **F** 020 8565 4282
**E** peterl@avmagazine.co.uk
*Editor* Peter Lloyd

## Bandit A&R Newsletter

PO Box 22
Newport
Isle Of Wight
PO30 1LZ
**T** 01983 524110   **F** 08701 640388
**E** bandit@banditnewsletter.com
**W** banditnewsletter.com
*Manager Director* John Waterman

*Monthly newsletter featuring worldwide music
companies looking for new acts, songs or masters
Also Solent Records (same contact address/phone/
fax)
Email: md@solentrecords.co.uk
Website: solentrecrods.co.uk*

## BBC Music Magazine

BBC Worldwide
Woodlands
80 Wood Lane
London
W12 0TT
**T** 020 8576 3277   **F** 020 8576 3292
*Editor* Helen Wallace
*Associate Publisher* Jessica Gibson
*Advertising Director* Justin Tunstall

## Beat, The

54 Canterbury Rd
Penn
Wolverhampton
West Midlands
WV4 4EH
**T** 01902 652759/0973 133416   **F** as first telephone
**E** steve-morris@blueyonder.co.uk
**W** surf.to.the.beat
*Editor* Steve Morris

*Also see Roots and Branches (same contact details)*

## Between the Grooves

3 Tannsfeld Rd
London
SE6 5DQ
**T** 020 8488 3677   **F** 020 8473 6539
**E** betweenthegrooves@produxion.com
**W** betweenthegrooves.com
*Contact* Jonathan Sharif

*Free urban music magazine, profiling today's finest
soul and dance record labels
See also Natural Grooves (record company)*

## Big Issue, The

236–240 Pentonville Rd
London
N1 9JY
**T** 020 7526 3200   **F** 020 7526 3301
**E** london@bigissue.com   **W** bigissue.com
*Editor* Matthew Collin

## Billboard

Endeavour House
189 Shaftesbury Avenue
London
WC2H 8TJ
**T** 020 7420 6003   **F** 020 7420 6014
**E** eu.billboard.com   **W** billboard.com
*International Editor in Chief* Adam White
*International News Editor* Gordon Masson
*International Editor* Tom Ferguson
*European Advertising Director* Christine Chinetti

## Birmingham What's On

Midland Independent Magazines
28 Colmore Circus
Queensway
Birmingham
West Midlands
B4 6AX
**T** 0121 212 4141/0121 234 5806   **F** 0121 212 2468/
0121 234 5844   **w** mim.co.uk
*Manager Director* Roger Marshall
*Editor* Mike Davies
*Advertising Manager* Vicky Gwinnutt

## Blender

19 Bolsover St
London
W1P 7HJ
**T** 020 7631 1433   **F** 020 7436 1321

## Blues & Soul

153 Praed St
London
W2 1RL
**T** 020 7402 6869/020 7402 7708   **F** 020 7224 8227
**E** editorial@bluesandsoul.demon.co.uk
**w** bluesandsoul.co.uk
*Editor* Bob Killbourn

## Brass Band World

Peak Press Building
Eccles Rd
Chapel-en-le-Frith
High Peak
Cheshire
SK23 9RQ
**T** 01298 812816/812816   **F** 01298 815220
**E** info@bbworld.u-net.com
**w** brassbandworld.com
*Editor* R G Mulholland
*Advertising Manager* Liz Winter

## British Bandsman

Harold Charles House
64 London End
Beaconsfield
Bucks
HP9 2JD
**T** 01494 674411   **F** 01494 670932
**F** info@britishbandsman.com
**w** britishbandsman.com
*Contacts* Nicki Bland or Philip Morris

## British Music Yearbook

Rhinegold Publishing
241 Shaftesbury Avenue
London
WC2H 8EH
**T** 020 7333 1760   **F** 020 7333 1769
**E** bmyb@rhinegold.co.uk   **w** rhinegold.co.uk
*Editor* Louise Head

## British Theatre Directory

Richmond House Publishing Co Ltd
3 Richmond Bulidings
Dean St
London
W1V 5AE
**T** 020 7437 9556   **F** 020 7287 3463
**E** sales@rhpco.co.uk
**w** britishtheatredirectory.co.uk
*Editor* Spencer Block

## Broadcast

EMAP Media
33–39 Bowling Green Lane
London
EC1R 0DA
**T** 020 7505 8014/8040   **F** 020 7505 8050
*Editor* Steve Clarke

## CADS

Miller Freeman Entertainment
8 Montague Close
London
SE1 9UR
**T** 0171 940 8500   **F** 0171 921 5984
*Promotions Executive* Lousie Stevens

## Campaign

174 Hammersmith Rd
London
W6 7JP
**T** 020 8267 4656   **F** 020 8267 4915
*Editor* Stephano Hatfield

## Celebrity Bulletin, The

Room 203–209
93–97 Regent St
London
W1R 7TA
**T** 020 7439 9840   **F** 020 7494 3500
*Contact* Diane Oliver

## Cipher

184 Bridewater Rd
Alperton
Middx
HA0 1AR
**T** 020 8903 6530    **F** 020 8795 0502
**E** ciphermag@aol.com
*Publishing Editor* Joan L Smith

## City Life

164 Deansgate
Manchester
M60 2RD
**T** 0161 832 7200    **F** 0161 839 1488
**E** citylife@mcr-evening-news.co.uk
**W** manchesteronline.co.uk
*Editor* Chris Sharratt
*Advertising Manager* Phil McLoughlin

## Classical Guitar Magazine

1–2 Vance Court
Trans Britannia Enterprise Park
Blaydon on Tyne
Tyne & Wear
NE21 5NH
**T** 0191 414 9000    **F** 0191 414 9001
**E** classicalguitar@ashleymark.co.uk
**W** classicalguitarmagazine.com
*Managing Director* Maurice J Summerfield

*Published by Ashley Mark Publishing Company*

## Clubscene

PO Box 11
Bathgate
Lothian
EH48 1RX
**T** 01506 636038/07785 222205    **F** 01506 633900
**E** mail@clubscene.co.uk    **W** clubscene.co.uk
*Managing Director* Bill Grainger
*Editor* Marc Macgillivary

## Contemporary Music Review

Harwood Academic Publishers
PO Box 23327
London
SE16 4ZP
**T** 020 7740 1382    **F** 020 7252 3510
**E** info@gbhap.com    **W** gbhap.com/contemporary_music_review/
*Contact* Oona Campbell
*Editors* Peter Nelson and Nigel Osborne

## Country Music International

5 Lower Farm Barns
Bucknell
Bicester
Oxon
OX27 7LT
**T** 01869 325407    **F** 01869 324777
**E** rondale@epinet.co.uk
**W** countrymusicinternational.com
*Editor* Alan Walsh
*Advertising Manager* Vicky Gwinnutt

## Country Music News & More!

Pebble View Publishing
8 Pebble View Walk
Hopton on Sea
Norfolk
NR31 9SG
**T** 01502 732040    **F** 01502 731800
**E** mickgreen@countrymusic20.freeserve.co.uk
**W** morecountry.8m.com
*Editor* Mick Green

## Country Music People

1–3 Love Lane
London
SE18 6QT
**T** 020 8854 7217    **F** 020 8855 6370
**E** info@countrymusicpeople.com
**W** countrymusicpeople.com
*Editor* Craig Baguley

## Country Music Round Up

PO Box 111
Waltham
Grimsby
DN37 0YN
**T** 01472 821707/01522 750150    **F** 01472 821808
**E** cmru@usa.net
*Editor/Publisher* John Emptage

## Crack, The

Crack House
1 Pink Lane
Newcastle Upon Tyne
NE1 5DW
**T** 0191 230 3038   **F** 0191 230 4484
**E** rmeddes@hotmail.com   **W** the-crack.co.uk
*Editor* Bev Stephenson
*Advertising Manager* Mandy Baxter

*Monthly, 20,000 circulation*
*Covers North-East England and features local,*
*national and international bands*

## CyberNoise

2a Beecham Rd
Reading
Berks
RG30 2RD
**T** 0118 9651 384
*Contact* Graham Needham

## Daily Record & Sunday Mail

40 Anderston Quay
Glasgow
G3 8DA
**T** 0141 248 7000/0141 242 3120
**E** j.dingwall@dailyrecord.co.uk
*Pop editor & Showbiz* John Dingwall
*Editor* Martin Clarke

## Daily Star

Ludgate House
245 Blackfriars Rd
London
SE1 9UX
**T** 020 7928 8000   **F** 020 7922 7962
**E** bentodd@dailystar.co.uk
*Editor* Peter Hill
*Advertising Manager* Andy Whelan
*Pop Editor* Ben Todd

## Deluxe

Exmouth House
Pine St
London
EC1R 0JL
**T** 020 7689 9999
*Music Editor* Andrew Male
*Editor* Andrew Harrison
*Advertising Manager* Sarah Jacombs

## DJ

Craven House
121 Kingsway
London
WC2B 6PA
**T** 020 7721 8120   **F** 020 7721 8121
**E** djmag@compuserve.com   **W** djmag.com
*Editor* Chris Mellor
*Ad. Manager* Matt Dicks

## Dotmusic

4th Floor
8 Montague Close
London Bridge
London
SE1 9UR
**T** 020 7940 8563   **F** 020 7940 8504
**E** andy@dotmusic.com   **W** dotmusic.com
*Editor* Andy Strickland
*Commercial Manager* Hanif Virani
(hanif@dotmusic.com)
*Executive Producer* Justin Parfitt
( justin@dotmusic.com)

## Echoes

4th Floor
27 Maddox St
London
W1R 9LE
**T** 020 7436 1302/1305   **F** 020 7436 1308
*Editor* Chris Wells
*Advertising Manager* Paul Phillips

## Encore . . . The Magazine for the Theatre Professional

240 Tolworth Rise South
Surbiton
Surrey
KT5 9NB
**T** 020 8330 3707   **F** 020 8330 3707
*Editor* Peter G Foot

*Published monthly (posted on 1st of month)*
*Circulation: 1400*
*Subscription: £20 pa*
*Distributed to theatres, concert halls, arts centres,*
*arenas and production houses throughout the*
*country*

## ep magazine
Vigilante Publications
Huntingdon House
35 Field Rd
Reading
Berks
RG1 6AP
**T** 0118 958 1878  **F** 0870 7345174
**E** epmagazine@vigilante.co.uk  **w** vigilante.co.uk
*Editor* Jon Ewing

## Face, The
Exmouth House
Pine St
London
EC1R 0JL
**T** 020 7689 9999  **F** 020 7689 0300
*Editor* Johnny Davis
*Ad. Manager* Sarah Jacombs

## Financial Times – Music & Copyright
Maple House
149 Tottenham Court Rd
London
W1P 9LL
**T** 020 7896 2000  **F** 020 7896 2235
**E** info.media@ft.com  **w** media.ft.com

## Folk Music Journal
English Folk Dance and Song Society
Cecil Sharp House
2 Regent's Park Rd
London
NW1 7AY
**T** 020 7485 2206  **F** 020 7284 0534
**E** michael.heaney@ulib.ox.ac.uk  **w** efdss.org
*Contact* Mike Heaney

*The foremost scholarly journal for traditional music,
dance and song
Published annually in December
Subscriptions and purchase: sheilafinn@emfdss.org*

## Fono
Miller Freeman Entertainment
8 Montague Close
London
SE1 9UR
**T** 020 7940 8515  **F** 020 7401 8035
**E** fono@dotmusic.co.uk
*Editor* Martin Talbot

*International Sales Manager* Matthew Tyrrell
*Senior Sales Executive* Archie Carmichael
*Publisher* Steve Redmond

## Foresight/Foresight Newsletter
Profile Press Agency
32–38 Saffron Hill
London
EC1N 8ST
**T** 020 7405 4455  **F** 020 7430 1089
**E** paul@profilegroup.co.uk  **w** fifi.co.uk
*Researcher* Paul Weatherley

## Fresh Direction
4 Heathgate Place
75 Agincourt Rd
London
NW3 2NU
**T** 020 7424 0400  **F** 020 7424 0100
**E** freshdirection@btinternet.com
**w** freshdirection.co.uk
*Editor* Paul Russell

## fRoots
PO Box 337
London
N4 1TW
**T** 020 8340 9651  **F** 020 8348 5626
**E** froots@froots.demon.co.uk
**w** froots.demon.co.uk
*Editor* Ian Anderson
*Editor's Assistant* Vanessa Lawlery

*Monthly, formerly Folk Roots, established for over 20
years as the UK's leading roots music journal*

## Future Hits
Miller Freeman Entertainment
8 Montague Close
London
SE1 9UR
**T** 020 7940 8605  **F** 020 7407 7081

## Future Music
Future Publishing
30 Monmouth St
Bath
BA1 2BW
**T** 01225 442244  **F** 01225 462986

**Green Sheet, The**
United Business Media International Ltd
8 Montague Close
London
SE1 9UR
**T** 020 7940 8571   **F** 020 7407 7087
**E** sabbott@ubminternational.com
*Editor* Simon Abbott

*The industry's A&R bible*


**Guitar Magazine**
Focus House
Dingwall Avenue
Croydon
CR9 2TA
**T** 020 8686 2599   **F** 020 8774 0934
**E** dave_hunter@ipcmedia.com   **w** ipcmedia.com
*Editor* Dave Hunter


**Guitarist**
Future Publishing
30 Monmouth St
Bath
BA1 2BW
**T** 01225 442244   **F** 01225 732334
**E** neville.marten@futurenet.co.uk
**w** guitarist@futurenet.co.uk
*Editor* Neville Marten
*Advertising Manager* Rob Last


**Heat**
Mappin House
Winsley St
London
W1 7AR
**T** 020 7436 1515   **F** 020 7817 8847
**E** heat@emap.com
*Editor* Mark Frith

*Circulation (Dec. 2000): 172,311*


**Hip Hop Connection**
Future Publishing
30 Monmouth St
Bath
BA1 2BW
**T** 01225 442244   **F** 01223 509041
**E** hhc@musicians-net.co.uk
**w** musicians-net.co.uk
*Editor* Andy Cowan


**Hit Music**
Miller Freeman Entertainment
8 Montague Close
London
SE1 9UR
**T** 020 7940 8560   **F** 020 7407 7092
*Editor* Tony Brown


**Hokie Pokie**
Millham Lane
Dulverton
Somerset
TA22 9HQ
**T** 01398 324114/07831 103194
**F** as first telephone number
**E** hokie.pokie@bigfoot.com
*Editor* Andrew Quarrie


**Hot Air**
John Brown Contract Publishing
The New Boathouse
136–142 Bramley Rd
London
W10 6SR
**T** 020 7565 3000
*Editor* Alex Finer


**Hot Press**
13 Trinity St
Dublin 2
Ireland
**T** 00 353 1 679 5077   **F** 00 353 1 679 5097
**E** hotpress@iol.ie   **w** hot-press.com
*Editor* Niall Stokes
*Advertising Manager* Marie Smyth


**I-D Magazine**
Universal House
251–255 Tottenham Court Rd
London
W1P 0EA
**T** 020 7813 6170   **F** 020 7813 6179
**E** editor@i-dmagazine.co.uk
*Editor* Avril Mair
*Advertising Manager* Andrew Creighton

## Implant
Vision Publishing
Second Floor A
14 King Square
Bristol
BS2 8JJ
**T** 0117 914 3306/07976 842279
**W** vision.netgates.co.uk
*Contact* Rachel Patey, Colin Steven

## Inside Multimedia
Tossa House
Main Rd
Smalley
Derby
Derbyshire
DE7 6EF
**T** 01332 881779   **F** 01332 780008
*Editor* John Barker

## International Arts Manager
Arts Publishing International
Lime Wharf
Vyner St
London
E2 9DJ
**T** 020 8709 9050   **F** 020 8709 9080
**E** editorial@api.co.uk
*Editor* Mike Farish
*Publisher* Martin Huber
*Staff Writer* Eva Johansson

*International performing arts periodical (10 issues per year)*

## Irish Music Scene
Bunbeg
Letterkenny
Co. Donegal
Ireland
**T** 00 353 753 1176   **E** donalkoboyle@eircom.net
*Editor* Kieran O'Fearraigh
*Reporter* Donnie Gall
*Managing Editor* Donal K O'Boyle

*Irish Music Scene also supplies a syndicated music column throughout Ireland*

## Jazz Journal International
Jazz Journal Ltd
3–3a Forest Rd
Loughton
Essex
IG10 1DR
**T** 020 8532 0456/0678   **F** 020 8532 0440
*Publisher/Editor* Eddie Cook

*Monthly, now in 54th year, with reviews, features, events diary etc and the annual Critics' Poll*

## Jazz Rag, The
PO Box 944
Birmingham
B16 8UT
**T** 0121 454 7020   **F** 0121 454 9996
**E** bigbearmusic@compuserve.com
**W** bigbearmusic.com
*Editor* Jim Simpson
*Advertising Manager* Catherine Ewart
*News* Ron Simpson
*Reviews Editor* Wilma Vanse

## Jazz UK
26 The Balcony
Castle Arcade
Cardiff
CF10 1BY
**T** 029 2066 5161   **F** 029 2066 5160
**E** jazzuk.cardiff@virgin.net   **W** jazzservices.org.uk
*Editor* John Fordham

*Free bi-monthly available through clubs, pubs, shops etc, with 30,000 print run and the most extensive jazz listings in the UK, edited by the Guardian's jazz critic*

## Jazzwise Magazine/Jazzwise Publications
2b Gleneagle Mews
London
SW16 6AE
**T** 020 8769 7725   **F** 020 8677 7128
**E** charles.alexander@talk21.com
*Contact* Charles Alexander

*The UK's leading monthly jazz magazine, edited by Stephen Graham, was launched in 1997. Features include over 100 CD reviews per issue Jazzwise Publications is a mail-order specialist for printed jazz music. Catalogue available*

*Jazzwise runs an annual jazz summer school in Richmond during the last week of July*

## Jocky Slut
Unit 4c
Beehive Mill
Jersey St
Manchester
M4 6JG
**T** 0161 950 4215   **F** 0161 950 4217
**E** e.slut@jockslut.demon.co.uk
*Editors* Paul Bennie and John Burgess

## Just Seventeen
EMAP Elan
Endeavour House
189 Shaftesbury Avenue
London
WC2H 8JG
**T** 020 7208 3408   **F** 020 7208 3590
**E** sam.baker@secm.emap.com
*Editor* Sam Baker

## Keep It Live!
144 Westgate
Guisborough
Cleveland
TS14 6NB
**T** 01468 665669   **E** keepit.live@virgin.net
**W** freespace.virgin.net/keepit.live/index.htm
*Contacts* Colin McCosh and Heather Jack

## Kerrang!
EMAP Metro
Mappin House
4 Winsley St
London
W1R 7AR
**T** 020 7436 1515/020 7312 8106   **F** 020 7312 8910
*Editor* Phil Alexander

## Keyboard Player
27 Russell Rd
Enfield
Middlesex
EN1 4TN
**T** 020 8367 2938   **F** 020 8367 2359
**W** keyboardplayer.com
*Editor* Steve Miller

## Knowledge
Vision Publishing
2nd Floor A
14 King Square
Bristol
BS2 8JJ
**T** 0117 914 3305/07966 486785
**E** editor@knowledgemag.co.uk
*Contact* Colin Steven
*Advertising Manager* Rachel Patey

## Knowledge, The
Miller Freeman Info. Services
Riverbank House
Angel Lane
Tonbridge
Kent
TN9 1SE
**T** 01732 377400   **F** 01732 367301
*Assistant Marketing Manager* Debbie O'Neill
*Group Publishing Director* Les Kelly
*Associate Publisher* Elaine Soni

## Lighting & Sound Intenational
PLASA Media
38 St Leonards Rd
Eastbourne
East Sussex
BN21 3UT
**T** 01323 418400   **F** 01323 646905
**E** ruth@plasa.org   **W** plasa.org
*Editor* Ruth Rossington
*Advertising Manager* Barry Howse

*Established 1985*

## Live And Kicking Magazine
BBC Worldwide
80 Wood Lane
London
W12 0TA
**T** 020 8576 2447   **F** 020 8576 2763
**E** jeremy.mark@bbc.co.uk
*Editor in Chief* Jeremy Mark
*Advertising Manager* Alfie Lewis

## Live!

Nexus House
Azalea Drive
Swanley
Kent
BR8 8HY
**T** 01322 660070   **F** 01322 615636
**E** 113251.662@compuserve.com
*Contact* Justine Smart

## Loaded

IPC Magazines
Kings Reach Tower
Stamford St
London
SE1 9LS
**T** 020 7261 5562   **F** 020 7261 5557
**E** loadweb@ipc.co.uk   **w** uploaded.com
*Editor* Keith Kendrick

## M8

11 Lynedoch Place
Glasgow
G3 6AB
**T** 0141 353 1118   **F** 0141 353 1448
**E** m8ken@dircon.co.uk
*Editor* Jerry Ross
*Ad. Manager* David Faulds

## M8 Magazine

11 Lynedoch Place
Glasgow
G3 6AV
**T** 0141 353 1118   **F** 0141 353 1448
**E** davidm8mag@aol.com   **w** m8magazine.com
*Contact* David Faulds

*Independent dance magazine*

## Making Music

Nexus House
Azalea Drive
Swanley
Kent
BR8 8HU
**T** 01322 660070   **F** 01322 616319/01322 615636
**E** makingmusic@cerbernet.co.uk
**w** cerbernet.co.uk.makingmusic
*Editor* Richard Chapman

## Metal Hammer

Dennis Publishing
19 Bolsover St
London
W1P 7HJ
**T** 020 7631 1433   **F** 020 7917 7655
**E** editor.metalhammer@dennis.co.uk
**w** metalhammer.co.uk
*Editor* Robyn Doreian
*Advertising Manager* Christian Ingham

## MI Pro

The Swan Agency
35 High St
Marlow
Bucks
SL7 1AU
**T** 01628 487820   **F** 01628 487822
**E** news@mi-pro.com
*Editor* Gez Kahan

*Monthly business publication specializing in musical instruments*
*Circulation ( July-December 2000): 4,961*
*£30 for 12 issues*

## Ministry

103 Gaunt St
London
SE1 6DP
**T** 020 7378 6528   **F** 020 7403 5348
*Editor* Scott Manson
*Advertising Manager* Chris Green

## Mixmag

EMAP Metro
Mappin House
4 Winsley St
London
W1N 7AR
**T** 020 7436 1515   **F** 020 7312 8977/020 7323 0276
**E** mixmag@ecm.emap.com   **w** techno.de/mixmag
*Managing Editor* Andrew Harrison
*Advertising Manager* Peter Fox

## Mixology

The Music Village
11b Osiers Rd
London
SW19 1NL
**T** 020 8870 0011   **F** 020 8870 8170

E martin@mixology.demon.co.uk
w musicfactory.co.uk
*Editor* Martin Smith

## Mojo

EMAP Metro
Mappin House
4 Winsley St
London
W1N 7AR
T 020 7436 1515   F 020 7312 8296
E mojo@ecm.emap.com   w mojo4music.com
*Editor* Paul Trynka

*Circulation ( Jan 2001): 84,010*
*Enquiries about writing for Mojo – request Writers'*
*Guidelines*
*Enquiries about reviews should be addressed to the*
*Reviews Editor*

## Music & Media

50–51 Bedford Row
London
WC1R 4LR
T 020 7822 8300   F 020 7242 9136
w billboard.com
*Editor In Chief* Emmanuel Legrand
*Managing Editor* Tom Ferguson
*News Editor* Lucy Aitken
*Advertising Director* Christine Chinetti

## Music Business International (MBI)

Miller Freeman Entertainment, UK Ltd
8 Montague Close
London
SE1 9UR
T 020 7940 8512   F 020 7407 7094
E mbi@dotmusic.com
*Editor* Ajax Scott
*Publishing Director* Steve Redmond
*Managing Editor* Hamish Champ

*Also publishers of MBI World Directory*

## Music Current

c/o Scottish Music Information Centre
Glasgow
G12 9LR
T 0141 334 6393   F 0141 337 1161

E smic@glasgow.almac.co.uk   w music.gla.ac.uk/
htmlfolder/resources/smic
*Contact* Alasdair Pettinger

## Music Journal

10 Stratford Place
London
W1C 1AA
T 020 7629 4413   F 020 7408 1538
E neil@ism.org   w ism.org
*Editor* Neil Hoyle

*Monthly journal of the ISM (Incorporated Society of*
*Musicians) open to professional musicians (and*
*student members), promoting their interests and*
*providing assistance on all aspects of the musician's*
*life. Full details from Stratford Place address*

## Music Mart

40 Scarletts Rd
Old Heath
Colchester
Essex
CO1 2HA
T 01206 795640   F 01206 869060
E stevedwright@compuserve.com
w musicmart-mag.co.uk
*Editor* Steve Wright
*Advertising Manager* Lisa Aston (0121 233 8730)

*Monthly aimed at home-based and semi-pro*
*musicians as well as professionals*
*Reviews of all types of instruments and equipment*

## Music Master

Retail Entertainment Data
Paulton House
8 Shepherdess Walk
London
N1 7LB
T 020 7566 8216   F 020 7566 8316
E info@redpublishing.co.uk
w redpublishing.co.uk

## Music News Asia

245 Old Marylebone Rd
London
NW1 5QT
T 020 7723 2277   F 020 7723 2288
*Editor* Ian Gittins

## Music Teacher

Rhinegold Publishing
241 Shaftesbury Avenue
London
WC2H 8TF
**T** 020 7333 1747   **F** 020 7333 1769
**E** music.teacher@rhinegold.co.uk
**W** rhinegold.co.uk
*Editor* Lucien Jenkins

*Monthly publication of relevance to people involved
in school music and instrumental music*

## Music Week

Miller Freeman Entertainment
8 Montague Close
London
SE1 9UR
**T** 020 7940 8500   **F** 020 7407 7094
**E** (initial.surname)@unmf.com
*Editor* Ajax Scott
*Publisher* Steve Redmond
*Special Projects Editor* Chas De Whalley

*Also publishers of Music Week Directory*

## Music365

52 Gloucester Park
London
W1H 3HJ
**T** 020 7505 7800   **F** 020 7505 7765
**E** brendon@music365.co.uk   **W** music365.com
*Editor* Brendon Fitzgerald
*Ad. Manager* Julian Marszalek

## Musical Opinion

2 Princes Rd
St Leonards on Sea
East Sussex
TN37 6EL
**T** 01424 715167   **F** 01424 712214
**E** musicalopinion2@aol.com
**W** musicalopinion.com
*Editor* Denby Richards

## Musical Times, The

The Musical Times Publications
22 Gibson Square
London
N1 0RD
**T** 020 7354 0627
*Editor* Antony Bye

## Musician

Rhinegold Publishing
241 Shaftesbury Avenue
London
WC2H 8EH
**T** 020 7333 1733   **F** 020 7333 1736
**E** 100546.1127@compuserve.com
*Managing Director* Brian Blain

## Muzik

IPC Magazines
King's Reach Tower
Stamford St
London
SE1 9LS
**T** 020 7261 5993/020 7261 5482   **F** 020 7261 7100/
020 7261 5504   **E** muzik@ipc.co.uk
*Editor* Ben Turner
*Advertising Manager* Saint-John Betteridge

## New Musical Express

IPC Music Magazines
King's Reach Tower
Stamford St
London
SE1 9LS
**T** 020 7261 5813   **F** 020 7261 5185   **W** nme.com
*Editor* Steve Sutherland

## Night Magazine

Suite 2
Waterloo Place
Watson Square
Stockport
Cheshire
SK1 3AZ
**T** 0161 429 7803   **F** 0161 480 8896
*Contact* Matt Turner

## Nightshift

Oxford Music Central
Second Floor
65 George St
Oxford
OX1 2BE
**T** 01865 798793   **F** as telephone
**W** nightshift.oxfordmusic.net
*Contact* Dale Kattack

*Monthly freesheet for the Oxfordshire live music scene*

## Noize Unlimited

Riff Raff Productions
PO Box 1900
London
N5 1EP
**T** 020 7226 4695   **F** 020 7609 2361
**E** riffraff@compuserve.com
*Contact* Mark Crampton

## One to One

United Business Media International Ltd
8 Montague Close
London
SE1 9UR
**T** 020 7940 8500   **F** 020 7401 8036
**E** tfrost@ubminternational.com
**W** oto-online.com
*Editor* Tim Frost

*The international magazine for the CD, DVD, video and cassette manufacturing markets. Also produces the DVD/CD Plant Guide and the Gold Book (industry directories)*

## Overload Media

PO Box 41
Bristol
BS16 3ZB
**T** 0117 965 4018   **F** as telephone
**E** input@overloadmedia.co.uk
**W** overloadmedia.co.uk
*Editor* Ali Wade

*Quarterly covering 'electronic music and wired culture', with a web version updated weekly Free, but there is a subscription to cover postage*

## Popular Music

Cambridge University Press
The Edinburgh Building
Shaftesbury Rd
Cambridge
Cambs
CB2 2RU
**T** 01223 325757   **F** 01223 315052
*Editors*: Lucy Green and David Laing

## Promo

United Business Media International Ltd
8 Montague Close
London
SE1 9UR
**T** 020 7940 8546   **F** 020 7407 7081
**E** dknight@ubminternational.com
*Editor* David Knight

## Q

EMAP Metro
4 Winsley St
London
W1N 7AR
**T** 020 7436 1515   **F** 020 7312 8247
**E** andy.pemberton@ecm.emap.com
**W** qonline.co.uk
*Editor* Andy Pemberton

## Record Collector

45 St. Mary's Rd
London
W5 5RQ
**T** 020 8579 1082   **F** 020 8566 2024
**E** editor@rcmag.demon.co.uk
**W** recordcollectermag.co.uk
*Editor* Andy Davis
*Ad. Manager* James Masterson

## Record Information Services

Unit 8 (Hasmick)
Forest Hill Industrial Estate
London
SE3 2LX
**T** 020 8291 6777   **F** 020 8291 0081
*Contact* Paul Pelletier

## Roots and Branches

54 Canterbury Rd
Penn
Wolverhampton
West Midlands
WV4 4EH
**T** 01902 652759    **F** as telephone
**E** steve-morris@blueyonder.co.uk
**W** surf.to.the.beat
*Editor* Steve Morris

*Also see The Beat (same contact details)*

## Showcase Publications

38c The Broadway
London
N8 9SU
**T** 020 8348 2332    **F** 020 8340 3750
**E** info@showcase-music.com
**W** showcase-music.com
*Editor* Kay Chestnutt

## Sketch Press

54 Carlton Place
Glasgow
G5 9TW
**T** 0141 418 0053    **F** 0141 418 0054
*Contact* Joolz MacCaskill

## Sky

EMAP
Mappin House
4 Winsley St
London
W1N 7AR
**T** 020 7436 1515    **F** 020 7312 8248
**E** sky@ecm.emap.com
*Editor* Michael Hogan
*Advertising Manager* Julian Elvin

## Smash Hits

EMAP Metro
Mappin House
4 Winsley St
London
W1N 7AR
**T** 020 7436 1515    **F** 020 7636 5792
**E** smash_hits@emap.com    **W** smashhits.net
*Editor* Emma Jones

*Fortnightly*

*UK's oldest pop magazine*
*Circulation: 221,000*
*Also publishes Smash Brits, the official Brits*
*magazine*
*Also Smash Hits radio and TV show on Sky One and*
*SHtv channel (launched June)*

## SongLink International

23 Belsize Crescent
London
NW3 5QY
**T** 020 7794 2540/07956 270592    **F** 020 7794 7393
**E** david@songlink.demon.co.uk    **W** songlink.com
*Editor and Publisher* David Stark

*Newsletter for publishers and song-writers, listing*
*artists and labels looking for material.*

## Songsearch Monthly

Wheel Close House
Delves Lane
Consett
Co. Durham
DH8 7ER
**T** 01207 580565/01207 583918    **F** 01736 763328/
01207 592308    **E** songmag@aol.com
*Editor* Colin Eade

## Songwriter

International Songwriter's Association
PO Box 46
Limerick City
Ireland
**T** 00 353 61 228837/020 7486 5353
**F** 00 353 61 229464/020 7486 2094
**E** jliddane@songwriter.iol.ie    **W** songwriter.co.uk
*Manager Director* James D Liddane
*Editor* Anna Sinden

## Songwriting and Composing

Sovereign House
12 Trewartha Rd
Praa Sands
Penzance
Cornwall
TR20 9ST
**T** 01736 762826/07721 449477    **F** 01736 763328
**E** songmag@aol.com    **W** songwriters-guild.co.uk
*Editor* Roderick G Jones

*Magazine published by the Guild of International*
*Songwriters and Composers*
*Contact them for membership details*

## Soul Trade/Garage Trade

63a Bruce Grove
London
N17 6RN
**T** 020 8621 0389    **F** as telephone
**E** karen@soultrade.co.uk    **w** soultrade.co.uk
*Editor* Karen-Joy Langley

*Bi-monthly for the independent soul and reggae scene*
*Same address/phone/fax for Hot FX (graphic and*
*web design), DJ Promos and Video Promos (all soul*
*and reggae)*

## Sound On Sound

Media House
Trafalgar Way
Bar Hill
Cambridge
CB3 8SQ
**T** 01954 789888    **F** 01954 789895
**E** info@sospubs.co.uk    **w** sound-on-sound.com
*Editor* Paul White

## Stage, The

47 Bermondsey St
London
SE1 3XT
**T** 020 7403 1818    **F** 020 7357 9287
*Editor* Brian Attwood

## Stirrings – Folk & Acoustic Music

28 Montgomery Avenue
Sheffield
South Yorkshire
S7 1NZ
**T** 0114 258 9182    **F** 0114 281 7922
**E** editor@stirrings.co.uk    **w** stirrings.co.uk
*Contact* Trevor Sommers

## Straight No Chaser

6 Hoxton Square
London
N1 6NU
**T** 020 7613 1594    **F** 020 7613 5506/1703
**E** snc.chaser@freeuk.com
*Editor* Paul Bradshaw

## Studio Sound

United Business Media International Ltd
8 Montague Close
London
SE1 9UR
**T** 020 7940 8500    **F** 020 7407 7102
**E** tgoodyer@ubminternational.com
**w** studio-sound.com
*Editor* Tim Goodyer
*Executive Editor* Zenon Schoepe

*International monthly for professional audio*
*personnel, covering all aspects of audio for recording,*
*broadcast and audio-for-video post-production*
*Circulation: c.16,000*

## Swinstead Publishing

1a Zetland House
8–26 Scrutton St
London
EC2A 4HJ
**T** 020 7729 3773    **F** 020 7729 8312
**E** adamdewhurst@sleazenation.com
**w** sleazenation.com and jockeyslut.com
*Marketing Director* Adam Dewhurst

## Time Out

Universal House
251 Tottenham Court Rd
London
W1A 0AB
**T** 020 7813 3000    **F** 020 7813 6158    **w** timeout.com
*Music Editor* Ross Fortune

*For folk and roots contact John Crosby*
*(folklistings@timeout.com)*

## Tip Sheet, The

7a Soring St
London
W2 3RA
**T** 020 7262 6666    **F** 020 7262 8477
**E** tips@tipsheet.co.uk    **w** tipsheet.co.uk
*Contact* Callaghan O'Rourke

*Weekly subscription-only info and discussion*
*newssheet published together with promotional CD,*
*instrumental in breaking such bands as Ace of Base,*
*Hanson and Atomic Kitten*

**Top**
Tower Records
62–64 Kensington High St
London
W8 4PE
T 020 7938 5388   F 020 7937 5024
E mail@topmag.demon.co.uk   W topmag.co.uk
*Editor* Hugh Fielder
*Publisher* Jon Newey

**Top Of The Pops Magazine**
BBC Worldwide
Room A1136
80 Wood Lane
London
W12 0TT
T 020 8433 3910   F 020 8433 2694
E totp.magazine@bbc.co.uk   W beeb.com/totp
*Editor* Corinna Shaffer
*Publisher* Alfie Lewis
*Advertising Manager* Phil Stringer

**Trade Winds**
c/o Sterns
74–75 Warren St
London
W1P 5PA
T 020 7387 5550   F 020 7388 2756
E info@sternsmusic.com   W sternsmusic.com
*Contact* Trevor Herman

**TV Hits**
Attic Futura
17–18 Berners St
London
W1P 3DD
T 020 7664 6400   F 020 7323 1854
*Editor* Allison Lower

**Uncut**
IPC Music Magazines
Kings Reach Tower
Stamford St
London
SE1 9LS
T 020 7261 6992   F 020 7261 5573
*Editor* Allan Jones

**Venue**
64–65 North Rd
St Andrews
Bristol
BS6 5AQ
T 0117 942 8491   F 0117 942 0369
E editor@venue.co.uk   W venue.co.uk
*Editor* John Mitchell
*Advertising Manager* Nigel Locker

**What's On In London**
180–182 Pentonville Rd
London
N1 9LB
T 020 7278 4393   F 020 7837 5838
E whatson@globalnet.co.uk
*Editor* Michael Darvell

**White Book, The**
Inside Communications
Bank House
23 Warwick Rd
Coventry
West Midlands
CV1 2EW
T 024 7655 9658   F 024 7663 1185
E (name)@mrn.co.uk   W whitebook.co.uk
*Editor* Sarah Hutchinson

**Wire, The**
45–46 Poland St
London
W1V 3DF
T 020 7439 6422/020 7494 1340   F 020 7287 4767
E info@thewire.co.uk   W thewire.co.uk
*Publisher and Editor-in-Chief* Tony Herrington
*Advertising Manager* Andy Tate